Scott Foresman • Addison Wesley

enVisionMATH™

Authors

Randall I. Charles
Professor Emeritus
Department of Mathematics
San Jose State University
San Jose, California

Janet H. Caldwell
Professor of Mathematics
Rowan University
Glassboro, New Jersey

Mary Cavanagh
Mathematics Consultant
San Diego County Office of Education
San Diego, California

Dinah Chancellor
Mathematics Consultant with Carroll ISD
Southlake, Texas
Mathematics Specialist with Venus ISD
Venus, Texas

Juanita V. Copley
Professor
College of Education
University of Houston
Houston, Texas

Warren D. Crown
Associate Dean for Academic Affairs
Graduate School of Education
Rutgers University
New Brunswick, New Jersey

Francis (Skip) Fennell
Professor of Education
McDaniel College
Westminster, Maryland

Alma B. Ramirez
Sr. Research Associate
Math Pathways and Pitfalls WestEd
Oakland, California

Kay B. Sammons
Coordinator of Elementary Mathematics
Howard County Public Schools
Ellicott City, Maryland

Jane F. Schielack
Professor of Mathematics
Associate Dean for Assessment and
Pre K-12 Education, College of Science
Texas A&M University
College Station, Texas

William Tate
Edward Mallinckrodt Distinguished
University Professor in Arts & Sciences
Washington University
St. Louis, Missouri

John A. Van de Walle
Professor Emeritus, Mathematics Education
Virginia Commonwealth University
Richmond, Virginia

Consulting Mathematicians

Edward J. Barbeau
Professor of Mathematics
University of Toronto
Toronto, Canada

Sybilla Beckmann
Professor of Mathematics
Department of Mathematics
University of Georgia
Athens, Georgia

David Bressoud
DeWitt Wallace Professor of Mathematics
Macalester College
Saint Paul, Minnesota

Gary Lippman
Professor of Mathematics and Computer Science
California State University East Bay
Hayward, California

PEARSON

Glenview, Illinois • Boston, Massachusetts • Chandler, Arizona • Upper Saddle River, New Jersey

Consulting Authors

Charles R. Allan
Mathematics Education Consultant
(Retired)
Michigan Department of Education
Lansing, Michigan

Verónica Galván Carlan
Private Consultant Mathematics
Harlingen, Texas

Stuart J. Murphy
Visual Learning Specialist
Boston, Massachusetts

Grant Wiggins
Researcher and Educational Consultant
Hopewell, New Jersey

ELL Consultants/Reviewers

Jim Cummins
Professor
The University of Toronto
Toronto, Canada

Alma B. Ramirez
Sr. Research Associate
Math Pathways and Pitfalls WestEd
Oakland, California

National Math Development Team

Cindy Bumbales
Teacher
Lake in the Hills, IL

Ann Hottovy
Teacher
Hampshire, IL

Deborah Ives
Supervisor of Mathematics
Ridgewood, NJ

Lisa Jasumback
Math Curriculum Supervisor
Farmington, UT

Rebecca Johnson
Teacher
Canonsburg, PA

Jo Lynn Miller
Math Specialist
Salt Lake City, UT

Patricia Morrison
Elementary Mathematics Specialist K-5
Upper Marlboro, MD

Patricia Horrigan Rourke
Mathematics Coordinator
Holliston, MA

Elise Sabaski
Teacher
Gladstone, MO

Math Advisory Board

John F. Campbell
Teacher
Upton, MA

Enrique Franco
Coordinator Elementary Math
Los Angeles, CA

Gladys Garrison
Teacher
Minot AFB, ND

Pat Glubka
Instructional Resource Teacher
Brookfield, UT

Shari Goodman
Math Specialist
Salt Lake City, UT

Cathy Massett
Math Facilitator
Cobb County SD, GA

Mary Modene
Math Facilitator
Belleville, IL

Kimya Moyo
Math Manager
Cincinnati, OH

Denise Redington
Teacher
Chicago, IL

Arlene Rosowski
Supervisor of Mathematics
Buffalo, NY

Darlene Teague
Director of Core Data
Kansas City, MO

Debbie Thompson
Elementary Math Teaching Specialist
Wichita, KS

Michele Whiston
Supervisor
Curriculum, Instruction, and Assessment
Mobile County, AL

Scott Foresman • Addison Wesley
enVisionMATH™

ISBN-13: 978-0-328-61098-3
ISBN-10: 0-328-61098-4

6 7 8 9 10 11 V057 17 16 15 14

Scott Foresman • Addison Wesley

enVisionMATH™

Topic Titles

Virginia Contents

MATH STRAND COLORS

- Number and Operations
- Algebra
- Geometry
- Measurement
- Data Analysis and Probability
- Problem Solving

For each Topic, the relevant VA Mathematics Standards of Learning (SOL) are listed below the Topic title.

Topic 3 Subtraction Number Sense

SOL 3.2, 3.4

Topic 4 Subtracting Whole Numbers to Solve Problems

SOL 3.2, 3.4

Topic 5 Multiplication Meanings and Facts

SOL 3.5, 3.6, 3.20.a, 3.20.b

Topic 6 Multiplication Fact Strategies: Use Known Facts
SOL 3.5, 3.6

Topic 7 Division Meanings
SOL 3.6

Topic 8 Division Facts
SOL 3.2, 3.5

Topic 9 Patterns and Relationships
SOL 3.19

Topic 10 Solids and Shapes
SOL 3.14, 3.15

Topic 11 Congruence and Symmetry
SOL 3.16

VA Virginia Handbook
Virginia Skills and Practice

Topic 12 Understanding Fractions
SOL 3.3.a, 3.3.b, 3.3.c, 3.7

Topic 13 Decimals and Money

SOL Prepares for 4.3.a, 4.3.d, 4.4.d, 4.5.c

Topic 14 Customary Measurement

SOL 3.9.a, 3.9.b, 3.9.c

Topic 15 Metric Measurement

SOL 3.9, 3.9.a, 3.9.b, 3.9.c

Topic 16 Perimeter, Area, and Volume

SOL 3.9.d, 3.10.a, 3.10.b

Topic 17 Time and Temperature

SOL 3.11.a, 3.11.b, 3.12, 3.13

Topic 18 Multiplying Greater Numbers

SOL 3.6

Topic 19 Dividing with 1-Digit Numbers

SOL 3.6

Topic 20 Data, Graphs, and Probability

SOL 3.17.a, 3.17.b, 3.17.c, 3.18

VA Virginia Handbook

enVisionMATH Across the U.S.A.

Problem Solving Using
Number and Operations

New Jersey and Outdoor Movies

One of the first drive-in movie theaters opened in 1933. It was in Camden, New Jersey. People could sit in their cars and watch movies. It cost 25¢ to park a car. The first three people in the car paid 25¢ each.

Arizona's Raccoon Relatives

Two animals from the raccoon family live in Arizona. They are the raccoon and the ringtail. The ringtail is Arizona's state mammal. A raccoon can weigh more than 25 pounds. A ringtail weighs about 2 pounds.

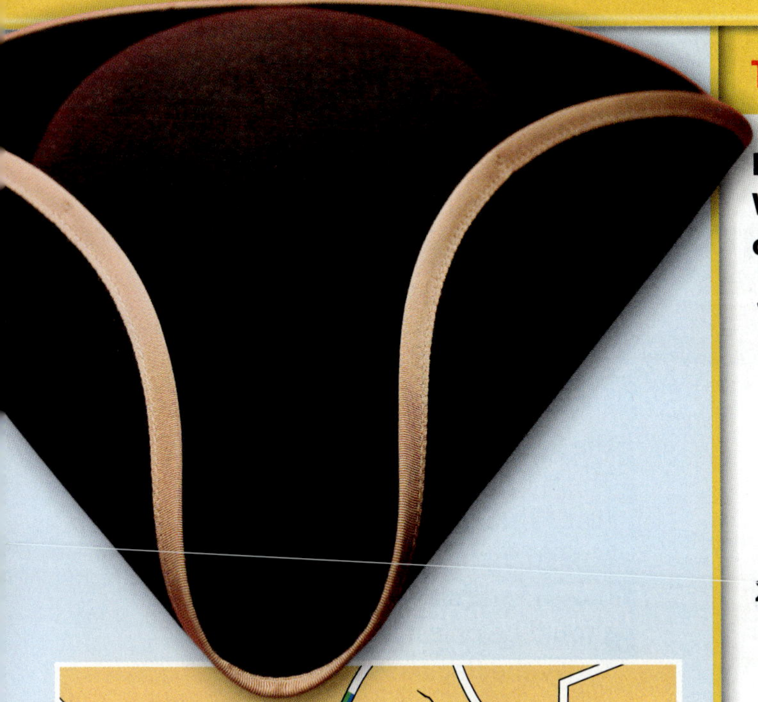

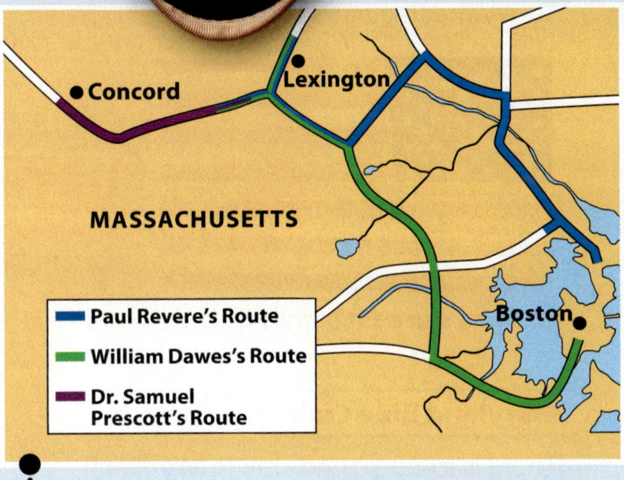

The British Are Coming!

In 1775 two men warned people in Massachusetts that British soldiers were coming. They rode horses from Boston to Lexington. They stopped at houses to give the alarm. Their ride took about two hours. Another man rode from Lexington to warn the town of Concord.

The distance from Boston to Lexington is about 15 miles. Today it would take about 30 minutes to drive a car from Boston to Lexington, a distance of about 15 miles. It would take about 20 minutes to drive about 8 miles from Lexington to Concord.

TEST PREP

Directions: Carefully read questions 1–20. Write your answers on a separate sheet of paper.

1. Rena and Jo paid 80¢ to watch a movie at the Camden drive-in. The two tickets only cost 75¢. How much money should they get back?

A 0¢ **B** 5¢ **C** 25¢ **D** 50¢

2. Eric drove alone to the Camden drive-in. How much money did he pay to park the car and watch the movie?

A 25¢ **B** 50¢ **C** 75¢ **D** $1.00

3. Suppose one ringtail weighs 2 pounds. How many pounds would five ringtails weigh all together?

A 3 pounds **B** 5 pounds **C** 7 pounds **D** 10 pounds

4. Suppose there is a raccoon that is 42 inches long and a ringtail that is 24 inches long. How much shorter is the ringtail than the raccoon?

A 8 inches **B** 18 inches **C** 22 inches **D** 66 inches

5. Pilar drove 15 miles from Boston to Lexington. Then she drove 8 miles to Concord. How many miles was her total trip?

A 7 miles **B** 15 miles **C** 23 miles **D** 40 miles

6. Alexi drove for 30 minutes from Boston to Lexington. June drove for 20 minutes from Lexington to Concord. How many more minutes did Alexi drive than June?

A 10 minutes **B** 20 minutes **C** 40 minutes **D** 50 minutes

enVisionMATH Across the U.S.A.

Problem Solving Using Geometry

U.S. flag in 1777

The United States Flag

The first official U.S. flag was called the Stars and Stripes. It had 13 stars. There was one star for each of the first 13 states. In 1818 a law was passed that the flag should always have 13 stripes. It also said that there should be one star for each state. Today the flag has 50 stars.

U.S. flag since 1960

Maryland Blue Crab

There is a 400-pound crab in Maryland! The crab is made of many glass pieces. It is at the airport in Baltimore. The glass crab shows travelers one of Maryland's state animals.

7. What is the shape of the U.S. flag?

A Rectangle
B Triangle
C Square
D Circle

8. Name a solid figure that has a side in the shape of the U.S. flag.

A Sphere
B Cone
C Cylinder
D Rectangular prism

9. The shape of the piece of glass shown as part of the crab's claw is a triangle. How many sides and angles does a triangle have?

A 3 sides, 3 angles
B 3 sides, 4 angles
C 3 sides, 5 angles
D 3 sides, 6 angles

Problem Solving Using **Measurement**

Let Freedom Ring

The Liberty Bell is a symbol of freedom. It has been at the Liberty Bell Center in Philadelphia, Pennsylvania, since 2003. The metal of the bell is 3 inches thick at the bottom. The bell is about 3 feet tall.

Sunlight in Michigan

Lansing, Michigan, can get more than 15 hours of sunlight in summer. In winter, Lansing may only get about 9 hours of sunlight. That's a difference of more than 6 hours!

State Capitol Building in Lansing, Michigan

10. The Liberty Bell is about 3 feet tall. Which object is longer than 3 feet?

A Toothbrush
B Eraser
C Spoon
D Car

11. The metal of the Liberty Bell is about 3 inches thick at the bottom. Which object is about 3 inches long?

A Umbrella
B Bathtub
C Belt
D Crayon

12. Look at the clock. It shows the time the sun set in Lansing, Michigan, on February 19, 2007. What time does the clock show?

A 3:06 P.M.
B 3:30 P.M.
C 6:03 P.M.
D 6:15 P.M.

enVisionMATH Across the U.S.A.

Problem Solving Using Data Analysis and Probability

©1910 USPS

©1962 USPS

©1999 USPS

U.S. Postage

In 1919 it cost 2¢ to mail a letter in the United States. Since then the cost has gone up many times. In May 2007 it cost 41¢ to mail a letter.

13. Ana has five stamps in a box. Four of them are 2¢ stamps. One of them is a 39¢ stamp. What is the likelihood Ana will choose a 39¢ stamp from the box?

A Certain
B Likely
C Unlikely
D Impossible

14. Ana has ten stamps in a box. All ten stamps are 2¢ stamps. What is the likelihood Ana will choose a 2¢ stamp from the box?

A Certain
B Likely
C Unlikely
D Impossible

15. Look at the graph of state animals. How many states chose the white-tailed deer?

A 3
B 4
C 10
D 17

16. Look at the graph of state animals. How many more states chose the white-tailed deer than the black bear?

A 4
B 6
C 10
D 14

State Symbols

Every state in the United States has state symbols such as state plants, rocks, or animals. Many states have a state animal. Some states picked the same animal. The pictograph shows the three animals that were picked by the most states.

Top Three State Animals

Bison	★ ★ ★
Black Bear	★ ★ ★ ★
White-tailed Deer	★ ★ ★ ★ ★ ★ ★ ★ ★ ★

Each ★ = 1 state.

white-tailed deer

Missouri Caves

There are many caves in Missouri. The longest cave is about 28 miles long. Some animals live in these caves.

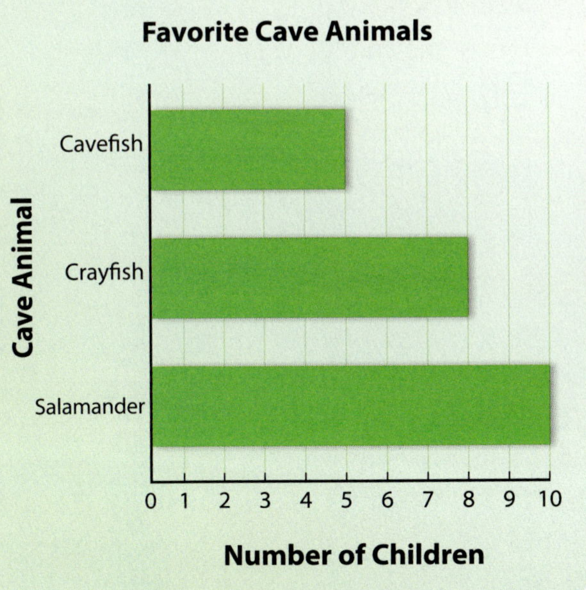

17. Look at the graph of cave animals. How many children chose the cavefish as their favorite cave animal?

A 1
B 3
C 5
D 10

18. Look at the graph of cave animals. How many more children chose the salamander as their favorite cave animal than the crayfish?

A 2
B 8
C 10
D 18

Problem Solving Using Algebra

Jim Henson

Jim Henson was born in Mississippi in 1936. His family moved to Maryland when he was in fifth grade. He made the first characters on *Sesame Street®*. One of them was the 98-inch-tall Big Bird®. Jim Henson called these characters "Muppets®." The Muppets® first appeared on *Sesame Street®* in 1969.

19. Big Bird® is 98 inches tall. He stands on a step that is 7 inches above the ground. Which number sentence tells how far the top of Big Bird's® head is above the ground in inches?

A $98 + 7 = \square$
B $98 - 7 = \square$
C $98 \times 7 = \square$
D $98 \div 7 = \square$

20. Big Bird® is about 8 feet tall. Jody is 5 feet tall. Which number sentence tells about how much taller Big Bird® is than Jody?

A $8 + 5 = \square$
B $8 - 5 = \square$
C $8 \times 5 = \square$
D $8 \div 5 = \square$

Problem-Solving Handbook

Scott Foresman · Addison Wesley

enVisionMATH™

Problem-Solving Handbook

Use this Problem-Solving Handbook throughout the year to help you solve problems.

Don't give up!

Everybody can be a good problem solver!

There's almost always more than one way to solve a problem!

Don't trust key words.

Pictures help me understand!

Explaining helps me understand!

Problem-Solving Process

Read and Understand

What am I trying to find?
- Tell what the question is asking.

What do I know?
- Tell the problem in my own words.
- Identify key facts and details.

Plan and Solve

What strategy or strategies should I try?

Can I show the problem?
- Try drawing a picture.
- Try making a list, table, or graph.
- Try acting it out or using objects.

How will I solve the problem?

What is the answer?
- Tell the answer in a complete sentence.

Strategies

- Show What You Know
  - Draw a Picture
  - Make an Organized List
  - Make a Table
  - Make a Graph
  - Act It Out/ Use Objects
- Look for a Pattern
- Try, Check, Revise
- Write a Number Sentence
- Use Reasoning
- Work Backward
- Solve a Simpler Problem

Look Back and Check

Did I check my work?
- Compare my work to the information in the problem.
- Be sure all calculations are correct.

Is my answer reasonable?
- Estimate to see if my answer makes sense.
- Make sure the question was answered.

Using Bar Diagrams

Use a bar diagram to show how what you know and what you want to find are related. Then choose an operation to solve the problem.

Problem 1

Carrie helps at the family flower store in the summer. She keeps a record of how many hours she works. How many hours did she work on Monday and Wednesday?

Carrie's Work Hours

Data

Days	Hours
Monday	5
Tuesday	3
Wednesday	6
Thursday	5
Friday	5

Bar Diagram

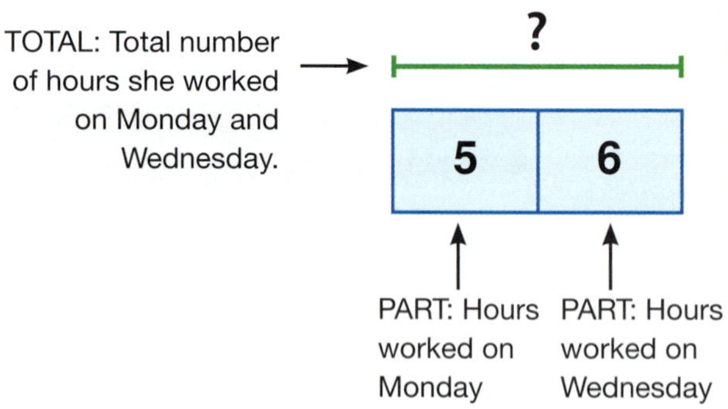

5 + 6 = ☐

Think I can add to find the total.

Problem 2

Kim is saving to buy a sweatshirt from the college her brother attends. She has $9. How much more money does she need to buy the sweatshirt?

Bar Diagram

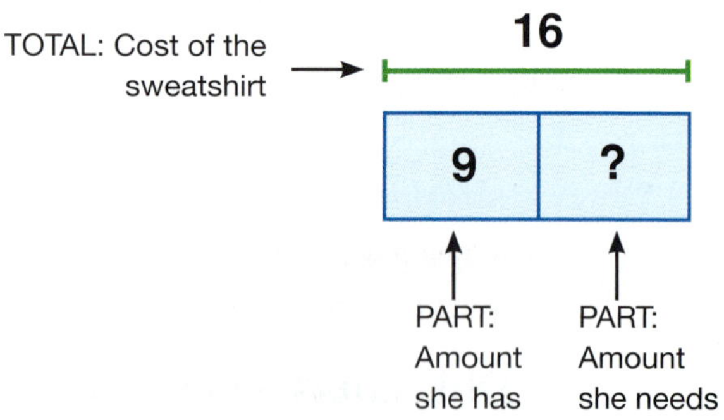

16 − 9 = ☐

Think I can subtract to find the missing part.

Pictures help me understand!

Don't trust key words!

Problem 3

Tickets to a movie on Saturday cost only $5 each no matter what age you are. What is the cost of tickets for a family of four?

Bar Diagram

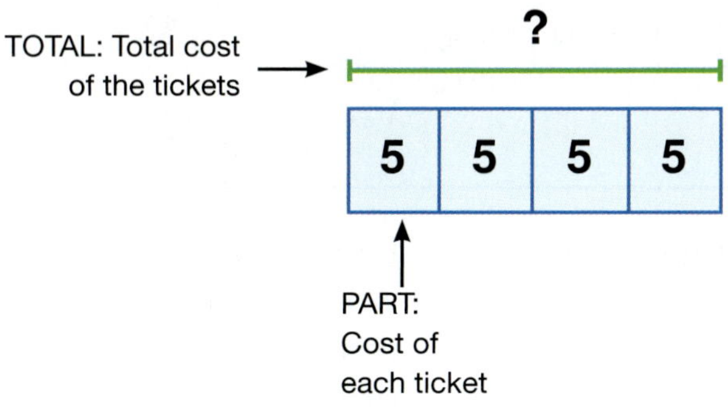

$4 \times 5 = \square$

Think: I can multiply because the parts are equal.

Problem 4

Twelve students traveled in 3 vans to the zoo. The same number of students were in each van. How many students were in each van?

Bar Diagram

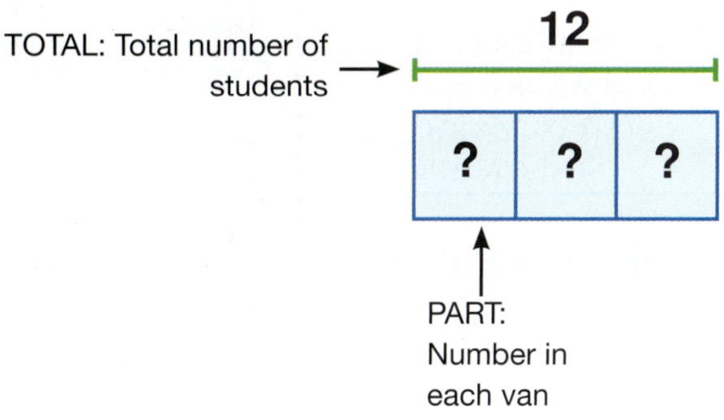

$12 \div 3 = \square$

Think: I can divide to find how many are in each part.

Problem-Solving Strategies

Strategy	Example	When I Use It
Draw a Picture	The race was 5 kilometers. Markers were at the starting line and the finish line. Markers showed each kilometer of the race. Find the number of markers used.	Try drawing a picture when it helps you visualize the problem or when the relationships such as joining or separating are involved.

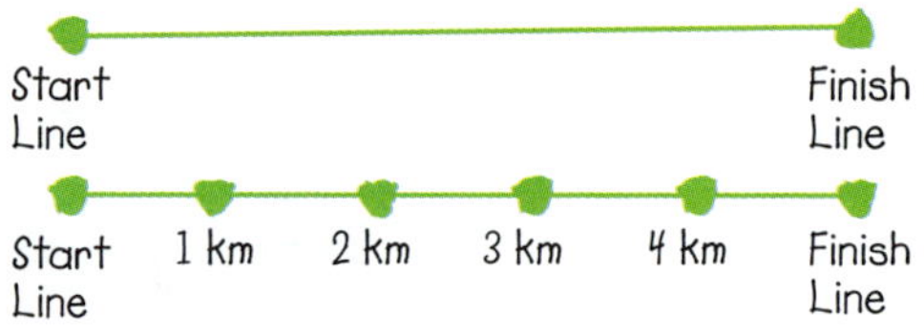

Strategy	Example	When I Use It
Make a Table	Phil and Marcy spent all day Saturday at the fair. Phil rode 3 rides each half hour and Marcy rode 2 rides each half hour. How many rides had Marcy ridden when Phil rode 24 rides?	Try making a table when: • there are 2 or more quantities, • amounts change using a pattern.

Rides for Phil	3	6	9	12	15	18	21	24
Rides for Marcy	2	4	6	8	10	12	14	16

Strategy	Example	When I Use It
Look for a Pattern	The house numbers on Forest Road change in a planned way. Describe the pattern. Tell what the next two house numbers should be.	Look for a pattern when something repeats in a predictable way.

Everybody can be a good problem solver!

Strategy	Example	When I Use It
Make an Organized List	How many ways can you make change for a quarter using dimes and nickels? 1 quarter = 1 dime + 1 dime + 1 nickel 1 dime + 1 nickel + 1 nickel + 1 nickel 1 nickel + 1 nickel + 1 nickel + 1 nickel + 1 nickel	Make an organized list when asked to find combinations of two or more items.
Try, Check, Revise	Suzanne spent $27, not including tax, on dog supplies. She bought two of one item and one of another item. What did she buy? $\$8 + \$8 + \$15 = \$31$ $\$7 + \$7 + \$12 = \$26$ $\$6 + \$6 + \$15 = \$27$	Use Try, Check, Revise when quantities are being combined to find a total, but you don't know which quantities. **Dog Supplies Sale!** Leash .... $8 Collar .... $6 Bowls .... $7 Medium Beds .... $15 Toys $12
Write a Number Sentence	Maria's new CD player can hold 6 discs at a time. If she has 54 CDs, how many times can the player be filled without repeating a CD? Find $54 \div 6 = \blacksquare$.	Write a number sentence when the story describes a situation that uses an operation or operations.

Even More Strategies

Strategy	Example	When I Use It
Act It Out	How many ways can 3 students shake each other's hand? 	Think about acting out a problem when the numbers are small and there is action in the problem you can do.
Use Reasoning	Beth collected some shells, rocks, and beach glass. **Beth's Collection** 2 rocks 3 times as many shells as rocks 12 objects in all  How many of each object are in the collection?	Use reasoning when you can use known information to reason out unknown information.
Work Backward	Tracy has band practice at 10:15 A.M. It takes her 20 minutes to get from home to practice and 5 minutes to warm up. What time should she leave home to get to practice on time? 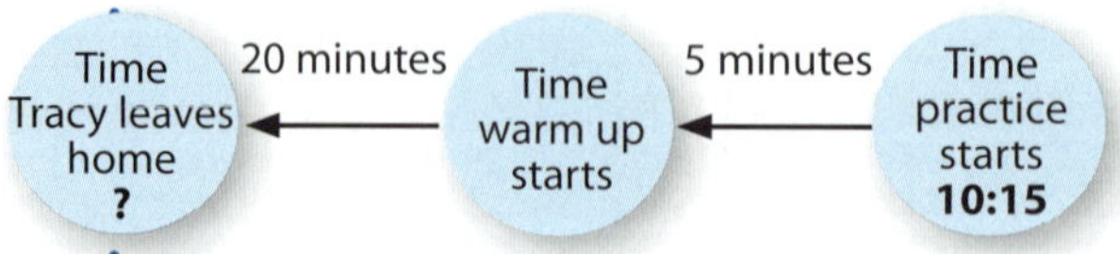 	Try working backward when: • you know the end result of a series of steps, • you want to know what happened at the beginning.

I can think about when to use each strategy.

Strategy	Example	When I Use It
Solve a Simpler Problem 	Each side of each triangle in the figure at the left is one centimeter. If there are 12 triangles in a row, what is the perimeter of the figure? I can look at 1 triangle, then 2 triangles, then 3 triangles.  perimeter = 3 cm 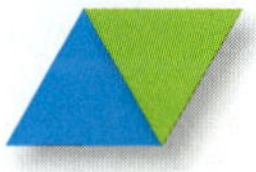 perimeter = 4 cm  perimeter = 5 cm	Try solving a simpler problem when you can create a simpler case that is easier to solve.
Make a Graph	Mary was in a jump rope contest. How did her number of jumps change over the five days of the contest? 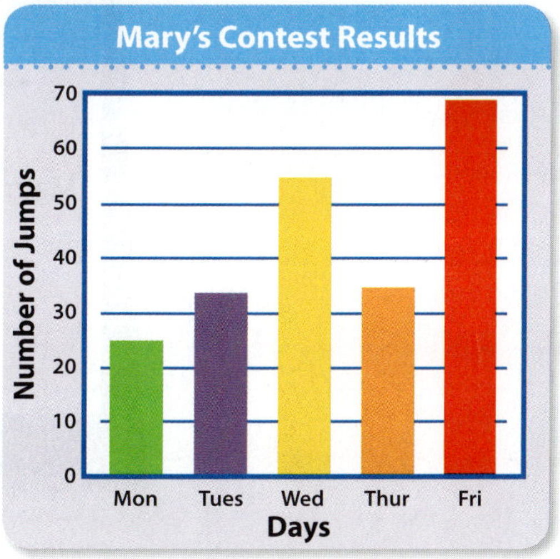	Make a graph when: • data for an event are given, • the question can be answered by reading the graph.

Writing to Explain

Here is a good math explanation.

Writing to Explain What happens to the area of the rectangle if the lengths of its sides are doubled?

■ = $\frac{1}{4}$ of the whole rectangle

The area of the new rectangle is 4 times the area of the original rectangle.

Tips for Writing Good Math Explanations....

A good explanation should be:

- correct
- simple
- complete
- easy to understand

Math explanations can use:

- words
- pictures
- numbers
- symbols

Explaining helps me understand!

This is another good math explanation.

Writing to Explain Use blocks to show 3×24. Draw a picture of what you did with the blocks.

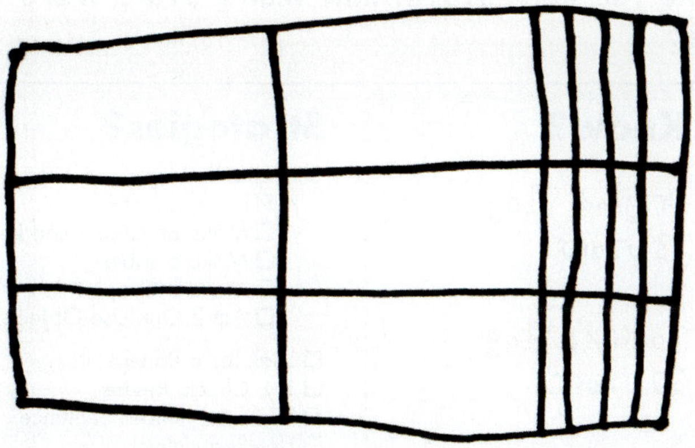

First we made a row of 24 using 2 tens and 4 ones. Then we made 2 more rows. Then we said 3 rows of 2 tens is 3 x 2 tens = 6 tens or 60. Then we said 3 rows of 4 ones is 3 x 4 = 12. Then we added the parts 60 + 12 = 72 So, 3 x 24 = 72.

Problem-Solving Recording Sheet

Name Jane

Teaching Tool 1

Problem-Solving Recording Sheet

Problem:
On June 14, 1777, the Continental Congress approved the design of a national flag. The 1777 flag had 13 stars, one for each colony. Today's flag has 50 stars, one for each state. How many stars were added to the flag since 1777?

Find?

Number of stars added to the flag

Know?

Original flag
13 stars

Today's flag
50 stars

Strategies?

Show the Problem
- ☑ Draw a Picture
- ☐ Make an Organized List
- ☐ Make a Table
- ☐ Make a Graph
- ☐ Act It Out/Use Objects

- ☐ Look for a Pattern
- ☐ Try, Check, Revise
- ☑ Write a Number Sentence
- ☐ Use Reasoning
- ☐ Work Backward
- ☐ Solve a Simpler Problem

Show the Problem?

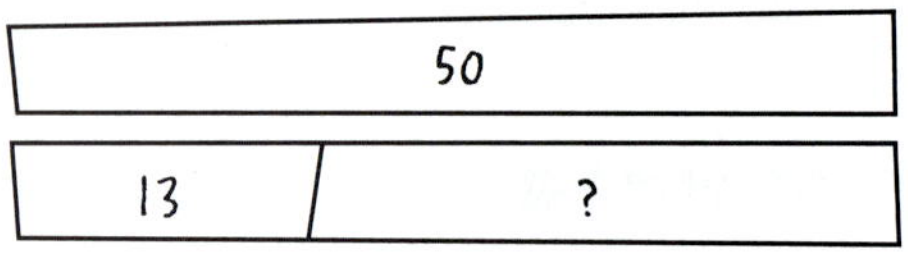

Solution?

I am comparing the two quantities.
I could add up from 13 to 50. I can also subtract 13 from 50. I'll subtract.

$$\begin{array}{r} 50 \\ -\ 13 \\ \hline 37 \end{array}$$

Answer?

There were 37 stars added to the flag from 1777 to today.

Check? Reasonable?

37 + 13 = 50 so I subtracted correctly.

50 - 13 is about 50 - 10 = 40
40 is close to 37. 37 is reasonable.

Teaching Tools • 1

Here's a way to organize my problem-solving work.

Name Benton

Teaching Tool
1

Problem-Solving Recording Sheet

Problem:

Suppose your teacher told you to open your math book to the facing pages whose page numbers add to 85. To which two pages would you open your book?

Find?

Two facing page numbers

Know?

Two pages.
Facing each other.
Sum is 85.

Strategies?

Show the Problem
- ☑ Draw a Picture
- ☐ Make an Organized List
- ☐ Make a Table
- ☐ Make a Graph
- ☐ Act It Out/Use Objects

- ☐ Look for a Pattern
- ☑ Try, Check, Revise
- ☑ Write a Number Sentence
- ☐ Use Reasoning
- ☐ Work Backward
- ☐ Solve a Simpler Problem

Show the Problem?

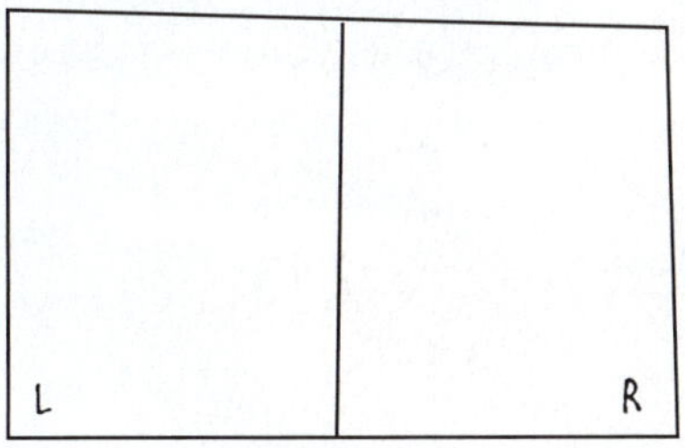

L + R = 85
L is 1 less than R

Solution?

I'll try some numbers in the middle.
40 + 41 = 81, too low
How about 46 and 47?
46 + 47 = 93, too high
Ok, now try 42 and 43.
42 + 43 = 85.

Answer?

The page numbers are 42 and 43.

Check? Reasonable?

I added correctly.
42 + 43 is about 40 + 40 = 80
80 is close to 85.
42 and 43 is reasonable.

Teaching Tools • 1

Topic 1

Numeration

1 How many dominos were used to set a world record for domino-toppling? You will find out in Lesson 1-3.

2 How much did the world's largest pumpkin weigh? You will find out in Lesson 1-2.

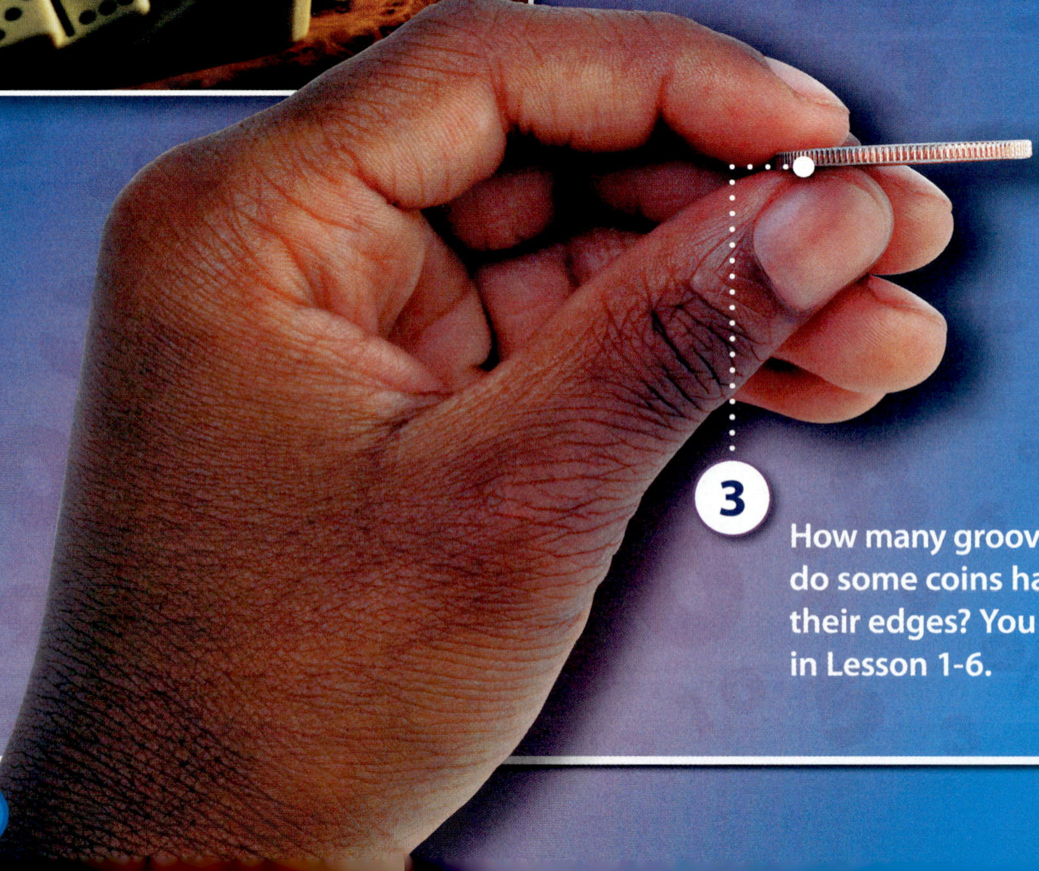

3 How many grooves, or reeds, do some coins have around their edges? You will find out in Lesson 1-6.

4

How tall is the Great Pyramid in Egypt? You will find out in Lesson 1-5.

Review What You Know!

Vocabulary

Choose the best term from the box.

- hundreds
- numbers
- ones
- tens

1. The number 49 has 4 ___?___.

2. The number 490 has 4 ___?___.

3. The number 54 has 4 ___?___.

Place Value

Write each number.

4. 3 tens 5 ones

5. 9 tens

6. forty-six

7. ninety-eight

Money

Write the value of each coin.

8. 

9. 

10. 

Skip count to find the missing amounts.

11. 5¢, 10¢, ___, ___, 25¢

12. 10¢, ___, 30¢, 40¢, ___

Compare Numbers

13. **Writing to Explain** Which is greater, 95 or 59? How do you know?

14. Write these numbers in order from least to greatest:

14 54 41

Virginia

Lesson 1-1

Prepares for 3.1.a The student will read and write six-digit numerals and identify the place value and value of each digit.

Hundreds

Hands-On: place-value blocks

How can you read and write a number in the hundreds?

All numbers are made from the digits, 0, 1, 2, 3, 4, 5, 6, 7, 8, and 9.

Place value is the value of the place a digit has in a number.

Bicycles with chains have been used for more than 125 years.

Another Example How can you show numbers on a place-value chart?

The place-value chart shows the value of each digit in 850.

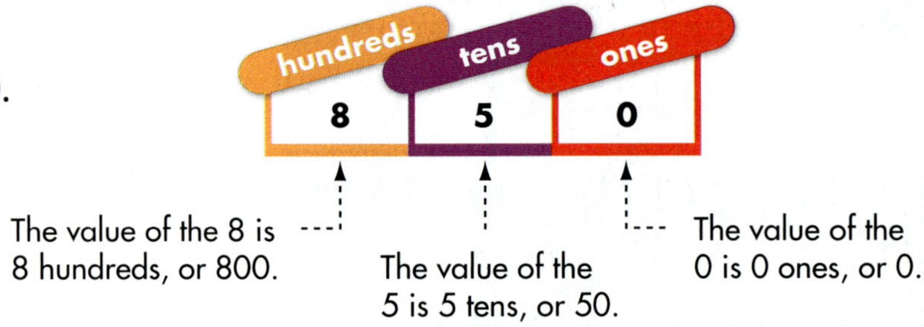

Explain It

1. In expanded form, 850 can be written as 800 + 50. Why are there only 2 addends in this expanded form?

Guided Practice*

Do you know HOW?

For **1–3**, write each number in standard form.

1. 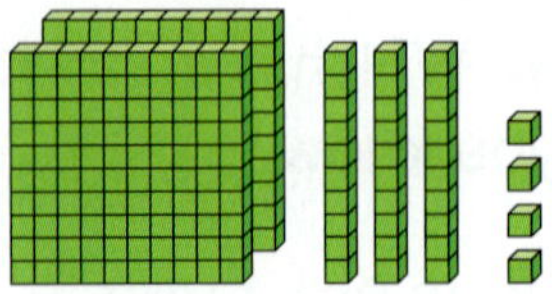

2. 600 + 50 + 3

3. eight hundred seventy-nine

4. Write 156 in expanded form.

Do you UNDERSTAND?

5. How does a place-value chart show the value of a number?

6. The example at the top of the page uses the number 125. What is the value of each digit in 125?

7. How do you know that 37 and 307 do not name the same number?

DIGITAL Animated Glossary, eTools **www.pearsonsuccessnet.com**

*For another example, see Set A on page 28.

You can show 125 in different ways.

One way you can show 125 is to use place-value blocks.

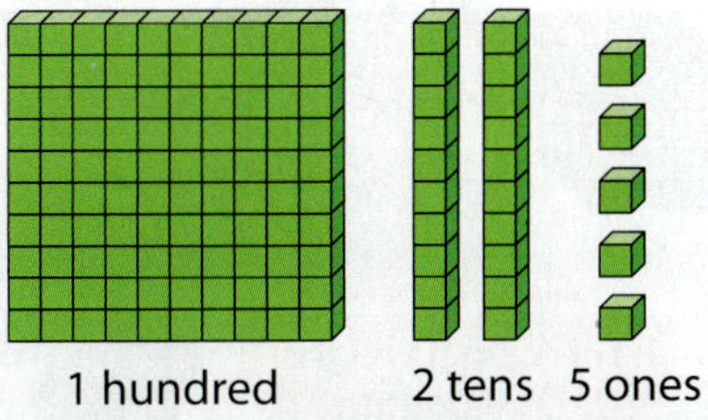

A number written in a way that shows only its digits is in **standard form**.

125

A number written as the sum of the values of its digits is in **expanded form**.

100 + 20 + 5

A number written in words is in **word form**.

one hundred twenty-five

Independent Practice

Write each number in standard form.

8. 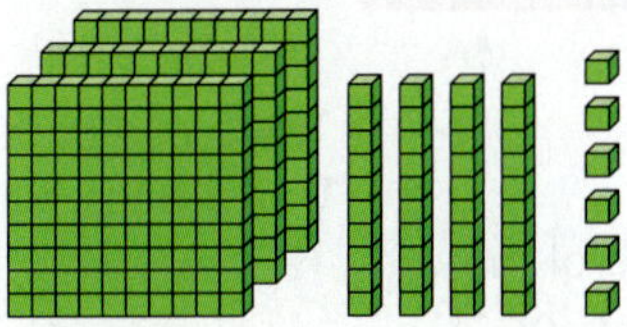

9. 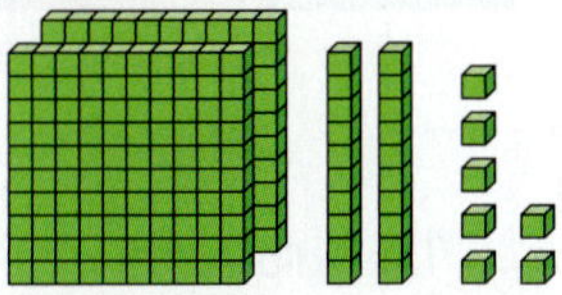

10. 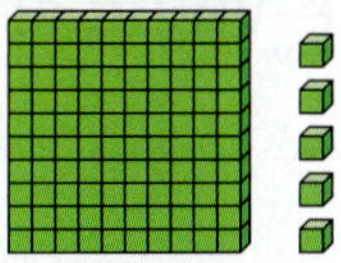

11. 900 + 80 + 5

12. 400 + 70 + 8

13. three hundred four

Write each number in expanded form and word form.

14. 707

15. 683

16. 894

17. 520

18. 251

19. 402

Problem Solving

20. **Reasoning** The sum of the digits in a three-digit number is 4. The ones digit is 3. What is the number?

21. **Algebra** Find the value of the missing number.
389 = ☐ + 80 + 9

22. **Writing to Explain** Which digit has the greatest value in 589? Explain.

23. Which is the standard form of 700 + 50?

SOL Prep

A 570 **B** 1,200 **C** 750 **D** 705

24. **Number Sense** What is the greatest three-digit number? the least?

Virginia

Lesson 1-2

Prepares for 3.1.a The student will read and write six-digit numerals and identify the place value and value of each digit.

Thousands

Hands-On place-value blocks

How can you read and write 4-digit numbers?

Ten hundreds equal one thousand.

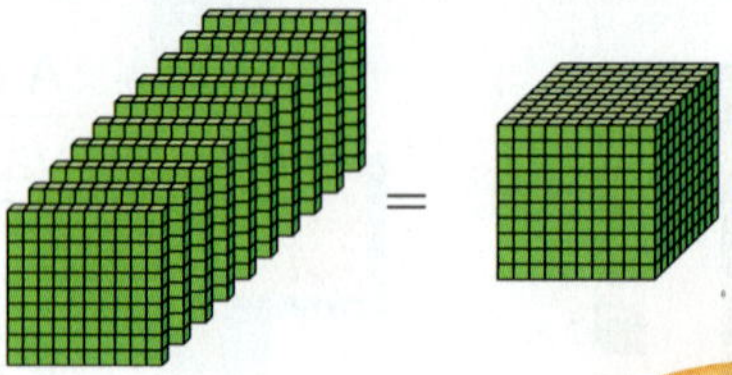

Did you know that a two-humped camel weighs between 1,000 and 1,450 pounds?

This camel weighs 1,350 pounds.

Another Example

How can you show 1,350 on a place-value chart?

thousands	hundreds	tens	ones
1,	3	5	0

The value of the 1 is 1 thousand, or 1,000.

The value of the 3 is 3 hundreds, or 300.

The value of the 5 is 5 tens, or 50.

The value of the 0 is 0 ones, or 0.

Explain It

1. If you showed 1,305 in a place-value chart, how would it look different from the example above?

Guided Practice*

Do you know HOW?

Write each number in standard form.

1. 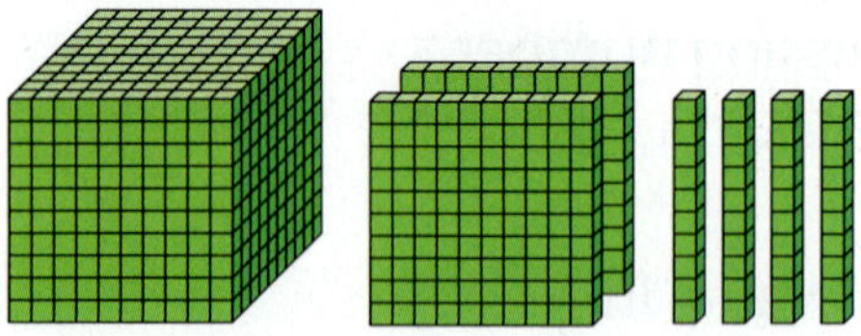

2. 8,000 + 500 + 30 + 9

3. two thousand, four hundred sixty-one

4. four hundred one

Do you UNDERSTAND?

5. Explain the value of each digit in 6,802.

6. Write a 4-digit number that has a tens digit of 5, a hundreds digit of 2, and 6 for each of the other digits.

7. Suppose another animal is three hundred pounds heavier than the camel in the photo. How would you write that weight in expanded form?

DIGITAL eTools **www.pearsonsuccessnet.com**

*For another example, see Set A on page 28.

You can show 1,350 in different ways.

place-value blocks:

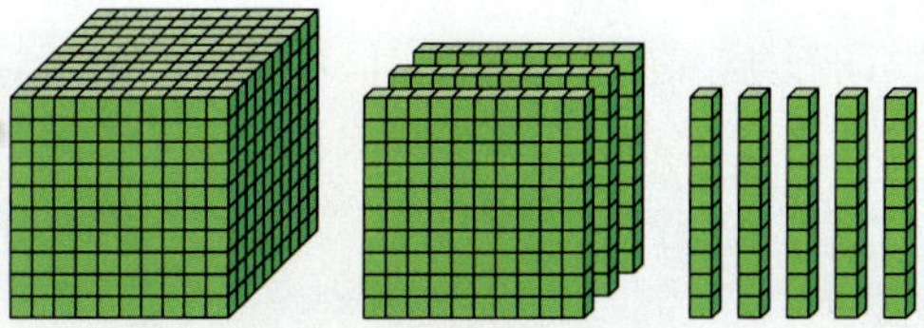

1 thousand 3 hundreds 5 tens 0 ones

expanded form: 1,000 + 300 + 50

standard form: 1,350

Write a comma between the thousands and the hundreds.

word form: one thousand, three hundred fifty

Write a comma between the thousands and the hundreds.

Independent Practice

For **8–10**, write each number in standard form.

8.

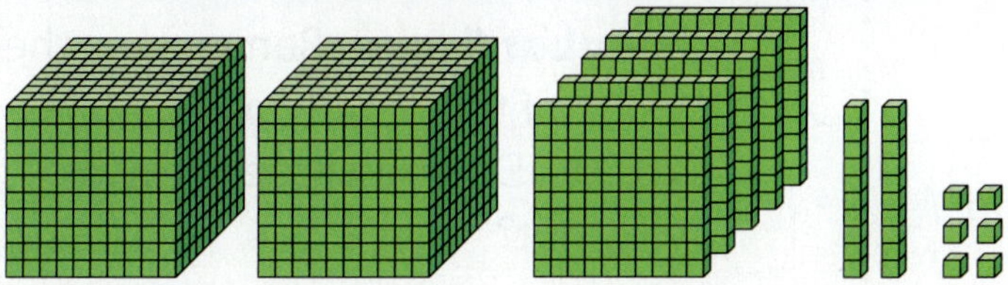

9. 4,000 + 600 + 50 + 8

10. 7,000 + 200 + 1

For **11** and **12**, write each number in expanded form.

11. six thousand, two hundred four

12. 5,033

For **13–17**, write the place of the underlined digit. Then write its value.

13. 4,$\underline{8}$65 **14.** 3,2$\underline{4}$5 **15.** $\underline{9}$,716 **16.** 5,3$\underline{0}$9 **17.** $\underline{7}$,240

Problem Solving

18. Number Sense Write the greatest possible number and the least possible number using the four digits 5, 2, 8, and 1.

19. In 2005, the world's largest pumpkin weighed 1,469 pounds. Write that number in word form.

20. Which is the word form of 2,406?

A twenty-four thousand, six

B two thousand, four hundred six

C two thousand, forty-six

D two hundred forty-six

21. Writing to Explain Sam used place-value blocks to show the number 3,124. Then he added 2 more thousand cubes. What was the new number? Explain.

Virginia

Lesson 1-3

3.1.a The student will read and write six-digit numerals and identify the place value and value of each digit.

Greater Numbers

How can you read and write greater numbers?

Capitol Reef National Park in Utah covers 241,904 acres of land.

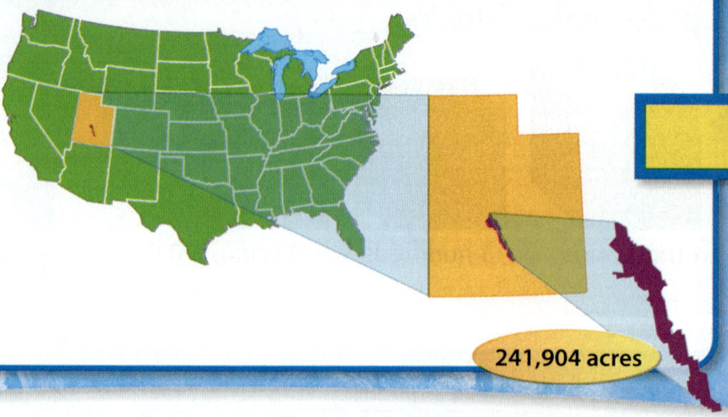

Guided Practice*

Do you know HOW?

For **1–3**, write each number in standard form.

1. three hundred forty-two thousand, six hundred seven

2. ninety-eight thousand, three hundred twenty

3. 500,000 + 40,000 + 600 + 90 + 3

4. What is the value of the 9 in 379,050?

Do you UNDERSTAND?

5. **Number Sense** Ramos says the value of the digit 7 in 765,450 is 70,000. Do you agree? Why or why not?

6. **Writing to Explain** Describe how 130,434 and 434,130 are alike and how they are different.

Independent Practice

Write each number in standard form.

7. twenty-seven thousand, five hundred fifty

8. 800,000 + 20,000 + 6,000 + 300 + 50

Write each number in expanded form.

9. 46,354

10. 395,980

Write the place of the underlined digit. Then write its value.

11. 404,705 **12.** 163,254 **13.** 45,391 **14.** 983,971 **15.** 657,240

DIGITAL Animated Glossary **www.pearsonsuccessnet.com**

For another example, see Set B on page 28.

How can you show 241,904 in different ways?

place-value chart:

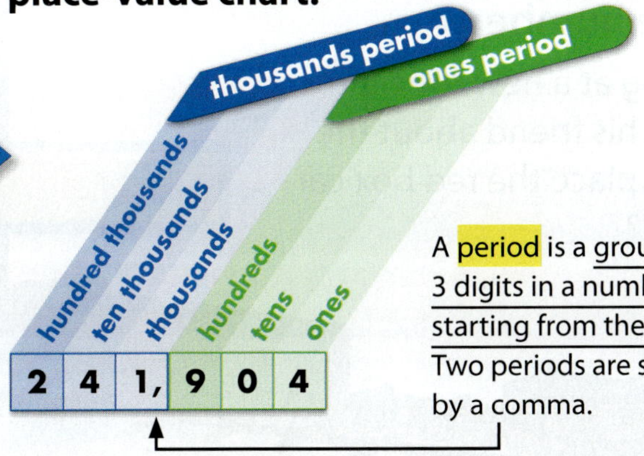

A period is a group of 3 digits in a number, starting from the right. Two periods are separated by a comma.

standard form:
241, 904

expanded form:
200,000 + 40,000 + 1,000 + 900 + 4

word form: two hundred forty-one thousand, nine hundred four

Algebra Find each missing number.

16. 26,305 = 20,000 + □ + 300 + 5

17. 801,960 = 800,000 + 1,000 + □ + 60

18. 400,000 + □ + 30 + 2 = 470,032

19. 618,005 = □ + 10,000 + 8,000 + 5

20. 300,000 + □ + 600 + 3 = 304,603

21. 200,000 + 4,000 + 60 + 3 = □

Problem Solving

For **22–24**, use the table.

22. Write the population of each city in the table in expanded form.

23. Write the population of Columbus, OH in word form.

Data

City Populations

City	Number of People
Austin, TX	681,804
Jacksonville, FL	777,704
Columbus, OH	730,008

24. Which cities listed in the table have more than seven hundred thousand people?

25. A new world record was once set when 303,628 dominos fell. Write 303,628 in expanded form.

26. Which is the word form of the number 805,920?

A eighty-five thousand, ninety-two

B eight hundred five thousand, ninety-two

C eight thousand, five hundred ninety-two

D eight hundred five thousand, nine hundred twenty

Virginia

Lesson 1-4

Reviews 2.2.b The student will write the ordinal number.

Ways to Name Numbers

How can you use and name numbers?

In the hobby shop, Jack is looking at a new toy train that has 38 cars. He wants to tell his friend about the train. How can he describe what place the red box car is in? What place is the last car in?

Other Examples

What are different ways to name the number 1,200?

one thousand, two hundred

1 thousand = 10 hundreds

twelve hundred

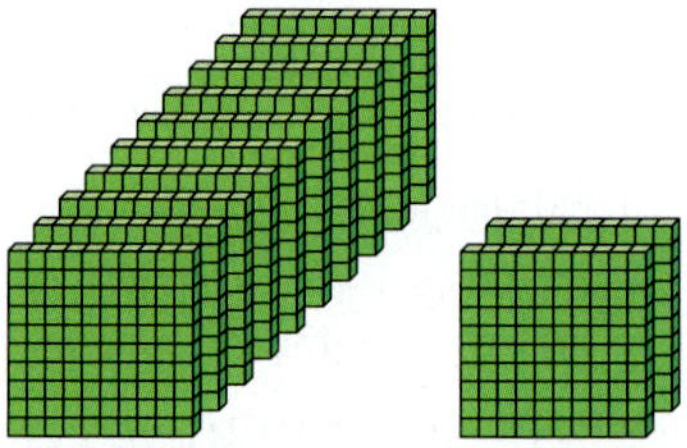

Guided Practice*

Do you know HOW?

Write the ordinal number and ordinal word form of each number.

1. 8

2. 63

Name each number in two ways.

3. 2,400

4. 8,300

Do you UNDERSTAND?

5. Reasoning In the example above, how are the two names for 1,200 the same? different?

6. Lon ran in a race. Sixty people finished the race in front of him. In what place did Lon finish?

Independent Practice

In **7–10**, write the ordinal number and ordinal word form of the number.

7. 18

8. 71

9. 80

10. 93

DIGITAL Animated Glossary **www.pearsonsuccessnet.com**

**For another example, see Set C on page 28.*

An ordinal number is used to show the order of people or objects.

Ordinal Number: 4th

Ordinal Word Form: fourth

The red box car is fourth.

There are 38 cars in the train.

Ordinal Number: 38th

Ordinal Word Form: thirty-eighth

The last car is the 38th car in the train.

Here are some other examples of ordinal numbers.

9th	12th	70th	91st
ninth	twelfth	seventieth	ninety-first

In **11–14**, name the number in two ways.

11. 5,200 **12.** 6,400 **13.** 9,800 **14.** 4,500

Problem Solving

Use the table at the right for **15** and **16**.

15. Beth wrote down the address she heard—Fifteen thousand, one hundred eight Allen Street. Which place is located at this address?

16. Write two names for the number in the address of Gibson's Market.

Data

Place	Address
Ace Sporting Goods	1518 Allen Street
Central Post Office	15008 Allen Street
Gibson's Market	3900 Allen Street
Tops Bowling Center	15108 Allen Street

17. Ron counted 39 people waiting in line ahead of him. Write the ordinal number and ordinal word form for Ron's place in line.

18. Maris named odd numbers starting with 1. Which is the eighth number in her count?

1, 3, 5, 7, 9, 11, 13, 15, 17, 19, 21

19. **Number Sense** The population of Leon County is 239,452. The population of Dakota County is 355,904. Which county has fewer than three hundred thousand people?

20. Which is another way to write the number 6,200?

A six hundred two

B six hundred two thousand

C sixty-two hundred

D sixty thousand, two hundred

Virginia

Lesson 1-5

3.1.c The student will compare two whole numbers between 0 and 9,999, using symbols (>, <, or =) and words (greater than, less than, or equal to).

Comparing Numbers

How do you compare numbers?

When you compare two numbers you find out which number is greater and which number is less.

Which is taller, the Statue of Liberty or its base?

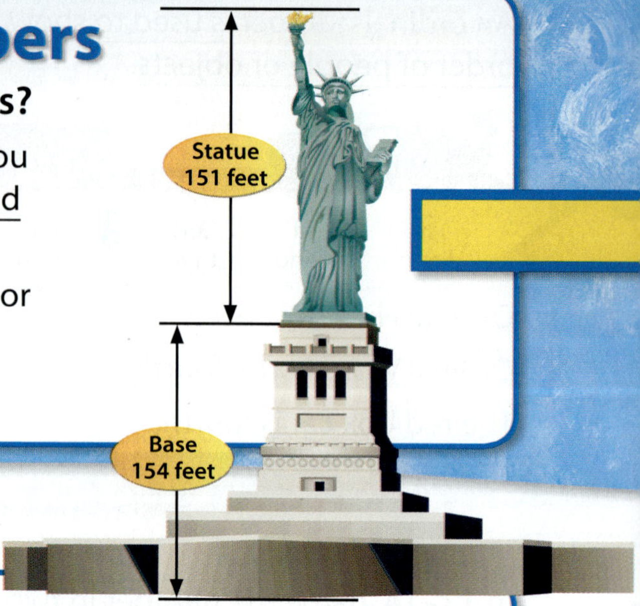

Another Example

How can you use place-value charts and number lines to compare numbers?

Compare 3,456 and 3,482 using a place-value chart. Then show these two numbers on a number line.

On a place-value chart, line up the digits by place value. Compare the digits starting from the left.

thousands	hundreds	tens	ones
3,	**4**	**5**	**6**
3,	**4**	**8**	**2**
↑ same	↑ same	↑ different 5 tens < 8 tens	

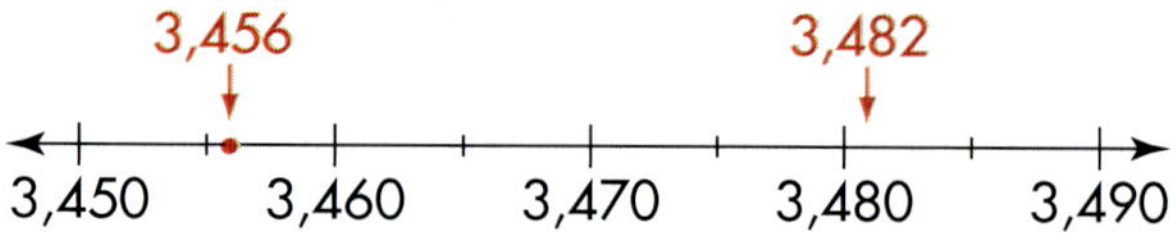

On the number line, 3,456 is to the left of 3,482.

So 3,456 **is less than** 3,482.

3,456 < 3,482

Explain It

1. In this example, why don't you need to compare the digit in the ones place?
2. Why can't you tell which number is greater by just comparing the first digit in each number?

DIGITAL Animated Glossary **www.pearsonsuccessnet.com**

You can use symbols.

Data

Symbol	Meaning
<	is less than
>	is greater than
=	is equal to

You can compare 151 and 154 with place value.

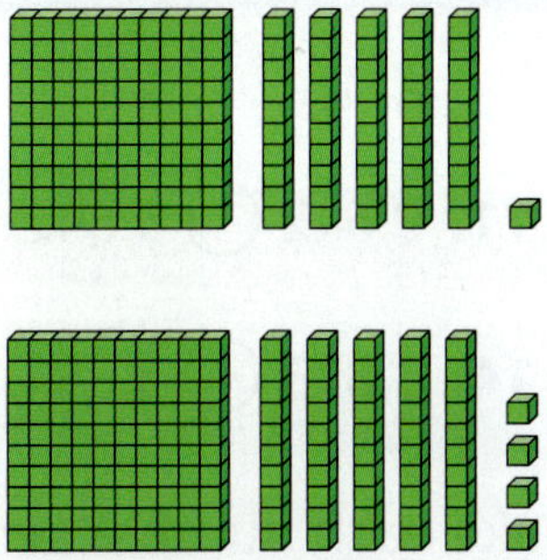

154 is greater than 151.

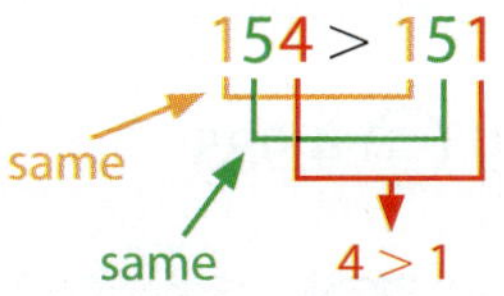

The place-value blocks also show that 151 is less than 154.

151 < 154

So, the base is taller than the statue.

Guided Practice*

Do you know HOW?

Compare the numbers. Use <, >, or =.

1.

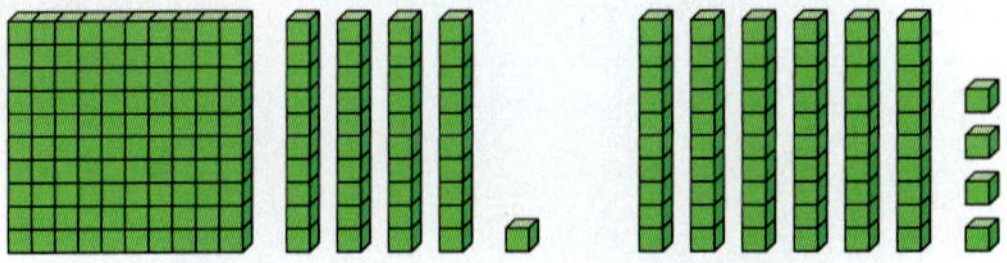

141 ◯ 64

2.

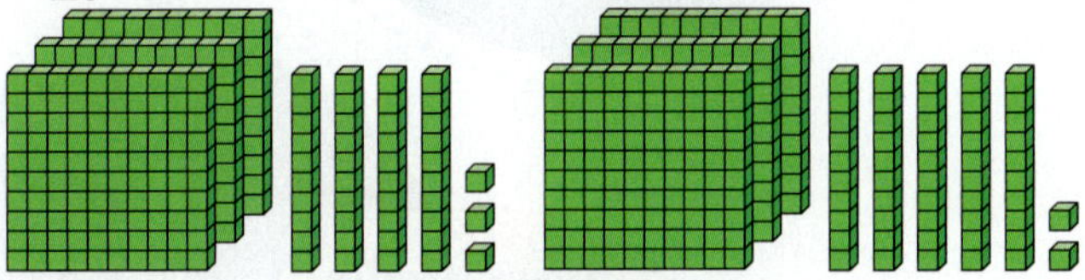

343 ◯ 352

3. 2,561 ◯ 2,261

4. 6,807 ◯ 6,807

Do you UNDERSTAND?

5. Number Sense Cara says that since 4 is greater than 1, the number 496 is greater than the number 1,230. Do you agree? Why or why not?

6. Writing to Explain The total height of the Statue of Liberty is 305 feet. The Washington Monument is 555 feet tall. Which is taller? Explain how you know.

7. Draw a number line to compare the numbers.

1,462 ◯ 1,521

Independent Practice

Compare the numbers. Use <, >, or =.

8.

93 ◯ 120

9.

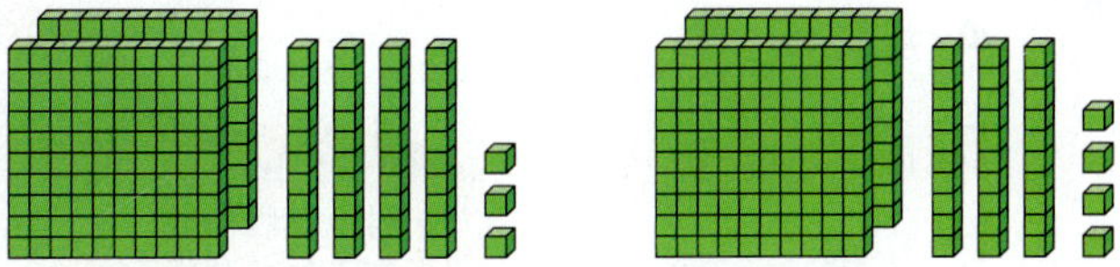

243 ◯ 234

For another example, see Set D on page 29.

Independent Practice

Compare the numbers. Use <, >, or =.

10. 679 ◯ 4,985 **11.** 9,642 ◯ 9,642 **12.** 5,136 ◯ 5,163

13. 8,204 ◯ 8,402 **14.** 3,823 ◯ 3,853 **15.** 2,424 ◯ 2,242

Write the missing digits to make each number sentence true.

16. □24 > 896 **17.** 6□7 < 617 **18.** 29□ = 2□0

19. □,000 < 1,542 **20.** 3,□12 > 3,812 **21.** 2,185 > 2,□85

Problem Solving

Use the pictures for **22** and **23**.

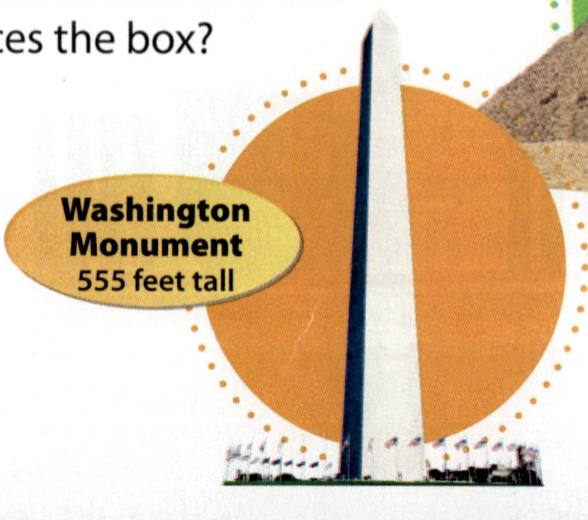

22. **Writing to Explain** Which is taller, the Washington Monument or the Great Pyramid in Egypt? How do you know?

23. Which is taller, the Gateway Arch or the Space Needle?

24. **Reasoning** Mark is thinking of a 3-digit number. Rory is thinking of a 4-digit number. Whose number is greater? How do you know?

25. **Number Sense** Suppose you are comparing 1,272 and 1,269. Do you need to compare the ones digits? Which number would be farther to the right on the number line? Explain.

26. Which number sentence is true if the number 537 replaces the box?

SOL Prep

A 456 > □

B □ = 256

C 598 < □

D □ > 357

Algebra Connections

Number Patterns

Remember that skip counting can be used to make a number pattern. Skip counting can also be used to find missing numbers in a given pattern.

Examples: 2, 4, 6, 8, ▢, 12

Think Can you skip count by a certain number to get each number in the pattern?

Skip count by 2s for this pattern.

2, 4, 6, 8, 10, 12

Copy and complete. Write the number that completes each pattern.

1. 3, 6, 9, 12, ▢, 18

2. 14, ▢, 18, 20, 22, 24

3. 20, 30, ▢, 50, 60, 70

4. 25, 50, 75, 100, 125, ▢

5. 3, 8, 13, 18, 23, ▢

6. 9, 19, 29, ▢, 49, 59

7. 7, 9, 11, ▢, 15, 17

8. 12, ▢, 20, 24, 28

9. 90, 80, 70, ▢, 50, 40

10. 22, 20, 18, 16, ▢, 12

11. 86, 81, ▢, 71, 66, 61

12. 150, ▢, 100, 75, 50, 25

For **13** and **14**, copy and complete each pattern. Use the pattern to help solve the problem.

13. Rusty saw that the house numbers on a street were in a pattern. First he saw the number 101. Then he saw the numbers 103, 105, and 107. There was a missing number, and then the number 111. What was the missing number?

101, 103, 105, 107, ▢, 111

14. Alani was skip counting the pasta shapes she made. The numbers she said were 90, 95, 100, 105, 110, 115. She needed to say one more number in the count to finish counting the pasta. How many pasta shapes did Alani make?

90, 95, 100, 105, 110, 115, ▢

15. **Write a Problem** Copy and complete the number pattern below. Write a real-world problem to match the number pattern.

5, 10, 15, 20, 25, 30, ▢

Virginia

Lesson 1-6

Extends 3.1.c The student will compare two whole numbers between 0 and 9,999, using symbols (>, <, or =) and words (greater than, less than, or equal to).

Ordering Numbers

How can you order numbers?

When you order numbers, you write them from greatest to least or from least to greatest.

Three rivers are shown on the map. Write their lengths in order from greatest to least.

Guided Practice*

Do you know HOW?

For **1** and **2**, order the numbers from least to greatest.

1. 769 679 697

2. 359 368 45

For **3** and **4**, order the numbers from greatest to least.

3. 4,334 809 4,350

4. 1,137 1,573 1,457

Do you UNDERSTAND?

5. **Writing to Explain** The length of another river has a 2 in the hundreds place. Can this river be longer than the Colorado? Why or why not?

6. Copy and complete the number line below to show the numbers 315, 305, and 319 in order.

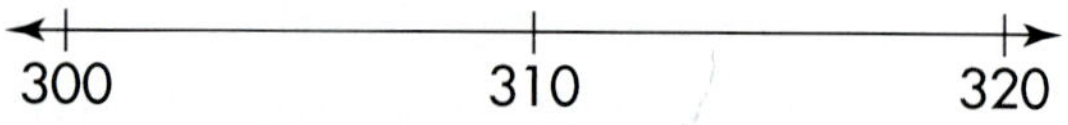

Independent Practice

For **7–9**, order the numbers from least to greatest.

7. 6,743 6,930 6,395 **8.** 995 1,293 1,932 **9.** 8,754 8,700 8,792

For **10–12**, order the numbers from greatest to least.

10. 2,601 967 2,365 **11.** 3,554 3,454 3,459 **12.** 5,304 5,430 5,403

13. Copy and complete the number line below to show 1,020, 965, and 985 in order.

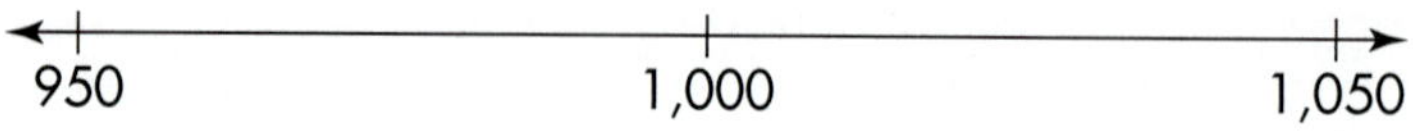

DIGITAL Animated Glossary www.pearsonsuccessnet.com

*For another example, see Set D on page 29.

You can use a place-value chart to help you.

thousands	hundreds	tens	ones
1,	4	5	0
2,	3	4	8
2,	3	1	5

1 < 2
So 1,450 is the least number.

3 = 3

4 > 1
So 2,348 is the greatest number.

The lengths of the rivers in order from greatest to least are:
Mississippi: 2,348 miles;
Missouri: 2,315 miles;
Colorado: 1,450 miles.

Problem Solving

Use the pictures for **14–17**.

14. Which animal weighs 100 pounds more than a moose?

15. Number Sense A ton is equal to 2,000 pounds. Which animals weigh less than 1 ton?

16. Write the names of the animals in the order of their weights from least to greatest.

17. Reasonableness Margo says the camel weighs about fifteen hundred pounds. Do you agree or disagree?

18. Writing to Explain Describe how you would write the numbers below from least to greatest.

3,456 3,654 2,375

19. Which number is between 5,695 and 6,725?

SOL Prep

A 5,659 **B** 6,735 **C** 6,632 **D** 6,728

20. The grooves around the outside of some coins are called reeds. Look at the table at the right. List the coins from the table in order from least to greatest number of reeds.

Data

Coin	Number of Reeds
Susan B. Anthony Dollar	133
Half dollar	150
Quarter	119
Dime	118

Virginia

Lesson 1-7

3.8 The student will determine, by counting, the value of a collection of bills and coins whose total value is $5.00 or less, compare the value of the bills and coins, and make change.

Counting Money

Hands-On
play money

How do you count money?

Here are some familiar bills and coins.

5 dollars
$5 or $5.00

1 dollar
$1 or $1.00

half dollar
50¢ or $0.50

quarter
25¢ or $0.25

dime
10¢ or $0.10

nickel
5¢ or $0.05

penny
1¢ or $0.01

Another Example How can you show the same amount of money in different ways?

You can show money amounts in more than one way.
Here are two ways to show $2.56.

One Way

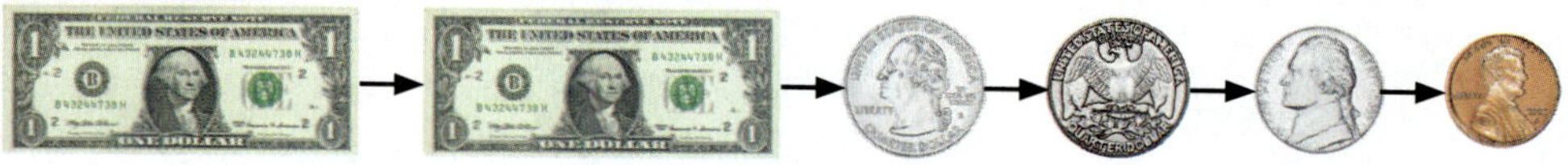

$1.00 $2.00 $2.25 $2.50 $2.55 **$2.56**

Another Way

$1.00 $1.50 $2.00 $2.25 $2.35 $2.45 $2.55 **$2.56**

Explain It

1. Could you show $2.56 without using pennies? Explain.
2. How could you show $2.56, using the least number of bills and coins?
3. How do you use skip counting when you count money?

This toy costs one dollar and ninety-five cents.

A dollar sign shows money amounts.

A decimal point separates dollars and cents.

Greg has the money shown below. Does he have enough money to buy the toy giraffe?

To count money, start with the bill or coin of greatest value. Then count on to find the total value.

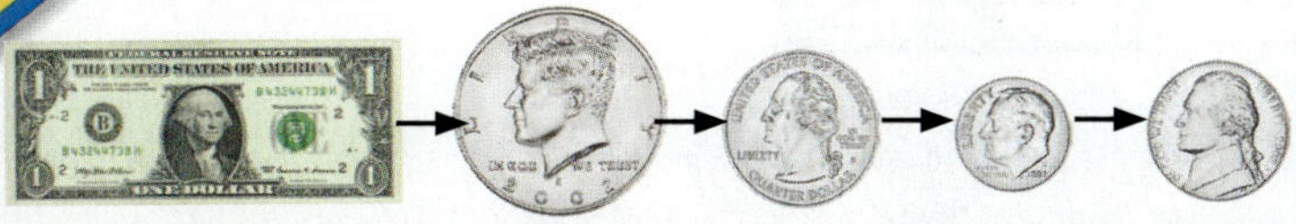

$1.00 → $1.50 → $1.75 → $1.85 → **$1.90**

Write: $1.90

Say: one dollar and ninety cents

No, Greg does not have enough money.

Guided Practice*

Do you know HOW?

Write the total value in dollars and cents.

1. 

2. 

3. 

Do you UNDERSTAND?

4. How could you show $7.95 using the least number of bills and coins?

5. What coins and bills could you use to show $2.65 two ways?

6. **Number Sense** If you have 195 pennies, do you have enough money to buy the toy giraffe shown above?

Independent Practice

Write the total value in dollars and cents.

7. 

8. 

DIGITAL Animated Glossary, eTools **www.pearsonsuccessnet.com**

*For another example, see Set E on page 29.

Independent Practice

Write the total value in dollars and cents.

9.

10.

11. 1 one-dollar bill, 1 half dollar, 3 nickels

12. 1 one-dollar bill, 2 half dollars, 1 quarter, 4 dimes, 4 nickels

13. 1 five-dollar bill, 1 one-dollar bill, 2 quarters, 3 dimes, 4 pennies

14. 1 five-dollar bill, 3 quarters, 2 dimes, 2 nickels

Compare the amounts. Write <, >, or =.

15. $1.01 ◯ 1 one-dollar bill

16. $0.83 ◯ 3 quarters, 1 dime

17. 9 dimes, 2 nickels ◯ $0.95

18. $1.60 ◯ 2 half dollars, 3 quarters

19. 10 quarters ◯ $2.50

20. $3.15 ◯ 4 half dollars, 4 quarters

Problem Solving

21. Look at the top of page 19. Keisha says Greg needs 5 more coins to have enough to buy the toy. Reni says he needs only 1 more coin. Explain who is correct.

22. **Reasoning** Bob has 3 quarters, 1 dime, and 1 nickel. What coin does he need to make $1.00?

23. Show two ways to make $3.62. Draw rectangles to represent bills. Draw circles with letters to represent coins.

24. Tyler has 5 coins worth $0.65. All of the coins are either quarters or dimes. How many of each coin does he have?

25. Use the picture at the right. Each minute, the U.S. Treasury Department produces 30,000 coins. Are more coins or bills produced in 1 minute?

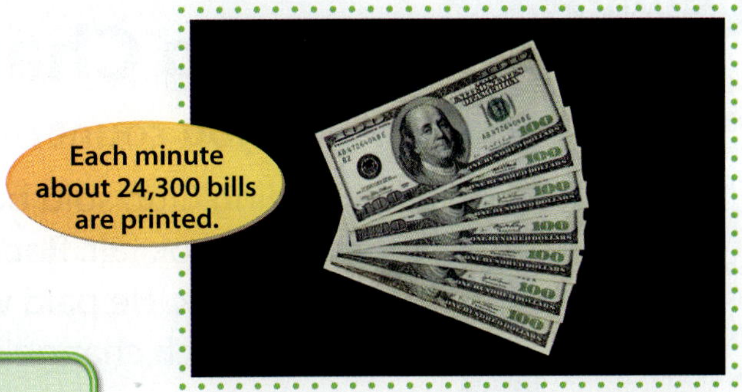

Use the table for **26–28**.

Ticket Prices for Gateway Arch

Attraction	Adults (17 and up)	Youth (13–16)	Child (3–12)
Tram Ride	$10.00	$7.00	$3.00
Movie	$7.00	$4.00	$2.50

26. Suppose you had only half dollars and quarters. How many half dollars are needed to buy a child's ticket for the tram ride? How many quarters are needed?

27. If you were using quarters only, how many would you need for a child's movie ticket? If you were using dimes only, how many would you need?

28. **Reasoning** When the Gateway Arch opened in July 1967, the total cost for 2 adult tram tickets and 1 child's tram ticket was $2.50. What can you buy at the arch for that amount now?

29. What is the total value of the 6 coins below?

SOL Prep

A $0.81

B $0.96

C $1.21

D $1.06

30. What is the total value of the 8 coins below?

SOL Prep

A $1.02

B $1.20

C $1.07

D $ 0.92

Virginia

Lesson 1-8

3.8 The student will determine, by counting, the value of a collection of bills and coins whose total value is $5.00 or less, compare the value of the bills and coins, and make change.

Making Change

How do you count on to make change?

The Reading Club sold bookmarks at the school book fair. Rodrigo bought one bookmark. He paid with two $1 bills. How much change should he get?

Another Example

Paula bought a notebook for $2.59. She paid with a $5 bill. How much change should she get?

Cost | Amount Paid

$2.59 → $2.60 → $2.70 → $2.75 → $3.00 → $4.00 → **$5.00**

Paula's change should be $2.41.

Guided Practice*

Do you know HOW?

In **1** and **2**, list coins and bills to make the change. Write the amount of the change.

1. Cost: $0.94
Amount paid: $1.00

2. Cost: $2.35
Amount paid: $5.00

Do you UNDERSTAND?

3. **Reasoning** In the notebook example, why does it make sense to start with a penny?

4. Tamara bought some bookmarks for $3.75. She paid with a $5 bill. How much change should she get?

Independent Practice

In **5–7**, list coins and bills to make the change. Write the amount of the change.

5. Cost: $0.79
Amount paid: $1.00

6. Cost: $2.37
Amount paid: $3.00

7. Cost: $3.21
Amount paid: $5.00

*For another example, see Set E on page 29.

Step 1

Start with the cost. Count on from the cost to the amount paid. Use coins that will make skip counting easy.

Cost			Amount Paid
$1.25 →	$1.50 →	$1.75 →	**$2.00**

Step 2

Find the total value of the coins you counted. There were 3 quarters.

3 quarters = $0.75

Rodrigo's change should be $0.75.

Problem Solving

Use the table at the right for **8–10**.

Data

Item	Price
Sharpener	$0.67
Eraser	$1.42
Marker	$1.38
Pencil	$0.56
Sticker	$0.15

8. **Writing to Explain** Arun paid for a sticker with a $1 bill. The change he received was all nickels. How many nickels did he get? Explain how you found your answer.

9. Mariko bought a marker. She paid with 2 one-dollar bills. List coins and bills that could be her change.

10. Wally paid for an eraser with a $5 bill. List coins and bills that could be his change.

11. **Reasonableness** Last year, the store sold 1,421 pencils. Walt said that was more than 14 hundred pencils. Is he correct? Explain.

12. A community collected $126,578 to help build a garden. What is the value of the 2 in $126,578?

13. **Algebra** Keri bought a pen. She paid with a $1 bill. This is the change she got. How much did the pen cost?

14. **SOL Prep** Rose bought a carton of milk that cost $2.39. She paid with a $5 bill. Which should be her change?

A $7.39 **C** $2.61

B $2.71 **D** $2.41

15. What are two different ways that $3.65 could be given as change?

Virginia

Lesson 1-9

Extends 3.1.a The student will read and write six-digit numerals and identify the place value and value of each digit.

Problem Solving

Make an Organized List

Randy is playing a game called *Guess the Number*. What are all the possible numbers that fit the clues shown at the right?

You can make an organized list to find all the possible numbers.

Clues

- It is a 3-digit even number.
- The digit in the hundreds place is greater than 8.
- The digit in the tens place is less than 2.

Guided Practice*

Do you know HOW?

Make an organized list to solve.

1. Rachel has a quarter, a dime, a nickel, and a penny. She told her brother he could take two coins. List all the different pairs of coins her brother can take.

Do you UNDERSTAND?

2. **Writing to Explain** How did making an organized list help you solve Problem 1?

3. **Write a Problem** Write and solve a real-world problem by making an organized list.

Independent Practice

For **4** and **5**, make an organized list to solve.

4. List all the 4-digit numbers that fit these clues.

- The thousands digit is less than 2.
- The hundreds digit is greater than 5.
- The tens digit and ones digit both equal 10 − 5.

5. Jen, Meg, and Emily are standing in line at the movies. How many different ways can they line up? List the ways.

Stuck? Try this....

- What do I know?
- What am I asked to find?
- What diagram can I use to help understand the problem?
- Can I use addition, subtraction, multiplication, or division?
- Is all of my work correct?
- Did I answer the right question?
- Is my answer reasonable?

*For another example, see Set F on page 29.

Plan

What the clues tell us:

The hundreds digit is 9.	The tens digit is 0 or 1.	The ones digit is 0, 2, 4, 6, or 8.
greater than 8	less than 2	even number

Solve

Make an organized list to find all the possible numbers.

900	910
902	912
904	914
906	916
908	918

For **6–8**, use the table.

Sandwich Choices

Bread Choices	Filling Choices
White	Ham
Rye	Tuna
	Turkey

6. How many different kinds of sandwiches can you choose if you want white bread?

7. How many different kinds of sandwiches can you choose if you don't want turkey?

8. Suppose wheat bread was added as a bread choice. How many different kinds of sandwiches could you choose then?

9. Jeremy has tan pants and black pants. He also has three shirts: blue, green, and red. List all the different outfits that Jeremy can wear.

10. Dennis bought a 3-pound bag of apples for $3. He also bought some grapes for $4. How much did Dennis spend?

11. How many different ways can you make 15 cents using dimes, nickels, or pennies?

SOL Prep

A 15 ways **C** 6 ways

B 9 ways **D** 3 ways

12. Carla bought 4 sheets of poster board. Each sheet cost $2. She paid with a $10 bill. Carla cut each sheet into 2 pieces. How many pieces does Carla have?

Tip *There is extra information in the problem.*

13. Reasoning What is this 3-digit number?

- The hundreds digit is 3 less than 5.
- The tens digit is greater than 8.
- The ones digit is 1 less than the tens digit.

1. The place-value blocks show the number of students at a school. How many students are there? (1-1)

A 2,054

B 254

C 250

D 245

2. On Friday, 1,593 people watched the play *Cinderella*. On Saturday, 1,595 people watched, and on Sunday, 1,586 people watched. Which lists these numbers in order from least to greatest? (1-6)

A 1,586 1,593 1,595

B 1,586 1,595 1,593

C 1,593 1,595 1,586

D 1,595 1,593 1,586

3. The cashier gave Hector the money shown below as change. How much change did he receive? (1-7)

A $3.82

B $7.67

C $7.82

D $7.87

4. What is the value of the 9 in the number 295,863? (1-3)

A 90

B 9,000

C 90,000

D 900,000

5. The place-value chart shows the depth, in feet, of the deepest lake in the United States, Crater Lake. Which is another way to write this number? (1-2)

thousands	hundreds	tens	ones
1,	9	3	2

A 100 + 900 + 30 + 2

B 1,000 + 90 + 30 + 2

C 1,000 + 900 + 30

D 1,000 + 900 + 30 + 2

6. Which is the word form of the number 530,450? (1-3)

A Five hundred thirty thousand, forty-five

B Five hundred thirty thousand, four hundred fifty

C Five hundred thirty, four fifty

D Fifty-three thousand, four hundred fifty

7. Which is greater than 4,324? (1-5)

A 4,342

B 4,322

C 4,314

D 3,424

8. Which shows 61 written in ordinal word form? (1-4)

A sixty-first

B sixty-one

C sixteenth

D sixty-oneth

9. Susan is thinking of a number between 3,674 and 5,628. Which of the following could be Susan's number? (1-6)

A 5,629

B 3,673

C 3,629

D 5,575

10. Which is another way to write 3,700? (1-4)

A thirty-seven thousand

B thirty-seven hundred

C three thousand, seven

D three thousand, seventy

11. Which is the standard form of 700 + 8? (1-1)

A 78

B 708

C 780

D 7,008

12. Which group of coins shows 67¢? (1-7)

A

B

C

D

13. Alex, Eric, Josh, and Tony are playing tennis. How many different groups of 2 can they make? (1-9)

A 12

B 8

C 6

D 2

14. The book costs $3.78. Becky gave the cashier $4.00. Which coins are her correct change? (1-8)

A 2 pennies, 2 nickels

B 2 pennies, 2 nickels, 2 dimes

C 2 pennies, 1 nickel, 1 dime

D 2 pennies, 2 dimes

Set A, pages 4–7

Write the number below in standard form, expanded form, and word form.

thousands	hundreds	tens	ones
4,	0	1	6

Standard form: 4,016

Expanded form: 4,000 + 10 + 6

Word form: four thousand, sixteen

Remember that the digit 0 is sometimes needed to hold a place in a number.

Write each number in standard form.

1. 1,000 + 5 **2.** 300 + 20 + 7

Write each number in expanded form and word form.

3. 8,214 **4.** 620

Set B, pages 8–9

Find the value of the 4 in 847,193.

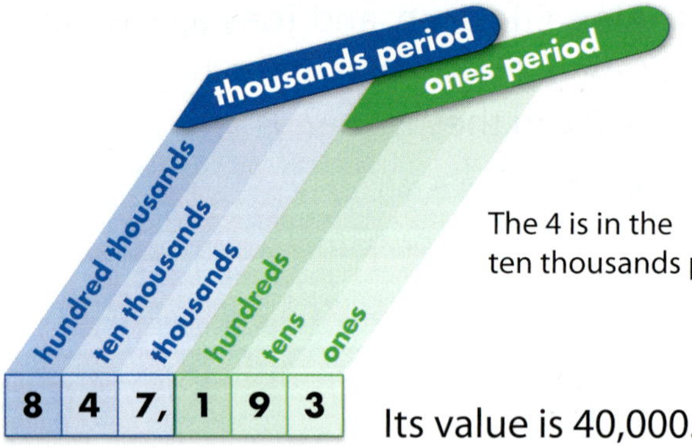

The 4 is in the ten thousands place.

Its value is 40,000.

Remember that 10 thousands equal 1 ten thousand.

Write the place of each underlined digit. Then write its value.

1. 341,791 **2.** 829,526

3. 570,890 **4.** 215,003

5. 197,206 **6.** 473,069

7. 628,174 **8.** 782,413

Set C, pages 10–11

The blue car is in the 6th place.

Ordinal Number: 6th **Ordinal Word Form:** sixth

Name 1,300 in two different ways.

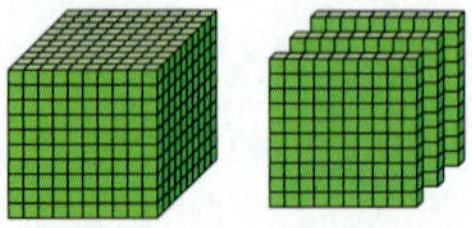

1 thousand + 3 hundreds
one thousand, three hundred

10 hundreds + 3 hundreds
thirteen hundred

Remember that ordinal numbers end with -st, -nd, -rd, or -th.

Write the ordinal number and ordinal word form of each number.

1. 8 **2.** 41

Name each number in two ways.

3. 1,700 **4.** 3,600

Set D, pages 12–14, 16–17

Compare 7,982 and 7,682.
Line up the digits by place value.
Compare the digits starting from the left.

7,	9	8	2
7,	6	8	2
↑ same	↑ different: 9 hundreds > 6 hundreds		

7,982 > 7,682

Remember, when ordering numbers, compare one place at a time.

Compare. Use <, >, or =.

1. 479 ◯ 912 **2.** 1,156 ◯ 156

Write the numbers in order from greatest to least.

3. 393 182 229

4. 1,289 2,983 1,760

Set E, pages 18–23

Write the total value in dollars and cents.

$5.00, $5.25, $5.35, $5.40, $5.45, $5.46

The total is $5.46.

Find the change. Start with the cost. Use coins to count up to the amount paid.

Cost → Amount Paid

$1.60 → $1.65 → $1.75 → **$2.00**

The change is $0.40.

Remember to count on from the bill or coin with the greatest value.

Write the total value in dollars and cents.

1. 

List coins and bills to make the change. Write the amount of the change.

2. Cost: $3.49
Amount paid: $5.00

Set F, pages 24–25

When you make an organized list to solve problems, follow these steps.

Step 1 Carefully read the clues or information from the problem.

Step 2 Choose one clue or piece of information and use it to start your list.

Step 3 Repeat step 2 until you have used all of the clues or information to make an organized list.

Remember that each item on your list must match all of the clues.

1. Pedro has a red marble, a blue marble, a yellow marble, and a green marble. He told Frank to take two marbles. How many different pairs of marbles can Frank take? List the pairs.

Topic 2

Adding Whole Numbers

1 The Kingda Ka is the tallest roller coaster in the world. How tall is the Kingda Ka? You will find out in Lesson 2-8.

2 How many spines does a lionfish have? You will find out in Lesson 2-1.

3 The faces of four presidents are carved in Mount Rushmore. What is the length of George Washington's face? You will find out in Lesson 2-9.

4 How many steps lead to the top of the Leaning Tower of Pisa? You will find out in Lesson 2-4.

Review What You Know!

Vocabulary

Choose the best term from the box.

- hundreds
- ones
- sum
- tens

1. In 259, the 2 is in the ? place.

2. In 259, the 9 is in the ? place.

3. The answer in addition is the ?.

Place Value

Copy and complete.

4. 35 = ☐ tens ☐ ones

5. 264 = ☐ hundreds ☐ tens ☐ ones

6. 302 = ☐ hundreds ☐ tens ☐ ones

Addition Facts

Write each sum.

7. 3 + 5 **8.** 1 + 8 **9.** 6 + 4

10. 4 + 3 **11.** 8 + 2 **12.** 6 + 6

13. 7 + 6 **14.** 8 + 6 **15.** 9 + 9

16. Janika bought 3 books on Monday and 6 books on Tuesday. How many books did she buy in all?

17. **Writing to Explain** Derrick has 4 red, 2 blue, 2 green, 2 yellow, and 2 orange balloons. Explain how to skip count to find how many balloons he has in all.

Virginia

Lesson 2-1

3.20.a The student will investigate the identity and the commutative properties for addition and multiplication. **(Also 3.20.b)**

Addition Meaning and Properties

What are some ways to think about addition?

You can use addition to join groups.

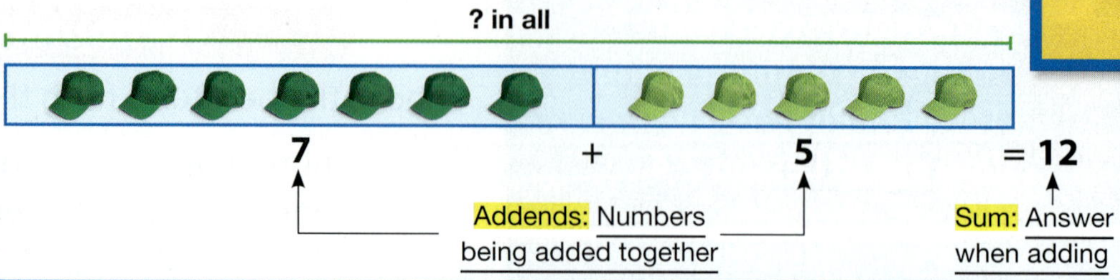

Another Example What is another way to think about addition?

Marda has two pieces of ribbon. One is 4 inches long and the other is 3 inches long. How many inches of ribbon does Marda have all together?

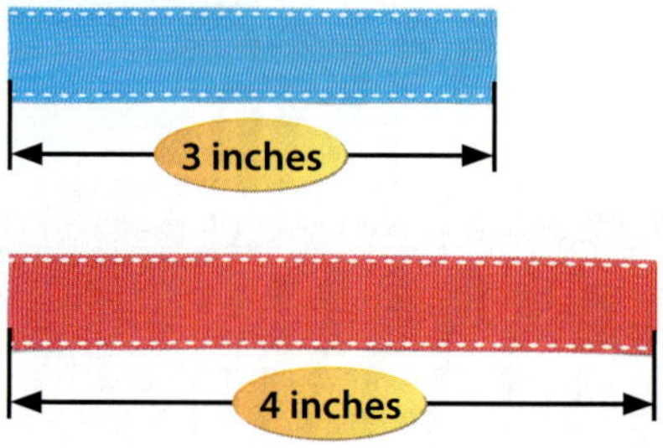

You can use a number line to think about addition.

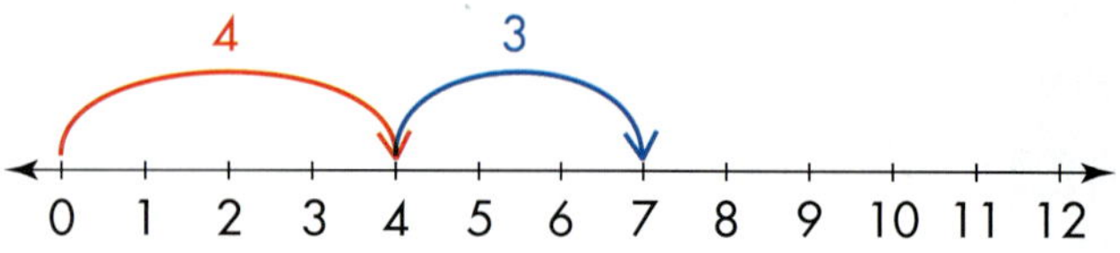

4 + 3 = 7

All together, Marda has 7 inches of ribbon.

Guided Practice*

Do you know HOW?

Write each missing number.

1. ☐ + 9 = 9

2. 4 + 6 = 6 + ☐

3. (2 + ☐) + 6 = 2 + (3 + 6)

Do you UNDERSTAND?

4. Why does it make sense that the Commutative Property is also called the order property?

5. **Writing to Explain** Ralph says you can rewrite (4 + 5) + 2 as 9 + 2. Do you agree? Why or why not?

DIGITAL Animated Glossary **www.pearsonsuccessnet.com**

*For another example, see Set A on page 62.

Commutative (Order) Property of Addition: You can add numbers in any order and the sum will be the same.

$$7 + 5 = 5 + 7$$

Identity (Zero) Property of Addition: The sum of zero and any number is that same number.

$$5 + 0 = 5$$

Associative (Grouping) Property of Addition: You can group addends in any way and the sum will be the same.

(3 + 4) + 5 = 12

3 + (4 + 5) = 12

$$(3 + 4) + 5 = 3 + (4 + 5)$$

Parentheses, (), show what to add first.

Independent Practice

Write each missing number.

6. ☐ + 8 = 8 + 2

7. 19 + ☐ = 19

8. (3 + ☐) + 2 = 2 + 8

9. 4 + (2 + 3) = 4 + ☐

10. 7 + 3 = ☐ + 7

11. ☐ + 25 = 25

12. (3 + ☐) + 6 = 3 + (4 + 6)

13. (6 + 2) + ☐ = 8 + 7

14. (7 + ☐) + 6 = 7 + 6

15. (5 + 6) + 3 = ☐ + (5 + 6)

Problem Solving

16. Reasoning What property of addition is shown in the number sentence 3 + (6 + 5) = (6 + 5) + 3? Explain.

17. Draw objects of 2 different colors to show that 4 + 3 = 3 + 4.

18. A lionfish has 13 spines on its back, 2 near the middle of its underside, and 3 on its underside near its tail. Write two different number sentences to find how many spines a lionfish has in all. What property did you use?

19. Which number sentence matches the picture?

A 3 + 8 = 11

B 11 + 0 = 11

C 11 − 8 = 3

D 11 − 3 = 8

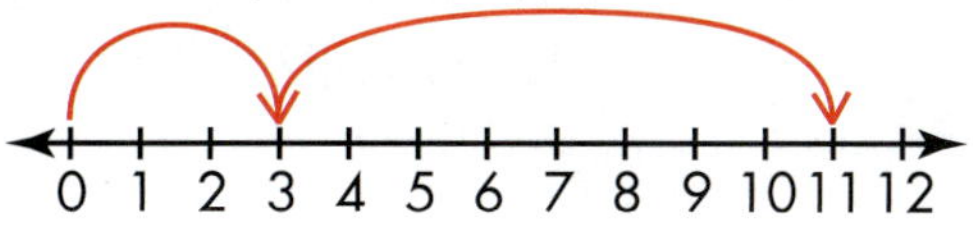

Virginia

Lesson 2-2

Reviews 2.6.b The student, given two whole numbers whose sum is 99 or less, will find the sum, using various methods of calculation.

Adding on a Hundred Chart

How can you add on a hundred chart?

Follow these steps to add 17 + 30.

- Start at 17.
- Count down three rows to add 30.
- You end up at 47.

17 + 30 = 47

1	2	3	4	5	6	7	8	9	10
11	12	13	14	15	16	17	18	19	20
21	22	23	24	25	26	27	28	29	30
31	32	33	34	35	36	37	38	39	40
41	42	43	44	45	46	47	48	49	50

Another Example How can you add on a hundred chart by counting backward?

Follow these steps to add 44 + 29:

- Start at 44.
- Move down 3 rows to add 30. You added 30 to 44. But you only needed to add 29, so you need to subtract 1.
- Move left 1 space.
- You end up at 73.

44 + 29 = 73

1	2	3	4	5	6	7	8	9	10
11	12	13	14	15	16	17	18	19	20
21	22	23	24	25	26	27	28	29	30
31	32	33	34	35	36	37	38	39	40
41	42	43	44	45	46	47	48	49	50
51	52	53	54	55	56	57	58	59	60
61	62	63	64	65	66	67	68	69	70
71	72	73	74	75	76	77	78	79	80
81	82	83	84	85	86	87	88	89	90
91	92	93	94	95	96	97	98	99	100

Guided Practice*

Do you know HOW?

Use a hundred chart to add.

1. 34 + 20

2. 78 + 19

3. 53 + 26

4. 68 + 18

5. 37 + 16

6. 44 + 29

7. 26 + 38

8. 57 + 35

Do you UNDERSTAND?

9. Reasoning Look at the examples at the top of pages 34 and 35. Compare the steps used to find each sum. How are they the same? How are they different?

10. Allie's mom bought 21 red apples and 18 green apples. How many apples did she buy in all?

*For another example, see Set B on page 62.

Follow these steps to add 56 + 35.

- Start at 56.
- Move down 3 rows to add 30.
- Move right 4 spaces to add 4 more. So far, you have added 34 to 56.
- To add 1 more, go down to the next row and move right 1 space.

51	52	53	54	55	56	57	58	59	60
61	62	63	64	65	66	67	68	69	70
71	72	73	74	75	76	77	78	79	80
81	82	83	84	85	86	87	88	89	90
91	92	93	94	95	96	97	98	99	100

You end up at 91.

56 + 35 = 91

Independent Practice

Use a hundred chart to add.

11. 48 + 50 **12.** 75 + 15 **13.** 73 + 20 **14.** 55 + 34

15. 38 + 15 **16.** 22 + 17 **17.** 68 + 16 **18.** 55 + 29

Number Sense Compare. Use <, >, or =.

19. 23 + 50 ◯ 23 + 65 **20.** 37 + 40 ◯ 47 + 30 **21.** 65 + 34 ◯ 65 + 43

22. 25 + 35 ◯ 35 + 45 **23.** 71 + 20 ◯ 61 + 20 **24.** 82 + 16 ◯ 72 + 26

Problem Solving

25. A horned lizard laid 37 eggs in one place. To the nearest ten, about how many eggs did the lizard lay?

26. **Reasoning** You have learned to add 9 to a number by first adding 10 and then subtracting 1. How could you add 99 to a number using mental math? Try using your method to find 24 + 99.

27. Which number is missing in the pattern below?

SOL Prep

0, 50, 100, ▢, 200

A 190 **C** 175

B 180 **D** 150

Virginia

Lesson 2-3

Reviews 2.6.b The student, given two whole numbers whose sum is 99 or less, will find the sum, using various methods of calculation.

Using Mental Math to Add

How can you add with mental math?

Dr. Gomez recorded how many whales, dolphins, and seals she saw. How many whales did she see during the two weeks?

Find 25 + 14.

Data

Marine Animals Seen

Animal	Week 1	Week 2
Whales	25	14
Dolphins	28	17
Seals	34	18

Another Example How can you make tens to add mentally?

How many dolphins did Dr. Gomez see during the two weeks?

You can make a ten to help you find 28 + 17.

Think

- Break apart 17.
  17 = 2 + 15
- Add 2 to 28
  2 + 28 = 30
- Add 15 to 30.
  30 + 15 = 45

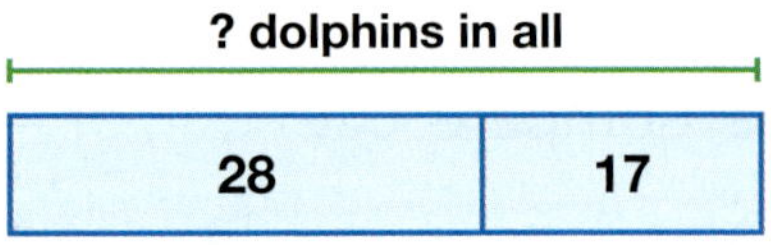

28 + 17 = 45

Dr. Gomez saw 45 dolphins.

Explain It

1. How does knowing that 17 = 2 + 15 help you find 28 + 17 mentally?
2. What is another way to make a 10 to add 28 + 17?

One Way

Break apart one of the addends.

Think
- Break apart 14.
  14 = 10 + 4
- Add 10 to 25.
  25 + 10 = 35
- Add 4 to 35.
  35 + 4 = 39

25 + 14 = 39

Dr. Gomez saw 39 whales.

Another Way

Break apart both addends.

Think
- Break apart both addends.
  25 = 20 + 5   14 = 10 + 4
- Add the tens. Add the ones.
  20 + 10 = 30   5 + 4 = 9
- Then add the tens and ones.
  30 + 9 = 39

25 + 14 = 39

Dr. Gomez saw 39 whales.

Guided Practice*

Do you know HOW?

1. Make a ten to add 38 + 26.

38 + 26
26 = 2 + 24
38 + ☐ = 40
40 + ☐ = 64
38 + 26 = ☐

2. Use breaking apart to add 25 + 12.

25 + 12
12 = 10 + 2
25 + 10 = ☐
☐ + 2 = 37
25 + 12 = ☐

Do you UNDERSTAND?

3. **Reasoning** Compare the One Way and Another Way examples above. How are they the same? How are they different?

4. **Number Sense** To find 37 + 28, you could add 37 + 30 = 67. Then what should you do next?

5. Use breaking apart or making tens to find how many seals Dr. Gomez saw during the two weeks. Explain which method you used.

Independent Practice

Leveled Practice Use breaking apart to add mentally.

6. 72 + 18
18 = 10 + ☐
72 + ☐ = 82
82 + ☐ = 90
72 + 18 = ☐

7. 34 + 25
25 = 20 + ☐
34 + ☐ = 54
☐ + 5 = 59
34 + 25 = ☐

8. 53 + 36
36 = ☐ + 6
53 + ☐ = 83
☐ + 6 = 89
53 + 36 = ☐

*For another example, see Set C on page 62.

Independent Practice

Leveled Practice Make a ten to add mentally.

9. 47 + 9
9 = ___ + 6
47 + ___ = 50
___ + 6 = 56
47 + 9 = ___

10. 55 + 37
37 = 5 + ___
___ + 5 = 60
60 + ___ = 92
55 + 37 = ___

11. 49 + 29
29 = ___ + 28
49 + ___ = 50
50 + ___ = 78
49 + 29 = ___

Find each sum using mental math.

12. 35 + 26
13. 50 + 42
14. 43 + 4
15. 71 + 13

16. 52 + 44
17. 7 + 54
18. 63 + 12
19. 62 + 34

20. 37 + 9
21. 5 + 38
22. 65 + 15
23. 33 + 23

Problem Solving

24. How long can a python be?

25. What is the total length of the iguana?

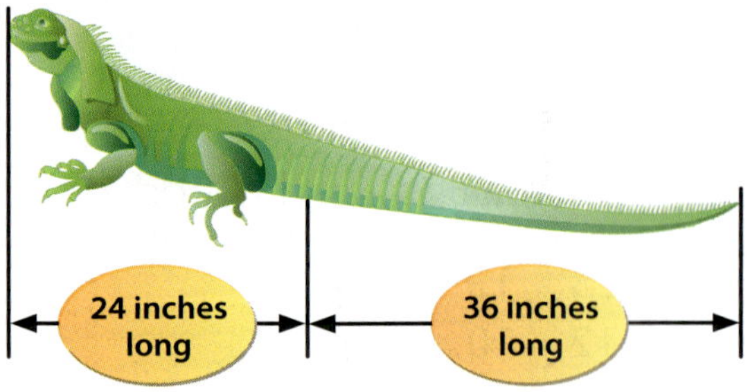

26. **Writing to Explain** Is Bill's work right? If not, tell why and write a correct answer.

Find 38 + 7.
I'll think of 7 as 2 + 5.
38 + 2 = 40
40 + 7 = 47
So, 38 + 7 is 47.

27. How is the number 4,038 written in word form?

A four hundred thirty-eight
B four thousand, three hundred eight
C four thousand, thirty-eight
D forty thousand, thirty-eight

Going Digital

Adding with Mental Math

Use eTools
Place-Value Blocks

Show two ways to make a ten to add 27 + 38.

Step 1 Go to the Place-Value Blocks eTool. Click on the Two-part workspace icon. In the top space, show 27 with place-value blocks. Show 38 in the bottom space.

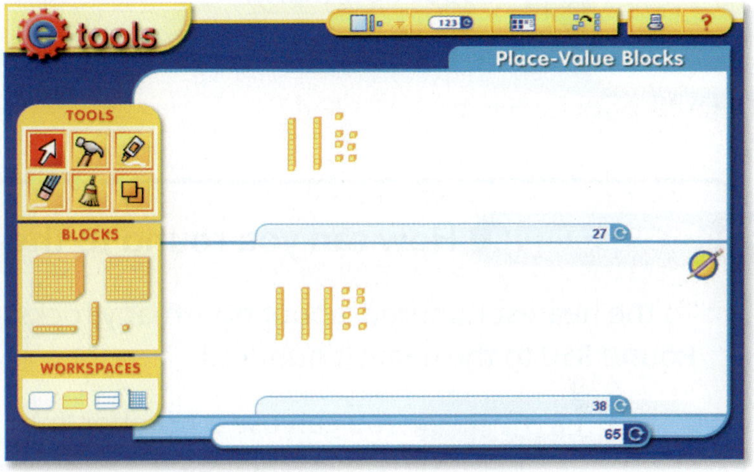

Step 2 Use the arrow tool to select ones from the bottom space and drag them to the top space. Do this until you make a ten on top. The odometers show that you have 30 + 35 = 65. So, 27 + 38 = 65, and 30 + 35 = 65.

Step 3 Use the arrow tool to move the blocks back to show 27 + 38. Then select ones from the top space and drag them to the bottom space until you make a ten on the bottom. The odometers show that you have 25 + 40 = 65. So, 27 + 38 = 65, and 25 + 40 = 65.

Practice

Use the Place-Value Blocks eTool. Find two ways to make a ten to add.

1. $47 + 29 = \square + \square = 76$
$47 + 29 = \square + \square = 76$

2. $58 + 36 = \square + \square = 94$
$58 + 36 = \square + \square = 94$

Virginia

Lesson 2-4

3.1.b The student will round whole numbers, 9,999 or less, to the nearest ten, hundred, and thousand.

Rounding

How can you round numbers?

To the nearest 10, about how many rocks does Tito have?

Round 394 to the nearest ten. To round, replace a number with a number that tells about how many.

Another Example How can you round to the nearest hundred?

To the nearest hundred, about how many rocks does Donna have? Round 350 to the nearest hundred.

One Way You can use a number line.

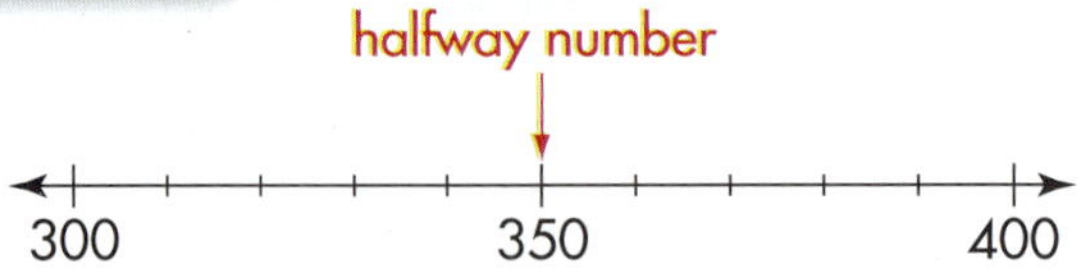

If a number is halfway between, round to the greater number.

350 is halfway between 300 and 400, so 350 rounds to 400.

Another Way You can use place value.

Find the digit in the rounding place. Then look at the next digit to the right.

hundreds place
↓
350
↓↓↓
400

Since 5 = 5, increase the digit in the hundreds place by one. Then change all the digits to the right to zero.

So, 350 rounds to 400. Donna has about 400 rocks.

Explain It

1. If you round 350 to the nearest ten, would you still say that Donna has about 400 rocks? Why or why not?
2. Explain why 350 is the least number that rounds to 400.

One Way

You can use a number line.

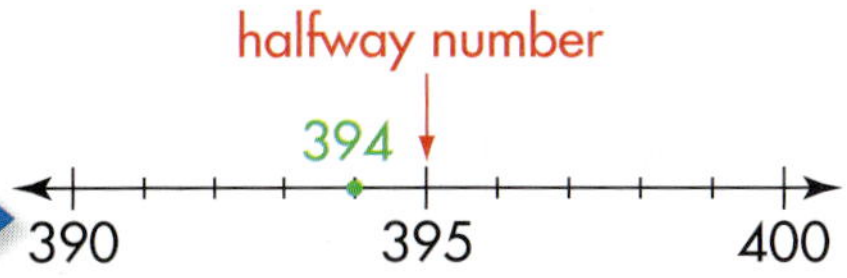

394 is closer to 390 than 400, so 394 rounds to 390.

Tito has about 390 rocks.

Another Way

You can use place value.

- Find the digit in the rounding place.
- Look at the next digit to the right. If it is 5 or greater, add 1 to the rounding digit. If it is less than 5, leave the rounding digit alone.
- Change all digits to the right of the rounding place to 0.

tens place

394 Since $4 < 5$, leave the digit in the tens place as it is.

390

So, 394 rounds to 390.

Tito has about 390 rocks.

Guided Practice*

Do you know HOW?

Round to the nearest ten.

1. 37 **2.** 63 **3.** 85

4. 654 **5.** 305 **6.** 752

Round to the nearest hundred.

7. 557 **8.** 149 **9.** 552

10. 207 **11.** 888 **12.** 835

Do you UNDERSTAND?

13. Number Sense What number is halfway between 250 and 260?

14. Reasoning If Tito adds one more rock to his collection, about how many rocks will he have, rounded to the nearest ten? rounded to the nearest hundred? Explain your answer.

15. Writing to Explain Tell what you would do to round 46 to the nearest ten.

Independent Practice

Round to the nearest ten.

16. 45 **17.** 68 **18.** 98 **19.** 24 **20.** 55

21. 249 **22.** 732 **23.** 235 **24.** 805 **25.** 703

26. Reasoning Round 996 to the nearest ten. Explain your answer.

DIGITAL Animated Glossary **www.pearsonsuccessnet.com**

For another example, see Set C on page 62.

Independent Practice

Round to the nearest hundred.

27. 354 **28.** 504 **29.** 470 **30.** 439 **31.** 682

32. 945 **33.** 585 **34.** 850 **35.** 702 **36.** 870

37. **Reasoning** Round 954 to the nearest hundred. Explain your answer.

Problem Solving

38. **Number Sense** Write a number that rounds to 200 when it is rounded to the nearest hundred.

39. **Writing to Explain** Describe the steps you would follow to round 439 to the nearest ten.

40. **Number Sense** Suppose you are rounding to the nearest hundred. What is the greatest number that rounds to 600? What is the least number that rounds to 600?

41. **Number Sense** A 3-digit number has the digits 2, 5, and 7. To the nearest hundred, it rounds to 800. What is the number?

42. To the nearest hundred dollars, a computer game costs $100. Which could **NOT** be the actual cost of the game?

SOL Prep

A $89 **C** $110

B $91 **D** $150

43. What is the standard form of 700 + 40?

SOL Prep

A 740 **C** 470

B 704 **D** 407

44. There are 293 steps to the top of the Leaning Tower of Pisa in Italy. To the nearest hundred, about how many steps are there?

Algebra Connections

Greater, Less, or Equal

Remember that the two sides of a number sentence can be equal or unequal. A symbol >, <, or = tells how the sides compare. Estimation or reasoning can help you tell if one side is greater.

Tip

>	<	=
is greater than	*is less than*	*is equal to*

Example: 6 + 2 ○ 8 + 1

Think Is 6 + 2 more than 8 + 1?

Since 6 + 2 = 8, 8 is already less than 8 + 1. Write "<."

6 + 2 ⓧ 8 + 1, with < written in the circle: 6 + 2 (<) 8 + 1

Copy and complete. Replace the circle with <, >, or =. Check your answers.

1. 3 + 4 ○ 2 + 7
2. 9 + 1 ○ 5 + 4
3. 5 + 3 ○ 6 + 3
4. 2 + 9 ○ 1 + 8
5. 4 + 6 ○ 4 + 7
6. 8 + 6 ○ 9 + 5
7. 18 + 2 ○ 16 + 4
8. 15 + 5 ○ 10 + 8
9. 14 + 4 ○ 12 + 4
10. 17 + 3 ○ 20 + 1
11. 21 + 2 ○ 19 + 2
12. 27 + 3 ○ 26 + 4

For **13** and **14**, copy and complete each number sentence. Use it to help solve the problem.

13. Al and Jiro had some toy animals. Al had 8 lizards and 3 frogs. Jiro had 11 lizards and 2 frogs. Who had more toy animals?

Al's toys ↓ Jiro's toys ↓

☐ + ☐ ○ ☐ + ☐

14. The number below each block tells how many are in a set. Val used all of the small and large cylinders. Jen used all of the small and large cubes. Who used more blocks?

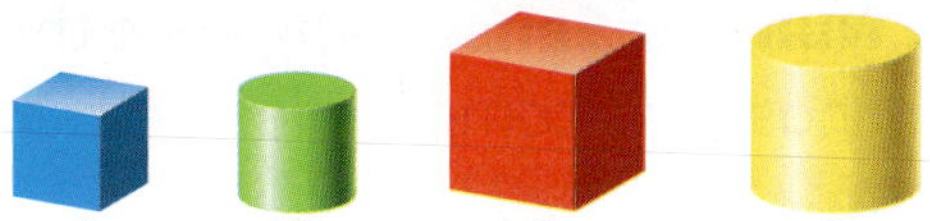

6 8 9 9

Val ↓ Jen ↓

☐ + ☐ ○ ☐ + ☐

15. **Write a Problem** Write a problem using this number sentence: 9 + 2 > 4 + 5.

Virginia

Lesson 2-5

3.4 The student will estimate solutions to and solve single-step and multistep problems involving the sum or difference of two whole numbers, each 9,999 or less, with or without regrouping.

Estimating Sums

How can you estimate sums?

Do the two pandas together weigh more than 500 pounds?

You can estimate to find out about how much the two pandas weigh.

Estimate 255 + 322.

Another Example **What is another way to estimate sums?**

You can use compatible numbers to estimate.

Compatible numbers are numbers that are close to the addends, but easy to add mentally.

Use compatible numbers to decide if the pandas together weigh more than 500 pounds.

$$\begin{array}{r} 255 \\ +\ 322 \\ \hline \end{array} \longrightarrow \begin{array}{r} 250 \\ +\ 325 \\ \hline 575 \end{array}$$

250 + 325 is about 575.
575 > 500

The pandas together weigh more than 500 pounds.

Explain It

1. **Number Sense** Why were the numbers 250 and 325 chosen as compatible numbers in the example above?
2. By rounding to the nearest ten, everyone gets the same estimated sum. Is this true if compatible numbers are used to estimate the sum? Explain.

One Way

Round to the nearest hundred.

$$\begin{array}{r} 255 \\ +\ 322 \\ \hline \end{array} \longrightarrow \begin{array}{r} 300 \\ +\ 300 \\ \hline 600 \end{array}$$

255 + 322 is about 600.
600 > 500

The pandas together weigh more than 500 pounds.

Another Way

Round to the nearest ten.

$$\begin{array}{r} 255 \\ +\ 322 \\ \hline \end{array} \longrightarrow \begin{array}{r} 260 \\ +\ 320 \\ \hline 580 \end{array}$$

255 + 322 is about 580.
580 > 500

The pandas together weigh more than 500 pounds.

Guided Practice*

Do you know HOW?

Round to the nearest ten to estimate.

1. 28 + 46 **2.** 75 + 17

Round to the nearest hundred to estimate.

3. 114 + 58 **4.** 198 + 426

Use compatible numbers to estimate.

5. 136 + 437 **6.** 654 + 253

Do you UNDERSTAND?

7. Writing to Explain Which estimate in the example above is closer to the actual sum? Explain your thinking.

8. How could you use rounding to estimate 487 + 354?

9. Number Sense If both addends are rounded down, will the estimate be greater or less than the actual sum?

Independent Practice

In **10–13**, round to the nearest ten to estimate.

10. 18 + 43 **11.** 75 + 72 **12.** 39 + 102 **13.** 376 + 295

In **14–17**, round to the nearest hundred to estimate.

14. 403 + 179 **15.** 462 + 251 **16.** 64 + 403 **17.** 539 + 399

In **18–21**, use compatible numbers to estimate.

18. 75 + 26 **19.** 167 + 27 **20.** 108 + 379 **21.** 145 + 394

DIGITAL Animated Glossary
www.pearsonsuccessnet.com

*For another example, see Set C on page 62.

Independent Practice

Reasonableness Estimate to decide if each answer is reasonable. Write *yes* or *no*. Then explain your thinking.

22. 32 + 58 = 70

23. 83 + 46 = 129

24. 55 + 64 = 99

25. 105 + 23 = 308

26. 713 + 118 = 831

27. 328 + 365 = 693

Problem Solving

In **28–30**, use the table at the right.

28. Which city is farthest from Indianapolis?

29. Mr. Tyson drove from Indianapolis to Cincinnati and back again. To the nearest ten miles, about how many miles did he drive?

30. Mr. Tyson drove from Chicago to Indianapolis to Louisville. To the nearest 10 miles, about how many miles in all did he drive?

Data: **Distance from Indianapolis, IN**

City	Miles Away
Chicago, IL	187 miles
Cincinnati, OH	112 miles
Columbus, OH	175 miles
Louisville, KY	114 miles

31. Dorinne paid for a pair of socks with a $5 bill. If the socks cost $2.67, what should her change be?

32. **Number Sense** Why might you round to the nearest ten instead of the nearest hundred when you estimate a sum?

33. How could you use rounding to estimate 268 + 354?

34. Write the number 3,500 in word form in two different ways.

35. How could you use compatible numbers to estimate 229 + 672?

36. Think About the Process Jared has 138 marbles. Manny has 132 marbles. Which number sentence is best to estimate how many marbles they have in all?

SOL Prep

A 38 + 32 = 70

B 100 + 100 = 200

C 108 + 102 = 210

D 140 + 130 = 270

Mixed Problem Solving

Math and Literature

Read the story and then answer the questions.

We Can't Wait!

Jamie and her sisters stared out of the front window of their home. They were talking about all the good stories their grandmother always tells them when she visits. About 10 minutes ago, their dad had called home from the airport. He said that he was exactly 26 blocks away. He needed to make one more stop 12 blocks farther away. Then he would come home.

When Dad finally came around the street corner, the sisters jumped off the sofa and ran to the door. Dad arrived at the door with some grocery bags, a suitcase, and a special visitor. Soon the family would be hearing many good stories.

1. What conclusion can you draw?

2. When the sisters were staring out of the window, their dad had called about 10 minutes ago. Write a number of minutes that rounds to 10 minutes.

3. To the nearest 10 blocks, about how many blocks away from home was Dad when he called home?

4. To the nearest 10 blocks, about how many blocks did Dad travel from his last stop to home?

5. Look at the table below.

   Write the distances in order from least to greatest.

Data

Place	Distance from Home
Bakery	38 blocks
Bank	12 blocks
Grocery Store	21 blocks
Toy Store	26 blocks

6. **Strategy Focus** Solve the problem. Use the strategy Make an Organized List.

   Jamie earned some money doing chores. She wants to put 70 cents in her bank. What are two different ways she could use coins to make 70 cents?

Lesson 2-6

3.4 The student will estimate solutions to and solve single-step and multistep problems involving the sum or difference of two whole numbers, each 9,999 or less, with or without regrouping.

Adding 2-Digit Numbers

Hands-On
place-value blocks

How can you use addition to solve problems?

How many ears of corn are there in all?

- Add to find the total. **58 + 47 = ☐**
- Estimate first. 58 + 47 is about 110. **60 + 50 = 110**

Guided Practice*

Do you know HOW?

Estimate. Then find each sum. Place-value blocks may help.

1. 42 + 59

2. 64 + 22

3. 93 + 28

4. 57 + 52

5. 47 + 9

6. 84 + 28

Do you UNDERSTAND?

7. Look at the What You Write step in the example above. Why is there a 1 above the 5 in the tens place?

8. Look at the pumpkins above.

a Estimate the total weight of the pumpkins.

b Write and solve a number sentence to find the actual total weight of the pumpkins.

Independent Practice

Estimate. Then find each sum.

9. 77 + 52

10. 19 + 24

11. 57 + 8

12. 72 + 26

13. 75 + 39

14. 33 + 45

15. 88 + 16

16. 24 + 54

17. 17 + 37

18. 59 + 13

19. 83 + 9

20. 71 + 19

21. 45 + 34

DIGITAL eTools www.pearsonsuccessnet.com

*For another example, see Set D on page 63.

What You Think

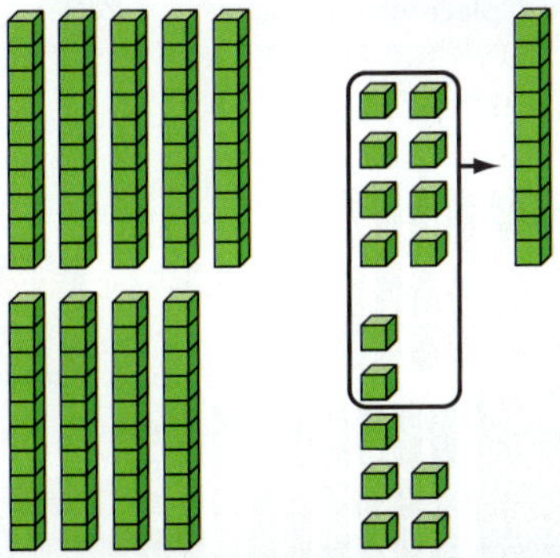

58 + 47 = □

- Add the ones.
  8 ones + 7 ones = 15 ones
  Regroup.
  15 ones = 1 ten 5 ones
- Add the tens.
  1 ten + 5 tens +
  4 tens = 10 tens
  Regroup.
  10 tens = 1 hundred

What You Write

$$\begin{array}{r} {}^{1} \\ 58 \\ +\ 47 \\ \hline 105 \end{array}$$

105 is close to 110, so 105 is reasonable.

There are 105 ears of corn in all.

Problem Solving

In **22** and **23**, use the table at the right.

22. Follow the steps below to find how many points the Hoop Troop scored all together in Games 1 and 2.

a Write a number sentence to show how to solve the problem.

b Estimate the answer.

c Solve the problem.

d Is your answer reasonable? Explain.

Data

The Hoop Troop

Games	Points Scored
Game 1	66
Game 2	57
Game 3	64

23. List the Hoop Troop's scores in order from the fewest to the most points.

24. **Reasonableness** Stan added 36 + 29 and got 515. Explain why his answer is not reasonable.

25. **Number Sense** What is the greatest possible sum of two 2-digit numbers? Explain.

26. Colleen ran 18 miles last week. She ran 26 miles this week. She plans to run 28 miles next week. Which number sentence would find how many miles she has run so far?

A 18 + 28 = □ **B** 18 + 26 = □ **C** 18 + 26 + 28 = □ **D** 28 − 18 = □

In **27** and **28**, use the pictures.

27. If the truck is first, which toy is fourth?

28. The jump rope costs $3.79. How much change should Susan get if she pays with a $5 bill?

Virginia

Lesson 2-7

3.4 The student will estimate solutions to and solve single-step and multistep problems involving the sum or difference of two whole numbers, each 9,999 or less, with or without regrouping.

Models for Adding 3-Digit Numbers

Hands-On
place-value blocks

How can you add 3-digit numbers with place-value blocks?

You can add whole numbers by using place value to break them apart.

Find 143 + 285.

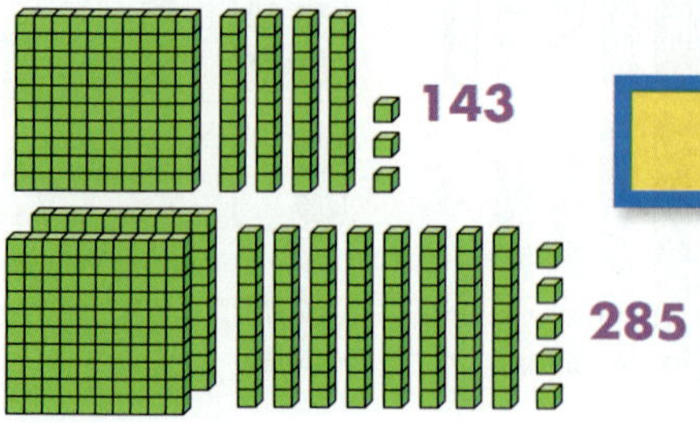

Another Example **How do you add with two regroupings?**

Find 148 + 276.

Step 1

Add the ones.
8 ones + 6 ones = 14 ones

Regroup.
14 ones = 1 ten 4 ones

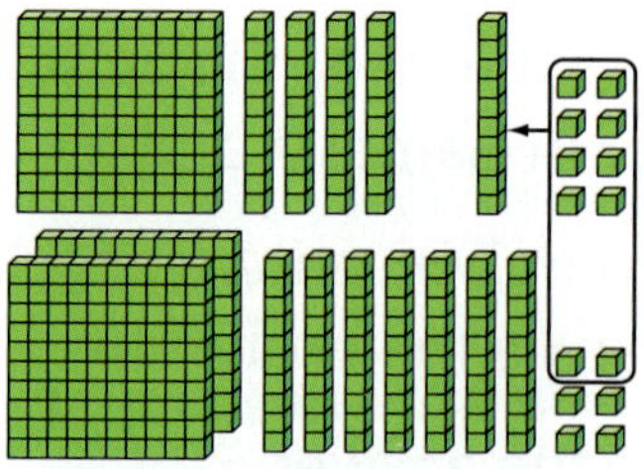

Step 2

Add the tens.
1 ten + 4 tens + 7 tens = 12 tens

Regroup.
12 tens = 1 hundred 2 tens

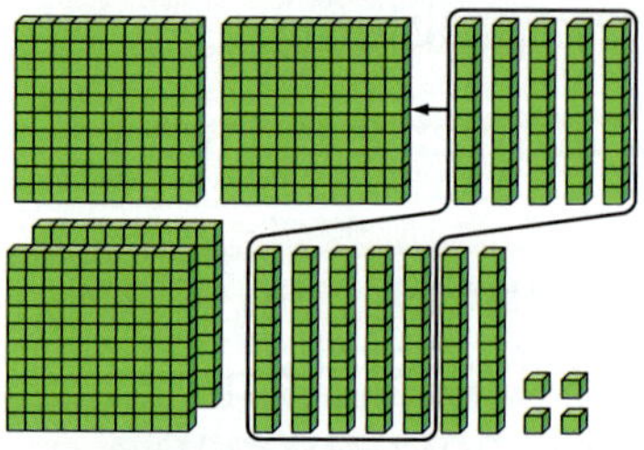

Step 3

Add the hundreds.
1 hundred + 1 hundred + 2 hundreds = 4 hundreds

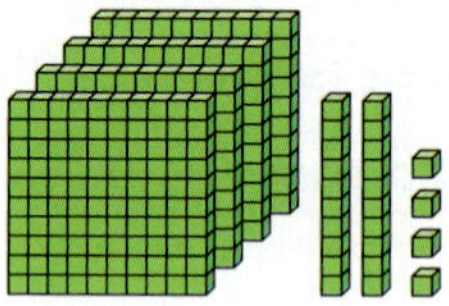

So, 148 + 276 = 424.

Explain It

1. Why did you need to regroup two times?
2. **Number Sense** Why didn't you regroup hundreds?

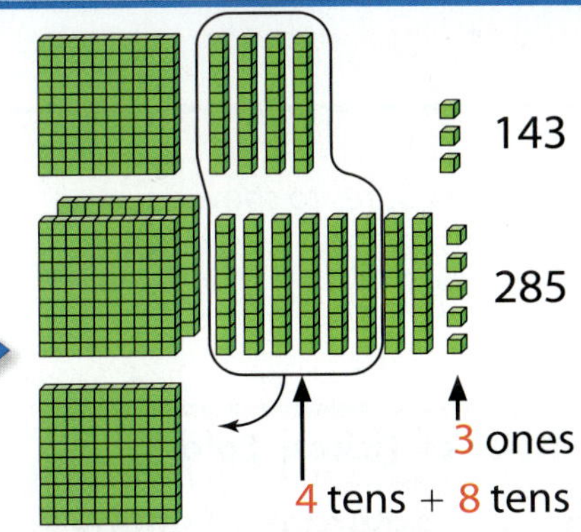

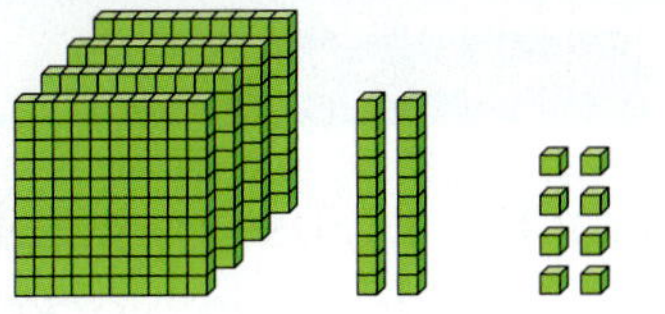

Guided Practice*

Do you know HOW?

1. Write the problem and find the sum.

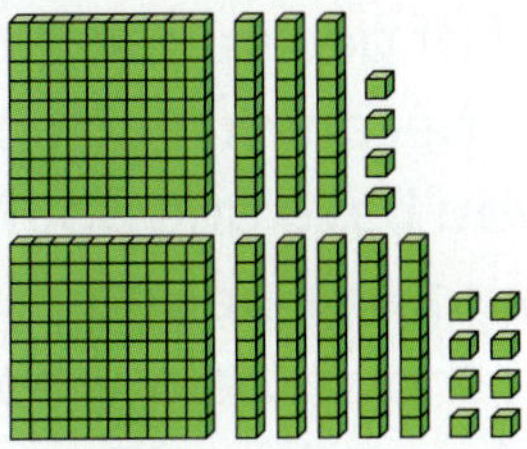

Use place-value blocks or draw pictures to find each sum.

2. 256 + 162

3. 138 + 29

Do you UNDERSTAND?

4. How do you know when you need to regroup?

5. Mr. Wu drove 224 miles yesterday. He drove 175 miles today. Use place-value blocks or draw pictures to find how many miles he drove in all.

Independent Practice

Write each problem and find the sum.

6. 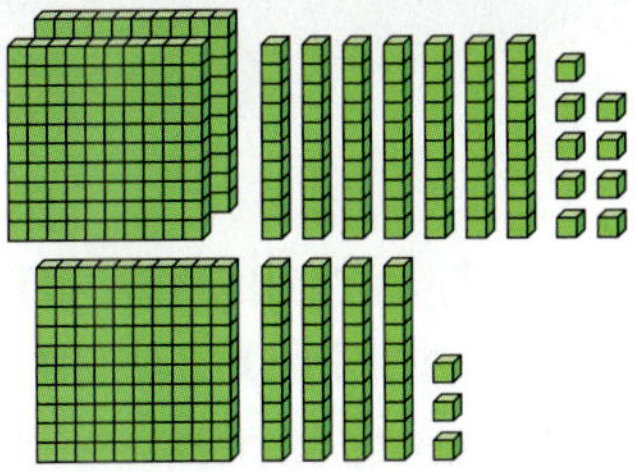

7. 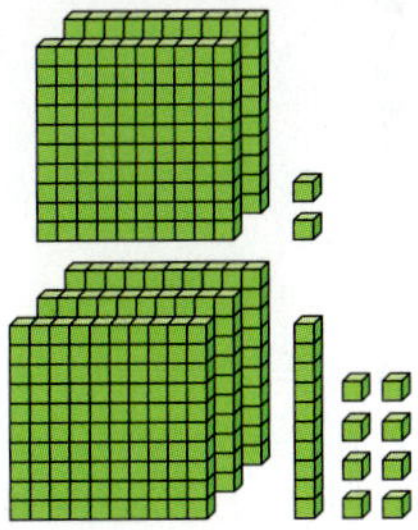

Find each sum. Use place-value blocks or draw pictures to help.

8. 635 + 222

9. 337 + 152

10. 359 + 211

11. 358 + 243

DIGITAL eTools **www.pearsonsuccessnet.com**

**For another example, see Set E on page 63.*

Problem Solving

For **12–15**, use the table at the right. Use place-value blocks or draw a picture to help.

Tip: You can draw squares to show hundreds, lines to show tens, and ×s to show ones.

Number of Tickets Sold (Data)

Ride	Saturday	Sunday
Ferris Wheel	368	406
Roller Coaster	486	456
Swings	138	251

12. Estimate about how many tickets in all were sold for the three rides on Saturday.

13. **Writing to Explain** Without adding, how can you tell whether more tickets were sold in the two days for the Ferris wheel or the swings?

14. How many Ferris wheel tickets were sold in the two days?

15. How many roller coaster tickets were sold in the two days?

16. **Number Sense** Mike wants to use place-value blocks to show 237 + 153. He has 8 tens blocks. Is that enough to show the sum? Explain.

17. One kind of pecan tree produces about 45 pecans in each pound of nuts. If you have one pound of these pecans and one pound of the kind of pecan shown below, how many pecans do you have?

18. **Writing to Explain** Is the sum of two 3-digit numbers always a 3-digit number? Explain how you know.

19. SOL Prep Which number sentence do these place-value blocks show?

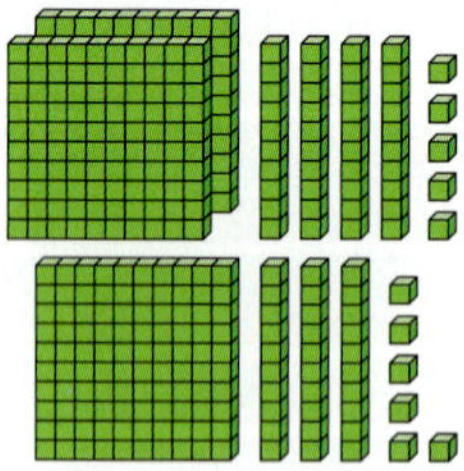

A 254 + 163 = 417

B 245 + 136 = 381

C 245 + 163 = 408

D 254 + 136 = 390

20. At a busy airport, 228 flights landed between noon and 3:00 P.M. On the same day 243 flights landed at that airport between 3 P.M. and 6 P.M. How many flights in all landed between noon and 6 P.M.?

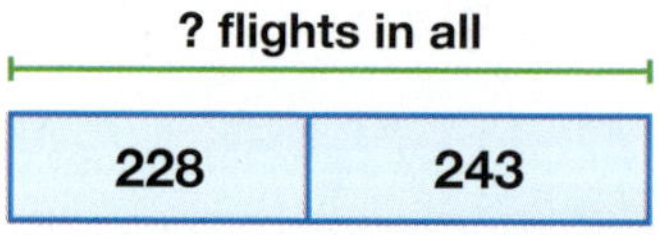

Going Digital

Adding with Regrouping

Use eTools

Place-Value Blocks

Use the Place-Value Blocks eTool to add 367 + 175 by regrouping.

Step 1 Go to the Place-Value Blocks eTool. Click on the Two-part workspace icon. In the top space, show 367 with place-value blocks. Show 175 in the bottom space.

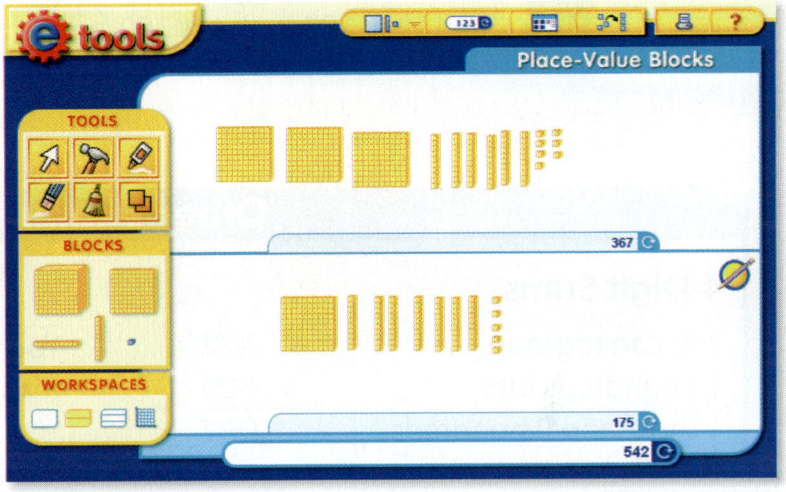

Step 2 Use the arrow tool to move the ones from 175 to the top space. Then use the glue tool to select 10 ones. Click on the group of 10 ones to make one ten.

Step 3 Use the arrow tool to move the tens from 175 to the top space. Use the glue tool to select 10 tens. Click on the group of 10 tens to make one hundred.

Step 4 Use the arrow tool to move the hundred from 175 to the top space. Look at the blocks to find the sum, 367 + 175 = 542.

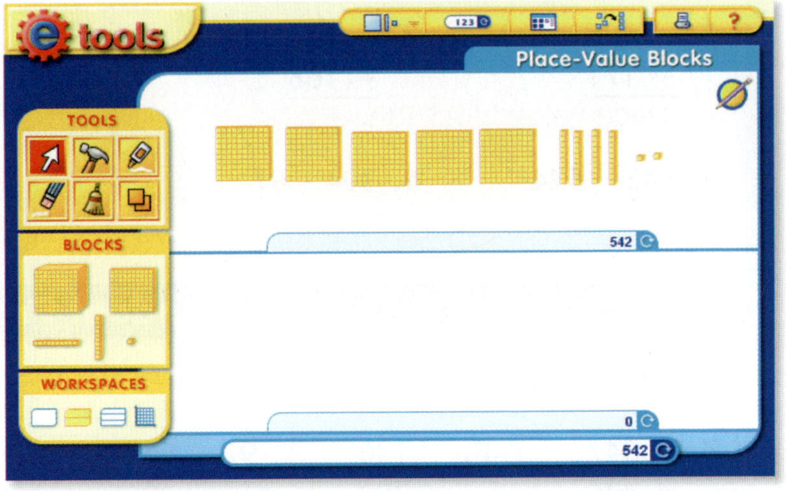

Practice

Use the Place-Value Blocks eTool to find the sums by regrouping.

1. 248 + 374 **2.** 459 + 178 **3.** 566 + 293 **4.** 675 + 189

Virginia

Lesson 2-8

3.4 The student will estimate solutions to and solve single-step and multistep problems involving the sum or difference of two whole numbers, each 9,999 or less, with or without regrouping.

Adding 3-Digit Numbers

How can you use addition to solve problems?

Jason's family drove from Niagara Falls to Albany. How far did they drive in all?

Find 119 + 187.

Estimate by rounding. 100 + 200 = 300
So, 119 + 187 is about 300.

Other Examples

4-Digit Sums

You can regroup 10 hundreds into 1 thousand 0 hundreds.

$$\begin{array}{r} 472 \\ +\ 625 \\ \hline 1{,}097 \end{array}$$

You can regroup ones, tens, and hundreds.

$$\begin{array}{r} {\scriptsize 1\ 1\ } \\ 568 \\ +\ 864 \\ \hline 1{,}432 \end{array}$$

Guided Practice*

Do you know HOW?

Estimate. Then find each sum. Use place-value blocks or drawings to help.

1. $\begin{array}{r} 126 \\ +\ 171 \\ \hline \end{array}$

2. $\begin{array}{r} 415 \\ +\ 168 \\ \hline \end{array}$

3. 645 + 524

4. 394 + 97

Do you UNDERSTAND?

5. Reasonableness In the example about Jason's family, is the answer 306 miles reasonable? Explain.

6. Ms. Lane drove 278 miles on Tuesday and 342 miles on Wednesday. Write and solve a number sentence to find how far she drove in all.

Independent Practice

For **7–15**, estimate. Then find each sum.

7. $\begin{array}{r} 347 \\ +\ 325 \\ \hline \end{array}$

8. $\begin{array}{r} 136 \\ +\ 252 \\ \hline \end{array}$

9. $\begin{array}{r} 564 \\ +\ 283 \\ \hline \end{array}$

10. $\begin{array}{r} 731 \\ +\ 344 \\ \hline \end{array}$

11. $\begin{array}{r} 324 \\ +\ 589 \\ \hline \end{array}$

12. 324 + 68

13. 709 + 94

14. 496 + 874

15. 526 + 307

*For another example, see Set E on page 63.

Step 1

Add the ones.

9 ones + 7 ones = 16 ones

Regroup.

16 ones = 1 ten 6 ones

$$\begin{array}{r} {}^{1} \\ 119 \\ +\ 187 \\ \hline 6 \end{array}$$

Step 2

Add the tens.

1 ten + 1 ten + 8 tens = 10 tens

Regroup.

10 tens = 1 hundred 0 tens

$$\begin{array}{r} {}^{1}\,{}^{1} \\ 119 \\ +\ 187 \\ \hline 06 \end{array}$$

Step 3

Add the hundreds.

1 hundred + 1 hundred + 1 hundred = 3 hundreds

$$\begin{array}{r} {}^{1}\,{}^{1} \\ 119 \\ +\ 187 \\ \hline 306 \end{array}$$

They drove 306 miles in all.

Problem Solving

For **16–19**, use the table at the right.

16. a Write a number sentence to find how many labels the first and second grade collected in all.

b Estimate the answer.

c Solve the problem.

d Is your answer reasonable? Explain.

Soup Labels Collected (Data)

Grades	Number
Grade 1	385
Grade 2	294
Grade 3	479
Grade 4	564

17. Number Sense Without finding the exact sum, how do you know that Grades 2 and 3 together collected more labels than Grade 4?

18. Write the number of labels collected from least to greatest.

19. Which number sentence shows how many labels Grades 1 and 4 collected in all?

A 385 + 479 = ▢

B 385 + 564 = ▢

C 294 + 479 + 564 = ▢

D 385 + 294 + 479 + 564 = ▢

20. The tallest roller coaster in the world is called Kingda Ka. It is 192 feet higher than the first Ferris wheel. How tall is Kingda Ka?

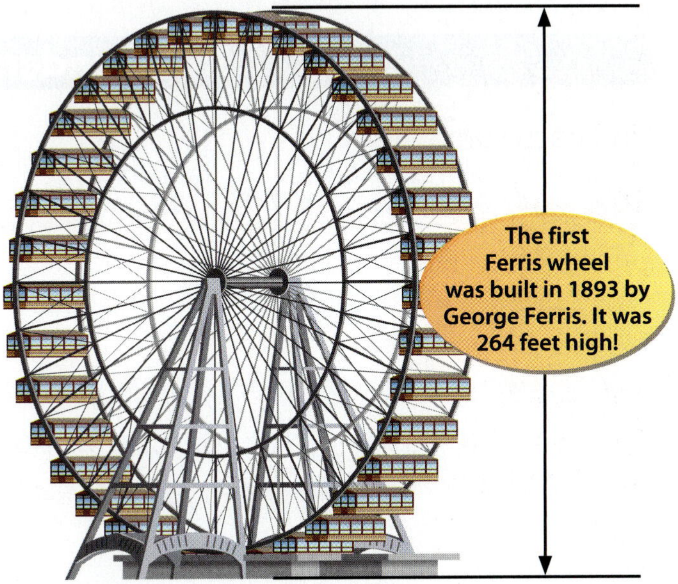

Virginia

Lesson 2-9

Extends 3.4 The student will estimate solutions to and solve single-step and multistep problems involving the sum or difference of two whole numbers, each 9,999 or less, with or without regrouping.

Adding 3 or More Numbers

How can you use addition to solve problems?

Different kinds of birds are for sale at a pet store. How many birds are for sale in all?

- Find 137 + 155 + 18.
- Estimate: 140 + 160 + 20 = 320

Guided Practice*

Do you know HOW?

Find each sum.

1.
$$\begin{array}{r} 36 \\ 47 \\ +\ 35 \\ \hline \end{array}$$

2.
$$\begin{array}{r} 247 \\ 362 \\ +\ \ 49 \\ \hline \end{array}$$

3.
$$\begin{array}{r} 273 \\ 82 \\ +\ 124 \\ \hline \end{array}$$

4.
$$\begin{array}{r} 59 \\ 506 \\ 302 \\ +\ \ 24 \\ \hline \end{array}$$

5. 9 + 46 + 24

6. 385 + 97 + 34

Do you UNDERSTAND?

For **7–9**, look at the example above.

7. Why is there a 2 above the tens place in Step 2?

8. **Reasonableness** How can you tell that 310 birds is a reasonable answer?

9. Suppose the pet store gets 46 lovebirds to sell. Write and solve a number sentence to show how many birds are for sale now.

Independent Practice

Find each sum.

10.
$$\begin{array}{r} 64 \\ 42 \\ +\ 88 \\ \hline \end{array}$$

11.
$$\begin{array}{r} 307 \\ 37 \\ +\ 234 \\ \hline \end{array}$$

12.
$$\begin{array}{r} 602 \\ 125 \\ +\ 231 \\ \hline \end{array}$$

13.
$$\begin{array}{r} 246 \\ 54 \\ 233 \\ +\ 205 \\ \hline \end{array}$$

14.
$$\begin{array}{r} 303 \\ 128 \\ 63 \\ +\ 149 \\ \hline \end{array}$$

15. 164 + 68 + 35

16. 32 + 9 + 46 + 8

17. 125 + 36 + 124 + 239

*For another example, see Set E on page 69.

Step 1

Line up ones, tens, and hundreds.

```
  137
  155
+  18
-----
```

Step 2

Add the ones. Regroup.

```
    2
  137
  155
+  18
-----
    0
```

Step 3

Add the tens. Regroup.

```
   12
  137
  155
+  18
-----
   10
```

Step 4

Add the hundreds.

```
   12
  137
  155
+  18
-----
  310
```

In all, 310 birds are for sale.

Problem Solving

Calories are used to measure the energy in food. Use the picture for **18** and **19**.

18. Karin had cereal, a glass of milk, and a banana for breakfast. Follow these steps to find how many calories were in the food she ate.

a Write a number sentence to show how to solve the problem.

b Estimate the answer.

c Solve the problem.

d Use the estimate to explain why your answer is reasonable.

19. Compare the number of calories in a glass of milk with the number of calories in a banana. Use >, <, or =.

20. **Reasonableness** Meg said that 95 + 76 + 86 is greater than 300. Explain why her answer is not reasonable.

21. Use the picture to find the size of President Washington's head carved in Mt. Rushmore.

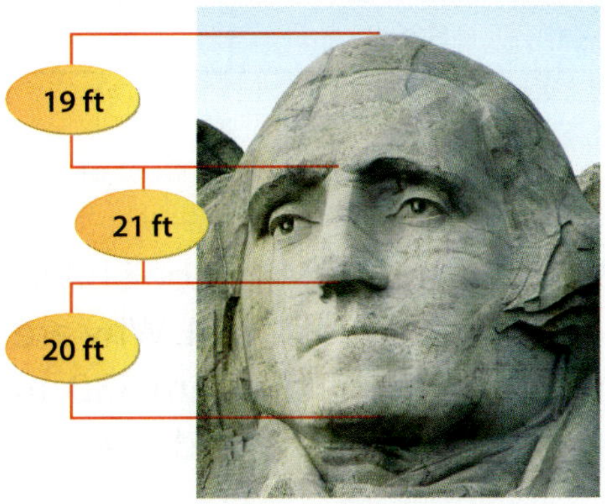

22. Ramos has 225 pennies, 105 nickels, and 65 dimes. How many coins does he have?

A 385 coins

B 395 coins

C 980 coins

D 3,815 coins

Virginia

Lesson 2-10

Extends 3.4 The student will estimate solutions to and solve single-step and multistep problems involving the sum or difference of two whole numbers, each 9,999 or less, with or without regrouping.

Problem Solving

Draw a Picture

David wants to buy some soccer souvenirs. How much money does David need to buy shorts and a shirt?

Guided Practice*

Do you know HOW?

1. Use the picture above. Cal bought a poster and a pennant. Copy and complete the diagram to find how much money he spent.

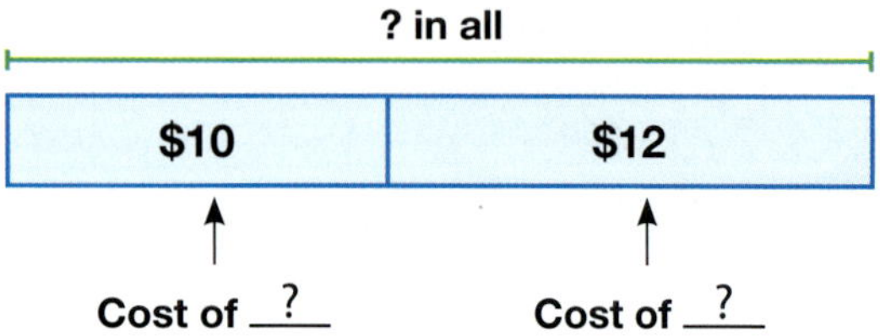

Do you UNDERSTAND?

2. Look at the diagram for Problem 1.

a What does each box show?

b What does the line above the whole rectangle show?

3. **Write a Problem** Write and solve a problem that can be solved by drawing a picture.

Independent Practice

4. David's dad spent $27 for tickets to the baseball game. He also spent $24 on food. **About** how much did he spend?

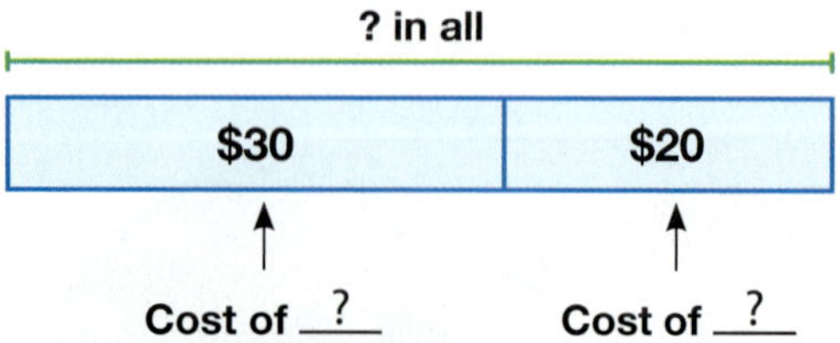

5. **Writing to Explain** Look back at the diagram for Problem 4. Why are the numbers in the diagram $30 and $20 instead of $27 and $24?

Stuck? Try this....

- What do I know?
- What am I asked to find?
- What diagram can I use to help understand the problem?
- Can I use addition, subtraction, multiplication, or division?
- Is all of my work correct?
- Did I answer the right question?
- Is my answer reasonable?

*For another example, see Set F on page 63.

Plan and Solve

Draw a diagram to show what you know.

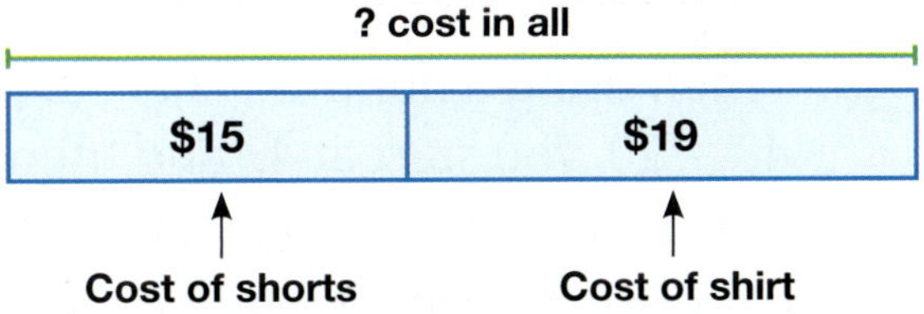

You know the parts. Add to find the total.

$15 + $19 = ▢

$15 + $19 = $34

Think $15 + $20 = $35
$20 is $1 more than $19.

David needs $34 to buy shorts and a shirt.

Check

Make sure the answer is reasonable.

Estimate.

$15 + $19 is about
$20 + $20, or $40.

The answer is reasonable because $34 is close to $40.

The table at the right shows the pets owned by third graders at Smith School. Use the table for **6–8**. For **6** and **7**, copy and complete the diagram. Answer the question.

Data

Students' Pets

Pets	**Number of Students**
Cats	18
Dogs	22
Fish	9
Hamsters	7
Snakes	2

6. How many students have fish or hamsters?

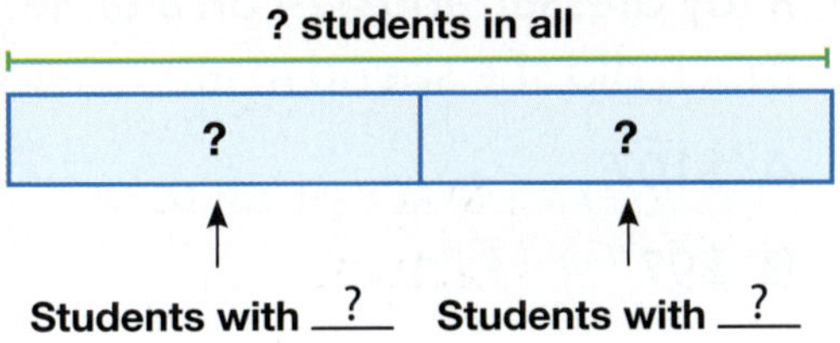

7. How many students have cats, dogs, or snakes?

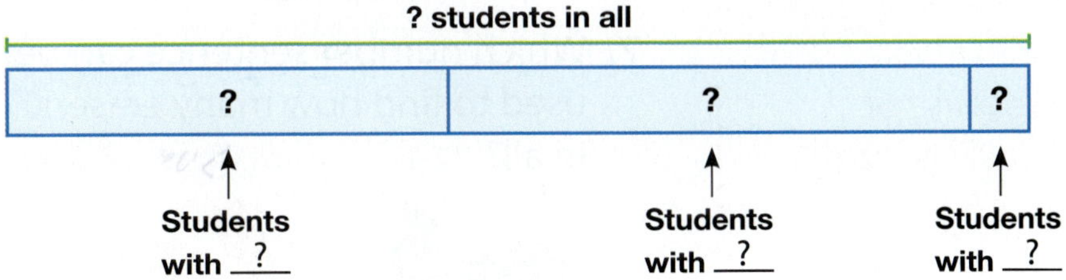

8. Draw a diagram to find about how many students have cats or dogs.

9. **Estimation** At the aquarium, Janet counted 12 sand sharks, 9 zebra sharks, and 11 nurse sharks. About how many sharks did Janet count?

A 50 sharks **B** 30 sharks **C** 20 sharks **D** 15 sharks

VA SOL Test Prep

1. To the nearest ten pounds, Riley weighs 90 pounds. Which could be her weight? (2-4)

A 84 pounds

B 86 pounds

C 95 pounds

D 98 pounds

2. Which addition sentence is shown? (2-7)

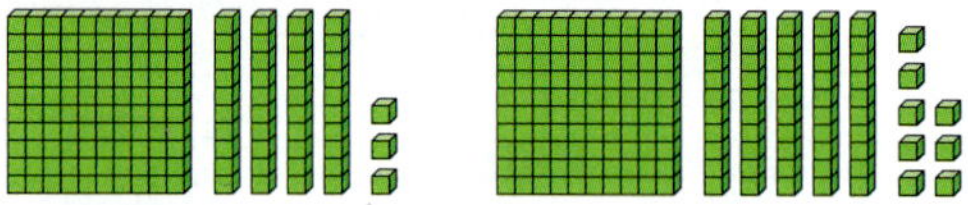

A $143 + 157 = \square$

B $143 + 158 = \square$

C $143 + 147 = \square$

D $8 + 14 = \square$

3. Rex has 252 football cards and 596 baseball cards. Which number sentence shows the best estimate of how many cards Rex has in all, using compatible numbers? (2-5)

A $300 + 550 = 850$

B $300 + 500 = 800$

C $250 + 550 = 800$

D $250 + 600 = 850$

4. Between 6 A.M. and 10 A.M., 389 trucks and 599 cars crossed a bridge. How many vehicles is this in all? (2-8)

A 878

B 888

C 978

D 988

5. When using a hundred chart to find $43 + 20$, you start at 43 and then do which of the following steps? (2-2)

21	22	23	24	25	26	27	28	29	30
31	32	33	34	35	36	37	38	39	40
41	42	43	44	45	46	47	48	49	50
51	52	53	54	55	56	57	58	59	60
61	62	63	64	65	66	67	68	69	70

A Count down 2 rows.

B Count to the right 2 squares.

C Count to the left 2 squares.

D Count up 2 rows.

6. Tricia spent \$35 on a toy bed, \$48 on a toy dresser, and \$24 on a table. How much did she spend in all? (2-9)

A \$107

B \$97

C \$83

D \$72

7. Which number sentence can be used to find how many erasers in all? (2-1)

A $8 + 6 = 14$

B $9 + 6 = 15$

C $9 + 5 = 14$

D $3 + 6 = 9$

Topic 2

VA SOL Test Prep

8. Mr. Kipper's class collected \$453 for the local animal shelter. What is \$453 rounded to the nearest hundred? (2-4)

A \$500

B \$460

C \$450

D \$400

9. Ava swam for 39 minutes on Saturday and 49 minutes on Sunday. To find $39 + 49$, Ava made a ten, as shown below. What is the missing number? (2-3)

$39 + 49 = 40 + \square = 88$

A 29

B 30

C 47

D 48

10. Kent has 28 butterflies, 16 beetles, and 12 grasshoppers in his collection. How many butterflies and beetles does he have? (2-6)

A 28

B 40

C 44

D 56

11. The Aztec Ruins monument has about 318 acres. Capulin Volcano has about 793 acres. Which is reasonable for the total size for these two national monuments in New Mexico? (2-8)

A 1,211 acres, because $318 + 793$ is about $400 + 800 = 1{,}200$

B 1,111 acres, because $318 + 793$ is about $300 + 800 = 1{,}100$

C 1,011 acres, because $318 + 793$ is about $300 + 700 = 1{,}000$

D 911 acres, because $318 + 793$ is about $300 + 600 = 900$

12. Cindy picked 9 roses and then 14 daisies. Which number correctly replaces the question mark in the diagram? (2-10)

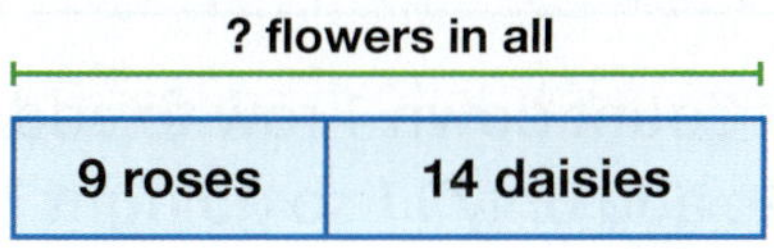

A 5

B 23

C 33

D 113

13. Kaitlyn read a 48-page book. Her sister read a 104-page book. Which is the best estimate for the total number of pages the sisters read? (2-5)

A 150

B 140

C 120

D 100

Set A, pages 32–33

Write the missing number.

Use the Associative Property of Addition.

(2 + □) + 1 = 2 + (5 + 1)
(2 + 5) + 1 = 2 + (5 + 1)

You can group addends in any way and the sum will be the same.

Use the Commutative Property of Addition.

7 + □ = 6 + 7
7 + 6 = 6 + 7

You can add numbers in any order and the sum will be the same.

Remember the Identity Property of Addition: the sum of any number and zero is that same number.

Write each missing number.

1. (2 + 3) + 5 = 2 + (3 + □)
2. □ + 0 = 6
3. (1 + □) + 6 = 1 + (4 + 6)

Set B, pages 34–35

Use a hundred chart to add 14 + 11.

1	2	3	4	5	6	7	8	9	10
11	12	13	14	15	16	17	18	19	20
21	22	23	24	25	26	27	28	29	30
31	32	33	34	35	36	37	38	39	40

Start at 14. Count down 1 row to add 10.
You need to add only 11 so go right 1 space.
14 + 11 = 25

Remember that to add on a hundred chart, first add the tens.

Use a hundred chart to add.

1. 37 + 20
2. 52 + 17
3. 18 + 45
4. 52 + 30
5. 8 + 29
6. 12 + 15

Set C, pages 36–38, 40–42, 44–46

Round 867 to the nearest hundred.

hundreds place
↓
867
↓↓↓
900

Since 6 > 5, increase the digit in the hundreds place by one. Then change all the digits to the right to zero.

867 rounds to 900.

Estimate 478 + 134.

Use compatible numbers.

478 → 470
+ 134 → + 130
600

Remember that you can break apart addends to use mental math.

Find each sum using mental math.

1. 30 + 56
2. 45 + 19

In **3–8**, estimate each sum.
Round to the nearest hundred.

3. 367 + 319
4. 732 + 110

Round to the nearest ten.

5. 98 + 42
6. 459 + 213

Use compatible numbers.

7. 372 + 123
8. 211 + 164

Set D, pages 48–49

Find 96 + 68. Estimate: 100 + 70 = 170

Then, add.

$$\begin{array}{r} {}^{1} \\ 96 \\ +\ 68 \\ \hline 164 \end{array}$$

6 + 8 = 14 ones
Regroup into 1 ten 4 ones.
1 ten + 9 tens + 6 tens = 16 tens

164 is close to 170, so 164 is reasonable.

Remember to add ones first. Regroup if necessary. Then add tens.

Estimate. Then find each sum.

1. $\begin{array}{r} 38 \\ +\ 47 \\ \hline \end{array}$

2. $\begin{array}{r} 77 \\ +\ 56 \\ \hline \end{array}$

3. 55 + 89

4. 58 + 33

Set E, pages 50–52, 54–57

Find 125 + 168.

Show 125 and 168 with place-value blocks.

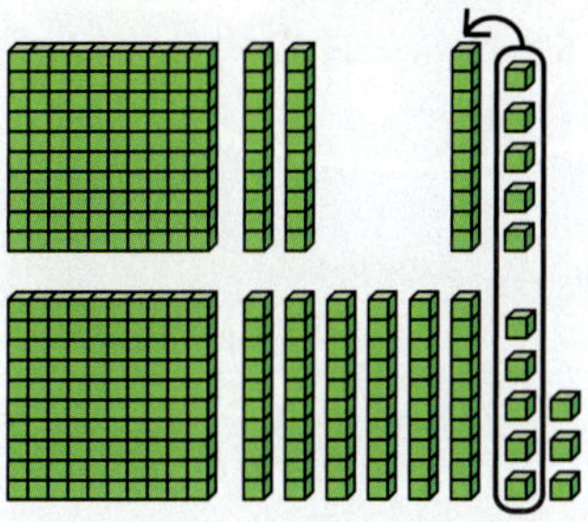

5 ones + 8 ones = 13 ones
Regroup.
13 ones = 1 ten 3 ones

1 ten + 2 tens + 6 tens = 9 tens

1 hundred + 1 hundred = 2 hundreds

So, 125 + 168 = 293.

Find 43 + 187 + 238.
Estimate: 40 + 190 + 240 = 470

$$\begin{array}{r} {}^{1}\,{}^{1} \\ 43 \\ 187 \\ +\ 238 \\ \hline 468 \end{array}$$

Line up ones, tens, and hundreds. Then add each column. Regroup as needed.

The answer 468 is close to 470, so 468 is reasonable.

Remember to add ones, then tens, then hundreds.

Find each sum. Use place-value blocks or draw a picture to help.

1. 265 + 116

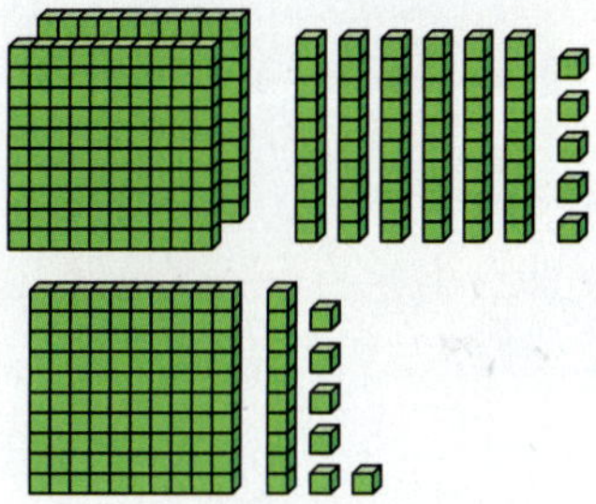

Find each sum.

2. $\begin{array}{r} 718 \\ +\ 156 \\ \hline \end{array}$

3. $\begin{array}{r} 139 \\ 209 \\ +\ 55 \\ \hline \end{array}$

Set F, pages 58–59

Ty's dad spent $26 for tickets to a game and $18 for snacks. How much did he spend in all?

$26 + $18 = ▢
$26 + $18 = $44

Remember to draw pictures to show the information you know.

Draw a picture and then solve.

1. Jason had 35 trading cards. Then he bought 27 more. How many does he have in all?

Topic 3

Subtraction Number Sense

1 How much longer was a *Brachiosaurus* than a *Tyrannosaurus rex*? You will find out in Lesson 3-4.

2 In recent years, how many missions from NASA's Jet Propulsion Lab have studied comets? You will find out in Lesson 3-1.

3 How fast can a cheetah run? You will find out in Lesson 3-2.

4 The giant Rafflesia plant has the largest flower in the world. How large is it? You will find out in Lesson 3-3.

Review What You Know!

Vocabulary

Choose the best term from the box.

- add
- round
- skip count
- subtract

1. To take away a part from a whole, you can _?_.

2. You can _?_ to find a number that is close to the actual number.

3. To join parts together, you can _?_.

Subtraction Facts

Find each difference.

4. 9 − 5 **5.** 11 − 3 **6.** 16 − 7

Addition Facts

Find each sum.

7. 4 + 8 **8.** 9 + 8 **9.** 6 + 7

Rounding

Writing to Explain

10. To what two numbers can you round 78? Explain why there is more than one way to round 78.

11. Is the sum of 5 + 8 the same as or different from the sum of 8 + 5? Explain.

Virginia

Lesson 3-1

3.2 The student will recognize and use the inverse relationships between addition/subtraction and multiplication/division to complete basic fact sentences. The student will use these relationships to solve problems.

Subtraction Meanings

Hands-On
counters

When do you subtract?

Ms. Aydin's class is making school flags to sell at the school fair.

The table shows how many flags several students have made so far.

Data

Flags for School Fair

Student	Number Made
Brent	12
Devon	9
Keisha	11
Ling	14
Pedro	7
Rick	8

Another Example Subtract to find a missing addend.

Rick plans on making 13 flags. How many more flags does he need?

The parts and the whole show how addition and subtraction are related.

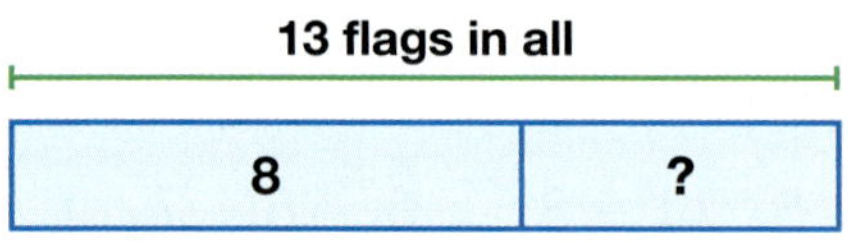

$8 + \square = 13$

You can write a fact family when you know the parts and the whole.

A fact family is a group of related facts using the same numbers.

$5 + 8 = 13$ $\quad$ $13 - 8 = 5$

$8 + 5 = 13$ $\quad$ $13 - 5 = 8$

The missing part is 5. This means Rick needs to make 5 more flags.

Guided Practice*

Do you know HOW?

Use the table to write and solve a number sentence.

1. How many more flags has Ling made than Devon?

2. How many more flags must Pedro make to have 15 in all? to have the same number as Ling?

Do you UNDERSTAND?

3. Ling sold 8 of the flags she had made. Write a number sentence to find how many flags she has left. Then solve the problem.

4. **Write a Problem** Write and solve a word problem that can be solved by subtracting.

DIGITAL Animated Glossary, eTools
www.pearsonsuccessnet.com

*For another example, see Set A on page 82.

Subtract to take some away and find how many are left.

Brent sold 5 of the flags he made. How many flags did he have left?

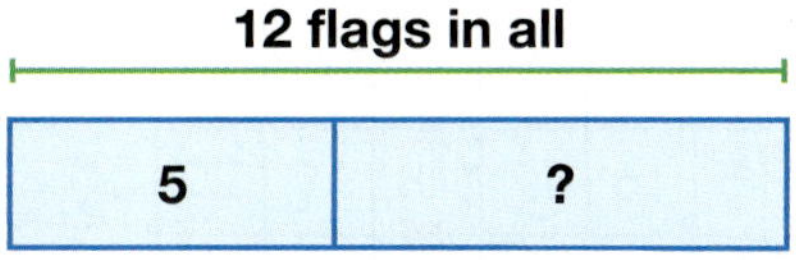

$12 - 5 = 7$

Brent had 7 flags left.

Subtract to compare amounts.

How many more flags did Keisha make than Pedro?

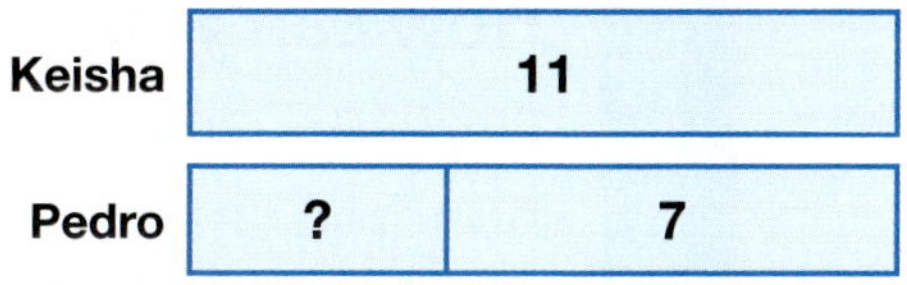

$11 - 7 = 4$

Keisha made 4 more flags than Pedro.

Independent Practice

Write a number sentence for each situation. Solve.

5. Pat has 15 pins. Chris has 9 pins. How many more pins does Pat have than Chris?

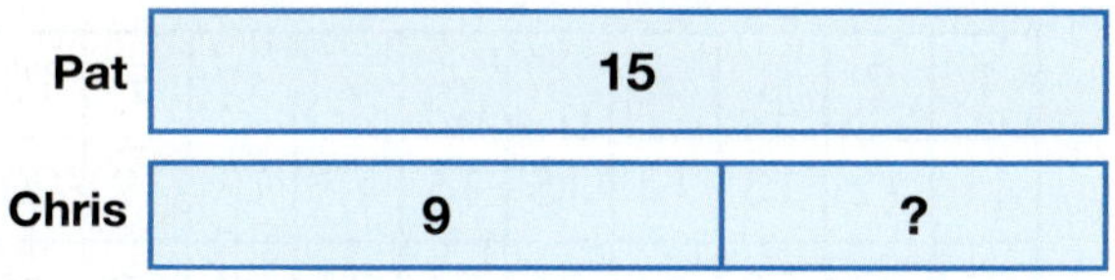

6. How many more orange flags than green flags are there?

Problem Solving

7. Ching had 12 pies to sell. After she sold some of the pies, she had 4 pies left. How many pies had Ching sold?

8. A pole holding a state flag is 10 feet tall. The height of the flag is 4 feet. How many feet taller is the pole than the flag?

9. The Jet Propulsion Lab had 9 missions between 2003 and 2006. Two of these missions were to study comets. How many of these missions did not study comets?

10. Kevin has 17 spelling words to learn this week. He already knows how to spell 9 of the words. How many words does he still need to learn?

11. Rob had 17 pens. After he gave some of them to his friend, he had 8 pens. Which number sentence shows one way to find how many pens Rob gave to his friend?

A $17 + 8 = \square$ **B** $8 - 1 = \square$ **C** $17 - 1 = \square$ **D** $17 - \square = 8$

Virginia

Lesson 3-2

Reviews 2.7.b The student, given two whole numbers, each of which is 99 or less, will find the difference, using various methods of calculation.

Subtracting on a Hundred Chart

How can you subtract on a hundred chart?

Find 38 − 20 on a hundred chart.

Start at 38. To count back 2 tens, move up 2 rows.

38 − 20 = 18

1	2	3	4	5	6	7	8	9	10
11	12	13	14	15	16	17	18	19	20
21	22	23	24	25	26	27	28	29	30
31	32	33	34	35	36	37	38	39	40
41	42	43	44	45	46	47	48	49	50

Another Example **How can you use counting on to find differences?**

The difference is the answer when subtracting two numbers.

Find 43 − 19.

Think 19 + ☐ = 43.

Start at 19.
Move right one square to count on to the next ten.
20

Count on by tens by moving down.
Move two rows.
30, 40

Then count on by ones until you reach 43.
41, 42, 43

You counted on: 1 + 20 + 3 = 24.

So, 43 − 19 = 24.

1	2	3	4	5	6	7	8	9	10
11	12	13	14	15	16	17	18	19	20
21	22	23	24	25	26	27	28	29	30
31	32	33	34	35	36	37	38	39	40
41	42	43	44	45	46	47	48	49	50
51	52	53	54	55	56	57	58	59	60
61	62	63	64	65	66	67	68	69	70
71	72	73	74	75	76	77	78	79	80
81	82	83	84	85	86	87	88	89	90
91	92	93	94	95	96	97	98	99	100

Explain It

1. Why do you stop at 20 when you first count on from 19?
2. Why do you add 1 + 20 + 3?

Find 85 − 19.

Think 85 − 20 = ☐

Start at 85 on the hundred chart.

Count back 2 tens to subtract 20.
To do this, move up two rows.
75, 65

Since you subtracted 1 more than 19, add 1 by moving to the right one square.
65 + 1 = 66

So, 85 − 19 = 66.

51	52	53	54	55	56	57	58	59	60
61	62	63	64	65	66	67	68	69	70
71	72	73	74	75	76	77	78	79	80
81	82	83	84	85	86	87	88	89	90
91	92	93	94	95	96	97	98	99	100

Guided Practice*

Do you know HOW?

Use a hundred chart to subtract.

1. 72 − 40

2. 86 − 30

3. 54 − 29

4. 95 − 39

5. 37 − 18

Do you UNDERSTAND?

6. **Writing to Explain** When you move up 2 rows on a hundred chart, how many are you subtracting? Explain.

7. How is subtracting ten on a hundred chart different from adding ten on a hundred chart?

8. Janey has 75 cents. She wants to buy a sticker that costs 39 cents. How much money would she have left? Explain how to use a hundred chart to find the answer.

Independent Practice

Use a hundred chart to subtract.

9. 75 − 30 **10.** 53 − 20 **11.** 68 − 40 **12.** 27 − 10

13. 84 − 50 **14.** 96 − 60 **15.** 47 − 19 **16.** 53 − 28

17. 65 − 39 **18.** 81 − 58 **19.** 76 − 29 **20.** 94 − 38

21. 96 − 17 **22.** 79 − 15 **23.** 81 − 26 **24.** 77 − 48

DIGITAL Animated Glossary www.pearsonsuccessnet.com

*For another example, see Set B on page 82.

Problem Solving

Use the table for **25–27**.

25. A cottonwood tree in Max's yard is 30 feet shorter than an average cottonwood tree. How tall is the tree in his yard?

26. Write the average heights of the trees from shortest to tallest.

Data

State Trees

State	Kind of Tree	Average Height
Kansas	Cottonwood	75 feet
Michigan	Eastern white pine	70 feet
New York	Sugar maple	80 feet

27. A sugar maple tree in the local park is 92 feet tall. How many feet taller is the tree in the park than an average sugar maple tree?

28. **Writing to Explain** A white pine tree is 52 feet tall. Suppose that during the next 7 years, it grows a total of 10 feet. How tall would it be then? Explain how you found your answer.

29. **Reasonableness** Liam used a hundred chart to find 92 − 62. He said the difference is 40. Is his answer reasonable? Why or why not?

Tip *What addition sentence can help?*

30. The workers in the lunchroom made 234 ham sandwiches and 165 tuna sandwiches. They also made 150 cheese pizzas and 125 veggie pizzas. How many sandwiches did they make in all?

31. For short distances, an elephant can run as fast as 15 miles per hour. How much faster can a cheetah run than an elephant?

A cheetah can run short distances as fast as 70 miles an hour.

32. John is 56 inches tall. John's father is 72 inches tall. How much taller is John's father than John? Explain how you found your answer.

33. Maya had 15 small rocks. She had 9 large rocks. Which number sentence shows one way to find how many more small rocks than large rocks Maya had?

A 15 − 9 = ☐

B 15 + 6 = ☐

C 15 + 9 = ☐

D 24 − 15 = ☐

Algebra Connections

Addition and Subtraction Number Sentences

The symbol = means "is equal to."
In a number sentence, the symbol = tells you that the value on the left is equal to the value on the right.

Examples: $29 = 20 + 9$

$6 = 11 - 5$

$9 + 4 = 13$

Think The value on the left side of the number sentence is equal to the value on the right side.

Copy and complete. Write the number that makes the number sentence true.

1. $9 + \square = 11$ **2.** $10 = 3 + \square$ **3.** $17 - \square = 9$

4. $5 + \square = 13$ **5.** $8 = 12 - \square$ **6.** $14 = 5 + \square$

7. $10 = 10 + \square$ **8.** $6 + \square = 26$ **9.** $19 + \square = 29$

10. $50 + \square = 60$ **11.** $30 = 40 - \square$ **12.** $25 = 5 + \square$

13. $10 + \square = 17$ **14.** $42 = 45 - \square$ **15.** $13 - \square = 0$

For **16** and **17**, copy and complete the number sentence below each problem. Use it to solve the problem.

16. Nate had 10 river stones. Chen had 26 river stones. How many more river stones did Chen have than Nate?

$10 + \square = 26$

17. Tania collected 10 more leaves than Gwen. Tania collected 37 leaves. How many leaves did Gwen collect?

$\square + 10 = 37$

18. **Write a Problem** Write and solve a problem to match the number sentence below.

$48 = 20 + \square$

Virginia

Lesson 3-3

Reviews 2.7.b The student, given two whole numbers, each of which is 99 or less, will find the difference, using various methods of calculation.

Using Mental Math to Subtract

How can you subtract with mental math?

The store is having a sale on jackets. A jacket is on sale for $17 less than the original price. What is the sale price?

You can use mental math to subtract and solve this problem.

Guided Practice*

Do you know HOW?

In **1–8**, find each difference using mental math.

1. 26 − 18
2. 34 − 19
3. 73 − 16
4. 45 − 27
5. 67 − 28
6. 83 − 39
7. 46 − 18
8. 49 − 19

Do you UNDERSTAND?

9. Writing to Explain In the One Way example above, why do you add 3 to 32 instead of subtract 3 from 32?

10. Suppose a coat has an original price of $74 and it is on sale for $18 less than the original price. What is the sale price of the coat? How can you use mental math to solve this problem?

Independent Practice

In **11–30**, find each difference using mental math.

11. 28 − 19
12. 46 − 18
13. 39 − 17
14. 68 − 11
15. 52 − 9
16. 75 − 12
17. 29 − 18
18. 49 − 18
19. 64 − 15
20. 43 − 16
21. 97 − 14
22. 86 − 13
23. 31 − 14
24. 98 − 17
25. 57 − 18
26. 72 − 19
27. 53 − 39
28. 27 − 19
29. 82 − 27
30. 73 − 39

**For another example, see Set C on page 83.*

One Way

52 − 17 = ▢

It's easier to subtract 20.

52 − 20 = 32

If you subtract 20, you subtract 3 more than 17. You must add 3 to the answer.

32 + 3 = 35

52 − 17 = 35

The sale price is $35.

Another Way

52 − 17 = ▢

Make a simpler problem by changing each number in the same way.

You can change 17 to 20 because it's easy to subtract 20. So, add 3 to both 17 and 52.

52 − 17 = ▢

↓ +3 ↓ +3

55 − 20 = 35

52 − 17 = 35

Problem Solving

31. Number Sense The giant Rafflesia flower can be as wide as shown in the picture. One petal can be 18 inches wide. How can you use mental math to find how much wider the whole flower is than one petal?

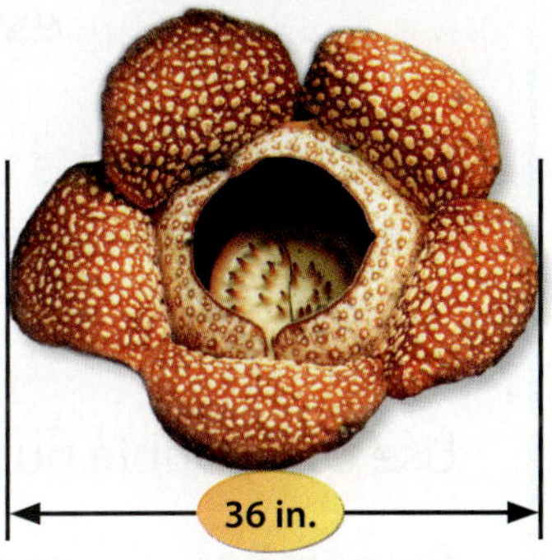

32. Writing to Explain To subtract 57 − 16, Tom added 4 to each number, while Saul added 3 to each number. Will both methods work to find the correct answer? Explain.

In **33** and **34**, use the photo below.

33. a What is the sale price of the jeans? Describe one way you can use mental math to find the answer.

b Maria bought two pairs of jeans. What was the total sale price of the jeans Maria bought?

34. Which number sentence shows the original price of two pairs of jeans?

A 46 + 46 = ▢

B 46 + 18 = ▢

C 18 + 18 = ▢

D 46 − 18 = ▢

35. Eva saved $38. She bought a book for $17. Which number sentence shows one way to find how much money Eva had left?

A 38 + 17 = ▢

B 38 − 17 = ▢

C ▢ − 38 = 17

D ▢ − 17 = 38

Virginia

Lesson 3-4

3.4 The student will estimate solutions to and solve single-step and multistep problems involving the sum or difference of two whole numbers, each 9,999 or less, with or without regrouping.

Estimating Differences

How can you estimate differences?

All of the tickets for a concert were sold. So far, 126 people have arrived at the concert. About how many people who have tickets have not arrived?

Since you need to find *about* how many, you can estimate.

Estimate 493 − 126 by rounding.

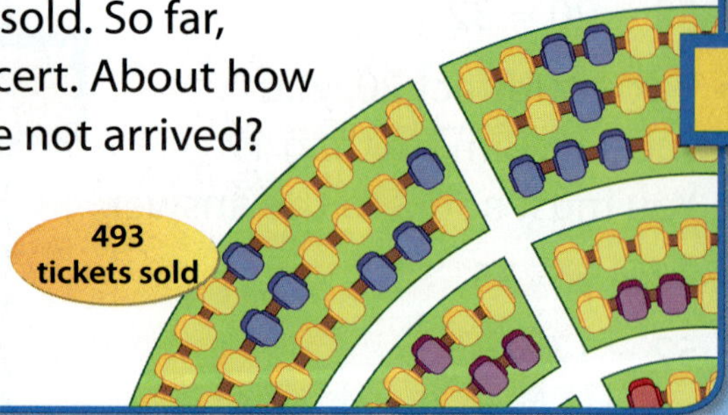

Another Example How can you use compatible numbers to estimate differences?

The Perry family is taking a car trip. The trip is 372 miles long. So far, the family has traveled 149 miles. About how many miles are left to travel?

Use compatible numbers to estimate 372 − 149.

Remember: Compatible numbers are numbers that are close and easy to work with.

$$\begin{array}{r} 372 \\ -\ 149 \\ \hline \end{array} \longrightarrow \begin{array}{r} 375 \\ -\ 150 \\ \hline 225 \end{array}$$

The Perry family still has about 225 miles to travel.

Explain It

1. How are the numbers 375 and 150 easy to work with?
2. Use a different pair of compatible numbers to estimate 372 − 149.
3. Is an estimate enough to solve this problem? Why or why not?

One Way

You can round each number to the nearest hundred.

$$\begin{array}{r} 493 \\ -\ 126 \\ \hline \end{array} \quad \rightarrow \quad \begin{array}{r} 500 \\ -\ 100 \\ \hline 400 \end{array}$$

About 400 people have not yet arrived.

Another Way

You can round each number to the nearest ten.

$$\begin{array}{r} 493 \\ -\ 126 \\ \hline \end{array} \quad \rightarrow \quad \begin{array}{r} 490 \\ -\ 130 \\ \hline 360 \end{array}$$

About 360 people have not yet arrived.

Guided Practice*

Do you know HOW?

In **1** and **2**, round to the nearest hundred to estimate each difference.

1. 321 − 112 **2.** 255 − 189

In **3** and **4**, round to the nearest ten to estimate each difference.

3. 579 − 214 **4.** 216 − 97

In **5** and **6**, use compatible numbers to estimate each difference.

5. 328 − 207 **6.** 472 − 148

Do you UNDERSTAND?

7. **Writing to Explain** In the problem above, which way of rounding gives an estimate that is closer to the actual difference? Explain why.

8. The theater sold 415 tickets to the comedy show. So far, 273 people have arrived at the show. About how many more people are expected to arrive? Tell which estimation method you used and how you found your answer.

Independent Practice

In **9–11**, round to the nearest hundred to estimate each difference.

9. 186 − 75 **10.** 704 − 369 **11.** 291 − 93

In **12–17**, round to the nearest ten to estimate each difference.

12. 88 − 32 **13.** 149 − 95 **14.** 361 − 117

15. 75 − 41 **16.** 86 − 38 **17.** 227 − 121

*For another example, see Set D on page 83.

Independent Practice

In **18–23**, use compatible numbers to estimate each difference.

18. 77 − 28 **19.** 202 − 144 **20.** 611 − 168

21. 512 − 205 **22.** 342 − 153 **23.** 904 − 31

Problem Solving

Use the table for **24–27**.

Grand Concert Hall

Day of Concert	Number of Tickets Sold
Wednesday	506
Thursday	323
Friday	251
Saturday	427
Sunday	

24. The concert hall sold 28 fewer tickets for the Sunday concert than for the Friday concert. About how many tickets were sold for the Sunday concert?

25. About how many tickets in all were sold for Thursday and Friday?

26. **Think About the Process** About how many more tickets were sold for the Wednesday concert than for the Friday concert? Write a number sentence that uses numbers rounded to the nearest ten to estimate how many more. Explain your answer.

27. SOL Prep Which number sentence shows the best way to estimate how many fewer tickets were sold for the Friday concert than the Thursday concert?

A 400 − 200 = 200

B 300 − 300 = 0

C 325 − 200 = 125

D 325 − 250 = 75

28. **Writing to Explain** About how many feet longer was a *Brachiosaurus* than a *T. rex*? Use compatible numbers to estimate. Explain why you chose the numbers you used.

Mixed Problem Solving

Math and Science

The length of one year on a planet is the total time for the planet to make one complete trip around the Sun.

1. About how many fewer Earth days is a year on Mercury than a year on Earth?

2. About how many more Earth days is a year on Mars than a year on Earth?

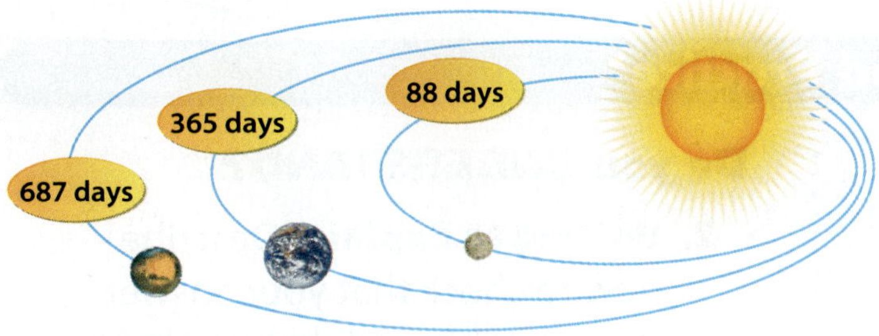

Data

Length of Year	
Planet	**Length of Year** (in Earth Days)
Mercury	88
Venus	225
Earth	365
Mars	687
Jupiter	4,330
Saturn	10,756
Uranus	30,687
Neptune	60,190

3. Which planet has a digit 6 with a value of sixty thousand in the length of its year?

4. Which planet has a year that is about six thousand Earth days more than Jupiter's?

5. Which space object listed in the table at the right has an average surface temperature closest to Mercury's?

6. Write the average surface temperatures in order from least to greatest.

Data

Space Object	Average Surface Temperature
Mercury	332°F
Earth	59°F
The Moon	225°F
Venus	854°F

7. **Strategy Focus** Solve. Use the strategy Make an Organized List.

   Meg's favorite planet has at least 5 letters in its name. The length of its year is less than 10,000 Earth days. List all the planets that fit these clues.

Lesson 3-5

3.4 The student will estimate solutions to and solve single-step and multistep problems involving the sum or difference of two whole numbers, each 9,999 or less, with or without regrouping.

Problem Solving

Reasonableness

Al had the marbles shown at the right. He gave 18 marbles to his brother. How many marbles does Al have left?

After you solve a problem, ask yourself:

- Is the answer reasonable?
- Did I answer the right question?

53 marbles in all

18 marbles	?

Guided Practice*

Do you know HOW?

1. Rosita is reading a book that is 65 pages long. She has 27 pages left to read. How many pages has she already read?

65 pages in all

?	27

Do you UNDERSTAND?

2. **Writing to Explain** Describe how to check that your answer is reasonable and that you have answered the right question.

3. **Write a Problem** Write and solve a problem. Check that your answer is reasonable.

Independent Practice

Solve. Then check that your answer is reasonable.

4. James is reading a book that is 85 pages long. He read 35 pages yesterday and 24 pages today. How many pages did James read in the two days?

? pages in all

35	24

5. Kyle had 56 model cars. He gave his brother 36 of them. How many model cars does Kyle have now?

Stuck? Try this....

- What do I know?
- What am I asked to find?
- What diagram can I use to help understand the problem?
- Can I use addition, subtraction, multiplication, or division?
- Is all of my work correct?
- Did I answer the right question?
- Is my answer reasonable?

*For another example, see Set E on page 83.

Jim's Answer

53 − 18 = 35
Al's brother has 35 marbles.

53 − 18 is about 50 − 20, or 30.

35 is close to 30, so 35 is reasonable.

The number 35 is reasonable, but Jim did not answer the right question.

Sally's Answer

53 − 18 = 45
Al has 45 marbles left.

53 − 18 is about 50 − 20, or 30.

45 is not close to 30, so 45 is not reasonable.

Sally answered the right question, but the number 45 is not reasonable.

Pablo's Answer

53 − 18 = 35
Al has 35 marbles left.

53 − 18 is about 50 − 20, or 30.

35 is close to 30, so 35 is reasonable.

The number 35 is reasonable, and Pablo did answer the right question.

Independent Practice

Use the table to solve **6–8**. Estimate, then check that your answer is reasonable.

Total Points Scored

Games	Points
Game 1	68
Game 2	74
Game 3	89

Data

6. How many points were scored all together in Games 1 and 2?

? points in all

68	**74**

7. There were 39 points scored in the first half of Game 1. How many points were scored in the second half?

68 points in all

39	**?**

8. **Estimation** About how many points were scored all together in the three games?

? points in all

70	**70**	**90**

9. Carl practices the piano 45 minutes each day. Today, he practiced 15 minutes after school and 10 minutes before dinner. How much time does he still need to practice?

SOL Prep

A 70 minutes
B 60 minutes
C 35 minutes
D 20 minutes

10. Carrie has 15 pennies. Her brother has 10 more pennies than Carrie. How many pennies do they have in all?

SOL Prep

A 40 pennies
B 25 pennies
C 10 pennies
D 5 pennies

1. Mario wants to have 15 insects in his collection. He has 8 insects. Which number sentence shows a way to find how many more insects Mario needs to collect? (3-1)

A 15 − 7 = ☐

B 15 − ☐ = 7

C 8 + 15 = ☐

D 8 + ☐ = 15

2. Tom had $41. He spent $17. Which is the best estimate of how much he had left? (3-4)

A $60

B $30

C $20

D $10

3. To find 67 − 19 on a hundred chart, Casie started at 67 and then moved up 2 rows. What should she do next? (3-2)

31	32	33	34	35	36	37	38	39	40
41	42	43	44	45	46	47	48	49	50
51	52	53	54	55	56	57	58	59	60
61	62	63	64	65	66	67	68	69	70

A Move right 1 square.

B Move left 1 square.

C Move right 9 squares.

D Move left 9 squares.

4. Which number sentence is shown? (3-1)

A 3 + 7 = 10

B 17 − 7 = 10

C 7 + 3 = 10

D 10 − 7 = 3

5. There are 263 children at summer camp. There are 114 boys. Which is the best estimate for the number of girls? (3-4)

A 250

B 150

C 120

D 100

6. Rosa has 9 pens. Kim has 4 pens. Which number sentence shows how many more pens Rosa has than Kim? (3-1)

A 9 + 4 = 13

B 13 − 4 = 9

C 9 − 5 = 4

D 9 − 4 = 5

7. Which is the best estimate for 392 − 84? (3-4)

A 500

B 400

C 300

D 200

8. Tropical Fish Warehouse had 98 goldfish on Monday. By Friday, they had sold 76 of the goldfish. How many goldfish had not been sold? Use mental math to solve. (3-3)

A 22

B 32

C 38

D 174

9. A zoo has 32 kinds of snakes and 22 kinds of lizards. Which number sentence shows the best way to estimate how many more kinds of snakes than lizards are in the zoo? (3-4)

A $30 - 20 = 10$

B $30 + 20 = 50$

C $40 - 20 = 20$

D $40 - 30 = 10$

10. Stacy has 16 spelling words. She already knows how to spell 9 of the words. How many words does she still need to learn how to spell? (3-1)

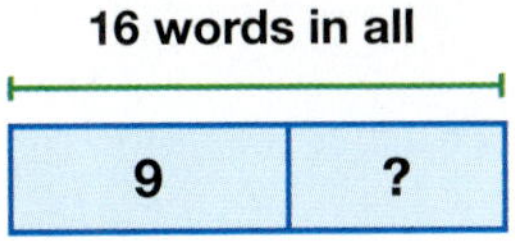

A 25

B 9

C 7

D 6

11. Lee drove 348 miles on Monday and 135 miles on Tuesday. Which is the most reasonable answer for how much farther he drove on Monday than on Tuesday? (3-5)

A 113 miles

B 213 miles

C 313 miles

D 483 miles

12. To subtract $62 - 17$ mentally, Talia subtracted $62 - 20 = 42$ first. What should she do next? (3-3)

A Add $42 + 2$.

B Add $42 + 3$.

C Subtract $42 - 2$.

D Subtract $42 - 3$.

13. Mia had $83. She spent $49. To find how much money she has left, Mia used counting on.

$49 + 1 = 50$

$50 + 30 = 80$

$80 + 3 = 83$

How much money does Mia have left? (3-2)

A $49

B $46

C $44

D $34

VA SOL Reteaching

Set A, pages 66–67

Write a number sentence for the situation. Solve.

Anthony has 10 flags. He gives 7 flags to his friends to wave during a parade on the 4th of July. How many flags does Anthony have left?

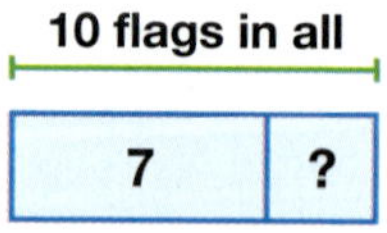

10 − 7 = 3

Anthony has 3 flags left.

Remember that you can subtract to find how many are left, to compare, or to find a missing addend.

Write a number sentence for each situation. Solve.

1. A band has eight members. Five of the band members sing. How many do not sing?
2. Juanita had 13 flowers. She gave one flower to each of her friends. She had 4 flowers left. How many flowers did Juanita give to her friends?
3. The ceiling in a room is 12 feet high. A ladder is 8 feet tall. How much higher is the ceiling than the top of the ladder?

Set B, pages 68–70

Use a hundred chart to find 76 − 18.

51	52	53	54	55	56	57	58	59	60
61	62	63	64	65	66	67	68	69	70
71	72	73	74	75	76	77	78	79	80
81	82	83	84	85	86	87	88	89	90
91	92	93	94	95	96	97	98	99	100

Start at 76.

Count up 2 rows to subtract 20.

Go right 2 spaces because you only need to subtract 18.

76 − 18 = 58

Remember to first subtract the tens. Then move to the right or left if necessary to adjust the ones.

Use a hundred chart to subtract.

1. 88 − 20
2. 53 − 30
3. 52 − 14
4. 36 − 19
5. 66 − 43
6. 72 − 16

Set C, pages 72–73

Use mental math to find 83 − 16.

Change each number in the same way to make a simpler problem.

20 is easier to subtract than 16.
So, add 4 to each number and then subtract.

83 + 4 = 87 and 16 + 4 = 20

87 − 20 = 67 so 83 − 16 = 67

Remember to change each number in the same way.

Find each difference using mental math.

1. 56 − 14 **2.** 31 − 5

3. 74 − 12 **4.** 97 − 34

Set D, pages 74–76

Estimate 486 − 177.

One Way

$$\begin{array}{rcr} 486 & \longrightarrow & 500 \\ -\ 177 & \longrightarrow & -\ 200 \\ & & 300 \end{array}$$

Round each number to the nearest hundred.

Another Way

$$\begin{array}{rcr} 486 & \longrightarrow & 500 \\ -\ 177 & \longrightarrow & -\ 175 \\ & & 325 \end{array}$$

Use compatible numbers.

Remember to check place value when rounding.

For **1–6**, estimate each difference.

Round to the nearest hundred.

1. 367 − 319 **2.** 872 − 110

Round to the nearest ten.

3. 78 − 54 **4.** 952 − 227

Use compatible numbers.

5. 472 − 228 **6.** 911 − 347

Set E, pages 78–79

Carla is reading a book that has 87 pages. She has read 49 pages. How many pages does she have left to read?

Estimate: 87 − 49 is about 90 − 50, or 40.
87 − 49 = 38.

Carla has 38 pages left to read. The answer is reasonable because 38 is close to the estimate of 40.

Remember that you can use an estimate to check if your answer is reasonable.

1. Lucy has 45 tulips. There are 27 red tulips. The rest are yellow. How many yellow tulips does Lucy have?

2. Cody had 43 toys. He gave Ty 27 of them. How many toys does Cody have now?

Topic 4

Subtracting Whole Numbers to Solve Problems

1 How much fresh and processed fruit does a person eat in a year? You will find out in Lesson 4-5.

2 The world's largest "basket" is a building in Newark, Ohio. How big is this basket? You will find out in Lesson 4-4.

3 How many days do students in Japan attend school each year? You will find out in Lesson 4-3.

4 How much taller would this statue be if President Lincoln were standing? You will find out in Lesson 4-2.

Review What You Know!

Vocabulary

Choose the best term from the box.

- difference
- estimate
- order
- regroup

1. When you trade 1 ten for 10 ones, you ___?___.

2. The answer in subtraction is the ___?___.

3. When you find an answer that is close to the exact answer, you ___?___.

Estimating Differences

Round to the nearest ten to estimate each difference.

4. 255 − 104 **5.** 97 − 61 **6.** 302 − 38

Round to the nearest hundred to estimate each difference.

7. 673 − 250 **8.** 315 − 96 **9.** 789 − 713

Compatible Numbers

Writing to Explain

10. Use compatible numbers to estimate the difference 478 − 123. Explain why the numbers you chose are compatible.

11. How is rounding to estimate an answer different from using compatible numbers?

Virginia

Lesson 4-1

Reviews 2.7.b The student, given two whole numbers, each of which is 99 or less, will find the difference, using various methods of calculation.

Models for Subtracting 2-Digit Numbers

Hands-On
place-value blocks

How can you subtract with place-value blocks?

Whole numbers can be subtracted using place value. Subtract the ones first. Then subtract the tens. When needed, a ten can be traded for 10 ones.

Find 43 − 18.

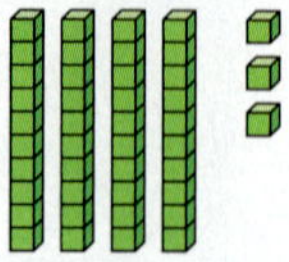

Show 43 with place-value blocks.

Guided Practice*

Do you know HOW?

In **1–6**, use place-value blocks or draw pictures to subtract.

1. 42 − 15

2. 34 − 18

3. 57 − 23

4. 25 − 16

5. 36 − 8

6. 50 − 18

Do you UNDERSTAND?

7. Why is a small 3 written above the 4 in the tens place in the example? Why is a small 13 written above the 3 in the ones place? What do you subtract to get 5 ones in the difference?

8. Nelson had 52 books in his bookcase. He gave away 38 of the books to the community center. How many books did Nelson still have in his bookcase?

Independent Practice

In **9–18**, use place-value blocks or draw pictures to subtract.

Tip *You can draw lines to show tens and Xs to show ones. This picture shows 27.*

9. 21 − 17

10. 32 − 19

11. 28 − 17

12. 38 − 9

13. 43 − 24

14. 46 − 19

15. 54 − 42

16. 51 − 39

17. 63 − 37

18. 76 − 49

DIGITAL eTools www.pearsonsuccessnet.com

*For another example, see Set A on page 104.

Step 1

Subtract the ones.
3 ones < 8 ones
Regroup 1 ten
into 10 ones.

$$\begin{array}{r} {\scriptstyle 3\ 13} \\ \not{4}\ \not{3} \\ -\ 1\ 8 \\ \hline \end{array}$$

1 less ten   10 more ones

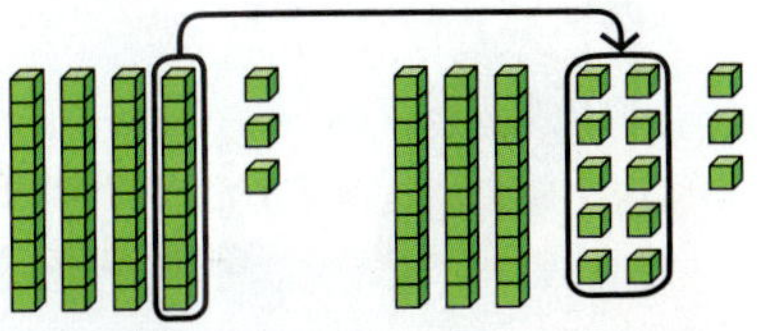

4 tens 3 ones = 3 tens 13 ones

Step 2

Subtract the ones.
13 − 8 = 5 ones

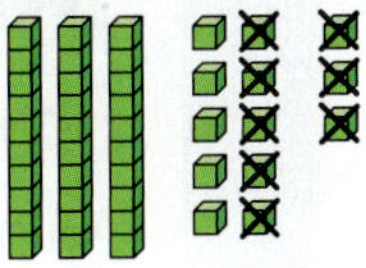

$$\begin{array}{r} {\scriptstyle 3\ 13} \\ \not{4}\ \not{3} \\ -\ 1\ 8 \\ \hline 5 \end{array}$$

Subtract the tens.
3 tens − 1 ten = 2 tens

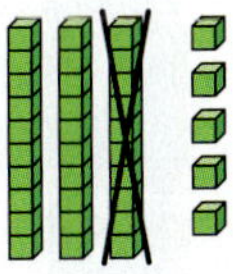

$$\begin{array}{r} {\scriptstyle 3\ 13} \\ \not{4}\ \not{3} \\ -\ 1\ 8 \\ \hline 2\ 5 \end{array}$$

43 − 18 = 25

Problem Solving

For **19** and **20**, use the map at the right.

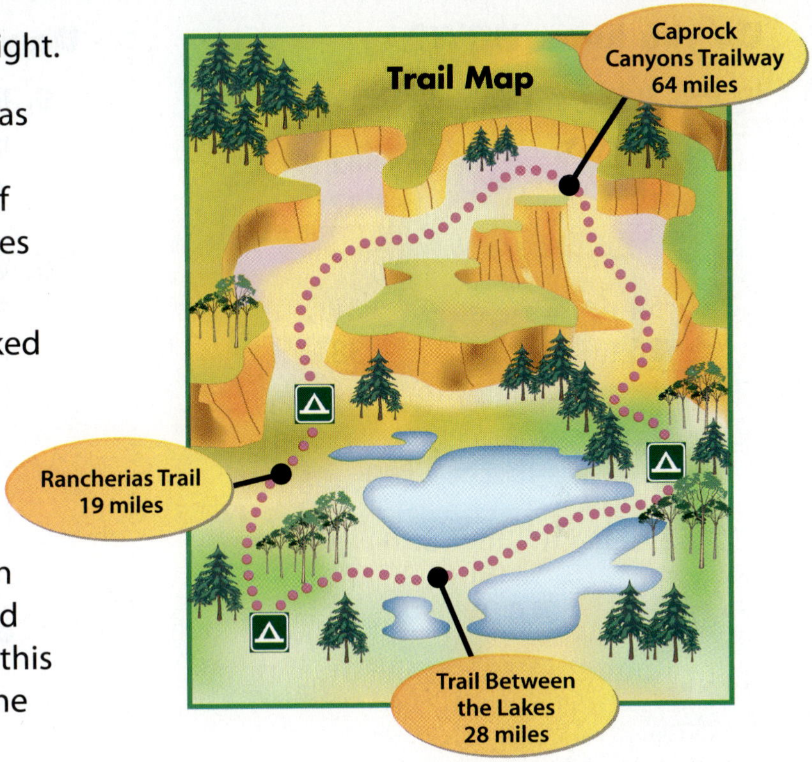

19. Hal wants to hike the Rancherias Trail and the Trail Between the Lakes. So far, he has hiked all of the Rancherias Trail and 19 miles of the Trail Between the Lakes.

a How many miles has Hal hiked so far?

b How many miles does Hal have left?

20. Tamara hiked the Trail Between the Lakes last month. She hiked the Caprock Canyons Trailway this month. How many miles did she hike in all?

21. **Writing to Explain** To subtract 34 − 18, Max said that 34 is equal to 2 tens and 14 ones. Is he correct? Explain how you know.

22. SOL Prep Ms Jones had 52 colored pencils in a package. She gave 25 of the pencils to her first art class and 18 of the pencils to her second art class. She put the rest of the pencils in a box. How many pencils are in the box?

A 95   **C** 19

B 27   **D** 9

Virginia

Lesson 4-2

3.4 The student will estimate solutions to and solve single-step and multistep problems involving the sum or difference of two whole numbers, each 9,999 or less, with or without regrouping.

Subtracting 2-Digit Numbers

How can you use subtraction?

Animal rescue workers have released 16 of the eagles they have cared for. How many eagles are left?

Find 34 − 16. Use compatible numbers to estimate.

35 − 15 = 20

Guided Practice*

Do you know HOW?

In **1–8**, subtract.

1. 35 − 19

2. 42 − 17

3. 54 − 26

4. 61 − 38

5. 47 − 9

6. 73 − 25

7. 62 − 34

8. 47 − 25

Do you UNDERSTAND?

9. In the example above, why is regrouping needed? What was regrouped?

10. Workers at the park have cared for 52 falcons. If 28 falcons are still at the park, how many of the falcons have left?

a Write a number sentence.

b Estimate the answer.

c Solve the problem.

d Use the estimate to explain why your answer is reasonable.

Independent Practice

In **11–20**, subtract.

11. 26 − 19

12. 45 − 17

13. 37 − 18

14. 56 − 38

15. 83 − 61

16. 75 − 48

17. 22 − 13

18. 31 − 14

19. 53 − 6

20. 48 − 29

*For another example, see Set B on page 104.

Subtract the ones.

6 ones > 4 ones
Regroup 1 ten 4 ones into 14 ones.

14 − 6 = 8 ones

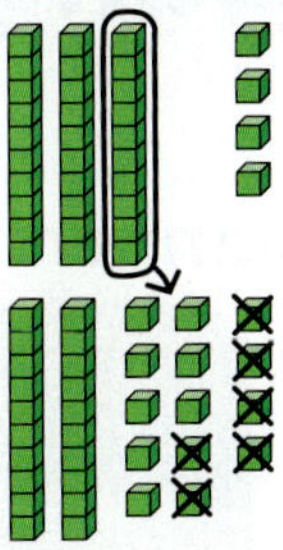

```
  2 14
  3̸ 4̸
− 1 6
─────
    8
```

Subtract the tens.

2 tens − 1 ten = 1 ten

34 − 16 = 18

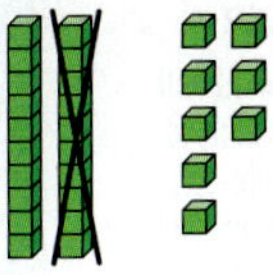

```
  2 14
  3̸ 4̸
− 1 6
─────
  1 8
```

18 eagles are left.

The answer is reasonable because 18 is close to the estimate of 20.

Problem Solving

For **21** and **22**, use the table at the right.

Kind of Bird	Number Taken In	Number Released
Hawk	51	34
Kite	32	19
Owl	43	27

Data: Animal Rescue Park

21. Follow the steps below to find how many owls are left at the rescue park.

a Write a number sentence that can be used to solve the problem.

b Estimate the answer.

c Solve the problem.

d Use the estimate to explain why your answer is reasonable.

22. How many fewer kites than hawks have been released from the animal rescue park?

23. Reasonableness Trista subtracted 75 − 48 and got 37. Explain why her answer is not reasonable.

24. This statue would be 25 feet tall if President Lincoln was standing. How much taller is this than the statue in the picture?

25. A sweater costs $29. A shirt costs $18. Meg has $36. Which number sentence can be used to find how much money Meg would have left if she bought the sweater?

A 29 + 36 = ☐

B 29 − 18 = ☐

C 36 − 29 = ☐

D 36 − 18 = ☐

26. Writing to Explain Do you need to regroup to find 64 − 37? Explain your answer.

3.4 The student will estimate solutions to and solve single-step and multistep problems involving the sum or difference of two whole numbers, each 9,999 or less, with or without regrouping.

Models for Subtracting 3-Digit Numbers

Hands-On
place-value blocks

How can you subtract 3-digit numbers with place-value blocks?

Use place value to subtract the ones first, the tens next, and then the hundreds.

Find 237 − 165.

Show 237 with place-value blocks.

Guided Practice*

Do you know HOW?

In **1–6**, use place-value blocks or draw pictures to subtract.

1. 249 − 187

2. 261 − 134

3. 158 − 76

4. 384 − 182

5. 173 − 158

6. 325 − 213

Do you UNDERSTAND?

7. In the example above, why do you need to regroup 1 hundred into 10 tens?

8. Colby saved $256 doing jobs in the neighborhood. He bought a computer printer for $173. How much money did he have left? Draw a picture to help you subtract.

Independent Practice

In **9–18**, use place-value blocks or draw pictures to subtract.

Tip *You can draw squares to show hundreds, lines to show tens, and Xs to show ones. This picture shows 127.*

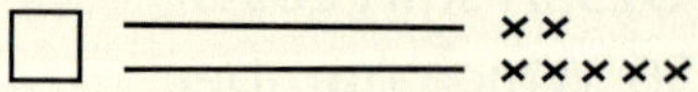

9. 347 − 263

10. 196 − 149

11. 218 − 117

12. 251 − 132

13. 423 − 291

14. 123 − 81

15. 265 − 84

16. 539 − 275

17. 376 − 153

18. 417 − 308

DIGITAL eTools www.pearsonsuccessnet.com

*For another example, see Set C on page 104.

Subtract the ones.

7 > 5, so no regrouping.

7 ones − 5 ones = 2 ones

$$\begin{array}{r} 237 \\ -\,165 \\ \hline 2 \end{array}$$

Subtract the tens.

3 tens < 6 tens, so regroup.
1 hundred = 10 tens

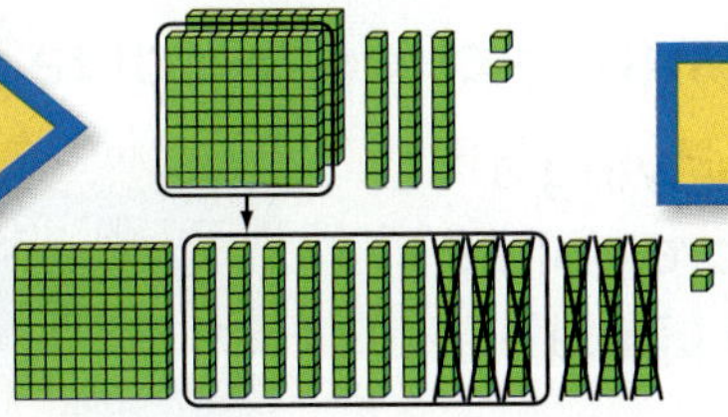

13 tens − 6 tens = 7 tens

$$\begin{array}{r} {\scriptstyle 1\ 13}\ \ \\ \not{2}\,\not{3}\,7 \\ -\,1\,6\,5 \\ \hline 7\,2 \end{array}$$

Subtract the hundreds.

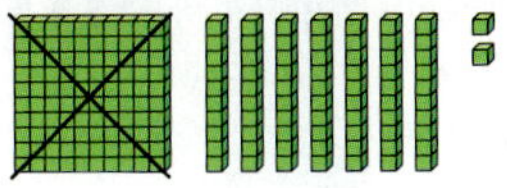

1 hundred − 1 hundred = 0 hundreds

$$\begin{array}{r} {\scriptstyle 1\ 13}\ \ \\ \not{2}\,\not{3}\,7 \\ -\,1\,6\,5 \\ \hline 7\,2 \end{array}$$

Problem Solving

For **19–21**, use the table at the right.

19. The Wen family drove from Cincinnati to Cleveland. Then the family drove to Chicago. How many miles did the family drive in all?

Data

Trip Distances

Trip	Miles
Cleveland to Chicago	346
Cincinnati to Cleveland	249
Washington, D.C., to Cleveland	372

20. The Miller family is driving from Washington, D.C., to Cleveland and then to Cincinnati. So far the Millers have traveled 127 miles. How many miles are left in their trip?

21. Writing to Explain Which city is farther from Cleveland, Chicago or Washington, D.C.? How much farther? Explain your answer.

22. In the United States, students go to school about 180 days per year. Students in Japan go to school about 60 days more per year than students in the United States. About how many days per year do students in Japan attend school?

23. An amusement park ride can hold 120 people. There were 116 people on the ride and 95 people waiting in line. Which number sentence can be used to find how many people in all were on the ride or waiting in line?

A 116 − 95 = ☐

B 120 + 116 + 95 = ☐

C 116 + 95 = ☐

D 120 − 95 = ☐

Virginia

Lesson 4-4

3.4 The student will estimate solutions to and solve single-step and multistep problems involving the sum or difference of two whole numbers, each 9,999 or less, with or without regrouping.

Subtracting 3-Digit Numbers

Hands-On
place-value blocks

How can you use subtraction to solve problems?

Mike and Linda are playing a game. How many more points does Mike have than Linda?

Find 528 − 341.

Estimate: 530 − 340 = 190

Another Example How do you subtract with two regroupings?

Find 356 − 189.

Estimate: 400 − 200 = 200

Step 1

Subtract the ones. Regroup if needed.

6 ones < 9 ones. So, regroup 1 ten into 10 ones.

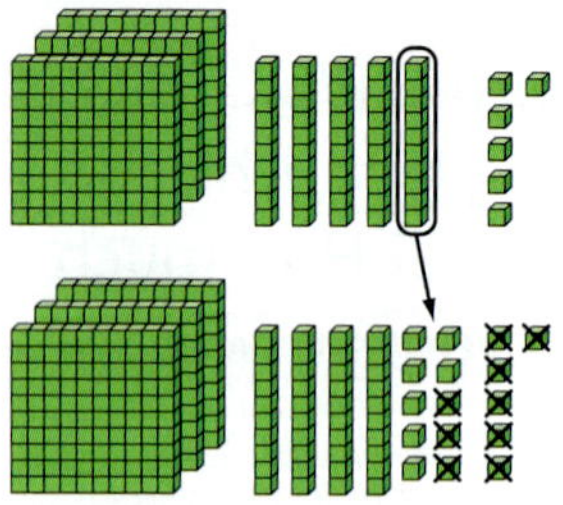

```
   4 16
 3 5̸ 6̸
− 1 8 9
-------
      7
```

Step 2

Subtract the tens. Regroup if needed.

4 tens < 8 tens. So, regroup 1 hundred into 10 tens.

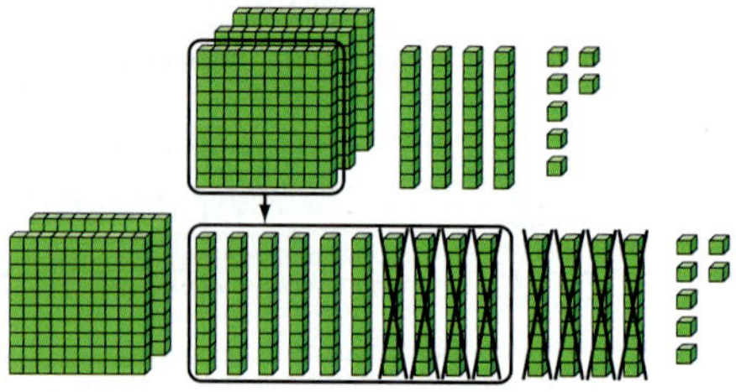

```
   14
 2 4̸ 16
 3̸ 5̸ 6̸
− 1 8 9
-------
    6 7
```

Step 3

Subtract the hundreds.

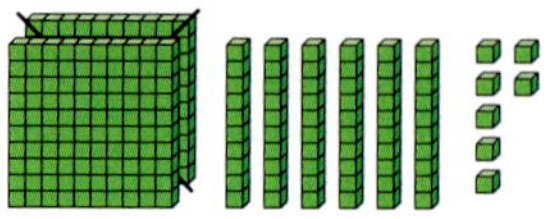

```
   14
 2 4̸ 16
 3̸ 5̸ 6̸
− 1 8 9
-------
  1 6 7
```

The answer 167 is reasonable because it is close to the estimate.

Explain It

1. Why do you need to regroup both a ten and a hundred?
2. How is 3 hundreds 5 tens 6 ones the same as 3 hundreds 4 tens 16 ones? How is 3 hundreds 4 tens 16 ones the same as 2 hundreds 14 tens 16 ones?

Subtract the ones.

8 ones > 1 one
You do not regroup.

8 ones − 1 one = 7 ones

$$\begin{array}{r} 528 \\ -\ 341 \\ \hline 7 \end{array}$$

Subtract the tens.

Since 2 tens < 4 tens, regroup 1 hundred into 10 tens.

12 tens − 4 tens = 8 tens

$$\begin{array}{r} \overset{4}{\not5}\,\overset{12}{\not2}\,8 \\ -\ 3\ 4\ 1 \\ \hline 8\ 7 \end{array}$$

Subtract the hundreds.

4 hundreds − 3 hundreds = 1 hundred

$$\begin{array}{r} \overset{4}{\not5}\,\overset{12}{\not2}\,8 \\ -\ 3\ 4\ 1 \\ \hline 1\ 8\ 7 \end{array}$$

Mike has 187 more points.

187 is close to the estimate of 190. The answer is reasonable.

Guided Practice*

Do you know HOW?

In **1–6**, subtract. Use place-value blocks, if you wish.

1. $\begin{array}{r} 374 \\ -\ 176 \\ \hline \end{array}$

2. $\begin{array}{r} 431 \\ -\ 145 \\ \hline \end{array}$

3. $\begin{array}{r} 568 \\ -\ 269 \\ \hline \end{array}$

4. $\begin{array}{r} 327 \\ -\ 238 \\ \hline \end{array}$

5. 574 − 86

6. 410 − 257

Do you UNDERSTAND?

7. In the example above, explain how to decide if regrouping is needed.

8. At the end of their game, Lora had 426 points, and Lou had 158 points. How many more points did Lora have than Lou?

a Write a number sentence.

b Estimate the answer.

c Solve the problem.

d Explain why your answer is reasonable.

Independent Practice

Estimate. Then find each difference. Check answers for reasonableness.

9. $\begin{array}{r} 385 \\ -\ 296 \\ \hline \end{array}$

10. $\begin{array}{r} 276 \\ -\ 97 \\ \hline \end{array}$

11. $\begin{array}{r} 516 \\ -\ 238 \\ \hline \end{array}$

12. $\begin{array}{r} 629 \\ -\ 453 \\ \hline \end{array}$

13. $\begin{array}{r} 948 \\ -\ 569 \\ \hline \end{array}$

DIGITAL eTools **www.pearsonsuccessnet.com**

*For another example, see Set D on page 105.

Independent Practice

Estimate and subtract. Check answers for reasonableness.

14. 392 − 195

15. 754 − 476

16. 819 − 652

17. 123 − 84

18. 435 − 367

19. 236 − 78

20. 568 − 362

21. 147 − 58

22. 952 − 794

Problem Solving

For **23–25**, use the table at the right.

23. Follow the steps below to find how many more swimmers signed up for the first session at Oak Pool than for the first session at Park Pool.

a Write a number sentence that can be used to solve the problem.

b Estimate the answer.

c Solve the problem.

d Explain why your answer is reasonable.

Swim Class Enrollment

Pool	Number of Swimmers	
	1st session	2nd session
Oak	763	586
Park	314	179
River	256	63

24. At River Pool, late enrollments added 29 swimmers to the second session. The total number of swimmers enrolled in the second session is how many fewer than in the first?

Tip *What addition sentence can help?*

25. **Write a Problem** Write a problem using the data in the table. Include too much information.

26. The world's largest basket is the building in the photo. It is 186 feet tall from the base to the top of the handles. What is the height of the handles?

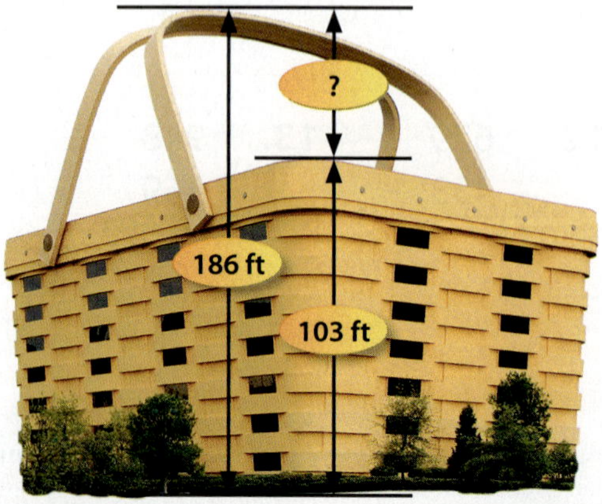

27. Ana made 14 hats. After giving some hats to Ty's family and some to Liv's family, she had 3 hats left. If she gave Ty's family 6 hats, which of these shows one way to find how many hats Ana gave to Liv's family?

A 14 + 3 − 6 = ▢

B 14 − 3 − 6 = ▢

C 14 − 3 + 6 = ▢

D 14 + 3 + 6 = ▢

Algebra Connections

Using Properties to Complete Number Sentences

The properties of addition can help you find missing numbers.

Commutative (Order) Property You can add numbers in any order and the sum will be the same. Example: $4 + 3 = 3 + 4$

Identity (Zero) Property The sum of any number and zero is that same number. Example: $9 + 0 = 9$

Associative (Grouping) Property You can group addends in any way and the sum will be the same. Example: $(5 + 2) + 3 = 5 + (2 + 3)$

Example: $26 + \square = 26$

Think: 26 plus what number is equal to 26?

You can use the Identity Property.

$26 + 0 = 26$

Example:

$36 + (14 + 12) = (36 + \square) + 12$

Think: What number makes the two sides equal?

Use the Associative Property.

$36 + (14 + 12) = (36 + 14) + 12$

Copy and complete. Write the missing number.

1. $19 + \square = 19$
2. $15 + 32 = 32 + \square$
3. $28 + (17 + 32) = (28 + \square) + 32$
4. $\square + 27 = 27$
5. $\square + 8 = 8 + 49$
6. $(16 + 14) + \square = 16 + (14 + 53)$
7. $(\square + 9) + 72 = 96 + (9 + 72)$
8. $\square + 473 = 473$

For **9** and **10**, copy and complete the number sentence. Use it to help solve the problem.

9. Vin walked 9 blocks from home to the library. Then he walked 5 blocks farther to the store. Later he walked the same path back to the library. How many more blocks would he need to walk to his home?

   $9 + 5 = 5 + \square$
   $\square$ blocks

10. Bo scored 7 points in each of two tosses in a game. Then he made one more toss. He had the same total score as Ed. Ed scored 8 points in one toss and 7 points in each of two tosses. How many points did Bo score on his last toss?

    $7 + 7 + \square = 8 + 7 + 7$
    $\square$ points

Virginia

Lesson 4-5

3.4 The student will estimate solutions to and solve single-step and multistep problems involving the sum or difference of two whole numbers, each 9,999 or less, with or without regrouping.

Subtracting Across Zero

How do you subtract from a number with one or more zeros?

How much more does the club need?

Find: 305 − 178

305: 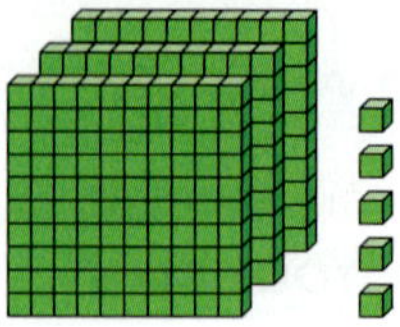

Another Example: How do you subtract from a number with two zeros?

Find 600 − 164.

Subtract the ones.
0 ones < 4 ones
So, regroup.

```
 5 10
 6̸ 0̸ 0
-1 6 4
```

You can't regroup 0 tens.
So, regroup 1 hundred.
6 hundreds 0 tens =
5 hundreds 10 tens

```
    9
 5 10̸ 10
 6̸ 0̸  0̸
-1 6  4
```

Now regroup tens.
10 tens 0 ones = 9 tens 10 ones
Subtract the ones, the tens, and then the hundreds.

```
    9
 5 10̸ 10
 6̸ 0̸  0̸
-1 6  4
 4 3  6
```

Guided Practice*

Do you know HOW?

In **1–6**, find each difference.

1. 402 − 139

2. 300 − 157

3. 607 − 439

4. 820 − 167

5. 200 − 74

6. 501 − 186

Do you UNDERSTAND?

7. In the examples above, why do you write 10 above the 0 in the tens place?

8. Lia says that she needs to regroup every time she subtracts from a number with a zero. Do you agree? Explain.

*For another example, see Set E on page 105.

Regroup to subtract the ones. There are no tens in 305 to regroup. Regroup 1 hundred.

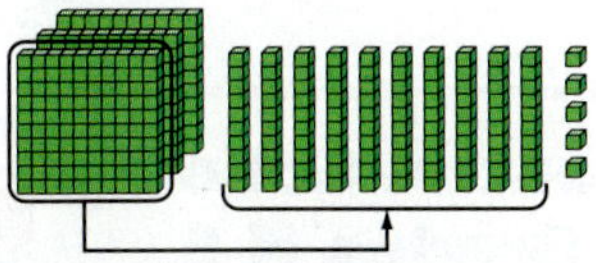

305 is the same as
2 hundreds 10 tens
5 ones.

```
 2 10
 3̸ 0̸ 5
- 1 7 8
```

Regroup the tens.

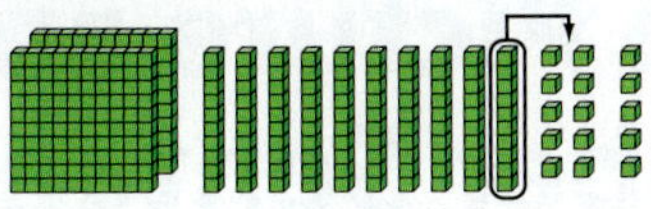

305 is the same as
2 hundreds 9 tens
15 ones.

```
    9
 2 1̸0̸ 15
 3̸ 0̸ 5̸
- 1 7 8
```

Subtract the ones, the tens, and then the hundreds.

```
    9
 2 1̸0̸ 15
 3̸ 0̸ 5̸
- 1 7 8
  1 2 7
```

The Art club needs $127.

Independent Practice

In **9–18**, find each difference.

9. 203 − 157 **10.** 400 − 371 **11.** 304 − 95 **12.** 401 − 282 **13.** 500 − 64

14. 600 − 439 **15.** 306 − 248 **16.** 705 − 123 **17.** 800 − 74 **18.** 900 − 506

Problem Solving

19. The average person eats about 126 pounds of fresh fruit in a year. Write a number sentence to help you find how many pounds of processed fruit you eat. Then solve.

20. Writing to Explain The Art Club needs 605 beads. A large bag of beads has 285 beads. A small bag of beads has 130 beads. Will one large bag and one small bag be enough beads? Explain.

21. Dina counted 204 items on the library cart. There were 91 fiction books, 75 nonfiction books, and some magazines. Which number sentence shows one way to find the number of magazines?

A 204 − 91 − 75 = ☐ **C** 204 − 91 + 75 = ☐

B 204 + 91 + 75 = ☐ **D** 204 + 91 − 75 = ☐

Virginia

Lesson 4-6

Reviews 2.21 The student will solve problems by completing numerical sentences involving basic facts for addition and subtraction. The student will create story problems, using the numerical sentences.

Problem Solving

Draw a Picture and Write a Number Sentence

There are two lunch periods at Central School. If 221 students eat during the first lunch period, how many students eat during the second lunch period?

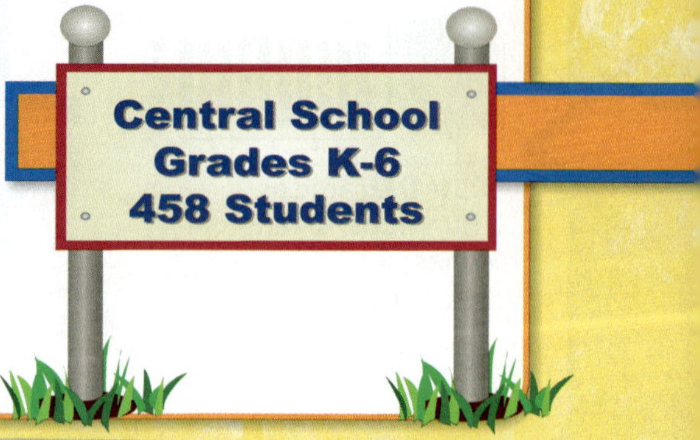

Another Example Are there other types of subtraction situations?

There are 85 students in Grade 2. That is 17 more students than in Grade 3. How many students are in Grade 3?

Plan and Solve

Draw a diagram to show what you know.

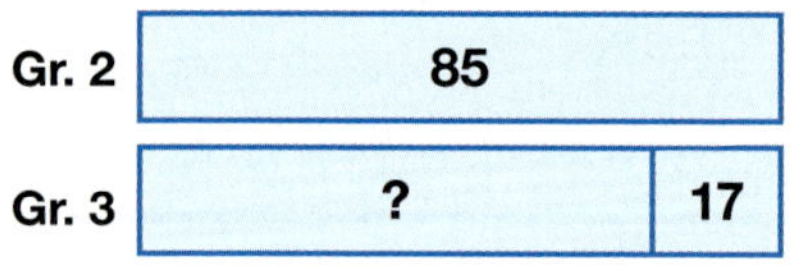

There are 17 more students in Grade 2 than in Grade 3. Subtract to find the number of students in Grade 3.

Write a number sentence.

$85 - 17 = \square$

Answer

$$\begin{array}{r} \scriptstyle 7\ 15 \\ \not{8}\,\not{5} \\ -\ 1\ 7 \\ \hline 6\ 8 \end{array}$$

There are 68 students in Grade 3.

Check

Make sure the answer is reasonable.

85 − 17 is about 90 − 20, or 70.

68 is close to 70, so 68 is reasonable.

The number 68 is reasonable, and the question in the problem was answered.

Explain It

1. Harry wrote $17 + \square = 85$ for the diagram above. Is his number sentence correct? Why or why not?
2. Grade 4 has 72 students. There are 12 more students in Grade 5 than in Grade 4. Would you add or subtract to find the number of students in Grade 5? Write and solve a number sentence.

Plan and Solve

Draw a picture to show what you know.

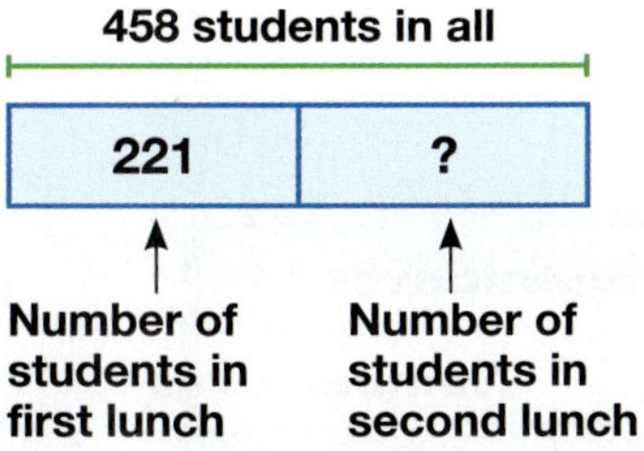

You know the total and one part. Write a subtraction sentence: 458 − 221 = ▢.

Answer

$$\begin{array}{r} 458 \\ -\ 221 \\ \hline 237 \end{array}$$

There are 237 students who eat during the second lunch period.

Check

Make sure the answer is reasonable.

458 − 221 is about 460 − 220, or 240.

237 is close to 240, so 237 is reasonable.

The number 237 is reasonable and the right question was answered.

Guided Practice*

Do you know HOW?

1. A total of 254 people entered a bicycle race. So far 135 people have finished the race. How many people are still racing?

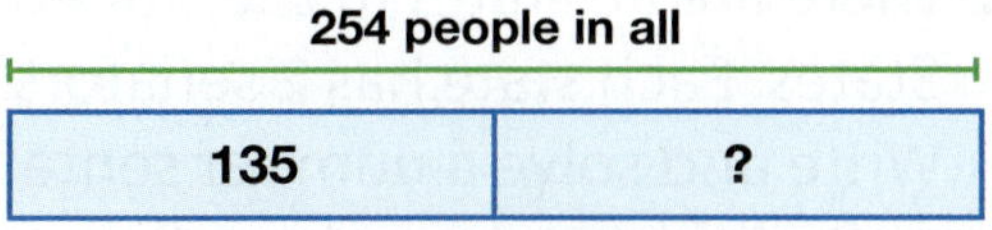

Do you UNDERSTAND?

2. **Writing to Explain** How do you know what operation to use to solve Problem 1?

3. **Write a Problem** Write a problem that can be solved by adding or subtracting. Then give your problem to a classmate to solve.

Independent Practice

4. The height of Capote Falls is 175 feet. The height of Madrid Falls is 120 feet. Write and solve a number sentence to find how much taller Capote Falls is than Madrid Falls.

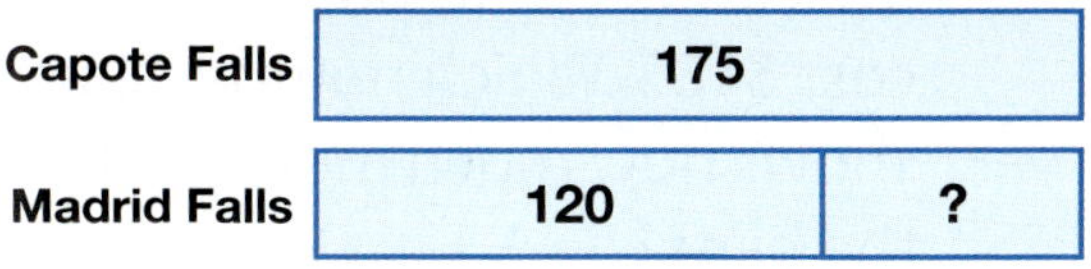

Stuck? Try this....

- What do I know?
- What am I asked to find?
- What diagram can I use to help understand the problem?
- Can I use addition, subtraction, multiplication, or division?
- Is all of my work correct?
- Did I answer the right question?
- Is my answer reasonable?

*For another example, see Set F on page 105.

Independent Practice

In the United States House of Representatives, the number of representatives each state has depends upon the number of people who live in the state.

Use the table at the right for **5–7**.

Data

U.S. Representatives	
State	**Number**
California	53
Florida	25
Michigan	15
Texas	32

5. Copy and complete the diagram below. New York has 14 more representatives than Michigan. How many representatives does New York have?

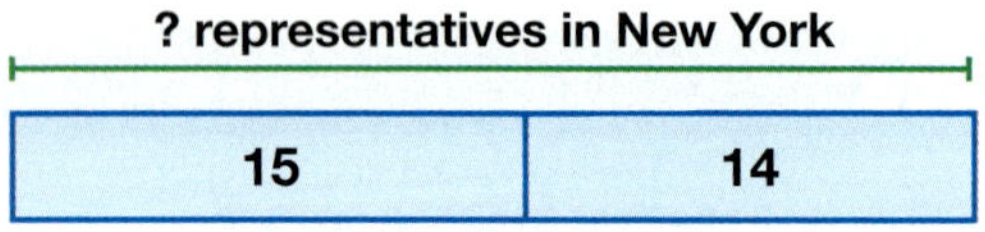

6. Draw a diagram to find how many more representatives Texas has than Florida.

7. How many representatives are there all together from the four states listed in the chart?

8. When the House of Representatives started in 1789, there were 65 members. Now there are 435 members. How many more members are there now?

9. There are 50 states in the United States. Each state has 2 senators. Write and solve a number sentence to find the total number of senators.

Think About the Process

10. Max exercised 38 minutes on Monday and 25 minutes on Tuesday. Which number sentence shows how long he exercised on the two days?

A 40 + 30 = ■

B 40 − 30 = ■

C 38 − 25 = ■

D 38 + 25 = ■

11. Nancy had $375 in the bank. She took $200 out to buy a scooter that cost $185. Which number sentence shows how much money is left in the bank?

A $375 + $185 = ■

B $375 − $185 = ■

C $375 − $200 = ■

D $375 + $185 + $200 = ■

Going Digital

Subtracting with Regrouping

Use e tools

Place-Value Blocks

Use the Place-Value Blocks eTool to subtract 324 − 168.

Step 1 Go to the Place-Value Blocks eTool. Click on the two-part workspace icon. In the top space, show 324 with place-value blocks.

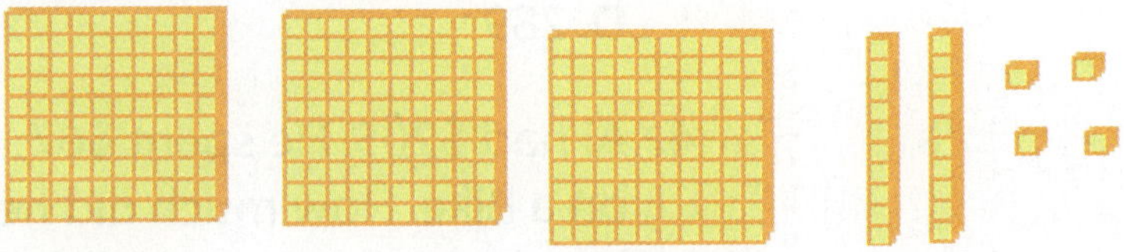

Step 2 Use the hammer tool to break one of the tens blocks into 10 ones. Then use the arrow tool to take away 8 ones and move them to the bottom workspace.

Step 3 Use the hammer tool to break one of the hundreds blocks into 10 tens. Then take away the 6 tens in 168 and move them to the bottom workspace.

Step 4 Use the arrow tool to take away the hundred block in 168. To find the difference, look at all of the blocks that are left.

324 − 168 = 156

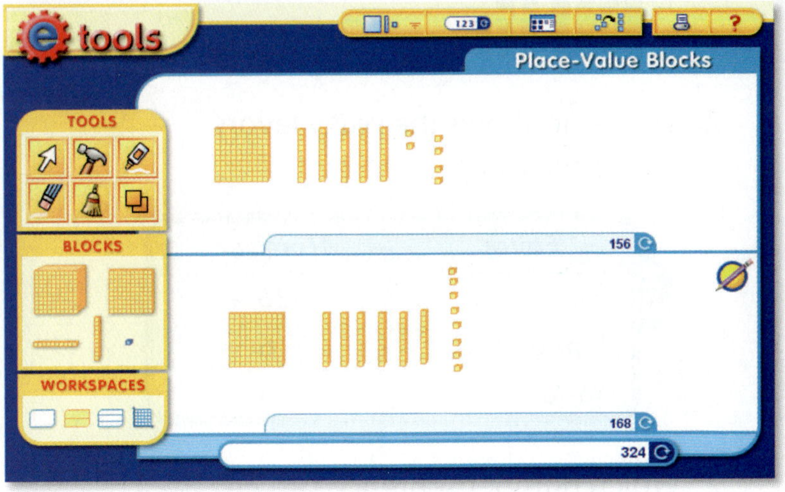

Practice

Use the Place-Value Blocks eTool to subtract.

1. 445 − 176 **2.** 318 − 142 **3.** 546 − 259 **4.** 600 − 473

1. Tracey knows that she will need to regroup to solve 52 − 18. Which picture shows how she should regroup 52? (4-1)

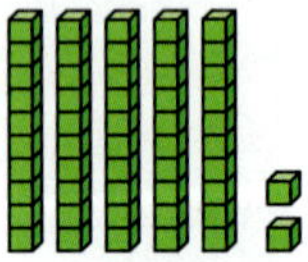

A 

B 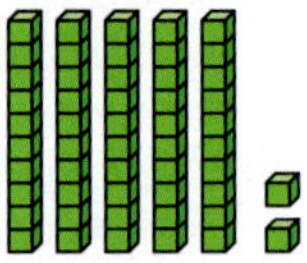

C 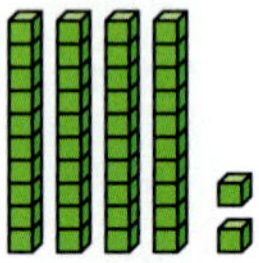

D 

2. The table shows the party favors Zac purchased.

Favor	Number
Pencil	36
Kazoo	16
Yo-Yo	8

Which number sentence can be used to find how many more pencils than yo-yos Zac purchased? (4-2)

A 36 − 8 = $\square$

B 36 + 8 = $\square$

C 36 − 16 = $\square$

D 36 + 16 = $\square$

3. Cristina scored 485 points on a video game. Olivia scored 196 points. How many more points did Cristina score than Olivia? (4-4)

A 681

B 389

C 299

D 289

4. Al had $205. He spent $67 on a bike. How much did he have left? (4-5)

A $162

B $148

C $138

D $38

5. Mr. Chavez needs to order trophies for the band members. The table shows how many girls and how many boys are in the band.

Band Members	
Boys	32
Girls	28

Which of the following best describes the band members? (4-2)

A There are 4 more boys than girls in the band.

B There are 4 more girls than boys in the band.

C There are 32 more boys than girls in the band.

D There are 28 more girls than boys in the band.

6. Mrs. Wesley bought 325 drinks for a picnic. She bought 135 cartons of milk, 95 bottles of water, and some bottles of juice. Which number sentence shows one way to find how many bottles of juice she bought? (4-4)

A 325 − 135 + 95 = ☐

B 325 − 135 − 95 = ☐

C 325 + 135 − 95 = ☐

D 325 + 135 + 95 = ☐

7. What regrouping is shown? (4-3)

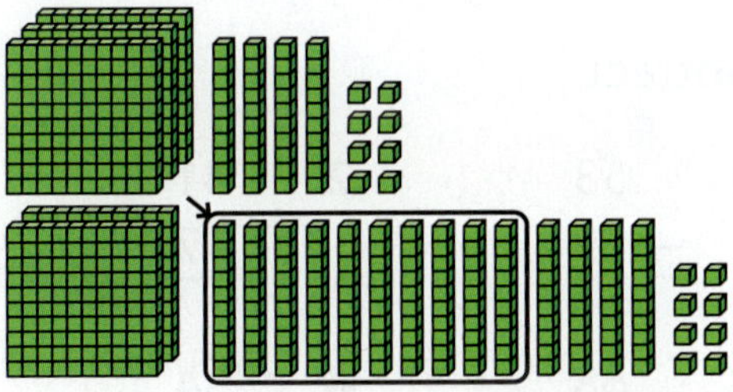

A 3 hundreds 4 tens 8 ones as 2 hundreds 3 tens 18 ones

B 3 hundreds 4 tens 8 ones as 2 hundreds 14 tens 8 ones

C 2 hundreds 4 tens 8 ones as 1 hundreds 14 tens 8 ones

D 2 hundreds 4 tens 8 ones as 2 hundreds 3 tens 18 ones

8. Texas has 254 counties. Georgia has 159 counties. How many more counties does Texas have than Georgia? (4-4)

A 195

B 145

C 105

D 95

9. Which picture shows the problem? Nessie saw 23 deer and 17 squirrels at a national park. How many more deer did she see than squirrels? (4-6)

A

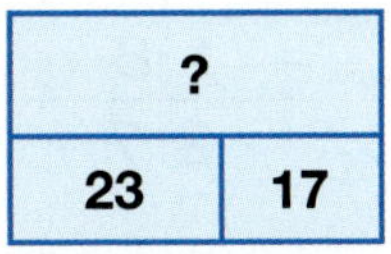

B

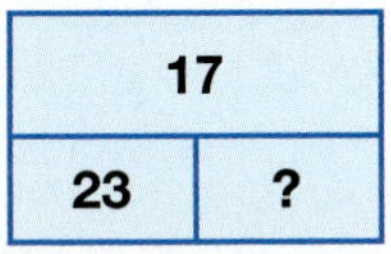

C

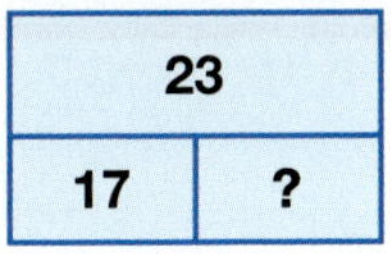

D

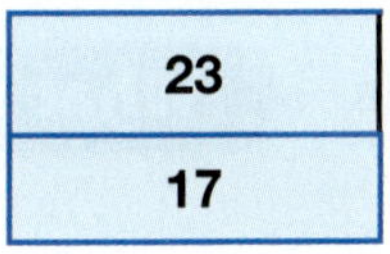

10. Ray had $41. He spent $14 for swim goggles and $19 for admission. How much money did Ray have left? (4-2)

A $27

B $12

C $8

D $5

11. Trisha had 300 milliliters of water in a beaker. She poured 237 milliliters of the water from the beaker into a test tube. How much water was left in the beaker? (4-5)

A 173 milliliters

B 163 milliliters

C 137 milliliters

D 63 milliliters

VA SOL Reteaching

Set A, pages 86–87

Find 45 − 18.

```
   3 15
   4̸ 5̸
 - 1 8
 -----
   2 7
```

Remember that you can regroup 1 ten as 10 ones.

Use place-value blocks or draw pictures to subtract.

1. 52 − 17

2. 38 − 25

3. 83 − 34

4. 75 − 53

Set B, pages 88–89

Find 31 − 17.

Estimate: 30 − 20 = 10

What You Think

31 = 3 tens 1 one

17 = 1 ten 7 ones

7 ones > 1 one, so regroup.

3 tens 1 one = 2 tens 11 ones

What You Write

```
   2 11
   3̸ 1̸
 - 1 7
 -----
   1 4
```

31 − 17 = 14

14 is close to 10, so the answer is reasonable.

Remember to check your answer by comparing it to your estimate.

Subtract.

1. 53 − 29

2. 41 − 17

3. 68 − 49

4. 34 − 28

5. 92 − 42

6. 70 − 54

Set C, pages 90–91

Find 236 − 127.

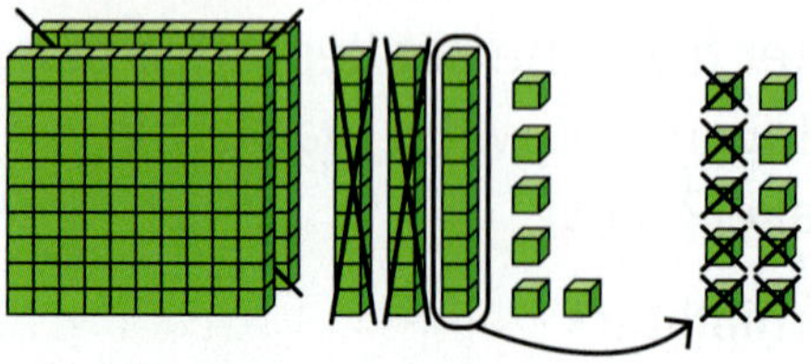

```
     2 16
   2 3̸ 6̸
 - 1 2 7
 -------
   1 0 9
```

Remember to subtract ones, then tens, and then hundreds.

Use place-value blocks or draw pictures to subtract.

1. 435 − 217

2. 255 − 161

3. 521 − 196

4. 332 − 108

Set D, pages 92–94

Find 312 − 186.

Estimate: 300 − 200 = 100

0 12 3 ~~1~~ ~~2~~ − 1 8 6 ——— 6	Regroup tens.
10 2 ~~0~~ 12 ~~3~~ ~~1~~ ~~2~~ − 1 8 6 ——— 1 2 6	Regroup hundreds.

126 is close to 100, so the answer is reasonable.

Remember that sometimes you must regroup twice.

Estimate. Subtract and check answers for reasonableness.

1. 221 − 134
2. 397 − 138
3. 611 − 125
4. 854 − 296

Set E, pages 96–97

Find 306 − 129.

Estimate: 300 − 100 = 200

2 10 ~~3~~ ~~0~~ 6 − 1 2 9 ———	There are no tens. Regroup hundreds.
9 2 ~~10~~ 16 ~~3~~ ~~0~~ ~~6~~ − 1 2 9 ——— 1 7 7	Regroup tens.

177 is close to 200, so the answer is reasonable.

Remember that when you need to regroup tens, but have 0 tens, regroup hundreds first.

Find each difference.

1. 308 − 125
2. 105 − 47
3. 200 − 136
4. 602 − 384

Set F, pages 98–100

At the school picnic, 234 students took part in the events. Of those students, 136 students were in the potato sack races. The other students were in the 3-legged races. How many students were in the 3-legged races?

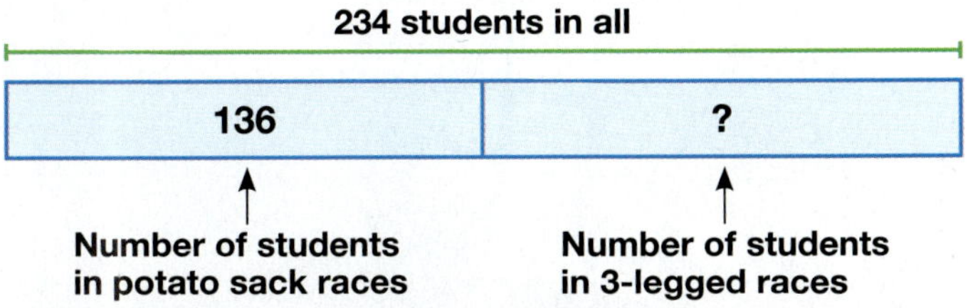

You know the total and one part, so you can subtract to find the other part: 234 − 136 = ▢.

234 − 136 = 98
98 students were in the 3-legged races.

Remember that drawing a picture of the problem can help you write a number sentence.

Draw a picture. Write a number sentence and solve.

1. A total of 293 people entered a running race. So far, 127 people have finished the race. How many people are still racing?

Topic 5

Multiplication Meanings and Facts

1 Monarch butterflies have bright orange wings. How many wings does each monarch butterfly have? You will find out in Lesson 5-4.

2 An armadillo needs more sleep than a horse. How many more hours of sleep does an armadillo need? You will find out in Lesson 5-3.

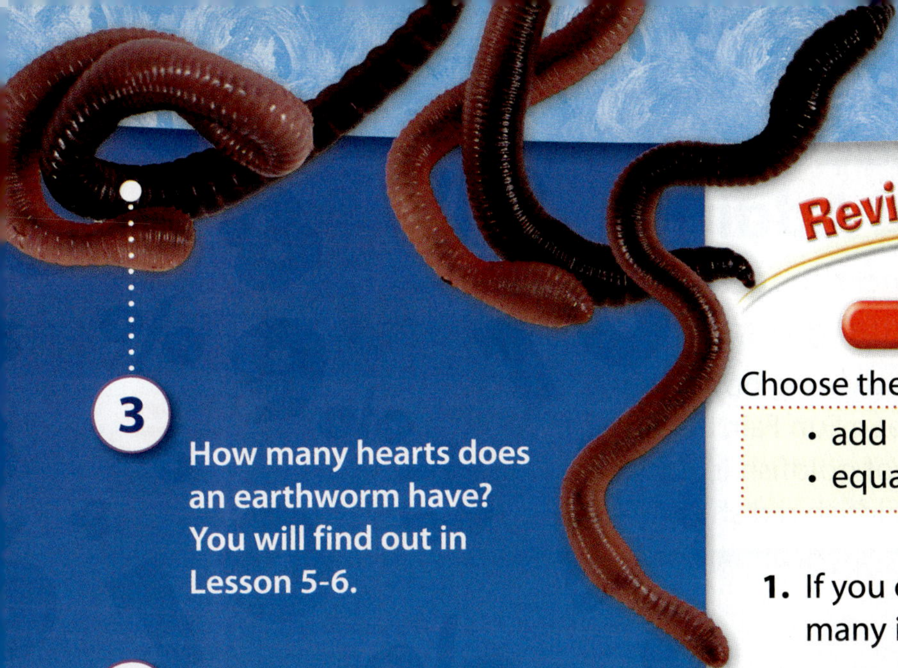

3 How many hearts does an earthworm have? You will find out in Lesson 5-6.

4 How many wheels are on the bikes of a unicycle relay team? You will find out in Lesson 5-9.

Review What You Know!

Vocabulary

Choose the best term from the box.

- add
- skip count
- equal groups
- subtract

1. If you combine groups to find how many in all, you __?__.

2. __?__ have the same number of items.

3. When you say the numbers 2, 4, 6, 8, you __?__.

Equal Groups

Are the groups equal? Write *yes* or *no*.

4. 

5. 

Adding

Find each sum.

6. $5 + 5 + 5$

7. $7 + 7$

8. $3 + 3 + 3$

9. $2 + 2 + 2 + 2$

10. $6 + 6 + 6$

11. $9 + 9 + 9$

Repeated Addition

12. **Writing to Explain** Draw a picture to show how to solve $8 + 8 + 8 = \square$. Then copy and complete the number sentence.

Virginia

Lesson 5-1

3.6 The student will represent multiplication and division, using area, set, and number line models, and create and solve problems that involve multiplication of two whole numbers, one factor 99 or less and the second factor 5 or less.

Multiplication as Repeated Addition

How can you find the total number of objects in equal groups?

Jessie used 3 bags to bring home the goldfish she won at a Fun Fair. She put the same number of goldfish in each bag. How many goldfish did she win?

Hands-On
counters

Guided Practice*

Do you know HOW?

Copy and complete. Use counters.

1.

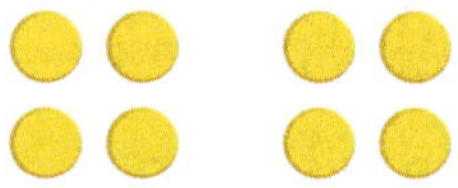

2 groups of □
4 + 4 = □
2 × □ = □

2.

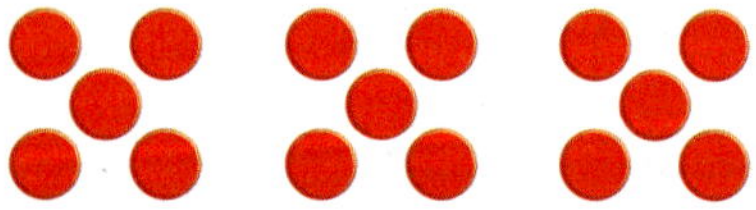

□ groups of 5
5 + □ + □ = □
3 × □ = □

Do you UNDERSTAND?

3. Can you write 3 + 3 + 3 + 3 as a multiplication sentence? Explain.

4. Can you write 3 + 5 + 6 = 14 as a multiplication sentence? Explain.

5. Write an addition sentence and a multiplication sentence to solve this problem:

Jessie bought 4 packages of colorful stones to put in the fish bowl. There were 6 stones in each package. How many stones did Jessie buy?

Independent Practice

Copy and complete. Use counters or draw a picture to help.

6.

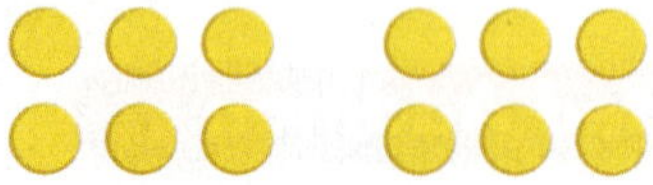

2 groups of □
6 + □ = □
2 × □ = □

7.

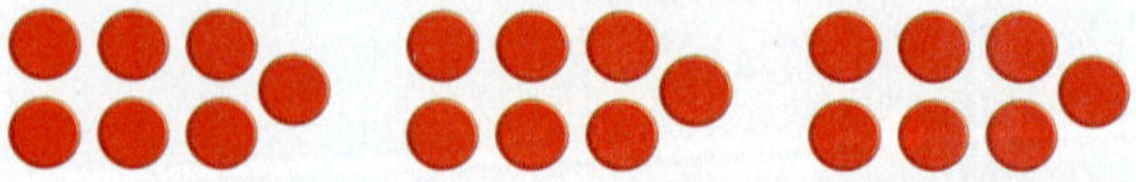

3 groups of □
7 + □ + □ = □
3 × □ = □

DIGITAL Animated Glossary, eTools
www.pearsonsuccessnet.com

For another example, see Set A on page 136.

The counters show 3 groups of 8 goldfish.

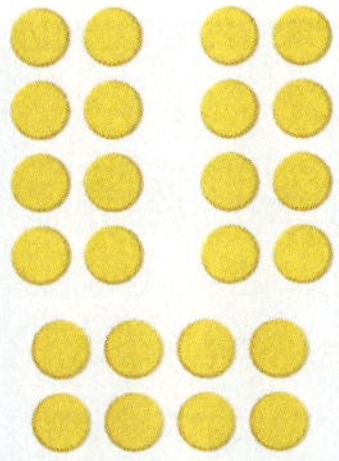

You can use addition to join equal groups.
8 + 8 + 8 = 24

Multiplication is an operation that gives the total number when you join equal groups.

What You Say 3 times 8 equals 24

What You Write 3 × 8 = 24

(3 = factor, 8 = factor, 24 = product)

Factors are the numbers that are being multiplied. The **product** is the answer to a multiplication problem.

Addition sentence:
8 + 8 + 8 = 24

Multiplication sentence:
3 × 8 = 24

So, 8 + 8 + 8 = 3 × 8.

Jessie won 24 goldfish.

Copy and complete each number sentence. Use counters or draw a picture to help.

8. 2 + 2 + 2 + 2 = 4 × □

9. □ + □ + □ = 3 × 7

10. 9 + □ + □ = □ × 9

11. 6 + 6 + 6 + 6 + 6 = □ × □

Algebra Write +, −, or × for each □.

12. 4 □ 3 = 12

13. 3 □ 6 = 9

14. 4 □ 4 = 0

15. 6 □ 4 = 10

16. 5 □ 3 = 2

17. 2 □ 4 = 8

Problem Solving

18. What number sentence shows how to find the total number of erasers?

A 5 + 5 = □

B 15 − 5 = □

C 15 + 5 = □

D 3 × 5 = □

19. Write an addition sentence and a multiplication sentence to solve the problem below.

Maria has 6 new flashlights. Each flashlight takes 3 batteries. How many batteries will Maria need for the flashlights?

20. Writing to Explain Luke says that you can add or multiply to join groups. Is he correct? Explain.

21. Which picture shows 3 groups of 2?

SOL Prep

A 

B 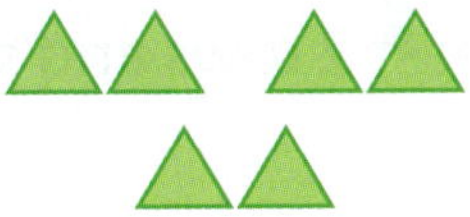

C 

D 

Virginia

Lesson 5-2

3.6 The student will represent multiplication and division, using area, set, and number line models, and create and solve problems that involve multiplication of two whole numbers, one factor 99 or less and the second factor 5 or less. **(Also 3.20.a, 3.20.b)**

Arrays and Multiplication

Hands-On
counters

How does an array show multiplication?

Dana keeps her entire CD collection in a holder on the wall. The holder has 4 rows. Each row holds 5 CDs. How many CDs are in Dana's collection?

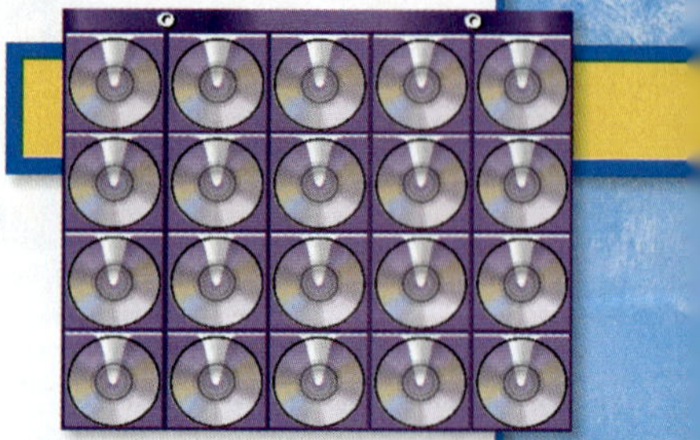

The CDs are in an array. An array shows objects in equal rows.

Another Example Does order matter when you multiply?

Libby and Sydney both say their poster has more stickers. Who is correct?

$4 + 4 + 4 = 12$
$3 \times 4 = 12$

Libby's poster has 12 stickers.

$3 + 3 + 3 + 3 = 12$
$4 \times 3 = 12$

Sydney's poster has 12 stickers.

Both poster boards have the same number of stickers.

$$\mathbf{3 \times 4 = 12} \text{ and } \mathbf{4 \times 3 = 12}$$

The Commutative (Order) Property of Multiplication says you can multiply numbers in any order and the product is the same. So, $3 \times 4 = 4 \times 3$.

Explain It

1. Miguel has 5 rows of stickers. There are 3 stickers in each row. Write an addition sentence and a multiplication sentence to show how many stickers he has.
2. Show the Commutative Property of Multiplication by drawing two arrays. Each array should have at least 2 rows and show a product of 6.

The counters show 4 rows of 5 CDs.

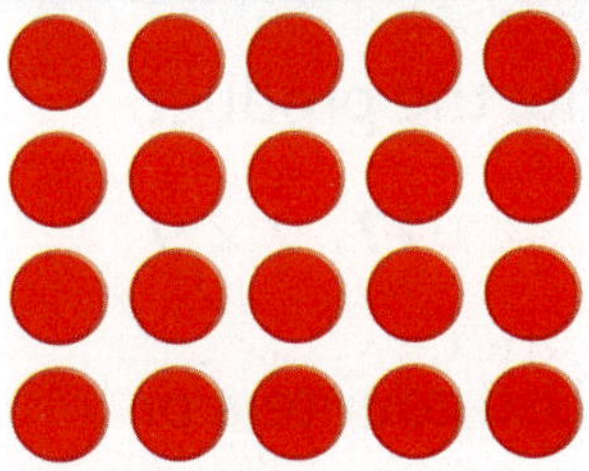

Each row is a group. You can use addition to find the total.

5 + 5 + 5 + 5 = 20

Multiplication can also be used to find the total in an array.

What You Say 4 times 5 equals 20

What You Write 4 × 5 = 20

(4: number of rows; 5: number in each row)

There are 20 CDs in Dana's collection.

Guided Practice*

Do you know HOW?

In **1** and **2**, write a multiplication sentence for each array.

1. 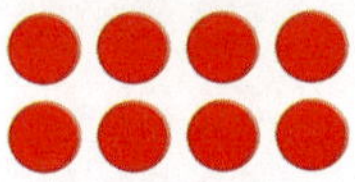

2. 

In **3** and **4**, draw an array to show each multiplication fact. Write the product.

3. 3 × 6

4. 5 × 4

In **5** and **6**, copy and complete each multiplication sentence. Use counters or draw an array to help.

5. 5 × ☐ = 10
2 × ☐ = 10

6. 4 × 3 = ☐
3 × ☐ = 12

Do you UNDERSTAND?

7. Look at the example above. What does the first factor in the multiplication sentence tell you about the array?

8. **Writing to Explain** Why is the Commutative Property of Multiplication sometimes called the *order property*?

9. Scott puts some sports stickers in rows. He makes 6 rows with 5 stickers in each row. If he put the same stickers in 5 equal rows, how many would be in each row?

Independent Practice

In **10–12**, write a multiplication sentence for each array.

10. 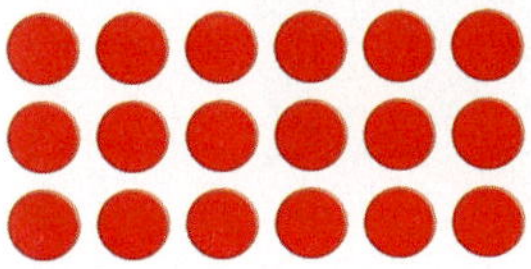

11. 

12. 

*For another example, see Set A on page 136.

Independent Practice

In **13–17**, draw an array to show each multiplication fact. Write the product.

13. 3×3 **14.** 5×6 **15.** 1×8 **16.** 4×3 **17.** 2×9

In **18–23**, copy and complete each multiplication sentence. Use counters or draw an array to help.

18. $4 \times \square = 8$
$2 \times \square = 8$

19. $6 \times 4 = \square$
$4 \times \square = 24$

20. $5 \times \square = 40$
$\square \times 5 = 40$

21. $3 \times 9 = 27$
$9 \times 3 = \square$

22. $7 \times 6 = 42$
$6 \times 7 = \square$

23. $9 \times 8 = 72$
$8 \times 9 = \square$

Problem Solving

24. Writing to Explain How do the arrays at the right show the Commutative Property of Multiplication?

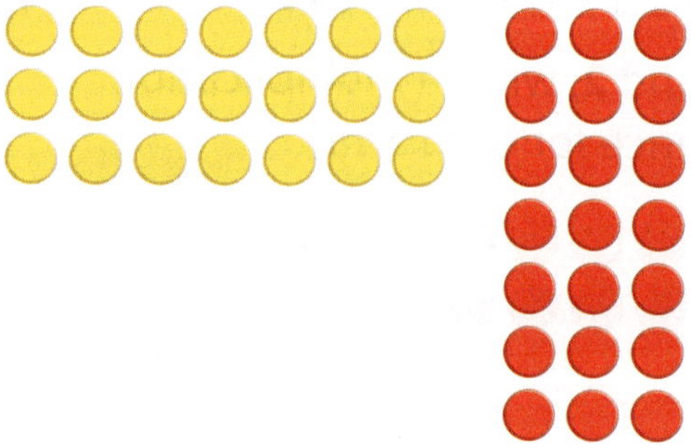

25. Number Sense How does an array show equal groups?

26. Taylor says that the product for 7×2 is the same as the product for 2×7. Is he correct? Explain.

27. Reasoning Margo has 23 pictures. Can she use all of the pictures to make an array with exactly two equal rows? Why or why not?

28. Dan bought the stamps shown at the right. Which number sentence shows one way to find how many stamps Dan bought?

A $4 + 5 = \square$

B $5 \times 4 = \square$

C $5 + 4 = \square$

D $5 - 4 = \square$

Mixed Problem Solving

Math and Art

Josie used stars and circles to make the artwork on the right. Answer the questions about her artwork.

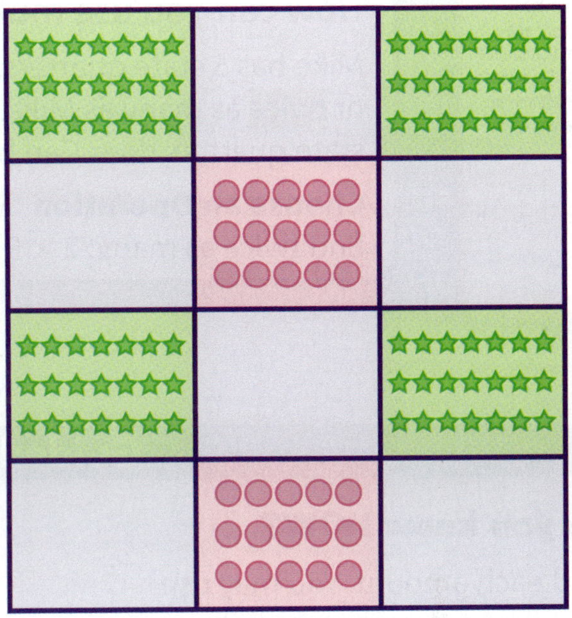

1. Describe the patterns you see in the artwork.

2. How many rows are in each array of stars?

3. Look at one array of circles. How many circles are in each row of the array?

4. Look at one array of stars. Write a number sentence for the array.

5. How many circles did Josie use in her artwork?

6. How many more stars than circles did Josie make?

7. The picture above shows Josie's artwork with 4 rows. Before she started, Josie made a table to plan how many of each shape she would need for different numbers of rows.

   Copy and complete Josie's table.

Data

Shapes Needed to Make Artwork

Total Number of Rows	Total Number of Stars	Total Number of Circles
2	42	15
4	84	30
6	126	45
8		

8. If Josie makes her artwork with 10 rows, how many stars will she use in all? how many circles?

9. Mark made 56 stars. He made 18 circles. How many shapes did he make in all?

10. **Strategy Focus** Solve. Use the strategy Write a Number Sentence.

    Maggie made a pattern using a total of 92 shapes. Of the 92 shapes Maggie used, 44 were circles and the rest were stars. How many stars did Maggie use?

Virginia

Lesson 5-3

3.6 The student will represent multiplication and division, using area, set, and number line models, and create and solve problems that involve multiplication of two whole numbers, one factor 99 or less and the second factor 5 or less.

Using Multiplication to Compare

Hands-On
counters

How can you use multiplication to compare?

Mike has 5 state quarters. Carl has two times as many, or twice as many as Mike. How many state quarters does Carl have?

Mike's quarters

Choose an Operation Multiply to find twice as many: $2 \times 5 = \square$

Guided Practice*

Do you know HOW?

Find each amount. You may use drawings or counters to help.

1. 3 times as many as 3

2. 2 times as many as 6

3. Twice as many as 3

Do you UNDERSTAND?

4. **Number Sense** Barry says you can add 5 + 5 to find how many state quarters Carl has. Is he correct? Why or why not?

5. Carl has 4 silver dollars. Mike has twice as many as Carl. How many silver dollars does Mike have?

Independent Practice

In **6–11**, find each amount. You may use drawings or counters to help.

6. 2 times as many as 7

7. 3 times as many as 8

8. Twice as many as 6

9. 4 times as many as 5

10. Twice as many as 9

11. 5 times as many as 4

In **12–15**, which coin or bill matches each value?

12. 2 times as much as 1 nickel

13. 10 times as much as 1 dime

14. 5 times as much as 1 nickel

15. 10 times as much as 1 nickel

dime quarter half dollar one dollar

DIGITAL Animated Glossary, eTools
www.pearsonsuccessnet.com

For another example, see Set A on page 136.

What You Think

Mike has 5 state quarters.

Carl has 2 times as many.

2 times as many is 10.

What You Write

$2 \times 5 = 10$

factors — product

or

$$\begin{array}{r} 5 \\ \times\ 2 \\ \hline 10 \end{array}$$

5 ← factor
2 ← factor
10 ← product

Carl has 10 state quarters.

Problem Solving

Number Sense For **16–17**, copy and complete.

16. 6 is twice as many as ☐.

17. 8 is eight times as many as ☐.

18. **Reasoning** Carol has 4 dolls. Her sister has twice as many. How many dolls do they have in all?

19. **Writing to Explain** How could this picture help you solve **Exercise 18**?

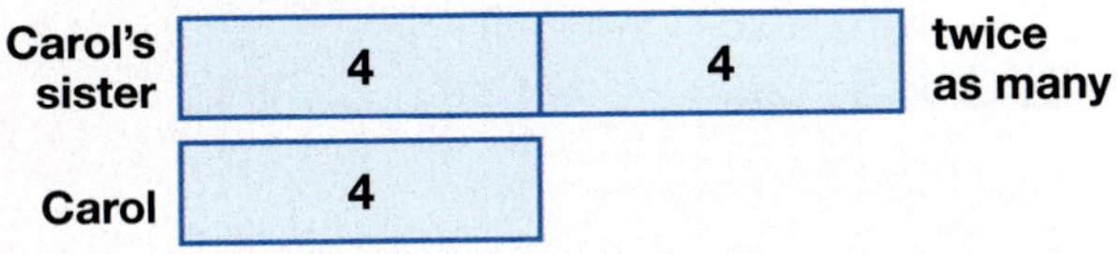

20. A horse needs about 3 hours of sleep each day. An armadillo needs 6 times as much sleep as a horse. About how many hours of sleep does an armadillo need each day?

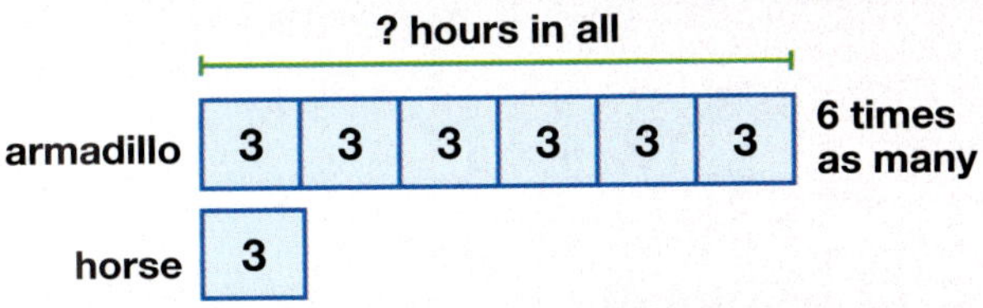

21. Two of the U. S. coins that are worth one dollar are shown below. The Susan B. Anthony coin was first issued in 1979. The Sacagawea coin was issued 21 years later. When was the Sacagawea coin issued?

22. What number sentence shows how to find twice as many marbles?

A $8 + 8 + 8 = $ ☐ **B** $1 \times 8 = $ ☐ **C** $2 \times 8 = $ ☐ **D** $3 \times 8 = $ ☐

Virginia

Lesson 5-4

Extends 3.6 The student will represent multiplication and division, using area, set, and number line models, and create and solve problems that involve multiplication of two whole numbers, one factor 99 or less and the second factor 5 or less.

Writing Multiplication Stories

How can you describe a multiplication fact?

Stories can be written to describe multiplication facts.

Write a multiplication story for $3 \times 6 = \square$.

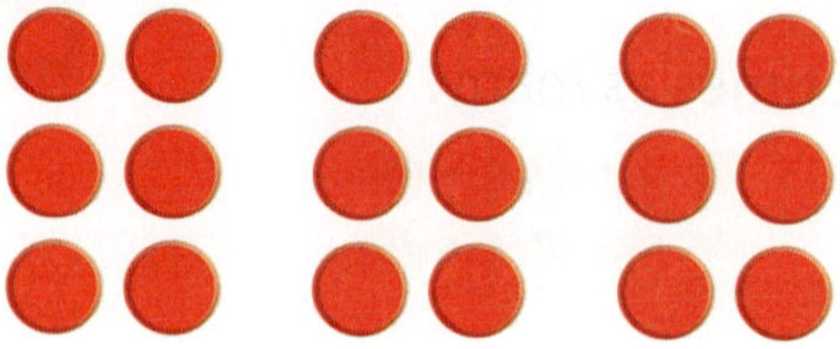

Guided Practice*

Do you know HOW?

In **1–4**, write a multiplication story for each problem. Draw a picture or use objects to find each product.

1. 2×6

2. 3×5

3. 4×2

4. 3×8

Do you UNDERSTAND?

5. How would the story about Randy change if the multiplication sentence $2 \times 6 = \square$ was used?

6. How would the story about Eliza change if the multiplication sentence $3 \times 5 = \square$ was used?

7. **Number Sense** Could the story about carrots also be an addition story? Explain.

Independent Practice

Write a multiplication story for each problem. Draw a picture or use objects to find each product.

8. 7×3

9. 2×9

10. 4×5

Write a multiplication story for each picture. Use the picture to find the product.

11.

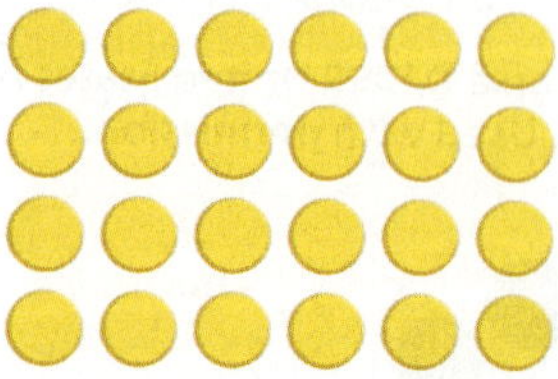

12.

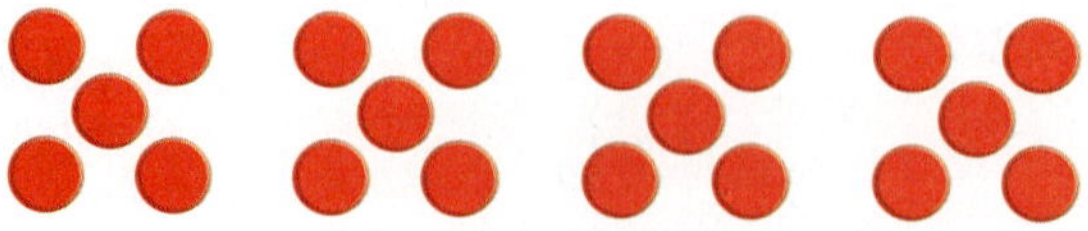

*For another example, see Set B on page 136.

Equal Groups

Randy has 3 packs of 6 buttons. How many buttons does he have?

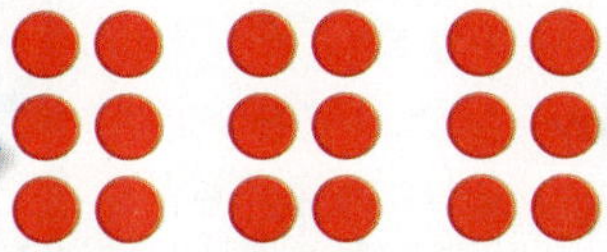

$3 \times 6 = 18$

Randy has 18 buttons.

An Array

Eliza planted 6 lilies in each of 3 rows. How many lilies did she plant?

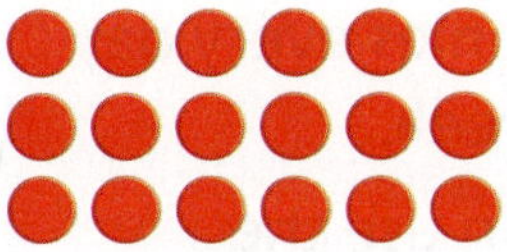

$3 \times 6 = 18$

Eliza planted 18 lilies.

"Times as Many"

Kanisha has 6 carrots. Jack has 3 times as many. How many carrots does Jack have?

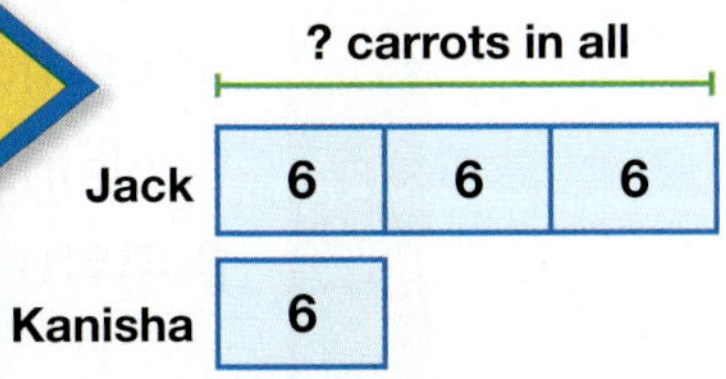

$3 \times 6 = 18$

Jack has 18 carrots.

Problem Solving

Number Sense For **13–15**, describe each story as an addition story, a subtraction story, or a multiplication story.

13. Kay has 6 pencils. She gave 4 of them to her friend. How many pencils does Kay have left?

14. Kay has 6 pencils. She bought 4 more pencils at the school store. How many pencils does Kay have now?

15. Kay has 6 bags of pencils. There are 2 pencils in each bag. How many pencils does Kay have?

16. SOL Prep A soccer team traveled to a soccer game in 4 vans. All four vans were full. Each van held 7 players. How many players went to the game?

A 47 **C** 24

B 28 **D** 11

17. **Algebra** Steve has some packages of balloons. There are 8 balloons in each package. He has 24 balloons in all. Draw a picture to find how many packages of balloons Steve has.

18. A group of 12 monarch butterflies is getting ready to migrate. How many wings will be moving when the group flies away?

Virginia

Lesson 5-5

Extends 3.19 The student will recognize and describe a variety of patterns formed using numbers, tables, and pictures, and extend the patterns, using the same or different forms.

Problem Solving

Writing to Explain

Gina's dad gave her 2 pennies on Monday. He promised to double that number of pennies every day after that for one week.

Explain how you can use the pattern to complete the table.

Data

Day	Number of pennies
Monday	2
Tuesday	4
Wednesday	8
Thursday	16
Friday	32
Saturday	
Sunday	

Another Example

Jackie got on an elevator on the first floor. She went up 5 floors. Then she went down 2 floors. Then she went up 4 floors and got off the elevator. What floor is Jackie on?

Use *words, pictures, numbers,* or *symbols* to write a math explanation.

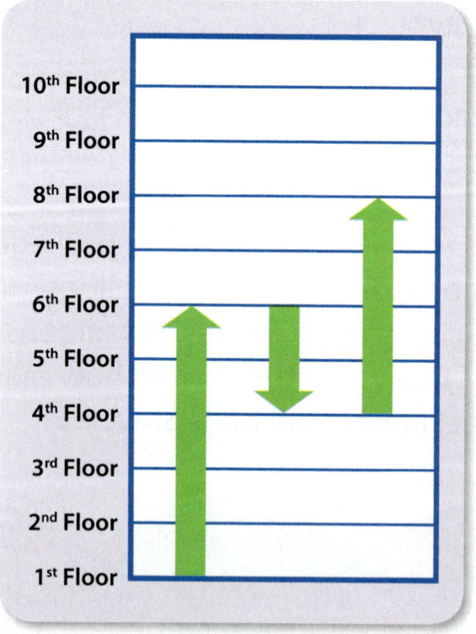

Jackie started on the first floor. Then she went up 5 floors.

$1 + 5 = 6$

Then she went down 2 floors.

$6 - 2 = 4$

Then she went up 4 floors and got off the elevator.

$4 + 4 = 8$

Jackie is on the eighth floor.

Explain It

1. Why is drawing a picture a good way to explain this problem?
2. How do the number sentences explain the problem?

Complete the table. Use *words, pictures, numbers,* or *symbols* to write a math explanation.

The number of pennies doubles each day. That means that Gina will get 2 times as many pennies as she got the day before.

So, I need to double 32.
32 + 32 = 64 pennies
Gina will get 64 pennies on Saturday.

Then, I need to double 64.
64 + 64 = 128 pennies
Gina will get 128 pennies on Sunday.

Data

Day	Number of Pennies
Monday	2
Tuesday	4
Wednesday	8
Thursday	16
Friday	32
Saturday	64
Sunday	128

Guided Practice*

Do you know HOW?

1. Brian bought 3 packs of baseball cards. There are 4 cards in each pack. How many baseball cards did he buy? Explain how you can solve this problem.

Do you UNDERSTAND?

2. If the pattern in the table above continued, how many pennies would Gina get next Monday?

3. **Write a Problem** Write a problem. Explain how to solve it using words, pictures, numbers, or symbols.

Independent Practice

4. Pam is setting up tables and chairs. She puts 4 chairs at each table.

   a Explain how the number of chairs changes as the number of tables changes.

   b Copy and complete the table.

Number of Tables	1	2	3	4	5
Number of Chairs	4	8	12		

5. Aaron cut a log into 5 pieces. How many cuts did he make? Explain how you found the answer.

Stuck? Try this....

- What do I know?
- What am I asked to find?
- What diagram can I use to help understand the problem?
- Can I use addition, subtraction, multiplication, or division?
- Is all of my work correct?
- Did I answer the right question?
- Is my answer reasonable?

*For another example, see Set B on page 136.

Independent Practice

6. Copy and complete the table below. Then describe how the table helps you explain the pattern.

Cost of School Play Tickets

Number of Tickets	Cost
1	$5
2	$10
3	$15
4	▢
5	▢

7. If Margo continues the pattern in the table, what is the first day she will exercise for 1 hour? Explain how you know.

Margo's Exercise Schedule

Day	Minutes
Monday	20 minutes
Tuesday	30 minutes
Wednesday	40 minutes
Thursday	▢ minutes
Friday	▢ minutes

8. Hank earns $4 for raking lawns and $6 for mowing lawns. How much will Hank earn if he mows and rakes 2 lawns?

9. a Describe the pattern below.

   81, 82, 84, 87, 91

   b Write the next two numbers in the pattern and explain how you found them.

10. Jake planted trees in a row that is 20 feet long. He planted a tree at the beginning of the row. Then he planted a tree every 5 feet. How many trees did he plant in this row? Draw a picture to explain.

Think About the Process

11. Alexandra bought 5 bags of oranges. There were 6 oranges in each bag. Then she gave 4 oranges away. Which number sentence shows how many oranges Alexandra bought?

   A $5 + 6 = \square$

   B $5 \times 6 = \square$

   C $(5 \times 6) - 4 = \square$

   D $(5 + 6) - 4 = \square$

12. Tara ran 5 miles on Monday and 4 miles on Tuesday. Teresa ran 3 miles on Monday and 6 miles on Tuesday. Which number sentence shows how far Tara ran in all?

   A $3 + 6 = \square$

   B $5 + 4 = \square$

   C $5 - 4 = \square$

   D $5 + 4 + 3 + 6 = \square$

Enrichment

Venn Diagrams

In the 1880s, British mathematician John Venn used diagrams with shapes, such as rings or circles, to show how groups of data relate.

Each shape in a **Venn diagram** is named for the group it represents. Shapes overlap, or **intersect,** because some of the data can belong to more than one group.

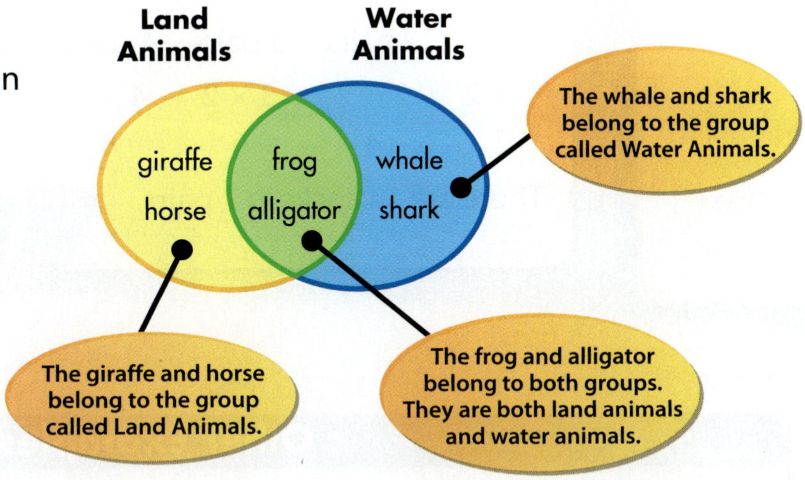

Practice

For **1–4**, use the Venn diagram at the right.

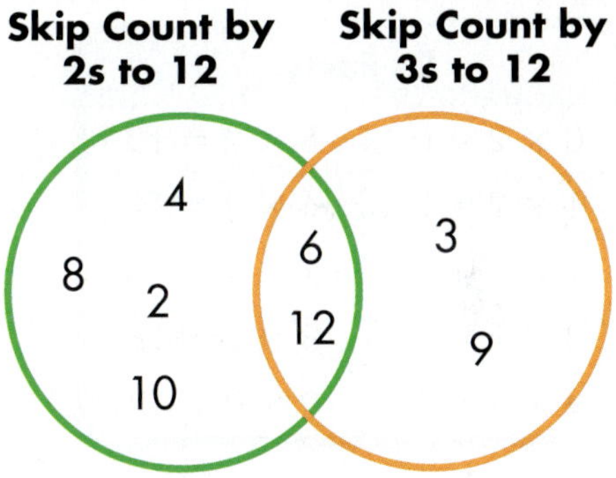

1. Which numbers do you name only when you count to 12 by 2s?

2. Which numbers do you name only when you count to 12 by 3s?

3. Which numbers do you name when you count to 12 by both 2s and 3s? How can you tell from the Venn diagram?

4. If you continued counting to 18, where would you place 14? 15? 18?

5. Jamie skip counted by 3s to 36. Oscar skip counted by 4s to 36.

a. Which numbers did Jamie and Oscar both say?

b. Jamie and Oscar used their skip-count numbers to make a Venn diagram. How many numbers did they write in the section where the circles intersect?

6. Use the lists below to make a Venn diagram.

Skip Count to 24

by 4s	by 6s
4	6
8	12
12	18
16	24
20	
24	

Virginia

Lesson 5-6

3.5 The student will recall multiplication facts through the twelves table, and the corresponding division facts.

2 and 5 as Factors

How can you use patterns to multiply by 2 and 5?

How many socks are in 7 pairs of socks? Find 7×2.

1 pair	2 pairs	3 pairs	4 pairs	5 pairs	6 pairs	7 pairs
1×2	2×2	3×2	4×2	5×2	6×2	7×2
2	4	6	8	10	12	14

There are 14 socks in 7 pairs.

Other Examples

What are the patterns in multiples of 2 and 5?

The products for the 2s facts are multiples of 2.
The products for the 5s facts are multiples of 5.
Multiples are the products of a number and other whole numbers.

Data

2s Facts	
$0 \times 2 = 0$	$5 \times 2 = 10$
$1 \times 2 = 2$	$6 \times 2 = 12$
$2 \times 2 = 4$	$7 \times 2 = 14$
$3 \times 2 = 6$	$8 \times 2 = 16$
$4 \times 2 = 8$	$9 \times 2 = 18$

Data

5s Facts	
$0 \times 5 = 0$	$5 \times 5 = 25$
$1 \times 5 = 5$	$6 \times 5 = 30$
$2 \times 5 = 10$	$7 \times 5 = 35$
$3 \times 5 = 15$	$8 \times 5 = 40$
$4 \times 5 = 20$	$9 \times 5 = 45$

Patterns for 2s Facts

- Multiples of 2 are even numbers. Multiples of 2 end in 0, 2, 4, 6, or 8.
- Each multiple of 2 is 2 more than the one before it.

Patterns for 5s Facts

- Each multiple of 5 ends in 0 or 5.
- Each multiple of 5 is 5 more than the one before it.

Explain It

1. Is 83 a multiple of 2? a multiple of 5? How do you know?
2. **Reasoning** How can patterns help you find 10×2?

How many fingers are on 7 gloves?

Choose an Operation Find 7×5.

$1 \times 5 = 5$
$2 \times 5 = 10$
$3 \times 5 = 15$
$4 \times 5 = 20$
$5 \times 5 = 25$
$6 \times 5 = 30$
$7 \times 5 = 35$

There are 35 fingers on 7 gloves.

Guided Practice*

Do you know HOW?

Find each product.

1. 2×6 **2.** 2×3 **3.** 7×2

4. 5×3 **5.** 5×5 **6.** 6×5

7. 4×2 **8.** 5×2 **9.** 8×5

Do you UNDERSTAND?

10. How can you skip count to find the number of socks in 9 pairs? in 10 pairs?

11. How can you skip count to find how many fingers are on 9 gloves? on 10 gloves?

12. **Number Sense** Bert says that 2×8 is 15. How can you use patterns to know that his answer is wrong?

Independent Practice

For **13–22**, find each product.

13. 2×2 **14.** 5×2 **15.** 3×5 **16.** 8×2 **17.** 9×5

18. 3×5 **19.** 2×4 **20.** 4×5 **21.** 9×2 **22.** 5×7

23. Find 5 times 6.

24. Multiply 2 by 5.

25. Find the product of 7 and 5.

26. Find 6×2.

DIGITAL Animated Glossary **www.pearsonsuccessnet.com**

For another example, see Set C on page 137.

Independent Practice

Algebra Compare. Use <, >, or =.

27. $2 \times 5 \bigcirc 5 \times 2$ **28.** $4 \times 5 \bigcirc 4 \times 6$ **29.** $2 \times 5 \bigcirc 2 \times 4$

30. $6 \times 5 \bigcirc 5 \times 5$ **31.** $9 \times 5 \bigcirc 5 \times 9$ **32.** $7 \times 2 \bigcirc 2 \times 9$

Problem Solving

For **33–35**, use the table at the right.

33. How much does it cost to bowl three games without renting shoes?

34. Maru rented some bowling shoes. She also bowled two games. How much money did she spend?

35. Wendy paid for 2 games with a twenty-dollar bill. How much change did she get back?

Data

Bowling	
Cost per game	$5
Daily shoe rental	$2

36. **Writing to Explain** Eric has some nickels. He says they are worth exactly 34 cents. Can you tell if he is correct or not? Why or why not?

38. Use the picture below. How many hearts do 3 earthworms have?

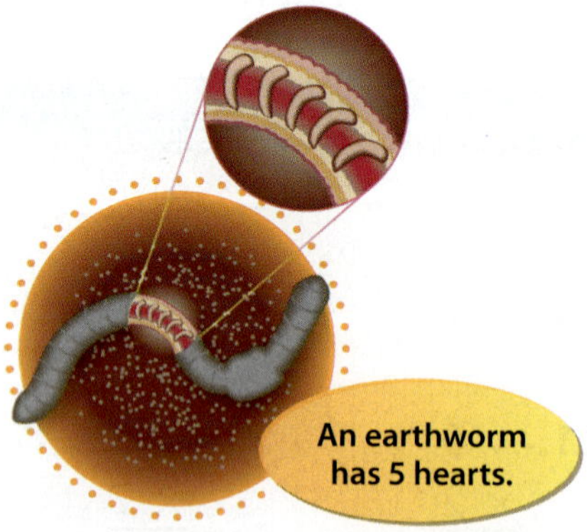

37. SOL Prep April has the coins shown below.

April counted the value of these coins in cents. Which list shows numbers she would have named?

A 5, 10, 16, 20, 25, 26

B 5, 10, 15, 22, 25, 32

C 5, 10, 15, 20, 25, 30

D 10, 15, 22, 25, 30, 35

39. **Algebra** What two 1-digit factors could you multiply to get a product of 30?

40. Jake went bowling. On his first turn, he knocked down 2 pins. On his second turn, he knocked down twice that many. So far, how many pins in all has he knocked down?

Going Digital

Meanings of Multiplication

Use eTools

Counters

Step 1 Go to the Counters eTool. Select a counter shape. Make 4 groups of counters with 3 counters in each group. The odometer tells how many counters in all. Write a number sentence: $4 \times 3 = 12$.

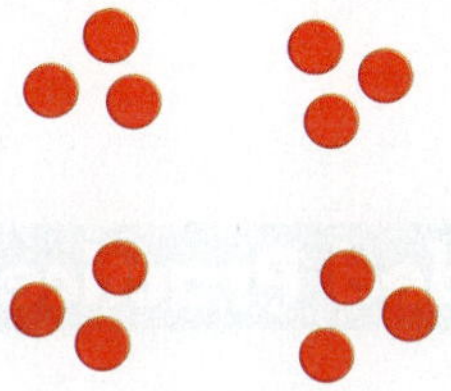

Step 2 Use the broom tool to clear the workspace. Show 3 groups with 8 counters in each and write a number sentence: $3 \times 8 = 24$.

Step 3 Select the array workspace. Drag the button to show 7 rows with 6 counters in each row. Write a number sentence: $7 \times 6 = 42$.

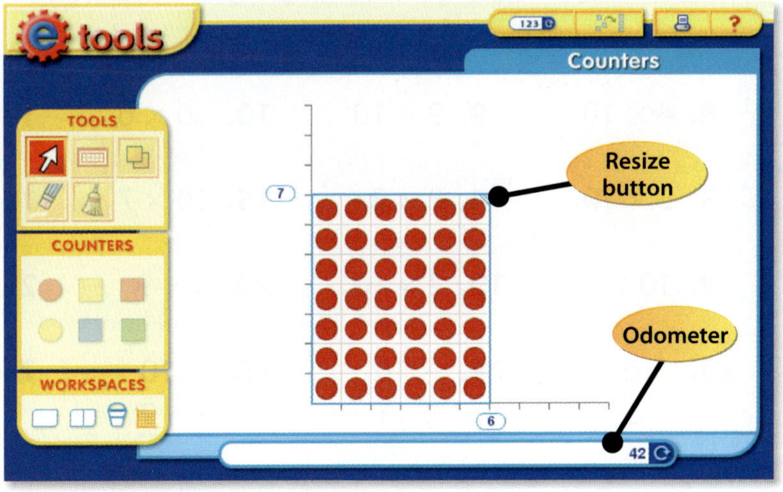

Practice

Use the Counters eTool to draw counters. Write a number sentence.

1. 5 groups with 3 counters in each

2. 7 groups with 4 counters in each

3. 8 rows with 6 counters in each

4. 9 rows with 5 counters in each

Virginia

Lesson 5-7

3.5 The student will recall multiplication facts through the twelves table, and the corresponding division facts.

10 as a Factor

What are the patterns in multiples of 10?

Greg wants to train for a race that is 10 weeks away. The chart shows his training schedule. How many miles will Greg run to train for the race?

Data

Weekly Schedule

Activity	Miles
Swimming	4 miles
Running	10 miles
Biking	9 miles

Choose the Operation

Find 10×10.

Guided Practice*

Do you know HOW?

Find each product.

1. 2×10

2. 6×10

3. 10×1

4. 10×3

5. 10×7

Do you UNDERSTAND?

6. **Writing to Explain** Is 91 a multiple of 10? Explain.

7. How many miles will Greg bike in 10 weeks?

Independent Practice

Find each product.

8. 4×10 **9.** 9×10 **10.** 10×6 **11.** 5×5 **12.** 10×10

13. 5×10 **14.** 8×2 **15.** 10×7 **16.** 2×5 **17.** 6×10

18. 10×10 **19.** 2×10 **20.** 5×9 **21.** 3×10 **22.** 10×8

23. 6×5 **24.** 10×1 **25.** 10×9 **26.** 2×9 **27.** 10×5

28. 10×2 **29.** 7×2 **30.** 10×4 **31.** 10×8 **32.** 0×6

33. 5×8 **34.** 10×0 **35.** 10×3 **36.** 5×7 **37.** 10×7

*For another example, see Set C on page 137.

10s Facts	
0 × 10 = 0	5 × 10 = 50
1 × 10 = 10	6 × 10 = 60
2 × 10 = 20	7 × 10 = 70
3 × 10 = 30	8 × 10 = 80
4 × 10 = 40	9 × 10 = 90
	10 × 10 =

Use patterns to find the product.

- Write the factor you are multiplying by 10.
- Write a zero to the right of that factor. A multiple of 10 will always have a zero in the ones place.

$10 \times 10 = 100$

Greg will run 100 miles.

Problem Solving

Use the table at the right for **38** and **39**. It shows the food that was bought for 70 third graders for a school picnic.

Food Item	Number of Packages	Number in Each Package
Hot dogs	8	10
Rolls	10	9
Juice boxes	7	10

38. Find the total number of each item bought.

a Hot dogs

b Rolls

c Juice boxes

39. How many extra juice boxes were bought?

40. Writing to Explain Look at the table at the top of page 126. Greg multiplied 5 × 10 to find how many more miles he biked than swam in the 10 weeks. Does that make sense? Why or why not?

41. Strategy Focus Solve. Use the strategy Draw a Picture.

Mai had 3 packs of pens. Each pack had 10 pens. She gave 5 pens to Ervin. How many pens did she have left?

42. Number Sense Raul has only dimes in his pocket. Could he have exactly 45 cents? Explain.

43. Kimmy bought 7 tickets for a concert. Each ticket cost $10. What was the total cost of the tickets Kimmy bought?

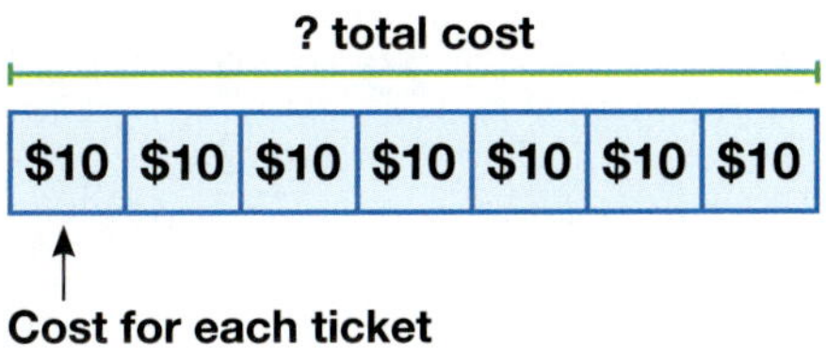

44. Which sign makes the number sentence true?

8 ☐ 5 = 40

A +

B −

C ×

D ÷

Virginia

Lesson 5-8

3.5 The student will recall multiplication facts through the twelves table, and the corresponding division facts.

9 as a Factor

How can patterns be used to find 9s facts?

The owner of a flower shop puts 9 roses in each package. How many roses are in 8 packages?

Use patterns to find 8×9.

Data

9s Facts

$0 \times 9 = 0$
$1 \times 9 = 9$
$2 \times 9 = 18$
$3 \times 9 = 27$
$4 \times 9 = 36$
$5 \times 9 = 45$
$6 \times 9 = 54$
$7 \times 9 = 63$
$8 \times 9 = \square$
$9 \times 9 = \square$

Guided Practice*

Do you know HOW?

Find each product.

1. 9×2 **2.** 5×9 **3.** 7×9

4. 4×9 **5.** 2×8 **6.** 6×9

7. 3×9 **8.** 5×5 **9.** 8×9

Do you UNDERSTAND?

10. Writing to Explain Use the patterns above to find 9×9. Then explain how you found the product.

11. Number Sense Paul thinks that 3×9 is 24. Use a 9s pattern to show that he is wrong.

Independent Practice

Find each product.

12. 9×0 **13.** 5×8 **14.** 9×4 **15.** 8×9

16. 9×9 **17.** 1×9 **18.** 5×9 **19.** 2×9

20. 7×9 **21.** 5×2 **22.** 6×5 **23.** 9×1

24. 6×9 **25.** 9×5 **26.** 9×7 **27.** 9×2

28. 7×9 **29.** 8×2 **30.** 0×9 **31.** 2×3

*For another example, see Set C on page 137.

One Way

Use these patterns. Start with $1 \times 9 = 9$.

The ones digit decreases by 1 each time. So the ones digit in the product after 63 is 2.

The tens digit increases by 1 each time. So the tens digit in the product after 63 is 7.

$8 \times 9 = 72$

There are 72 roses in 8 packages.

Another Way

Use these patterns to find the product.

The tens digit is 1 less than the factor being multiplied by 9.

$8 - 1 = 7$

$8 \times 9 = 72$

The digits of the product have a sum of 9.

$7 + 2 = 9$

There are 72 roses in 8 packages.

Algebra Copy and complete. Use +, −, or ×.

32. $2 \times 6 = 10 \square 2$ **33.** $5 \times 7 = 45 \square 10$ **34.** $9 \times 9 = 80 \square 1$

35. $20 - 2 = 2 \square 9$ **36.** $9 \square 3 = 30 - 3$ **37.** $9 \square 1 = 2 \square 5$

Problem Solving

The library is having a used book sale. For **38–41**, use the table at the right.

38. How much do 4 hardcover books cost?

39. How much more would Chico spend if he bought 3 books on CDs rather than 3 hardcover books?

Data

Library Book Sale	
Paperback Books	$2
Hardcover Books	$5
Books on CDs	$9

40. Maggie bought only paperback books. The clerk told her she owed $15. How does Maggie know that the clerk made a mistake?

41. **Writing to Explain** Mr. Lee bought 2 books on CDs and 9 paperback books. Did he spend more on CDs or on paperback books? Tell how you know.

42. The owner of a flower shop counted the flowers in groups of 9. Which list shows the numbers he named?

SOL Prep

A 9, 19, 29, 39, 49, 59 **C** 18, 27, 36, 45, 56, 65

B 6, 12, 18, 24, 36, 42 **D** 9, 18, 27, 36, 45, 54

Virginia

Lesson 5-9

3.5 The student will recall multiplication facts through the twelves table, and the corresponding division facts. **(Also 3.20.a, 3.20.b)**

Multiplying with 0 and 1

What are the patterns in multiples of 1 and 0?

Kira has 8 plates with 1 orange on each plate.
How many oranges does Kira have?

Find 8×1.

Guided Practice*

Do you know HOW?

Find each product.

1. 1×7 **2.** 5×0 **3.** 5×1

4. 0×0 **5.** 1×1 **6.** 8×1

7. 7×0 **8.** 1×9 **9.** 0×6

Do you UNDERSTAND?

10. **Writing to Explain** How can you use the properties above to find 375×1 and 0×754?

11. Draw an array to show that $1 \times 8 = 8$.

12. Chad has 6 plates. There is 1 apple and 0 grapes on each plate. How many apples are there? How many grapes are there?

Independent Practice

Find each product.

13. 0×4 **14.** 1×6 **15.** 1×3 **16.** 3×0 **17.** 4×1

18. 0×9 **19.** 1×3 **20.** 1×7 **21.** 0×7 **22.** 8×0

23. 8×1 **24.** 0×2 **25.** 1×2 **26.** 9×0 **27.** 0×1

DIGITAL Animated Glossary **www.pearsonsuccessnet.com**

**For another example, see Set E on page 137.*

8 groups with 1 in each group equals 8 in all.

$8 \times 1 = 8$

Kira has 8 oranges.

1 plate with 8 oranges also equals 8 oranges.

$1 \times 8 = 8$

The **Identity (One) Property of Multiplication**: when you multiply a number and 1, the product is that number.

If Kira has 4 plates with 0 oranges on each plate, she has 0 oranges.

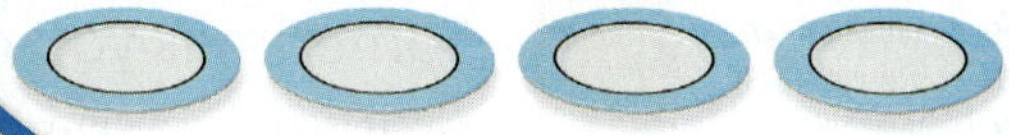

$4 \times 0 = 0$

If $4 \times 0 = 0$ then $0 \times 4 = 0$.

The Zero Property of Multiplication: when you multiply a number and 0, the product is 0.

Algebra Copy and complete. Write <, >, or = for each ◯.

28. 1×6 ◯ 8×0 **29.** 8×1 ◯ 1×9 **30.** 1×4 ◯ 4×1

31. 0×654 ◯ 346×0 **32.** 2×9 ◯ 9×1 **33.** 0×754 ◯ 5×1

Algebra Copy and complete. Write ×, +, or − for each ☐.

34. 4 ☐ 1 = 4
4 ☐ 1 = 5
4 ☐ 1 = 3

35. 4 ☐ 0 = 4
4 ☐ 0 = 0

36. 6 ☐ 1 = 5
6 ☐ 1 = 6
6 ☐ 1 = 7

Problem Solving

37. What is the missing factor?

SOL Prep

$548 \times \square = 548$

A 0 **B** 1 **C** 2 **D** 4

38. Writing to Explain The product of two factors is 0. One of the factors is 0. Can you tell what the other factor is? Explain your answer.

39. A unicycle relay team has 4 riders. Each rider has one unicycle. If each unicycle has 1 wheel, how many wheels does the team have?

40. Reasoning Why do you think the Identity Property of Multiplication is sometimes called the One Property of Multiplication?

41. Tickets for a school concert are free to students. The cost is $1 for each adult. What is the total cost of tickets for 2 adults and 5 students?

SOL Prep

A $7 **B** $5 **C** $2 **D** $1

42. The children in the 3rd-grade classes are having a bicycle parade. There are 5 rows of bikes with 8 bikes in each row. How many bikes in all are in the parade?

Virginia

Lesson 5-10

3.6 The student will represent multiplication and division, using area, set, and number line models, and create and solve problems that involve multiplication of two whole numbers, one factor 99 or less and the second factor 5 or less.

Problem Solving

Two-Question Problems

Sometimes you must use the answer to one problem to solve another problem.

Problem 1: Four girls and five boys went to the movies. How many children went to the movies?

Problem 2: Children's movie tickets cost $5 each. What was the total cost of the tickets for these children?

Guided Practice*

Do you know HOW?

1a. A movie ticket for an adult costs $9. How much do 3 adult tickets cost?

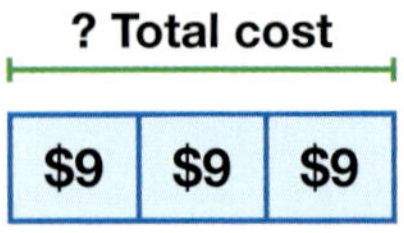

b. Mr. Jones paid for 3 adult tickets with $40. How much change will he get?

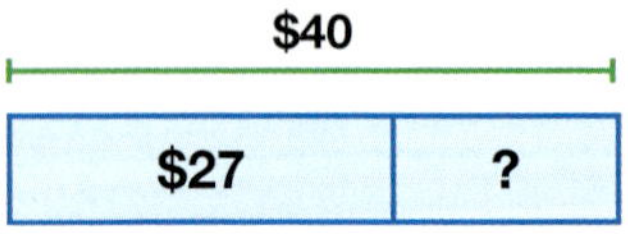

Do you UNDERSTAND?

2. What operations were used to solve Problems 1a and 1b? Tell why.

3. **Writing to Explain** Why must you solve Problem 1a before solving Problem 1b?

4. **Write a Problem** Write 2 problems that use the answer from the first problem to solve the second one.

Independent Practice

5a. Jared bought a baseball cap for $12 and a T-shirt for $19. How much did the items cost all together?

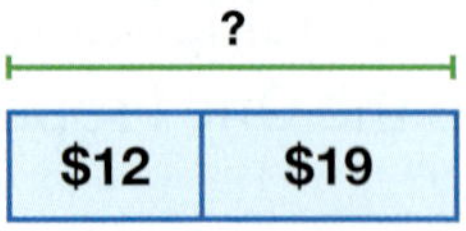

b. Suppose Jared paid with a $50 bill. How much change should he get?

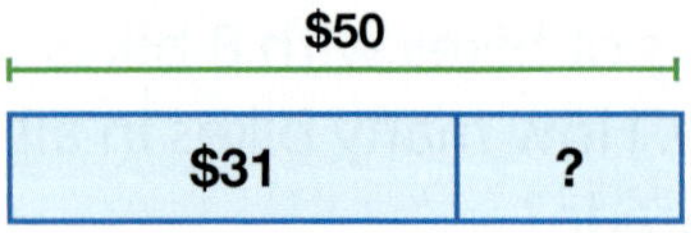

Stuck? Try this....

- What do I know?
- What am I asked to find?
- What diagram can I use to help understand the problem?
- Can I use addition, subtraction, multiplication, or division?
- Is all of my work correct?
- Did I answer the right question?
- Is my answer reasonable?

**For another example, see Set E on page 137.*

Solve

Problem 1

Four girls and five boys went to the movies. How many children went to the movies?

? Children in all

4 girls	5 boys

$4 + 5 = 9$

Nine children went to the movies.

Solve

Problem 2

Children's movie tickets cost $5 each. What was the total cost of the tickets for these children?

? Total cost

$5	$5	$5	$5	$5	$5	$5	$5	$5

$9 \times \$5 = \$45$

The total cost of the tickets was $45.

Independent Practice

Cara and some friends bought gifts in a museum shop. The gifts were from Hawaii. In **6–8**, use the answer from the first problem to solve the second problem.

6a. Cara bought a poster and a shirt. How much did her gifts cost?

b. Cara gave the clerk $30. How much change should she get?

7a. Dan bought 3 cups. How much did Dan spend on cups?

b. Dan also bought a CD. How much did Dan spend in all?

8a. Teri bought the most expensive and the least expensive gift. How much did she spend?

b. Teri's sister bought a CD. How much did the two girls spend in all?

9. On Monday, Roberta swam 10 laps. On Tuesday, she swam twice as many laps as on Monday. Which pair of number sentences can be used to find:

a how many laps Roberta swam on Tuesday?
b how many laps Roberta swam in all?

A $2 \times 10 = 20$
$20 + 10 = 30$

B $2 \times 10 = 20$
$20 - 10 = 10$

C $10 + 2 = 12$
$12 + 10 = 22$

D $10 + 2 = 12$
$12 - 10 = 2$

1. Which has the same value as 5×2? (5-1)

A $5 + 2$

B $2 + 2 + 2 + 2$

C $2 + 2 + 2 + 5$

D $2 + 2 + 2 + 2 + 2$

2. Which number sentence shows how to find 4 times as many books as the number of books shown below? (5-3)

A $4 + 8 = 12$

B $4 \times 8 = 32$

C $4 \times 9 = 36$

D $5 \times 8 = 40$

3. Which story could be solved with 7×8? (5-4)

A Ben bought 7 bags of apples. Each bag had 8 apples. How many apples did Ben buy?

B Rob has 7 red fish and 8 orange fish. How many fish does Rob have in all?

C Tao had 8 math problems to solve. He has solved 7 of them. How many does he have left?

D Max has 7 pages in his album. He has 8 pictures. How many pictures can he put on each page?

4. Which number makes the second number sentence true? (5-2)

$9 \times 7 = 63$

$7 \times \square = 63$

A 63

B 56

C 9

D 7

5. The 3rd graders at Willow School were put in 9 groups of 10. How many 3rd graders were there? (5-7)

A 19

B 90

C 99

D 900

6. Alice is buying paper cups for the picnic. Each package has 8 cups. How does the number of cups change as the number of packages increases by 1? (5-5)

Packages	1	2	3	4	5
Cups	8	16	24	32	40

A There are 40 more cups for each additional package.

B There are 40 fewer cups for each additional package.

C There are 8 more cups for each additional package.

D There are 8 fewer cups for each additional package.

7. Which symbol makes the number sentence true? (5-9)

$5 \times 0 \bigcirc 2 \times 1$

A $>$

B $<$

C $=$

D $\times$

8. For the 4th of July, Ron put flags in his yard as shown below. Which number sentence could be used to find how many flags Ron put in his yard? (5-2)

A $5 + 4 = \square$

B $4 \times 5 = \square$

C $4 + 5 = \square$

D $5 - 4 = \square$

9. Rosa bought all of the ribbon shown below. How many yards of ribbon did she buy? (5-6)

A 8

B 12

C 15

D 18

10. Todd has 7 aquariums. Each aquarium has 9 fish. What is the total number of fish? (5-8)

A 63

B 62

C 27

D 21

11. Len has 3 rolls of quarters. Ryan has 8 rolls. How many more rolls does Ryan have than Len? Each roll has $10 worth of quarters. In these rolls of quarters, how much more money does Ryan have than Len? (5-10)

A Ryan has 11 more rolls, so he has $110 more than Len.

B Ryan has 5 more rolls, so he has $55 more than Len.

C Ryan has 5 more rolls, so he has $50 more than Len.

D Ryan has 6 more rolls, so he has $60 more than Len.

12. Which of these best describes all of the snake lengths? (5-6)

Data

Snake	Length in Feet
Black Mamba	14
King Cobra	16
Taipan	10

A They are all greater than 12.

B They are all less than 15.

C They are all multiples of 5.

D They are all multiples of 2.

Set A, pages 108–112, 114–115

Find the total number of squares.

There are 3 groups of 2 squares.

Use addition to join groups: 2 + 2 + 2 = 6

Draw an array to show 3 × 2.

This array shows 3 rows of 2.

2 + 2 + 2 = 6 or 3 × 2 = 6.

Find twice as many as 6. Multiply by 2 to find *twice as many*.

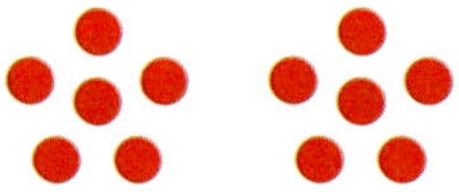

2 × 6 = 12

Remember that multiplication is a quick way of joining equal groups or comparing groups. Use the Commutative (order) Property of Multiplication.

Copy and complete.

1. 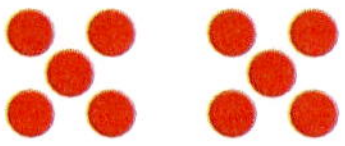

2 groups of ___
5 + ___ = ___
2 × ___ = ___

Draw an array to show each fact. Write the product.

2. 2 × 4 **3.** 3 × 5 **4.** 4 × 4

Find each amount. You may use drawings or counters to help.

5. 5 times as many as 4

6. Twice as many as 7

Set B, pages 116–120

Write a multiplication story for 3 × 5. Draw a picture to help find the product.

Jessica is putting pretzels into 3 bags. She will put 5 pretzels in each bag. How many pretzels does Jessica have in all?

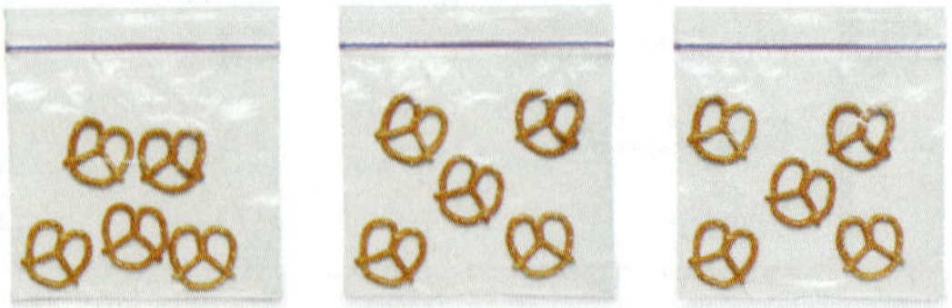

Jessica has 3 bags of pretzels. There are 5 pretzels in each bag.

5 + 5 + 5 = 15

Jessica has 15 pretzels.

Remember that another person should be able to follow your explanation.

Write a multiplication story for each problem. Solve. Explain your answer.

1. 3 × 9 **2.** 5 × 6 **3.** 7 × 2

Solve. Explain your answer.

4. Jack is setting up tables for a party. Each table has 6 chairs. How many chairs does he need for 10 tables?

Set C, pages 122–124, 126–129

Find 8×5.

You can use patterns to multiply by 5s.

- You can skip count: 5, 10, 15, 20, and so on.
- Each multiple of 5 ends with a 0 or a 5.
- Each multiple of 5 is 5 more than the one before it.

$8 \times 5 = 40$

Remember that making a table and using a pattern can help you to multiply by 2, 5, 9, or 10.

Find each product.

1. 2×4 **2.** 5×4 **3.** 5×9

4. 10×4 **5.** 9×4 **6.** 9×10

Set D, pages 130–131

Identity Property of Multiplication:
When you multiply a number and 1, the product is that number.

$1 \times 6 = 6$ $12 \times 1 = 12$

Zero Property of Multiplication:
When you multiply a number and 0, the product is 0.

$0 \times 6 = 0$ $12 \times 0 = 0$

Remember that you can think about an array with 1 row when you multiply by 1.

Find each product.

1. 7×0 **2.** 1×10 **3.** 0×9

4. 3×1 **5.** 7×0 **6.** 1×5

Set E, pages 132–133

In two-question problems, you must solve one problem before you can solve the other.

Problem 1: A family of 2 adults and 3 children went to an air show. How many family members went to the air show?
$2 + 3 = 5$

Problem 2: Each pass to the air show cost \$10. How much did the family spend on passes for the air show?
$5 \times \$10 = \$50$

The family spent a total of \$50.

Remember to solve the first problem before you try to solve the second problem.

1. a For lunch, Julia bought a sandwich for \$8 and a glass of juice for \$3. How much did her lunch cost?

b Julia paid with a \$20 bill. How much change will she get?

Topic 6

Multiplication Fact Strategies: Use Known Facts

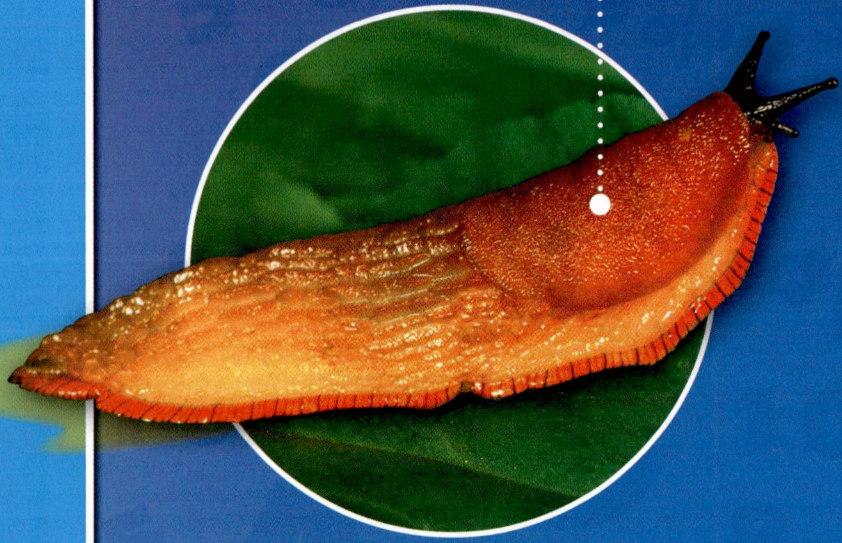

1 How many feelers do slugs have? You will find out in Lesson 6-2.

2 How many train layouts are at the National Toy Train Museum? You will find out in Lesson 6-3.

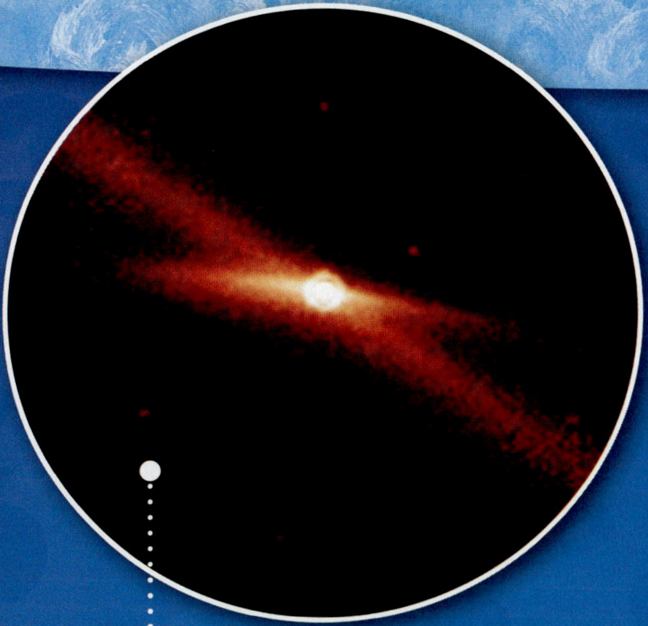

3

How long does Comet Encke take to orbit the Sun? You will find out in Lesson 6-1.

4

How much did miners pay for a glass of water during the California Gold Rush? You will find out in Lesson 6-4.

Review What You Know!

Vocabulary

Choose the best term from the box.

- addend
- array
- factor
- multiply

1. When you put together equal groups to get the total number, you _?_.

2. When numbers are multiplied, each number is called a(n) _?_.

3. When you display objects in rows and columns, you make a(n) _?_.

Multiplication

Find each product.

4. 3×2 **5.** 4×5 **6.** 7×2

7. 6×1 **8.** 8×0 **9.** 5×9

Arrays

Draw an array for each multiplication fact.

10. 6×2 **11.** 4×9

12. Write a multiplication number sentence for the array shown at the right. Explain why you used the numbers you did.

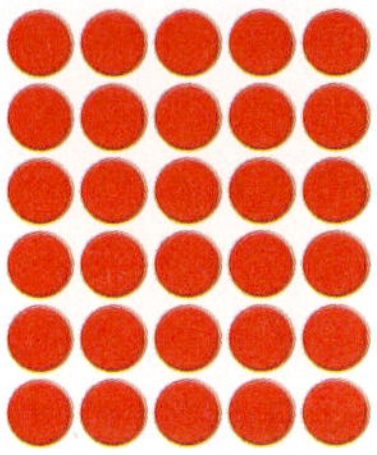

13. **Writing to Explain** Is an array for 2×9 the same as or different from an array for 9×2? Draw a picture and explain your answer.

Virginia

Lesson 6-1

3.5 The student will recall multiplication facts through the twelves table, and the corresponding division facts.

3 as a Factor

Hands-On
counters

How can you break apart arrays to multiply with 3?

The canoes are stored in 3 rows. There are 6 canoes in each row. What is the total number of canoes stored?

Find 3×6.

Choose an Operation Multiply to find the total for an array.

Guided Practice*

Do you know HOW?

In **1–6**, multiply. You may use counters or draw pictures to help.

1. 3×4

2. 3×10

3. 3×5

4. 3×9

5. $\begin{array}{r} 12 \\ \times\ 3 \\ \hline \end{array}$

6. $\begin{array}{r} 3 \\ \times\ 6 \\ \hline \end{array}$

Do you UNDERSTAND?

7. How can you use $2 \times 8 = 16$ to find 3×8?

8. Selena arranged plants in 3 rows at the community garden. She put 6 plants in each row. How many plants in all did Selena arrange into the rows?

Independent Practice

In **9–28**, find the product. You may draw pictures to help.

9. 3×2

10. 4×9

11. 10×3

12. 2×9

13. 1×3

14. 8×3

15. 2×7

16. 5×3

17. 0×3

18. 3×8

19. $\begin{array}{r} 7 \\ \times 3 \\ \hline \end{array}$

20. $\begin{array}{r} 9 \\ \times 8 \\ \hline \end{array}$

21. $\begin{array}{r} 3 \\ \times 3 \\ \hline \end{array}$

22. $\begin{array}{r} 5 \\ \times 4 \\ \hline \end{array}$

23. $\begin{array}{r} 3 \\ \times 9 \\ \hline \end{array}$

24. $\begin{array}{r} 1 \\ \times 3 \\ \hline \end{array}$

25. $\begin{array}{r} 6 \\ \times 3 \\ \hline \end{array}$

26. $\begin{array}{r} 9 \\ \times 5 \\ \hline \end{array}$

27. $\begin{array}{r} 3 \\ \times 4 \\ \hline \end{array}$

28. $\begin{array}{r} 3 \\ \times 7 \\ \hline \end{array}$

DIGITAL
eTools
www.pearsonsuccessnet.com

**For another example, see Set A on page 160.*

What You Show

Find 3 × 6.

Use 1s facts and 2s facts to help multiply with 3.

Make an array for each multiplication sentence.

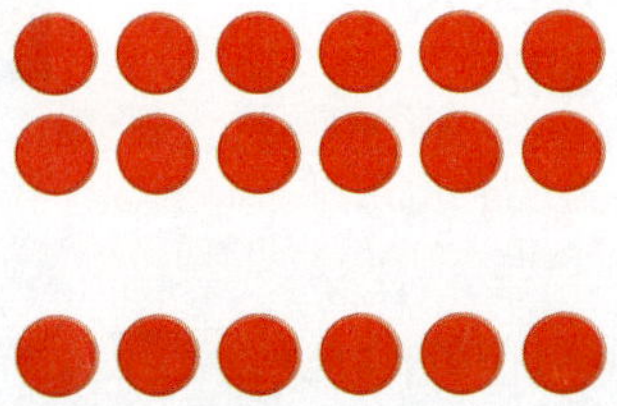

$2 \times 6 = 12$

$1 \times 6 = 6$

$12 + 6 = 18$

What You Think

3 × 6 is 3 rows of 6. That is 2 sixes plus 1 more six.

2 sixes are 12.
1 six is 6.

$12 + 6 = 18$

$3 \times 6 = 18$

There are 18 canoes in all.

Problem Solving

For **29** and **30**, use the table at the right.

29. What is the total number of stamps in a package of car stamps and a package of outer space stamps?

30. Cara bought 1 package of reptile stamps. What is the total number of reptile stamps she bought? Draw an array.

Data

Number of Stamps in Different Packages

Kind of Stamp	Number of Rows	Number in Each Row
Dinosaurs	3	7
Cars	3	9
Outer Space	3	8
Reptiles	5	6

31. Number Sense Suppose you need to find 3 × 9.

a What two multiplication facts can help you find 3 × 9?

b How could you use 3 × 9 to help you find 9 × 3?

32. SOL Prep It takes about 3 years for Comet Encke to orbit the Sun. About how many years will it take Comet Encke to orbit the Sun 5 times?

A About 5 years

B About 10 years

C About 15 years

D About 20 years

33. SOL Prep Mr. Torres had packages of tomatoes on the counter. Each package had 3 tomatoes in it.

If Mr. Torres counted the tomatoes in groups of 3, which list shows numbers he could have named?

A 6, 12, 16, 19

B 6, 9, 12, 15

C 3, 6, 10, 13

D 3, 7, 11, 15

Virginia

Lesson 6-2

3.5 The student will recall multiplication facts through the twelves table, and the corresponding division facts.

4 as a Factor

Hands-On
counters

How can you use doubles to multiply with 4?

Anna painted piggy banks to sell at the student art show. She painted a bank on each of the 7 days of the week for 4 weeks. How many piggy banks did she paint in all?

Find 4×7.

Choose an Operation Multiply to find the total for an array.

Guided Practice*

Do you know HOW?

In **1–6**, multiply. You may use counters or draw pictures to help.

1. 4×6

2. 5×4

3. 4×9

4. 1×4

5. $\begin{array}{r} 1 \\ \times 4 \\ \hline \end{array}$

6. $\begin{array}{r} 10 \\ \times \ 4 \\ \hline \end{array}$

Do you UNDERSTAND?

7. Besides the way shown above, what is another way to break apart 4×7 using facts you know?

8. If you know $2 \times 8 = 16$, how can you find 4×8?

9. Nolan made lamps to sell at the school art show. He made 9 lamps each week for 4 weeks. How many lamps did Nolan make in all?

Independent Practice

In **10–29**, find the product. You may draw pictures to help.

10. 4×8 **11.** 3×8 **12.** 4×3 **13.** 6×4 **14.** 9×6

15. 4×4 **16.** 5×9 **17.** 1×4 **18.** 0×4 **19.** 2×10

20. 3×4 **21.** 2×8 **22.** 4×5 **23.** 7×4 **24.** 4×1

25. $\begin{array}{r} 2 \\ \times 4 \\ \hline \end{array}$ **26.** $\begin{array}{r} 7 \\ \times 4 \\ \hline \end{array}$ **27.** $\begin{array}{r} 9 \\ \times 4 \\ \hline \end{array}$ **28.** $\begin{array}{r} 10 \\ \times \ 7 \\ \hline \end{array}$ **29.** $\begin{array}{r} 4 \\ \times 8 \\ \hline \end{array}$

DIGITAL eTools **www.pearsonsuccessnet.com**

*For another example, see Set B on page 160.

What You Show

Find 4×7.

To multiply by 4, you can think of a 2s fact, then double it.

You can make arrays.

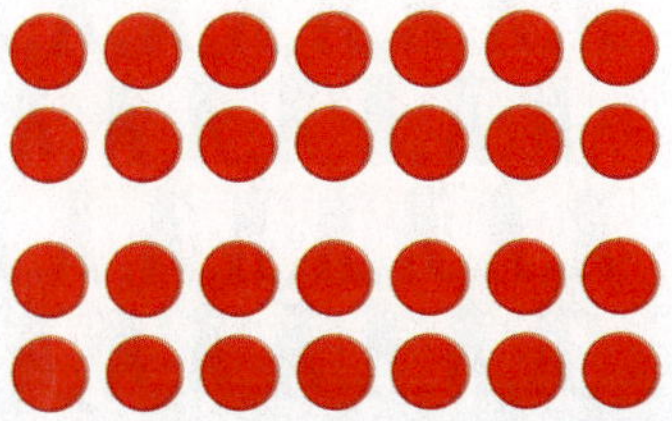

$2 \times 7 = 14$

$2 \times 7 = 14$

$14 + 14 = 28$

What You Think

4×7 is 4 rows of 7. That is 2 sevens plus 2 sevens.

2 sevens are 14.

$14 + 14 = 28$

So, $4 \times 7 = 28$.

Anna painted 28 piggy banks in all.

Problem Solving

For **30** and **31**, use the table at the right for the supplies James needs to buy for the Trail Walk trip.

30. What is the total number of cereal bars he needs to buy?

31. How many more apples than juice drinks does James need?

Data

Trail Walk Trip Supplies

Item	Number of Packages Needed	Number of Items in Each Package
Apples	2	8
Cereal Bars	4	6
Juice Drinks	4	3

32. Martin studied slugs in science class. He learned that each slug has 4 feelers. That evening, he saw 8 slugs. How many feelers did the slugs have in all?

33. **Writing to Explain** Lila had 9 weeks of rock climbing lessons. She had 4 lessons each week. Explain why Lila can use 4×9 to find the product of 9×4.

34. Which of these best describes all the numbers on the shirts?

A They are all even numbers.

B They are all multiples of 3.

C They are all greater than 10.

D They are all 2-digit numbers.

35. SOL Prep Bess had boxes of candles on the table. Each box had 4 candles in it.

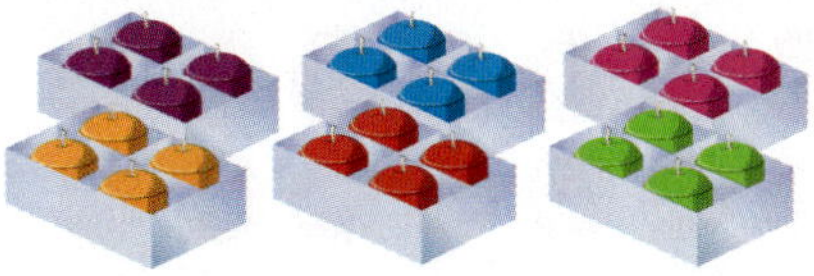

If Bess counted the candles in groups of 4, which list shows numbers she could have named?

A 8, 12, 16, 20

B 8, 12, 14, 18

C 4, 6, 12, 14

D 4, 8, 10, 14

Virginia

Lesson 6-3

3.5 The student will recall multiplication facts through the twelves table, and the corresponding division facts.

6 and 7 as Factors

Hands-On
counters

How can you break apart arrays to multiply?

The members of the band march in 6 equal rows. There are 8 band members in each row. How many are in the band?

Find 6×8.

Choose an Operation Multiply to find the total for an array.

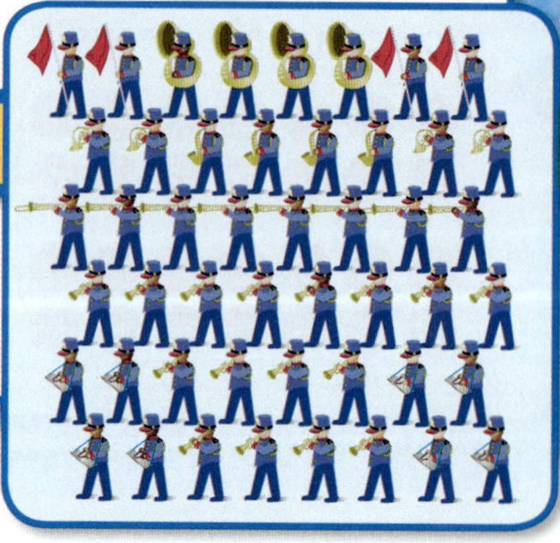

Another Example

How can you break apart arrays to multiply by 7?

The singers in the chorus are standing in equal rows. There are 8 singers in each row. There are 7 rows. How many singers are in the chorus?

What You Show

Find 7×8.

Use 5s facts and 2s facts to help multiply with 7. Make an array for each multiplication sentence.

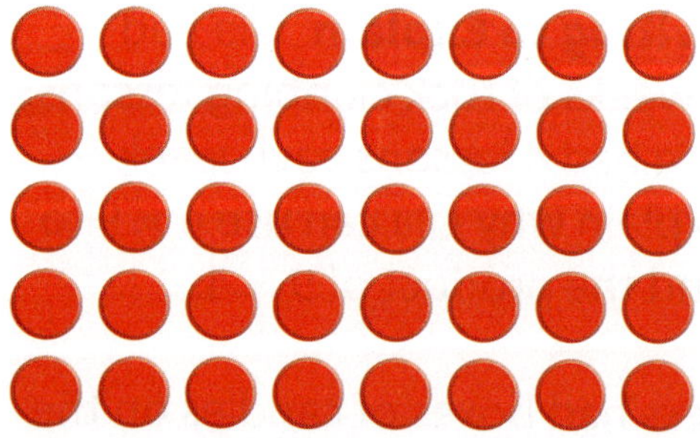

$5 \times 8 = 40$

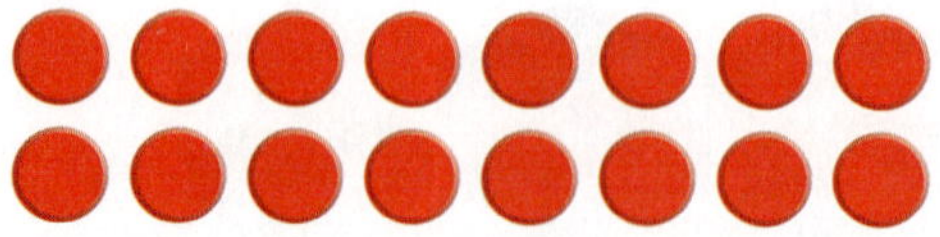

$2 \times 8 = 16$

What You Think

7×8 is 7 rows of 8.

That is 5 eights plus 2 eights.

5 eights are 40.
2 eights are 16.

$40 + 16 = 56$

So, $7 \times 8 = 56$.

The chorus has 56 singers.

Explain It

1. What other multiplication facts might help to find 7×8?
2. How could you use 5×7 and 2×7 to find 7×7?

What You Show

Find 6×8.

Use 5s facts and 1s facts.

Make an array for each multiplication sentence.

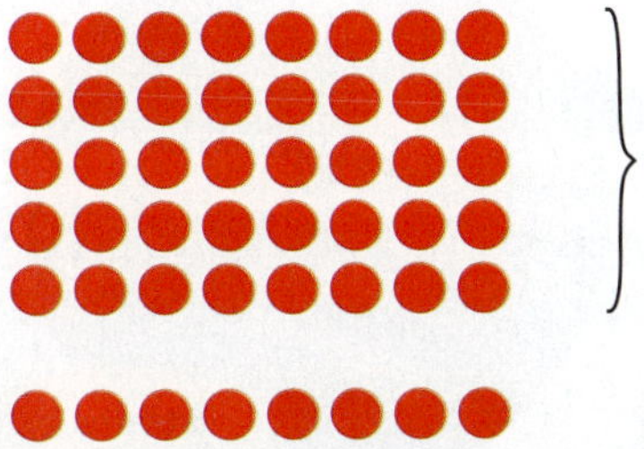

$5 \times 8 = 40$

$1 \times 8 = 8$

What You Think

6×8 is 6 rows of 8. That is 5 eights plus 1 more eight.

5 eights are 40.
8 more is 48.
$40 + 8 = 48$

So, $6 \times 8 = 48$.

The band has 48 members.

Guided Practice*

Do you know HOW?

In **1–6**, multiply. You may draw pictures or use counters to help.

1. 6×10

2. 7×6

3. $\begin{array}{r} 7 \\ \times\ 6 \\ \hline \end{array}$

4. $\begin{array}{r} 9 \\ \times\ 7 \\ \hline \end{array}$

5. Find 4 times 7.

6. Multiply 6 and 5.

Do you UNDERSTAND?

7. Writing to Explain Draw a picture of two arrays that show that 6×9 is equal to 5×9 plus 1×9. Explain your drawing.

8. The students who are graduating are standing in 7 equal rows. There are 9 students in each row. How many students are graduating?

Independent Practice

In **9–23**, find the product. You may draw pictures to help.

9. 6×7 **10.** 7×9 **11.** 9×6 **12.** 8×7 **13.** 6×4

14. 6×6 **15.** 10×7 **16.** 8×6 **17.** 7×7 **18.** 7×3

19. $\begin{array}{r} 5 \\ \times\ 7 \\ \hline \end{array}$ **20.** $\begin{array}{r} 3 \\ \times\ 6 \\ \hline \end{array}$ **21.** $\begin{array}{r} 4 \\ \times\ 7 \\ \hline \end{array}$ **22.** $\begin{array}{r} 7 \\ \times\ 8 \\ \hline \end{array}$ **23.** $\begin{array}{r} 10 \\ \times\ 6 \\ \hline \end{array}$

DIGITAL eTools www.pearsonsuccessnet.com

*For another example, see Set C on page 160.

Problem Solving

24. The National Toy Train Museum has 5 large layouts for trains. One day, each layout had the same number of trains. Use the picture on the right to find how many trains were on display at the museum that day.

25. **Number Sense** Marge says that 1×0 is equal to $1 + 0$. Is she correct? Why or why not?

26. Miguel had baskets of oranges. Each held 6 oranges.

SOL Prep

If Miguel counted the oranges in groups of 6, which list shows the numbers he would have named?

A 6, 12, 21, 26, 32

B 6, 11, 16, 21, 26

C 12, 16, 20, 24, 28

D 6, 12, 18, 24, 30

27. **Writing to Explain** Nan made the arrays shown to find 6×3. Explain how to change the arrays to find 7×3. Use objects and draw a picture.

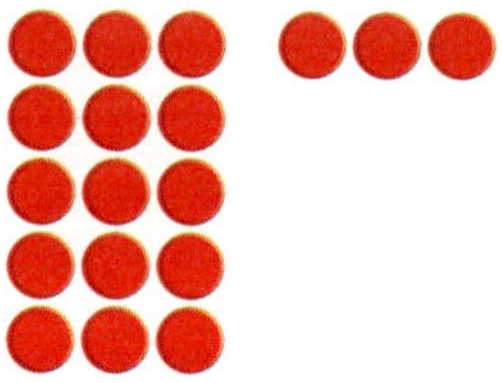

For **28** and **29**, use the drawings of the trains below.

28. A group of tourists needs 7 rows of seats in Car 5 of the Réseau train.

a How many seats will this group need?

b How many seats are left on this train for other passengers?

29. **Estimation** Use rounding to the nearest ten to find about how many seats in all are on the Réseau and the Sud-Est trains.

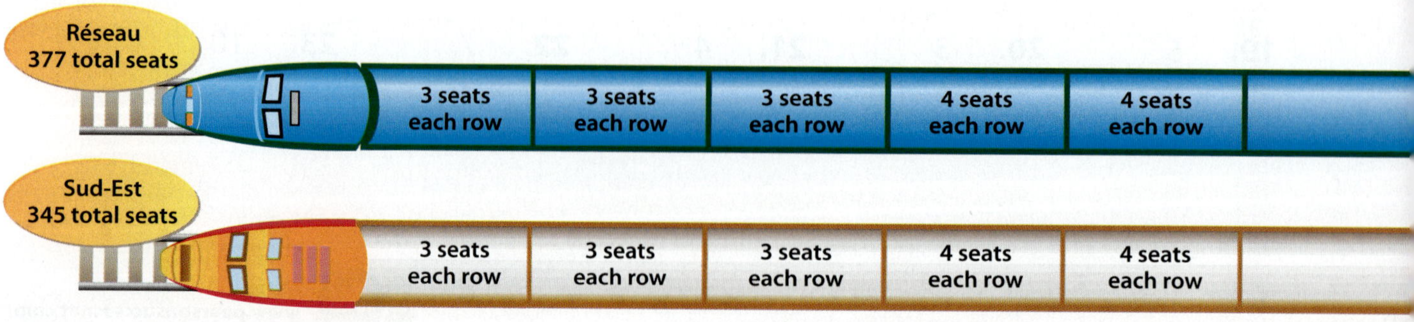

Algebra Connections

Missing Operations

In a number sentence with the = symbol, both sides of the number sentence must have the same value. An operation symbol such as +, −, or × tells how to find that value. Reasoning can help you decide which operation symbol is missing.

Example: $72 = 8 \square 9$

Think: 72 is equal to 8 (plus or minus or multiplied by) 9?

Since $8 \times 9 = 72$, write "×."

$72 = 8 \boxed{\times} 9$

Copy and complete. Replace the square with +, −, or ×. Check your answers.

1. $9 \square 36 = 45$

2. $24 \square 17 = 7$

3. $16 = 2 \square 8$

4. $8 = 32 \square 24$

5. $7 \square 5 = 35$

6. $50 = 12 \square 38$

7. $18 = 9 \square 2$

8. $64 \square 36 = 28$

9. $30 = 6 \square 5$

10. $47 \square 37 = 84$

11. $63 = 9 \square 7$

12. $12 \square 1 = 12$

For **13** and **14**, copy and complete the number sentence below each problem. Use it to help find your answer.

13. Lisa had some pens left after she gave 27 pens to her friends. She started with a package of 36 pens. What operation can you use to find the number of pens Lisa had left?

$9 = 36 \square 27$

14. The picture below shows the number of each kind of button in a package. What operation can you use to find the total number of buttons in one package?

$45 = 5 \square 9$

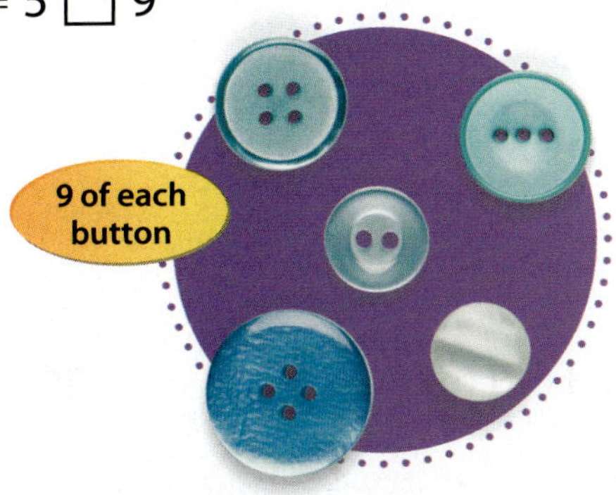

15. **Write a Problem** Write a problem using the number sentence below.

$48 = 26 + 22$

Virginia

Lesson 6-4

3.5 The student will recall multiplication facts through the twelves table, and the corresponding division facts.

8 as a Factor

How can you use doubles to multiply with 8?

At the school fun fair, students try to toss a table tennis ball into a bowl. There are 8 rows of bowls. There are 8 bowls in each row. How many bowls are there in all?

Choose an Operation Multiply to find the total for an array. Find 8×8.

Guided Practice*

Do you know HOW?

In **1–6**, multiply.

1. 8×7

2. 8×4

3. 6×8

4. 10×8

5. 9×8

6. 8×3

Do you UNDERSTAND?

7. How could the fact that $5 \times 8 = 40$ help you find 8×8?

8. How can you use 4×7 to find 8×7?

9. Mrs. Reyes needs to order bricks for her garden. She needs 8 rows of bricks. Each row will have 7 bricks. How many bricks in all should Mrs. Reyes order?

Independent Practice

In **10–27**, find the product.

10. 8×4 **11.** 1×8 **12.** 2×9 **13.** 5×7 **14.** 8×2

15. 8×6 **16.** 5×9 **17.** 8×5 **18.** 0×8 **19.** 4×9

20. 10×8 **21.** 3×7 **22.** 8×8 **23.** 2×4 **24.** 9×8

25. Find 6 times 9. **26.** Multiply 8 and 1. **27.** Find 9 times 8.

*For another example, see Set C on page 160.

One Way

Use 2s facts to find 8×8.

8×8 is 4 groups of 2 eights.

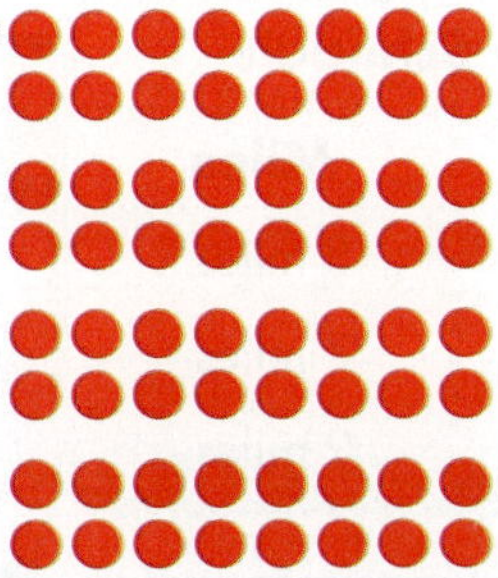

$2 \times 8 = 16$

$2 \times 8 = 16$

$2 \times 8 = 16$

$2 \times 8 = 16$

$16 + 16 + 16 + 16 = 64$

Another Way

Double a 4s fact to find 8×8.

8×8 is 4 eights plus 4 eights.

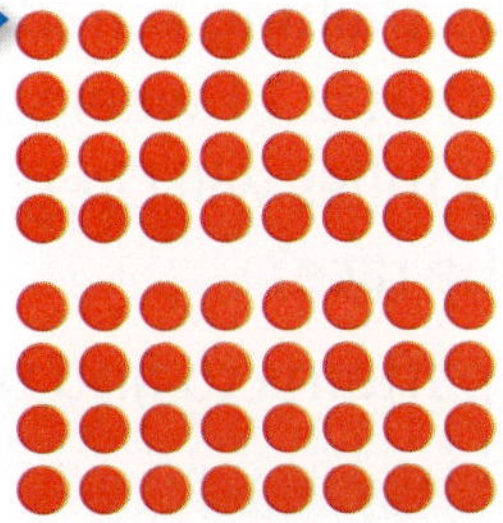

$4 \times 8 = 32$

$4 \times 8 = 32$

Double the product.

$32 + 32 = 64$

So, $8 \times 8 = 64$.

There are 64 bowls in all.

Problem Solving

For **28–30**, find the total number of tiles.

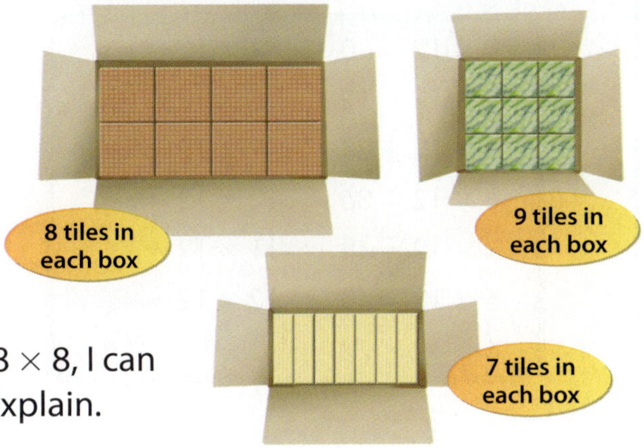

28. Mischa bought 8 boxes of orange tiles.

29. Aaron bought 6 boxes of yellow tiles.

30. Liz bought 7 boxes of green tiles.

31. **Writing to Explain** Sophi says, "To find 8×8, I can find 2×8 and double it." Do you agree? Explain.

For **32** and **33**, use the table at the right.

32. **Algebra** The total amount of money Nate spent at the clothing sale is $(2 \times \$9) + \$42$. What did he buy?

33. Willa bought a shirt and a sweater. She had $14 left. How much money did she start with?

Data

Clothing Sale	
Shirt	$23
Belt	$9
Sweater	$38
Pair of jeans	$42

34. Ms. Vero had boxes of crayons in a closet. Each box had 8 crayons in it. If Ms. Vero counted the crayons in groups of 8, which list shows the numbers she would have named?

A 8, 16, 28, 32, 40, 48

B 8, 14, 18, 24, 32, 40

C 16, 20, 24, 28, 32, 36

D 8, 16, 24, 32, 40, 48

35. During the California Gold Rush, miners sometimes paid $10 for a glass of water. What was the total cost if 8 miners each bought one glass of water?

Virginia

Lesson 6-5

3.5 The student will recall multiplication facts through the twelves table, and the corresponding division facts. **(Also 3.6)**

11 and 12 as Factors

What are the patterns in multiples of 11 and 12?

Greg's training schedule is for a race that is 11 weeks away. How many miles will Greg swim to train for the race?

Use patterns to find the product 8×11.

Data

Weekly Schedule

Activity	Miles
Swimming	8 miles
Running	7 miles
Biking	9 miles

Another Example What are the patterns in multiples of 12?

Data

$0 \times 12 = 0$	$7 \times 12 =$ ☐
$1 \times 12 = 12$	$8 \times 12 =$ ☐
$2 \times 12 = 24$	$9 \times 12 =$ ☐
$3 \times 12 = 36$	$10 \times 12 =$ ☐
$4 \times 12 = 48$	$11 \times 12 =$ ☐
$5 \times 12 = 60$	$12 \times 12 =$ ☐
$6 \times 12 = 72$	

To multiply any factor by 12, first multiply that factor by 10. Then multiply that factor by 2 and add the two products.

Example: $3 \times 12 = (3 \times 10) + (3 \times 2)$

Find: 7×12.

$7 \times 10 = 70$ and $7 \times 2 = 14$

$70 + 14 = 84$

So, $7 \times 12 = 84$.

Guided Practice*

Do you know HOW?

Use patterns to find each product.

1. 8×12 **2.** 9×12

3. 9×11 **4.** 11×11

Do you UNDERSTAND?

5. Writing to Explain How can you use a pattern to find 12×11?

6. How many miles will Greg bike in 12 weeks?

Independent Practice

Use patterns to find each product.

7. 7×11 **8.** 11×9 **9.** 6×11 **10.** 12×11 **11.** 8×11

12. 11×12 **13.** 10×12 **14.** 11×5 **15.** 10×11 **16.** 12×12

*For another example, see Set D on page 161.

$0 \times 11 = 0$	$6 \times 11 = 66$
$1 \times 11 = 11$	$7 \times 11 = 77$
$2 \times 11 = 22$	$8 \times 11 =$ ☐
$3 \times 11 = 33$	$9 \times 11 =$ ☐
$4 \times 11 = 44$	$10 \times 11 =$ ☐
$5 \times 11 = 55$	$11 \times 11 =$ ☐

Look at the patterns in the table.

$2 \times 11 = 20 + 2$ (where $20 = 2 \times 10$)

$3 \times 11 = 30 + 3$ (where $30 = 3 \times 10$)

To multiply any factor by 11, first multiply that factor by 10. Then add that factor to the product.

$8 \times 10 = 80 \rightarrow 80 + 8 = 88 \rightarrow 8 \times 11 = 88$

Greg will swim 88 miles.

Problem Solving

Use the table at the right for **17** and **18**. It shows the food that was bought for 96 third graders for a school picnic.

Food Item	Number of Packages	Number in Each Package
Hot Dogs	8	12
Rolls	12	9
Juice Boxes	12	11

17. Find the total number of each item bought.

a Hot dogs

b Rolls

c Juice boxes

18. How many extra juice boxes were bought?

19. **Writing to Explain** Look at the table at the top of page 150. Greg multiplied 2×11 to find how many more miles he biked than he ran in 11 weeks. Does that make sense? Why or why not?

20. **Strategy Focus** Solve. Use the strategy Draw a Picture.

Mai had 3 packs of pens. Each pack had 11 pens. She gave 5 pens to Ervin. How many pens did she have left?

21. **Number Sense** Raul has only dimes in his pocket. Could he have exactly 45 cents? Explain.

22. **Algebra** Which symbol makes the number sentence true?

$8 \square 5 = 40$

A $+$ **B** $-$ **C** $\times$ **D** $\div$

23. Suppose a worker building one of the first railroads hammered 10 spikes into each railroad tie. How many spikes did he need for 7 ties?

Virginia

Lesson 6-6

Extends 3.6 The student will represent multiplication and division, using area, set, and number line models, and create and solve problems that involve multiplication of two whole numbers, one factor 99 or less and the second factor 5 or less.

Multiplying with 3 Factors

How can you multiply 3 numbers?

Drew is joining 3 sections of a quilt. Each section has 2 rows with 4 squares in each row. How many squares in all are in these 3 sections?

Find $3 \times 2 \times 4$.

Guided Practice*

Do you know HOW?

In **1–6**, multiply. You may use objects or draw a picture to help.

1. $2 \times 4 \times 2$

2. $3 \times 4 \times 3$

3. $2 \times 2 \times 3$

4. $2 \times 5 \times 2$

5. $3 \times 2 \times 4$

6. $2 \times 6 \times 2$

Do you UNDERSTAND?

7. In the example above, if you find 3×4 first, do you get the same product? Explain.

8. Sara has 4 quilt pieces. Each piece has 3 rows with 3 squares in each row. How many squares are in Sara's quilt pieces?

Independent Practice

In **9–16**, find the product. You may draw a picture to help.

9. $2 \times 3 \times 2$

10. $5 \times 2 \times 2$

11. $3 \times 6 \times 1$

12. $3 \times 3 \times 2$

13. $2 \times 2 \times 2$

14. $2 \times 3 \times 4$

15. $3 \times 3 \times 3$

16. $6 \times 2 \times 2$

In **17–22**, write the missing number.

17. $3 \times (2 \times 5) = 30$, so $(3 \times 2) \times 5 = \square$

18. $5 \times (7 \times 2) = (7 \times 2) \times \square$

19. $4 \times (2 \times 2) = 16$, so $(4 \times 2) \times 2 = \square$

20. $8 \times (3 \times 6) = (8 \times 3) \times \square$

21. $(7 \times 3) \times 4 = \square \times (3 \times 4)$

22. $5 \times (2 \times 9) = (5 \times \square) \times 9$

DIGITAL Animated Glossary **www.pearsonsuccessnet.com**

For another example, see Set E on page 161.

One Way

Find 3×2 first.

$(3 \times 2) \times 4$

$6 \quad \times 4 = 24$

6 rows, 4 squares in each row

There are 24 squares in all.

Another Way

Find 2×4 first.

$3 \times (2 \times 4)$

$3 \times \quad 8 = 24$ 3 sections, 8 squares in each section

There are 24 squares in Drew's quilt.

The **Associative (Grouping) Property of Multiplication** says that you can change the grouping of the factors and the product will be the same.

Problem Solving

For **23–25**, find the total number of eggs.

23. There are 8 mockingbird nests at a park. Each nest has 5 eggs.

24. At another park, there are 3 mockingbird nests with 4 eggs in each nest, and 2 more nests with 3 eggs in each.

25. **Estimation** About how many eggs would you find in 10 nests?

26. **Reasonableness** Anita says the product of $5 \times 2 \times 3$ is less than 20. Do you agree? Explain.

For **27** and **28**, use the table at the right.

27. Ellis bought 3 packs of baseball cards and 2 packs of basketball cards. How many cards did he buy in all?

28. Mandy bought 1 pack of each of the four kinds of cards. What is the total number of cards she bought?

Data

Sports Card Sale

Kind of Cards	Number of Cards in Each Pack
Baseball	8
Basketball	5
Football	7
Hockey	6

SOL Prep

29. Which number makes this number sentence true?

$4 \times (3 \times 2) = (4 \times \square) \times 2$

A 12 **B** 7 **C** 3 **D** 2

Lesson 6-7

Prepares for 4.4.d
The student will solve single-step and multistep addition, subtraction, and multiplication problems with whole numbers.

Problem Solving

Multiple-Step Problems

Some word problems have hidden questions that need to be answered before you can solve the problem.

Keisha bought 2 yards of felt to make some puppets. Tanya bought 6 yards of felt. The felt cost $3 a yard. How much did the two girls spend on felt?

Another Example

Keisha plans to make 3 puppets. Tanya will make 3 times as many puppets as Keisha. Each puppet needs 2 buttons for its eyes. How many buttons will Tanya need?

Find and solve the hidden question.

How many puppets will Tanya make?

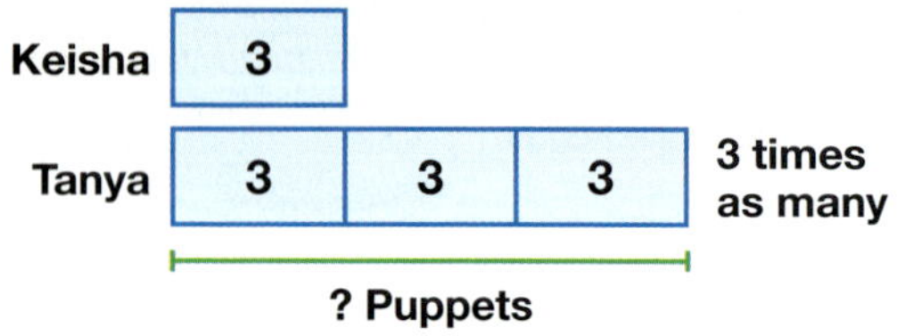

3×3 puppets $= 9$ puppets

Tanya will make 9 puppets.

Use the answer to the hidden question to solve the problem.

How many buttons will Tanya need?

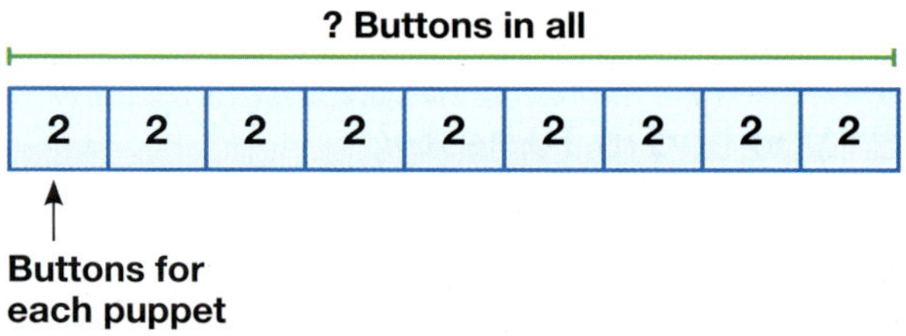

9×2 buttons $= 18$ buttons

Tanya will need 18 buttons.

Explain It

1. Philip wrote $3 + 3 + 3 = \square$ instead of $3 \times 3 = \square$ for the diagram for the hidden question. Is his number sentence correct? Why or why not?
2. **Number Sense** What number sentences could you write to find how many buttons both girls need? Explain your thinking.

Find and solve the hidden question.

How much felt did the girls buy in all?

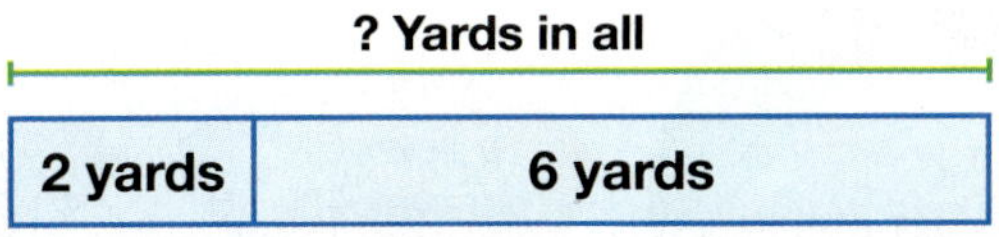

2 yards + 6 yards = 8 yards

The girls bought 8 yards of felt.

Use the answer to the hidden question to solve the problem.

How much did the girls spend in all?

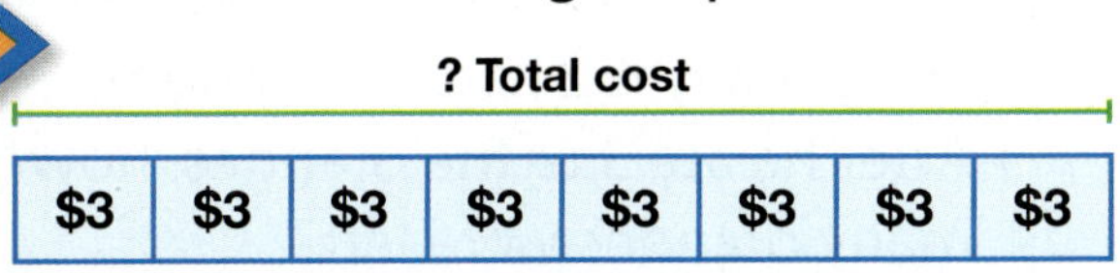

$8 \times \$3 = \$24$

The two girls spent $24 on felt.

Guided Practice*

Do you know HOW?

1. Keisha bought glue for $3, sequins for $6, and lace for $4 to decorate her puppets. She paid for these items with a $20 bill. How much change should she get?

Tip *The hidden question is "What is the total cost of the three items?"*

Do you UNDERSTAND?

2. Describe another way to solve the problem above about buying felt.

3. **Write a Problem** Write a problem that has a hidden question. Then solve your problem.

Independent Practice

4. The library has 4 videos and some books about dinosaurs. There are 5 times as many books as videos. After 3 of the books were checked out, how many were left? The diagram below helps you answer the hidden question. Draw a diagram and solve the problem.

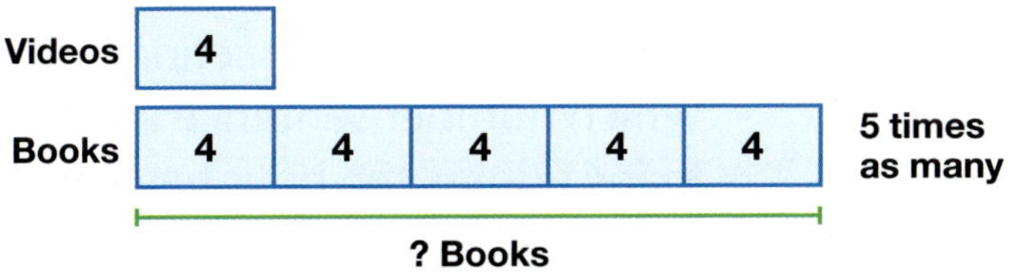

Stuck? Try this....

- What do I know?
- What am I asked to find?
- What diagram can I use to help understand the problem?
- Can I use addition, subtraction, multiplication, or division?
- Is all of my work correct?
- Did I answer the right question?
- Is my answer reasonable?

*For another example, see Set F on page 161.

Independent Practice

Use the pictures for **5–8**.

5. Craig bought 2 bags of oranges. After he ate 3 of the oranges, how many oranges were left?

Tip *First find how many oranges Craig bought.*

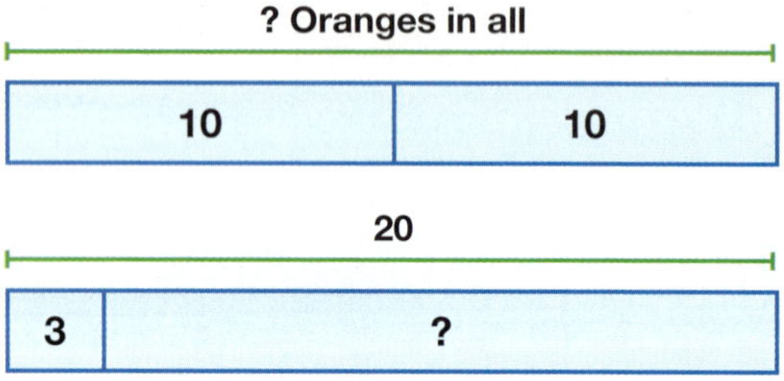

6. Delia bought 2 bags of lemons and 3 bags of apples. How much did she spend on fruit?

7. Mrs. Evans bought 2 bags of oranges and 2 bags of lemons. How many pieces of fruit did she buy?

8. Mr. Day bought a bag each of apples, oranges, and lemons. He paid with a $20 bill. What change should he get?

9. **Writing to Explain** Which costs more, 30 oranges or 30 lemons? How much more? Explain how you found your answer.

Think About the Process

10. Al had $38. He spent $4 on an action figure and $10 on a board game. Which number sentence shows how much money Al has left?

A $38 + $4 + $10 = ▢

B $38 − ($4 + $10) = ▢

C $38 − $4 = ▢

D 38 + $10 = ▢

11. Jose has 4 action figures. His brother has 3 times as many action figures. Which number sentence shows how many figures the boys have in all?

A $4 + 3 =$ ▢

B $4 \times 3 =$ ▢

C $4 - 3 =$ ▢

D $4 + (3 \times 4) =$ ▢

Going Digital

Using Known Facts

Use eTools

Counters

Use known facts to find 4 × 6 and 6 × 7.

Step 1 Go to the Counters eTool. Select the two-part workspace. Use 2 × 6 to find 4 × 6. Select a counter. Show two rows of 6 counters in the left side. Look at the odometer. You see that 2 × 6 = 12. Show the same rows on the right side. There are 4 rows of 6 counters in all. 4 × 6 = 24, and 12 + 12 = 24.

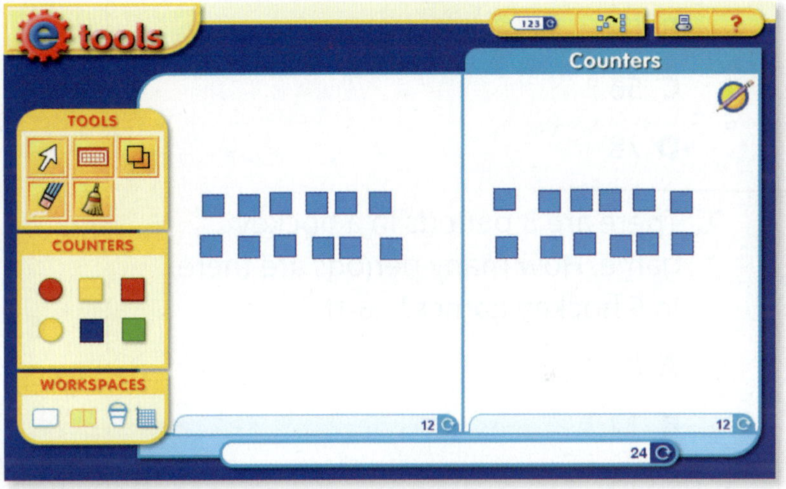

Step 2 Use the broom tool to clear one side of the workspace. Select the other side and use the broom tool again, to clear it. Use 5 × 7 and 1 × 7 to find 6 × 7. Show 5 rows of 7 counters on one side of the workspace. Look at the odometer to find that 5 × 7 = 35. Show 1 row of 7 counters on the other side. There are 6 rows of 7 counters in all. 6 × 7 = 42, and 35 + 7 = 42.

Practice

Use the Counters eTool and known facts to find each product. Explain how you found the product.

1. 4 × 9

2. 8 × 8

3. 6 × 8

4. 7 × 7

Topic 6

VA SOL Test Prep

1. Last summer, Martin walked the 8-mile Wolf Mountain Trail 7 times. How many total miles did he walk on the trail? (6-3)

A 15

B 54

C 56

D 78

2. There are 3 periods in a hockey game. How many periods are there in 5 hockey games? (6-1)

A 8

B 12

C 15

D 18

3. Which shows a way to find 4×6? (6-2)

A $4 + 6$

B $12 + 12$

C $6 + 6 + 6$

D $12 + 2$

4. Jon bought 3 packages of invitations. Each package had 8 invitations. He sent out 20 invitations. Which shows one way to find how many are left? (6-7)

A Multiply 3 by 8 and then subtract 20.

B Multiply 3 by 20 and then subtract 8.

C Multiply 5 by 8 and then add 20.

D Multiply 3 by 8 and then add 20.

5. If you count the muffins below in groups of 6, which list shows numbers you would name? (6-3)

A 6, 12, 16, 24

B 6, 12, 16, 22

C 12, 18, 24, 32

D 12, 18, 24, 30

6. Sven feeds his fish 2 food pellets 3 times a day. How many pellets does he feed them in 7 days? (6-6)

A 13

B 14

C 21

D 42

7. What number makes the number sentence true? (6-6)

$6 \times (9 \times 2) = (6 \times 9) \times \square$

A 2

B 6

C 9

D 54

8. The 3rd graders formed 11 groups with 10 in each group. How many 3rd graders were there in all? (6-5)

A 111

B 110

C 101

D 100

9. Mr. Hernandez bought 8 bags of limes. Each bag had 4 limes. How many limes did he buy? (6-2)

A 32

B 28

C 24

D 12

10. Mrs. Chavez put new light switch covers in her house. She put in 8 plastic covers and 7 wooden covers. Each cover uses 2 screws. How many screws did she use? (6-7)

A 14

B 15

C 16

D 30

11. A marching band was in a parade. The band members marched in 8 rows. There were 6 band members in each row. Which shows a way to find 8×6? (6-4)

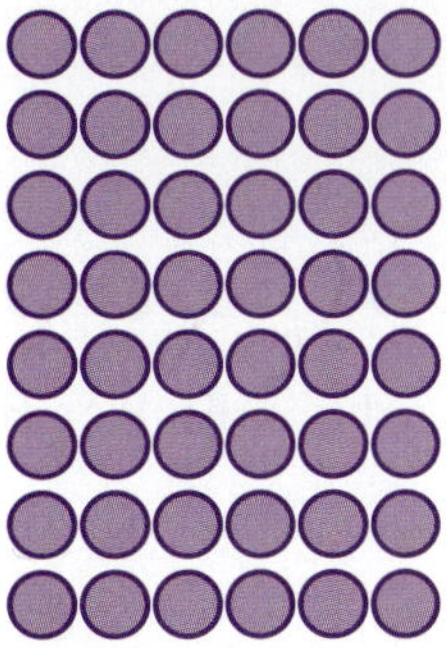

A $8 + 6$

B $24 + 24 + 24$

C $12 + 12 + 12 + 12$

D $16 + 16 + 16 + 16$

12. The Cougars basketball team has 8 players. The coach ordered 3 pairs of socks for each player. How many pairs did he order? (6-4)

A 16

B 24

C 32

D 48

13. Which of these best describes all the numbers on the mileage sign? (6-1)

A They are all greater than 18.

B They are all multiples of 5.

C They are all multiples of 3.

D They are all less than 30.

14. Which is a way to find 7×6? (6-3)

A $35 + 14$

B $30 + 12$

C $35 + 6$

D $30 + 14$

15. Mrs. Kent drives 12 miles 6 times a week for her part-time job. How many miles is this in all? (6-5)

A 18 miles

B 36 miles

C 48 miles

D 72 miles

Set A, pages 140–141

Find 3×7.

You can break an array into facts you know.

$3 \times 7 = 3$ groups of 7
That is 2 sevens plus 1 more seven.

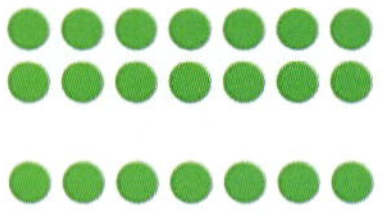

$2 \times 7 = 14$
$1 \times 7 = 7$
$14 + 7 = 21$

So, $3 \times 7 = 21$.

Remember that you can use facts you already know to help you multiply.

Find the product.

1. 3×8 **2.** 6×3 **3.** 4×3

4. 3×3 **5.** 3×5 **6.** 10×3

Set B, pages 142–143

Find 4×7.

Think of a 2s fact, then double the product.

$4 \times 7 = 4$ groups of 7.

$2 \times 7 = 14$
$2 \times 7 = 14$
$14 + 14 = 28$

So, $4 \times 7 = 28$.

Remember that you can draw arrays to solve multiplication facts.

Find the product.

1. 4×10 **2.** 3×4 **3.** 6×4

4. 8×4 **5.** 4×2 **6.** 9×4

Set C, pages 144–146, 148–149

Find 7×6.

$5 + 2 = 7$, so use 5s facts and 2s facts to multiply with 7.

$5 \times 6 = 30$
$2 \times 6 = 12$
$30 + 12 = 42$

So, $7 \times 6 = 42$.

To find 8×6, you can double a 4s fact.
Find 4×6. Then double the product.
$4 \times 6 = 24$, and $24 + 24 = 48$.
So, $8 \times 6 = 48$.

Remember that you can use known facts to multiply with 6, 7 and 8.

Find the product.

1. 7×9 **2.** 8×7 **3.** 6×9

4. 3×6 **5.** 7×4 **6.** 8×6

7. 8×7 **8.** 6×2 **9.** 3×8

Set D, pages 150–151

Find 5×12. Use a pattern.

Multiply the factor that is not 12 by 10.
$5 \times 10 = 50$

Then multiply the same factor by 2.
$5 \times 2 = 10$

Then add the two products.
$50 + 10 = 60$

$5 \times 12 = 60$

Remember that you can use a 10s fact plus another fact to help.

Use patterns to find each product.

1. 11×4
12×4

2. 11×7
12×7

3. 6×12

4. 11×12

Set E, pages 152–153

Find $4 \times 5 \times 2$.

The Associative Property of Multiplication says that you can change the grouping of the factors, and the product will be the same.

One Way

$(4 \times 5) \times 2$

$20 \times 2 = 40$

Another Way

$4 \times (5 \times 2)$

$4 \times 10 = 40$

So, $4 \times 5 \times 2 = 40$.

Remember you may draw a picture to help you multiply 3 factors.

Find the product.

1. $3 \times 2 \times 5$

2. $5 \times 3 \times 4$

3. $1 \times 9 \times 8$

4. $7 \times 2 \times 5$

5. $6 \times 3 \times 4$

6. $4 \times 3 \times 2$

Set F, pages 154–156

Some problems have hidden questions.

Jeff charged \$10 to wash a car and \$7 to walk a dog. How much money did Jeff earn for washing 6 cars and walking 1 dog?

Find and solve the hidden question.
How much money did Jeff earn washing 6 cars?
$6 \times \$10 = \$60$
Then solve the problem.
How much money did Jeff earn in all?
$\$60 + \$7 = \$67$
Jeff earned \$67.

Remember to carefully read the order in which things happen.

1. At the fair, Bonnie wants to get 2 rings and 1 pen. Each ring costs 8 tickets, and each pen costs 6 tickets. How many tickets does she need in all?

2. Mrs. Green bought 2 bags of apples. Each bag had 10 apples. She used 4 apples. How many apples did she have left?

Topic 7

Division Meanings

1 How many strings are on the guitars used by Tejano musicians? You will find out in Lesson 7-2.

2 These three astronauts orbited the Moon on Apollo 11. How many astronauts in all orbited the Moon on Apollo space missions? You will find out in Lesson 7-1.

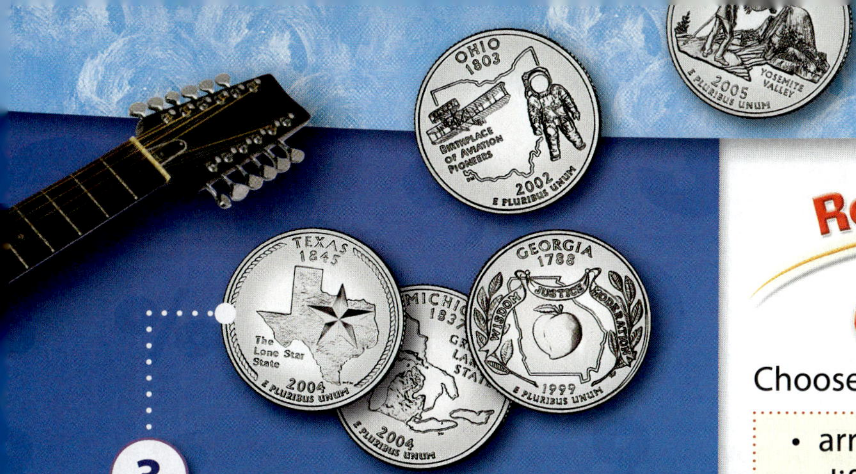

3 In 1999, the United States Mint began circulating new state quarters. How many states have new quarters every year? You will find out in Lesson 7-3.

4 About how many baseballs are used during one inning of a major league game? You will find out in Lesson 7-4.

Review What You Know!

Vocabulary

Choose the best term from the box.

- array
- difference
- factor
- product

1. The answer in multiplication is the __?__.

2. In $3 \times 5 = 15$, 5 is a(n) __?__.

3. When objects are placed in equal rows they form a(n) __?__.

Subtraction

Subtract.

4. 21 − 7	**5.** 15 − 5	**6.** 27 − 9
14 − 7	10 − 5	18 − 9
7 − 7	5 − 5	9 − 9

Multiplication Facts

7. 5×4	**8.** 7×3	**9.** 3×8
10. 9×2	**11.** 6×5	**12.** 4×7
13. 6×7	**14.** 8×4	**15.** 5×9

Equal Groups

16. **Writing to Explain** The picture has 9 counters. Describe why this picture doesn't show equal groups. Then show how to change the drawing so it does show equal groups.

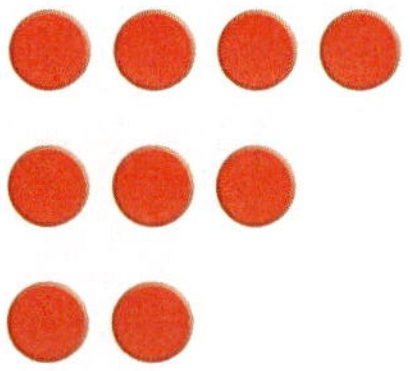

Virginia

Lesson 7-1

3.6 The student will represent multiplication and division, using area, set, and number line models, and create and solve problems that involve multiplication of two whole numbers, one factor 99 or less and the second factor 5 or less.

Division as Sharing

Hands-On
counters

How many are in each group?

Three friends have 12 toys to share equally. How many toys will each person get?

Think of putting 12 toys into 3 equal groups.

Division is an operation that is used to find how many equal groups or how many are in each group.

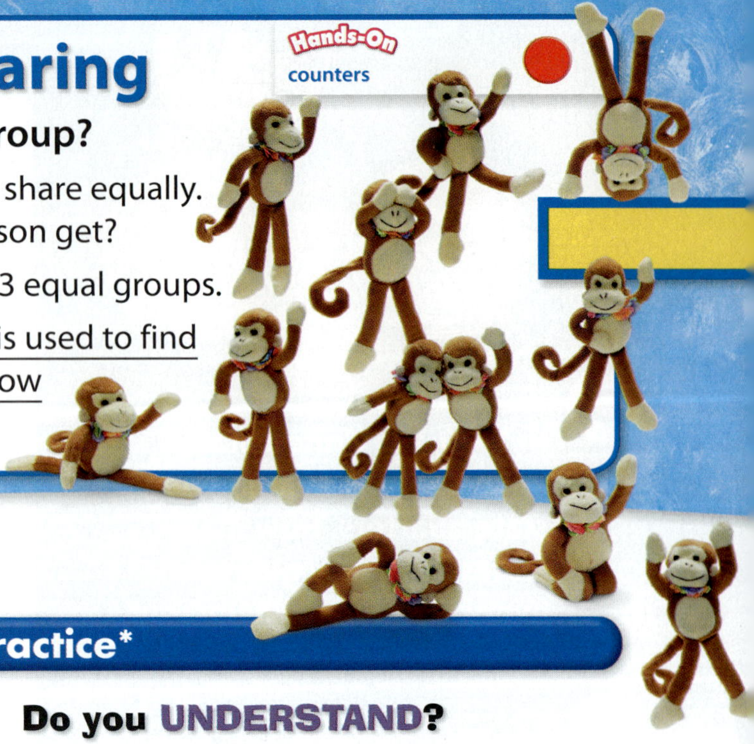

Guided Practice*

Do you know HOW?

Use counters or draw a picture to solve.

1. 15 bananas, 3 boxes
   How many bananas in each box?

2. 16 plants, 4 pots
   How many plants in each pot?

Do you UNDERSTAND?

3. Copy and complete the division sentence. Use the picture to help.

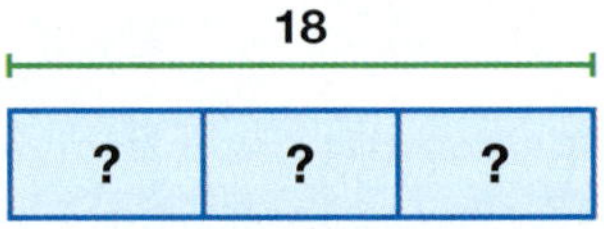

$18 \div 3 = \square$

4. Can 12 grapes be shared equally among 5 children? Explain.

Independent Practice

Use counters or draw a picture to solve.

5. 18 marbles, 6 sacks
   How many marbles in each sack?

6. 36 stickers, 4 people
   How many stickers for each person?

7. 16 crayons, 2 people
   How many crayons for each person?

8. 12 pictures, 4 pages
   How many pictures on each page?

9. 24 bottles, 4 cases
   How many bottles in each case?

10. 27 CDs, 9 packages
    How many CDs in each package?

Complete each division sentence.

11. 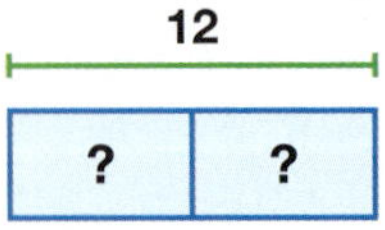

$12 \div 2 = \square$

12. 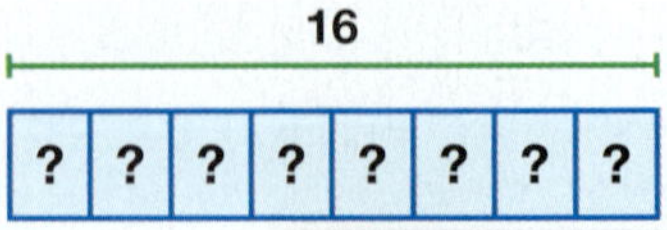

$16 \div 8 = \square$

DIGITAL Animated Glossary, eTools **www.pearsonsuccessnet.com**

*For another example, see Set A on page 180.

What You Think

Put one at a time in each group.

When all the toys are grouped, there will be 4 in each group.

What You Write

You can write a division sentence to find the number in each group.

12	÷	3	=	4
↑ Total		↑ Number of equal groups		↑ Number in each group

Each person will get 4 toys.

Problem Solving

13. **Writing to Explain** Jim is putting 18 pens into equal groups. He says that there will be more pens in each of 2 equal groups than in each of 3 equal groups. Is he correct? Explain.

14. Joy has 12 shells. She gives 2 to her mom. Then she and her sister share the rest equally. How many shells does Joy get? How many shells does her sister get?

15. Three astronauts were on each *Apollo* spacecraft. How many astronauts in all were on the nine *Apollo* spacecraft that orbited the Moon?

16. Max has the stickers shown. He wants to put an equal number of stickers on each of 2 posters. Which number sentence shows how to find the number of stickers Max should put on each poster?

A $14 + 2 = \square$

B $14 \times 2 = \square$

C $14 - 2 = \square$

D $14 \div 2 = \square$

17. The flag bearers march in 9 rows with 5 people in each row. Each person is carrying one flag. Write a number sentence to show how many flags there are.

3.6 The student will represent multiplication and division, using area, set, and number line models, and create and solve problems that involve multiplication of two whole numbers, one factor 99 or less and the second factor 5 or less.

Understanding Remainders

Hands-On
counters

How many are left over?

Luisa is packing soccer balls into crates. Each crate will hold 5 soccer balls. How many crates will she fill? Are any soccer balls left?

Choose an Operation You want to separate 23 into equal groups of 5, so you can divide.

Another Example What do you do with the remainder?

Sometimes a problem asks for the amount in the remainder. Sometimes a problem asks about the number of groups.

Ned has 27 soccer cards to put in an album. He can put 6 cards on each page.

Example A

How many pages can Ned fill?

Find how many groups of 6 there will be.

Ned can fill 4 pages.

Example B

How many pages will Ned work on?

Find how many groups are filled or started.

Ned will work on 5 pages.

Example C

How many cards will Ned put on the 5th page?

Find how many are left after 4 pages are filled.

Ned will put 3 cards on the 5th page.

Explain It

1. Why are the answers to the examples different?
2. Janie has 34 photos to put in an album. She can put 4 photos on each page. How many photos will be on the 9th page?

DIGITAL Animated Glossary, eTools
www.pearsonsuccessnet.com

Step 1

Show the total number of items.

Use counters to show 23.

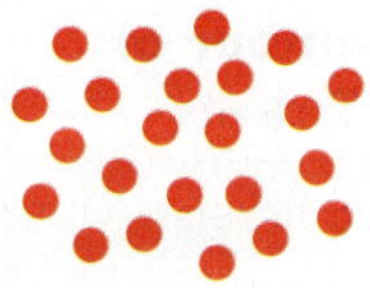

Step 2

Divide them into equal groups.

Make equal groups with 5 counters in each group.

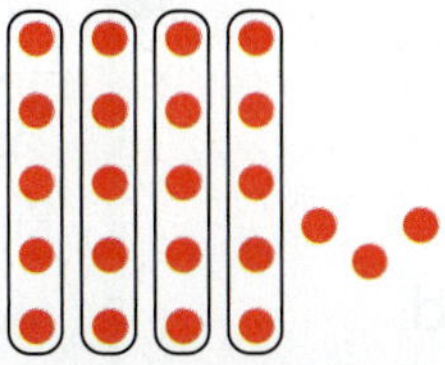

Step 3

Write the number of equal groups and the number left over.

$23 \div 5 = 4$ with 3 left over

Luisa will fill 4 crates. There will be 3 soccer balls left over.

The part that is left over when we divide is called the remainder.

Guided Practice*

Do you know HOW?

Use counters or draw a picture to find the number of groups and the number left over.

1. 17 oranges, 3 oranges in each box

$17 \div 3 =$ ☐ with ☐ left over

2. $9 \div 2 =$ ☐ with ☐ left over

Do you UNDERSTAND?

3. In the example above, how do you find the remainder?

4. Dave is packing 23 sweaters into boxes. Each box will hold 3 sweaters. How many boxes will he fill? How many sweaters will be left over?

Independent Practice

For **5–10**, find the number of groups and the number left over. Use counters or draw a picture to help.

5. 18 jars, 4 jars in each box
$18 \div 4 =$ ☐ with ☐ left over

6. 22 shirts, 6 shirts in each box
$22 \div 6 =$ ☐ with ☐ left over

7. 27 books, 7 books in each box
$27 \div 7 =$ ☐ with ☐ left over

8. $13 \div 2 =$ ☐ with ☐ left

9. $31 \div 8 =$ ☐ with ☐ left

10. $32 \div 9 =$ ☐ with ☐ left

11. 7 football cards, 3 cards on each page
How many pages can Alex complete?

12. 11 baseball cards, 4 cards on each page
How many cards are on the 3rd page?

13. 34 stickers, 5 stickers on each page
How many pages will have some stickers?

For another example, see Set B on page 180.

Problem Solving

Use the table for **14–16**.

14. Samuel has 45 prize tickets. How many marbles can he get?

15. Inez got 3 rings and 2 stickers. How many tickets did she use?

16. Milt had 28 prize tickets. He traded tickets for 3 yo-yos. How many prize tickets does he have left?

Data

Trade Tickets for Prizes!

Prize	Number of Tickets
Yo-yo	8 tickets
Ring	9 tickets
Marble	7 tickets
Sticker	4 tickets

17. **Strategy Focus** Solve. Use the Draw a Picture strategy.

Keiko makes necklaces like the one in the picture on the right. She has 19 blue beads and 13 red beads.

a How many more blue beads than red beads does Keiko have?

b How many necklaces can she make?

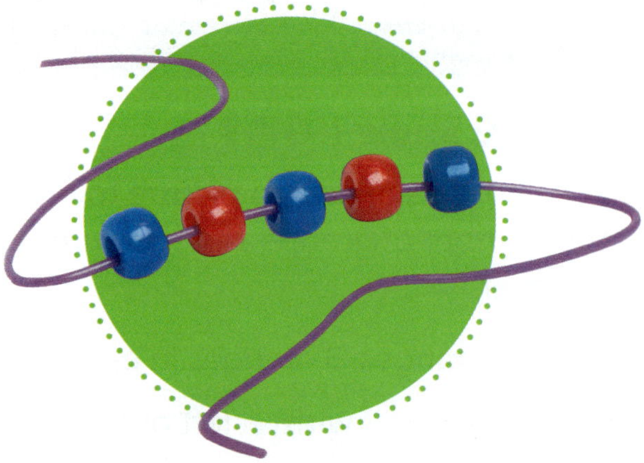

18. There are 38 students going to a museum. Each van can hold 8 students. How many vans will be needed?

19. Jack is making muffins. He will use 5 raisins to decorate each muffin. If he has 21 raisins, how many muffins can he decorate?

20. Jada bought a bag of 8 apples. She and her 3 sisters will share the apples equally. How many apples will each person get? Will there be any apples left over? If so, how many?

21. How many strings in all are used to make 4 guitars like the ones in the picture below?

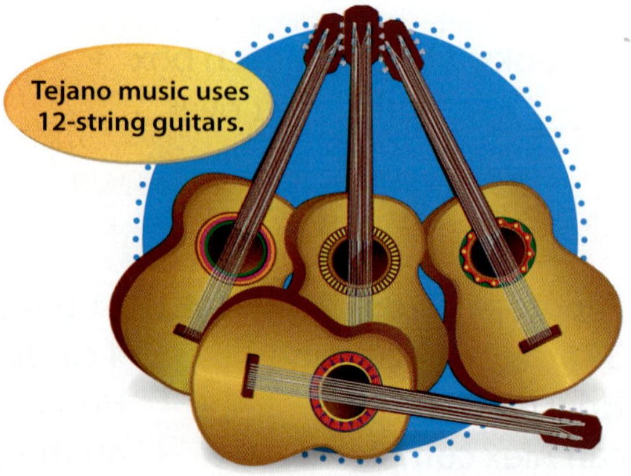

22. SOL Prep There are 39 children at a park. They want to make teams with 9 children on each team. How many teams can they make?

A 4 **C** 9

B 5 **D** 28

Mixed Problem Solving

Math and Science

Animals get special features, called inherited traits, from their parents. Use the table on the right to answer the questions.

Some Traits of Animals

Kind of Animal	Inherited Trait
Birds	2 eyes, 2 legs, 2 wings
Fish	2 eyes
Insects	2 antennas, 6 legs, 3 body parts
Apes	2 hands, 5 fingers on each hand, 2 legs, 5 toes on each foot, 2 eyes

1. A mother and her two babies are on a tree branch. They have six wings in all. Which kind of animal listed in the table could they be?

2. Two adult apes and two baby apes are near the water. How many fingers do the apes have in all?

3. One of these animals is on a tree branch. It has six legs in all. Which kind of animal listed in the table could it be?

4. Which has more legs—two birds or one insect? How many more?

5. Look at the table below.

Kind of Animal	Number of Body Parts	Number of Legs
Insect	3	6
Spider	2	8

Danny saw three of the same kind of animal on the sidewalk. He counted six body parts in all. Did Danny see 3 spiders or 3 insects?

6. **Strategy Focus** Solve. Use the strategy Draw a Picture.

Trini had 31 baby fish and 5 adult fish in a fish tank. She put 18 of the baby fish in another tank, and all of the adult fish in a third tank. How many baby fish are left in the first tank? Check if your answer is reasonable.

Virginia

Lesson 7-3

Extends 3.6 The student will represent multiplication and division, using area, set, and number line models, and create and solve problems that involve multiplication of two whole numbers, one factor 99 or less and the second factor 5 or less.

Division as Repeated Subtraction

Hands-On
counters

How many equal groups?

June has 10 strawberries to serve to her guests. If each guest eats 2 strawberries, how many guests can June serve?

Guided Practice*

Do you know HOW?

Use counters or draw a picture to solve.

1. 16 gloves
2 gloves in each pair
How many pairs?

2. 15 tennis balls
3 balls in each can
How many cans?

Do you UNDERSTAND?

3. Suppose June had 12 strawberries and each guest ate 2 strawberries. How many guests could she serve? Use counters or draw a picture to solve.

4. **Number Sense** Show how you can use repeated subtraction to find how many groups of 4 there are in 20. Then write the division sentence for the problem.

Independent Practice

Use counters or draw a picture to solve.

5. 12 wheels
4 wheels on each wagon
How many wagons?

6. 30 markers
5 markers in each package
How many packages?

7. 8 apples
4 apples in each bag
How many bags?

8. 18 pencils
2 pencils on each desk
How many desks?

DIGITAL
eTools
www.pearsonsuccessnet.com

*For another example, see Set A on page 180.

One Way

You can use repeated subtraction to find how many groups of 2 are in 10.

$10 - 2 = 8$
$8 - 2 = 6$
$6 - 2 = 4$
$4 - 2 = 2$
$2 - 2 = 0$

You can subtract 2, five times. There are five groups of 2 in 10.

There are no strawberries left.

June can serve 5 guests.

Another Way

You can write a division sentence to find the number of groups.

Write: $10 \div 2 = 5$

Read: Ten divided by 2 equals 5.

June can serve 5 guests.

Problem Solving

9. **Number Sense** Raymond has 16 model planes that he wants to display. Will he need more shelves if he puts 8 on a shelf or 4 on a shelf? Explain.

For **10–12**, match each problem to a picture or a repeated subtraction. Then write the division sentence to solve.

10. 24 books
6 in a box
How many boxes?

11. 24 books
3 in a box
How many boxes?

12. 24 books
8 in a box
How many boxes?

a

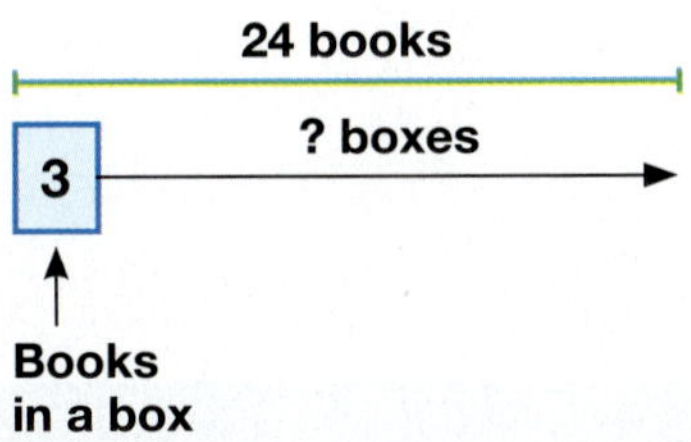

b $24 - 8 = 16$
$16 - 8 = 8$
$8 - 8 = 0$

c

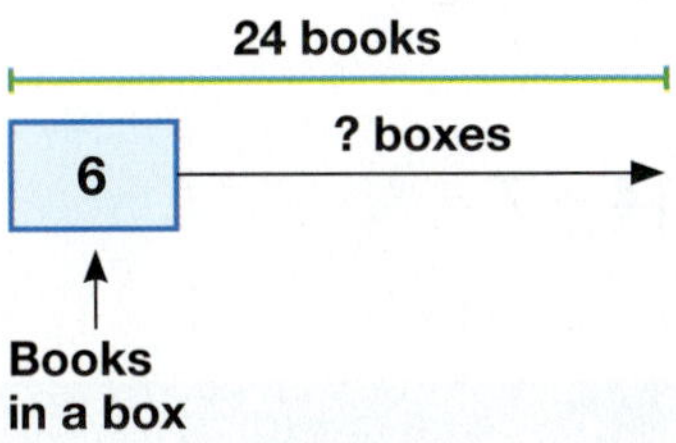

13. In 1999, the United States Mint began circulating state quarters. New quarters for 5 states are released each year. How many years will it take for quarters to be released for all 50 states? Write a number sentence to solve.

SOL Prep

14. Toni has 6 tulips and 6 daisies. She wants to put 4 flowers in each vase. Which number sentence shows how many vases she needs?

A $12 + 4 = 16$ **B** $12 - 4 = 8$ **C** $6 \times 4 = 24$ **D** $12 \div 4 = 3$

Virginia

Lesson 7-4

Prepares for 4.4.c The student will divide whole numbers, finding quotients with and without remainders.

Writing Division Stories

Hands-On
counters

What is the main idea of a division story?

Mrs. White asked her students to write a division story for 15 ÷ 3 = $\square$.

Mike and Kia decided to write stories about putting roses in vases.

Guided Practice*

Do you know HOW?

Write a division story for each number sentence. Then use counters or draw a picture to solve.

1. 8 ÷ 4 = $\square$

2. 10 ÷ 2 = $\square$

3. 20 ÷ 5 = $\square$

4. 14 ÷ 7 = $\square$

Do you UNDERSTAND?

5. How are Mike's and Kia's stories alike? How are the two stories different?

6. **Writing to Explain** When you write a division story, what two pieces of information do you need to include? What kind of information do you ask for?

Independent Practice

Write a division story for each number sentence. Then use counters or draw a picture to solve.

7. 18 ÷ 3 = $\square$ **8.** 25 ÷ 5 = $\square$ **9.** 16 ÷ 4 = $\square$ **10.** 30 ÷ 6 = $\square$

11. **Number Sense** Choose two of the stories you wrote for the exercises above. For each, tell whether you found the number in each group or the number of equal groups.

DIGITAL eTools www.pearsonsuccessnet.com

*For another example, see Set C on page 181.

Mike's Story

I have 15 roses. I want an equal number of roses in each of 3 vases. How many roses should I put in each vase?

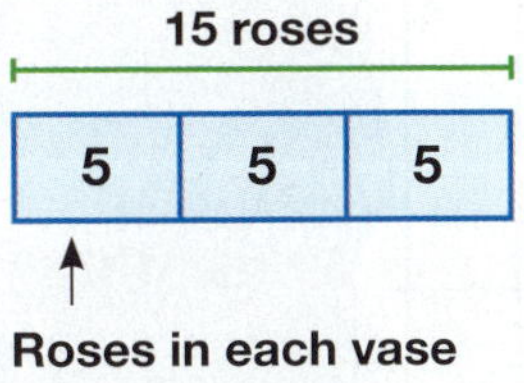

Main idea: How many are in each group?

$15 \div 3 = 5$

I should put 5 roses in each vase.

Kia's Story

I have 15 roses to put into vases. I want to put 3 roses into each vase. How many vases will I need?

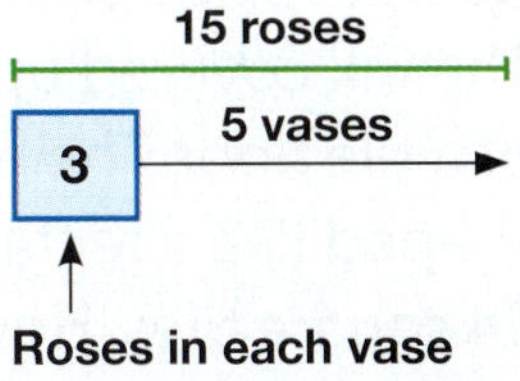

Main idea: How many groups are there?

$15 \div 3 = 5$

I will need 5 vases.

Problem Solving

The table shows the number of players needed for each kind of sports team. Use the table for **12–15**.

There are 36 third graders at sports camp who want to play on different teams.

Data

Sports Team	Number
Baseball	9 players
Basketball	5 players
Doubles Tennis	2 players

12. If everyone wants to play baseball, how many teams will there be?

13. **Writing to Explain** Could everyone play basketball at the same time? Why or why not?

14. Twenty of the third graders went swimming. The rest of them played doubles tennis. How many doubles tennis teams were there?

15. Two baseball teams are playing a game. At the same time, two basketball teams are playing a game. The rest of the campers are playing tennis. How many campers are playing tennis?

16. Carmen rides her bike to school from 3 to 5 times a week. Which is a reasonable number of times Carmen will ride her bike in 4 weeks?

A More than 28

B From 12 to 20

C From 14 to 28

D Fewer than 12

17. In one inning, each baseball was used for 7 pitches. Write a number sentence that shows the total number of pitches thrown that inning.

Virginia

Lesson 7-5

Extends 3.10.b The student will count the number of square units needed to cover a given surface in order to determine area.

Problem Solving

Use Objects and Draw a Picture

Hands-On

square tiles

grid paper

Naomi spilled some ink on her paper. The ink covered up part of her picture of a tile floor. The entire floor was shaped like a rectangle covered by 24 square tiles. How many tiles were in each row?

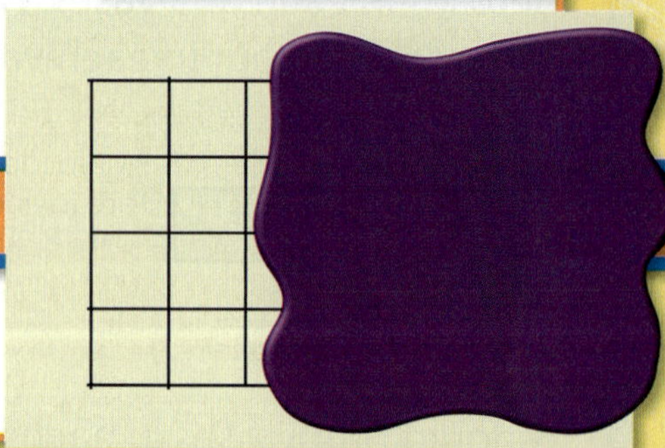

Another Example How can drawing a picture help you solve a problem?

Some ink spilled and covered up part of a picture of a tile floor. The tile floor was shaped like a rectangle. There were 21 square tiles in the whole floor. How many tiles were in each row?

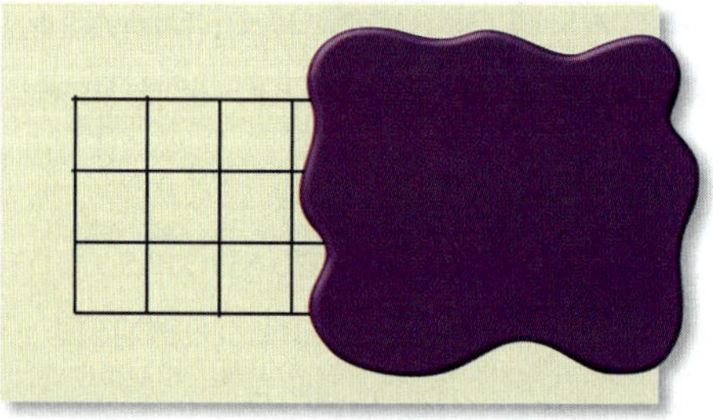

Plan

What strategy can I use?

I can draw a picture to show what I know.

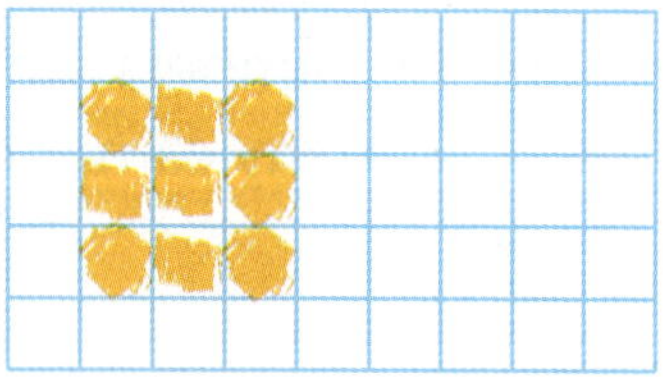

Solve

I can finish the picture to solve the problem.

There should be 21 squares in all.

$7 + 7 + 7 = 21$

There were 7 tiles in each row.

Explain It

1. How do you know how many tiles to draw to finish the picture in the problem above?
2. Explain how to check the solution to this problem.

DIGITAL eTools **www.pearsonsuccessnet.com**

Understand and Plan

What strategy can I use?

I can act it out by using objects to show what I know.

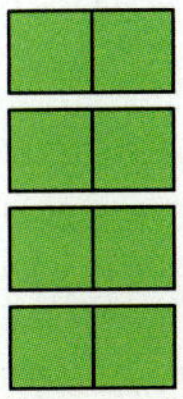

These tiles were not covered.

Solve

Now I will add tiles to each row to solve the problem. I'll add the same number of tiles to each row until there are 24 tiles in all.

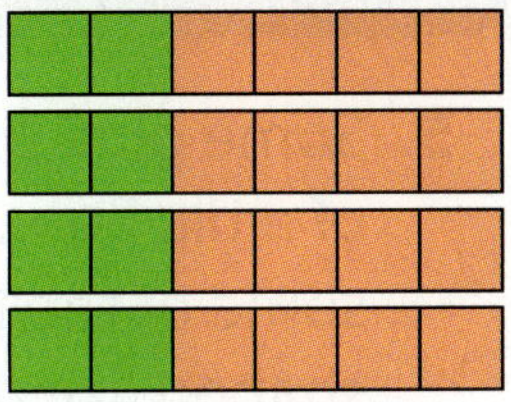

$6 + 6 + 6 + 6 = 24$

There were 6 tiles in each row.

Guided Practice*

Do you know HOW?

Solve. Use objects or draw a picture.

1. Paint covered part of a tile floor. The square floor had 16 tiles. How many tiles had paint on them?

Do you UNDERSTAND?

2. What strategy did you use to find the number of tiles covered by paint in Exercise 1?

3. **Write a Problem** Write and solve a problem that you can solve by using objects or drawing a picture.

Independent Practice

Solve. Use objects or draw a picture.

4. Kim painted part of a tiled section of a wall. The whole section of tiles was shaped like a rectangle. There were 27 square tiles. How many tiles were in each row?

Stuck? Try this....

- What do I know?
- What am I asked to find?
- What diagram can I use to help understand the problem?
- Can I use addition, subtraction, multiplication, or division?
- Is all of my work correct?
- Did I answer the right question?
- Is my answer reasonable?

For another example, see Set D on page 181.

Independent Practice

5. Some glue spilled on Ana's drawing of a tile floor. The glue covered up some of the tiles. The tile floor was shaped like a rectangle. There were 20 square tiles in the whole floor. How many of the tiles had glue on them?

6. Joyce wants to make a design using the pattern of square tiles shown below. She wants to use this pattern four times. How many white tiles does she need?

7. Jeff's family took a car trip for a summer vacation. The family drove 362 miles to a national park. Then the family drove 174 miles to hike in the mountains. How many miles did the family drive all together?

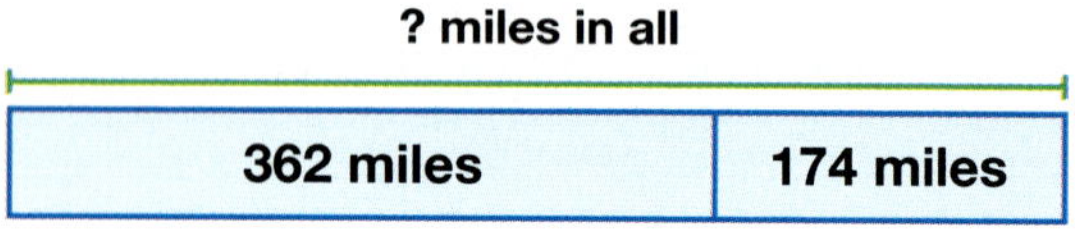

8. Mari needs to make 215 programs in all for the class play. So far, she has made 89 programs. How many more programs does she still need to make?

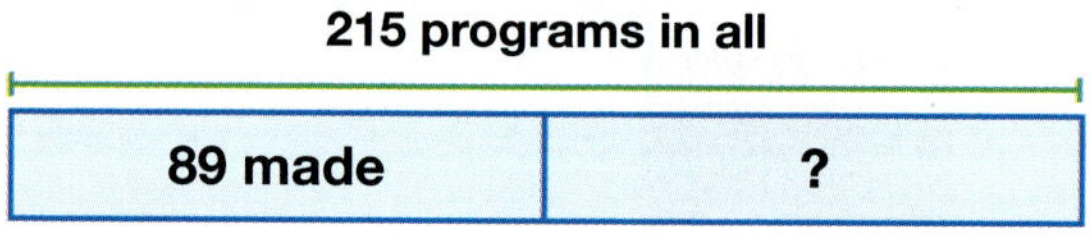

Think About the Process

9. Which of the following can be used to find how many days there are in 8 weeks?

A 8×7

B $8 \div 2$

C $8 + 7$

D $8 - 2$

10. Mrs. Clay bought 28 picture frames packed equally into 4 boxes. Which number sentence shows how to find the number of frames in each box?

A $28 - 4 = \square$

B $28 + 4 = \square$

C $28 \times 4 = \square$

D $28 \div 4 = \square$

Stop and Practice

Write each number in expanded form.

1. 7,409 **2.** 38,617 **3.** 926,054

Order the numbers from least to greatest.

4. 918 909 1,062 **5.** 934 1,121 1,119

6. 5,609 5,600 5,610 **7.** 8,736 8,832 8,734

Estimate and then find each sum. Check that your answer is reasonable.

8. $\begin{array}{r} 73 \\ +\ 59 \\ \hline \end{array}$ **9.** $\begin{array}{r} 386 \\ +\ 94 \\ \hline \end{array}$ **10.** $\begin{array}{r} 869 \\ +\ 253 \\ \hline \end{array}$ **11.** $\begin{array}{r} 925 \\ +\ 678 \\ \hline \end{array}$ **12.** $\begin{array}{r} 215 \\ +\ 499 \\ \hline \end{array}$

Estimate and then find each difference. Check that your answer is reasonable.

13. $\begin{array}{r} 64 \\ -\ 39 \\ \hline \end{array}$ **14.** $\begin{array}{r} 213 \\ -\ 95 \\ \hline \end{array}$ **15.** $\begin{array}{r} 502 \\ -\ 317 \\ \hline \end{array}$ **16.** $\begin{array}{r} 756 \\ -\ 359 \\ \hline \end{array}$ **17.** $\begin{array}{r} 308 \\ -\ 179 \\ \hline \end{array}$

Find each product.

18. 6×8 **19.** 10×1 **20.** $2 \times 2 \times 2$ **21.** 4×7 **22.** 9×0

Error Search Find each sum or difference that is not correct. Write it correctly and explain the error.

23. $\begin{array}{r} 95 \\ +\ 18 \\ \hline 103 \end{array}$ **24.** $\begin{array}{r} 207 \\ +\ 536 \\ \hline 743 \end{array}$ **25.** $\begin{array}{r} 630 \\ -\ 472 \\ \hline 228 \end{array}$ **26.** $\begin{array}{r} 849 \\ +\ 205 \\ \hline 1{,}044 \end{array}$ **27.** $\begin{array}{r} 534 \\ -\ 427 \\ \hline 107 \end{array}$

Number Sense

Estimating and Reasoning Write true or false for each statement. If it is false, explain why.

28. $67 + 45 < 100$

29. $8 \times 10 > 18$

30. $218 - 53 < 100$

31. $969 - 837 > 100$

32. $342 + 519 < 1{,}000$

33. $0 \times 9 > 1 \times 9$

VA SOL Test Prep

1. Martin has 12 pinecones. His birdfeeder design uses 3 pinecones. Which number sentence shows how many birdfeeders he can make? (7-3)

A $12 + 3 = 15$

B $12 \div 3 = 4$

C $12 - 3 = 9$

D $12 \times 3 = 36$

2. Which story could be solved with $20 \div 4$? (7-4)

A Harold caught 20 fish. All but 4 of them were catfish. How many of the fish were something other than catfish?

B Becky bought 20 bags of crystal beads. Each bag had 4 crystal beads. How many crystal beads did she buy?

C Batina has made 20 doll dresses. If she makes 4 more, how many doll dresses will she have made?

D Coach Sid has 20 baseballs. Each group needs 4 balls for the practice drill. How many groups can he form?

3. Five friends have 15 pencils to share equally. Which number sentence shows how many pencils each friend will get? (7-1)

A $15 \div 5 = 3$

B $15 + 5 = 20$

C $15 \times 5 = 75$

D $15 - 5 = 10$

4. Mrs. Vincent bought 16 kiwis for her 4 children to share equally. How many kiwis will each child get? (7-1)

A 3

B 4

C 5

D 12

5. Each fence board requires 4 nails. How many boards can Mason put up with one package of 30 nails? (7-2)

A 2

B 6

C 7

D 8

6. Which division sentence is shown by the repeated subtraction? (7-3)

$15 - 3 = 12$
$12 - 3 = 9$
$9 - 3 = 6$
$6 - 3 = 3$
$3 - 3 = 0$

A $15 \div 3 = 5$

B $15 \div 3 = 0$

C $18 \div 3 = 6$

D $18 \div 6 = 3$

7. The pet store had 24 parakeets to put equally in 8 cages. How many birds should be put in each cage? (7-1)

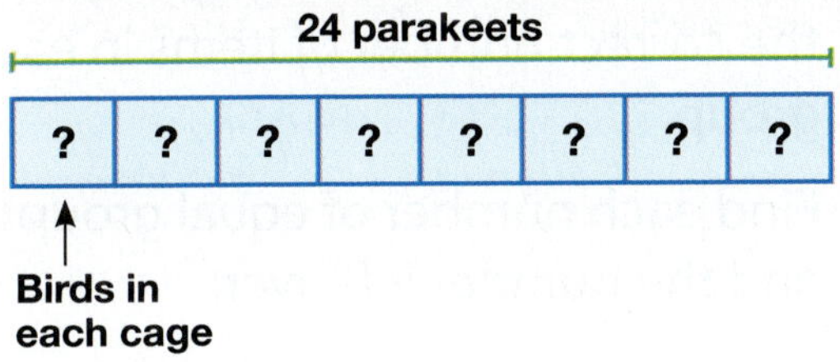

A 6

B 4

C 3

D 2

8. While on vacation, Ginny bought 22 postcards. She can put 4 postcards on each page in her memory book. How many postcards will Ginny put on the 6th page? (7-2)

A 6

B 5

C 4

D 2

9. Which story could be solved with $36 \div 6$? (7-4)

A Carla used 36 seashells to make 6 necklaces. Each necklace had the same number of shells. How many shells were on each necklace?

B Patrick planted 36 trees on Arbor Day. If he plants 6 more, how many trees will he have planted?

C The zoo's gift shop ordered 36 bags with 6 plastic animals in each. How many plastic animals did the gift shop order?

D Ray counted 36 coins in his bank. All but 6 of them were quarters. How many of the coins were something other than quarters?

10. The pictures below are examples of a triangle in several different positions.

Which of the following shapes can **NOT** be made by joining two of the triangles? (7-5)

A A rectangle

B A parallelogram

C A triangle

D A square

Set A, pages 164–165, 170–171

There are 12 toys. If 4 toys are put in each box, how many boxes are needed?

$12 - 4 = 8$ Use repeated subtraction to find
$8 - 4 = 4$ how many groups.
$4 - 4 = 0$ You can subtract 4 three times.

$12 \div 4 = 3$ You can also divide to find the number of groups.

Three boxes are needed.

Remember that you can also think of division as sharing equally.

Use counters or draw a picture to solve each problem.

1. 6 books
3 shelves
How many books are on each shelf?

2. 18 students
2 students in each group
How many groups are there?

Set B, pages 166–168

Tom has 14 apples to put into bags. Each bag holds 4 apples. How many bags can Tom fill? Are any apples left?

- Show the total number of items.
- Divide them into equal groups.
- Write the number of equal groups and the number left over.

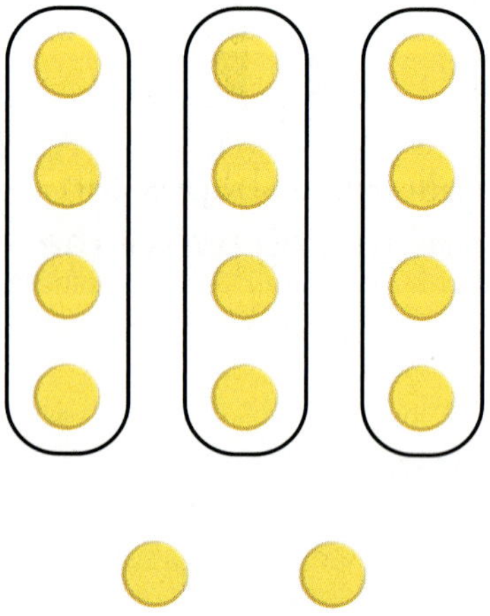

$14 \div 4 = 3$ with 2 left over

Tom can fill 3 bags. There will be 2 apples left over.

Remember to make sure you put the correct number of items in each group.

Find each number of equal groups and the number left over.

1. 21 books,
5 books in each box

$21 \div 5 = \square$ with $\square$ left over

2. 20 muffins,
3 muffins in each box

$20 \div 3 = \square$ with $\square$ left over

3. 40 stickers
6 stickers on each page

$40 \div 6 = \square$ with $\square$ left over

4. 23 days
7 days in each week

$23 \div 7 = \square$ with $\square$ left over

Set C, pages 172–173

Write a division story for $20 \div 5$.

If 20 children form 5 equal teams, how many children are on each team?

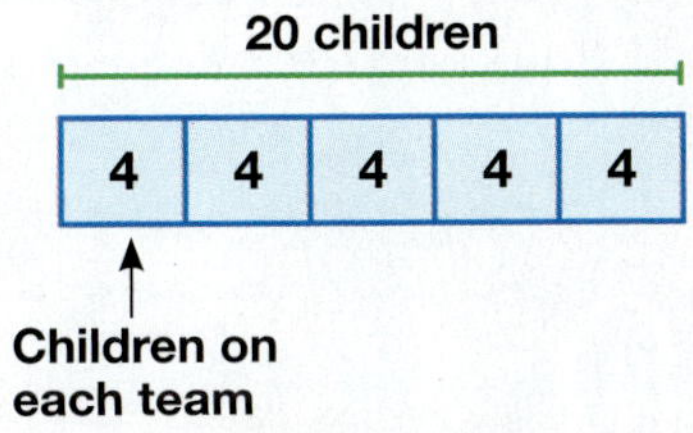

$20 \div 5 = 4$

There are 4 children on each team.

Remember that division stories can ask for the number in each group or the number of equal groups.

Write a division story for each number sentence. Draw a picture to help.

1. $15 \div 3 = \square$

2. $21 \div 7 = \square$

3. $24 \div 6 = \square$

4. $30 \div 5 = \square$

Set D, pages 174–176

Some blue paint spilled on a tile floor. The tile floor was in the shape of a square. There were 9 tiles in the whole floor. How many of the tiles had blue paint on them?

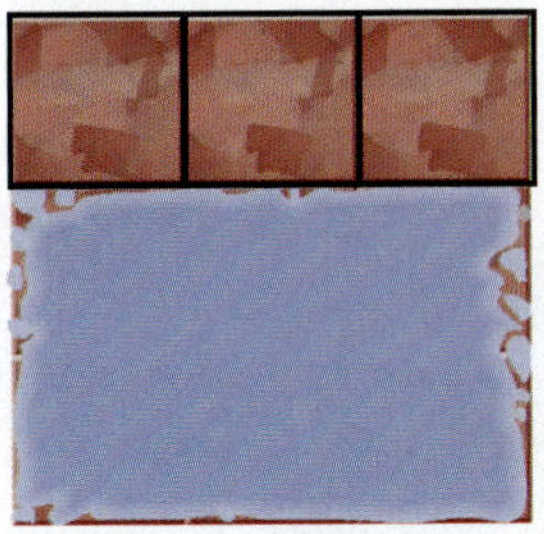

Draw a picture to show what you know.

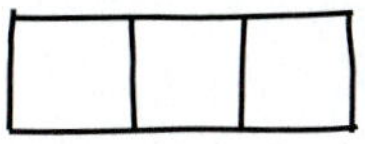

Finish the picture to solve. Show 9 tiles in all.

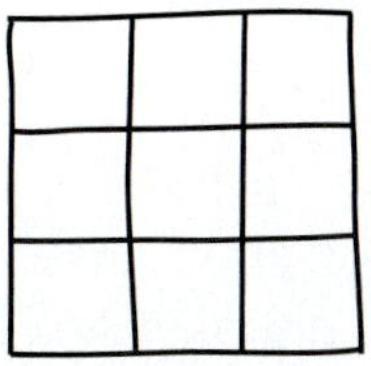

Six tiles had blue paint on them.

Remember to check that your picture matches the information in the problem.

1. Carmela painted over a part of some tiles. The whole group of tiles was in the shape of a rectangle. There were 28 tiles in the whole group. How many tiles did Carmela paint over?

Topic 8

Division Facts

1 A dollhouse was made for Queen Mary of England. How do the objects in the dollhouse compare in size to the objects in her real-life castle? You will find out in Lesson 8-5.

2 The public subway in London is called the Underground, or the Tube. How long is the East London tube line? You will find out in Lesson 8-4.

3 How much water might you use when you brush your teeth? You will find out in Lesson 8-2.

4 A mosaic is a type of art made with tiles. How does this mosaic show multiplication and division? You will find out in Lesson 8-1.

Review What You Know!

Vocabulary

Choose the best term from the box.

- addends
- factors
- difference
- product

1. The numbers you multiply are __?__.
2. The answer in a subtraction problem is the __?__.
3. The answer in a multiplication problem is the __?__.

Fact Families

Copy and complete each fact family.

4. $7 + 6 = \square$ $\quad 13 - 6 = \square$
   $6 + 7 = \square$ $\quad \square - 7 = 6$
5. $8 + \square = 17$ $\quad 17 - 8 = \square$
   $9 + 8 = \square$ $\quad \square - 9 = 8$
6. Write the fact family for 2, 6, and 8.

Multiplication

Copy and complete.

7. $6 \times 8 = \square \times 6$
8. $10 \times \square = 0$
9. $\square \times 1 = 7$
10. **Writing to Explain** Explain how to find how many items are in 3 groups if there are 4 items in each group. Draw a picture to help.

Virginia

Lesson 8-1

3.2 The student will recognize and use the inverse relationships between addition/subtraction and multiplication/division to complete basic fact sentences. The student will use these relationships to solve problems.

Relating Multiplication and Division

Hands-On
counters

How can multiplication facts help you divide?

This array can show multiplication and division.

Multiplication	Division
5 rows of 6 drums	30 drums in 5 equal rows
$5 \times 6 = 30$	$30 \div 5 = 6$
30 drums	6 drums in each row

Guided Practice*

Do you know HOW?

Copy and complete. Use counters or draw a picture to help.

1. $4 \times \square = 28$
$28 \div 4 = \square$

2. $6 \times \square = 36$
$36 \div 6 = \square$

3. $2 \times \square = 18$
$18 \div 2 = \square$

4. $8 \times \square = 32$
$32 \div 8 = \square$

Do you UNDERSTAND?

5. **Number Sense** What multiplication fact can help you find $54 \div 6$?

6. Look at the fact family for 5, 6, and 30. What do you notice about the products and the dividends?

7. **Writing to Explain** Is $4 \times 6 = 24$ part of the fact family for 3, 8, and 24? Explain.

Independent Practice

Copy and complete. Use counters or draw a picture to help.

8. $8 \times \square = 16$
$16 \div 8 = \square$

9. $5 \times \square = 35$
$35 \div 5 = \square$

10. $6 \times \square = 48$
$48 \div 6 = \square$

11. $9 \times \square = 36$
$36 \div 9 = \square$

12. $3 \times \square = 27$
$27 \div 3 = \square$

13. $8 \times \square = 56$
$56 \div 8 = \square$

14. $\square \times 7 = 42$
$42 \div 7 = \square$

15. $\square \times 8 = 72$
$72 \div 8 = \square$

16. $\square \times 9 = 45$
$45 \div 9 = \square$

17. Write the fact family for 5, 8, and 40.

DIGITAL
Animated Glossary, eTools
www.pearsonsuccessnet.com

**For another example, see Set A on page 202.*

A fact family shows how multiplication and division are related.

Fact family for 5, 6, and 30:

$5 \times 6 = 30$	$30 \div 5 = 6$
$6 \times 5 = 30$	$30 \div 6 = 5$

30 → dividend; 6 → divisor; 5 → quotient

The **dividend** is the number of objects to be divided.

The **divisor** is the number by which another number is divided.

The **quotient** is the answer to a division problem.

Problem Solving

18. Writing to Explain Why does the fact family for $2 \times 2 = 4$ have only two facts?

For **19** and **20**, write the rest of the fact family for each array.

19.

$3 \times 4 = 12$ $12 \div 3 = 4$

20.

$4 \times 5 = 20$ $20 \div 4 = 5$

21. There were 3 lines of clowns in a parade. Each line had 8 clowns in it. Near the end of the parade, 3 of the clowns had to leave. How many clowns were still in the parade?

22. Write a fact family to describe the array of tiles in the mosaic shown at the right.

23. What number makes this number sentence true?

SOL Prep

$\square \div 3 = 9$

A 3 **B** 12 **C** 18 **D** 27

Virginia

Lesson 8-2

3.5 The student will recall multiplication facts through the twelves table, and the corresponding division facts.

Fact Families with 2, 3, 4, and 5

What multiplication fact can you use?

Dee has 14 noisemakers. She puts the same number on each of 2 tables. How many will be on each table?

What You Think	What You Write
2 times what number is 14? $2 \times 7 = 14$	$14 \div 2 = 7$ There will be 7 noisemakers on each table.

Another Example **What is another way to write a division problem?**

Dee is making balloon animals for her party. She has 24 balloons. It takes 4 balloons to make each animal. How many balloon animals can she make?

4 times what number is 24?
$4 \times 6 = 24$

There are two ways to write a division problem.

$24 \div 4 = 6$

24 ↑ dividend; 4 ↑ divisor; 6 ↑ quotient

$4\overline{)24}$ with 6 above: 6 ← quotient; divisor → 4; 24 ← dividend

Dee can make 6 balloon animals.

Explain It

1. Copy and complete the fact family:

   $4 \times 6 = 24$
   $24 \div 4 = 6$

2. How do you know what multiplication fact to use to find $24 \div 4$?

3. **Number Sense** Dee says she could make more than 10 balloon animals if she was able to make an animal using only 3 balloons. Do you agree? Why or why not?

Dee has 40 stickers. She puts 5 stickers on each bag. How many bags can she decorate?

What You Think	What You Write
5 times what number is 40? $5 \times 8 = 40$	$40 \div 5 = 8$ Dee can decorate 8 bags.

Dee wants to put 15 cups in 3 rows on the table. How many cups will she put in each row?

What You Think	What You Write
3 times what number is 15? $3 \times 5 = 15$	$15 \div 3 = 5$ Dee will put 5 cups in each row.

Guided Practice*

Do you know HOW?

In **1–2**, copy and complete each fact family.

1. $2 \times 7 = 14$
$14 \div 2 = 7$

2. $5 \times 8 = 40$
$40 \div 5 = 8$

In **3–8**, find each quotient.

3. $27 \div 3$ **4.** $16 \div 4$ **5.** $40 \div 4$

6. $2\overline{)18}$ **7.** $4\overline{)28}$ **8.** $5\overline{)30}$

Do you UNDERSTAND?

9. Identify the dividend, divisor and quotient in Exercise 8.

10. **Number Sense** How can you tell without dividing that $15 \div 3$ will be greater than $15 \div 5$?

11. How can you use multiplication to help you find 36 divided by 4?

12. Dee has planned 4 games for her party. If she has 12 prizes, how many prizes can she give for each game?

Independent Practice

Find each quotient.

13. $10 \div 2$ **14.** $25 \div 5$ **15.** $21 \div 3$ **16.** $18 \div 3$

17. $2\overline{)16}$ **18.** $5\overline{)50}$ **19.** $3\overline{)24}$ **20.** $4\overline{)36}$

21. $12 \div 4$ **22.** $45 \div 5$ **23.** $4\overline{)16}$ **24.** $5\overline{)40}$

25. Find 12 divided by 2. **26.** Divide 20 by 5. **27.** Find 32 divided by 4.

For another example, see Set B on page 202.

Independent Practice

Algebra Find each missing number.

28. $2 \times \square = 8$

29. $15 \div 3 = \square$

30. $\square \div 3 = 2$

31. $7 \times 4 = \square$

32. $\square \times 5 = 40$

33. $32 \div \square = 8$

Number Sense Write $<$ or $>$ to compare.

34. $4 \times 2 \bigcirc 4 \div 2$

35. $2 \times 3 \bigcirc 6 \div 2$

36. $5 + 8 \bigcirc 5 \times 8$

Problem Solving

37. Writing to Explain Joey says, "I can't solve $8 \div 2$ by using the fact $2 \times 8 = 16$." Do you agree or disagree? Explain.

38. Anna wants to make one array with 2 rows of 8 tiles and another array with 3 rows of 5 tiles. How many tiles does she need all together?

39. You might use 2 gallons of water when you brush your teeth. There are 16 cups in 1 gallon. About how many cups of water might you use when brushing your teeth?

40. Bob has 15 pennies and 3 dimes. Miko has the same amount of money, but she has only nickels. How many nickels does Miko have?

41. Which number sentence is in the same fact family as $3 \times 6 = 18$?

SOL Prep

A $3 \times 3 = 9$

B $2 \times 9 = 18$

C $6 \div 3 = 2$

D $18 \div 6 = 3$

42. Mike bought 3 bags of marbles with 5 marbles in each bag. He gave 4 marbles to Marsha. How many marbles did Mike have left?

A 11

B 15

C 19

D 21

43. Sammy wants to buy one remote control car for $49 and three small cars for $5 each. What is the total amount he will spend?

44. Annie helped her friend set up 40 chairs for a meeting. They set up the chairs in 5 equal rows. Write a division sentence to show the number of chairs in each row. What multiplication fact could you use to help you divide?

Algebra Connections

Division and Number Sentences

Remember that the two sides of a number sentence can be equal or unequal. A symbol >, <, or = tells how the sides compare. Estimation or reasoning can help you tell if one side is greater without doing any computations.

Tip
> means *is greater than*
< means *is less than*
= means *is equal to*

Example: $10 \div 2 \bigcirc 8 \div 2$

Think Each whole is being divided into 2 equal groups. The greater whole will have a greater number of items in each group.

Since 10 is greater than 8, the quotient on the left side is greater. Write the symbol >.

$10 \div 2 \; (>) \; 8 \div 2$

Copy and complete by writing >, <, or =.

1. $20 \div 5 \bigcirc 25 \div 5$

2. $12 \div 3 \bigcirc 12 \div 4$

3. $3 \times 18 \bigcirc 3 \times 21$

4. $24 \div 2 \bigcirc 8$

5. $19 + 19 \bigcirc 2 \times 19$

6. $100 \bigcirc 5 \times 30$

7. $1 \times 53 \bigcirc 1 \times 43$

8. $9 \bigcirc 36 \div 4$

9. $9 \div 3 \bigcirc 18 \div 3$

10. $16 \div 2 \bigcirc 1 + 9$

11. $35 \div 5 \bigcirc 2 + 3$

12. $24 \div 4 \bigcirc 24 \div 2$

In **13** and **14**, copy and complete the number sentence below each problem. Use it to help explain your answer.

13. Mara and Bobby each have 40 pages to read. Mara will read 4 pages each day. Bobby will read 5 pages each day. Who needs more days to read 40 pages?

Mara ↓ Bobby ↓

$\square \div \square \bigcirc \square \div \square$

14. Tim had a board that was 12 feet long. He cut the board into 3 equal pieces. Ellen had a board that was 18 feet long. She cut the board into 3 equal pieces. Who had the longer pieces?

Tim ↓ Ellen ↓

$\square \div \square \bigcirc \square \div \square$

15. Write a Problem Write a problem described by $16 \div 2 > 14 \div 2$.

Virginia

Lesson 8-3

3.5 The student will recall multiplication facts through the twelves table, and the corresponding division facts.

Fact Families with 6 and 7

How do you divide with 6 and 7?

There are 48 dogs entered in a dog show. The judge wants 6 dogs in each group. How many groups will there be?

Choose an Operation Divide to find how many groups.

Guided Practice*

Do you know HOW?

1. Copy and complete the fact family.

$8 \times 6 = 48$
$48 \div 6 = 8$

In **2–10**, find each quotient.

2. $12 \div 6$ **3.** $30 \div 6$ **4.** $42 \div 6$

5. $14 \div 7$ **6.** $77 \div 7$ **7.** $63 \div 7$

8. $6\overline{)24}$ **9.** $6\overline{)54}$ **10.** $7\overline{)49}$

Do you UNDERSTAND?

11. **Number Sense** How can you tell without dividing that $42 \div 6$ will be greater than $42 \div 7$?

12. Write the fact family for 7, 8, and 56.

13. There are 54 children in 6 ballet classes. Each class is the same size. How many children are in each class?

Independent Practice

Find each quotient.

14. $18 \div 6$ **15.** $6 \div 6$ **16.** $21 \div 7$ **17.** $36 \div 6$ **18.** $84 \div 7$

19. $6\overline{)48}$ **20.** $5\overline{)30}$ **21.** $7\overline{)56}$ **22.** $7\overline{)35}$ **23.** $6\overline{)36}$

24. $6\overline{)42}$ **25.** $7\overline{)63}$ **26.** $6\overline{)18}$ **27.** $7\overline{)42}$ **28.** $3\overline{)21}$

29. Find 49 divided by 7. **30.** Divide 72 by 6. **31.** Find 56 divided by 7.

32. Find 60 divided by 6. **33.** Divide 28 by 7. **34.** Find 48 divided by 6.

*For another example, see Set C on page 202.

Find 48 ÷ 6.

What You Think	What You Write
What number times 6 is 48? $8 \times 6 = 48$	$48 \div 6 = 8$ There will be 8 groups.

Another dog was entered. There will now be 7 dogs in each group. How many groups will there be now?

Find 49 ÷ 7.

What You Think	What You Write
What number times 7 is 49? $7 \times 7 = 49$	$49 \div 7 = 7$ There will be 7 groups.

Problem Solving

Use the pictures below for **35–38**.

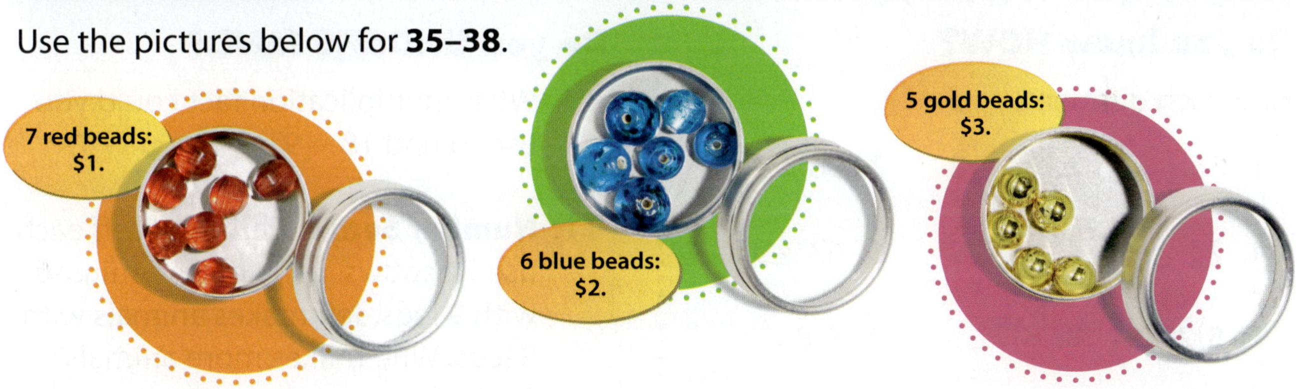

35. Rita needs 15 gold beads for an art project.

a How many packages of beads does she need?

b How much do the beads cost?

36. Eve bought 2 packages of red beads and 2 packages of blue beads.

a How many beads did she buy?

b How much did she spend?

37. **Writing to Explain** Guy bought 28 red beads and 18 blue beads. How many packages did he buy? Explain how you solved the problem.

38. **Number Sense** Andy bought exactly 35 beads, all the same color. Which color beads could he have bought? Explain your thinking.

39. SOL Prep There are 6 rafts on the river. Each raft holds 8 people. Which number sentence is in the fact family for these numbers?

A $48 - 6 = 42$ **C** $48 + 6 = 54$

B $48 \div 6 = 8$ **D** $48 - 8 = 40$

40. SOL Prep The school auditorium has 182 seats. People are sitting in 56 of the seats. Which is the best estimate of the number of seats that do **NOT** have people sitting in them?

A 20 **B** 120 **C** 240 **D** 250

Virginia

Lesson 8-4

3.5 The student will recall multiplication facts through the twelves table, and the corresponding division facts.

Fact Families with 8 and 9

What multiplication fact can you use?

John has 56 straws. How many spiders can he make?

Find $56 \div 8$.

What number times 8 is 56?

$7 \times 8 = 56$

John can make 7 spiders.

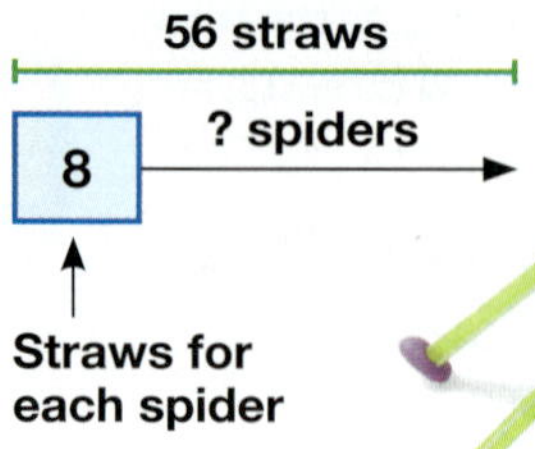

Guided Practice*

Do you know HOW?

Find each quotient.

1. $16 \div 8$ **2.** $64 \div 8$ **3.** $36 \div 9$

4. $27 \div 9$ **5.** $45 \div 9$ **6.** $63 \div 9$

7. $8\overline{)24}$ **8.** $8\overline{)72}$ **9.** $8\overline{)8}$

Do you UNDERSTAND?

10. What multiplication fact could you use to find $18 \div 9$?

11. **Number Sense** Carla and Jeff each use 72 straws. Carla makes animals with 9 legs. Jeff makes animals with 8 legs. Who makes more animals? Explain.

Independent Practice

Find each quotient.

12. $32 \div 8$ **13.** $28 \div 7$ **14.** $18 \div 9$ **15.** $48 \div 8$ **16.** $81 \div 9$

17. $5\overline{)45}$ **18.** $9\overline{)54}$ **19.** $7\overline{)56}$ **20.** $4\overline{)28}$ **21.** $8\overline{)56}$

22. $9\overline{)27}$ **23.** $9\overline{)72}$ **24.** $8\overline{)16}$ **25.** $8\overline{)64}$ **26.** $8\overline{)48}$

27. Find 90 divided by 9. **28.** Divide 40 by 8. **29.** Find 56 divided by 8.

30. Find 81 divided by 9. **31.** Divide 45 by 9. **32.** Find 88 divided by 8.

33. Write fact families for the numbers in **30** and **31**. How are the fact families different?

*For another example, see Set D on page 203.

Luz made 9 animals. She used 54 straws. She used the same number of straws for each animal. How many straws did Luz use for each animal?

Find $54 \div 9$.

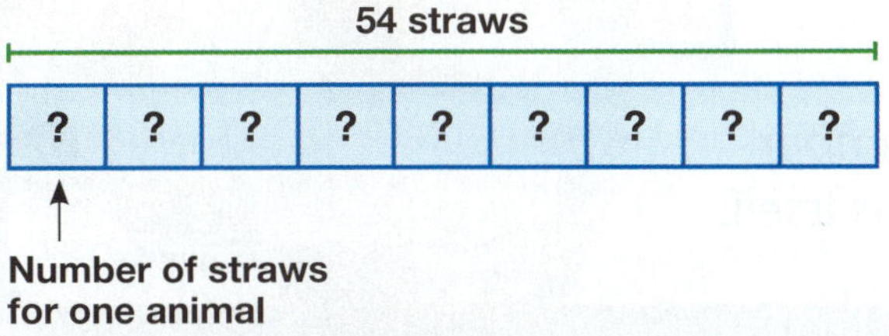

What You Think	What You Write
9 times what number is 54?	$54 \div 9 = 6$
$9 \times 6 = 54$	Luz used 6 straws for each animal.

Problem Solving

Algebra Write < or > to compare.

34. $36 \div 9$ ◯ 9

35. 65 ◯ 8×8

36. $63 \div 9$ ◯ 8

Use the ticket prices at the right for **37–39**.

37. Writing to Explain Mr. Stern bought 4 children's tickets and 2 adult tickets. How much more did he spend for the adult tickets than the children's tickets? Explain.

Data

Playhouse Ticket Prices

Type of Ticket	Price of Ticket
Child	$4
Youth	$8
Adult	$9

38. What is the total cost of 2 children's tickets and 2 adult tickets?

39. Reasoning The clerk at the playhouse sold $72 worth of adult tickets. Ten people bought adult tickets online. Did more people buy tickets at the playhouse or online? Tell how you know.

40. SOL Prep Which number sentence is **NOT** in the same fact family as the others?

A $8 \times 4 = 32$

B $32 \div 8 = 4$

C $2 \times 4 = 8$

D $4 \times 8 = 32$

41. The London Underground has 12 lines. The District line is 8 times as long as the East London line. Use the diagram to write a number sentence to find the length of the East London line.

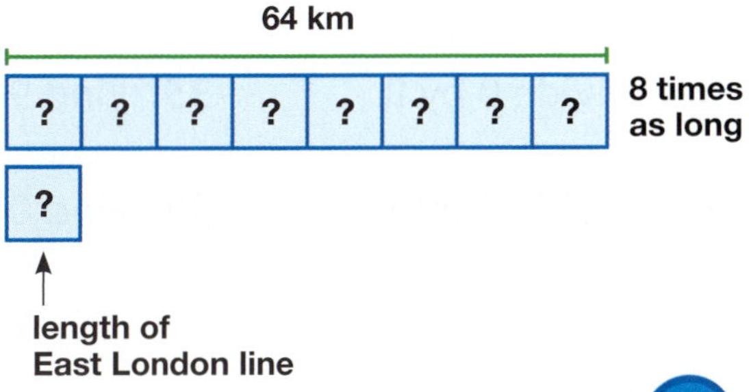

Virginia

Lesson 8-5

3.5 The student will recall multiplication facts through the twelves table, and the corresponding division facts.

Dividing with 0 and 1

How do you divide with 1 or 0?

Dividing by 1

Find 3 ÷ 1

What number times 1 is 3?

$3 \times 1 = 3$

So, $3 \div 1 = 3$.

Rule: Any number divided by 1 is itself.

Guided Practice*

Do you know HOW?

Find each quotient.

1. $8 \div 8$ **2.** $2 \div 1$ **3.** $0 \div 5$

4. $1\overline{)8}$ **5.** $6\overline{)6}$ **6.** $10\overline{)0}$

Do you UNDERSTAND?

7. How can you tell without dividing that $375 \div 375 = 1$?

8. **Writing to Explain** Describe how you can find $0 \div 267$, without dividing.

Independent Practice

Find each quotient.

9. $7 \div 7$ **10.** $0 \div 4$ **11.** $10 \div 1$ **12.** $0 \div 6$ **13.** $10 \div 10$

14. $4 \div 1$ **15.** $7 \div 1$ **16.** $0 \div 8$ **17.** $5 \div 5$ **18.** $5 \div 1$

19. $14 \div 2$ **20.** $70 \div 7$ **21.** $56 \div 7$ **22.** $24 \div 4$ **23.** $90 \div 9$

24. $6\overline{)36}$ **25.** $7\overline{)49}$ **26.** $8\overline{)64}$ **27.** $9\overline{)81}$ **28.** $5\overline{)20}$

29. $7\overline{)56}$ **30.** $8\overline{)48}$ **31.** $7\overline{)42}$ **32.** $5\overline{)25}$ **33.** $4\overline{)32}$

34. Divide 0 by 9. **35.** Find 9 divided by 9. **36.** Find 6 divided by 1.

37. Divide 3 by 3. **38.** Find 0 divided by 8. **39.** Find 7 divided by 1.

**For another example, see Set E on page 203.*

1 as a Quotient

Find $3 \div 3$.

Think: 3 times what number equals 3?

$3 \times 1 = 3$

So, $3 \div 3 = 1$.

Rule: Any number (except 0) divided by itself is 1.

Dividing 0 by a Number

Find $0 \div 3$.

Think: 3 times what number equals 0?

$3 \times 0 = 0$

So, $0 \div 3 = 0$.

Rule: 0 divided by any number (except 0) is 0.

Dividing by 0

Find $3 \div 0$.

Think: 0 times what number equals 3?

There is no such number.

So, $3 \div 0$ can't be done.

Rule: You cannot divide any number by 0.

Problem Solving

Algebra In **40–43**, copy and complete. Use $<$, $>$, or $=$.

40. $3 \div 3 \bigcirc 3 \times 0$

41. $17 \div 17 \bigcirc 1 \div 1$

42. $0 \div 6 \bigcirc 0 \div 1$

43. $6 \times 1 \bigcirc 6 \div 1$

Use the sign at the right for **44–47**.

44. Paul hiked one trail 3 times for a total distance of 12 miles. Which trail did he hike?

45. **Reasoning** Addie hiked 3 different trails for a total distance of 11 miles. Which trails did she hike?

46. Yoko hiked the blue trail once and the green trail twice. How many miles did she hike on the green trail?

47. **Writing to Explain** Marty hiked one trail 4 times. He hiked more than 10 miles but less than 16 miles. Which trail did he hike? Explain.

48. Objects in Windsor Castle are 12 times the size of the miniature versions in Queen Mary's dollhouse. How tall is a real-life painting if it is 1 inch tall in the dollhouse?

49. Which number will make the number sentence below true?

SOL Prep

$54 \div \square = 9$

A 5 **B** 6 **C** 7 **D** 8

Virginia

Lesson 8-6

Extends 3.2 The student will recognize and use the inverse relationships between addition/subtraction and multiplication/division to complete basic fact sentences. The student will use these relationships to solve problems.

Problem Solving

Draw a Picture and Write a Number Sentence

Jeff is setting up the sand-painting booth at the school carnival. He put the sand from one bag of sand into 5 buckets. If each bucket has the same amount of sand, how much sand is in each bucket?

Another Example Are there other types of division situations?

Alison is setting up the prize booth. She has 48 prizes. She will put 8 prizes in each row. How many rows can she make?

Plan and Solve

Use a diagram to show what you know.

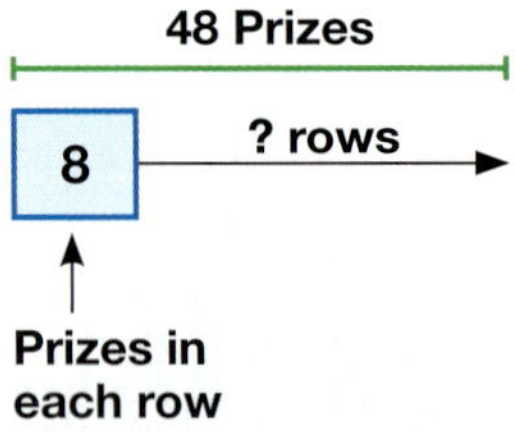

Answer

Write a number sentence

$48 \div 8 = 6$

Alison can make 6 rows.

Check

Make sure the answer is reasonable.

Use multiplication or repeated addition to check.

$6 \times 8 = 48$

or

$8 + 8 + 8 + 8 + 8 + 8 = 48$

Explain It

1. Explain how you can check the quotient in division by using either multiplication or addition.
2. **Number Sense** If Alison wants fewer than 6 rows of prizes, should she put more or fewer prizes in each row? Explain your thinking.

Plan and Solve

Use a diagram to show what you know.

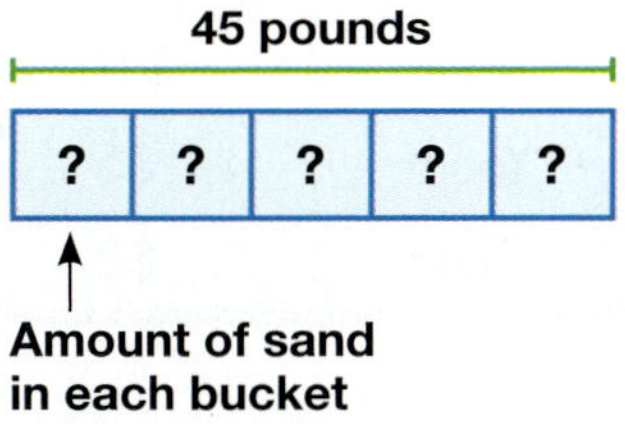

You know the total amount of sand and that there are 5 buckets. Divide to find how much sand is in each bucket.

Answer

Write a number sentence.

$45 \div 5 = 9$

There are 9 pounds of sand in each bucket.

Check

Make sure the answer is reasonable.

Use multiplication or repeated addition to check.

$5 \times 9 = 45$

or

$9 + 9 + 9 + 9 + 9 = 45$

Guided Practice*

Do you know HOW?

1. Larry and Pat made 18 posters. Each made the same number. How many did each make? Write a number sentence and solve.

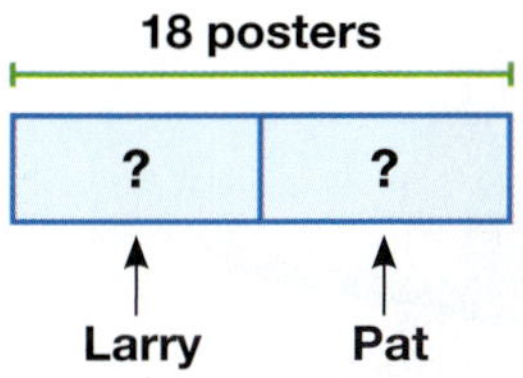

Do you UNDERSTAND?

2. What operation did you use for Problem 1? Tell why.

3. **Write a Problem** Write a real-world problem that you can solve by subtracting. Draw a diagram. Write a number sentence and solve.

Independent Practice

For **4** and **5**, draw a diagram to show what you know. Then write a number sentence and solve.

4. There are 8 cars on a Ferris wheel. Each car holds 3 people. How many people can ride the Ferris wheel at the same time?

5. There were 24 children in a relay race. There were 6 teams in all. How many children were on each team?

6. Austin is 8 years old. Grace is twice as old as Austin. How old is Grace?

Stuck? Try this....

- What do I know?
- What am I asked to find?
- What diagram can I use to help understand the problem?
- Can I use addition, subtraction, multiplication, or division?
- Is all of my work correct?
- Did I answer the right question?
- Is my answer reasonable?

*For another example, see Set F on page 203.

Independent Practice

Use the table at the right for **7** and **8**. Solve each problem.

Cost of Tickets	
Adult	$10
Youth	$5
Child	$3

7. Mr. Niglio bought 2 youth tickets and 2 adult tickets. He gave the clerk a $50 bill. How much change did he get back?

8. **Number Sense** Dan, Sue, and Joe each bought a different kind of ticket. Dan spent the least. Sue spent twice as much as Joe. How much did Joe spend?

For **9** and **10**, use the animal pictures at the right. Write a number sentence and solve.

9. About how many hours is a sloth awake each day?

Tip *There are 24 hours in a day.*

10. About how many hours is a koala bear awake each day?

Tip *There are 7 days in a week.*

Think About the Process

11. Alma bought 2 bracelets for $6 at the craft fair. Each bracelet cost the same amount. Which number sentence shows how to find the cost of each bracelet?

A $2 \times \$6 = \square$

B $2 + \$6 = \square$

C $\$6 - 2 = \square$

D $\$6 \div 2 = \square$

12. Tomas bought a book for $4, crayons for $2, and a pen for $1. He gave the clerk $10. Which number sentence shows how to find his change?

A $\$4 + \$2 + \$1 = \square$

B $\$4 \times \$2 \times \$1 = \square$

C $\$10 - \$6 = \square$

D $\$10 - (\$4 + \$2 + \$1) = \square$

Going Digital

Choosing an Operation and a Computation Method

The tallest building in a city is on Central Avenue. It is 921 feet tall. The second tallest building is on Main Street. It is 886 feet tall. How much taller is the building on Central Avenue than the building on Main Street?

Step 1 Choose an operation.

You are comparing the heights, so subtract. Find 921 − 886.

Step 2 Choose the best computation method. Decide whether to use mental math, paper and pencil, or a calculator.

Since there is more than 1 regrouping, use a calculator.

Step 3 Solve.

Press: 921 [−] 886 [ENTER =]

Display: 35

The building on Central Avenue is 35 feet taller than the building on Main Street.

Practice

For each problem, choose an operation. Then use the best computation method to solve.

1. The building on Central Avenue has 72 floors. An elevator stopped at every 9th floor as it came down from the top floor to the bottom. How many times did it stop?

2. An office building on Elm Street could be divided into 3 sections with 25 floors in each section. How many floors does the office building have?

3. The Plaza skyscraper is 579 feet tall. The Fountain skyscraper is 142 feet taller. How tall is the Fountain skyscraper?

4. The Morgan building is 1,002 feet tall. The Plaza Tower is 972 feet tall. How much taller is the Morgan building than the Plaza Tower?

VA SOL Test Prep

1. Which number makes both number sentences true? (8-1)

$9 \times \square = 54$
$54 \div 9 = \square$

A 8

B 7

C 6

D 5

2. Which number sentence is true? (8-5)

A $6 \div 6 = 0$

B $5 \div 1 = 1$

C $0 \div 4 = 4$

D $7 \div 1 = 7$

3. Nancy has 4 CDs. Each CD has 8 songs. Which number sentence is in the same fact family as $4 \times 8 = 32$? (8-2)

A $32 \div 4 = 8$

B $32 - 8 = 24$

C $8 - 4 = 4$

D $2 \times 4 = 8$

4. Gavin has 7 pages of his picture album filled. Each page has 6 pictures, for a total of 42 pictures. Which number sentence is **NOT** in the same fact family as the others? (8-3)

A $7 \times 6 = 42$

B $6 \times 7 = 42$

C $42 \div 7 = 6$

D $5 \times 7 = 35$

5. Mrs. Hendrix bought 45 pounds of modeling clay. She wants to divide it evenly among her 5 art classes. How many pounds of modeling clay will each class get? (8-2)

A 40

B 9

C 8

D 7

6. Beth bought a box of dog treats. The box had 48 treats. If Beth gives her dog 6 treats a day, how many days will the box of treats last? (8-3)

A 6

B 7

C 8

D 9

7. What number makes this number sentence true? (8-4)

$\square \div 9 = 8$

A 81

B 72

C 17

D 8

8. Peg put 18 rocks into 2 equal piles. How many rocks were in each pile? (8-2)

A 6

B 8

C 9

D 36

9. Neil has 30 nails and 6 boards. Which number sentence shows how many nails he can put in each board if he puts the same number in each? (8-6)

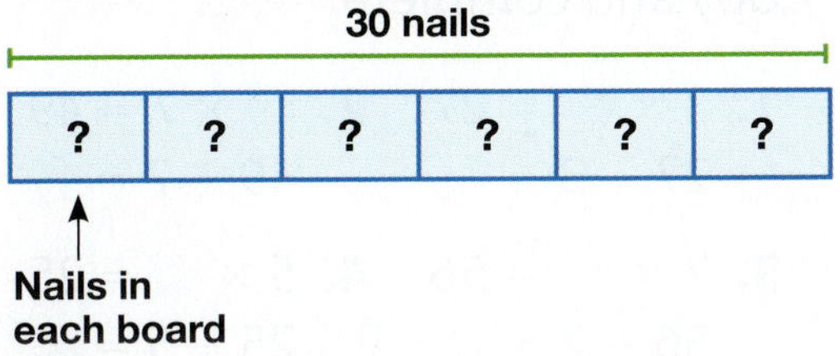

A $30 + 6 = 36$

B $30 - 6 = 24$

C $30 \div 6 = 5$

D $6 \times 30 = 180$

10. The drawing below shows how Janet planted 18 daisies in her flowerbed.

$6 \times 3 = 18$

Which division sentence can be written using the drawing of Janet's daisies? (8-1)

A $6 \div 3 = 2$

B $18 \div 9 = 2$

C $24 \div 3 = 8$

D $18 \div 6 = 3$

11. Mrs. Manchez bought 3 boxes of tissue. How many rooms will get a box of tissue if she puts 1 box in each room? (8-5)

A 9

B 3

C 1

D 0

12. A league has 7 basketball teams. Each team has 8 players, for a total of 56 players. Which number sentence is **NOT** in the same fact family as the others? (8-4)

A $9 \times 7 = 63$

B $8 \times 7 = 56$

C $56 \div 8 = 7$

D $7 \times 8 = 56$

13. Mr. Yarbrough bought 20 pounds of sand. Each bag contained 5 pounds of sand. Which number sentence shows how to find the number of bags of sand Mr. Yarbrough bought? (8-6)

A $20 \div 5 = 4$

B $5 \times 20 = 100$

C $20 - 5 = 15$

D $20 + 5 = 25$

14. What is $24 \div 8$? (8-4)

A 16

B 6

C 4

D 3

Topic 8

VA SOL Reteaching

Set A, pages 184–185

Use the array to help you find the fact family for 4, 7, and 28.

Multiplication	**Division**
$4 \times 7 = 28$	$28 \div 4 = 7$
$7 \times 4 = 28$	$28 \div 7 = 4$

Remember that a fact family shows how multiplication and division are related.

Copy and complete.

1. $3 \times \square = 27$
   $27 \div 3 = \square$
2. $\square \times 7 = 49$
   $49 \div 7 = \square$
3. $7 \times \square = 56$
   $56 \div 7 = \square$
4. $5 \times \square = 25$
   $25 \div 5 = \square$

Set B, pages 186–188

Hanna read 21 pages of a book in 3 days. If Hanna read the same number of pages each day, how many pages did she read each day?

Find $21 \div 3$.

Think: What number times 3 equals 21?

$7 \times 3 = 21$

Write: $21 \div 3 = 7$

Hanna read 7 pages each day.

Remember to think of a related multiplication fact to solve a division problem.

Find each quotient.

1. $27 \div 3$
2. $12 \div 2$
3. $32 \div 4$
4. $35 \div 5$
5. $50 \div 5$
6. $8 \div 2$
7. $20 \div 4$
8. $18 \div 3$

Set C, pages 190–191

Joseph has 24 spelling words to practice in the next 6 days. How many words does he need to practice each day?

Find $24 \div 6$.

Think: What number times 6 equals 24?

$4 \times 6 = 24$

Write: $24 \div 6 = 4$

Joseph has 4 words to practice each day.

Remember that division problems can be written in two ways.

Find the quotient.

1. $63 \div 7$
2. $36 \div 6$
3. $42 \div 6$
4. $60 \div 6$
5. $7\overline{)14}$
6. $6\overline{)30}$
7. $6\overline{)48}$
8. $7\overline{)42}$

Set D, pages 192–193

There are 36 students who want to play baseball. Each team needs 9 players. How many teams will there be?

Find $36 \div 9$.

Think What number times 9 equals 36?

$4 \times 9 = 36$

Write: $36 \div 9 = 4$

There will be 4 teams.

Remember that you can divide to find how many equal groups.

Find the quotient.

1. $64 \div 8$
2. $18 \div 9$
3. $9\overline{)54}$
4. $8\overline{)32}$
5. Divide 24 by 8.
6. Find 45 divided by 9.

Set E, pages 194–195

Find $8 \div 1$, $8 \div 8$, and $0 \div 8$.

When any number is divided by 1, the quotient is that number. $\mathbf{8 \div 1 = 8}$

When any number (except 0) is divided by itself, the quotient is 1. $\mathbf{8 \div 8 = 1}$

When zero is divided by any number (except 0), the quotient is 0. $\mathbf{0 \div 8 = 0}$

Remember that you cannot divide any number by 0.

Find each quotient.

1. $4 \div 1$
2. $7 \div 7$
3. $0 \div 5$
4. $1\overline{)5}$
5. $3\overline{)0}$
6. $9\overline{)9}$
7. $6\overline{)6}$
8. $1\overline{)7}$
9. $4\overline{)0}$

Set F, pages 196–198

Carl has 48 balloons to tie in 6 equal groups. How many balloons will be in each group?

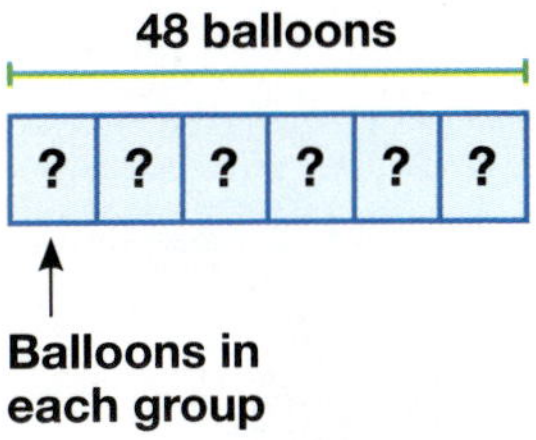

Draw a diagram to show what you know.

Write a number sentence.
$48 \div 6 = 8$
There will be 8 balloons in each group.

Remember to read carefully.

Draw a diagram and write a number sentence to solve.

1. A roller coaster has 10 cars that each hold 6 people. How many people can ride the roller coaster at one time?
2. There were 36 children on a field trip. The children formed 6 equal groups. How many children were in each group?

Topic 9

Patterns and Relationships

1 How many years will it take an animal symbol to repeat in the Chinese calendar? You will find out in Lesson 9-2.

2 How fast can a penguin swim? You will find out in Lesson 9-3.

3 Are the rocks of Stonehenge arranged in a pattern? You will find out in Lesson 9-6.

4

How many eggs can an ostrich hen lay in a year? You will find out in Lesson 9-4.

Review What You Know!

Vocabulary

Choose the best term from the box.

- compare
- multiply
- divide
- regroup

1. To put together equal groups to find the total number, you __?__.

2. To decide if 4 has more ones or fewer ones than 8, __?__ the numbers.

3. To separate into equal groups, you __?__.

Number Patterns

Write the missing number in each pattern.

4. 3, 6, 9, 12, ▢, 18 **5.** 4, 8, 12, ▢, 20, 24

6. 8, 7, 6, ▢, 4, 3 **7.** 30, 25, 20, 15, ▢, 5

Multiplication Facts

Find each product.

8. 4×3 **9.** 3×5 **10.** 7×2

11. 5×6 **12.** 2×4 **13.** 3×7

Division Facts

Find each quotient.

14. $20 \div 4$ **15.** $10 \div 5$ **16.** $18 \div 6$

17. $28 \div 4$ **18.** $24 \div 6$ **19.** $56 \div 8$

20. **Writing to Explain** Janelle bought 4 cans of tennis balls. There are 3 balls in each can. How many tennis balls did she buy? Explain how you solved the problem.

Virginia

Lesson 9-1

3.19 The student will recognize and describe a variety of patterns formed using numbers, tables, and pictures, and extend the patterns, using the same or different forms.

Repeating Patterns

How can you continue a repeating pattern?

Rashad is making patterns with shapes. What three shapes should come next in this pattern?

A repeating pattern is made up of shapes or numbers that form a part that repeats.

Guided Practice*

Do you know HOW?

1. Draw the next three shapes to continue the pattern.

2. Write the next three numbers to continue the pattern.
9, 2, 7, 6, 9, 2, 7, 6, 9

Do you UNDERSTAND?

3. In the example above, describe the pattern using words.

4. What is the 10th shape in the pattern below? How do you know?

Independent Practice

In **5–8**, draw the next three shapes to continue the pattern.

5. 

6. 

7. 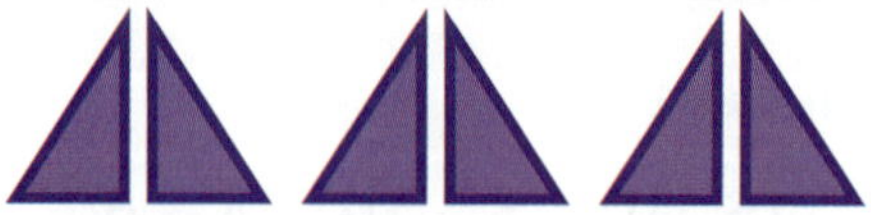

8. 

In **9–12**, write the next three numbers to continue the pattern.

9. 1, 1, 2, 1, 1, 2, 1, 1, 2

10. 5, 7, 4, 8, 5, 7, 4, 8, 5, 7, 4

11. 2, 8, 2, 9, 2, 8, 2, 9, 2, 8, 2, 9

12. 4, 0, 3, 3, 4, 0, 3, 3, 4, 0, 3

DIGITAL Animated Glossary **www.pearsonsuccessnet.com**

*For another example, see Set A on page 230.

Step 1

Find the part that repeats.

These 4 shapes make up the part that repeats.

Step 2

Continue the pattern.

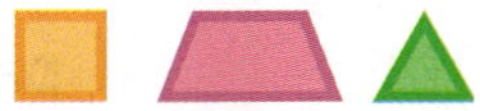

Problem Solving

13. Hilda is making a pattern with the shapes below. If she continues the pattern, what will the 11th shape in the pattern be? Draw a picture to show the shape.

14. Marcus is using shapes to make the pattern below. He wants the completed pattern to show the part that repeats 5 times. How many circles will be in Marcus' finished pattern?

15. Louisa put beads on a string to make a bracelet. She used a blue bead, then three green beads, then a blue bead, then three green beads, and so on, until she used 18 green beads. How many beads did she use in all?

16. **Estimation** A box of toy blocks has 108 blocks. Jiang used 72 of the blocks to make a building. About how many blocks are left in the box? Explain how you estimated.

17. The table shows the number of students in each grade at a school.

Which grade has more than 145 but fewer than 149 students?

A First **C** Second

B Third **D** Fourth

Data

Grade	Number of Students
First	142
Second	158
Third	146
Fourth	139

18. **Writing to Explain** Balloons are sold in bags of 30. There are 5 giant balloons in each bag. How many giant balloons will you get if you buy 120 balloons? Explain.

Virginia

Lesson 9-2

3.19 The student will recognize and describe a variety of patterns formed using numbers, tables, and pictures, and extend the patterns, using the same or different forms.

Number Sequences

What is the pattern?

The house numbers on a street are in a pattern. If the pattern continues, what are the next three numbers?

Guided Practice*

Do you know HOW?

In **1** and **2**, find a rule for the pattern. Use your rule to continue each pattern.

1. 

2. 48, 42, 36, 30, 24, ___, ___, ___

Do you UNDERSTAND?

3. In the example above, suppose 16 is the 1st number in the pattern. What is the 10th number?

4. Rudy is using "add 2" as his rule to make a pattern. He started with 4 and wrote the numbers below for his pattern. Which number does not belong in this pattern? Explain.

4, 6, 8, 9, 10, 12

Independent Practice

In **5–16**, find a rule for the pattern. Use your rule to continue each pattern.

5. 21, 18, 15, ___, ___

6. 4, 11, 18, ___, ___

7. 5, 10, 15, ___, ___

8. 5, 7, 9, ___, ___, 15

9. 250, 300, 350, ___, ___

10. 92, 80, 68, ___, ___

11. 790, 780, 770, ___, ___

12. 16, 27, 38, ___, ___

13. 96, 101, 106, ___, 116, ___

14. 43, 47, 51, ___, ___, 63

15. 120, 105, 90, ___, ___, 45

16. 99, 90, 81, 72, ___, ___

For another example, see Set B on page 230.

Step 1

Find a rule for the pattern.

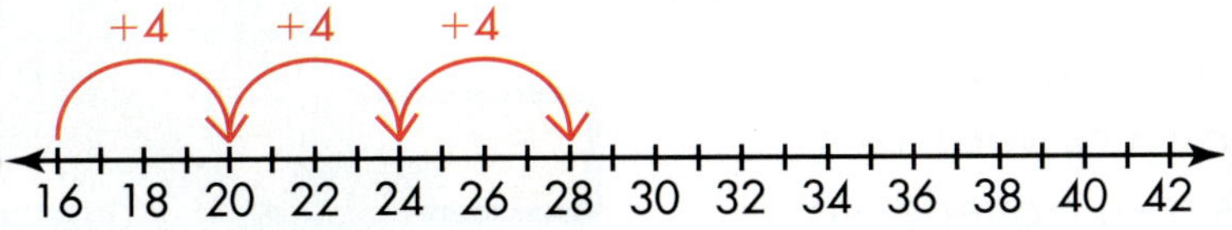

Each number is 4 more than the number before it.

Step 2

Use your rule to continue the pattern.

Rule: Add 4.

$28 + 4 = 32$

$32 + 4 = 36$

$36 + 4 = 40$

The next numbers in the pattern are 32, 36, and 40.

Problem Solving

17. Orlando delivers mail. He sees that one mailbox does not have a number. If the numbers are in a pattern, what is the missing number?

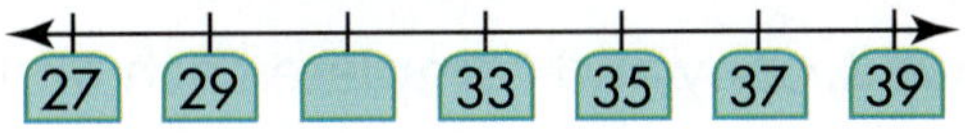

18. In the Chinese calendar, each year has an animal as a symbol. There are 12 animals. It was the year of the snake in 2001 and will be again in 2013. The year 2005 was the year of the rooster. When is the next year of the rooster?

19. Suppose you were born in the year of the snake. How old will you be the next time the year of the snake is celebrated?

20. **Reasoning** The numbers below are in a pattern.

SOL Prep

24, 27, 30, 33

Which number would be part of the pattern?

A 34 **C** 39

B 38 **D** 44

21. Mia counted the pencils in groups of 6.

SOL Prep

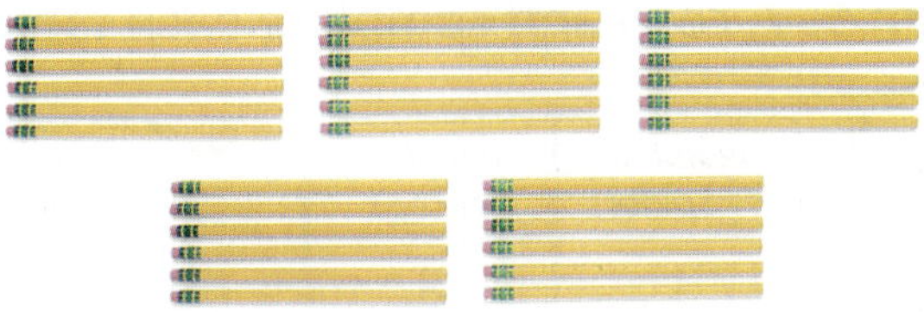

Which list shows numbers Mia named?

A 24, 36, 48, 52 **C** 6, 12, 24, 32

B 6, 24, 48, 56 **D** 12, 18, 24, 30

Virginia

Lesson 9-3

3.19 The student will recognize and describe a variety of patterns formed using numbers, tables, and pictures, and extend the patterns, using the same or different forms.

Extending Tables

What pairs of numbers fit a pattern?

There are 3 leaflets on 1 cloverleaf.
There are 9 leaflets on 3 cloverleaves.
There are 12 leaflets on 4 cloverleaves.
How many leaflets are there on 2 cloverleaves? on 5 cloverleaves?

Guided Practice*

Do you know HOW?

In **1** and **2**, copy and complete each table.

1.

Number of Boxes	Total Number of Hats
2	6
5	15
7	21
	27

2.

Number of Cars	2	3	5	9
Total Number of Wheels	8	12	20	

Do you UNDERSTAND?

3. In the example above, 4 and 12 are a pair of numbers that fit the pattern. Does the pair 6 and 16 fit the pattern? Explain.

4. Reasonableness A rule for this table is "add 5 to my age."

My Age	Joe's Age
5	10
8	13
9	15

Which number does not belong?

Independent Practice

In **5–7**, copy and complete each table.

5.

Number of Spiders	Number of Legs
1	8
2	
3	24
4	32
	56

6.

Regular Price	Sale Price
$29	$22
$25	$18
	$16
$22	
$19	$12

7.

Weight of Book in Ounces	9	11	12	16
Total Weight of Carton in Ounces	18	20	21	

8. For each table in 5–7, write another pair of numbers that could be in the table.

*For another example, see Set C on page 230.

Draw pictures to show what you know.

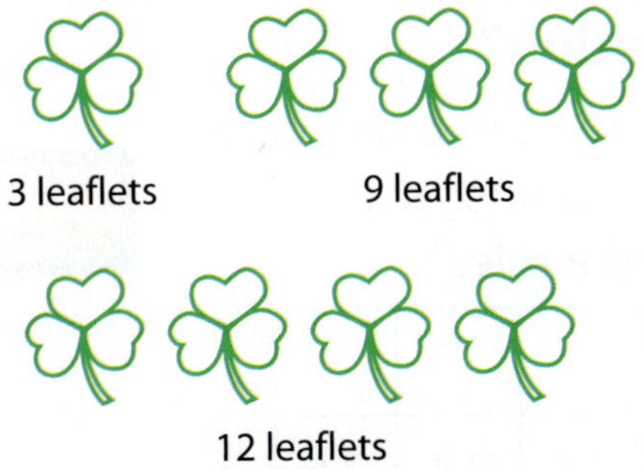

Fill in a table by using a rule.

Rule: Multiply by 3

Number of Cloverleaves	Number of Leaflets
1	3
2	6
3	9
4	12
5	15

Problem Solving

For **9** and **10**, the table at the right shows the number of batteries needed for different numbers of one kind of flashlight.

Data

Batteries for Flashlights

Number of Flashlights	Number of Batteries
1	3
4	12
7	21

9. How many batteries do 8 flashlights need? 10 flashlights?

10. **Writing to Explain** How many more batteries do 6 flashlights need than 4 flashlights? Explain how you found your answer.

11. **Number Sense** What is the greatest number you can make using each of the digits 1, 7, 0, and 6 once?

12. A penguin can swim 11 miles per hour. At this speed, how far can it swim in 3 hours? Use a table to help.

13. Alan has 35 fewer coins than Suzy has. Which of these shows the number of coins that Alan and Suzy could have?

SOL Prep

A Alan 65, Suzy 105
B Alan 105, Suzy 70
C Alan 105, Suzy 65
D Alan 70, Suzy 105

14. If the pattern at the right continues, how long will each side of the next square be?

SOL Prep

A 8 feet
B 9 feet
C 10 feet
D 11 feet

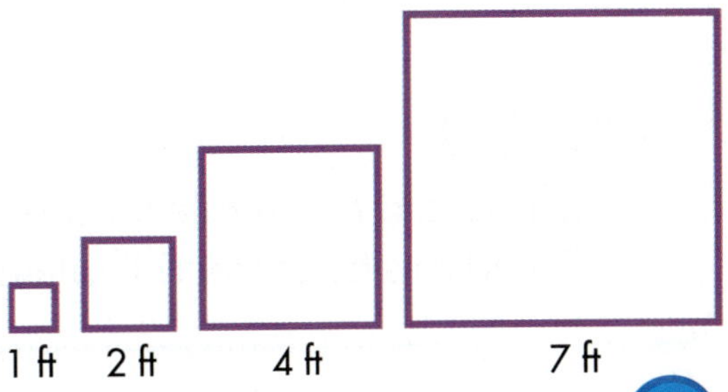

Virginia

Lesson 9-4

3.19 The student will recognize and describe a variety of patterns formed using numbers, tables, and pictures, and extend the patterns, using the same or different forms.

Writing Rules for Situations

What is a math rule for the situation?

Alex and his older brother Andy have the same birthday. If you know Alex's age, how can you find Andy's age? Look for a pattern in the table and find a rule.

Alex's age	2	4	6	7	9
Andy's age	8	10	12	13	15

Another Example **What other rules are there for pairs of numbers?**

Nell saves some of the money she earns. The table shows how much she earned and how much she saved for five days. What is a rule for the table? What are the missing numbers?

Earned	65¢	45¢	50¢	30¢	
Saved	50¢	30¢		15¢	25¢

Step 1

Find a rule for the table.

Look for a pattern.

Earned	65¢	45¢	50¢	30¢	
Saved	50¢	30¢		15¢	25¢

Each time, the amount saved is 15¢ less than the amount earned.

Rule: Subtract 15¢ from the amount earned.

Step 2

Check that your rule works for all pairs.

65¢ − 15¢ = 50¢
45¢ − 15¢ = 30¢
30¢ − 15¢ = 15¢

Your rule works for each pair.

What amount is 15¢ less than 50¢?
50¢ − 15¢ = 35¢

25¢ is 15¢ less than what amount?
25¢ = ▢ − 15¢   15¢ + 25¢ = 40¢

The missing amounts are 35¢ saved and 40¢ earned.

Explain It

1. David said that a rule for the table above is "Add 15¢." Could this be correct? Explain.

Step 1

Find a rule for the table.

Compare each pair of numbers. Look for a pattern.

Alex's age	2	4	6	7	9
Andy's age	8	10	12	13	15

In each pair, Andy's age is 6 more than Alex's age. You say a rule for the table is "add 6."

Step 2

Check that your rule works for all pairs.

Rule: Add 6.

$2 + 6 = 8$
$4 + 6 = 10$
$6 + 6 = 12$
$7 + 6 = 13$
$9 + 6 = 15$

Your rule works for each pair.

Guided Practice*

Do you know HOW?

In **1** and **2**, use the table below.

Hours Worked	4	8	7	2	6
Amount Earned	$24	$48	▢	$12	▢

1. Write a rule for the table.

2. What are the missing numbers?

Do you UNDERSTAND?

3. In the example above, what does the rule "add 6" mean in the problem?

4. Marty uses the rule "subtract 9" for his table. If the first number in Marty's table is 11, what is the second number in that pair?

Independent Practice

In **5–9**, find a rule for the table. Use your rule to complete the table.

5.

Earned	$15	$12	$17	$9	$11
Spent	$7	▢	$9	▢	$3

6.

Earned	$14	$18	$12	$16	$8
Saved	$7	$9	▢	▢	$4

7.

Price	$36	$28	$33	$40	$25
Discount	$24	$16	▢	$28	▢

8.

Number of Chairs	*Number of Legs*
3	12
2	8
5	20
7	▢
▢	36

9.

Number of Teams	*Number of Players*
4	20
3	15
5	▢
6	30
8	▢

**For another example, see Set C on page 230.*

Problem Solving

For **10** and **11**, use the table at the right.

10. The table shows the ages of a velvet mesquite tree and a saguaro cactus plant at a garden. When the velvet mesquite tree was 48 years old, how old was the saguaro cactus?

Plant's Age in Years

Velvet Mesquite Tree	Saguaro Cactus
1 year	36
15	50
67	102
48	

11. Reasonableness Phil says the saguaro cactus is about 100 years older than the velvet mesquite tree. Is his estimate reasonable? Explain.

12. Use the table below. How many eggs can 4 ostrich hens lay in one year? 5 ostrich hens?

Number of Ostrich Hens	1	2	3	4	5
Number of Eggs	50	100	150		

For **13** and **14**, the table shows the number of baskets that Betty needs for different numbers of apples. She needs to put an equal number of apples into each basket.

Betty's Apple Baskets

Number of Apples	28	56	7	21	14
Number of Baskets	4		1	3	2

13. How many baskets does Betty need for 56 apples?

A 8 **B** 7 **C** 6 **D** 5

14. What is a rule for the table?

A Subtract 24. **C** Divide by 7.

B Subtract 6. **D** Add 12.

15. An art museum has 47 paintings in one room and 24 paintings in another room. Which is the best estimate of the total number of paintings in these two rooms?

A 50 **C** 80

B 70 **D** 100

16. Esther is 8 years older than Manuel. Which of these shows the ages that Esther and Manuel could be?

A Esther 15, Manuel 23

B Esther 16, Manuel 15

C Esther 15, Manuel 7

D Esther 7, Manuel 15

Mixed Problem Solving

Math and Social Studies

In the 1800s and 1900s, several inventions helped to change life around the world. The time line shows the dates of some of these inventions and discoveries.

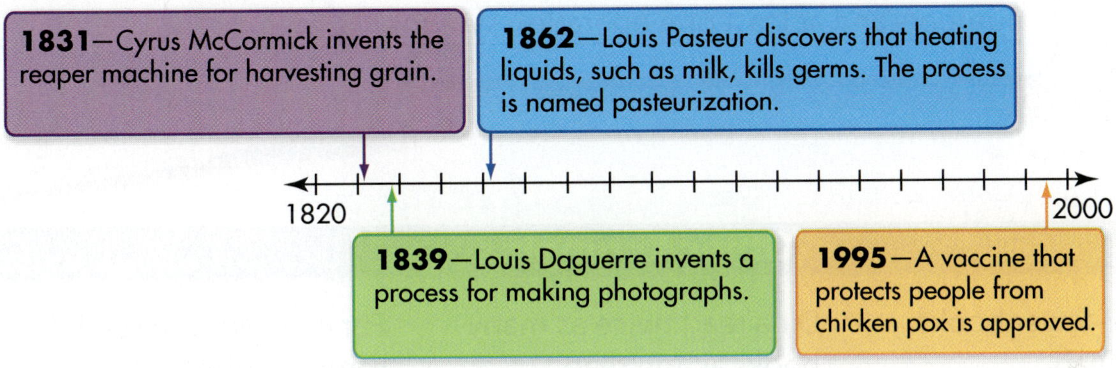

1. Which invention was made about 10 years before a process for making photographs was invented?

2. How many years after the discovery of pasteurization was the chicken pox vaccine approved?

3. Which invention or discovery was made before 1900 but after 1850?

4. How many years have passed since the year that a chicken pox vaccine was approved?

For **5** and **6**, use the table below.

Data

Year	Invention
1804	Steam Locomotive
1885	Gasoline-powered Automobile
1934	Diesel Train in U.S.

5. How many years passed between the first steam locomotive and U.S. diesel train?

6. How many years ago was the gasoline-powered automobile invented?

7. **Strategy Focus** Solve the problem. Use the strategy Make a Table.

The reaper machine could cut wheat and move it to the side for harvesting. One reaper machine could do the work of 5 people. How many reapers could do the work of 20 people?

Virginia

Lesson 9-5

Prepares for 5.18.b The student will write an open sentence to represent a given mathematical relationship, using a variable.

Translating Words to Expressions

How can you translate words to numerical expressions?

In a reading contest, Kara read 5 more books than Jon. What numerical expression shows how many books Kara read?

A numerical expression is made up of numbers and at least one operation symbol.

Other Examples

Teri read 3 fewer books than Jon read.

Word phrase
"3 fewer books than the 8 books Jon read"

Numerical expression
$8 - 3$

Dina read twice as many books as Jon read.

Word phrase
"twice as many as the 8 books Jon read"

Numerical expression
2×8

For 4 weeks, Jon read the same number of books each week.

Word phrase
"the 8 books Jon read, put into 4 equal groups"

Numerical expression
$8 \div 4$

Guided Practice*

Do you know HOW?

Write a numerical expression for each.

1. 18 less than 25

2. half of 14

Tip *"Half" means 2 equal groups.*

3. the total of 24, 16, and 32

Do you UNDERSTAND?

4. Jon read 7 fewer books than Jamal. Use the examples above to write a numerical expression to show how many books Jamal read.

5. **Reasoning** Does the word "fewer" always tell you to subtract? Explain.

Independent Practice

In **6–9**, write a numerical expression for each word phrase.

6. 7 times as many as 8

7. the product of 9 and 8

8. the difference of 56 and 48

9. the sum of 15, 24, and 18

*For another example, see Set D on page 231.

What You Think

Word phrase:

"5 more books than the 8 books Jon read"

To find 5 more than a number, use addition.

What You Write

To show the number of books Kara read, write "the sum of 8 and 5" as a numerical expression.

Numerical expression:

$8 + 5$

Problem Solving

In **10–17,** write a numerical expression for each word phrase.

10. 8 points taken away from 16 points

11. 28 players separated into 4 equal teams

12. $15 less than $35

13. 4 times as long as 9 inches

14. twice as old as 7 years old

15. 24 grapes shared equally by 4 people

16. the total of 18 children and 13 adults

17. 45 yards shorter than 120 yards

There are 10 cars in a parking lot. For **18–21,** write a numerical expression for the number of cars described in each word phrase.

18. 7 fewer cars

19. half the number of cars

20. 5 times as many cars

21. 12 more cars

22. **Geometry** Juana has a wooden block that is 12 inches long. Juana cut the block into 6 pieces that are all the same length. How long is each piece?

23. Walt bought 16 muffins packed equally into 4 boxes. Which numerical expression shows how to find the number of muffins in each box?

A $16 \div 4$

B 16×4

C $16 - 4$

D $16 + 4$

DIGITAL Animated Glossary **www.pearsonsuccessnet.com**

Virginia

Lesson 9-6

Prepares for 4.15 The student will recognize, create, and extend numerical and geometric patterns.

Geometric Patterns

Hands-On
grid paper
cubes

How can you describe block towers?

Talisa made three block towers. She recorded her pattern. If she continued the pattern, how many blocks would be in a 10-story tower? a 100-story tower?

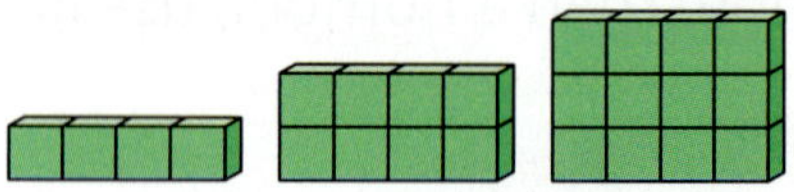

Stories:	1	2	3
Blocks:	4	8	12

Another Example Making Another Block Tower

Luis made three more block towers. He recorded his pattern. If he continued the pattern, how many blocks would a 5-story tower have?

Number of Stories	1	2	3
Number of Blocks	1	3	6

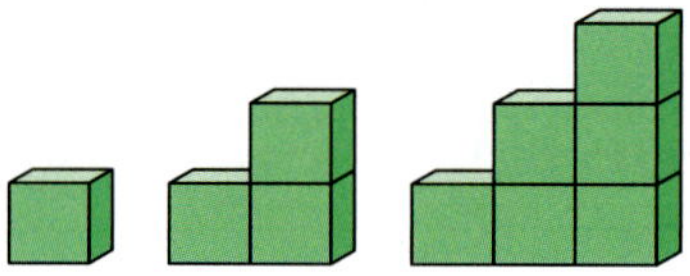

Build the next two towers.

Number of Stories	1	2	3	4	5
Number of Blocks	1	3	6		

A 4-story tower has 10 blocks, and a 5-story tower has 15 blocks.

Explain It

1. How many blocks would Luis need for a 6-story tower? Explain.
2. How many stories is a tower made of 36 blocks?

Build the next two towers.

Number of Stories	1	2	3	4	5
Number of Blocks	4	8	12		

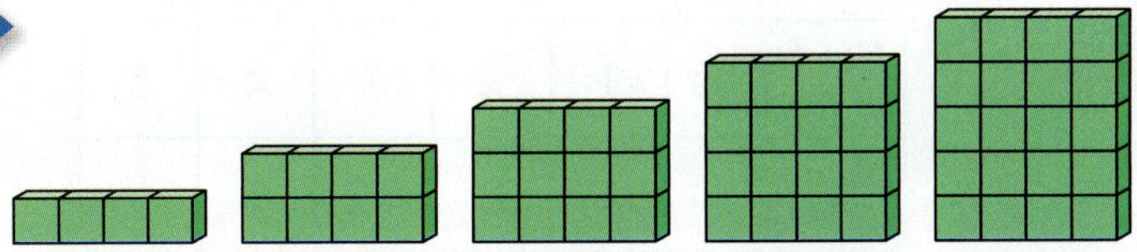

1 story
4 blocks

2 stories
8 blocks

3 stories
12 blocks

4 stories
16 blocks

5 stories
20 blocks

A rule for the pattern in the table is "multiply by 4."

$5 \times 4 = 20$
$10 \times 4 = 40$
$100 \times 4 = 400$

A 10-story tower would have 40 blocks.

A 100-story tower would have 400 blocks.

Guided Practice*

Do you know HOW?

In **1** and **2**, draw the next two towers in the pattern. Use grid paper. Find the missing numbers in each table.

1.

Number of Stories	1	2	3	4	5
Number of Blocks	2	4	6		

2.

Number of Stories	1	2	3	4	5	
Number of Blocks	2	3	4	5		7

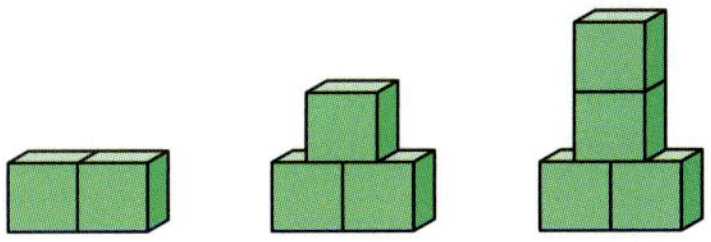

Do you UNDERSTAND?

3. In the example above, why does multiplication work to get from the first number to the second number in a number pair?

4. In Exercise 1, how many blocks would a 10-story tower have?

5. Lionel made the three block towers below. If he continued the pattern, how many blocks would a 100-story tower have?

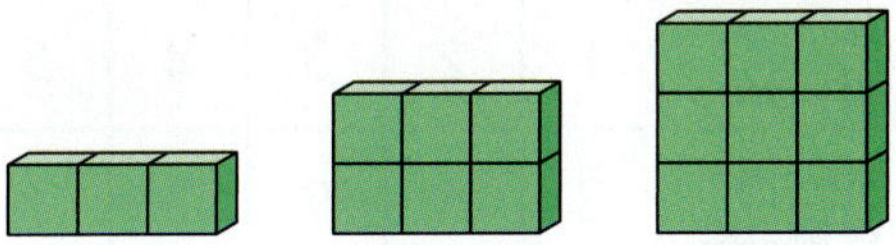

6. **Writing to Explain** How many blocks would you need to make a 15-story tower in Exercise 2? Explain how you know.

DIGITAL
eTools
www.pearsonsuccessnet.com

For another example, see Set C on page 230.

Independent Practice

In **7–10**, use patterns to find the missing numbers in each table. You may draw the next two figures on grid paper to help.

7.

Number of Stories	7	6	5	4	3
Number of Blocks	21	18	15		

8.

Number of Stories	1	2	3	4	5
Number of Blocks	4	8	12		

9.

Number of Rows	2	3	4	5	6
Number of Squares	3	5	7		

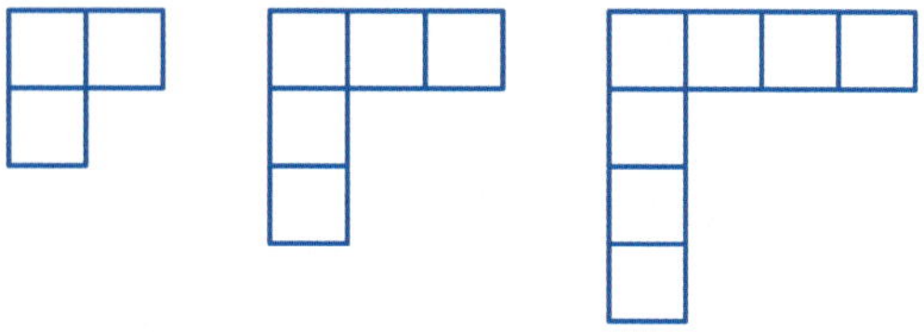

10.

Number of Rows	1	2	3	4	5
Number of Small Triangles	1	4	9		

In **11–13**, use the patterns in the block towers or squares to copy and complete each table.

11.

Number of Stories	1	2	3	4	5	
Number of Blocks	3	6	9			30

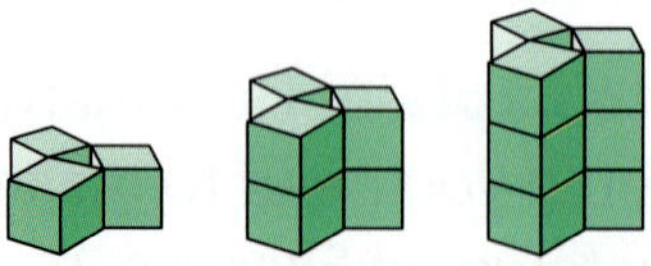

12.

Length of Each Side	1	2	4	6	9
Sum of All Sides	4	8	16		

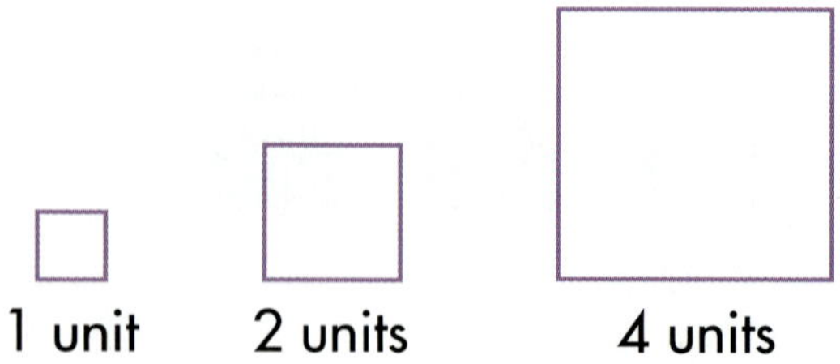

13.

Number of Stories	1	2	3	4	5
Number of Blocks	2	6	12		

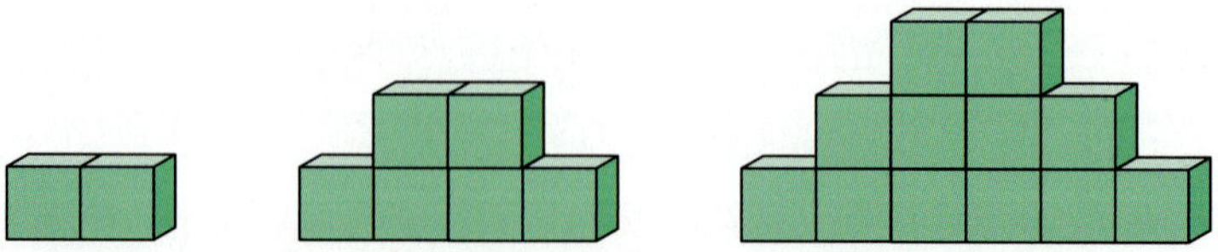

Problem Solving

14. Jon used 15 blocks to make a tower. Next he used 12 blocks to make a tower, and then 9 blocks to make a tower. If he continued the pattern, what rule could he use for this table?

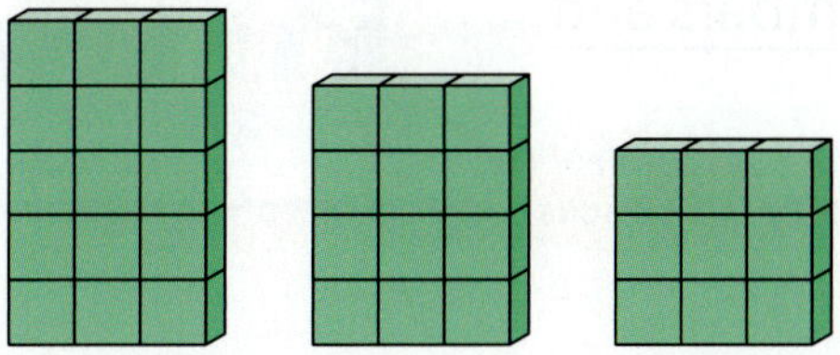

Number of Blocks	15	12	9	6	3
Number of Stories	5	4	3	2	1

15. SOL Prep Dean is making picture frames. He uses the same number of wood pieces in each frame. The table shows the number of wood pieces that he needs for different numbers of frames.

Number of Frames	6	7	8	9	10
Number of Wood Pieces	24	28	■	36	40

How many wood pieces does Dean need for 8 picture frames?

A 30 **C** 34

B 32 **D** 36

16. Stonehenge is an ancient monument in England made up of a pattern of rocks that looks like this:

Draw the shape that comes next.

17. Maura made these three block towers. If she continued the pattern, how many blocks would a 10-story tower have? How many blocks would a 100-story tower have?

18. **Algebra** What two 1-digit factors could you multiply to get a product of 48?

19. **Number Sense** Which product is greater, 9 × 15 or 9 × 17? Explain how you can tell without finding the products.

20. **Estimation** Lily has 75¢. A stamp costs 39¢. Does she have enough money to buy 2 stamps? Explain.

21. Leon ran twice as many laps around the track as Sam. Sam ran 6 laps. How many laps did they run in all?

22. **Writing to Explain** Eduardo spent \$3.78 on groceries. He paid with a \$5 bill. How do you know that his change included at least two pennies?

Virginia

Lesson 9-7

Prepares for 4.16.a The student will recognize and demonstrate the meaning of equality in an equation.

Equal or Unequal

How can you compare two expressions?

Max and Julie each have the books shown in the bookcase. If Max gets 2 more books and Julie gives away 3 of her books, how can you compare the numbers of books they will have?

A numerical expression contains numbers and at least one operation.

Other Examples

An equation is a number sentence that says two expressions are equal.

$5 + 3 = 10 - 2$
$8 = 8$

An inequality is a number sentence that uses $<$ or $>$. An inequality shows that two expressions are not equal.

$5 + 1 < 10 - 1$
$6 < 9$

$3 + 4 + 1 > 12 - 6$
$8 > 6$

Jerry, Yoko, and Eric each tried to find a number that would make the inequality $5 + \square > 10$ true. Whose number is correct?

Jerry	Yoko	Eric
$5 + 6 > 10$	$5 + 8 > 10$	$5 + 3 > 10$
$11 > 10$	$13 > 10$	$8 > 10$
True	True	False

Jerry's and Yoko's numbers are correct.

Guided Practice*

Do you know HOW?

Compare. Write $<$, $>$, or $=$ for each ◯.

1. $12 + 5$ ◯ $20 - 2$

2. $46 + 10$ ◯ 50

3. $27 + 8$ ◯ $6 + 29$

Do you UNDERSTAND?

4. Reasoning Find a third number that makes $5 + \square > 10$ true.

5. Tom had 9 rocks and then got 3 more. Ira had 11 rocks but lost 2 of them. Write a number sentence to compare their numbers of rocks.

*For another example, see Set E on page 231.

Step 1

Write an expression for each person's number of books.

Max	Julie
$6 + 2$	$12 - 3$

Step 2

Do the operation for each expression to find how the expressions compare.

Max	Julie
$6 + 2$	$12 - 3$
8	9

Step 3

Use $<$, $>$, or $=$ to compare the expressions.

$8 < 9$ so

$6 + 2 < 12 - 3$

Independent Practice

In **6–8**, compare. Write $<$, $>$, or $=$ for each $\bigcirc$.

6. $34 + 17 \bigcirc 45$ **7.** $18 + 9 \bigcirc 6 + 21$ **8.** $41 + 7 \bigcirc 53 - 4$

In **9–11**, write a number that makes each number sentence true.

9. $4 + \square = 12$ **10.** $16 - \square > 10$ **11.** $5 + \square < 18$

Problem Solving

For **12–14**, the table at the right shows the number of rocks in each friend's collection last month.

Data

Rock Collections

Name	Number of Rocks
Ana	29
Julio	32
Rashad	27
Sally	45

12. How many more rocks did Sally have than Ana?

13. This month, Rashad collected 7 more rocks and Ana gave away 3 rocks. Write a number sentence to compare their numbers of rocks.

14. This month, Sally gave away 6 rocks and Julio got 8 more rocks. Write a number sentence to compare their numbers of rocks.

15. **Estimation** Boris put 18 lemons on one shelf. He put 34 lemons on another shelf. About how many lemons in all did he put on the shelves?

16. Which symbol makes the number sentence true?

$34 - 17 \bigcirc 5 + 11$

A $+$ **B** $=$ **C** $<$ **D** $>$

DIGITAL Animated Glossary
www.pearsonsuccessnet.com

Virginia

Lesson 9-8

Prepares for 4.4.d The student will solve single-step and multistep addition, subtraction, and multiplication problems using whole numbers.

Problem Solving

Act It Out and Use Reasoning

Hands-On
counters

Juana collected old pennies, nickels, and dimes. Her collection has at least one of each kind of coin.

How many of each kind of coin does Juana have?

Juana's Collection
2 pennies
2 fewer nickels than dimes
10 coins in all

Another Example What are other kinds of relationships?

Ken's Collection of Dimes, Nickels, and Pennies
3 nickels
4 more dimes than nickels
15 coins in all

How many of each coin are in his collection?

Read and Understand

What do I know? There are 15 coins in all, and 3 of the coins are nickels.

There are 4 more dimes than nickels.

Use objects to show what you know.

Plan and Solve

Use reasoning to make conclusions.

Since there are 3 nickels, there are 12 pennies and dimes together.

Try 3 nickels, 7 dimes, and 5 pennies. Since $3 + 7 + 5 = 15$, this is correct.

There are 5 pennies, 3 nickels, and 7 dimes in the collection.

Explain It

1. Which number of coins in Ken's collection is given to you? Which information do you need to find?
2. Explain how you know 7 is the number of dimes in the solution above.

DIGITAL eTools www.pearsonsuccessnet.com

Read and Understand

What do I know? Juana has 10 coins in all, and 2 of the coins are pennies.

There are 2 fewer nickels than dimes.

Use objects to show what you know.

Plan and Solve

Use reasoning to make conclusions.

She has 2 pennies, so there are 8 nickels and dimes together.

Try 1 nickel and 7 dimes. $2 + 1 + 7 = 10$, but 1 nickel is not 2 fewer than 7.

Try 3 nickels and 5 dimes. Since $2 + 3 + 5 = 10$, this is correct.

There are 2 pennies, 3 nickels, and 5 dimes in Juana's collection.

Guided Practice*

Do you know HOW?

Find the number of each kind of stamp in the collection. Use counters.

1. Ricardo has 9 stamps in all. He has 2 nation stamps and 3 more inventor stamps than flower stamps.

Nation Stamps = ☐
Inventor Stamps = ☐
Flower Stamps = ☐

Do you UNDERSTAND?

2. What did you do to find the number of inventor stamps in Ricardo's collection?

3. **Write a Problem** Write a problem about coin collections that you can solve by using reasoning.

Independent Practice

Find the number of each kind of object in Anya's collection. Use counters or draw pictures to help.

4. **Anya's Collection of Minerals, Gemstones and Rocks**
6 minerals
3 fewer gemstones than rocks.
15 objects in all.

Minerals = ☐
Gemstones = ☐
Rocks = ☐

Stuck? Try this....

- What do I know?
- What am I asked to find?
- What diagram can I use to help understand the problem?
- Can I use addition, subtraction, multiplication, or division?
- Is all of my work correct?
- Did I answer the right question?
- Is my answer reasonable?

*For another example, see Set F on page 231.

Independent Practice

5. There are 10 fish in all in Percy's fish tank. Four of the fish are angel fish. There are 4 more mollie fish than tetra fish. How many of each kind of fish are in the tank?

6. Norah's dog weighs 9 pounds more than her cat. Her dog weighs 6 pounds less than Jeff's dog. Norah's cat weighs 7 pounds. How much does Jeff's dog weigh?

The students in Mr. Cole's class voted on which kind of collection their class should start. The graph shows the results. Use the graph for **7–9**.

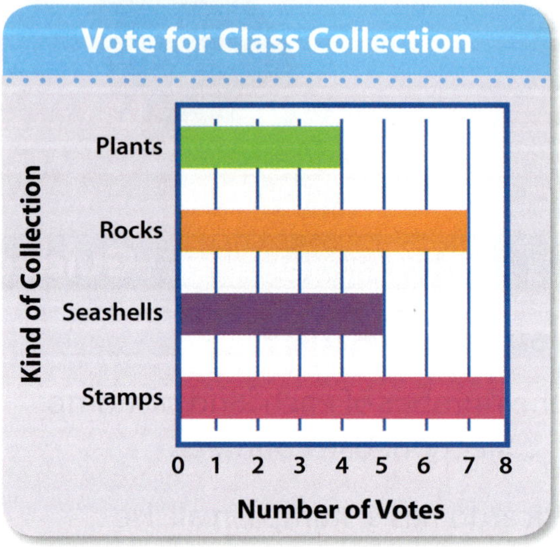

7. Which collection got five votes?

8. Which collection got the greatest number of votes?

9. How many more votes did the collection with the most of votes get than the collection with the fewest votes?

10. Isadora has 15 seashells in her collection. She has some oyster shells, some conch shells, and 6 clam shells. She has 2 fewer clam shells than oyster shells. How many conch shells does she have?

11. Lyn, Kurt, and Steve wrote a riddle about their ages. Lyn is 7 years older than Steve. Steve is 5 years old. The sum of their ages is 25 years. How old is Kurt?

12. Sondra wants to buy 2 plates and 3 towels. What is the total cost of her items?

Data

Item	Price
Flashlight	$9
Plate	$7
Towel	$4
Fishing net	$8
Umbrella	$3

13. Think About the Process At the town pet show, Dina saw 48 pets. There were 6 birds and 7 cats. The remaining pets were dogs. Which number sentence shows one way to find the number of pets that were dogs?

A $48 - 6 - 7 = \square$

B $48 + 6 \div 7 = \square$

C $48 - 6 \times 7 = \square$

D $6 \times 7 \times 48 = \square$

Going Digital

Extending Tables

Use e tools
Spreadsheet/Data/Grapher eTool
Use a rule to complete the table.

Number of Lions	1	2	3	4	5
Number of Legs	4	8		16	20

Step 1 Go to the Spreadsheet/Data/Grapher eTool. Use the arrow tool to select at least 2 rows and 6 columns. Set the number of decimal places at zero using the .00 pull-down menu. Enter *Lions*, *1*, *2*, *3*, *4*, *5* in row A. Enter *Legs* in the first column of row B.

Step 2 Try the rule "multiply by 4." Cell B2 is in column B, row 2. In cell B2, type = *4*B1*. This means "multiply 4 by the value in cell B1." The product will be shown in cell B2. In cell C2, type = *4*C1*. In cell D2, type = *4*D1* and so on for cells E2 and F2.

Step 3 Check that the numbers match those in the table above. This means the rule "multiply by 4" is correct. The missing number is 12.

F2 20

	A	B	C	D	E	F
1	Lions	1.00	2.00	3.00	4.00	5.00
2	Legs	4.00	8.00	12.00	16.00	20.00

Practice

Copy each table, find a rule, and fill in the missing cell.

1.

Bud's Age	2	4	6	9
Spot's Age	7	9		14

2.

Days	1	2	3	4
Toys Made	7		21	28

1. Football players came out of the tunnel in the pattern shown below.

What number belongs on the blank jersey? (9-2)

A 26

B 25

C 24

D 22

2. What are the next three numbers in this pattern? (9-1)

6, 5, 3, 1, 6, 5, 3, 1, 6, 5, 3

A 6, 3, 1

B 6, 5, 3

C 1, 5, 3

D 1, 6, 5

3. What rule can be used to find the number of legs on 7 grasshoppers? (9-4)

Number of Grasshoppers	3	5	7	9
Number of Legs	18	30		54

A Add 15.

B Divide by 5.

C Multiply by 5.

D Multiply by 6.

4. Kayla is cutting ribbon to go around cards. Each card is shaped like a triangle with all sides the same length. How many inches of ribbon does she need for a card with each side 7 inches long? (9-6)

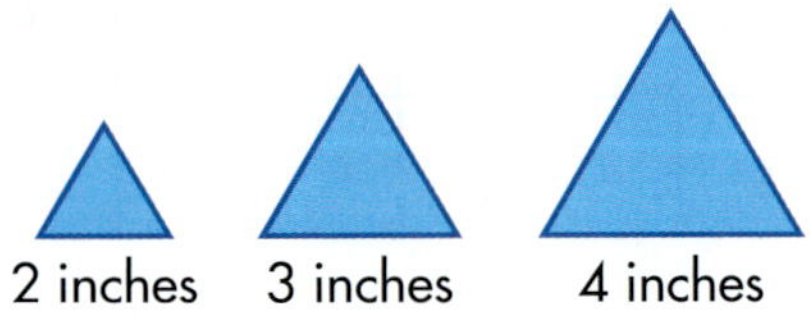

Side Length in Inches	2	3	4	7
Inches of Ribbon	6	9	12	

A 15

B 18

C 21

D 24

5. Coach Kim needs to form teams that all have the same number of players. The table shows the number of teams formed for different numbers of players.

Number of Players	24	32	40	72
Number of Teams	3	4		9

What rule can be used to find how many teams are formed if there are 40 players? (9-4)

A Divide by 8.

B Divide by 6.

C Subtract 21.

D Multiply by 6.

6. Hank had a party at the zoo. He used the table below to find the total price of admission for groups of different sizes.

Total Number of Children	*Total Admission Price*
3	$21
5	$35
7	▢
9	$63

What is the total cost of admission for 7 children? (9-3)

A $37

B $48

C $49

D $56

7. Joe has 18 pets. His pets are birds, hamsters, and 10 fish. He has 2 fewer birds than hamsters. How many birds does he have? (9-8)

A 2

B 3

C 4

D 5

8. Which is a rule for the pattern? (9-2)

29, 24, 19, 14, 9

A Subtract 4.

B Subtract 5.

C Add 4.

D Subtract 10.

9. Fran has 3 grapes. Ivan has 6 times as many grapes as Fran. Which numerical expression shows how to find the number of grapes Ivan has? (9-5)

A $6 + 3$

B $6 - 3$

C 6×3

D $6 \div 3$

10. Which symbol makes the number sentence true? (9-7)

$24 + 9 \bigcirc 36 - 4$

A $>$

B $<$

C $=$

D $\times$

11. Which numerical expression shows 2 feet shorter than 18 feet? (9-5)

A $2 - 18$

B $18 \div 2$

C $18 + 2$

D $18 - 2$

12. Which number makes the number sentence true? (9-7)

$9 + \square = 16$

A 25

B 7

C 6

D 5

Set A, pages 206–207

Draw the next three shapes to continue the pattern.

Find the part that repeats. 

Then continue the pattern. 

Remember to first find the part of the pattern that repeats.

Draw the next three shapes or numbers to continue the pattern.

1. 
2. 3, 5, 7, 9, 3, 5, 7, 9, 3, 5, 7

Set B, pages 208–209

Find a rule to use to continue the pattern.

24, 21, 18, 15, 12, ___, ___, ___,
−3 −3 −3 −3 −3 −3 −3

Rule: Subtract 3
The next numbers in the pattern are 9, 6, and 3.

Remember to check that your rule works with all of the given numbers.

Write a rule and continue the pattern.

1. 5, 7, 9, ___, ___, ___
2. 22, 18, 14, ___, ___, ___

Set C, pages 210–214, 218–221

If Sam continues the pattern, how many blocks would a 5-story tower have? a 10-story tower?

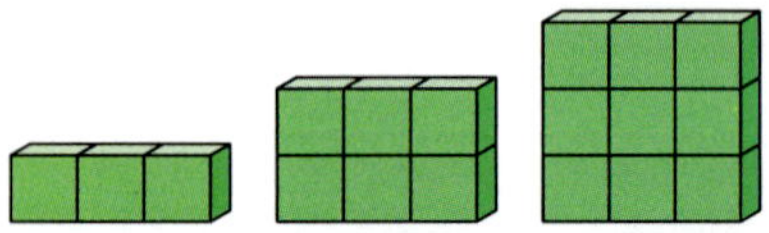

Stories	1	2	3
Blocks	3	6	9

A pattern in the table is multiply by 3. So, use 5×3 to find the number of blocks in a 5-story tower.
$5 \times 3 = 15$
There are 15 blocks in a 5-story tower.

A 10-story tower would have 10×3 or 30 blocks.

Remember to use the number pairs in a table to find a rule or make predictions.

In 1 and 2, write the missing numbers and a rule.

1.

Cars	1	2	3	4
Wheels	4	8		

2. Draw the next two figures in the pattern. Use grid paper.

Stories	1	2	3	4	5
Blocks	6	12	18		

Set D, pages 216–217

Some friends made posters for a music night. Kelli made 3 times as many posters as Rob. Suppose □ stands for the number of posters Rob made. Write a numerical expression to show how many posters Kelli made.

Think *Word phrase "3 times as many posters as Rob made"*

Numerical expression: $3 \times$ □

Remember that □ stands for a value in the problem.

1. Suppose □ stands for the number of friends who will share 16 peaches equally. Write a numerical expression to show how many peaches each friend will get.

Set E, pages 222–223

Compare the expressions.

$3 + 4 \bigcirc 8 - 2$

Do the operation for each expression,
$3 + 4 = 7$ $8 - 2 = 6$

Compare. $7 > 6$

$3 + 4 > 8 - 2$

Remember to do each operation.

Copy and complete. Use $>$, $<$, or $=$ to compare.

1. $18 - 11 \bigcirc 7 + 1$
2. $25 + 9 \bigcirc 46 - 12$

Write a number that makes the number sentence true.

3. $13 -$ □ > 9

Set F, pages 224–226

When you solve a problem by acting it out, follow these steps.

Step 1

Choose objects to act out the problem.

Step 2

Show what you know using the objects.

Step 3

Act out the problem.

Step 4

Find the answer.

Remember to decide what the objects represent before you begin.

Solve. Find the number of each kind of sticker in Ben's collection.

1. **Ben's Sticker Collection**
   - 3 kinds of stickers with 17 stickers in all
   - 6 star stickers
   - 3 fewer smiley face stickers than planet stickers

Topic 10

Solids and Shapes

1 A sculpture in Madrid, Spain, is made from 6 tons of bananas! Which solid figure best describes the shape of this sculpture? You will find out in Lesson 10-1.

2 Which geometric term describes the wings of a biplane? You will find out in Lesson 10-3.

3 Which polygons did famous architect Frank Lloyd Wright use in designing this building ? You will find out in Lesson 10-5.

4 When was this unusual bicycle designed? You will find out in Lesson 10-7.

Review What You Know!

Vocabulary

Choose the best term from the box.

- circle
- cube
- square
- triangle

1. A shape that has 4 sides all the same length is called a ___?___.

2. A solid that has six square faces is called a ___?___.

3. A shape with 3 sides is called a ___?___.

Name Solids and Shapes

Write the name of each figure.

4. 

5. 

6. 

7. 

Shapes

Write the number of sides each figure has.

8. 

9. 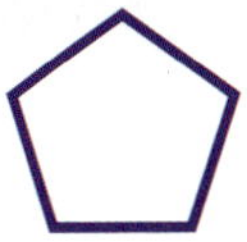

10. 

11. 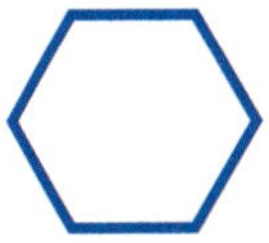

12. **Writing to Explain** Which solid rolls, a cone or a cube? Explain why it rolls.

Virginia

Lesson 10-1

3.14 The student will identify, describe, compare, and contrast characteristics of plane and solid geometric figures (circle, square, rectangle, triangle, cube, rectangular prism, square pyramid, sphere, cone, and cylinder) by identifying relevant characteristics, including the number of angles, vertices, and edges, and the number and shape of faces, using concrete models.

Solid Figures

What is a solid figure?

A solid figure is a geometric figure that has length, width, and height.

Some common solid figures and their names are shown at the right.

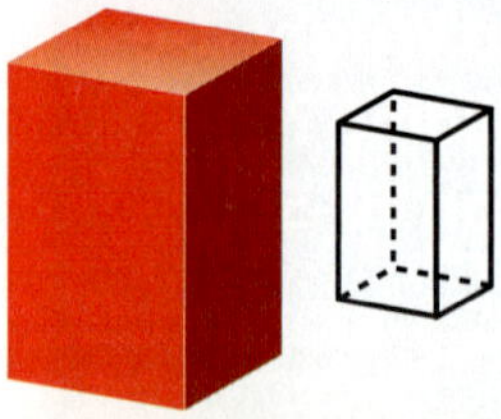

Rectangular prism

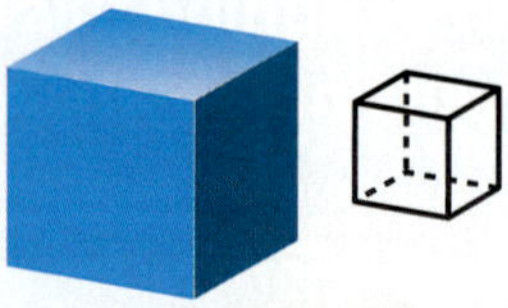

Cube

Another Example How do solid figures help you describe objects in the world around you?

Many things in the real world are shaped like the solid figures shown above. Name the solid figure each object looks like.

The clown's hat looks like a cone.

The cereal box looks like a rectangular prism.

The tennis ball looks like a sphere.

The glue stick looks like a cylinder.

Explain It

1. Explain why the clown's hat looks like a cone.
2. Why is it wrong to say that the cereal box looks like a cube?
3. Which of the 4 objects pictured can roll? Explain.

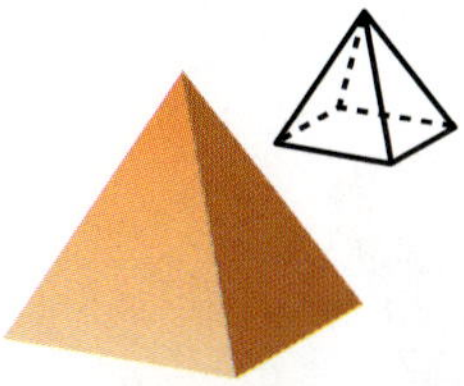
Pyramid

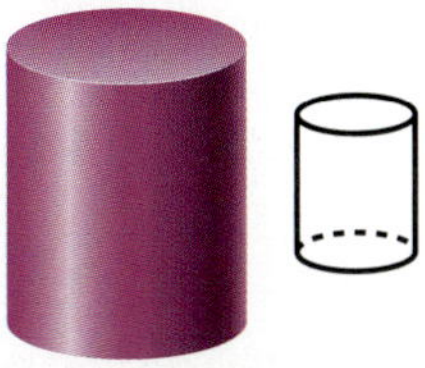
Cylinder

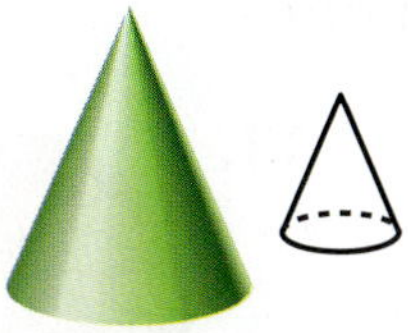
Cone

Sphere

Guided Practice*

Do you know HOW?

Name the solid figure.

1.

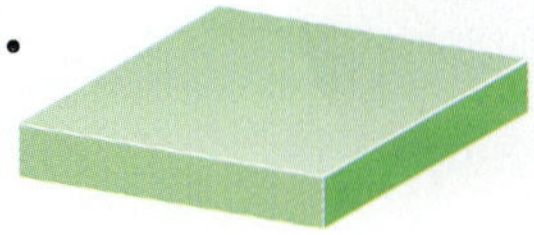

2.

Name the solid figure that each object looks like.

3.

4.

5.

6.

Do you UNDERSTAND?

For **7–10**, look at the solid figures above.

7. Which solid figure has no flat surfaces?

8. Which solid figures can roll? Which cannot roll?

9. How are the cone and the cylinder alike? How are they different?

10. How are the cone and the pyramid alike? How are they different?

11. Writing to Explain Look at the pictures below. Does the name of a solid figure change if the figure is turned on its side? Explain.

DIGITAL Animated Glossary
www.pearsonsuccessnet.com

For another example, see Set A on page 256.

Independent Practice

In **12–17**, name the solid figure.

12.

13.

14.

15.

16.

17.

In **18–26**, name the solid figure that each object looks like.

18.
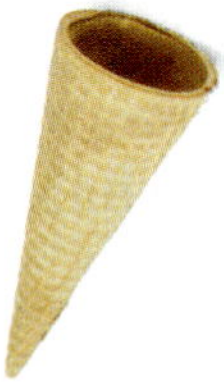

19.

20.

21.

22.

23.

24.

25.

26.

In **27–32**, name an object in your classroom or at home that is shaped like each solid figure.

27. Sphere

28. Cube

29. Cylinder

30. Rectangular prism

31. Pyramid

32. Cone

Problem Solving

33. Kayla used blocks to make this train. Give the solid figure name for each type of block. Tell how many blocks of each type Kayla used.

34. What solid figures do you get if you cut a cube as shown?

35. Three pizzas were cut into 8 slices each. Six friends ate all of the pizza, and each person ate the same number of slices. How many slices did each person eat?

36. **Writing to Explain** Spheres and cylinders are both solid figures that can roll. Why are so many sports played with objects shaped like spheres rather than objects shaped like cylinders?

37. What solid figure would you make if you stacked two rectangular prisms of the same size?

38. What solid figures can be stacked to make a round tower with a flat top?

39. Which solid figure name best describes the shape of the banana sculpture shown at the right?

SOL Prep

A Cylinder

B Pyramid

C Rectangular prism

D Sphere

40. **Number Sense** There are 10 girls and 9 boys in Catherine's class. Which number sentence can be used to find how many children are in the class?

A $10 \times 9 = \square$ **C** $10 - 9 = \square$

B $10 \div 9 = \square$ **D** $10 + 9 = \square$

Virginia

Lesson 10-2

3.14 The student will identify, describe, compare, and contrast characteristics of plane and solid geometric figures (circle, square, rectangle, triangle, cube, rectangular prism, square pyramid, sphere, cone, and cylinder) by identifying relevant characteristics, including the number of angles, vertices, and edges, and the number and shape of faces, using concrete models.

Relating Solids and Shapes

How can you describe parts of solid figures?

Some solid figures have faces, vertices, and edges.

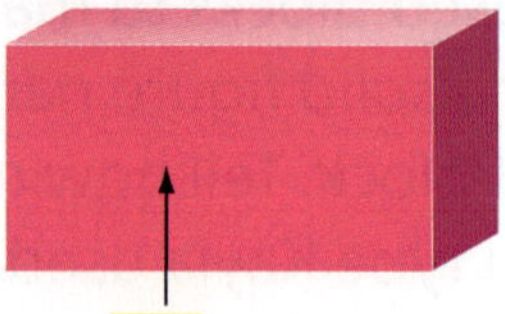

Each flat surface is a face.

A rectangular prism has 6 faces. The shape of each face is a rectangle.

Another Example How can you describe parts of solid figures that roll?

Flat surfaces of solid figures that can roll are called bases.

A cylinder has two flat surfaces.

A cylinder can roll.

So, the flat surfaces of a cylinder are called bases.

A cone has one vertex.

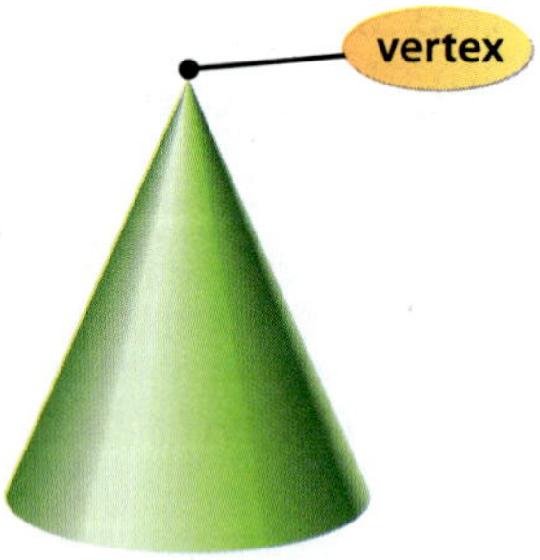

Explain It

1. Explain why the flat surface of a cone is called a base.
2. Do you think that the flat surfaces of a pyramid are called faces? Explain.

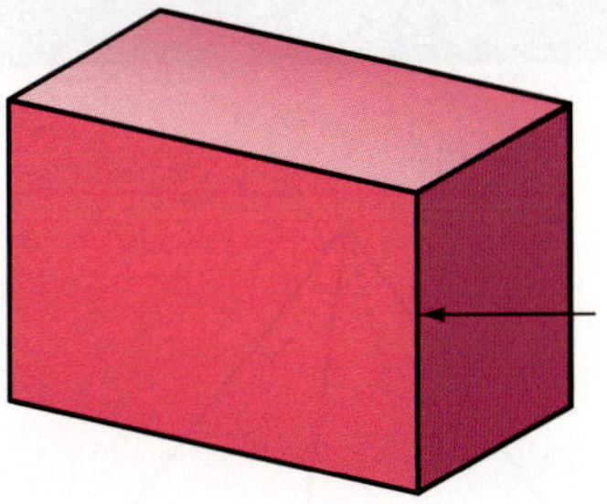

A rectangular prism has 12 edges.

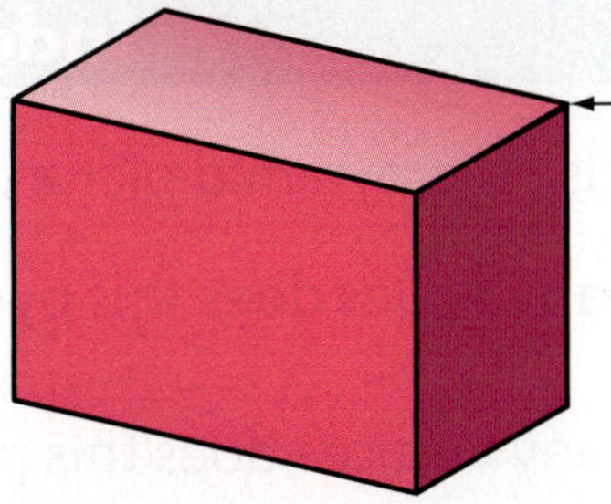

A rectangular prism has 8 vertices.

Guided Practice*

Do you know HOW?

For **1–6**, use the cube and cone pictured below.

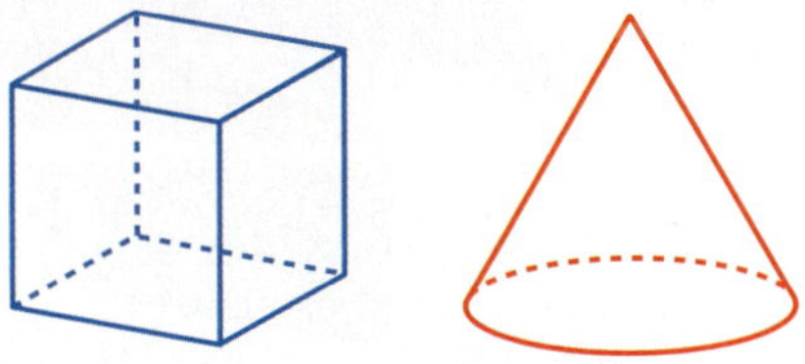

1. How many faces does the cube have in all?
2. What is the shape of each face of the cube?
3. How many edges does the cube have?
4. How many vertices does the cube have?
5. How many bases does the cone have?
6. How many vertices does the cone have?

Do you UNDERSTAND?

For **7–10**, use the solids pictured below.

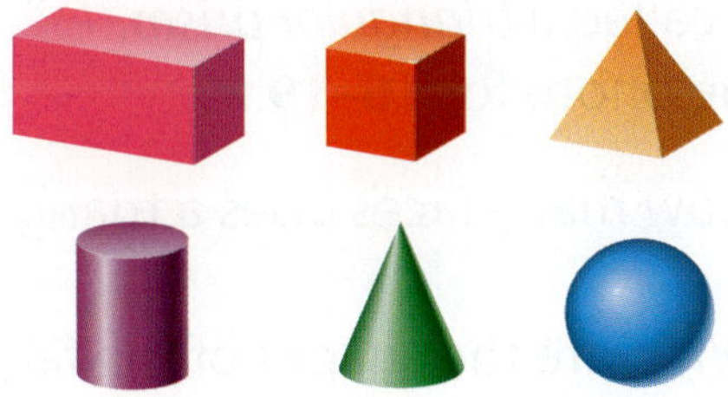

7. Which solid has faces that are all the same size and shape? What is the shape of the faces?
8. Which two solids have the same number of edges?
9. Which of these solid figures roll?
10. Besides the rectangular prism, which solid has 6 faces, 12 edges, and 8 vertices?

DIGITAL Animated Glossary **www.pearsonsuccessnet.com**

For another example, see Set B on page 256.

Independent Practice

For **11–14**, use the pyramid pictured at the right.

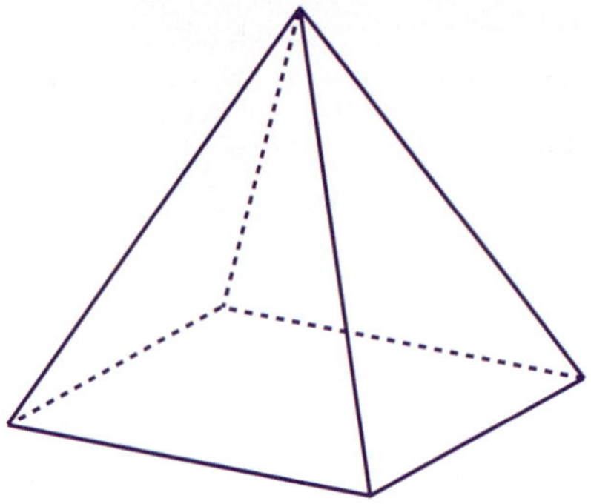

11. How many edges does this pyramid have?

12. How many vertices does this pyramid have?

13. How many faces does this pyramid have?

14. What are the shapes of the faces? How many faces of each shape are there?

Problem Solving

15. **Writing to Explain** Why does a cube have the same number of faces, edges, and vertices as a rectangular prism?

This wedge of cheese looks like a solid figure called a *triangular prism.* Use the photo for **16–19**.

16. How many faces does a triangular prism have?

17. What are the shapes of the faces?

18. How many vertices does a triangular prism have?

19. How many edges does a triangular prism have?

20. SOL Prep Tran bought a bag of 24 stickers. He plans to put one sticker on each face of this cube. How many stickers will be left over?

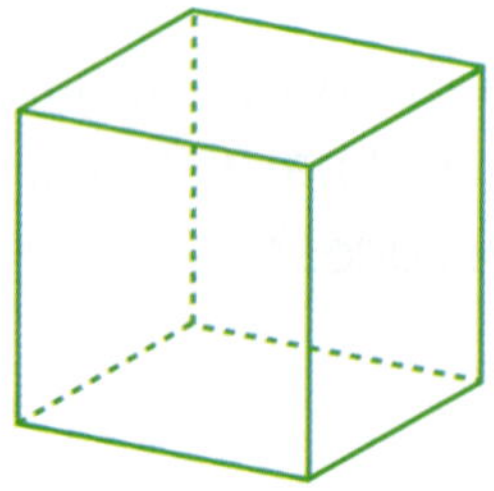

A 12 **C** 18

B 16 **D** 21

21. SOL Prep What is the total value of the 8 coins shown below?

A 36¢ **C** 56¢

B 46¢ **D** 71¢

Enrichment

Nets

A **net** is a flat pattern that can be folded to make a solid figure.

The pictures below show how to fold the net at the right into a rectangular prism.

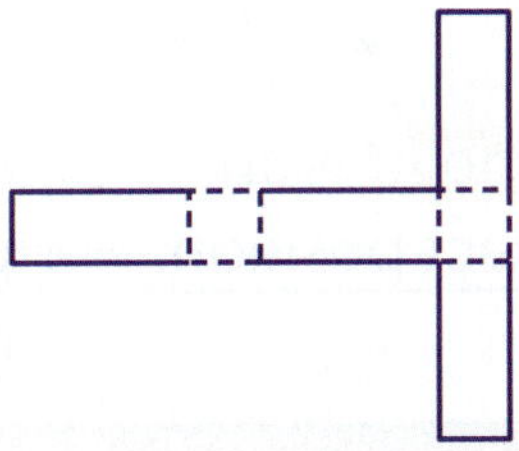

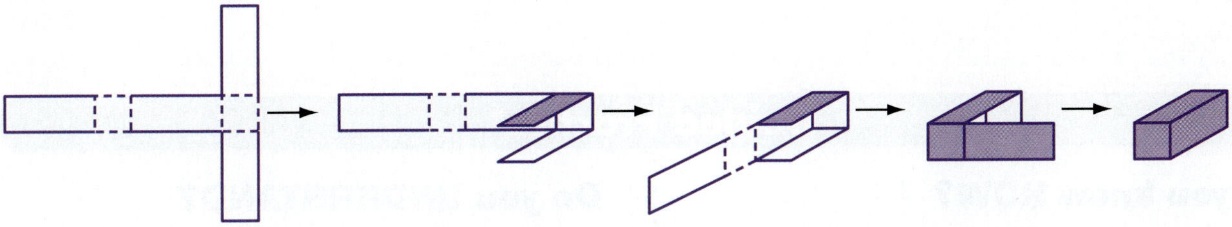

Practice

Match each net to the solid figure it makes below.

1.

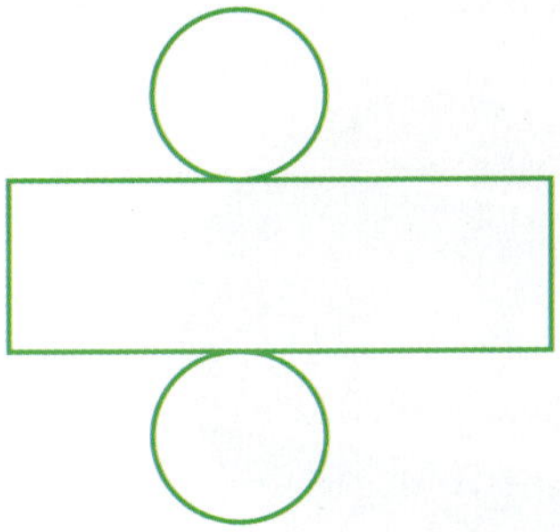

2.

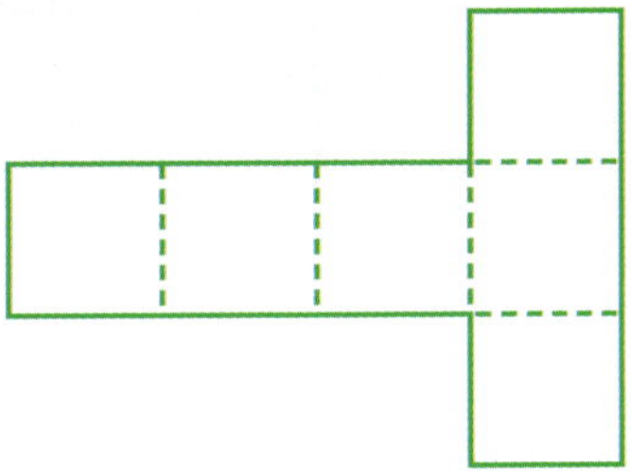

3.

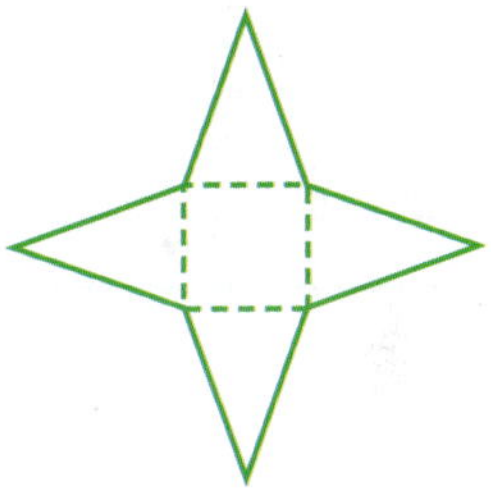

a.

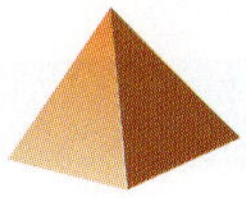

b.

c.

4. Draw a net for a cube. Use a design that is different from the net that matched Picture **c**. How many faces does a cube have? What is the shape of each face?

5. Bruce made the net below by tracing around each face of a solid figure. What solid figure did he use?

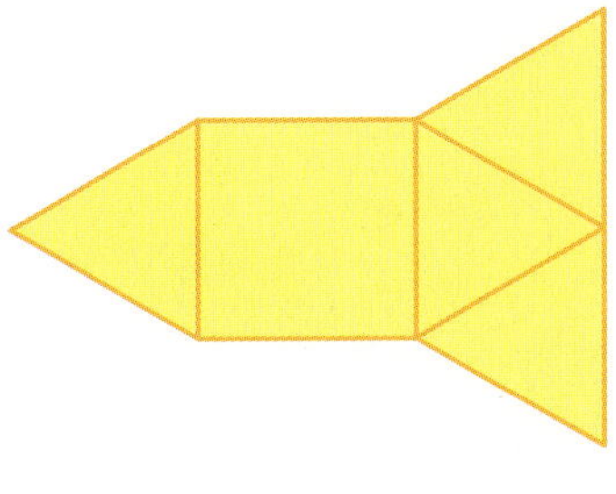

Virginia

Lesson 10-3

3.15 The student will identify and draw representations of points, line segments, rays, angles, and lines.

Lines and Line Segments

What is important to know about lines?

Lines and parts of lines are used to describe shapes and solid figures.

A **point** is an exact position.

A **line** is a set of points that is endless in two directions.

A **line segment** is a part of a line with two endpoints.

Guided Practice*

Do you know HOW?

Write the name for each.

1. 

2. 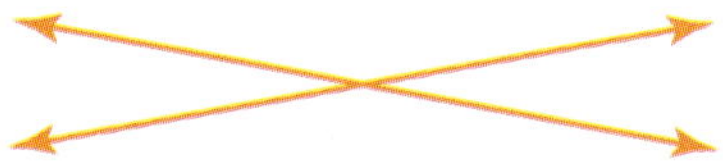

3. 

Do you UNDERSTAND?

4. What do the arrows in the drawing of a line tell you?

5. What type of lines do the railroad tracks look like?

Independent Practice

Write the name for each.

6. 

7. 

8. 

9. 

10. 

11. 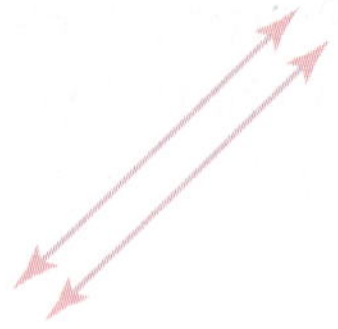

DIGITAL Animated Glossary **www.pearsonsuccessnet.com**

**For another example, see Set C on page 256.*

Intersecting lines cross at one point.

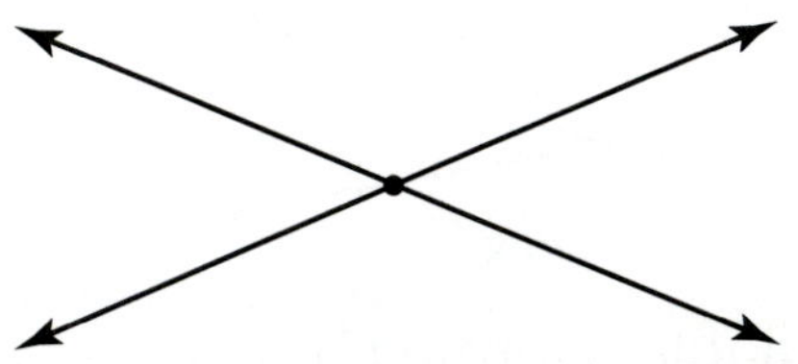

Parallel lines never cross.

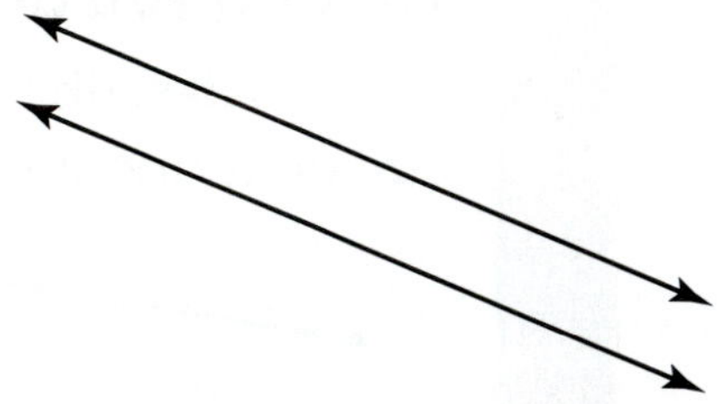

Draw and label a picture of each.

12. Line segment **13.** Line **14.** Parallel lines **15.** Intersecting lines

Problem Solving

For **16** and **17**, use the map at the right. Tell if the two streets named look like intersecting lines or parallel lines.

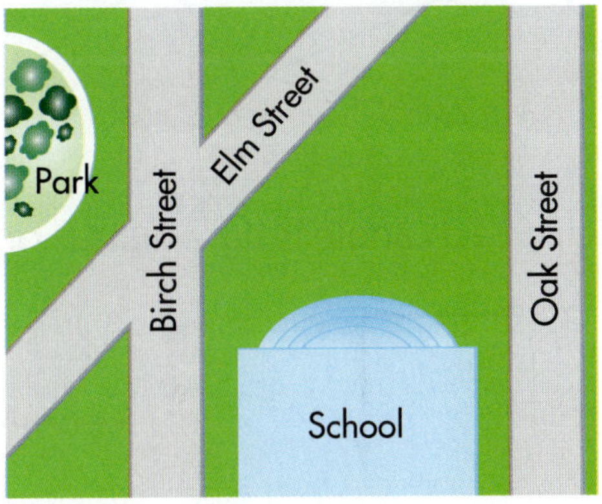

16. Oak Street and Birch Street

17. Birch Street and Elm Street

18. **Writing to Explain** Rosa bought 3 packs of 6 baseball cards. Luis bought 4 packs of 3 baseball cards. Who bought more baseball cards? Explain.

19. Look at the wings on the plane. What geometric term can you use to describe them?

20. Which best describes the place where these two lines intersect?

SOL Prep

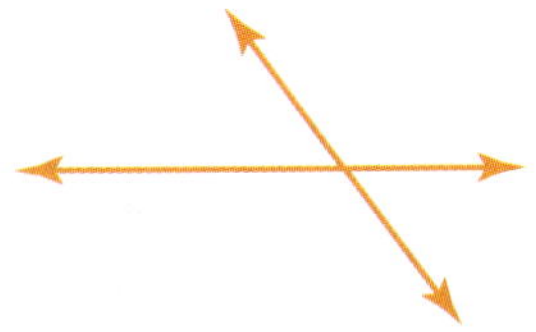

A Line

B Point

C Line segment

D Parallel line

Virginia

Lesson 10-4

3.15 The student will identify and draw representations of points, line segments, rays, angles, and lines.

Angles

How do you describe angles?

You can describe an angle by the size of its opening.

A **ray** is a part of a line with one endpoint.

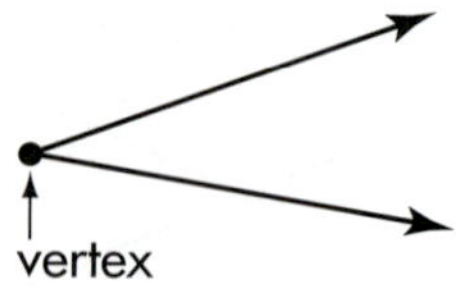

An **angle** is formed by two rays with the same endpoint. That endpoint is the **vertex** of the angle.

Guided Practice*

Do you know HOW?

Write the name for each.

1.
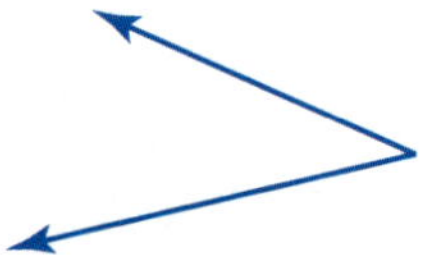

2.

Tell if each angle is right, acute, or obtuse.

3.
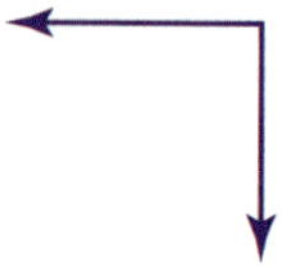

4.

Do you UNDERSTAND?

5. How can you use the corner of a note card to decide if an angle is acute, right, or obtuse?

6. Explain why these two rays do not form an angle.

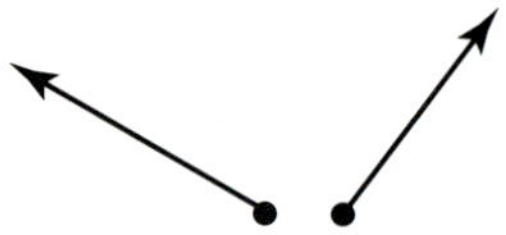

7. Describe something in your classroom that reminds you of perpendicular line segments.

Independent Practice

Tell if each angle is right, acute, or obtuse.

8.
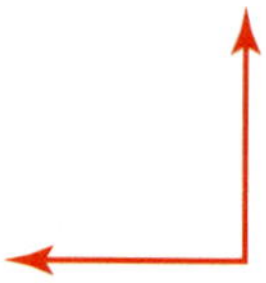

9.

10.

11.
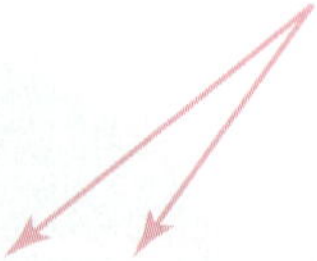

In **12–15**, draw a picture of each.

12. Obtuse angle **13.** Right angle **14.** Ray **15.** Acute angle

DIGITAL Animated Glossary **www.pearsonsuccessnet.com**

**For another example, see Set D on page 256.*

A right angle makes a square corner.

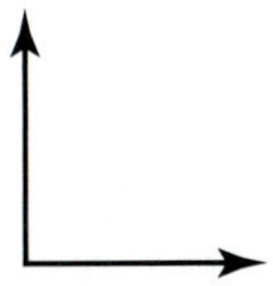

If two lines, line segments, or rays make a right angle, they are perpendicular.

An acute angle is an angle that is open less than a right angle.

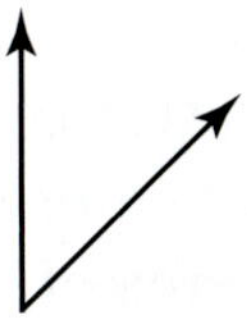

An obtuse angle is an angle that is open more than a right angle.

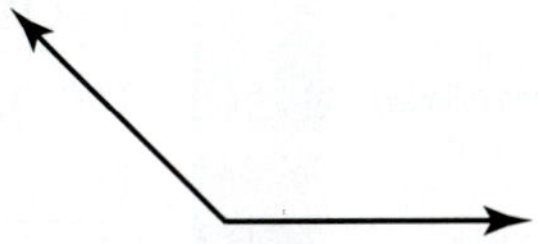

Problem Solving

In **16–18**, tell the time on each clock. Then tell what type of angle is formed by the hands of the clock.

16.

17.

18.

19. Writing to Explain Are all obtuse angles the same size? Draw a picture to explain your answer.

20. Which picture shows a pair of perpendicular line segments?

A

B

C

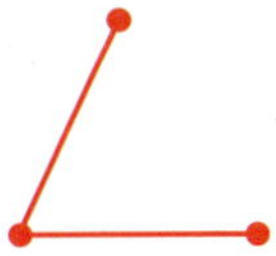

D

21. Reasoning Are these lines parallel or intersecting? Explain.

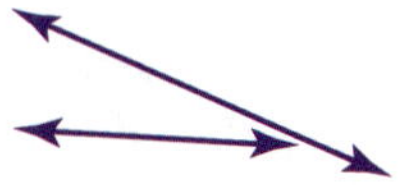

Tip *Remember that a line does not end.*

22. Which number is greater than 1,051?

SOL Prep

A 1,005 **C** 947

B 1,073 **D** 1,021

23. Dori counted 8 children waiting in line ahead of her at the drinking fountain. Write the ordinal number and the ordinal word form for Dori's place in line.

Virginia

Lesson 10-5

3.14 The student will identify, describe, compare, and contrast characteristics of plane and solid geometric figures (circle, square, rectangle, triangle, cube, rectangular prism, square pyramid, sphere, cone, and cylinder) by identifying relevant characteristics, including the number of angles, vertices, and edges, and the number and shape of faces, using concrete models.

Polygons

What is a polygon?

A polygon is a closed figure made up of line segments. Each line segment is a side of the polygon. The point where two sides meet is a vertex of the polygon.

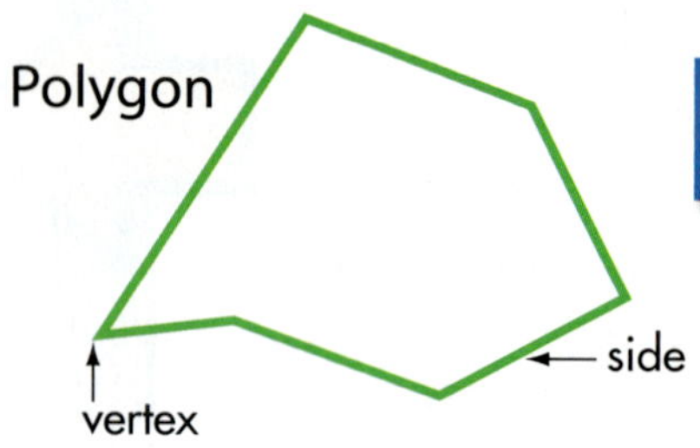

Guided Practice*

Do you know HOW?

Name the polygon.

1.

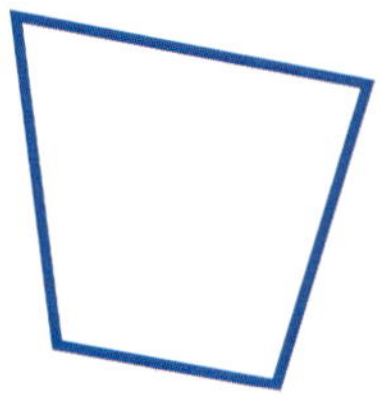

2.

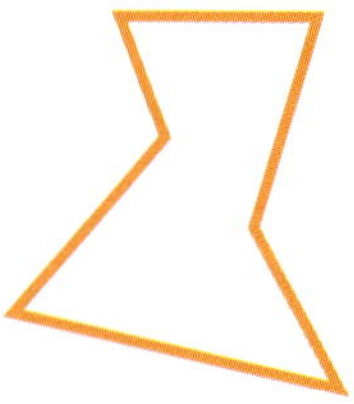

Is each figure a polygon? If it is not, explain why.

3.

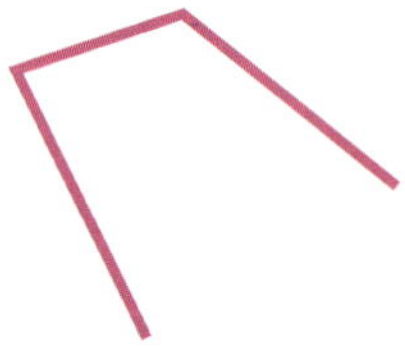

4.

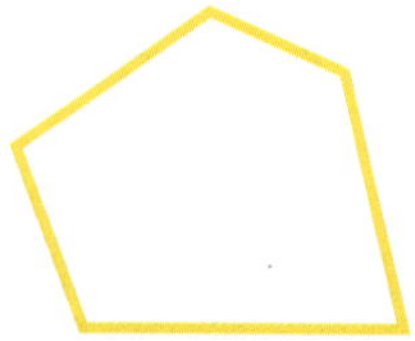

Do you UNDERSTAND?

Draw a polygon with 3 sides. Use the polygon for Exercises **5–7**.

5. How many vertices are there?

6. How many angles are there?

7. What is the name of the polygon?

8. Suppose that a polygon has 10 sides. How many angles does it have?

9. Describe an everyday object that is a model of a polygon. What is the name of the polygon?

Independent Practice

Name the polygon.

10.

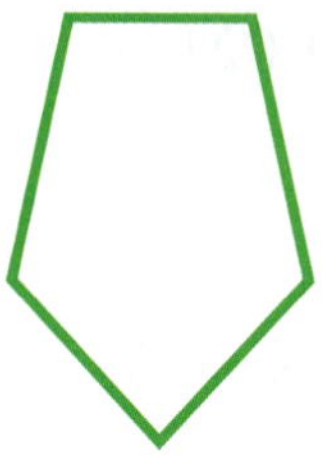

11.

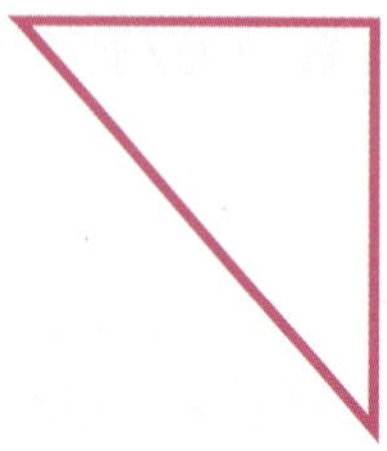

12.

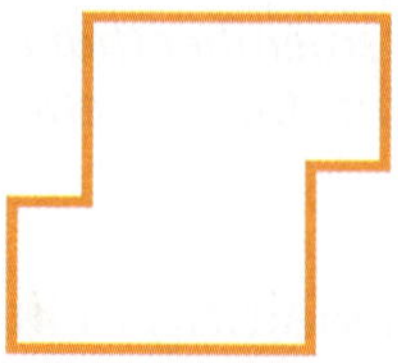

13.

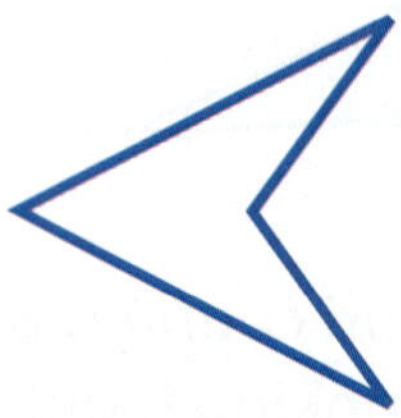

DIGITAL Animated Glossary **www.pearsonsuccessnet.com**

*For another example, see Set E on page 257.

Polygons are named for the number of sides they have. Two sides meet to form an angle at each vertex.

Some commonly used polygons are named and described in the table.

Data

Polygon	Number of Sides	Number of Vertices
Triangle	3	3
Quadrilateral	4	4
Pentagon	5	5
Hexagon	6	6
Octagon	8	8

Is each figure a polygon? If not, explain why.

14. 

15. 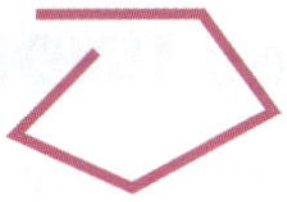

16. 

17. 

Problem Solving

In **18–21**, name the polygon that each traffic sign looks most like.

18. 

19. 

20. 

21. 

22. **Reasoning** Which polygon comes next in the pattern? Explain your answer.

23. What polygons were used to design this house?

24. Which polygon best represents the top of the box?

SOL Prep

A Quadrilateral **C** Pentagon

B Octagon **D** Hexagon

Virginia

Lesson 10-6

3.14 The student will identify, describe, compare, and contrast characteristics of plane and solid geometric figures (circle, square, rectangle, triangle, cube, rectangular prism, square pyramid, sphere, cone, and cylinder) by identifying relevant characteristics, including the number of angles, vertices, and edges, and the number and shape of faces, using concrete models.

Triangles

How can you describe triangles?

Triangles can be described by their sides.

Equilateral triangle

All three sides are the same length.

Isosceles triangle

At least two sides are the same length.

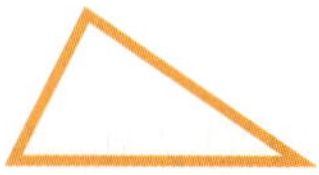

Scalene triangle

No sides are the same length.

Guided Practice*

Do you know HOW?

Tell if each triangle is equilateral, isosceles, or scalene.

1. 

2.

Tell if each triangle is right, acute, or obtuse.

3. 

4. 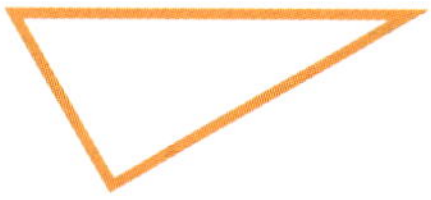

Do you UNDERSTAND?

5. How many acute angles are in an acute triangle?

6. How many obtuse angles are in an obtuse triangle?

7. Can a right triangle also be

a an isosceles triangle? Explain.

b an equilateral triangle? Explain.

8. Can an isosceles triangle also be equilateral? Explain.

Independent Practice

In **9–12**, tell if each triangle is equilateral, isosceles, or scalene. If a triangle has two names, give the name that best describes it.

9. 

10. 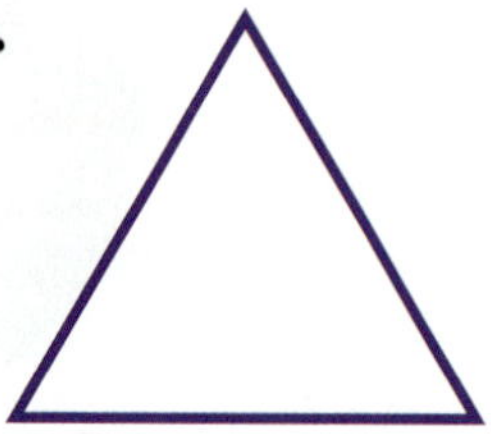

11. 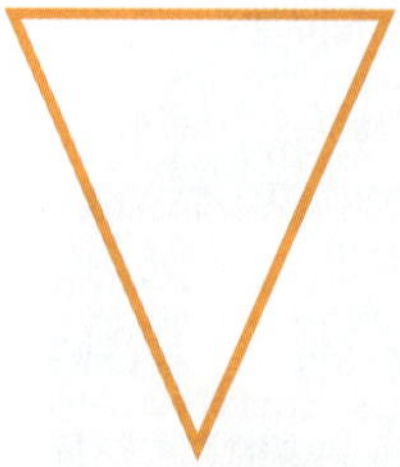

12. 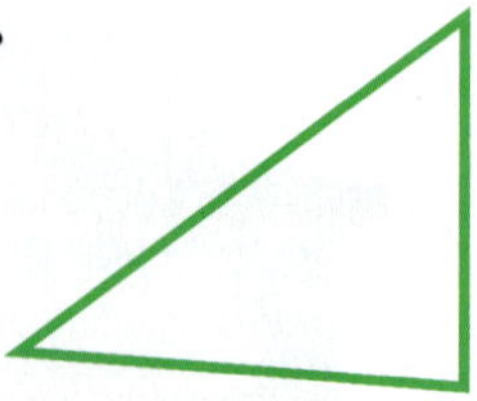

DIGITAL Animated Glossary **www.pearsonsuccessnet.com**

**For another example, see Set F on page 257.*

Triangles can be described by their angles.

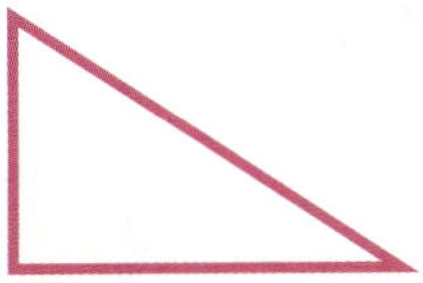

Right triangle
One angle is a right angle.

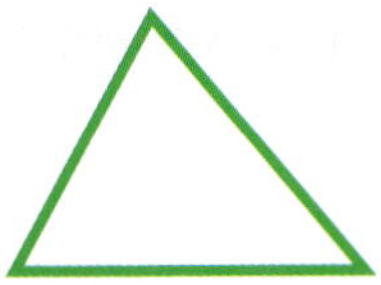

Acute triangle
All three angles are acute angles.

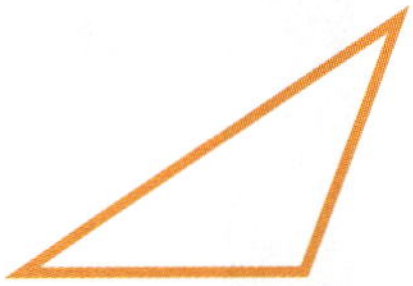

Obtuse triangle
One angle is an obtuse angle.

In **13–16**, tell if each triangle is right, acute, or obtuse.

13. 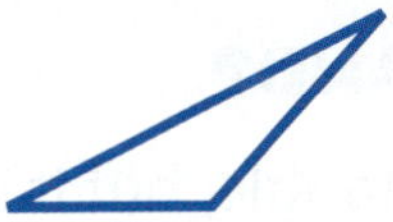 **14.** 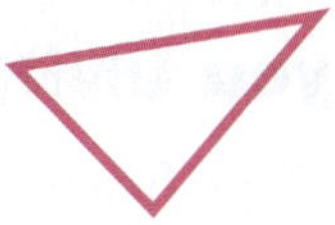 **15.** 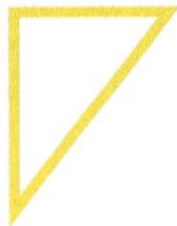 **16.** 

Problem Solving

For **17** and **18**, use the picture of the musical triangle.

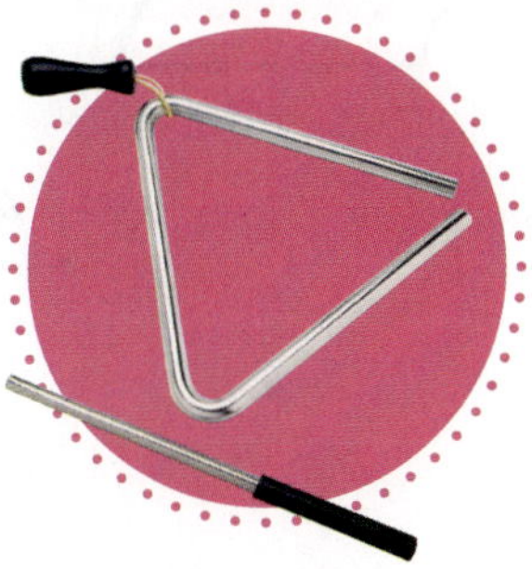

17. Does the musical triangle look most like an equilateral triangle, an isosceles triangle, or a scalene triangle?

18. **Reasoning** The shape of the musical triangle is not a geometric triangle. Explain why not.

19. Look at the sentence below. Write the word that will make it true.

An obtuse triangle has one obtuse angle and two __?__ angles.

20. Draw a picture to show how you could make one straight cut in a rectangle to form two right triangles.

21. Which pair of triangle names best describes this pennant?

SOL Prep

A Equilateral triangle, acute triangle

B Equilateral triangle, right triangle

C Isosceles triangle, acute triangle

D Isosceles triangle, obtuse triangle

22. **Writing to Explain** Why is it impossible for a triangle to have two right angles?

Virginia

Lesson 10-7

3.14 The student will identify, describe, compare, and contrast characteristics of plane and solid geometric figures (circle, square, rectangle, triangle, cube, rectangular prism, square pyramid, sphere, cone, and cylinder) by identifying relevant characteristics, including the number of angles, vertices, and edges, and the number and shape of faces, using concrete models.

Quadrilaterals

What are some special names for quadrilaterals?

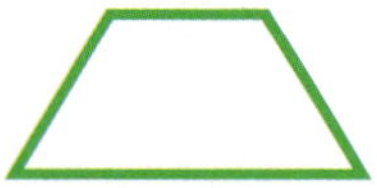

Trapezoid

Exactly one pair of parallel sides

Parallelogram

Two pairs of parallel sides

Opposite sides are the same length.
Opposite angles are the same size.

Guided Practice*

Do you know HOW?

In **1–4**, write as many special names as possible for each quadrilateral.

1. 

2. 

3.

4. 

Do you UNDERSTAND?

5. This figure is a rectangle, but it is not a square. Why?

6. Draw a parallelogram with all four sides the same length. What is its special name?

7. Why is a square a parallelogram?

Independent Practice

In **8–13**, write as many special names as possible for each quadrilateral.

8. 

9. 

10. 

11. 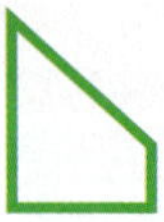

12.

13. 

DIGITAL Animated Glossary **www.pearsonsuccessnet.com**

For another example, see Set G on page 257.

Some quadrilaterals have more than one special name.

Rectangle

Four right angles

A *rectangle* is a special *parallelogram.*

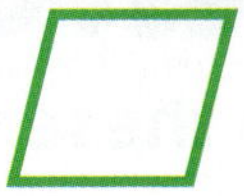

Rhombus

All sides the same length

A *rhombus* is a special *parallelogram.*

Square

Four right angles and all sides the same length

A *square* is a special *parallelogram.* It is a combination of a *rectangle* and a *rhombus.*

In **14–17**, write the name that best describes the quadrilateral. Draw a picture to help.

14. A rectangle with all sides the same length

15. A quadrilateral with only one pair of parallel sides

16. A parallelogram with four right angles

17. A rhombus with four right angles

Problem Solving

18. The bike in the photo was designed in 1997. What is the shape of the wheels? How is the shape different from the wheels on most bikes? How is a square different from a circle?

19. **Reasoning** I am a special quadrilateral with opposite sides the same length. What special quadrilateral could I be? (*Hint:* There is more than one correct answer.)

20. **Writing to Explain** How are a rectangle and a rhombus alike? How are they different?

21. Which picture shows more than $\frac{5}{8}$ of the square shaded?

SOL Prep

A 

B 

C 

D 

Virginia

Lesson 10-8

Extends 3.14 The student will identify, describe, compare, and contrast characteristics of plane and solid geometric figures (circle, square, rectangle, triangle, cube, rectangular prism, square pyramid, sphere, cone, and cylinder) by identifying relevant characteristics, including the number of angles, vertices, and edges, and the number and shape of faces, using concrete models.

Problem Solving

Make and Test Generalizations

What is the same in these three polygons?

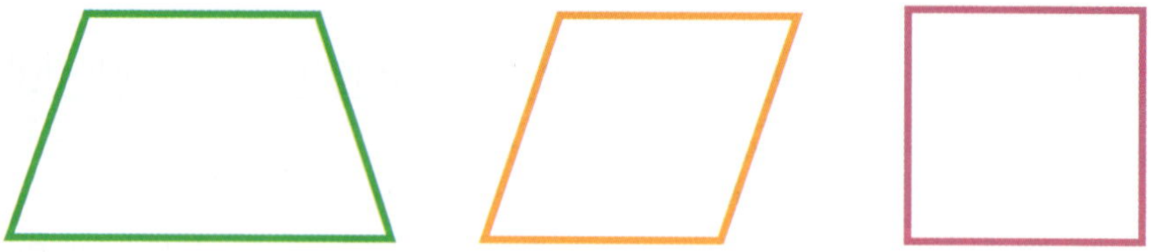

Guided Practice*

Do you know HOW?

Make and test a generalization for each set of polygons.

1. 

2. 

Do you UNDERSTAND?

3. Look at the polygons above. All sides of the second and third polygons **are** the same length. So why is the friend's generalization incorrect?

4. Draw a set of polygons that you can make a generalization about. Include a picture.

Independent Practice

In **5–7**, make a generalization for each set of polygons.

5. 

6. 

7. 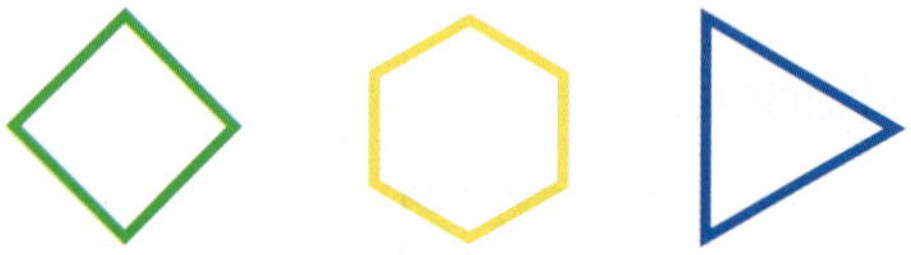

Stuck? Try this....

- What do I know?
- What am I asked to find?
- What diagram can I use to help understand the problem?
- Can I use addition, subtraction, multiplication, or division?
- Is all of my work correct?
- Did I answer the right question?
- Is my answer reasonable?

*For another example, see Set H on page 257.

Make a Generalization

Your friend says that the sides are all the same length.

You say that they all have 4 sides.

Test the Generalization

Notice that the top and bottom of this polygon are not the same length. Your friend's generalization is not correct!

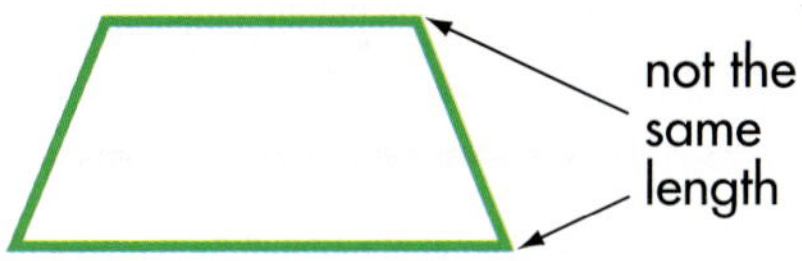

You see that the first polygon has 4 sides. The second has 4 sides. So does the third. Your generalization is correct!

8. Mr. Redbird makes tables that have 3 legs and tables that have 4 legs. The tables that he made this month have 18 legs in all. How many tables of each kind did he make?

9. Anna earns $4 for each hour that she babysits. She babysat for 2 hours last week and 5 hours this week. How much did she earn in all?

10. How are the four numbers 18, 24, 16, and 40 alike?

11. Compare each sum to its addends in these number sentences:

$34 + 65 = 99$ $\quad$ $8 + 87 = 95$ $\quad$ $435 + 0 = 435$

Make a generalization about addends and sums for whole numbers.

12. **Writing to Explain** Is this generalization true? If not, draw a picture to show why not.

If a shape is made up of line segments, then it is a polygon.

13. Ari gave his friends these clues about a secret number.

- The number has three digits.
- The hundreds digit is less than 3.
- The tens digit is twice the ones digit.
- The number is odd.

What are all the possible secret numbers?

14. SOL Prep What is the same in all these polygons?

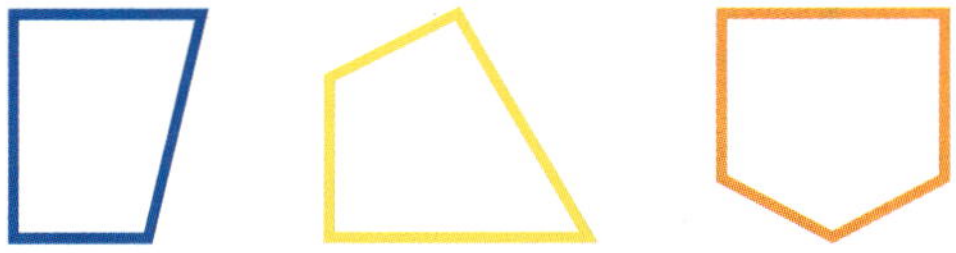

A All have a pair of parallel sides.

B All have two right angles.

C All have one acute angle.

D All have four sides.

Topic 10

VA SOL Test Prep

1. Evelyn packed her stuffed animals in the box shown below. Which solid best describes the box? (10-1)

A Cylinder

B Cube

C Pyramid

D Cone

2. The angles below are examples of acute angles. (10-4)

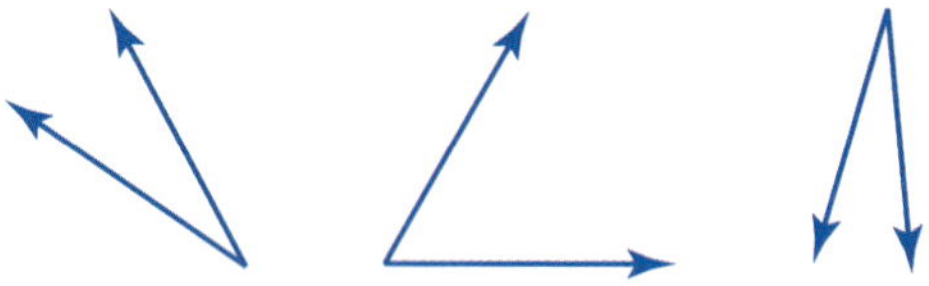

Which clock face below shows the hands in an acute angle?

A

B

C

D

3. Keenan bought a yo-yo in an unusually shaped box. Which best describes the shape of the top of the box? (10-5)

A Hexagon

B Pentagon

C Octagon

D Quadrilateral

4. Which best describes the triangles? (10-8)

A They are all acute triangles.

B They are all isosceles triangles.

C They are all obtuse triangles.

D They are all scalene triangles.

5. Which figure is a polygon? (10-5)

A

B

C

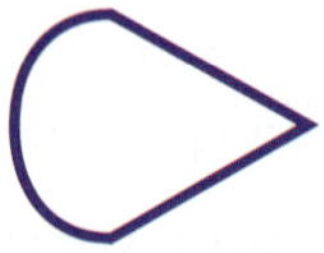

D

6. Four friends made quadrilateral shapes out of colored paper. Whose shape has only one set of parallel sides? (10-7)

A Melissa's

B Nigel's

C Pat's

D Rahmi's

7. Below is part of a nature trail map. Which two trails represent parallel lines? (10-3)

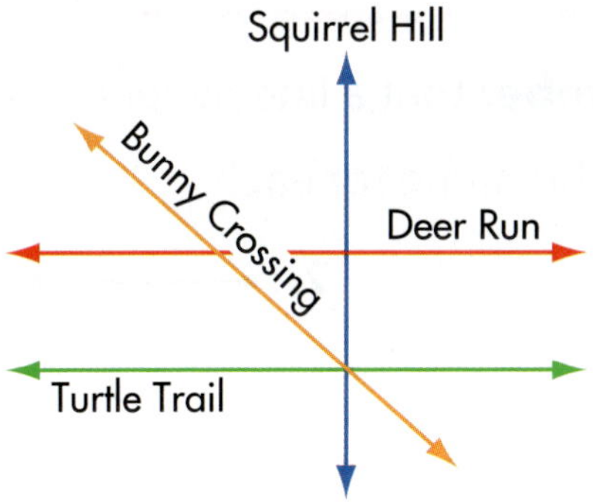

A Deer Run and Turtle Trail

B Deer Run and Squirrel Hill

C Bunny Crossing and Squirrel Hill

D Bunny Crossing and Deer Run

8. The students ran a course from the flag to the tree, to the trash can, and then back to the flag. What type of triangle did the course form? (10-6)

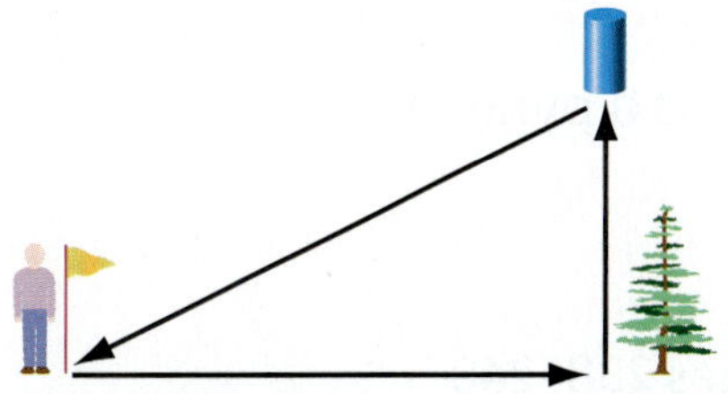

A Scalene

B Isosceles

C Equilateral

D Acute

9. What two quadrilaterals did Kim use to make up the rug design? (10-7)

A Rhombus and parallelogram

B Rhombus and trapezoid

C Parallelogram and trapezoid

D Parallelogram and hexagon

10. A decorative pillow is shaped like a rectangular prism with a tassel at each vertex. How many tassels are there? (10-2)

A 4

B 6

C 7

D 8

Set A, pages 234–236

Name this solid figure.

The figure has flat surfaces and a point at the top.

The figure is a pyramid.

Remember that some solid figures roll and some do not.

Name the solid figure.

1. 

2. 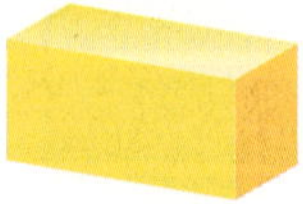

Set B, pages 238–240

How many faces, edges, and vertices does the following solid figure have?

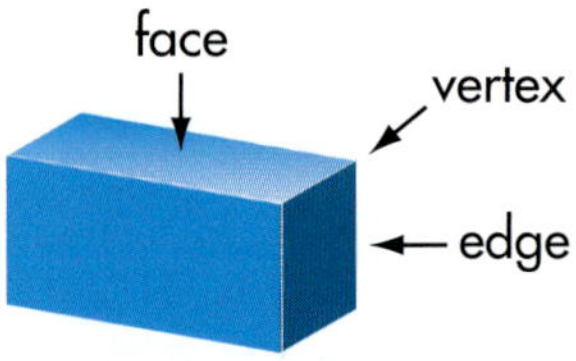

A rectangular prism has 6 faces, 12 edges, and 8 vertices.

Remember that a vertex is where three or more edges meet.

For **1** and **2**, use the cube below.

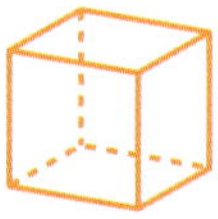

1. How many faces, edges, and vertices does this cube have?

2. Describe the shape of each face.

Set C, pages 242–243

Write the name for the following.

The lines cross at one point. They are intersecting lines.

Remember that a line never ends.

Write the name for each.

1.

2.

Set D, pages 244–245

Describe the angle as right, acute, or obtuse.

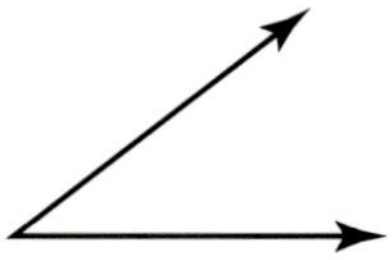

The angle is open less than a right angle.

It is an acute angle.

Remember that the opening of a right angle makes a square corner.

Describe each angle.

1. 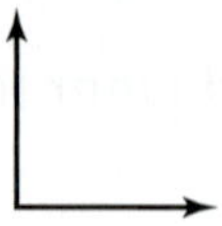

2. 

Set E, pages 246–247

Is the figure a polygon? If it is a polygon, give its name. If not, explain why.

The figure is closed and is made up of line segments. It is a polygon.

The figure has 5 sides. It is a pentagon.

Remember that a polygon is made up of line segments.

Is each figure a polygon? If so, give its name. If not, explain why.

1. 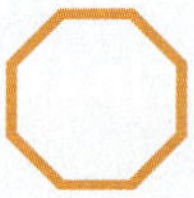

2. 

Set F, pages 248–249

Tell if the triangle below is equilateral, isosceles, or scalene. Then tell if the triangle is right, acute, or obtuse.

None of the sides are the same length. The triangle is a scalene triangle. One angle is an obtuse angle.

The triangle is an obtuse triangle.

Remember that no sides of a scalene triangle are the same length.

Describe each triangle by its sides and by its angles.

1. 

2. 

Set G, pages 250–251

Name the following quadrilateral.

Opposite sides are parallel and opposite sides have the same length.

The figure is a parallelogram.

Remember that all quadrilaterals have four sides.

Write as many special names as possible for each quadrilateral.

1. 

2. 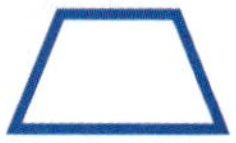

Set H, pages 252–253

Make and test a generalization for the set of polygons.

Make a generalization. *Each polygon has sides that are the same length.*

Test the generalization. *All of the polygons have sides that are the same length.*

Remember that a generalization must apply to the entire set.

Make and test a generalization for this set of polygons.

1. 

Topic 11

Congruence and Symmetry

1 Are snowflakes symmetric? You will find out in Lesson 11-3.

2 Are the windows of the Taj Mahal congruent? You will find out in Lesson 11-1.

3

Where is the line of symmetry in the picture of a mountain and its reflection? You will find out in Lesson 11-2.

4

Does fruit such as an orange, a grapefruit, or a starfruit have lines of symmetry? You will find out in Lesson 11-3.

Review What You Know!

Vocabulary

Choose the best term from the box.

- difference
- estimate
- line
- rounding

1. When you subtract two numbers, the answer is called the __?__.

2. When you replace a number with a number that tells about how many to the nearest ten, you are __?__ the number.

3. A __?__ is a straight path of points that is endless in both directions.

Repeating Patterns

Draw the next three shapes to continue each pattern.

4. 

5. 

Division Facts

Find each quotient.

6. 24 ÷ 3 **7.** 36 ÷ 9 **8.** 16 ÷ 4

9. 54 ÷ 6 **10.** 81 ÷ 9 **11.** 48 ÷ 8

12. **Writing to Explain** Is the figure below a polygon? Explain how you can draw the figure to make it a polygon.

Virginia

Lesson 11-1

3.16 The student will identify and describe congruent and noncongruent plane figures.

Congruent Figures and Motion

What are congruent figures?

Figures that have the same size and shape are **congruent** figures. You can move a figure to make a new figure that is congruent to it.

A **slide** or **translation** moves a figure up, down, left, or right.

Slide or Translation

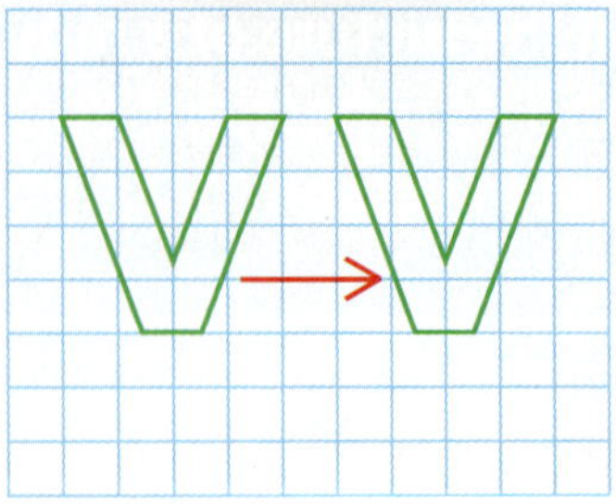

Another Example How can you decide if two figures are congruent?

To decide if two figures are congruent, trace one of the figures and place the tracing on top of the other figure.

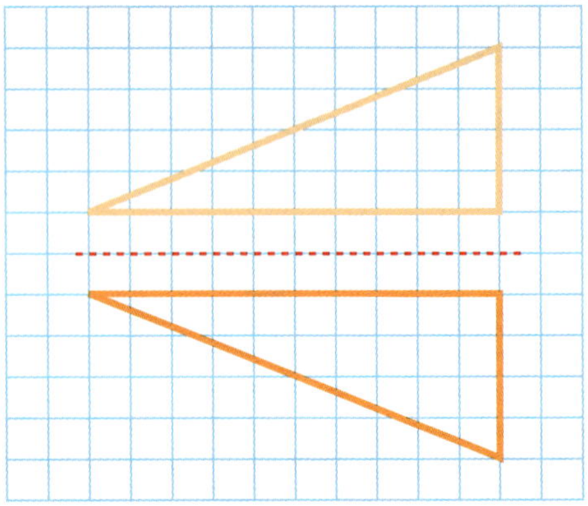

Yes, the figures are congruent.

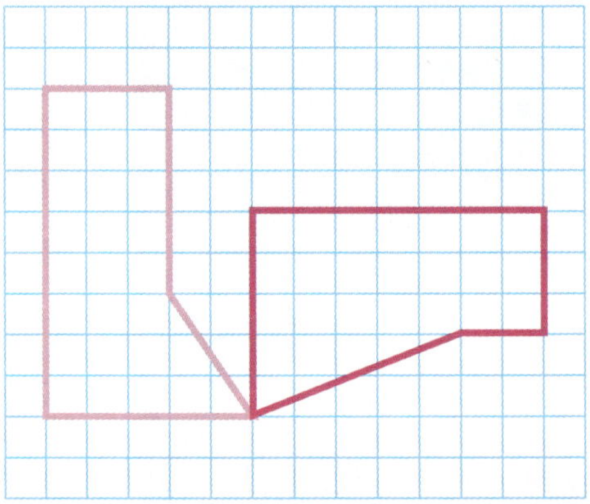

No, the figures are not congruent.

Explain It

1. Look at the two triangles. How could you move one triangle to match it to the other?
2. Look at the two pentagons. How could you move one to show that it does not match the other?

A flip or reflection picks up and moves a figure to give a mirror image.

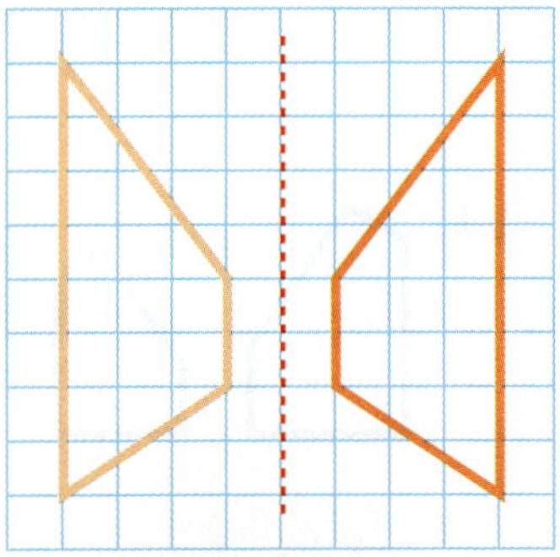

Flip or Reflection

A turn or rotation moves a figure around a point.

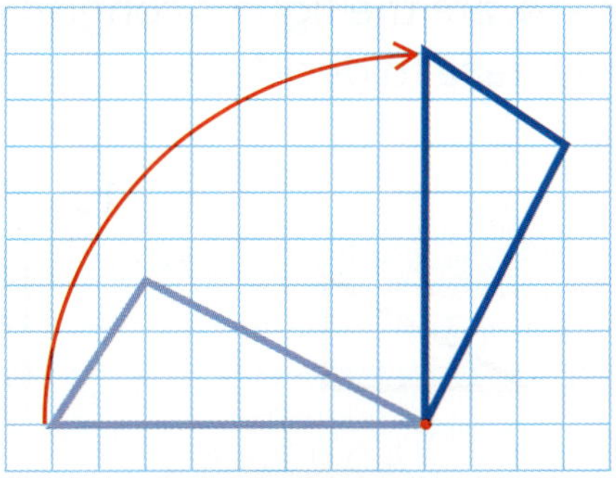

Turn or Rotation

Guided Practice*

Do you know HOW?

Write *slide, flip,* or *turn* for each.

1.

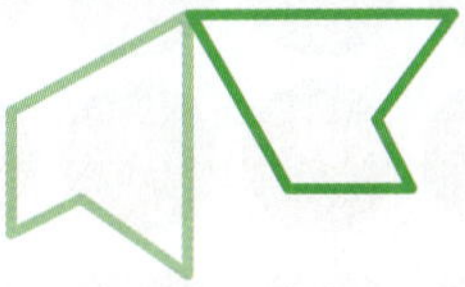

2.

Are the figures congruent? Write *yes* or *no*. You may trace to decide.

3.

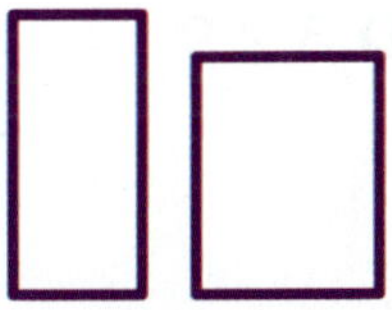

4.

Do you UNDERSTAND?

5. Could a triangle and a square be congruent? Explain your answer.

6. Are all triangles congruent? Explain your answer.

7. Are all squares congruent? Explain your answer.

8. Trace this pentagon. Then show what it would look like after reflecting it to the right.

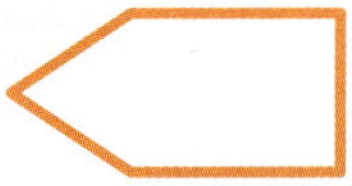

Independent Practice

For **9–11**, write *slide, flip,* or *turn* for each pair of congruent figures.

9.

10.

11.

DIGITAL Animated Glossary **www.pearsonsuccessnet.com**

For another example, see Set A on page 272.

Independent Practice

For **12–14**, are the figures congruent? Write *yes* or *no*.
You may trace to decide.

12. 

13. 

14. 

Problem Solving

15. Manny says the windows of the Taj Mahal are congruent because they are all shaped like the window in the picture below. Do you agree? Why or why not?

16. **Think About the Process** Samantha arranged some pennies in the pattern shown below. Which numerical expression best shows how she arranged them?

SOL Prep

A $3 + 6$

B $3 + 9$

C 3×6

D 3×9

17. Draw a rectangle. Then draw a line segment that divides the rectangle into two congruent figures. Describe the two figures.

18. **Writing to Explain** Are all rectangles congruent? Explain your answer.

19. Which figure below is congruent to the figure at the right?

SOL Prep

A 

B 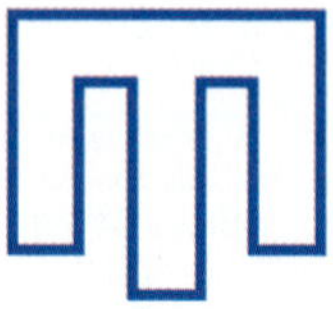

C 

D 

Going Digital

Motions

Use eTools

Geometry Shapes

Write *translation*, *reflection*, or *rotation* for each pair of figures.

Step 1 Go to the Geometry Shapes eTool. Click on the pentagon, and then click in the workspace twice to create two pentagons side-by-side.

Step 2 Click on the rotate tool and then click on the second pentagon until it looks like the second pentagon pictured above. This shows that the second pentagon is the result of rotating the first. Write *rotation*.

Step 3 Make two copies of the right triangle in the workspace. Click on the reflection (flip vertical) tool and then on the second triangle. This shows that the second triangle is a reflection of the first. Write *reflection*.

Step 4 Make two copies of the trapezoid in the workspace. Use the arrow tool to move the second trapezoid like the one pictured above. This shows that the second trapezoid is a translation of the first. Write *translation*. Use the broom tool to clear the workspace.

Practice

Write *translation, reflection,* or *rotation* for each pair of figures.

1.

2.

3.

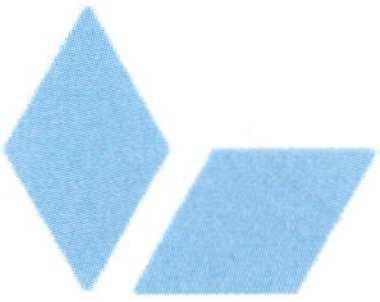

Virginia

Lesson 11-2

Reviews 2.15.b The student will identify and create figures with at least one line of symmetry.

Line Symmetry

What are symmetric figures?

A line of symmetry is a line on which a figure can be folded so the two parts match exactly. A symmetric figure has at least one line of symmetry.

A figure can have just one line of symmetry.

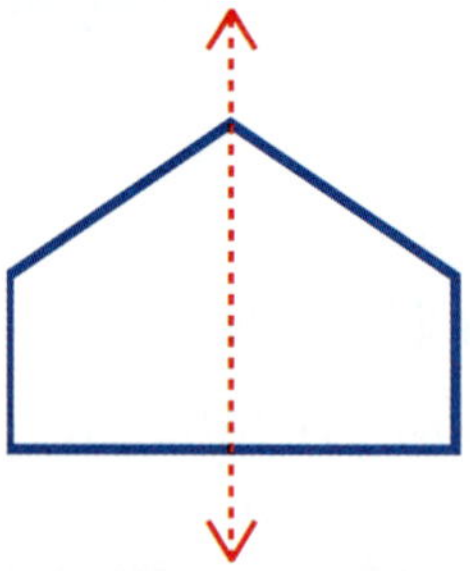

Guided Practice*

Do you know HOW?

Is the figure symmetric? Write *yes* or *no*. You may trace to decide.

1. 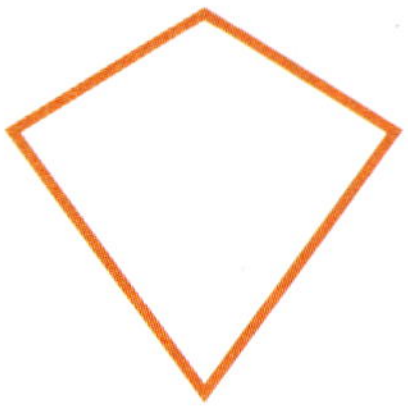

2. 

3. 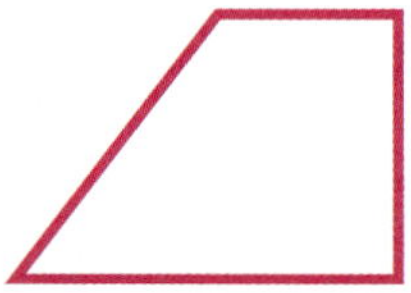

4. 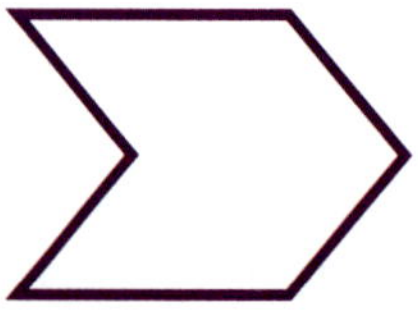

Do you UNDERSTAND?

5. Explain how you can test a figure to decide if it has a line of symmetry.

6. Is the dashed line a line of symmetry for the rectangle? Explain.

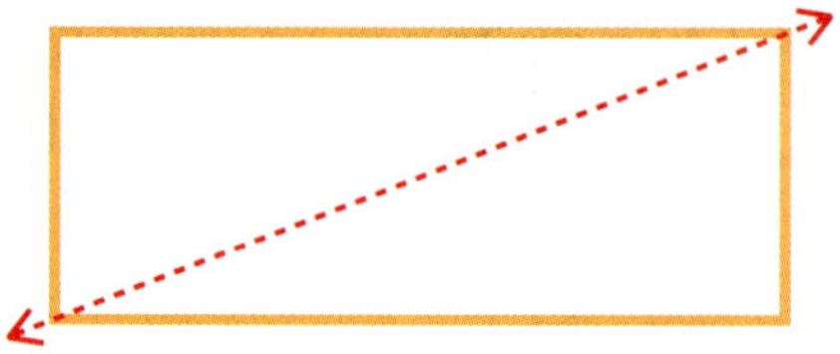

Independent Practice

Is the figure symmetric? Write *yes* or *no*. You may trace to decide.

7. 

8. 

9. 

10. 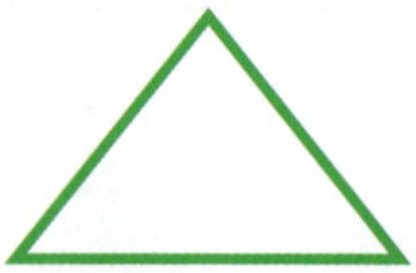

DIGITAL Animated Glossary **www.pearsonsuccessnet.com**

**For another example, see Set B on page 272.*

A figure can have no lines of symmetry.

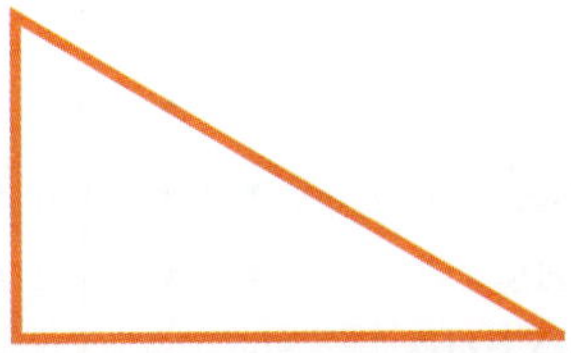

A figure can have more than one line of symmetry.

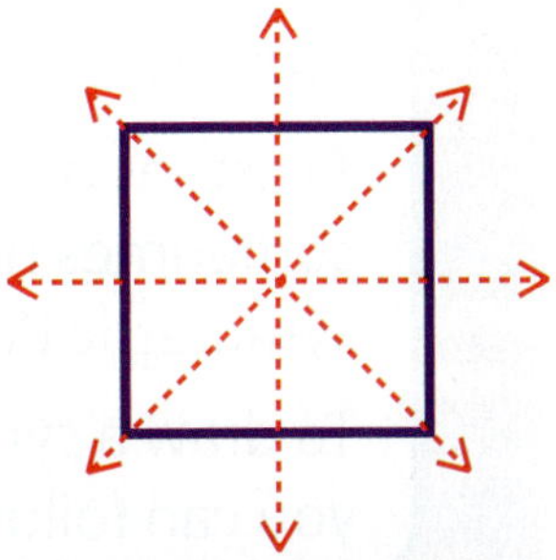

Tell whether each object is symmetric. Write *yes* or *no*.

11. 

12. 

13. 

14. 

Problem Solving

15. Trace this picture of a mountain and its reflection. Then fold your tracing and draw the line of symmetry.

16. Which figure below does **NOT** have at least one line of symmetry?

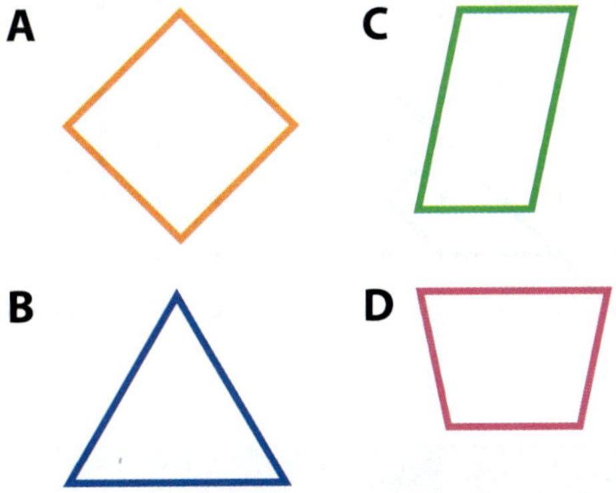

17. **Writing to Explain** You have learned that a square is a type of rectangle. Do all rectangles have the same number of lines of symmetry as all squares? Explain your answer.

18. Sue has some nickels, dimes, and quarters in her pocket.

- There are 3 quarters.
- There are 2 more dimes than nickels.
- There are 15 coins in all.

What is the total value of the coins?

Virginia

Lesson 11-3

Reviews 2.15.b The student will identify and create figures with at least one line of symmetry.

Drawing Shapes with Lines of Symmetry

Hands-On
grid paper

How can you draw a figure with a line of symmetry?

Artists and other workers sometimes need to draw symmetric figures.

To draw a symmetric figure, you can follow these steps.

Step 1

Draw a line segment as part of the line of symmetry.

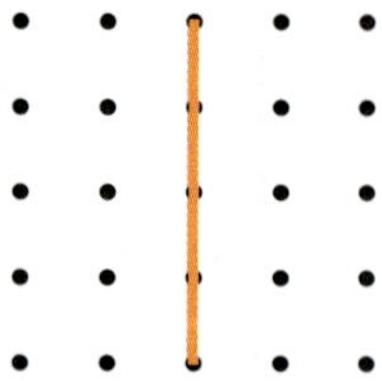

Guided Practice*

Do you know HOW?

Trace the figure onto dot paper or grid paper. Then complete it so the blue line segment is part of a line of symmetry.

1. 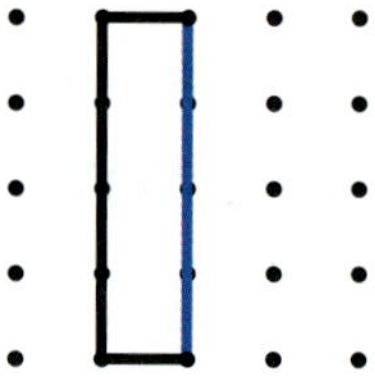

2. 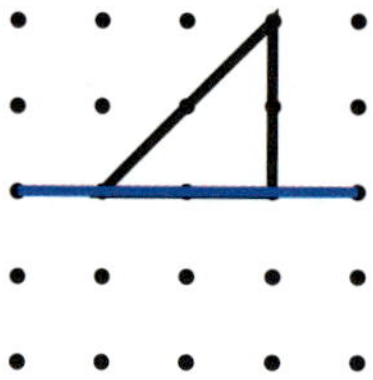

3. 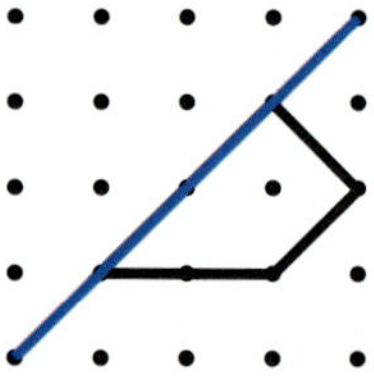

4. 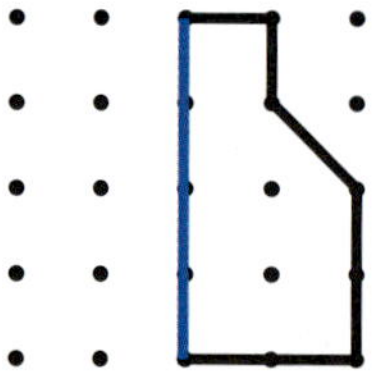

Do you UNDERSTAND?

5. The picture below shows two parts of a figure on dot paper.

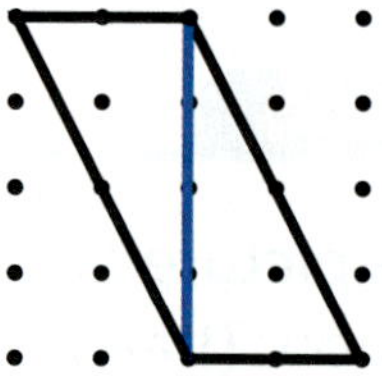

Explain why the blue line segment is not part of a line of symmetry.

6. How would you draw a figure that has two lines of symmetry?

Independent Practice

Trace the figure. Then complete it so the blue line segment is part of a line of symmetry. You may use dot paper or fold and trace.

7. 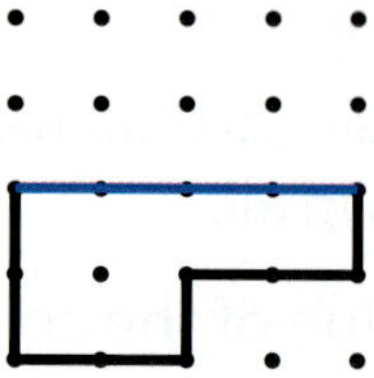

8. 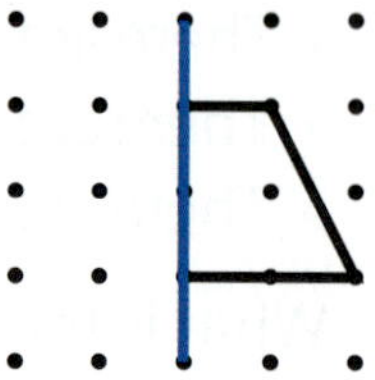

9. 

10. 

DIGITAL eTools www.pearsonsuccessnet.com

*For another example, see Set C on page 273.

Step 2

Draw the first part of the figure on one side of the line segment.

Step 3

Copy the first part exactly on the other side of the line segment.

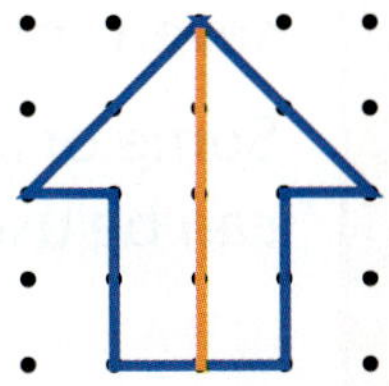

Problem Solving

11. **Estimation** Jeremy is reading a book that has 121 pages. He read 19 pages yesterday and 33 pages today. About how many more pages are left to read?

12. A perfectly formed snowflake has 6 sides and is symmetric.

Draw your own snowflake. Color the lines of symmetry on your drawing. How many lines of symmetry does it have?

13. **Writing to Explain** Explain how you can use this shape to make a symmetric quadrilateral. What type of quadrilateral will it be?

14. The picture shows a sliced ruby red grapefruit and an outline of part of the grapefruit sections.

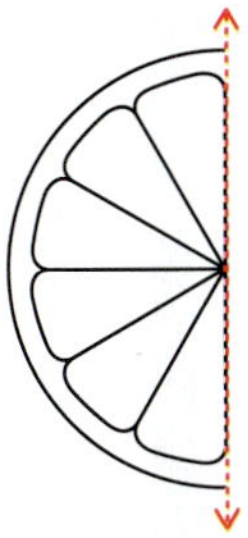

Trace the outline onto a sheet of paper. Complete the outline so the dashed line is a line of symmetry.

15. The green line segment is part of a line of symmetry. Which picture below shows the complete figure?

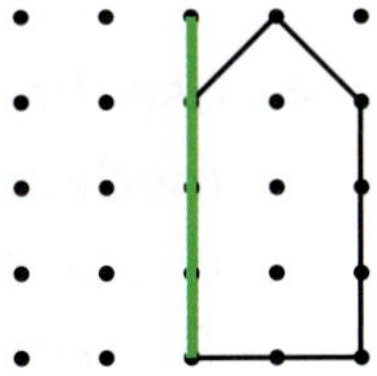

A

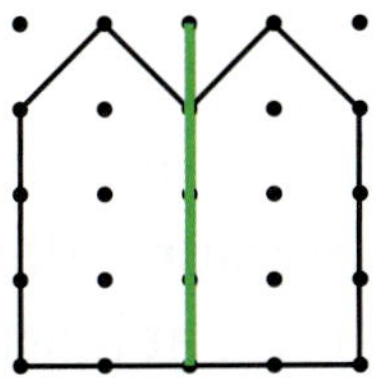

C

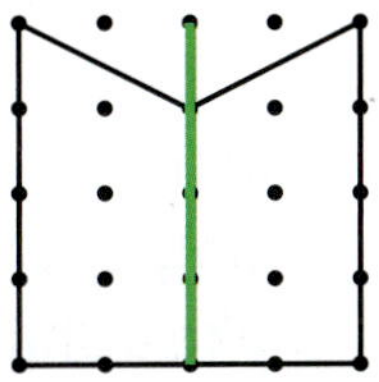

B

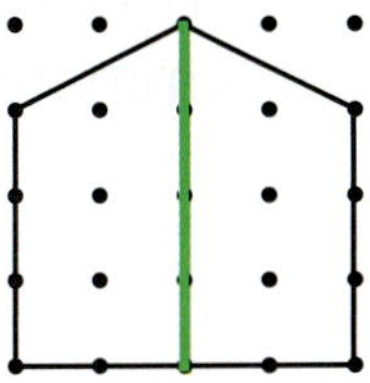

D

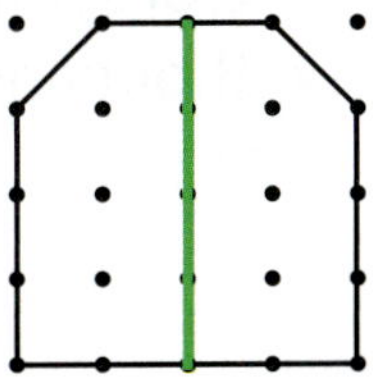

Virginia

Lesson 11-4

Reviews 2.15.b The student will identify and create figures with at least one line of symmetry.

Problem Solving

Use Objects

A tangram is a square made up of seven smaller shapes.

Some or all of the smaller shapes can be used to make other shapes.

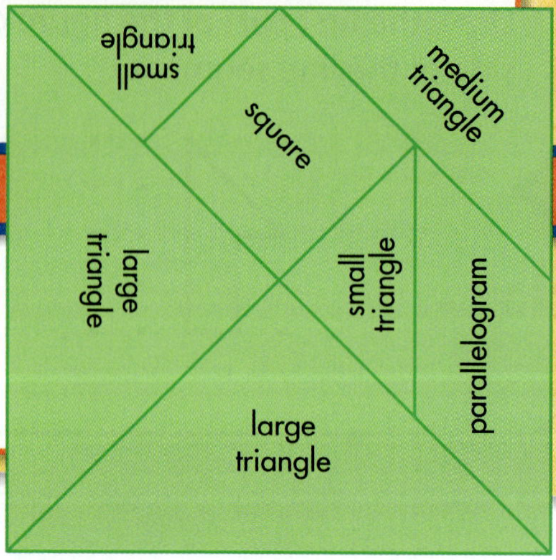

Guided Practice*

Do you know HOW?

Use tangram pieces to make the shapes described. Draw what you made.

1. Use the parallelogram and one small triangle. Make a shape that has at least one line of symmetry. Then make a shape without any lines of symmetry.

Do you UNDERSTAND?

For **2** and **3**, look at the problem above.

2. Where are the two lines of symmetry in the rectangle?

3. **Write a Problem** Write a problem that you can solve by making a shape from tangram pieces.

Independent Practice

For **4** and **5**, use tangram pieces to make the shapes described. Draw what you made.

4. Use the parallelogram and the medium triangle. Make a shape that has at least one line of symmetry. Then make a shape without any lines of symmetry.

5. Use the parallelogram, one small triangle, and the medium triangle. Make a shape that has at least one line of symmetry. Then make a shape without any lines of symmetry.

Stuck? Try this....

- What do I know?
- What am I asked to find?
- What diagram can I use to help understand the problem?
- Can I use addition, subtraction, multiplication, or division?
- Is all of my work correct?
- Did I answer the right question?
- Is my answer reasonable?

*For another example, see Set D on page 273.

Read and Understand

Make two different shapes using the two small triangles and the medium triangle.

- Make one shape that has at least one line of symmetry.
- Make the other shape without any lines of symmetry.

Plan and Solve

This shape is a rectangle. It has two lines of symmetry.

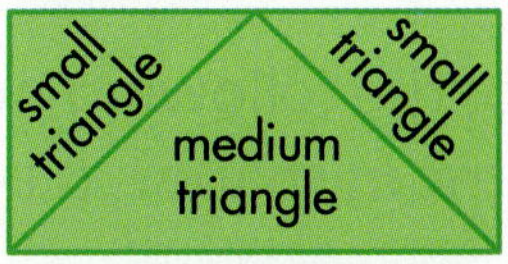

This shape is a parallelogram. It does not have a line of symmetry.

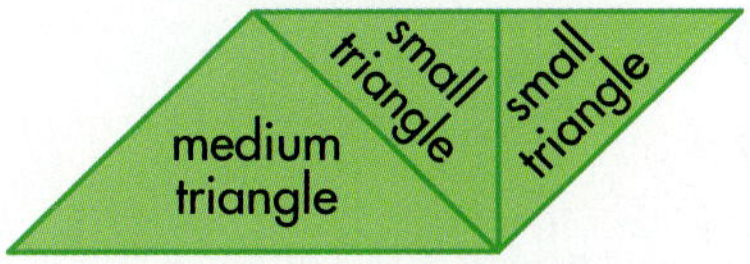

For **6–8**, use the two small triangles and the parallelogram to make each shape. For each shape, use all three pieces. Then draw what you made.

6. A rectangle **7.** A triangle **8.** A parallelogram

For **9–11**, use the two small triangles, the parallelogram, and the square. Make each shape using all four pieces. Then draw what you made.

9. A rectangle **10.** A parallelogram **11.** A hexagon

12. Writing to Explain Show and explain how you can make a triangle and two types of quadrilaterals using just the two small triangles.

13. Use all five triangles from a set of tangram shapes. Make at least three different shapes. Draw what you made.

14. Timothy sold some tickets to the school play. The tickets were numbered in order. The numbers started at 16 and ended at 45. How many tickets did Timothy sell?

15. Jessica is standing in a line of 10 people. There are twice as many people ahead of her as there are behind her. How many people are ahead of Jessica in the line?

16. David's mother brought 24 cartons of orange and grape juice to the class picnic. There were twice as many cartons of orange juice as cartons of grape juice. How many of each kind were there?

A 12 orange, 6 grape
B 12 grape, 6 orange
C 16 orange, 8 grape
D 16 grape, 8 orange

Topic 11

VA SOL Test Prep

1. Which of the following numbers is symmetric in shape? (11-2)

A 2

B 5

C 0

D 7

2. Which moves one arrow to match the other one? (11-1)

A Flip

B Symmetry

C Slide

D Turn

3. Below are examples of the small triangle tangram shape turned to several different positions.

Which of the following shapes can **NOT** be made by joining two of the triangles? (11-4)

A A square

B A parallelogram

C A triangle

D A trapezoid

4. Katherine designed the body of a kite.

Which shape is congruent to her kite design? (11-1)

A 

B 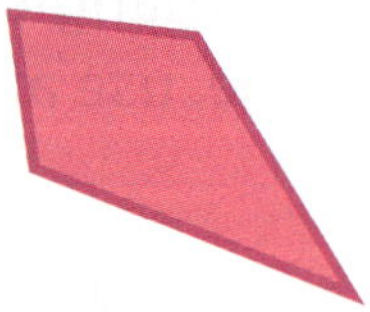

C 

D 

5. Which of the following shows a rotation (turn)? (11-1)

A 

B 

C 

D 

6. While on a nature hike, Nolan saw the items below. Which item does **NOT** show a line of symmetry? (11-2)

A

B

C

D

7. Which moves one flag to match the other one? (11-1)

A Slide

B Turn

C Congruent

D Flip

8. Danny drew the left half of his playground design on dot paper.

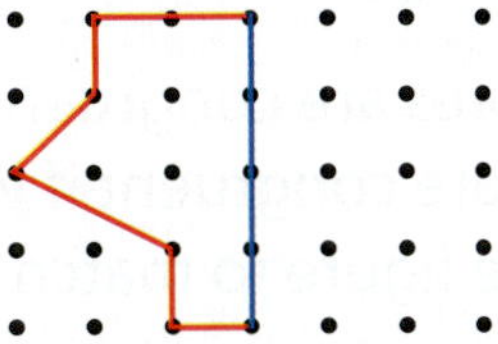

Which shows the right half of his design if the blue segment is part of a line of symmetry? (11-3)

A

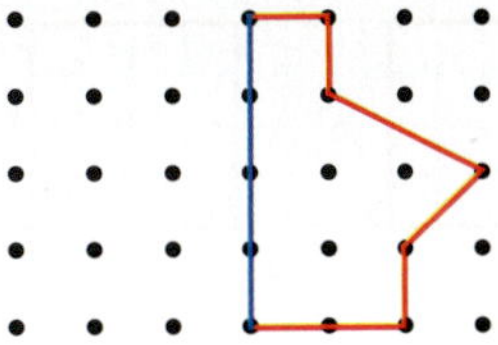

B

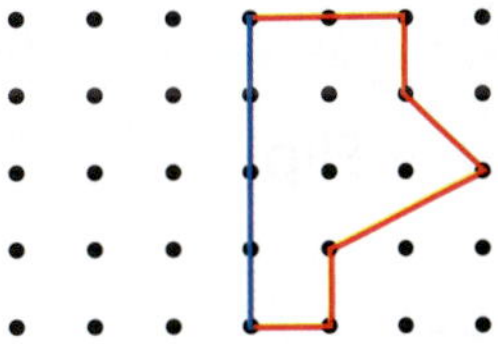

C

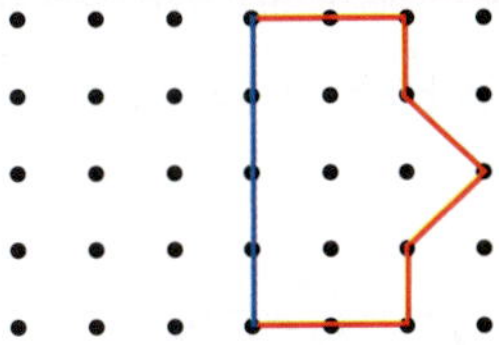

D

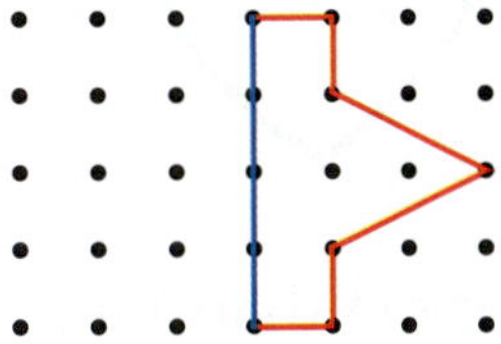

9. How many letters in the word below have at least one line of symmetry? (11-2)

TAXES

A 0

B 2

C 4

D 5

Set A, pages 260–262

Figures that have the same size and same shape are congruent figures.

You can check if figures are congruent by moving them. They are congruent if you can slide, flip, or turn one figure to match the other.

This reflection shows that these two figures are congruent.

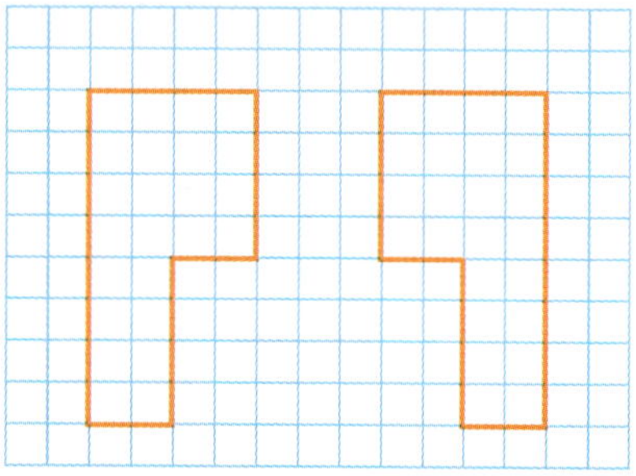

Flip

Remember that figures need to be the same shape and same size to be congruent.

Are the figures congruent? Write *yes* or *no*. If yes, write *slide*, *turn*, or *flip* for each.

1. 

2. 

Set B, pages 264–265

A symmetric figure has at least two parts that match exactly.

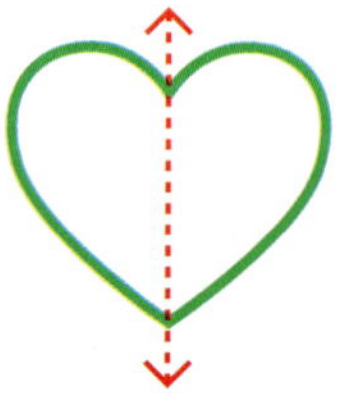

A figure can have more than 1 line of symmetry.

This figure has 5 lines of symmetry.

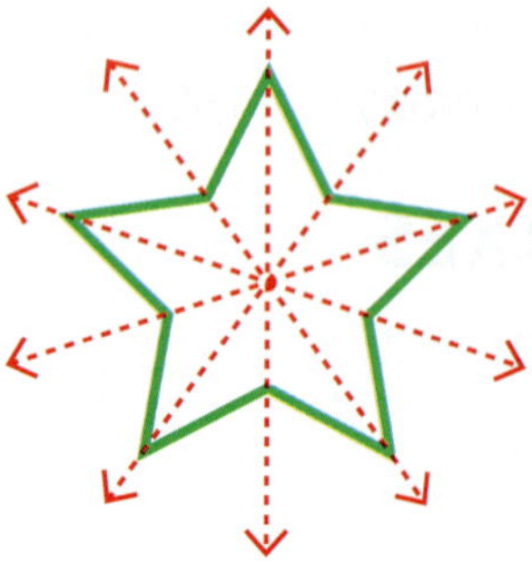

Remember that a symmetric figure has at least 1 line of symmetry, showing two parts that match exactly.

Tell whether each figure is symmetric. Write *yes* or *no*.

1. 

2. 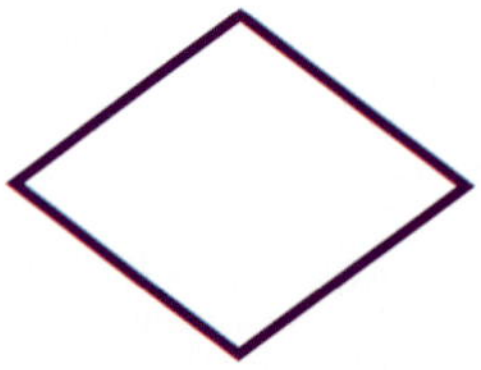

Set C, pages 266–267

To draw a symmetric figure, draw the first part of the figure on one side of a line segment.

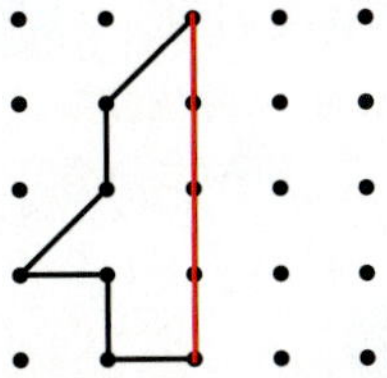

Copy the first part exactly on the other side of the line segment.

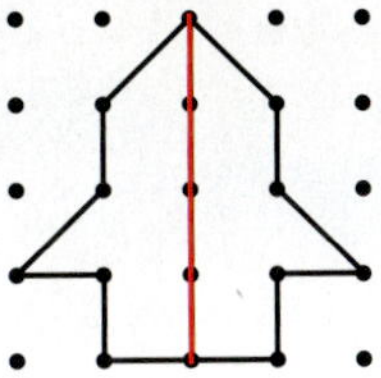

Remember to match each part of the figure exactly.

Copy the figure onto dot paper. Then complete it so the red line segment is part of a line of symmetry.

1. 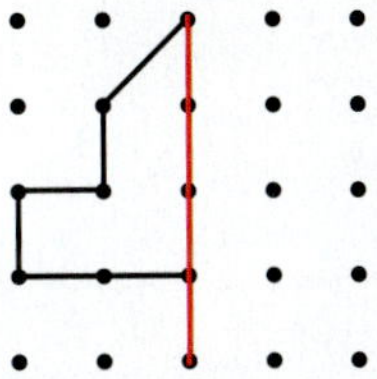

2. 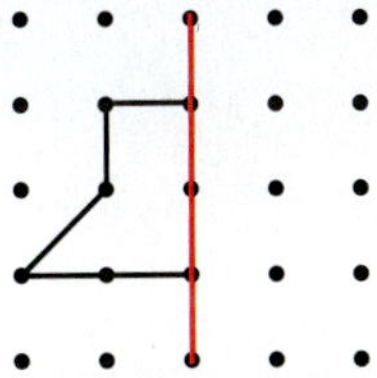

Set D, pages 268–269

Use the two large triangle tangram shapes. Make one shape that has at least one line of symmetry. Make another shape that does not have a line of symmetry.

This shape is a triangle. It has one line of symmetry.

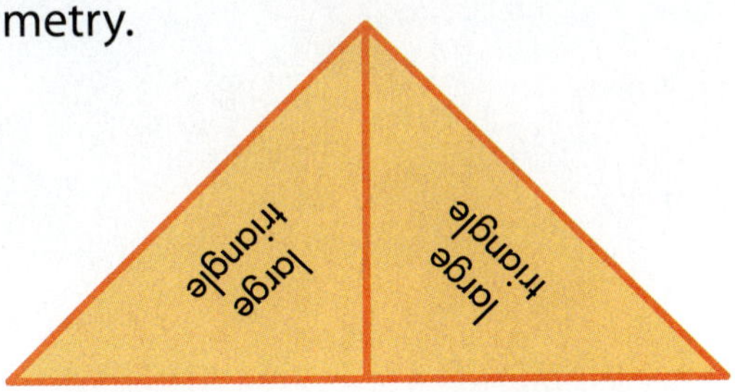

This shape is a polygon. It does not have a line of symmetry.

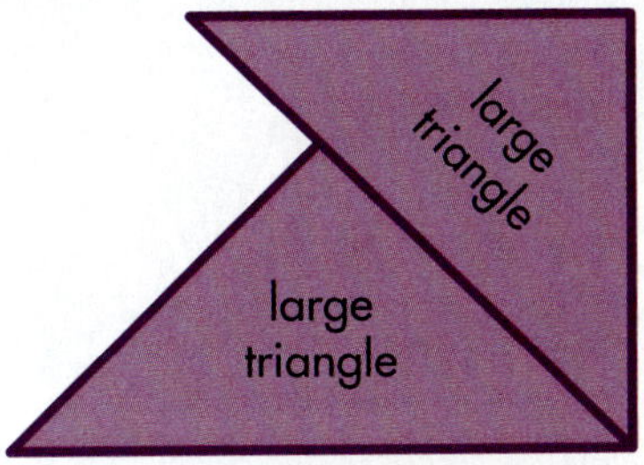

Remember to check that your new shape matches the directions given.

From a tangram, use the two small triangles and the square. Make the shape described. Draw what you made.

1. A shape with a line of symmetry
2. A parallelogram
3. A trapezoid

Scott Foresman·Addison Wesley

enVisionMATH™

Virginia

Virginia Handbook

Lessons

VA SOL Practice

Virginia

Lesson VA-1

3.8 The student will determine, by counting, the value of a collection of bills and coins whose total value is $5.00 or less, compare the value of the bills and coins, and make change.

Comparing Sets of Bills and Coins

How do you compare the values of sets of bills and coins?

Ed and Sue each have some bills and coins. Is the total value of Ed's bills and coins *greater than*, *less than*, or *equal to* Sue's?

Ed

Sue

Example Group each set of bills and coins in order from greatest to least. Count on to find the total value in dollars and cents.

Ed:

$1 $1.25 $1.35 $1.40 **$1.41**

Sue:

$1 $1.10 $1.20 $1.30 $1.35 **$1.36**

$1.41 > $1.36, so the total value of Ed's money is *greater than* Sue's.

Guided Practice

Do you know HOW?

For **1** and **2**, draw to solve.

1. Draw and label a different set of coins that has a value *equal to* the coins below.

2. Draw and label a set of bills and coins that has a value *less than* the bills and coins below.

Do you UNDERSTAND?

3. Writing to Explain Does a set with more coins always have a greater value than a set with fewer coins? Explain.

4. How does grouping bills and coins in order from greatest to least value help you find the value of the set?

5. Ann has a penny, two quarters, and one dollar bill. Is the total value of Ann's bills and coins *greater than*, *less than*, or *equal to* the value of Sue's bills and coins?

Independent Practice

For **6–9**, use the sets of bills and coins below.

Alex's Bills and Coins

Ben's Bills and Coins

Tia's Bills and Coins

Dale's Bills and Coins

6. Is the total value of Alex's bills and coins *greater than*, *less than*, or *equal to* Dale's?

7. Is the total value of Tia's bills and coins *greater than*, *less than*, or *equal to* Ben's?

8. The value of Jim's 4 bills and 1 coin is equal to the value of Tia's bills and coins. What bills and coin does Jim have?

9. Fiona has a different set of bills and coins that is equal in value to Dale's. What bills and coins might Fiona have?

Problem Solving

For **10** and **11**, use the chart at the right.

10. Is the value of Viv's coins *greater than*, *less than*, or *equal to* Jill's coins?

11. Jan has only nickels in her pocket. The total value of her coins is *equal to* the value of Viv's set of coins. How many nickels does Jan have?

12. **Writing to Explain** Brad bought 5 presents for $3 each. Koji bought 4 presents for $4 each. Who spent more money? Explain.

13. Which shows the number below in standard form?

700,000 + 6,000 + 50

A 700,650 **C** 760,050

B 706,050 **D** 765,000

Virginia

Lesson VA-2

3.1.b The student will round whole numbers, 9,999 or less, to the nearest ten, hundred, and thousand.

Rounding Whole Numbers

How can you round 4-digit numbers?

You can round a 4-digit number to the nearest thousand, hundred, or ten.

About how many pounds does Mr. Morgan's compact car weigh? Round to the nearest thousand.

One Way Use a number line.

3,611 is closer to 4,000 than to 3,000.

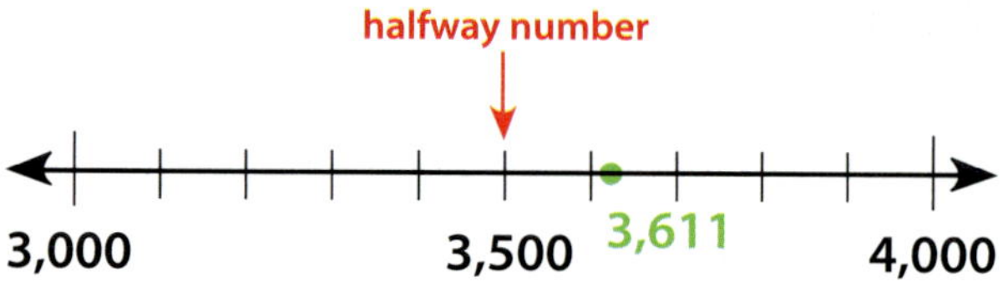

Another Way Use place value. Find the digit in the rounding place and look at the next digit to the right.

thousands place

3,611
↓↓
4,000

The digit 6 is greater than 5, so add one to the digit in the thousands place. Then change all the digits to the right to zero.

Rounded to the nearest thousand, the compact car weighs about 4,000 pounds.

Guided Practice

Do you know HOW?

Round each number to the nearest ten, hundred, and thousand.

1. 5,388
2. 1,509
3. 2,842
4. 9,199

Do you UNDERSTAND?

5. **Writing to Explain** Jill rounds a number to 2,500. Haley rounds the same number to 2,480. Why are their rounded numbers different?

6. Round the weight of Mr. Morgan's truck to the nearest ten, hundred, and thousand. Which estimate is closest to the actual weight?

Independent Practice

For **7–31**, round each number to the place of the underlined digit.

7. 1,451	**8.** 7,827	**9.** 5,355	**10.** 2,385	**11.** 4,674
12. 3,925	**13.** 9,849	**14.** 8,894	**15.** 6,063	**16.** 7,238
17. 2,155	**18.** 4,099	**19.** 5,543	**20.** 9,475	**21.** 8,802
22. 3,462	**23.** 6,345	**24.** 8,232	**25.** 2,795	**26.** 4,592
27. 1,309	**28.** 8,823	**29.** 6,629	**30.** 5,289	**31.** 9,329

Problem Solving

For **32** and **33**, use the chart at the right.

32. Which rivers are about 3,900 miles long when their lengths are rounded to the nearest hundred?

33. Reasoning Eva rounded the length of each river and got the same estimate for each river. Demario rounded the length of each river and got a different estimate for each. What can explain the difference?

Data

World's Longest Rivers

River	Approximate Length in Miles
Nile	4,132
Amazon	3,976
Yangtze	3,915
Mississippi-Missouri	3,902

34. Leah went to the store to buy pencils. Her total was $0.31. She paid with a $1 bill. How much change did Leah receive?

35. Number Sense A 4-digit number has the digits 1, 1, 9, and 9. When it is rounded to the nearest hundred, the result is 9,200. What is the number?

36. A builder ordered one thousand, six hundred nine bricks to build a patio and one thousand, seven hundred twelve bricks to build a garden path. Write both numbers in standard form.

37. An elephant weighs 5,608 pounds. What is its weight rounded to the nearest hundred?

A 5,500 pounds **C** 5,600 pounds

B 5,610 pounds **D** 6,000 pounds

Virginia

Lesson VA-3

3.4 The student will estimate solutions to and solve single-step and multistep problems involving the sum or difference of two whole numbers, each 9,999 or less, with or without regrouping.

Multistep Problems

How do you solve a problem with more than one step?

The students in Sara's school are making bows to sell at the fair. They bought 2,000 yards of ribbon. The students in grade 3 will use 245 yards and the students in grade 4 will use 260 yards. How many yards of ribbon will be left?

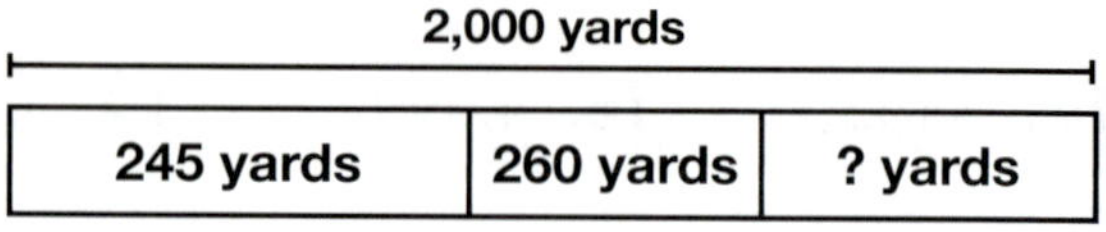

Example First find how much ribbon the students in grade 3 and grade 4 will use.

Add the two measurements of ribbon:

$$245 + 260 = 505 \text{ yards}$$

Then find how much ribbon is left for the students in other grades. Subtract 505 from the total number of yards of ribbon:

$$2000 - 505 = 1{,}495 \text{ yards}$$

There are 1,495 yards of ribbon left.

Guided Practice

Do you know HOW?

1. A piece of art is made of 3,165 tiles. The art has 142 black tiles, 725 white tiles, and 1,034 red tiles. All other tiles are blue. How many of the tiles are blue?

2. Dan rode his bike for 15 minutes in the morning and 25 minutes in the afternoon. Carl rode his bike for 35 minutes in the morning and 20 minutes in the afternoon. For how many more minutes did Carl ride his bike than Dan?

Do you UNDERSTAND?

3. **Writing to Explain** Bobby subtracted 3 times when he solved Exercise 1. Is that possible? Explain.

4. **Number Sense** The students in grade 5 will use 315 yards of ribbon. How many yards of ribbon are now left?

 Use after Lesson 2-8.

Independent Practice

Solve.

5. Philip needs to fold 36 napkins for a party. He has folded 8 napkins so far. His friend Terry has folded 12 napkins. How many napkins do they have left to fold?

6. Teresa is making necklaces. She bought glass beads for $6, clay beads for $3, and wooden beads for $5. She paid for all of the beads with a $20 bill. How much change did Teresa receive?

7. Mario has a collection of 181 CDs. He has 86 pop CDs and 43 rap CDs. The rest of the CDs are rock. How many of the CDs are rock?

8. The aquarium sold 1,605 tickets. Of the tickets, 1,104 were child tickets and 72 were teen tickets. The rest of the tickets sold were adult tickets. How many adult tickets were sold?

Problem Solving

For **9**, use the diagram at the right.

9. Mr. Min bought 5,250 feet of fence. He used 3,150 feet to fence the two long sides of his yard. He used 2,000 feet to fence the two shorter sides. How much fence did Mr. Min have left?

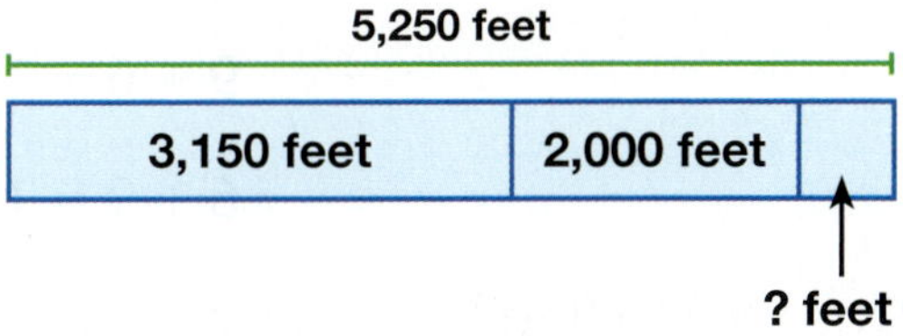

10. Richmond, Virginia is 102 miles from Alexandria, Virginia. There are 186 miles from Richmond, Virginia to Roanoke, Virginia. How much farther is it from Richmond to Roanoke than from Richmond to Alexandria?

11. Carole collects rubber bands, paper clips, and bottle caps. She has 2,130 rubber bands, 2,301 paper clips, and 1,332 bottle caps. Write the numbers of items Carole has in order from least to greatest.

12. How many faces does a cube have?

A 12

B 8

C 6

D 4

13. Max's Computer Store sold a computer for $1,050 and a printer for $900 less than the computer. How much did the computer and the printer cost in all?

A $105

B $1,200

C $1,350

D $1,950

Virginia

Lesson VA-4

3.2 The student will recognize and use the inverse relationships between addition/subtraction and multiplication/division to complete basic fact sentences. The student will use these relationships to solve problems.

Solving Problems Using Inverse Relationships

How can you use addition facts to solve subtraction problems?

Kito has 15 books on a shelf. Nine of the books are fiction, and the rest are nonfiction. How many nonfiction books does Kito have on the shelf?

Example Operations that undo each other are inverse operations.

Addition and subtraction have an inverse relationship. For example, adding 6 and subtracting 6 are inverse operations.

You can solve this problem in different ways.
You can use the fact family to help you solve addition and subtraction problems.

$9 + 6 = 15$ $15 - 6 = 9$

$6 + 9 = 15$ $15 - 9 = 6$

One way to find how many nonfiction books are on the shelf is to add:
9 plus what number is 15?
$9 + 6 = 15$

Another way is to subtract: $15 - 9 = 6$

Kito has 6 nonfiction books on the shelf.

Guided Practice

Do you know HOW?

Which addition sentence can help you find the difference? Then find each difference.

1. $10 - 8 =$ ▢
2. $16 - 7 =$ ▢
3. $14 - 6 =$ ▢
4. $13 - 4 =$ ▢

Do you UNDERSTAND?

5. Martina wrote $11 - 7 = 5$ on her math paper. How can she use addition to check her answer?

6. John scored 7 goals. Fred scored 16 goals. Write the fact family that can help you find how many more goals Fred scored than John.

Independent Practice

For **7–14**, find each difference. Use an inverse addition fact to help solve.

7. $11 - 6 =$ ▢ **8.** $10 - 2 =$ ▢ **9.** $15 - 5 =$ ▢ **10.** $15 - 7 =$ ▢

11. $12 - 3 =$ ▢ **12.** $12 - 6 =$ ▢ **13.** $13 - 6 =$ ▢ **14.** $11 - 2 =$ ▢

For **15–18**, write the related fact family. Then subtract.

15. $\begin{array}{r} 15 \\ -\ 8 \\ \hline \end{array}$ **16.** $\begin{array}{r} 13 \\ -\ 9 \\ \hline \end{array}$ **17.** $\begin{array}{r} 11 \\ -\ 3 \\ \hline \end{array}$ **18.** $\begin{array}{r} 14 \\ -\ 7 \\ \hline \end{array}$

For **19** and **20**, use the table at the right.

19. Write an addition fact to help find how much longer Tyler Road is than Adams Road. Solve.

20. Write an addition fact to help find how much longer Jackson Road is than Madison Road. Solve.

Data

Length of Roads

Road	Kilometers
Jackson	12
Adams	8
Madison	7
Tyler	17

Problem Solving

For **21**, use the picture at the right.

21. Kiara goes to the store. She has \$15 in her purse. She wants to buy two items that together cost exactly \$15. Which two items can she buy?

22. Ben's basketball team scored 18 points in the first half of a game. Ben scored 9 of the points. How many points did the other members of Ben's team score? Write an addition fact to help solve.

23. There are 26 monkeys at a zoo. There are 10 fewer apes than monkeys and 7 fewer lions than apes. How many lions are at the zoo?

24. DeAnna bought a book that cost \$4.13. She paid with a \$5 bill. List the coins and bills that could be DeAnna's change.

25. Which addition fact can you use to solve $14 - 5$?

A $5 + 9 = 14$ **C** $7 + 7 = 14$

B $7 + 5 = 12$ **D** $14 + 5 = 19$

Virginia

Lesson VA-5

3.6 The student will represent multiplication and division, using area, set, and number line models, and create and solve problems that involve multiplication of two whole numbers, one factor 99 or less and the second factor 5 or less.

Ways to Show Multiplication

How can you show multiplication in different ways?

Heather has 3 vases. She puts 5 flowers in each vase. How many flowers are in the 3 vases?

Example

Each model shows that 3×5 is the same as $5 + 5 + 5$.

Number Line	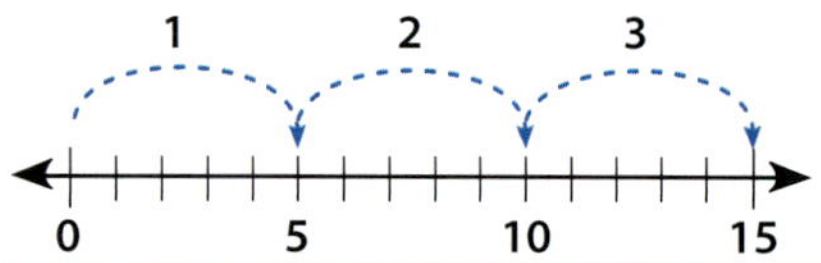	**3 jumps of 5**
Area Model	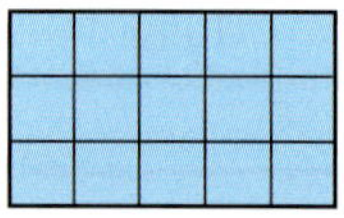	**3 rows with 5 squares in each row**
Set Model		**3 groups of 5**

There are 15 flowers in Heather's 3 vases.

Guided Practice

Do you know HOW?

1. Tina's area model has 6 rows with 7 squares in each row. How many squares are in Tina's model?

2. Five rafts were floating down a river. There were 4 people in each raft. Draw a number line to find how many people were in the rafts in all.

Do you UNDERSTAND?

3. **Strategy Focus** Draw a number line to find the product of 3×8.

4. At a flower shop, Heather saw 4 vases, with 12 flowers in each vase. Write an addition sentence to show how many flowers were in all of the vases.

Independent Practice

For **5–8**, write a multiplication sentence for each model.

5.

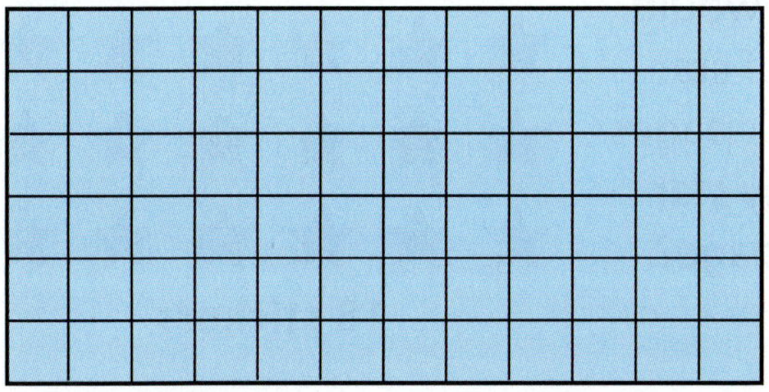

6.

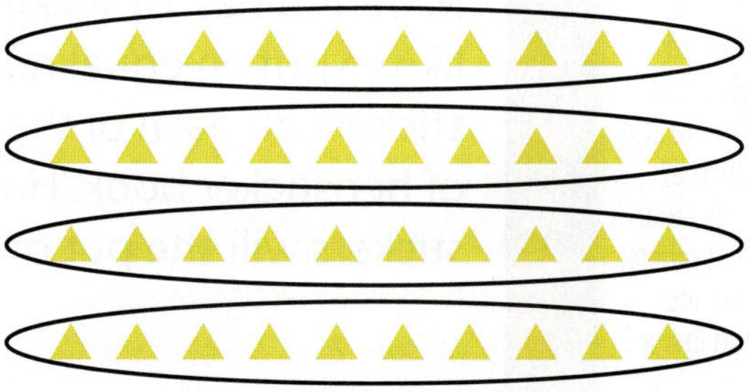

7.

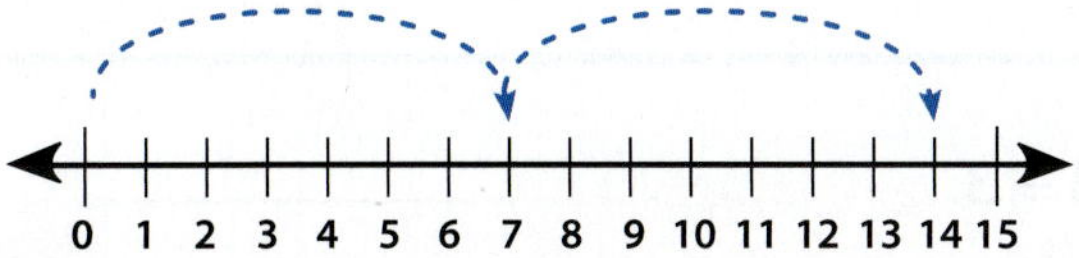

8.

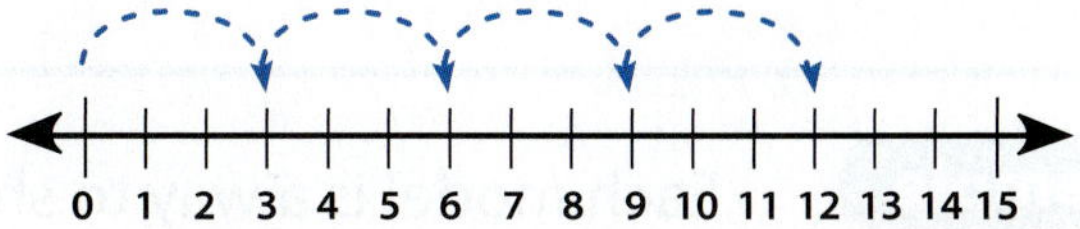

For **9–12**, write a repeated addition sentence to solve each problem.

9. 3×9 **10.** 2×12 **11.** 4×8 **12.** 5×11

Problem Solving

Use the table at the right for **13–15**.

13. How many books are there in 10 students' desks?

14. How many pencils are there in 7 students' desks?

15. **Write a Problem** Write a multiplication story problem about the items in students' desks. Solve.

Data: Items in Each Student's Desk

Item	Number
Crayons	12
Books	4
Pencils	5
Erasers	2

16. Daniel had the set of bills and coins below in his pocket. Write the total value in dollars and cents.

17. A fruit stand had 45 apples, 84 bananas, and 12 pineapples. How many apples, bananas, and pineapples did the fruit stand have in all?

A 129 **C** 141

B 139 **D** 146

Virginia

Lesson VA-6

3.6 The student will represent multiplication and division, using area, set, and number line models, and create and solve problems that involve multiplication of two whole numbers, one factor 99 or less and the second factor 5 or less.

Ways to Show Division

How can you show division in different ways?

Meredith has 18 stickers. She would like to put an equal number of star stickers on each of the 3 blank pages of her sticker book. How many star stickers will she put on each page?

18 stickers

Example Each model is a way to show 18 ÷ 3.

Number Line	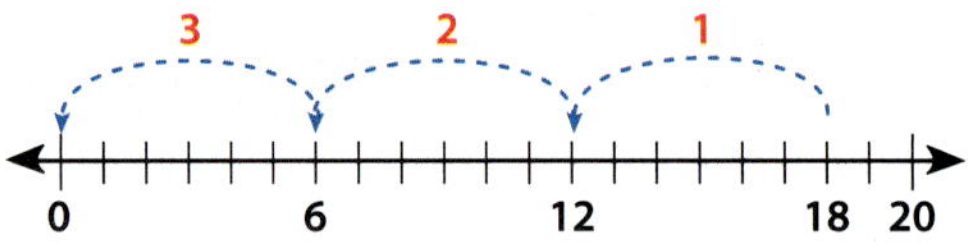	**3 jumps of equal length from 18 to 0**
Area Model	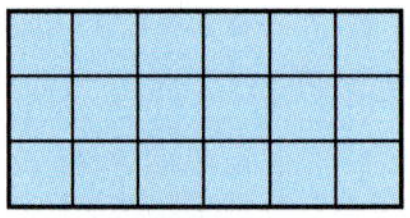	**18 squares arranged in 3 equal rows**
Set Model	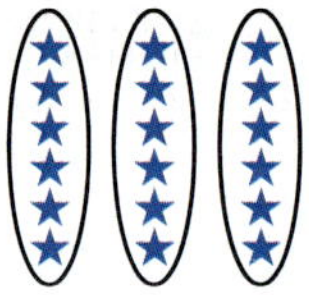	**18 divided into 3 equal groups**

Meredith will put 6 star stickers on each page.

Guided Practice

Do you know HOW?

1. Draw a number line to find 9 ÷ 3.

2. Use the set model to find 44 ÷ 11.

Do you UNDERSTAND?

3. **Draw a Picture** Draw a picture of a set model to show 30 ÷ 5.

4. Meredith buys 48 more stickers. She wants to put an equal number of these on each of 12 pages. How many stickers will she put on each page?

Independent Practice

For **5–8**, write a division sentence for each model.

5. 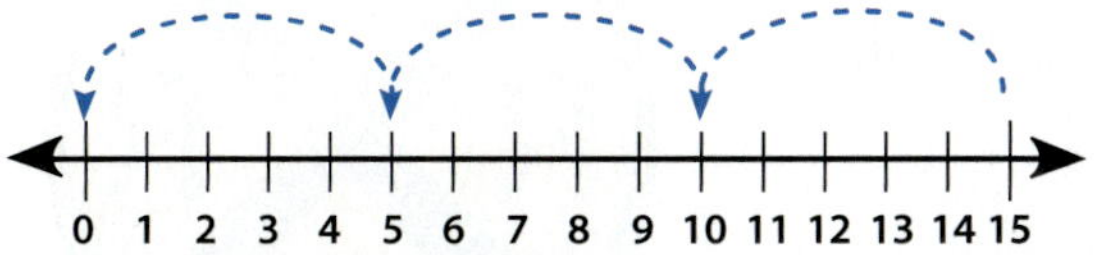

6. 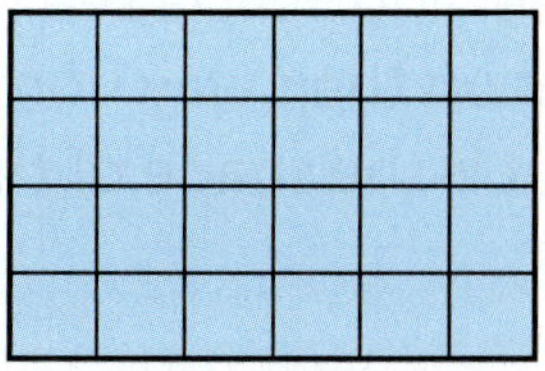

7. 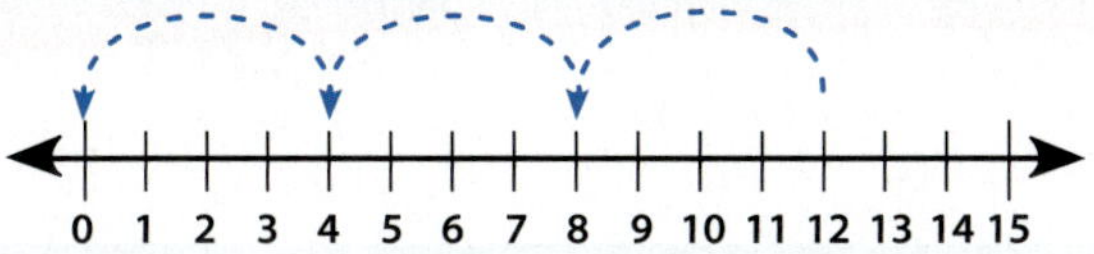

8. 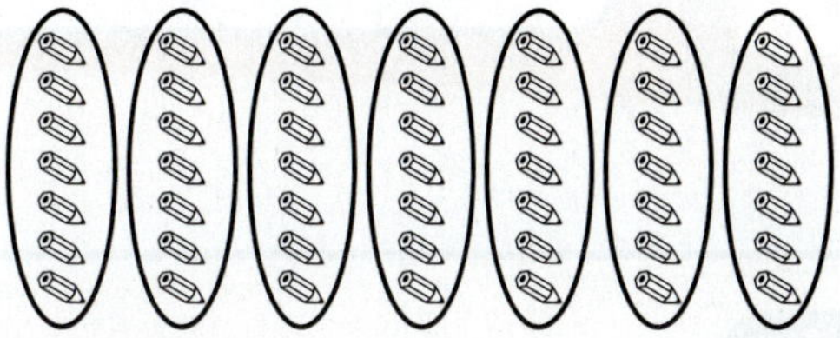

For **9** and **10**, draw a model to show the division sentence.

9. 32 ÷ 4 = 8

10. 10 ÷ 2 = 5

Problem Solving

Solve.

11. There were 2,548 people at a baseball game. To the nearest hundred, about how many people were at the baseball game?

12. Terrance put 90 crayons into 9 equal groups. What division sentence did he model?

13. **Strategy Focus** Show how to use a number line to solve 24 ÷ 8.

14. **Writing to Explain** Explain how to use an area model to show 45 ÷ 9.

15. Stella has a marble collection. She has 132 solid marbles and 368 striped marbles. How many solid and striped marbles does Stella have in all?

16. Deangelo bought an apple for $0.85, a turkey sandwich for $3.35, and a carton of milk for $0.55. He paid with a $5 bill. How much change should Deangelo receive?

17. Fred has 14 pennies and 2 pockets. He put an equal number of the pennies into each pocket. How many pennies did he put into each pocket? Use the number line below to solve.

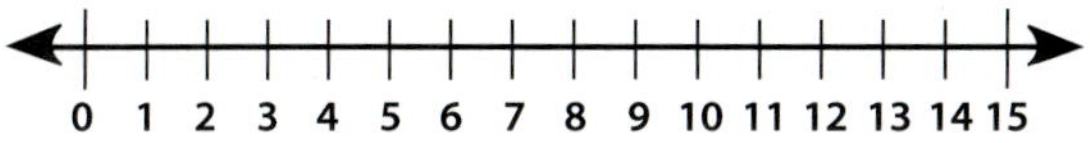

18. Clara bought 6 boxes of strawberries at the market. Each box had 12 strawberries in it. How many strawberries did Clara buy in all?

A 72 **C** 18

B 62 **D** 2

Virginia

Lesson VA-7

3.14 The student will identify, describe, compare, and contrast characteristics of plane and solid geometric figures (circle, square, rectangle, triangle, cube, rectangular prism, square pyramid, sphere, cone, and cylinder) by identifying relevant characteristics, including the number of angles, vertices, and edges, and the number and shape of faces, using concrete models.

Circles

How can you describe a circle?

Rafael and Felicia see the sign at the right on their way home from school. What is the shape of the sign?

Example

A circle is a closed shape made up of points that are all the same distance from the center.

A circle is not made up of line segments, and it does not have vertices. It is not a polygon.

The shape of the sign is a circle.

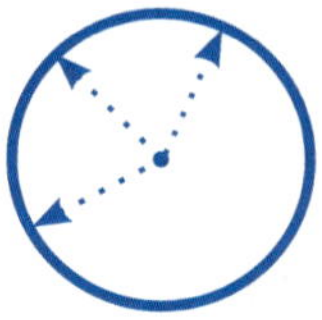
Circle

Not a circle
Some straight sides
Not closed

Guided Practice

Do you know HOW?

Is each figure a circle? If not, explain why.

1. 

2. 

3. 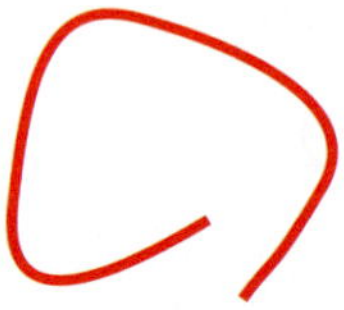

Do you UNDERSTAND?

4. Draw a polygon, a circle, and a shape that is neither a polygon nor a circle.

5. Which letter in the words below could be a circle?

RICHMOND, VIRGINIA

6. Rafael says the shape of the sign above is a polygon. Felicia says it is not a polygon. Which student is correct? Explain.

Independent Practice

Is each figure a circle? If not, explain why.

7. 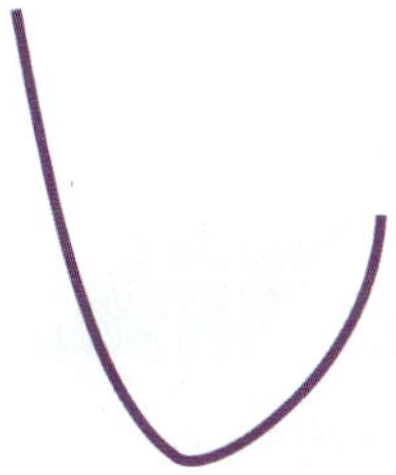

8. 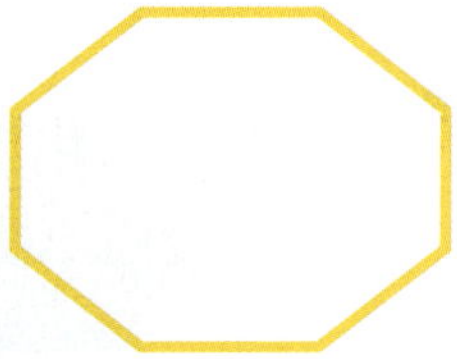

9. 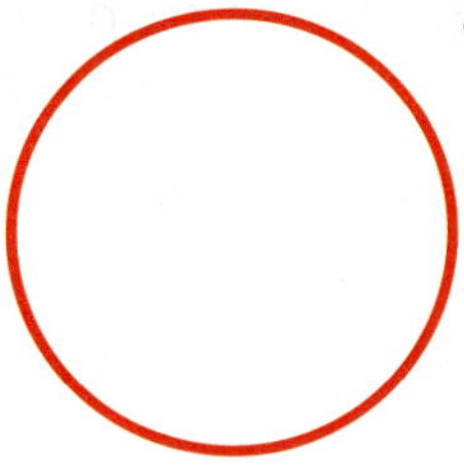

10. 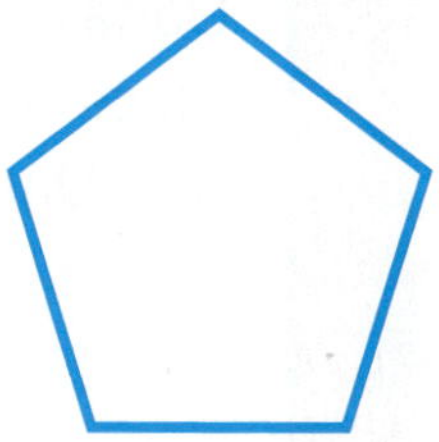

11. 

12. 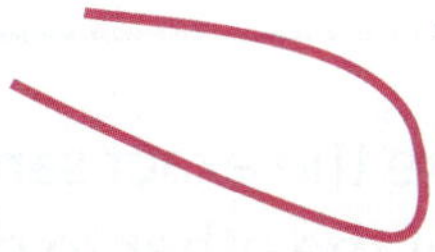

13. 

14. 

Problem Solving

15. Emma said that the two figures below are circles. Is she correct? Explain.

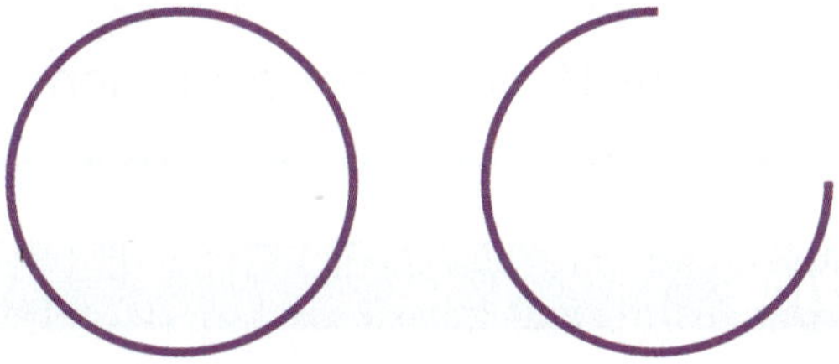

16. What multiplication sentence is shown by the model below?

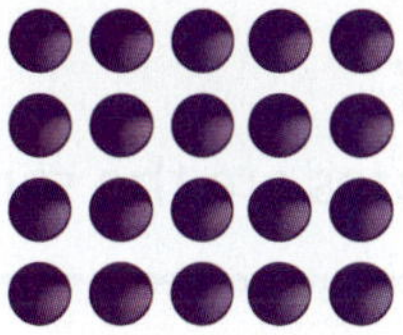

17. Draw a picture of an everyday object that is a circle.

18. Why do car tires need to have the shape of a circle?

19. Jackie created the table below to show the regular price and the sale price of clothes at a store. What is a rule for the table?

Regular Price	$23	$29	$34	$39	$52
Sale Price	$17	$23	$28	$33	$46

20. A teacher brought 10 packs of juice drinks on a class trip. Each pack held 6 juice drinks. If there were 52 students, and each student had 1 juice drink, how many juice drinks were left over?

A 4

B 8

C 16

D 60

Virginia

Lesson VA-8

3.16 The student will identify and describe congruent and noncongruent plane figures.

Congruent or Not?

How can you tell if two plane figures are congruent?

Dana cut two figures from a piece of fabric. Are the two figures that Dana cut congruent?

Dana's Figures

Example Two figures are congruent if they are the exact same shape and size. Trace one figure and place the tracing on top of the other to decide if they are congruent.

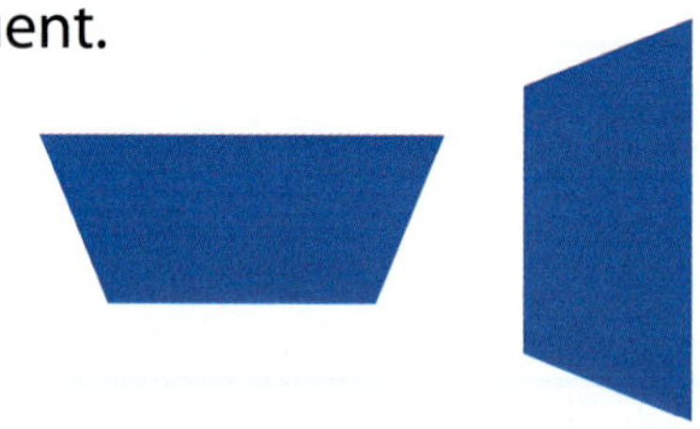

These trapezoids are congruent. Place the tracing of one on top of the other. They are the same shape and size.

These figures are **NOT** congruent. Place the tracing of one on top of the other. They are two different shapes.

Dana's figures are the same shape but not the same size. They are not congruent.

Guided Practice

Do you know HOW?

Are the figures congruent? Write *yes* or *no*.

1.

2. 

3. 

Do you UNDERSTAND?

4. Describe how you could draw two congruent triangles.

5. Draw two congruent figures, and two figures that are not congruent.

6. Dana wants to cut two more congruent figures from the piece of fabric. How can Dana make sure that the figures she cuts out are congruent?

Independent Practice

Are the figures congruent? Write *yes* or *no*. You may trace to decide.

7. 

8. 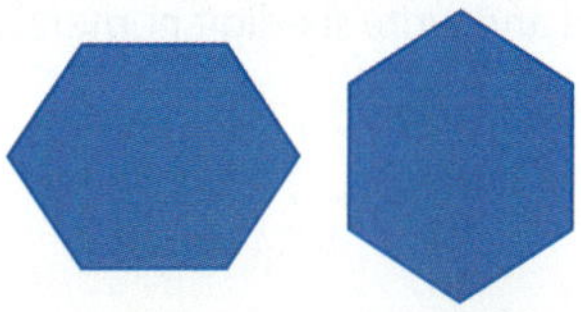

9. 

10.

11. 

12. 

13.

14. 

Problem Solving

Solve.

15. Writing to Explain James drew the triangles at the right. He says that the triangles he drew are congruent. Is James correct? Explain.

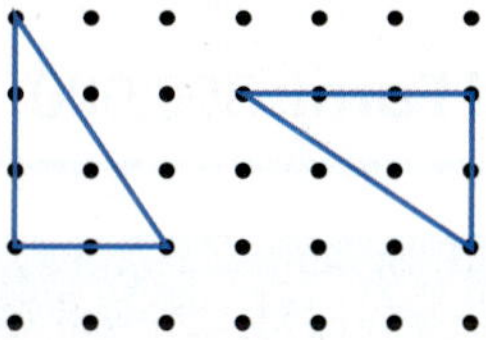

16. Mr. Greene brought 21 granola bars to work. If he eats 3 granola bars each week, in how many weeks will Mr. Greene finish his granola bars?

17. Miguel's rectangle is 6 inches long and 4 inches wide. Serena draws a congruent rectangle. What is the length and width of Serena's rectangle?

18. Reasoning Taryn traced a hexagon pattern block at the top of a sheet of paper. Then she moved the hexagon block and traced it again at the bottom of the paper. Are the shapes Taryn drew congruent? Explain.

19. Algebra Find the missing factor.

$\square \times (5 \times 2) = (3 \times 5) \times 2$

A 15

B 10

C 5

D 3

3.1.a The student will read and write six-digit numerals and identify the place value and value of each digit.

Place Value (See Lesson 1-3 for help.)

The value of any digit in a number depends upon its place in the number.

Example:

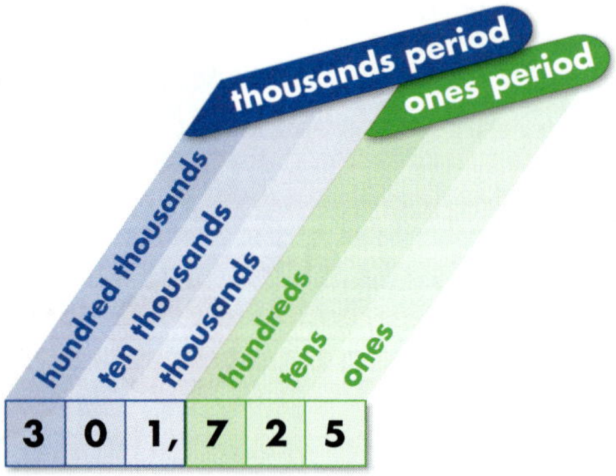

Standard Form: 301,725

Word Form: Three hundred one thousand, seven hundred twenty-five

Expanded Form: 300,000 + 1,000 + 700 + 20 + 5

Practice

For **1–4**, write each number in expanded form.

1. 820,346 **2.** 749,266 **3.** 661,420 **4.** 618,505

For **5–8**, write each number in word form.

5. 204,372 **6.** 152,693 **7.** 199,854 **8.** 703,121

For **9–12**, write each number in standard form.

9. Three hundred ninety-two thousand, six hundred ten

10. Two hundred six thousand, five hundred thirty-two

11. 500,000 + 60,000 + 4,000 + 700 + 20 + 5

12. 100,000 + 20,000 + 500 + 10 + 2

3.1.c The student will compare two whole numbers between 0 and 9,999, using symbols ($>$, $<$, or $=$) and words (*greater than*, *less than*, or *equal to*).

Comparing Whole Numbers (See Lesson 1-5 for help.)

When comparing numbers, always start with the digit in the greatest place value.

Example:

Compare 6,357 and 6,259.

thousands	hundreds	tens	ones
6,	3	5	7
6,	2	5	9
↑ same	↑ different		

$300 > 200$

So 6,357 ***is greater than*** 6,259.

$6,357 > 6,259$

Practice

For **1–9**, compare. Then write $>$, $<$, or $=$ for each ◯.

1. 2,716 ◯ 1,672 **2.** 8,019 ◯ 8,099 **3.** 2,500 ◯ 2,015

4. 5,233 ◯ 5,233 **5.** 2,908 ◯ 2,091 **6.** 4,619 ◯ 4,911

7. 8,125 ◯ 7,519 **8.** 7,082 ◯ 7,802 **9.** 6,017 ◯ 6,017

For **10–15**, compare. Then write *is greater than*, *is less than*, or *is equal to*.

10. 5,940 ________________ 5,490 **11.** 1,625 ________________ 6,125

12. 6,217 ________________ 6,217 **13.** 2,015 ________________ 2,001

14. 1,382 ________________ 2,381 **15.** 7,284 ________________ 7,824

VA SOL Practice

3.8 The student will determine, by counting, the value of a collection of bills and coins whose total value is $5.00 or less, compare the value of the bills and coins, and make change.

Counting Money (See Lesson 1-7 for help.)

You can find the value of a set of bills and coins by counting on.

Example:

Find the total value.
First, group the coins from greatest to least value.

Then, count on to find the total value.

$1.00 ⟶ $1.25 → $1.50 → $1.60 → $1.65

Practice

Write the total value in dollars and cents.

1. 

2. 

3. 

4. 

5. 2 quarters and 7 dimes

6. 2 nickels and 5 quarters

7. 1 one-dollar bill, 3 quarters, 3 half dollars, and 3 pennies

8. 4 one-dollar bills, 5 nickels, 1 penny, 1 quarter, and 4 dimes

3.20.a The student will investigate the identity and the commutative properties for addition and multiplication.

Properties of Addition (See Lesson 2-1 for help.)

The Commutative Property of Addition and the Identity Property of Addition can help you find a sum.

Examples:

If 3 + 8 = 11, what is the sum of 8 + 3?

Use the **Commutative Property**: You can add numbers in any order and the sum will be the same.
8 + 3 = 3 + 8

So, 8 + 3 = 11.

What is the sum of 7 + 0?

Use the **Identity Property**: The sum of any number and 0 is that same number.

So, 7 + 0 = 7.

Practice

For **1–12**, find each missing number.

1. 4 + 6 = 6 + ▢

2. 3 + 0 = ▢

3. ▢ + 8 = 8

4. ▢ + 9 = 9 + 8

5. 7 + 5 = ▢ + 7

6. ▢ = 20 + 0

7. 8 + 5 = ▢ + 8

8. ▢ + 43 = 43

9. 7 + ▢ = 6 + 7

10. 3 + 12 = ▢ + 3

11. ▢ + 7 = 7 + 9

12. 0 + ▢ = 17

13. Sam put the same number of marbles into two boxes. He put 23 red marbles and 26 blue marbles into one box. He put 26 red marbles and some blue marbles into the other box. How many blue marbles did Sam put in the second box?

For **14**, use the picture at the right.

14. Write an addition sentence that shows how many shells Gia has in each box and how many shells in all.

Gia's Shells

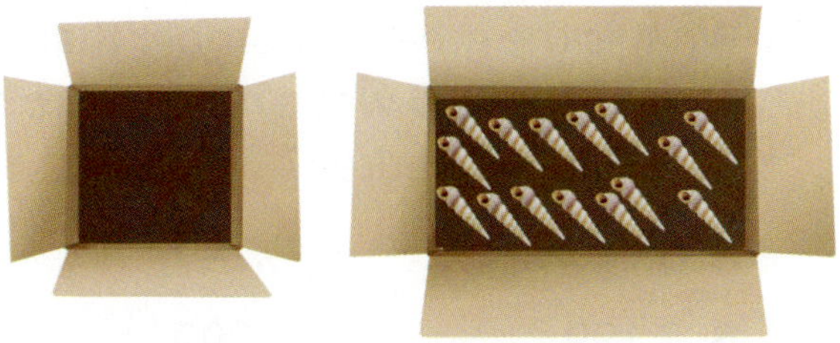

3.1.b The student will round whole numbers, 9,999 or less, to the nearest ten, hundred, and thousand.

Rounding Whole Numbers (See Lesson 2-4 for help.)

When you round, you replace an exact number with a number that tells about how many.

Examples:

Round 8,745 to the nearest thousand.

thousands place

8,745 ↓ 9,000

Since 7 > 5, add 1 to the rounding digit.

Round 8,745 to the nearest hundred.

hundreds place

8,745 ↓ 8,700

Since 4 < 5, do not change the rounding digit.

Round 8,745 to the nearest ten.

tens place

8,745 ↓ 8,750

Since the digit in the ones place is 5, add 1 to the rounding digit.

Practice

For **1–15**, round each number to the place of the underlined digit.

1. 6,$\underline{1}$32 **2.** 1,8$\underline{8}$5 **3.** $\underline{3}$,004 **4.** 7,5$\underline{5}$2 **5.** 8,$\underline{7}$67

6. 2,$\underline{4}$10 **7.** $\underline{6}$,636 **8.** 2,8$\underline{6}$5 **9.** 3,$\underline{7}$24 **10.** 7,3$\underline{6}$3

11. $\underline{4}$,253 **12.** 1,6$\underline{2}$3 **13.** $\underline{9}$,256 **14.** 3,$\underline{8}$36 **15.** $\underline{2}$,598

16. The Appalachian Trail is about 2,178 miles long. What is the length of the trail rounded to the nearest hundred miles?

17. Mount Rogers has a height of 5,729 feet above sea level. What is its height rounded to the nearest thousand feet?

18. What is the greatest number that rounds to 3,200 when rounded to the nearest hundred?

A 3,099 **C** 3,249

B 3,199 **D** 3,299

19. What is the least number that rounds to 7,000 when rounded to the nearest thousand?

A 6,000 **C** 6,599

B 6,500 **D** 6,999

3.4 The student will estimate solutions to and solve single-step and multistep problems involving the sum or difference of two whole numbers, each 9,999 or less, with or without regrouping.

Solving Problems Using Addition and Subtraction

(See Lesson 4-4 for help.)

When solving a problem, read all parts of the problem carefully.

Example: In a recent trip, John's mother flew a total of 5,273 miles. Her first flight was from Norfolk, VA to Minneapolis, MN, a distance of 1,296 miles. Her second flight was from Minneapolis, MN, to Phoenix, AZ, a distance of 1,643 miles. Then she flew from Phoenix, AZ back to Norfolk, VA. How many miles was her third flight?

Add to find the miles flown on the first two flights: 1,296 + 1,643 = 2,939 miles

Subtract to find the miles flown on the third flight: 5,273 − 2,939 = 2,334 miles

John's mother flew 2,334 miles on her flight from Phoenix, AZ to Norfolk, VA.

Practice

Solve.

1. The principal of Scott School bought 375 boxes of red paper, 300 boxes of green paper, 425 boxes of blue paper, 260 boxes of yellow paper. How many boxes of colored paper did the principal buy?

2. The Feathered Friends pet store sold 1,835 birds last year. Of the birds sold, 258 were cockatiels, 512 were parakeets, and the rest were finches. How many finches did the pet store sell?

3. Nora's mother bought her a coat for $74 and a pair of shoes for $35. She paid with $120. How much change did Nora's mother get back?

4. Jim took 164 pictures. He took 86 of the pictures at the park and the rest at the zoo. How many pictures did he take at the zoo?

5. The Snack Shop sold 265 egg salad sandwiches, 483 ham sandwiches, and 82 tuna salad sandwiches. How many sandwiches did they sell in all?

A 747 **C** 830

B 828 **D** 930

6. Ray and Lynn played a video game. Lynn scored 2,673 points. Ray scored 523 fewer points than Lynn. How many points did they score in all?

A 4,823 **C** 3,196

B 4,723 **D** 2,150

3.20.b The student will identify examples of the identity and commutative properties for addition and multiplication.

Properties of Multiplication (See Lesson 5-9 for help.)

You can use the Commutative Property of Multiplication or the Identity Property of Multiplication to help find products.

Examples:

If $5 \times 3 = 15$, what is the product of 3×5?

Use the **Commutative Property**: You can multiply numbers in any order and the product will be the same.

$5 \times 3 = 3 \times 5$

So, $3 \times 5 = 15$.

What is the product of 9×1?

Use the **Identity Property** of Multiplication: The product of any number times 1 is that same number.

So, $9 \times 1 = 9$.

Practice

For **1–6**, tell whether each multiplication sentence shows the Commutative Property or Identity Property of Multiplication.

1. $8 = 8 \times 1$

2. $7 \times 5 = 5 \times 7$

3. $2 \times 9 = 9 \times 2$

4. $6 \times 14 = 14 \times 6$

5. $23 \times 1 = 23$

6. $14 = 1 \times 14$

For **7–12**, find each missing number.

7. $\square = 1 \times 10$

8. $8 \times 9 = \square \times 8$

9. $\square = 1 \times 6$

10. $3 \times \square = 8 \times 3$

11. $\square \times 7 = 7 \times 9$

12. $8 \times 5 = 5 \times \square$

13. Lena set up 7 rows with 8 chairs in each. Then she set up 8 rows with 7 chairs in each. Write two multiplication sentences to show how Lena set up the chairs. Which property did you use?

14. William set up 1 row of 6 chairs for the school violin recital. Write a multiplication sentence to show how many chairs William set up in all. Which property of multiplication did you use?

3.6 The student will represent multiplication and division, using area, set, and number line models, and create and solve problems that involve multiplication of two whole numbers, one factor 99 or less and the second factor 5 or less.

Representing Multiplication and Division

(See Lesson 7-4 for help.)

You can show multiplication and division by drawing a diagram or by using a number line.

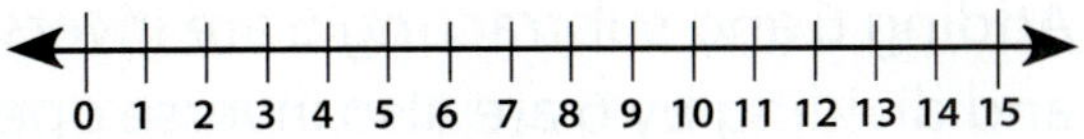

Examples:

What is 3 × 2?

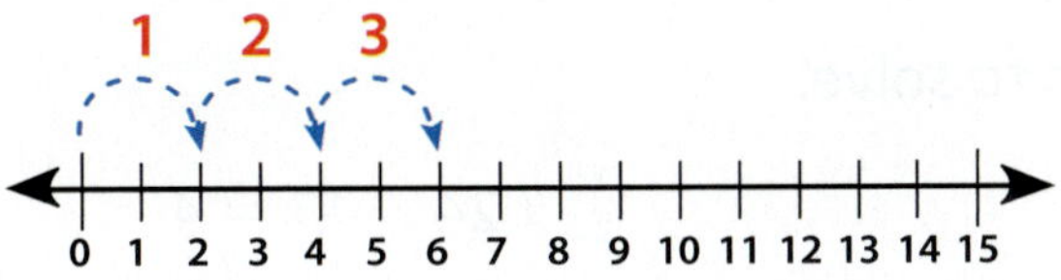

$3 \times 2 = 6$

What is 14 ÷ 2?

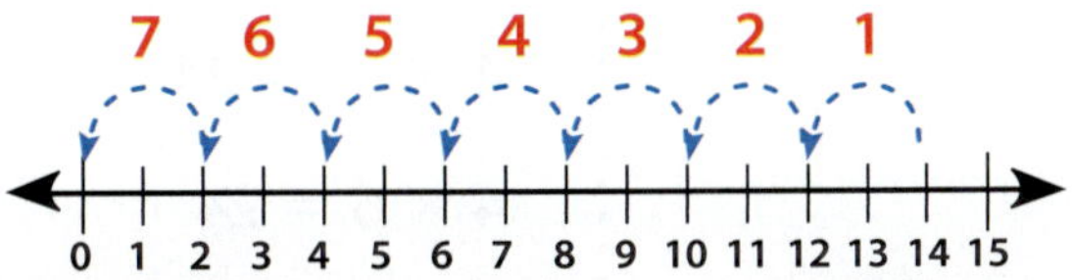

$14 \div 2 = 7$

Practice

For **1–4**, write the multiplication or division sentence that the model shows.

1.

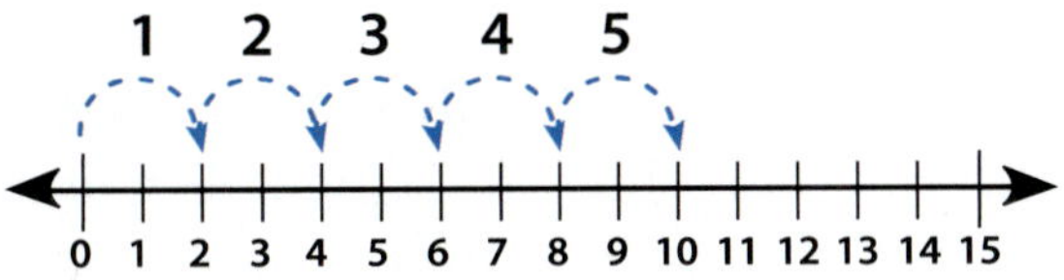

2.

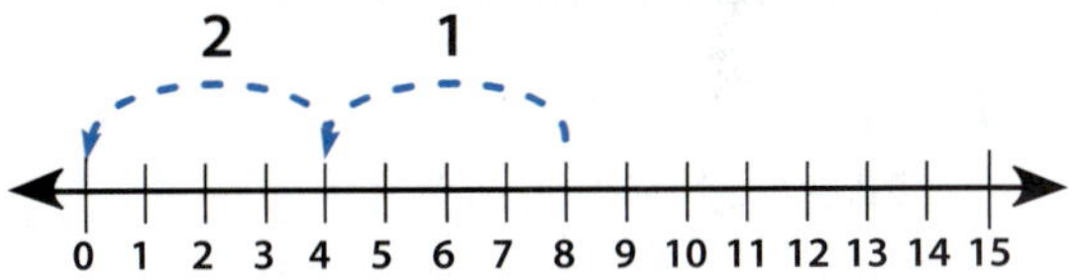

3.

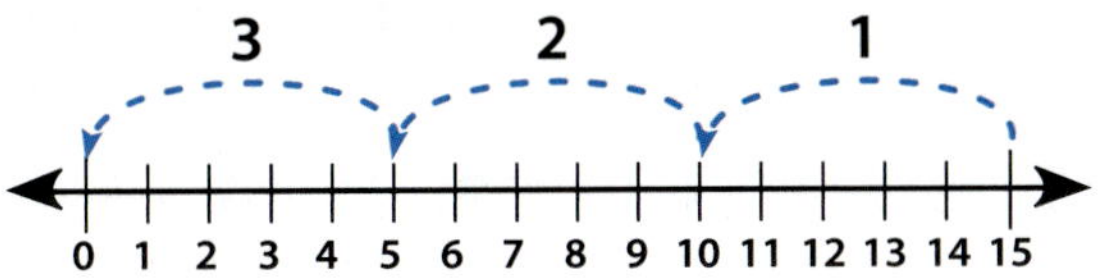

4.

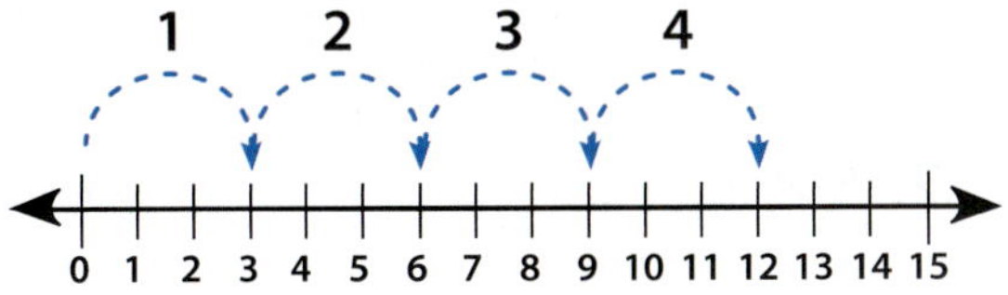

5. Eliza takes a 10 minute walk each day. If she walked 5 days this week, how many minutes did she walk in all?

6. Sam made 32 water balloons. He and 3 of his friends shared the balloons equally. How many water balloons did they each get?

7. Shea has 2 boxes on her desk. She has 11 pencils in each box. How many pencils does Shea have in all?

8. Bart uses 54 stickers to fill a sticker book. He puts 6 stickers on each page. How many pages does the sticker book have?

3.2 The student will recognize and use the inverse relationships between addition/subtraction and multiplication/division to complete basic fact sentences. The student will use these relationships to solve problems.

Inverse Relationships (See Lesson 8-1 for help.)

Adding 6 and subtracting 6 are inverse operations. Multiplying by 6 and dividing by 6 are also inverse operations.

Examples:

Use the inverse operation to solve.

$18 - \square = 12$

The inverse of subtraction is addition.

$12 + \square = 18$

$12 + 6 = 18$

So, $18 - 6 = 12$.

$24 \div \square = 4$

The inverse of division is multiplication.

$4 \times \square = 24$

$4 \times 6 = 24$

So, $24 \div 6 = 4$.

Practice

For **1–9**, copy and complete.

1. $12 \times \square = 24$
$24 \div 12 = \square$

2. $3 \times \square = 24$
$24 \div 3 = \square$

3. $4 \times \square = 24$
$24 \div 4 = \square$

4. $3 + \square = 12$
$12 - \square = 3$

5. $\square + 7 = 15$
$15 - 7 = \square$

6. $10 + \square = 14$
$14 - \square = 10$

7. $5 \times \square = 30$
$30 \div \square = 5$

8. $4 \times \square = 28$
$28 \div 4 = \square$

9. $\square \times 6 = 36$
$36 \div 6 = \square$

For **10–21**, simplify.

10. $30 - 15$

11. $48 - 36$

12. $25 - 17$

13. $56 \div 8$

14. $63 \div 7$

15. $27 \div 9$

16. $45 \div 5$

17. $81 \div 9$

18. $42 \div 6$

19. $28 \div 7$

20. $64 \div 8$

21. $49 \div 7$

3.5 The student will recall multiplication facts through the twelves table, and the corresponding division facts.

Related Multiplication and Division Facts

(See Lesson 8-4 for help.)

Since multiplication and division have an inverse relationship, you can use a related multiplication sentence to help solve a division problem.

Examples:

Find $72 \div 6$. Use related facts to help you.

$6 \times 12 = 72$ $\quad$ $12 \times 6 = 72$

$72 \div 12 = 6$ $\quad$ $72 \div 6 = 12$

Find $121 \div 11$.

$11 \times 11 = 121$ $\quad$ $121 \div 11 = 11$

Practice

For **1–3**, copy and complete the related facts.

1. $3 \times \square = 33$
$33 \div 3 = \square$

2. $4 \times \square = 48$
$48 \div \square = 4$

3. $9 \times \square = 108$
$108 \div 9 = \square$

For **4–15**, find each quotient.

4. $30 \div 6$

5. $48 \div 8$

6. $99 \div 9$

7. $44 \div 11$

8. $66 \div 6$

9. $108 \div 9$

10. $96 \div 12$

11. $60 \div 5$

12. $63 \div 9$

13. $22 \div 2$

14. $84 \div 12$

15. $56 \div 7$

16. The teacher wants to divide 24 students into 2 equal groups. How many students will be in each group?

17. Lea used 84 beads to make necklaces. She used 12 beads for each necklace. How many necklaces did Lea make?

VA SOL Practice

3.19 The student will recognize and describe a variety of patterns formed using numbers, tables, and pictures, and extend the patterns, using the same or different forms.

Patterns (See Lesson 9-4 for help.)

You can write a rule to describe and extend some patterns.

Example:

Look for a pattern in the table.

Number of Birds	3	5	2	4
Number of Wings	6	10	4	

A rule for the table is: **Multiply by 2.**

$3 \times 2 = 6 \qquad 5 \times 2 = 10 \qquad 2 \times 2 = 4$

The missing number is 8, because $4 \times 2 = 8$.

Practice

For **1** and **2**, write a rule for the table. Use your rule to find the missing numbers.

1.

Earned	\$3	\$6	\$10	\$7	\$2
Saved	\$2	\$5		\$6	

2.

Triangles	4	2	6	7	1
Sides	12	6			3

For **3–6**, write a rule. Then use your rule to find what comes next in the pattern.

3. 4, 8, 16, 32, 64,

4. 17, 23, 29, 35, 41,

5. 6, 11, 16, 21, 26,

6. 104, 95, 86, 77, 68,

For **7** and **8**, draw what comes next in the pattern.

7. 

8. 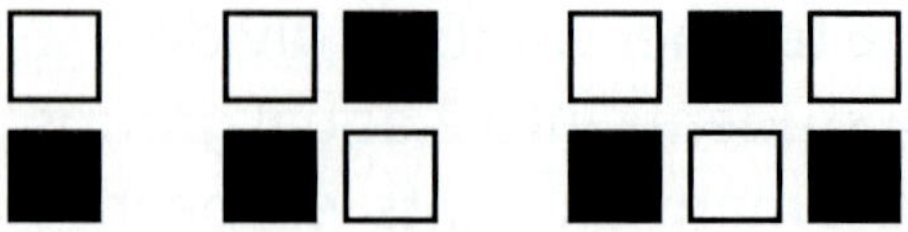

VA SOL Practice

3.14 The student will identify, describe, compare, and contrast characteristics of plane and solid geometric figures (circle, square, rectangle, triangle, cube, rectangular prism, square pyramid, sphere, cone, and cylinder) by identifying relevant characteristics, including the number of angles, vertices, and edges, and the number and shape of faces, using concrete models.

Solid Figures (See Lesson 10-2 for help.)

Solid figures have three dimensions: length, width, and height. Some solid figures have faces, edges, and vertices.

Example:

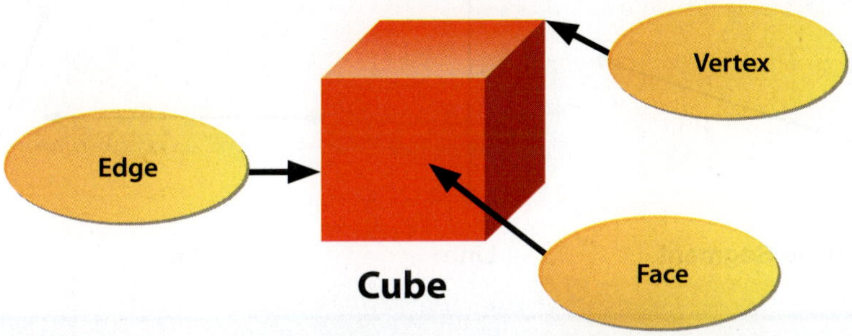

Practice

For **1–3**, identify the number of faces, edges, and vertices in each solid figure.

1. Cube

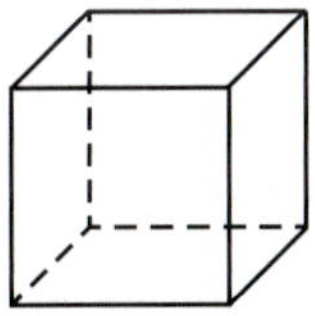

2. Rectangular Prism

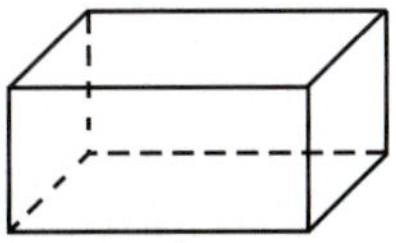

3. Square Pyramid

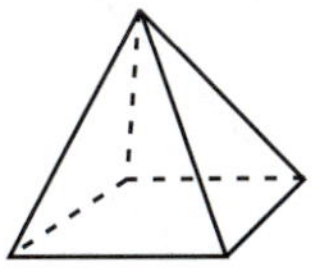

For **4–6**, name each solid figure.

4.

5.

6.

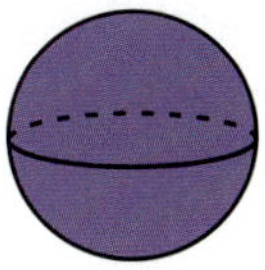

For **7** and **8**, name the solid figure that can be made.

7.

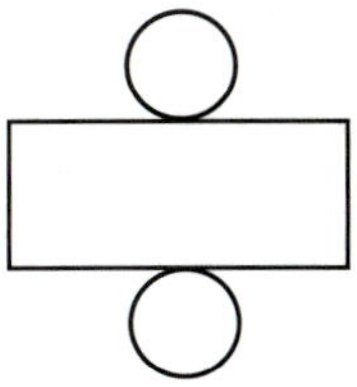

8.

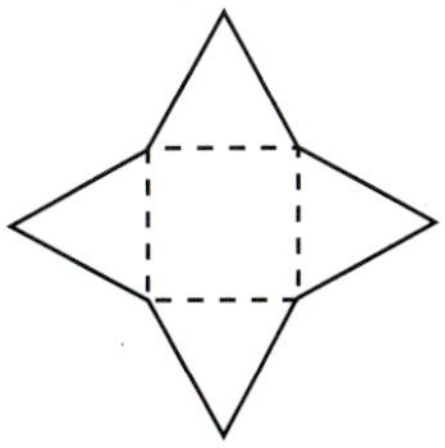

3.15 The student will identify and draw representations of points, line segments, rays, angles, and lines.

Points, Lines, and Angles (See Lesson 10-4 for help.)

You can identify lines and parts of lines.

Examples:

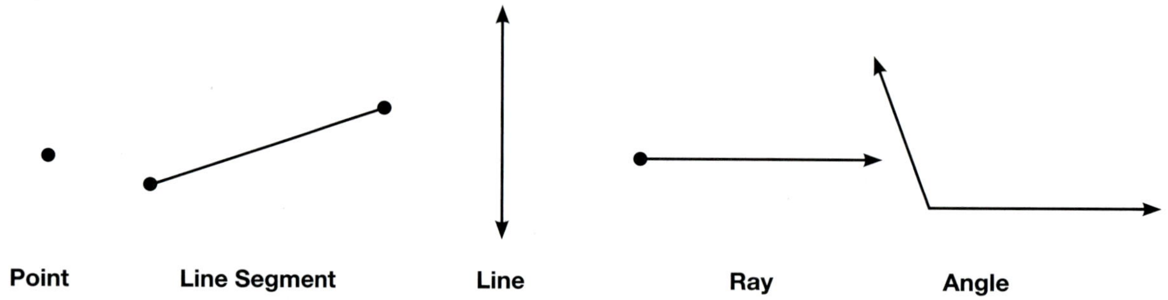

Practice

For **1–4**, write the name for each.

1. 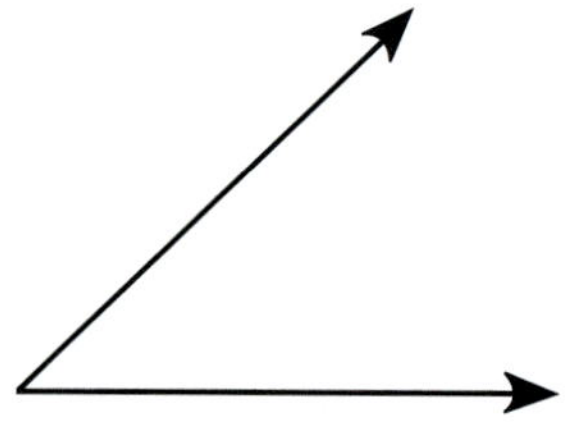

2. 

3. 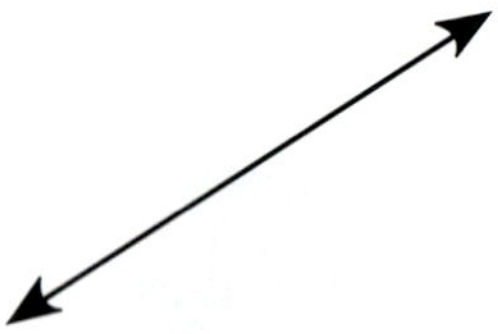

4. 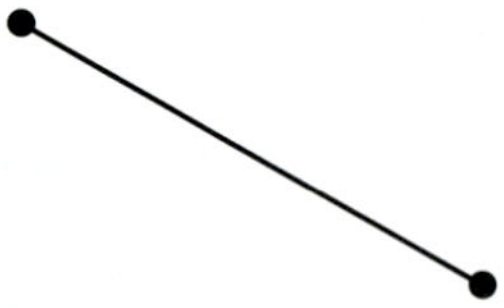

For **5–9**, draw an example of each.

5. Point

6. Angle

7. Ray

8. Line

9. Line Segment

3.14 The student will identify, describe, compare, and contrast characteristics of plane and solid geometric figures (circle, square, rectangle, triangle, cube, rectangular prism, square pyramid, sphere, cone, and cylinder) by identifying relevant characteristics, including the number of angles, vertices, and edges, and the number and shape of faces, using concrete models.

Plane Figures (See Lesson 10-7 for help.)

To describe a plane figure, you can identify its characteristics, such as the number of sides and angles.

Example:

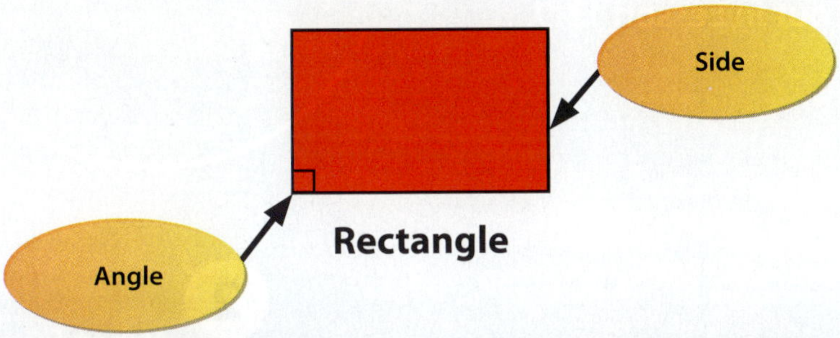

Practice

For **1–8**, use the plane figures below to solve.

1. Which plane figure has three sides and three angles?

2. Write *true* or *false*. A rectangle always has the same number of sides and angles.

3. How many sides and angles does a rectangle have?

4. How many sides and angles does a circle have?

5. Which two plane figures above have more than 3 sides?

6. Which plane figures above have 3 or fewer angles?

7. Trace the figures above, and label each figure with its name.

8. How are a rectangle and a square different?

Topic 12

Understanding Fractions

1 The tiger beetle and the caterpillar hunter beetle are helpful insects. Which type of beetle is longer? You will find out in Lesson 12-9.

2 What fraction of Earth's land surface is desert? You will find out in Lesson 12-5.

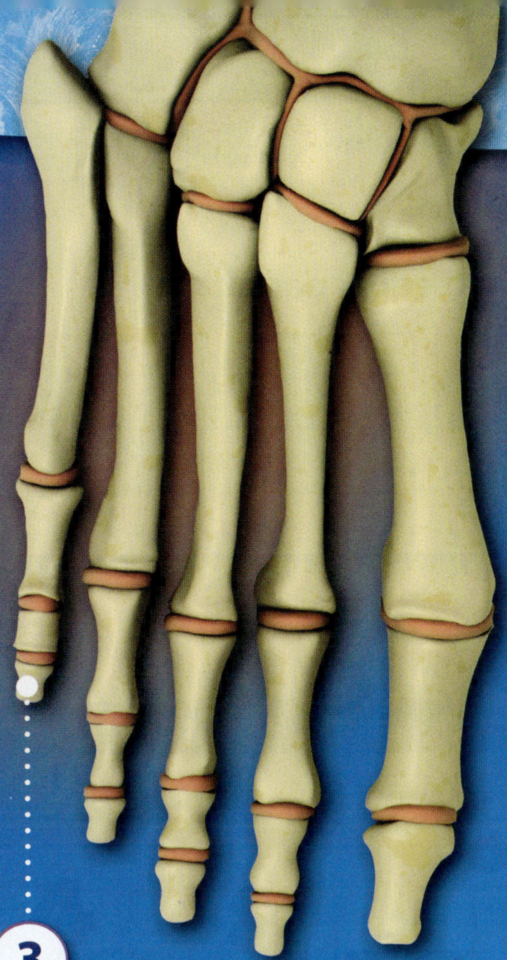

3 What fraction of the bones in your body are in your feet? You will find out in Lesson 12-4.

4 Is the flag of Nigeria made up of equal parts? You will find out in Lesson 12-1.

Review What You Know!

Vocabulary

Choose the best term from the box.

- compare
- greater
- less
- multiply

1. The number 219 is __?__ than the number 392.
2. The number 38 is __?__ than the number 19.
3. When you decide if 15 has more tens or fewer tens than 24, you __?__ the numbers.

Arrays

Find the product for each array.

4. 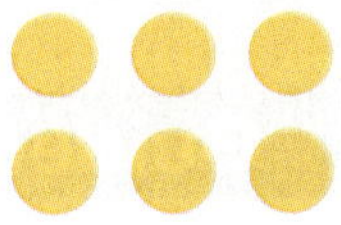

5. 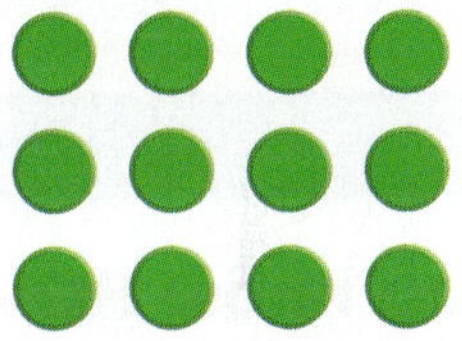

Compare Numbers

Compare. Write $>$, $<$, or $=$.

6. 427 ◯ 583	**7.** 910 ◯ 906
8. 139 ◯ 136	**9.** 4,500 ◯ 4,500
10. 693 ◯ 734	**11.** 1,050 ◯ 1,005

12. **Writing to Explain** Which number is greater, 595 or 565? Explain which digits you used to decide.

Virginia

Lesson 12-1

Reviews 2.3.a The student will identify the parts of a set and/or region that represent fractions for halves, thirds, fourths, sixths, eighths, and tenths.

Dividing Regions into Equal Parts

Hands-On
grid paper

How can you divide a whole into equal parts?

Show two ways to divide the grid paper into equal parts.

When a region is divided into two equal parts, the parts are called halves.

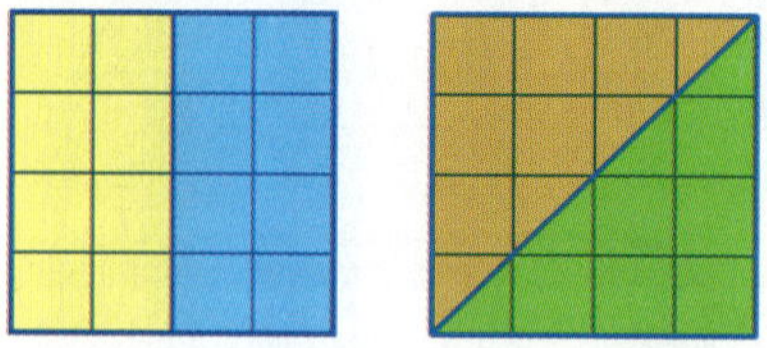

Other Examples

The parts do not need to be the same shape, but they must be equal in area.

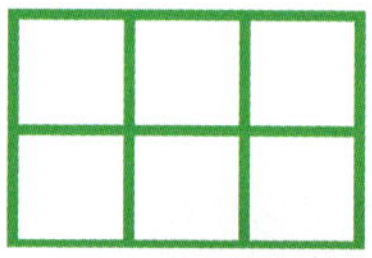

6 equal parts
sixths

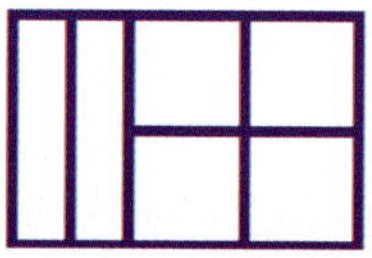

6 equal parts
sixths

10 equal parts
tenths

10 equal parts
tenths

Guided Practice*

Do you know HOW?

In **1–4**, tell if each shows equal or unequal parts. If the parts are equal, name them.

1. 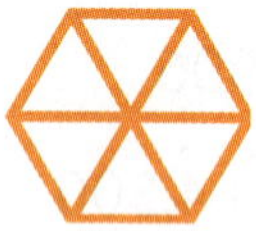

2. 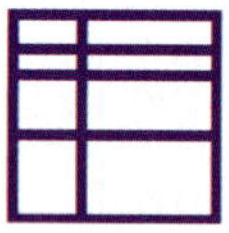

3. 

4. 

Do you UNDERSTAND?

5. In the examples on grid paper above, explain how you know the two parts are equal.

6. Use grid paper. Draw a picture to show sixths.

7. Amar divided his garden into equal areas, as shown below. What is the name of the equal parts of the whole?

DIGITAL
Animated Glossary, eTools
www.pearsonsuccessnet.com

*For another example, see Set A on page 302.

Here are some names of equal parts of a whole.

 2 equal parts **halves**	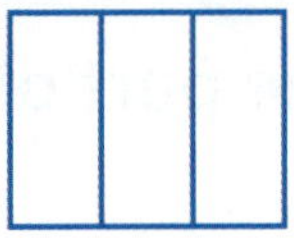 3 equal parts **thirds**	 4 equal parts **fourths**	 5 equal parts **fifths**
 6 equal parts **sixths**	 8 equal parts **eighths**	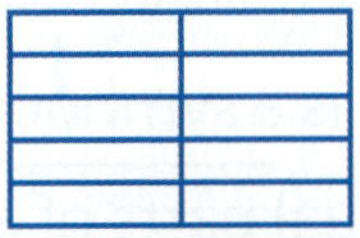 10 equal parts **tenths**	 12 equal parts **twelfths**

Independent Practice

In **8–11**, tell if each shows equal or unequal parts. If the parts are equal, name them.

8. 

9. 

10. 

11. 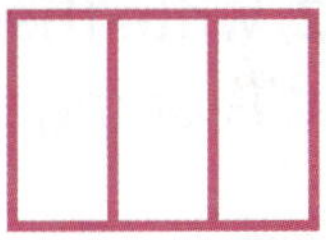

In **12–15**, use grid paper. Draw a region showing the equal parts named.

12. fourths **13.** halves **14.** tenths **15.** eighths

Problem Solving

In **16–18**, use the table of flags.

Flags of Different Nations

Nation	Flag
Mauritius	
Nigeria	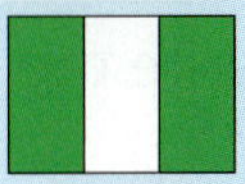
Poland	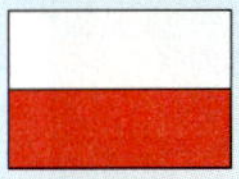
Seychelles	

16. Reasoning The flag of this nation has more than three parts. The parts are equal. Which nation is this?

17. The flag of Nigeria is made up of equal parts. What is the name of the parts of this flag?

18. Which flag does **NOT** have equal parts?

19. Which shape does **NOT** show equal parts?

A 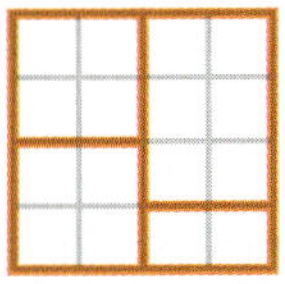

B 

C 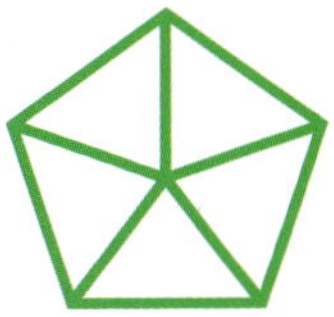

D 

Virginia

Lesson 12-2

3.3.a The student will name and write fractions (including mixed numbers) represented by a model. **(Also 3.3.b)**

Fractions and Regions

How can you show and name part of a region?

Mr. Kim made a pan of fruit bars. He served part of the pan of bars to friends. What part of the whole pan was served? What part was left?

A fraction is a symbol, such as $\frac{1}{2}$ or $\frac{2}{3}$, that names equal parts of a whole.

Guided Practice*

Do you know HOW?

In **1** and **2**, write the fraction of each figure that is orange.

1. 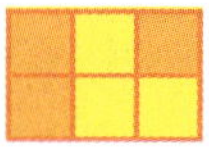

2. 

In **3** and **4**, draw a picture to show each fraction.

3. $\frac{3}{4}$

4. $\frac{4}{7}$

Do you UNDERSTAND?

5. In the example above, what fraction names all of the parts in the pan of bars?

6. Mrs. Gupta bought a pizza. The picture shows what part of it she ate. What fraction of the pizza did she eat? What fraction of the pizza was left?

Independent Practice

In **7–10**, write the fraction of each figure that is green.

7. 

8. 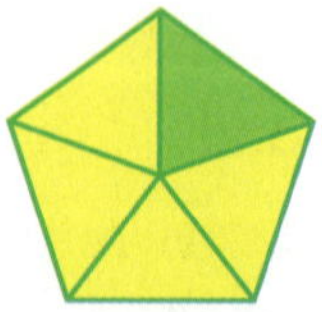

9. 

10. 

In **11–15**, draw a picture to show each fraction.

11. $\frac{1}{3}$ **12.** $\frac{2}{4}$ **13.** $\frac{1}{6}$ **14.** $\frac{7}{10}$ **15.** $\frac{2}{2}$

DIGITAL Animated Glossary **www.pearsonsuccessnet.com**

*For another example, see Set A on page 302.

What You Write

Numerator → $\frac{4}{9}$ ← 4 equal parts served
Denominator → ← 9 equal parts **in all**

Numerator → $\frac{5}{9}$ ← 5 equal parts left
Denominator → ← 9 equal parts **in all**

The numerator tells how many equal parts are described. It is the number above the fraction bar.

The denominator tells the total number of equal parts. It is the number below the bar.

What You Say

Four ninths of the pan of fruit bars was served.

Five ninths of the pan of fruit bars was left.

Problem Solving

For **16–19**, use the sign at the right.

Size of Pizza	Price
Small 	$7
Medium 	$9
Large 	$11

16. Ben and his friends ordered a medium pizza. Ben ate 1 slice of the pizza. What fraction of the pizza did Ben eat?

17. Aida's family bought a large pizza. The family ate 4 slices of the pizza. What fraction of the pizza was left?

18. Tami's family bought 3 small pizzas. Leo's family bought 2 medium pizzas. How much more did Tami's family spend than Leo's family?

19. Which costs more, 6 small pizzas or 4 large pizzas? How much more?

20. **Writing to Explain** A pan of cornbread is divided into 12 unequal parts. Alana serves 3 of the parts. Is it reasonable to say she has served $\frac{3}{12}$ of the cornbread? Explain.

21. Look at the grid at the right. What fraction of the grid is white?

SOL Prep

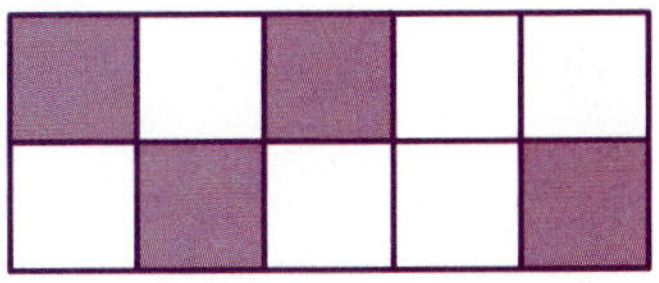

A $\frac{4}{6}$

B $\frac{6}{6}$

C $\frac{6}{10}$

D $\frac{2}{5}$

Virginia

Lesson 12-3

3.3.a. The student will name and write fractions (including mixed numbers) represented by a model. **(Also 3.3.b)**

Fractions and Sets

Hands-On counters

How can a fraction name part of a group?

A group of 12 people is in line for movie tickets. What fraction of the group of people are wearing red? What fraction of the people are not wearing red?

A fraction can name parts of a set, or group, of objects or people.

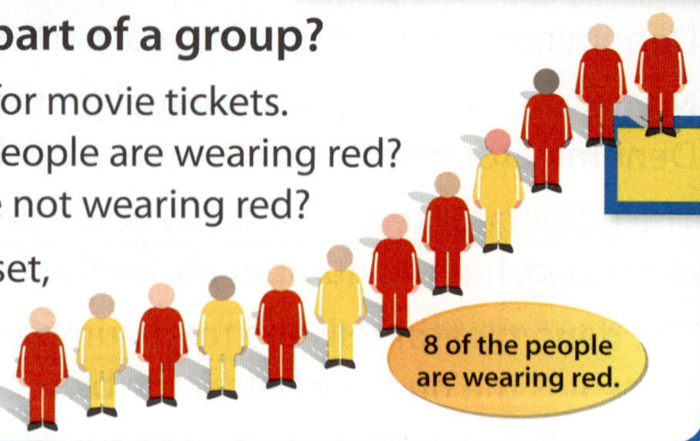

Guided Practice*

Do you know HOW?

In **1** and **2**, write the fraction of the counters that are red.

1. 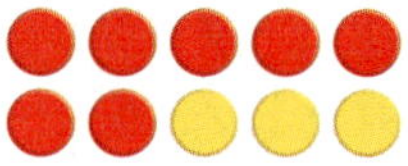

2. 

In **3** and **4**, draw counters to show the fraction given.

3. $\frac{4}{5}$

4. $\frac{3}{8}$

Do you UNDERSTAND?

5. In the example above, why is the denominator the same for the part of the group wearing red and for the part of the group not wearing red?

6. A group of 9 students is waiting for a bus. Six of them are wearing jackets. What fraction of the students in the group are wearing jackets? What fraction of the students are not wearing jackets?

Independent Practice

In **7–9**, write the fraction of the counters that are yellow.

7. 

8. 

9. 

In **10–12**, draw a picture of the set described.

10. 5 shapes, $\frac{3}{5}$ of the shapes are circles

11. 8 shapes, $\frac{5}{8}$ of the shapes are triangles

12. 2 shapes, $\frac{1}{2}$ of the shapes are squares

DIGITAL eTools **www.pearsonsuccessnet.com**

*For another example, see Set A on page 302.

What You Write

$\frac{8}{12}$ ← Number of people wearing red
← Total number of people

$\frac{4}{12}$ ← Number of people **not** wearing red
← Total number of people

What You Say

Eight twelfths of the people are wearing red.

Four twelfths of the people are not wearing red.

Problem Solving

For **13–15**, write the fraction of the group of buttons described.

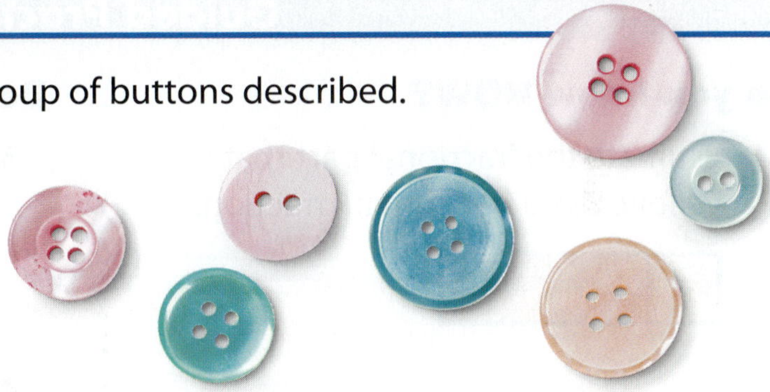

13. Pink buttons

14. Blue buttons

15. Buttons with only two holes

In **16** and **17**, draw a picture to show each fraction of a set.

16. Flowers: $\frac{3}{4}$ are yellow

17. Apples: $\frac{1}{2}$ are green

18. The picture below shows six statues of children. How many are statues of girls?

$\frac{3}{6}$ of the statues are statues of girls.

19. Number Sense A family of 5 is buying concert tickets. If $\frac{2}{5}$ of the tickets they buy are for adults, how many adult tickets does the family need?

20. What fraction of the flower petals have fallen off the flower?

SOL Prep

A $\frac{3}{5}$

B $\frac{2}{8}$

C $\frac{8}{10}$

D $\frac{2}{10}$

Virginia

Lesson 12-4

Extends 3.3.b The student will model fractions (including mixed numbers) and write the fractions' names.

Benchmark Fractions

How do you estimate parts?

Mr. Anderson is harvesting wheat on his farm. About what part of the wheat field does he still need to harvest?

Guided Practice*

Do you know HOW?

1. Estimate the fractional part that is yellow. Use a benchmark fraction.

2. What benchmark fraction should be written at point *P*?

Do you UNDERSTAND?

3. In the example above, what benchmark fraction can you use for the part of the wheat field that Mr. Anderson has harvested?

4. Geena is raking the leaves in her yard. About what part of the yard still needs to be raked?

Independent Practice

In **5–7**, estimate the fractional part that is green. Use a benchmark fraction.

5. 

6. 

7.

In **8–10**, what benchmark fraction is closest to each point? Choose from the benchmark fractions $\frac{1}{2}$, $\frac{1}{3}$, $\frac{2}{3}$, $\frac{1}{4}$, and $\frac{3}{4}$.

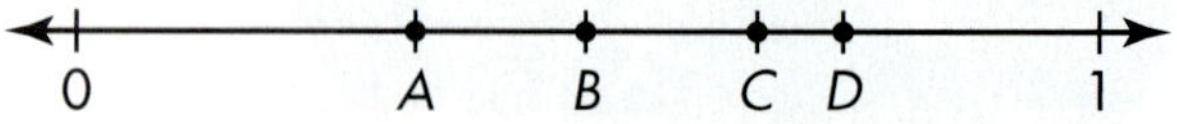

8. *A* **9.** *B* **10.** *C* **11.** *D*

DIGITAL Animated Glossary
www.pearsonsuccessnet.com

For another example, see Set B on page 302.

Step 1

You can use benchmark fractions to estimate fractional parts.

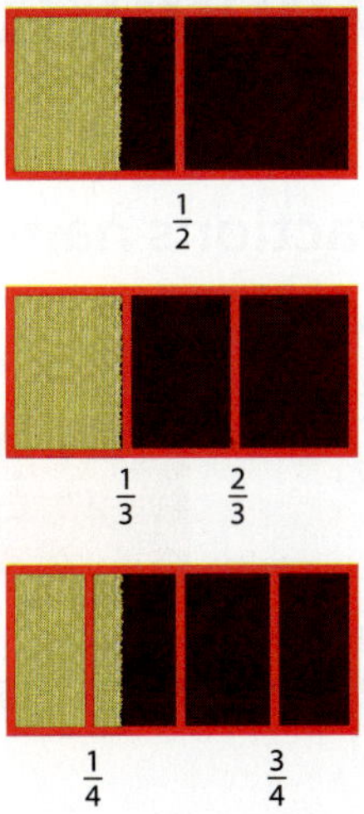

Benchmark fractions are commonly used fractions. Some benchmark fractions are $\frac{1}{4}$, $\frac{1}{3}$, $\frac{1}{2}$, $\frac{2}{3}$, and $\frac{3}{4}$.

Step 2

Find the benchmark fraction that is closest to the fraction in the problem.

The part of the field that still has wheat is closest to $\frac{1}{3}$.

Mr. Anderson still needs to harvest about $\frac{1}{3}$ of the wheat field.

Problem Solving

In **12–14**, estimate the part of each garden that has flowers.

12. Garden A

13. Garden B

14. Garden C

Use the table at the right for **15–17**.

15. In which months did the garden sell more tickets—May and June combined or July and August combined?

Data

Children's Garden Tickets Sold

Month	Tickets
May	583
June	947
July	815
August	726

16. **Estimation** About how many tickets in all were sold in the four months? Explain how you estimated.

17. Which shows the numbers in the table from least to greatest?

SOL Prep

A 583, 947, 815, 726

B 947, 815, 726, 583

C 947, 726, 815, 583

D 583, 726, 815, 947

18. What fraction of your body's bones are **NOT** in your feet? Use the picture at the right.

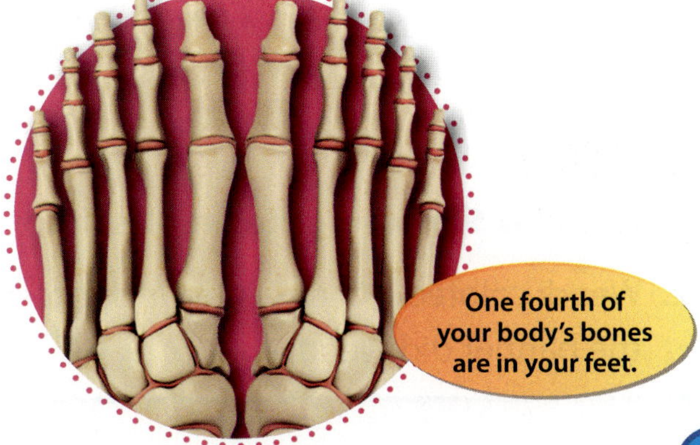

Virginia

Lesson 12-5

Prepares for 4.2.b The student will represent equivalent fractions.

Finding Equivalent Fractions

Hands-On
fraction strips

How can different fractions name the same part of a whole?

Sonya has decorated $\frac{1}{2}$ of the border. What are two other ways to name $\frac{1}{2}$?

$\frac{1}{2}$ of the border

Different fractions can name the same part of a whole.

Another Example How can you write a fraction in simplest form?

Division facts that you know will help you find equivalent fractions.

Mario has colored $\frac{4}{6}$ of a border. What is the simplest form of $\frac{4}{6}$?

The simplest form of a fraction is a fraction with a numerator and denominator that cannot be divided by the same divisor, except 1.

$\frac{4}{6}$ of the length of the border

One Way

Use models.

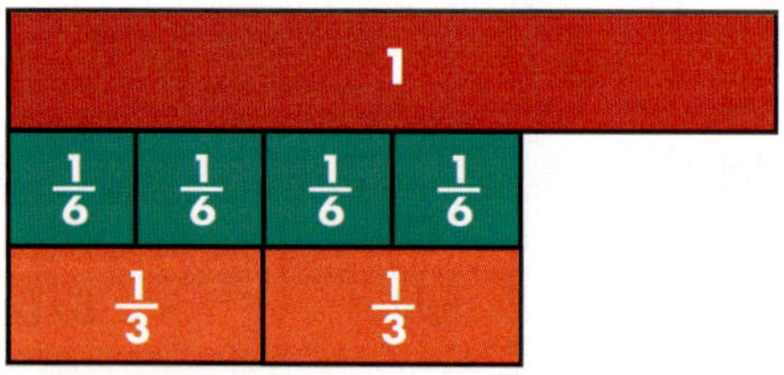

$\frac{4}{6} = \frac{2}{3}$

The simplest form of $\frac{4}{6}$ is $\frac{2}{3}$.

Another Way

Divide the numerator and denominator by the same number.

Find a divisor that both the numerator and denominator can be divided by evenly.

Both 4 and 6 can be evenly divided by 2.

$$\frac{4 \div 2}{6 \div 2} = \frac{2}{3}$$

The numerator and denominator of $\frac{2}{3}$ cannot be divided evenly by the same divisor except 1. The simplest form of $\frac{4}{6}$ is $\frac{2}{3}$.

Explain It

1. **Number Sense** Is $\frac{1}{3}$ the simplest form of $\frac{2}{6}$? Why or why not?
2. Wendi colored $\frac{2}{4}$ of a banner. In simplest form, what fraction of the banner did Wendi color?

$\frac{1}{2} = \frac{\square}{8}$ You can use fraction strips. The denominators of the fractions tell which fraction strips to use.

Find how many $\frac{1}{8}$s are equal to $\frac{1}{2}$.

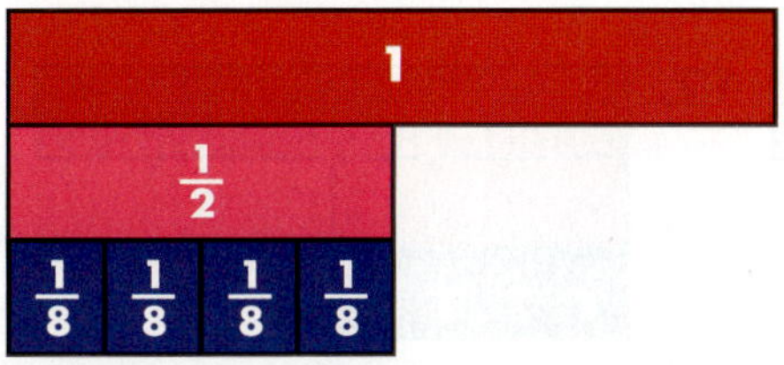

Four $\frac{1}{8}$ strips are equal to $\frac{1}{2}$, so $\frac{1}{2} = \frac{4}{8}$.
Another name for $\frac{1}{2}$ is $\frac{4}{8}$.

$\frac{1}{2} = \frac{\square}{6}$ You can use fraction strips. The denominator is 6 so use $\frac{1}{6}$ strips.

Find how many $\frac{1}{6}$s are equal to $\frac{1}{2}$.

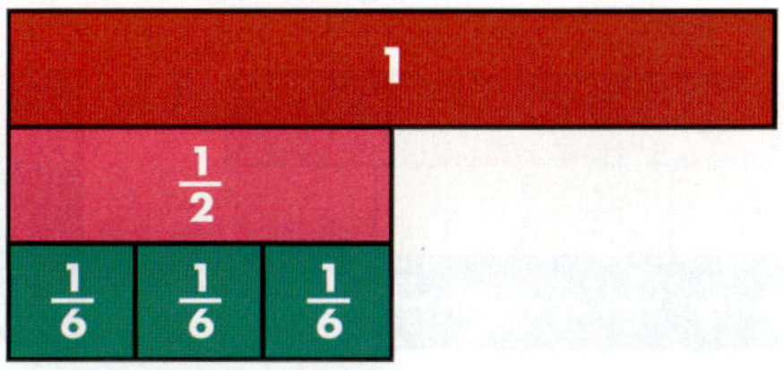

Three $\frac{1}{6}$ strips are equal to $\frac{1}{2}$, so $\frac{1}{2} = \frac{3}{6}$.
Another name for $\frac{1}{2}$ is $\frac{3}{6}$.

Guided Practice*

Do you know HOW?

1. Copy and complete the number sentence. Use fraction strips or make drawings on grid paper.

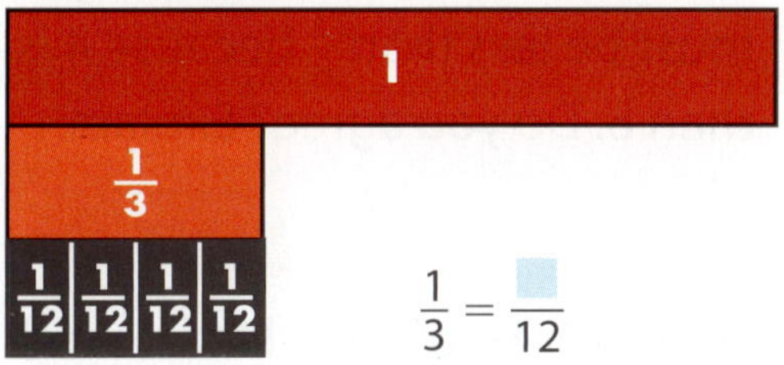

$\frac{1}{3} = \frac{\square}{12}$

Find the simplest form of each fraction.

2. $\frac{5}{10}$ **3.** $\frac{6}{9}$ **4.** $\frac{2}{4}$

Do you UNDERSTAND?

5. In the example above, what pattern do you see in the numerator and denominator of fractions that name $\frac{1}{2}$?

6. Vijay folded a rope into fourths. Then he showed $\frac{1}{4}$ of the length. Write $\frac{1}{4}$ one other way.

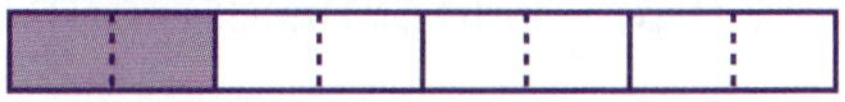

Independent Practice

In **7–9**, copy and complete each number sentence. Use fraction strips or make drawings on grid paper to help.

7.

$\frac{1}{4} = \frac{\square}{8}$

8.

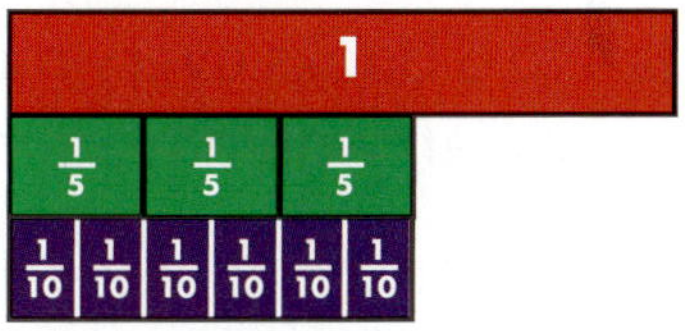

$\frac{3}{5} = \frac{\square}{10}$

9.

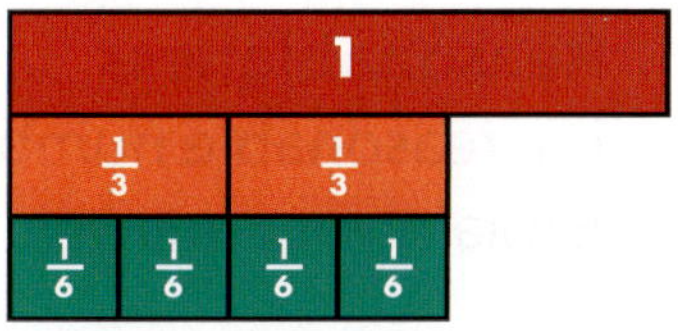

$\frac{2}{3} = \frac{\square}{6}$

DIGITAL Animated Glossary, eTools
www.pearsonsuccessnet.com

*For another example, see Set A on page 302.

Independent Practice

For **10–12**, copy and complete each number sentence. Use fraction strips or make drawings on grid paper to help.

10.

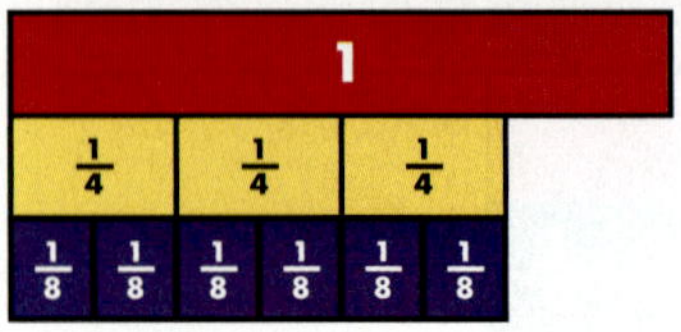

$\frac{6}{8} = \frac{\square}{4}$

11.

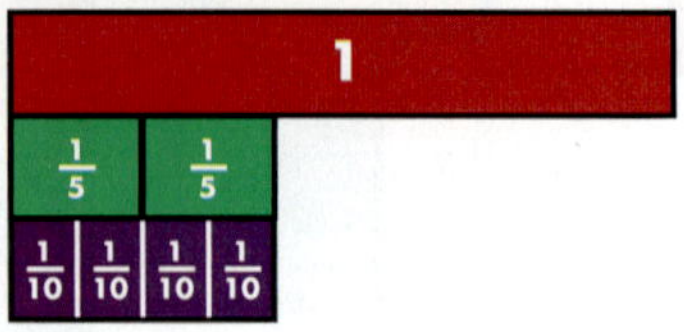

$\frac{2}{5} = \frac{\square}{10}$

12.

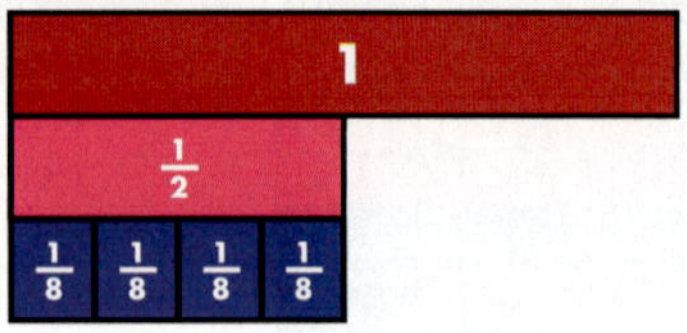

$\frac{1}{2} = \frac{\square}{8}$

For **13–20**, write each fraction in simplest form.

13. $\frac{3}{6}$ **14.** $\frac{9}{12}$ **15.** $\frac{8}{12}$ **16.** $\frac{5}{15}$

17. $\frac{2}{10}$ **18.** $\frac{7}{8}$ **19.** $\frac{8}{10}$ **20.** $\frac{6}{12}$

Problem Solving

21. Evie painted $\frac{1}{6}$ of a board. What is one other way to name $\frac{1}{6}$?

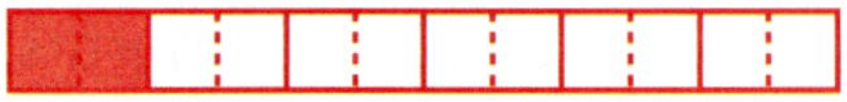

22. **Number Sense** Carlos said that $\frac{3}{4}$ must be less than $\frac{3}{8}$ because 4 is less than 8. Do you agree? Explain.

23. **Writing to Explain** How do you know that $\frac{2}{3}$ is in simplest form?

24. Two eighths of a necklace is red. What part of the necklace is not red?

25. The shaded part of which rectangle is a fraction equal to $\frac{1}{4}$?

SOL Prep

A 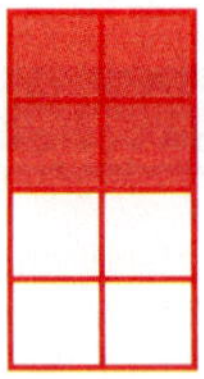 **B** 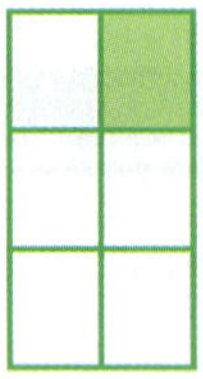 **C** 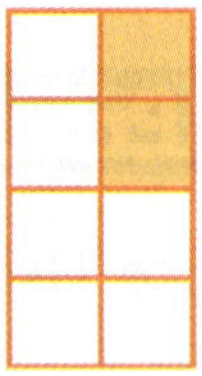 **D** 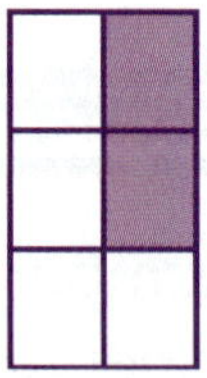

26. **Reasonableness** Jan reads 4 to 6 books every month. What is a reasonable number of books Jan would read in 7 months? Explain your answer.

27. In simplest form, what fraction of the Earth's land surface is desert? Use the picture.

SOL Prep

A $\frac{1}{2}$ **B** $\frac{1}{3}$ **C** $\frac{1}{5}$ **D** $\frac{4}{6}$

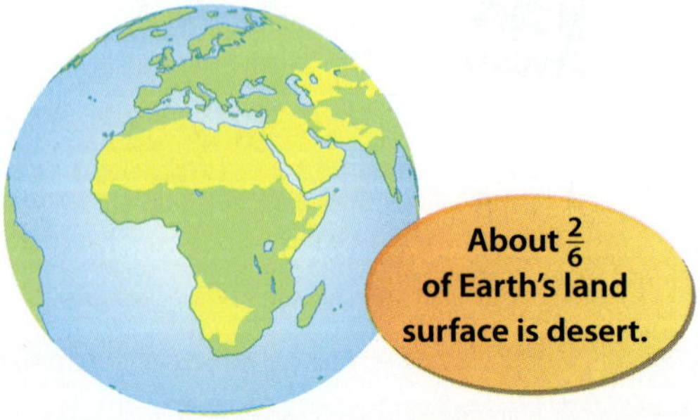

Enrichment

Circle Graphs

Kara earned $20 last week. The circle graph shows how she earned money and what part of the total was earned for each kind of job.

Kara's Earnings

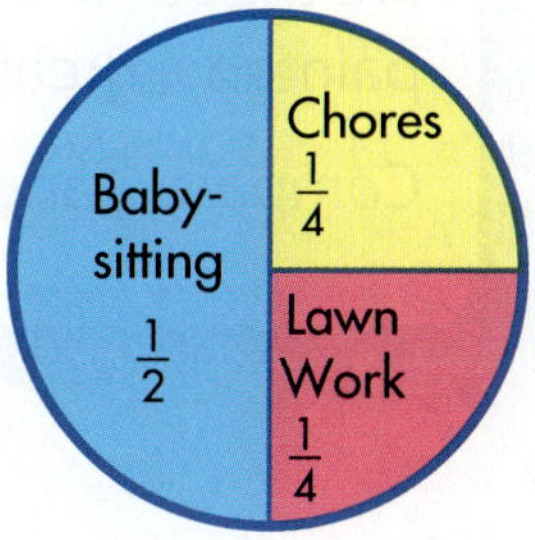

The part for babysitting is half of the circle. Kara earned more by babysitting than by doing chores or lawn work.

One half of the $20 Kara earned was from babysitting.

$\frac{1}{2} = \frac{10}{20}$ So, Kara earned $10 by babysitting.

One fourth of the amount Kara earned was from doing chores, and one fourth was from doing lawn work.

$\frac{1}{4} = \frac{5}{20}$ Kara earned $5 doing chores and $5 doing lawn work.

Practice

Tom spent a total of $12 on supplies for Hammy, his pet hamster. For **1–5**, use the circle graph that Tom made.

Supplies for Hammy

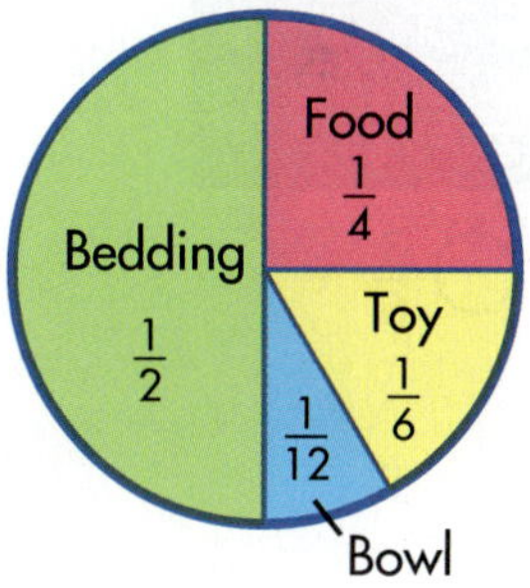

1. Which item cost one fourth of the total? How much money is that?

2. How much did Tom spend on bedding?

3. Which item cost one sixth of the total? How much money is that?

4. List the items Tom bought from least to greatest cost.

5. How could thinking about a clock help Tom make the circle graph for Hammy's supplies?

For **6** and **7**, use the table at the right that shows the voting results for class color.

Class Color (Data)

Color	Votes
Blue	9
Green	3
Silver	6

6. a. What is the total number of votes?

b. Write a fraction that describes the votes for each color.

7. Make a circle graph showing the votes.

Virginia

Lesson 12-6

3.3.c The student will compare fractions having like and unlike denominators, using words and symbols (>, <, or =).

Using Models to Compare Fractions

Hands-On
fraction strips

How can you compare fractions?

Nola and Edwin are painting two boards that are the same size and the same shape. Who painted a greater amount—Nola or Edwin?

Compare $\frac{1}{2}$ and $\frac{2}{5}$.

Nola painted $\frac{1}{2}$ of one board.

Edwin painted $\frac{2}{5}$ of the other board.

Guided Practice*

Do you know HOW?

In **1** and **2**, compare. Write >, <, or =. Use fraction strips to help.

1.

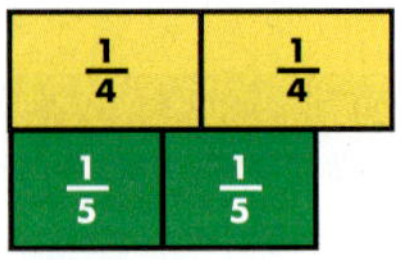

$\frac{2}{4} \bigcirc \frac{2}{5}$

2.

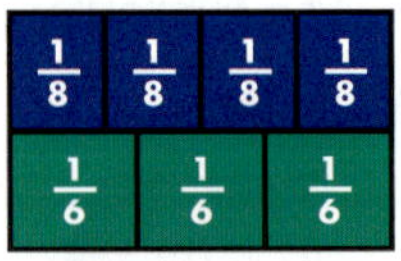

$\frac{4}{8} \bigcirc \frac{3}{6}$

Do you UNDERSTAND?

3. In the problem above about Zoe and Nat, can you tell who painted a greater area of board? Explain.

4. Bob and Irene are painting two walls that are the same size and shape. Irene painted $\frac{2}{3}$ of one wall. Bob painted $\frac{3}{4}$ of the other wall. Who painted a greater amount?

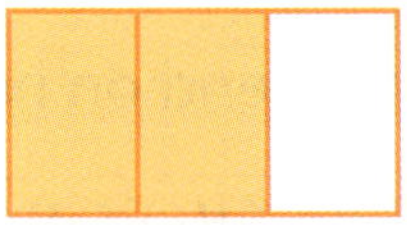

$\frac{2}{3}$

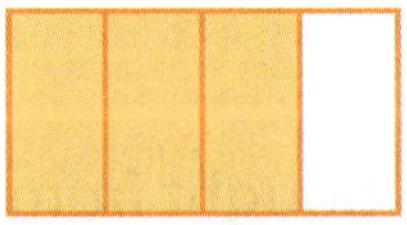

$\frac{3}{4}$

Independent Practice

In **5–7**, compare. Write >, <, or =. Use fraction strips to help.

5.

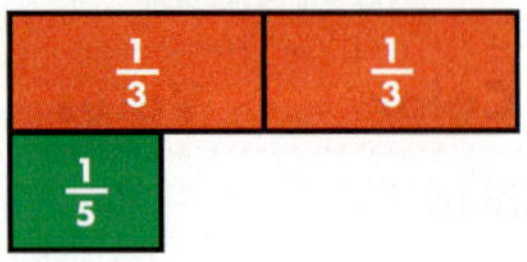

$\frac{2}{3} \bigcirc \frac{1}{5}$

6.

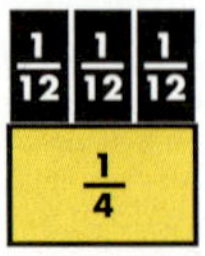

$\frac{3}{12} \bigcirc \frac{1}{4}$

7.

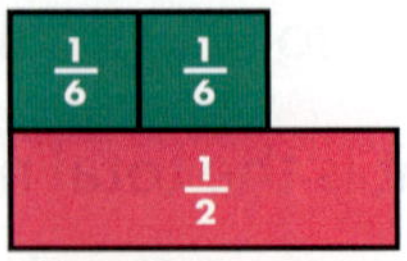

$\frac{2}{6} \bigcirc \frac{1}{2}$

DIGITAL
eTools
www.pearsonsuccessnet.com

*For another example, see Set C on page 302.

You can use fraction strips.

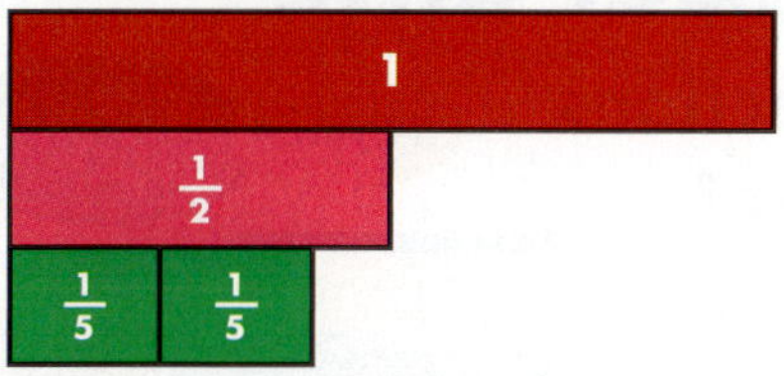

Compare the fraction strips.

$\frac{1}{2}$ is greater than $\frac{2}{5}$.

$\frac{1}{2} > \frac{2}{5}$

Nola painted a greater amount.

Zoe painted $\frac{1}{2}$ of one board. Nat painted $\frac{1}{2}$ of a board with a different area. Is the half Zoe painted equal to the half Nat painted?

Draw a picture.

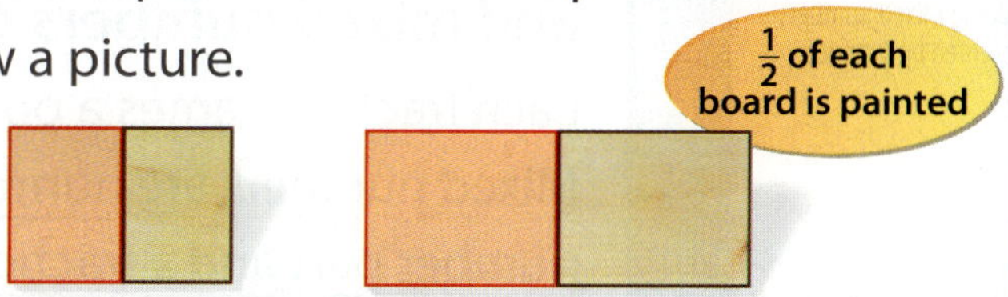

The boards have different areas. Zoe's half is not equal to Nat's half.

Problem Solving

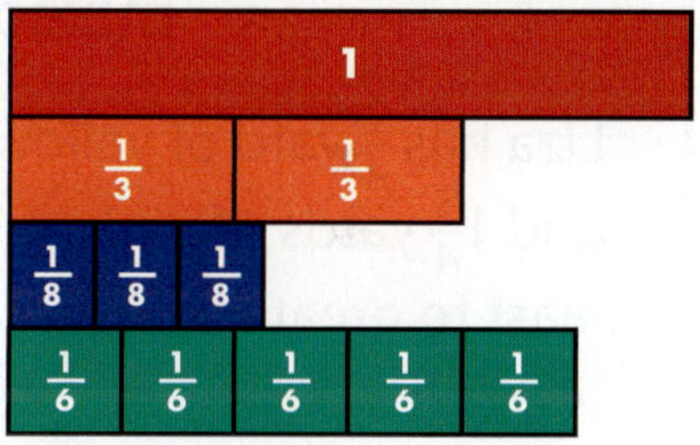

The fraction strips at the right represent three loaves of bread that Mrs. Rai sliced for a meal. The 1 strip represents a whole loaf. The other strips show how much of each loaf was left after the meal.

For **8** and **9**, copy and complete each number sentence to find the loaf with the greater amount left.

8. The loaf cut in sixths or the loaf cut in thirds

$\frac{5}{6} \bigcirc \frac{2}{3}$

9. The loaf cut in eighths or the loaf cut in thirds

$\frac{3}{8} \bigcirc \frac{2}{3}$

10. Writing to Explain Lupe ate $\frac{1}{3}$ of a sandwich. Jed ate $\frac{1}{3}$ of a different sandwich. Jed ate more than Lupe. How is that possible?

11. Kobe fed his hamster and his rabbit. He gave the rabbit 3 carrot pieces for each 2 carrot pieces he gave the hamster. If the hamster got 8 carrot pieces, how many carrot pieces did the rabbit get?

12. Which group shows more than $\frac{5}{7}$ of the shapes shaded?

SOL Prep

A 

C 

B 

D 

3.3.a. The student will name and write fractions (including mixed numbers) represented by a model.

Fractions on the Number Line

How can you locate and compare fractions and mixed numbers on a number line?

Each fraction names a point on a number line. Mixed numbers are numbers that have a whole number part and a fraction part. For example, $1\frac{3}{4}$ and $1\frac{1}{2}$ are mixed numbers.

Is there more red ribbon or more blue ribbon?

Another Example How can you order fractions and mixed numbers?

Liza has $\frac{3}{4}$ yard of yellow ribbon, $\frac{1}{2}$ yard of green ribbon, and $1\frac{3}{4}$ yards of pink ribbon. Write the lengths in order from least to greatest.

You can use a number line to order fractions and mixed numbers.

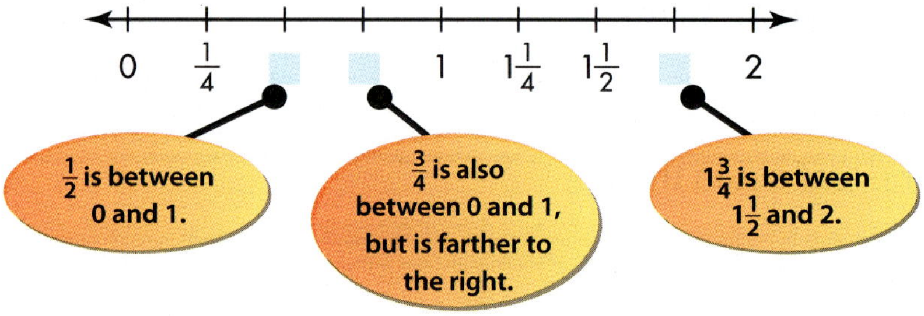

The order of the lengths of ribbon from least to greatest is $\frac{1}{2}$ yard, $\frac{3}{4}$ yard, $1\frac{3}{4}$ yards.

Explain It

1. Describe how you would order $\frac{3}{4}$, $2\frac{3}{4}$, and $2\frac{2}{4}$ from greatest to least.
2. Suppose there are two unit fractions and one mixed number between 1 and 2. Which of them is the greatest? Explain your reasoning.

Tip *The numerator of every unit fraction is 1.*

Use a number line to compare $1\frac{1}{2}$ and $1\frac{3}{4}$.

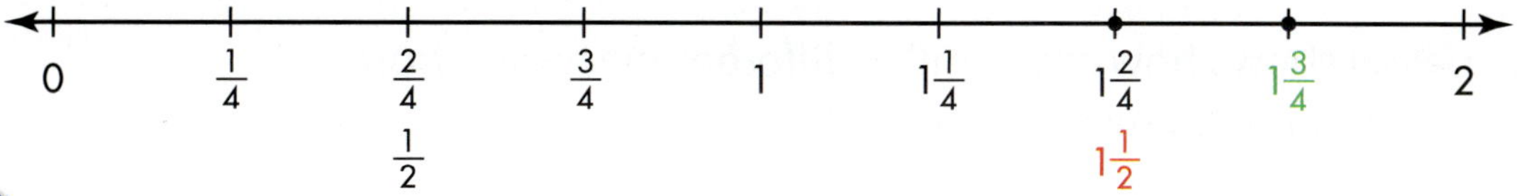

Another name for $\frac{2}{4}$ is $\frac{1}{2}$.

Another name for $1\frac{2}{4}$ is $1\frac{1}{2}$.

On the number line, $1\frac{3}{4}$ is farther to the right than $1\frac{1}{2}$.

$1\frac{3}{4} > 1\frac{1}{2}$

There is more blue ribbon than red ribbon.

Guided Practice*

Do you know HOW?

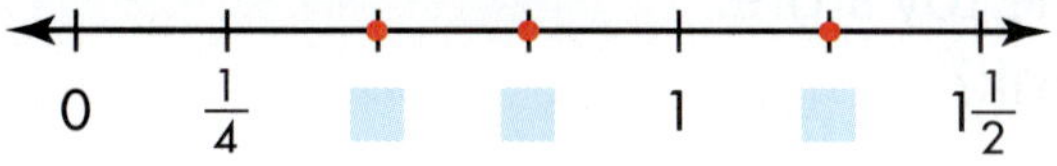

1. Write the missing fractions or mixed numbers for the number line above.

2. Write the answers for Exercise 1 in order from greatest to least.

Compare. Write <, >, or =. Use a number line to help.

3. $\frac{1}{2} \bigcirc \frac{3}{4}$ **4.** $4\frac{1}{2} \bigcirc 4\frac{2}{4}$

Do you UNDERSTAND?

5. In the example above, could you compare $1\frac{3}{4}$ and $1\frac{1}{2}$ by just comparing $\frac{3}{4}$ and $\frac{1}{2}$? Explain.

6. A number line is divided into fourths. What is the next mixed number to the right of $2\frac{2}{4}$?

7. **Number Sense** In Exercise 2, how do you know which fraction or mixed number is greatest?

Independent Practice

8. Copy and complete the number line by writing the missing fractions and mixed numbers.

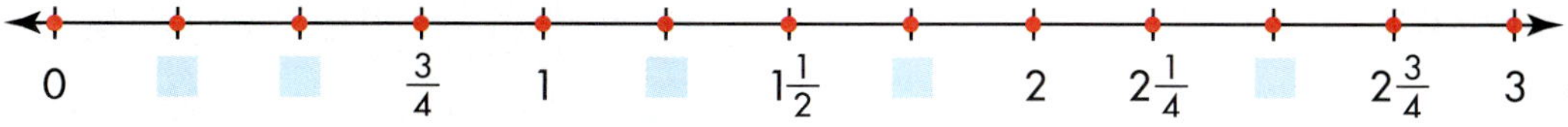

Compare. Write <, >, or =. Use a number line to help.

9. $\frac{2}{4} \bigcirc 1$ **10.** $\frac{2}{4} \bigcirc \frac{1}{2}$ **11.** $2\frac{3}{4} \bigcirc 2\frac{1}{4}$ **12.** $1\frac{3}{4} \bigcirc 2\frac{1}{3}$

13. Write $2\frac{1}{2}$, $\frac{1}{4}$, and $1\frac{3}{4}$ in order from least to greatest.

DIGITAL Animated Glossary www.pearsonsuccessnet.com

For another example, see Set D on page 303.

Problem Solving

The number line below shows how many miles different places are from Oliver's house. Use the number line for **14** and **15**.

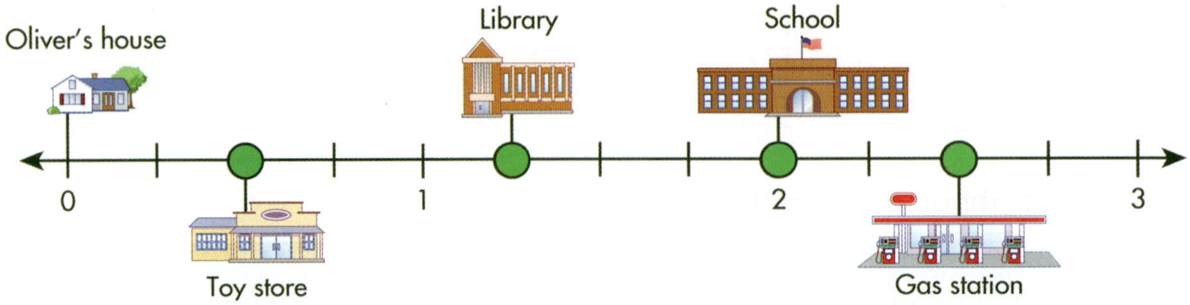

14. The school is 2 miles from Oliver's house. How many miles from Oliver's house are these places?

a library **b** toy store **c** gas station

15. A bank is twice as far from Oliver's house as the toy store. How many miles from Oliver's house is the bank?

16. **Geometry** Teresa drew this shape.

a How many acute angles does the shape have?

b What is the best name for this shape?

17. **Reasonableness** Mr. Smith has 38 sheets of drawing paper. Does he have enough paper to give 4 sheets to each of 9 students? Explain.

18. Which lettered point on the ruler below could represent the number of centimeters that the shore of Iceland grows in a year?

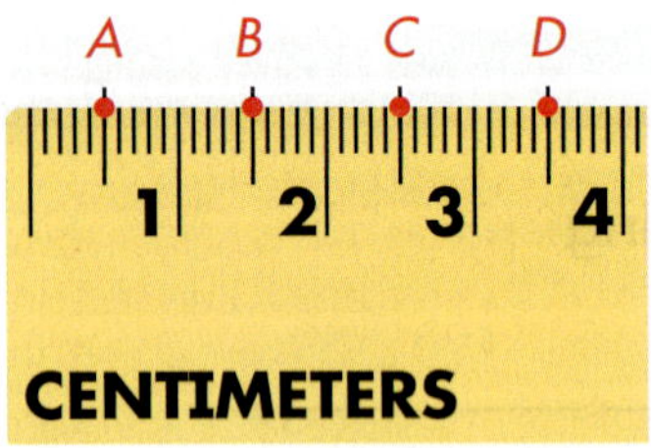

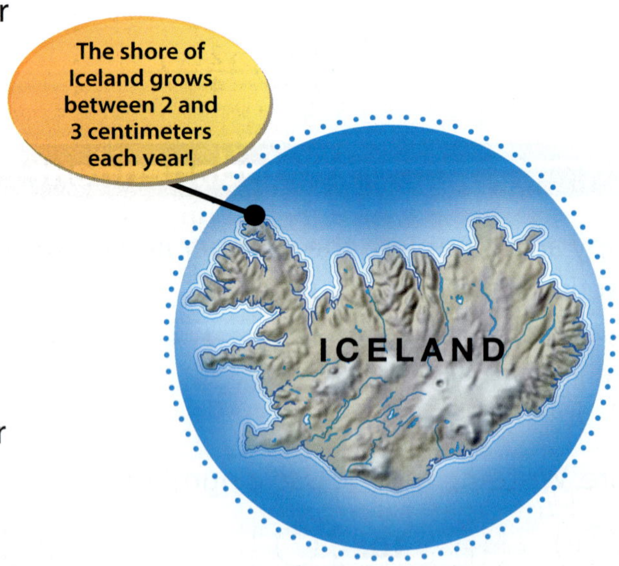

SOL Prep

19. Which number makes this number sentence true?

$\square \div 9 = 6$

A 18 **B** 28 **C** 36 **D** 54

Use the pictures and number line below for **20** through **23**.

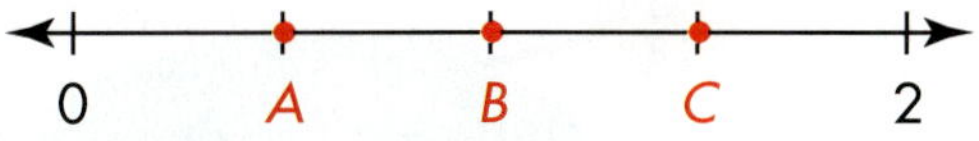

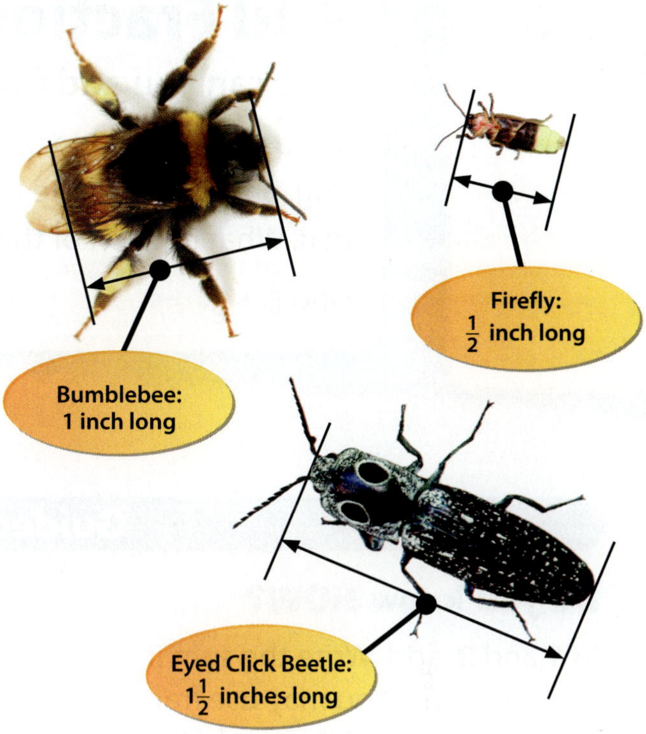

20. Write the name of the insect whose length in inches matches each lettered point on the number line.

a Point *A*

b Point *B*

c Point *C*

21. **Writing to Explain** How does the number line show which insect is the longest?

22. Which is longer—the firefly or the bumblebee?

23. Which insect is the shortest?

24. Show 3 different ways to divide a square into fourths.

25. What fraction of the letters in the word *TENNESSEE* are *E*s?

26. What kind of angle do the clock hands form at 4:00?

A acute **C** square

B obtuse **D** right

27. What number is missing from the pattern below?

SOL Prep

66	58	50	■

A 48 **B** 46 **C** 44 **D** 42

28. Janet had the coins and bills shown at the right. How much money did she have in all?

Virginia

Lesson 12-8

3.7 The student will add and subtract proper fractions having like denominators of 12 or less.

Using Models to Add Fractions

Hands-On
fraction strips $\frac{1}{8}$

How can you add fractions?

Mia used $\frac{3}{8}$ of the block of clay to make the frog. She used $\frac{1}{8}$ of the block to make the lily pad. What fraction of the block did she use in all?

Find $\frac{3}{8} + \frac{1}{8}$.

Guided Practice*

Do you know HOW?

In **1** and **2**, add. Write the sum in simplest form. You may use fraction strips or draw a picture to help.

1. $\frac{2}{5} + \frac{1}{5}$

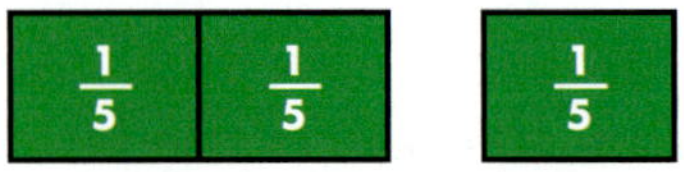

2. $\frac{2}{12} + \frac{4}{12}$

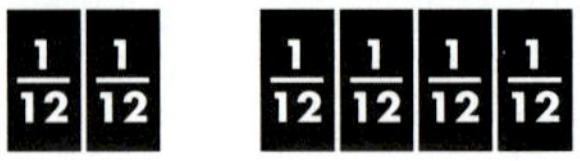

Do you UNDERSTAND?

3. Suppose you add two fractions with the same denominator. What can you say about the sum before you write it in simplest form?

4. Alonso used $\frac{2}{6}$ of a loaf of bread to make peanut butter sandwiches. He used $\frac{2}{6}$ of the loaf to make tuna sandwiches. What fraction of the bread loaf did he use in all?

Independent Practice

Leveled Practice In **5–14**, add. Write the sum in simplest form. You may draw a picture to help.

5. $\frac{3}{6} + \frac{2}{6}$

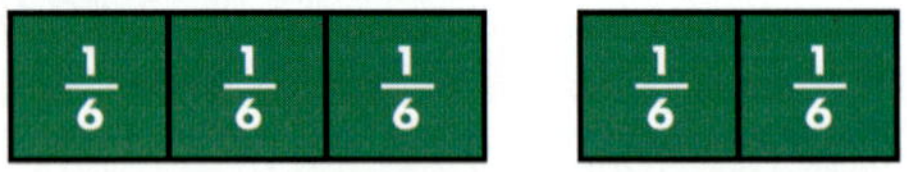

6. $\frac{2}{8} + \frac{4}{8}$

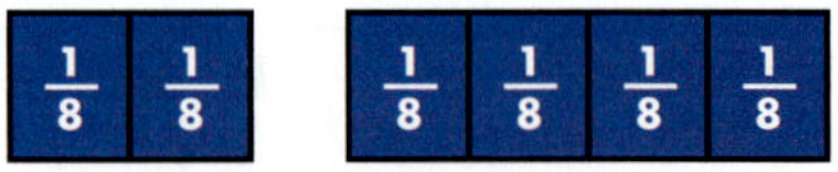

7. $\frac{1}{4} + \frac{2}{4}$

8. $\frac{1}{3} + \frac{1}{3}$

9. $\frac{3}{10} + \frac{5}{10}$

10. $\frac{2}{5} + \frac{1}{5}$

11. $\frac{3}{12} + \frac{5}{12}$

12. $\frac{1}{6} + \frac{2}{6}$

13. $\frac{5}{8} + \frac{2}{8}$

14. $\frac{4}{10} + \frac{3}{10}$

DIGITAL eTools **www.pearsonsuccessnet.com**

*For another example, see Set E on page 303.

Step 1

Add.

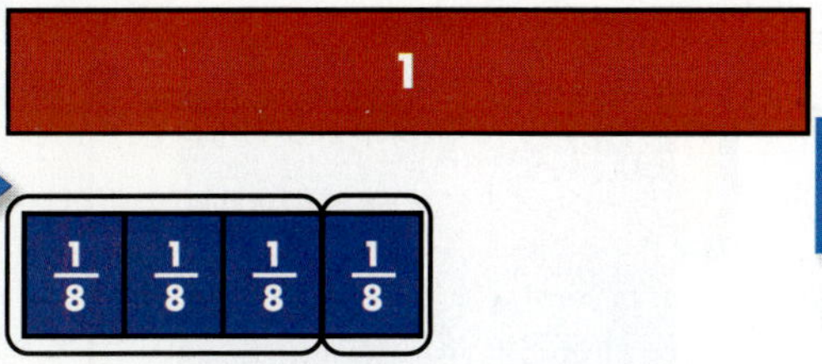

$\frac{3}{8} + \frac{1}{8} = \frac{4}{8}$

Step 2

Write the sum in simplest form.

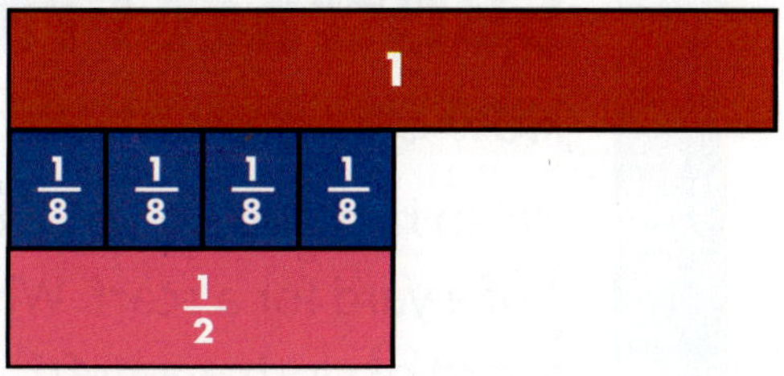

$\frac{4}{8} = \frac{1}{2}$

So, in simplest form, $\frac{3}{8} + \frac{1}{8} = \frac{4}{8}$, or $\frac{1}{2}$.

All together, Mia used $\frac{1}{2}$ of the block of clay.

Problem Solving

15. Ken ate $\frac{2}{4}$ of a large sandwich and Janet ate $\frac{1}{4}$ of it. Write an addition sentence that shows the fraction of the sandwich they ate all together.

16. Chad found 12 seashells. Four of them were bubble shells. The rest were jingle shells. In simplest form, what fraction of the shells were jingle shells?

17. Rashad colored $\frac{3}{5}$ of a flag red and $\frac{1}{5}$ of the same flag green. What fraction of the flag did he color in all?

18. SOL Prep Nia painted $\frac{4}{8}$ of a fence rail and Tracy painted $\frac{2}{8}$ of it. What simplest form fraction names the part of the rail they painted in all?

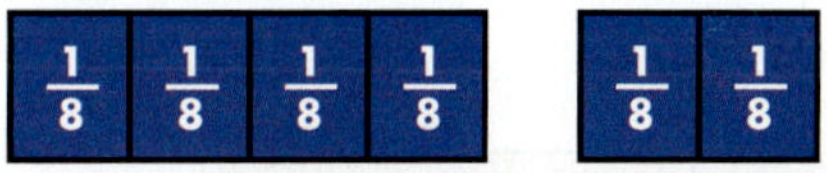

A $\frac{6}{4}$ **B** $\frac{3}{4}$ **C** $\frac{1}{2}$ **D** $\frac{2}{8}$

19. Diane's hair grew $\frac{2}{5}$ inch in one month and $\frac{3}{5}$ inch the next month. How much did it grow in the two months?

20. **Writing to Explain** Cassie drank $\frac{5}{8}$ of a glass of juice. Julie drank $\frac{3}{4}$ of the same size glass of juice. Who drank more juice? Explain.

21. SOL Prep Which fraction comes next in the pattern?

$\frac{1}{2}, \frac{2}{4}, \frac{3}{6}, \frac{4}{8}$, ▢

A $\frac{5}{15}$ **B** $\frac{3}{7}$ **C** $\frac{5}{10}$ **D** $\frac{5}{9}$

22. Estela cut a rectangle into sixths. Draw a picture of a rectangle divided into sixths. Use grid paper to help.

Virginia

Lesson 12-9

3.7 The student will add and subtract proper fractions having like denominators of 12 or less.

Using Models to Subtract Fractions

Hands-On fraction strips

How can you subtract fractions?

Helen had $\frac{5}{8}$ of a yard of cloth. She cut $\frac{1}{8}$ of a yard for a scarf. What fraction of a yard of cloth was left?

Choose an Operation $\frac{5}{8} - \frac{1}{8} = \square$

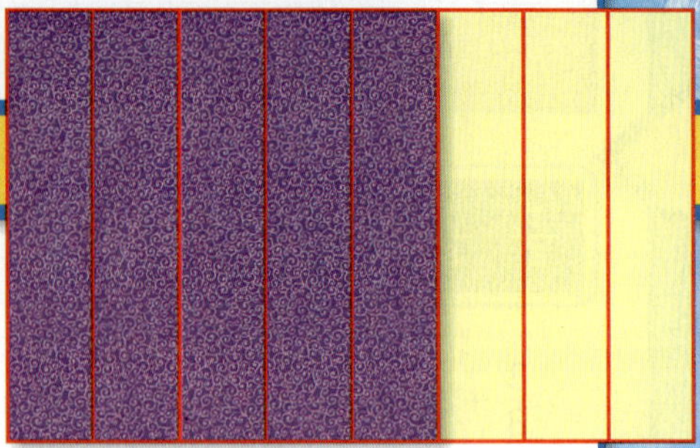

Guided Practice*

Do you know HOW?

In **1** and **2**, subtract. Write the difference in simplest form. You may use fraction strips or draw a picture to help.

1. $\frac{6}{8} - \frac{4}{8}$

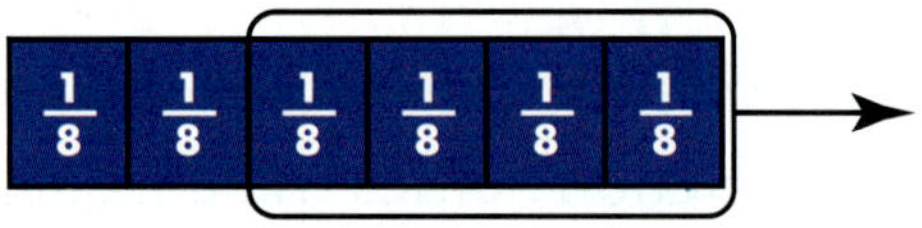

2. $\frac{3}{4} - \frac{1}{4}$

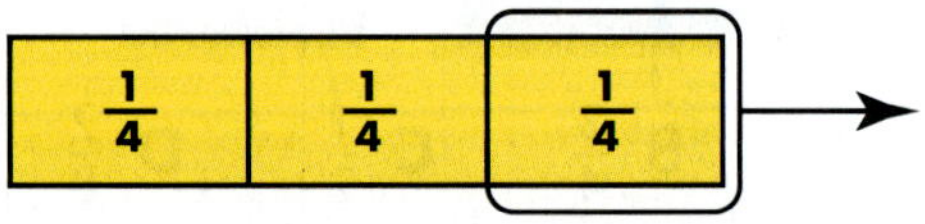

Do you UNDERSTAND?

3. Suppose you subtract two fractions with the same denominator. What can you say about the difference before you write it in simplest form?

4. Ethan lives $\frac{9}{10}$ of a mile from school. His friend Luis lives $\frac{3}{10}$ of a mile from school. How much farther from school does Ethan live than Luis? Write the answer in simplest form.

Independent Practice

Leveled Practice In **5–10**, subtract. Write the difference in simplest form. You may draw a picture to help.

5. $\frac{2}{3} - \frac{1}{3}$

6. $\frac{4}{6} - \frac{2}{6}$

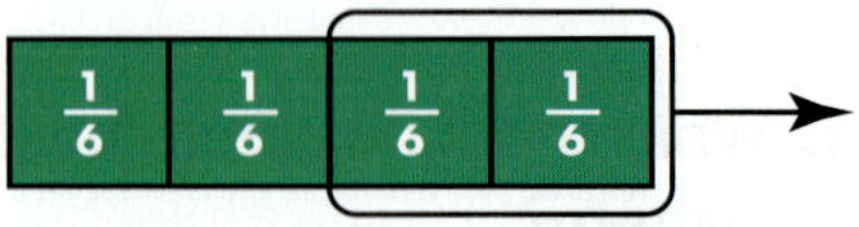

7. $\frac{4}{5} - \frac{2}{5}$

8. $\frac{7}{9} - \frac{4}{9}$

9. $\frac{10}{12} - \frac{4}{12}$

10. $\frac{3}{4} - \frac{2}{4}$

DIGITAL eTools **www.pearsonsuccessnet.com**

*For another example, see Set E on page 303.

Step 1

Subtract.

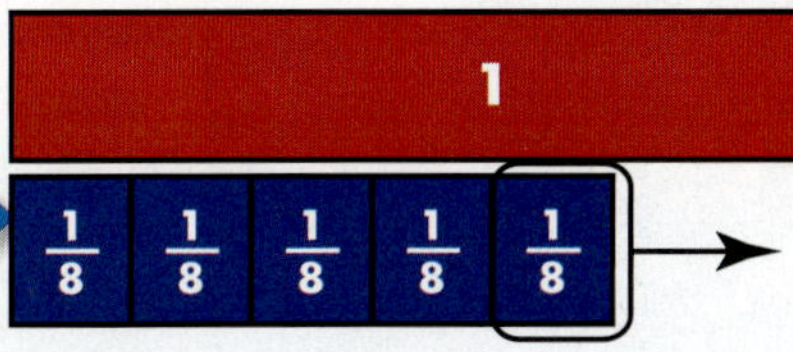

$\frac{5}{8} - \frac{1}{8} = \frac{4}{8}$

Step 2

Write the difference in simplest form.

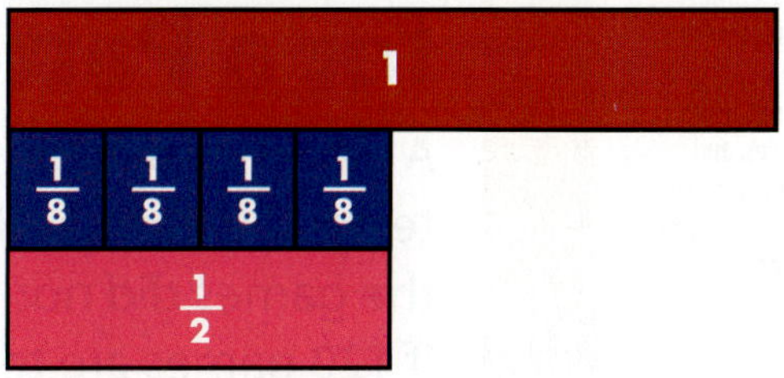

$\frac{4}{8} = \frac{1}{2}$

$\frac{5}{8} - \frac{1}{8} = \frac{4}{8}$, or $\frac{1}{2}$

One half yard of cloth was left.

Problem Solving

11. Selena had $\frac{3}{4}$ of a whole sheet of grid paper. She cut off $\frac{2}{4}$ of the whole sheet. Write a subtraction sentence that shows the fraction of the whole sheet that was left.

12. **Number Sense** There are 56 crayons. The crayons are placed onto 8 tables so that the same number of crayons is on each table. How many crayons in all would be on 3 tables?

13. Ted saw that there was $\frac{5}{8}$ of a pizza in the refrigerator. He ate $\frac{1}{8}$ of the pizza. What fraction of the original pizza was left? Write the fraction in simplest form.

14. SOL Prep A diner had $\frac{8}{12}$ of a supreme pizza on the warming shelf. Then Marion served $\frac{4}{12}$ of the pizza to customers. In simplest form, what fraction of the pizza was left?

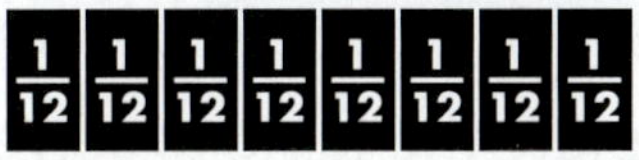

A $\frac{4}{4}$

B $\frac{1}{3}$

C $\frac{1}{4}$

D $\frac{2}{12}$

15. Use the pictures of beetles at the right. How much longer is the caterpillar hunter beetle than the tiger beetle?

Virginia

Lesson 12-10

Extends 3.19 The student will recognize and describe a variety of patterns formed using numbers, tables, and pictures, and extend the patterns, using the same or different forms.

Problem Solving

Make a Table and Look for a Pattern

A video game company tested 20 games. Three of the games did not work. If 120 games are tested, how many of them might not work?

Guided Practice*

Do you know HOW?

Copy and complete the table to solve.

1. Ms Simms is buying bags of blocks. Out of the 50 blocks in each bag, 3 are cubes. If she buys 250 blocks, how many cubes will she get?

Cubes	3				
Total Blocks	50				

Do you UNDERSTAND?

2. Look at the example above. If the video game store bought 50 games, about how many games might not work? Explain.

3. **Write a Problem** Write a problem that can be solved by making a table and using a pattern. Then solve the problem.

Independent Practice

Copy and complete the table to solve.

4. Erasers are sold in packages of 6. In each package, 2 of the erasers are pink. How many pink erasers will Andrea get if she buys 30 erasers?

Pink Erasers	2				
Total Erasers	6				

Stuck? Try this....

- What do I know?
- What am I asked to find?
- What diagram can I use to help understand the problem?
- Can I use addition, subtraction, multiplication, or division?
- Is all of my work correct?
- Did I answer the right question?
- Is my answer reasonable?

*For another example, see Set F on page 303

Plan

Make a table.

Then, write in the information you know.

Might Not Work	3					
Total Games	20					

Solve

Extend the table. Look for a pattern to help. Then find the answer in the table.

Might Not Work	3	6	9	12	15	18
Total Games	20	40	60	80	100	120

If 120 games are tested, 18 might not work.

Copy and complete the tables in **5** and **7**. Use the tables to help solve.

5. Sue planted 8 daffodil bulbs. Two of the bulbs didn't grow. Suppose that pattern continues and Sue plants 32 bulbs. How many bulbs most likely won't grow?

Didn't Grow	2			
Total Bulbs	8			

6. **Reasoning** Look back at Problem 5. Suppose Sue decided to plant 20 daffodil bulbs.

a How many bulbs would most likely not grow?

b How many bulbs would most likely grow?

7. Sue planted 12 tulip bulbs of mixed colors. When the bulbs grew, there were 4 red tulips. Suppose that pattern continues and Sue plants 48 bulbs. How many of the tulips will likely be red? How many will NOT be red?

Red Tulips	4			
Total Tulips	12			

8. **Reasoning** Tad planted 15 tulips in a row. He followed the pattern shown below. What is the color of the last tulip in the row?

9. **Number Sense** See Problem 8. Suppose Tad planted 30 tulips in this pattern. How many would be red?

10. Which equivalent fraction completes the pattern below?

SOL Prep

$\frac{1}{4}$ $\frac{2}{8}$ $\frac{3}{12}$ $\frac{\square}{\square}$

A $\frac{3}{14}$ **B** $\frac{4}{14}$ **C** $\frac{3}{16}$ **D** $\frac{4}{16}$

1. What is the name of the equal parts of the whole pizza? (12-1)

A Sixths

B Sevenths

C Eighths

D Ninths

2. The stage was divided into equal parts. What fraction names the part of the stage used for flute players? (12-2)

Trombones	Drums	Trombones
Clarinets	Trombones	Clarinets
Flutes	Triangles	Flutes

A $\frac{1}{9}$

B $\frac{2}{9}$

C $\frac{2}{7}$

D $\frac{3}{9}$

3. Blair bought the fruit shown below. What fraction of the pieces of fruit are oranges? (12-3)

A $\frac{5}{7}$

B $\frac{6}{12}$

C $\frac{5}{12}$

D $\frac{1}{5}$

4. Stacy rode her bike $\frac{1}{5}$ mile to her grandmother's house. Then she rode $\frac{3}{5}$ mile to her aunt's house. How far did Stacy ride? (12-8)

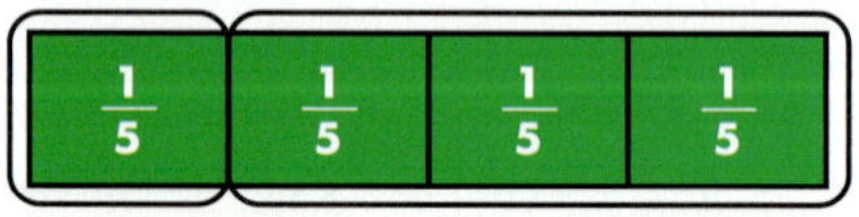

A $\frac{5}{4}$ miles

B $\frac{4}{5}$ mile

C $\frac{2}{5}$ mile

D $\frac{4}{10}$ mile

5. Which fraction is in simplest form? (12-5)

A $\frac{2}{3}$

B $\frac{6}{8}$

C $\frac{2}{4}$

D $\frac{9}{12}$

6. The number line shows four friends' guesses for the average length, in inches, of the striped bark scorpion. Ty's guess was correct. Which number did Ty guess? (12-7)

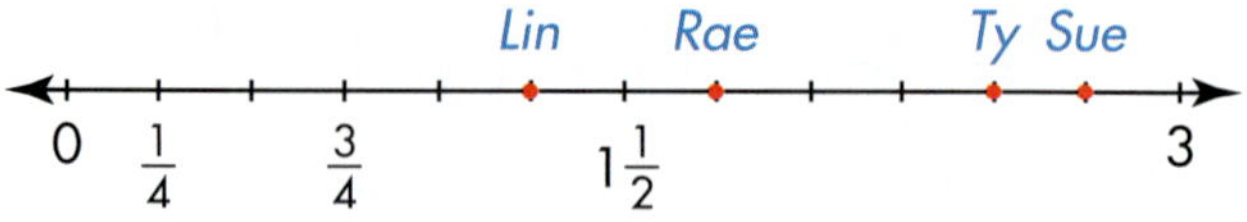

A $1\frac{1}{4}$

B $1\frac{3}{4}$

C $2\frac{1}{2}$

D $2\frac{3}{4}$

7. During the time allowed, Delia swam $\frac{3}{4}$ of the length of the pool. Loren swam $\frac{4}{5}$ of it. Use the models to find which is the correct symbol to compare the fractions. (12-6)

$\frac{3}{4} \bigcirc \frac{4}{5}$

A $=$

B $\times$

C $>$

D $<$

8. Allison is buying packages of sliced meat for the picnic. Each package has 20 slices of meat. Out of the 20 slices, 5 are turkey. If Allison buys 80 slices, how many are turkey? (12-10)

Turkey Slices	5	10	■	■
Total Slices	20	40	60	80

A 11

B 15

C 16

D 20

9. About how much of Trenton's garden is corn? (12-4)

A About $\frac{1}{2}$

B About $\frac{1}{3}$

C About $\frac{1}{4}$

D About $\frac{3}{4}$

10. Bethany bought $\frac{7}{8}$ yard of ribbon. She used $\frac{5}{8}$ yard to decorate a costume. In simplest form, how much ribbon does she have left? (12-9)

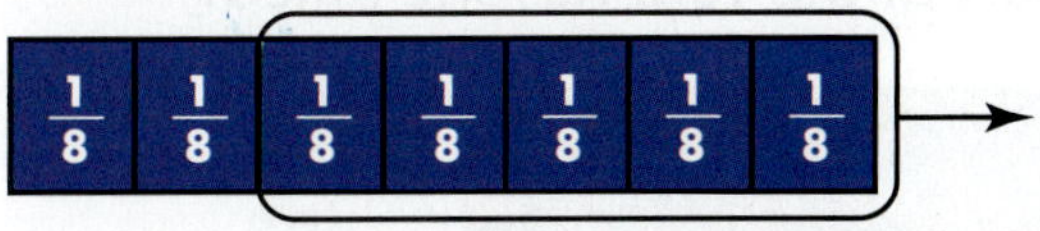

A $\frac{1}{4}$ yard

B $\frac{1}{3}$ yard

C $\frac{3}{4}$ yard

D $\frac{4}{3}$ yards

11. Rachel's scarf is $2\frac{1}{2}$ feet long. Elle's scarf is longer. Which could be the length of Elle's scarf? (12-7)

A $2\frac{3}{4}$ feet

B $1\frac{3}{4}$ feet

C 2 feet

D $2\frac{1}{4}$ feet

Set A, pages 276–281, 284–286

What fraction of the triangles are pink?

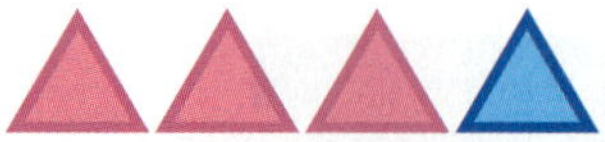

$\frac{\text{numerator}}{\text{denominator}} = \frac{\text{number of pink triangles}}{\text{total number of triangles}} = \frac{3}{4}$

$\frac{3}{4}$ of the triangles are pink.

What is another name for $\frac{3}{4}$?

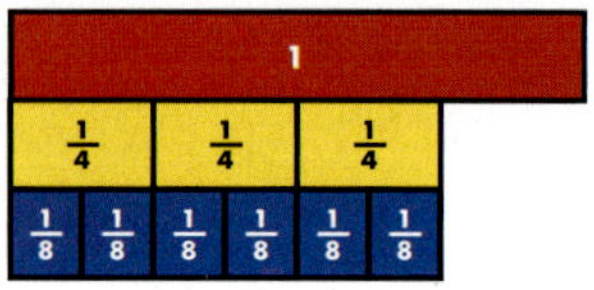

$\frac{3}{4} = \frac{\square}{8}$

$\frac{3}{4} = \frac{6}{8}$

Remember that fractions can name parts of a whole or a set.

Write the fraction that is red.

1. 

2. 

Copy and complete.

3. $\frac{2}{3} = \frac{\square}{6}$

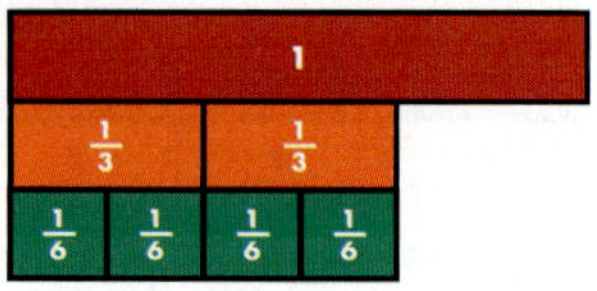

Set B, pages 282–283

Lisa is raking the leaves in her yard. About what part of the yard has she raked?

Find the benchmark fraction that is closest to the fraction in the problem.

Try $\frac{1}{2}$, $\frac{1}{3}$, $\frac{2}{3}$, $\frac{1}{4}$, or $\frac{3}{4}$.

Lisa has raked about $\frac{1}{4}$ of the yard.

Remember that benchmark fractions are commonly used fractions such as $\frac{1}{4}$, $\frac{1}{3}$, $\frac{1}{2}$, $\frac{2}{3}$, and $\frac{3}{4}$.

Estimate the fractional part that is yellow. Use a benchmark fraction.

1. 

2. 

Set C, pages 288–289

Compare $\frac{3}{8}$ and $\frac{1}{2}$.

$\frac{3}{8} \bigcirc \frac{1}{2}$

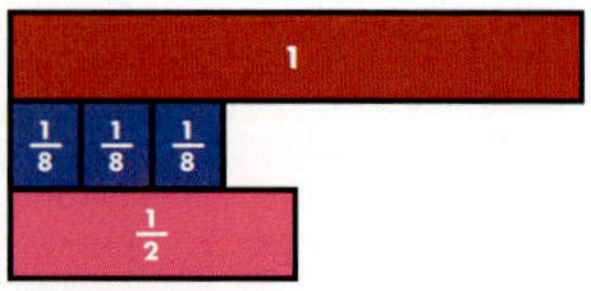

$\frac{3}{8} < \frac{1}{2}$

Remember that if two fractions have the same denominator, the fraction with the greater numerator is the greater fraction.

1. Compare. Write $<$, $>$, or $=$.

$\frac{7}{8} \bigcirc \frac{2}{5}$

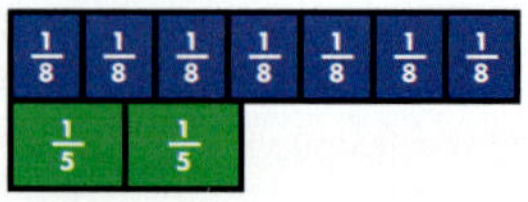

Set D, pages 290–293

What fraction and what mixed number are missing on the number line?

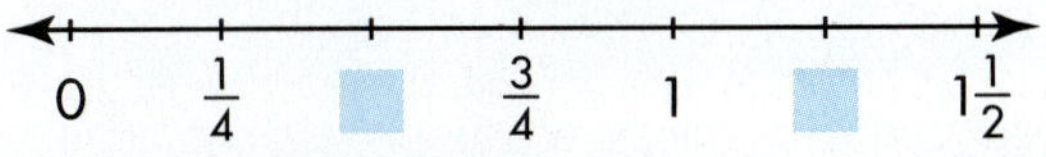

Each section of the number line is $\frac{1}{4}$.

So $\frac{2}{4}$, or $\frac{1}{2}$, and $1\frac{1}{4}$ are missing.

Which is greater, $1\frac{1}{4}$ or $\frac{3}{4}$?

Since $1\frac{1}{4}$ is farther to the right, $1\frac{1}{4} > \frac{3}{4}$.

Remember to look for a pattern in the fractions on your number line.

Write the missing fraction or mixed number for the number line.

1.

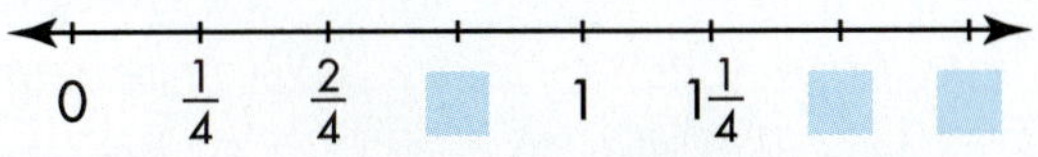

Compare. Write <, >, or =.

2. $\frac{1}{4}$ ◯ $\frac{1}{2}$

3. $5\frac{2}{4}$ ◯ $5\frac{1}{4}$

Set E, pages 294–297

Find the sum $\frac{1}{6} + \frac{3}{6}$ in simplest form.

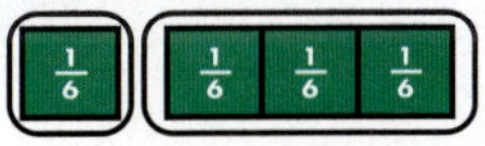

$\frac{1}{6} + \frac{3}{6} = \frac{4}{6}$ and $\frac{4}{6} = \frac{2}{3}$, so $\frac{1}{6} + \frac{3}{6} = \frac{2}{3}$

Find $\frac{6}{8} - \frac{2}{8}$ in simplest form.

$\frac{6}{8} - \frac{2}{8} = \frac{4}{8}$ and $\frac{4}{8} = \frac{1}{2}$, so $\frac{6}{8} - \frac{2}{8} = \frac{1}{2}$.

Remember to check your work.

Find each answer in simplest form.

1. $\frac{3}{10} + \frac{2}{10}$

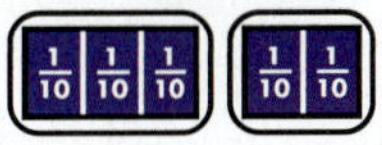

2. $\frac{5}{6} - \frac{3}{6}$

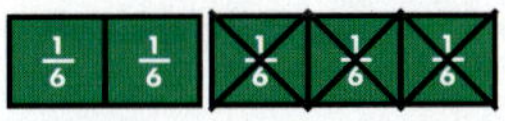

Set F, pages 298–299

Make a table and find a pattern to solve.

Each bag of 20 marbles has 4 green marbles. If Ed buys 80 marbles, how many are green?

Make a table. Look for a pattern.

Green	4	8	12	16
Total	20	40	60	80

16 marbles are green.

Remember that making a table can help you find a pattern.

1. Each box of pens has 2 red pens. How many red pens will you get if you buy 40 pens?

Red	2				
Total	8				

Topic 13 Decimals and Money

1 On March 1, 2002, the euro became the official money in several countries in Europe. What was the value of 1 U.S. dollar in euros? You will find out in Lesson 13-3.

2 In one minute, does the United States Treasury Department produce more coins or more bills? You will find out in Lesson 13-5.

3 How much does it cost the United States Mint to make a quarter? You will find out in Lesson 13-2.

Review What You Know!

Vocabulary

Choose the best term from the box.

- digits
- place
- one thousand
- tens

1. All of the numbers are made from __?__.
2. The number 328 has a 3 in the hundreds __?__.
3. Ten hundreds equal __?__.

Fractions

Name the equal parts of the whole.

4. 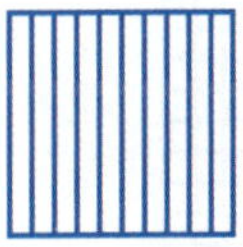

5. 

Fractions and Regions

Write the fraction that is blue.

6. 

7. 

Place Value

Write each number in standard form.

8. 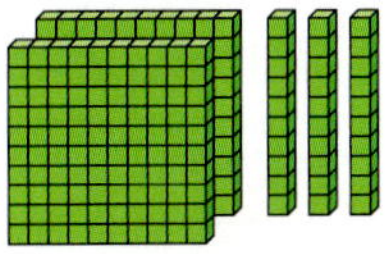

9. 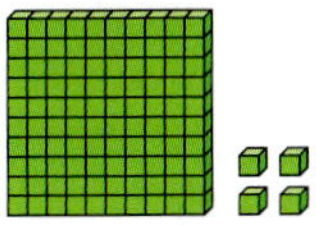

10. **Writing to Explain** Show the number 180 in a place-value chart. Explain how the chart helps show the value of a number.

Virginia

Lesson 13-1

Prepares for 4.3.d The student will, given a model, write the decimal and fraction equivalents.

Fractions and Decimals

How can you write a decimal and a fraction for the same part of a whole?

Amy has a set of ten markers. Three of the markers are green. What part of the set of markers is green?

Guided Practice*

Do you know HOW?

In **1** and **2**, write a fraction and a decimal for each shaded part.

1. 

2. 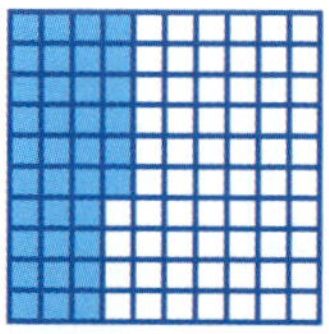

Do you UNDERSTAND?

In **3** and **4**, use the example above.

3. What part of the set is NOT green? Write your answer in three ways.

4. What part of the set is blue? Write your answer in three ways.

Independent Practice

In **5–12**, write a fraction and a decimal for each shaded part.

5. 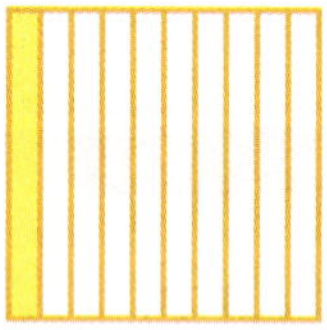

6. 

7. 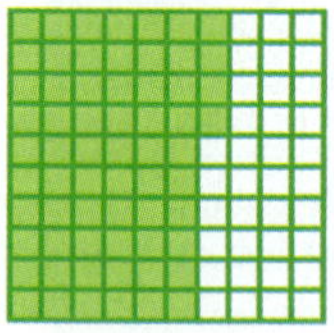

8. 

9. 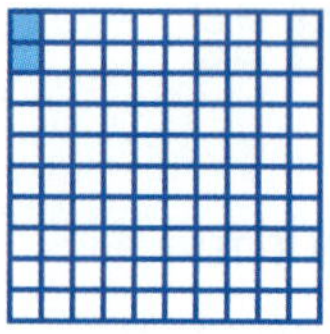

10. 

11. 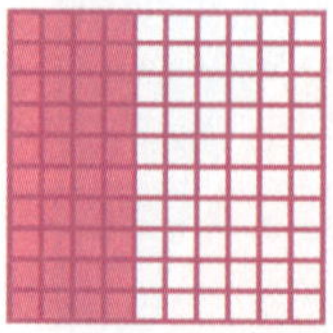

12. 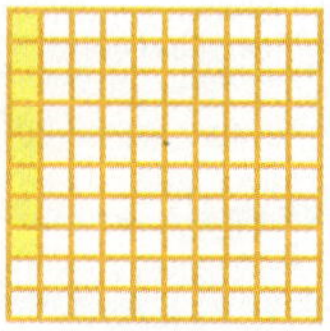

DIGITAL Animated Glossary **www.pearsonsuccessnet.com**

For another example, see Set A on page 324.

Tenths are ten equal parts of a whole or a set.

A decimal point is a dot used to separate ones from tenths in a number.

A decimal is a number with one or more digits to the right of the decimal point. Tenths can be written as a fraction or a decimal.

Three tenths of the set of markers is green. Three tenths can be written as $\frac{3}{10}$ or 0.3.

A tiled wall is made up of 100 tiles that are the same size and shape. Joel painted 27 of the tiles orange. What part of the whole wall did he paint orange?

Hundredths are one hundred equal parts of a whole or a set.

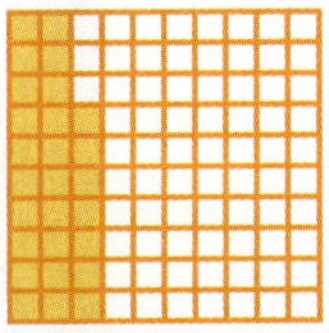

Joel painted $\frac{27}{100}$ or 0.27 of the wall.

In **13–15**, use the pictures below. Mike cut each kind of food he served at a party into tenths. For each kind of food, write a fraction and a decimal for the part that is left.

13. Rice

14. Pasta

15. Potatoes

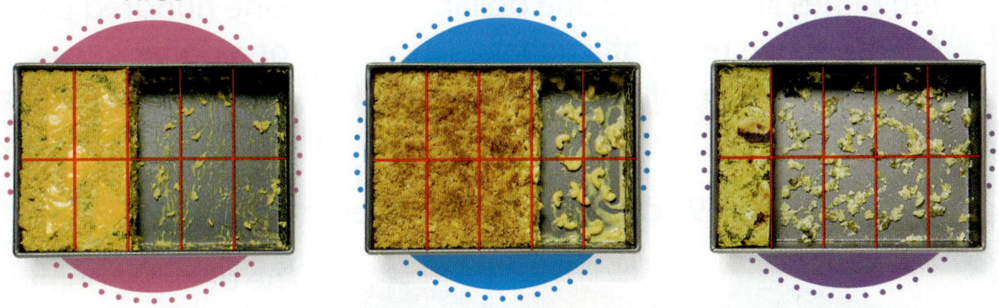

For **16** and **17**, use the sign at the right.

16. **Estimation** Which costs more, boots and one jacket or one winter coat? Use estimation to decide. Explain how you got your answer.

17. Mr. Murti wants to buy a winter coat for himself and one for his son. What is the total cost of the coats?

Data

Ace Clothing Shop Sale

Item	Cost
Boots	$129
Jacket	$87
Pants	$64
Winter Coat	$238

18. A fairy fly is the world's smallest insect. It is $\frac{1}{100}$ inch long. Write the length of a fairy fly as a decimal.

19. Jeremy shaded $\frac{4}{10}$ of the figure at the right. Which decimal equals $\frac{4}{10}$?

A 4.0 **B** 0.440 **C** 0.4 **D** 0.04

Lesson 13-2

Prepares for 4.3.a The student will read, write, represent, and identify decimals expressed through thousandths.

Using Money to Understand Decimals

Hands-On money

How are decimals and fractions related to money?

How could Ben pay for the popcorn with only dollars, dimes, and pennies?

dollar bill	quarter	dime	nickel	penny
1 dollar	25 cents	10 cents	5 cents	1 cent
$1 or $1.00	25¢ or $0.25	10¢ or $0.10	5¢ or $0.05	1¢ or $0.01

Another Example **What are other ways to write money amounts?**

You can use what you have learned about place value for whole numbers to help you understand place value for money amounts.

Ten dimes are equal to one dollar.
A dime is one tenth of a dollar.
Each dime has a value of $0.10 or 10¢.

One hundred pennies are equal to one dollar.
A penny is one hundredth of a dollar.
Each penny has a value of $0.01 or 1¢.

The amount $4.95 can be made in different ways.

The decimal point is read by saying *and*. So $4.95 is read as *4 dollars and 95 cents*.

$4.95 = 4 dollars + 9 dimes + 5 pennies ← **Expanded Form**
4.95 = 4 ones + 9 tenths + 5 hundredths

$4.95 = 4 dollars + 95 pennies
4.95 = 4 ones + 95 hundredths

Explain It

1. How is a dime one tenth of a dollar?
2. How is a penny one hundredth of a dollar?
3. Write the cost of the yarn in expanded form.

One Way

Ben can use 1 dollar, 2 dimes, and 4 pennies.

$1.24

Another Way

Ben can use 1 dollar and 24 pennies.

$1.24

Other Examples

Four quarters make a dollar. So each quarter is $\frac{1}{4}$ of a dollar.

Write $\frac{1}{4}$ of a dollar using a decimal point.

One quarter is $\frac{1}{4}$ of a dollar.

$\frac{1}{4} = \frac{25}{100}$

$\frac{1}{4}$ of a dollar = $0.25

Write $\frac{1}{2}$ of a dollar using a decimal point.

Two quarters are $\frac{1}{2}$ of a dollar.

$\frac{1}{2} = \frac{50}{100}$

$\frac{1}{2}$ of a dollar = $0.50

Write $\frac{3}{4}$ of a dollar using a decimal point.

Three quarters are $\frac{3}{4}$ of a dollar.

$\frac{3}{4} = \frac{75}{100}$

$\frac{3}{4}$ of a dollar = $0.75

Guided Practice*

Do you know HOW?

1. Copy and complete. $3.62 = ▢ dollars + ▢ dimes + ▢ pennies

3.62 = ▢ ones + ▢ tenths + ▢ hundredths

3.62 = ▢ ones + ▢ hundredths

2. Write one and four hundredths as a decimal.

Do you UNDERSTAND?

3. In the example above, what is another way to show $1.24?

4. How could you show $4.17 with only dollars, dimes, and pennies?

DIGITAL eTools www.pearsonsuccessnet.com

*For another example, see Set A on page 324.

Independent Practice

Leveled Practice In **5–10**, copy and complete.

5. $6.45 = ___ dollars + 4 dimes + 5 pennies or 6 dollars + 45 pennies
6.45 = 6 ones + ___ tenths + ___ hundredths or ___ ones + ___ hundredths

6. $8.09 = ___ dollars + ___ dimes + ___ pennies or ___ dollars + 9 pennies
8.09 = ___ ones + ___ tenths + ___ hundredths or ___ ones + ___ hundredths

7. $2.39 = ___ dollars + ___ dimes + ___ pennies or ___ dollars + ___ pennies
2.39 = ___ ones + ___ tenths + ___ hundredths or ___ ones + ___ hundredths

8. $5.07 = ___ dollars + ___ dimes + ___ pennies or ___ dollars + ___ pennies
5.07 = ___ ones + ___ tenths + ___ hundredths or ___ ones + ___ hundredths

9. $4.80 = ___ dollars + ___ dimes + ___ pennies or ___ dollars + ___ pennies
4.80 = ___ ones + ___ tenths + ___ hundredths or ___ ones + ___ hundredths

10. $9.65 = ___ dollars + ___ dimes + ___ pennies or ___ dollars + ___ pennies
9.65 = ___ ones + ___ tenths + ___ hundredths or ___ ones + ___ hundredths

In **11–14**, write each number with a decimal point.

11. seven and fifty-two hundredths

12. eight and twelve hundredths

13. one and ninety-six hundredths

14. three and six hundredths

Problem Solving

In **15** and **16**, draw a picture of bills and coins that equal the amount of each price.

Tip *Draw rectangles for dollars and circles with letters for coins.*

15.

16.

17. **Writing to Explain** Marnie has two dollars and fifteen pennies. Alfred has two dollars, one dime, and eight pennies. Who has a greater amount of money? Explain how you decided.

18. **Reasoning** Carl has two dollar bills, nine dimes, and 6 pennies. What coins does he need to make $3.00?

19. Tamiya has 23 pennies. How many hundredths of a dollar does she have?

20. Lars and Evelyn each have $1.38 in bills and coins. They have different coins. Show two ways to make $1.38. Draw a picture of each set of bills and coins.

21. Use a piece of grid paper. Draw a shape with one line of symmetry.

Use the table at the right for **22** and **23**.

22. Ms. Evans bought one quart of paint. She paid the exact price with six dollar bills and fourteen pennies. From which store did she buy the paint?

23. Mr. Park bought one quart of paint. He paid the exact price with dollars and coins. He used only one penny. From which store did he buy the paint?

Data

1 Quart of Paint

Store	Price
A-1 Supplies	$6.48
Crafts and More	$6.14
Paint Station	$6.04
Wagner's	$6.41

24. Draw another set of bills and coins to make the same amount as shown.

25. It costs the United States Mint about 4 hundredths of a dollar to make a quarter. Write 4 hundredths using a decimal point.

26. Which money amount represents $\frac{1}{4}$ of a dollar?

A $1.40
B $0.40
C $0.25
D $0.14

SOL Prep

27. Which money amount represents 4 dollars, 7 dimes, and 3 pennies?

A $4.38
B $4.73
C $40.73
D $47.03

Virginia

Lesson 13-3

Prepares for 4.5.c The student will add and subtract decimals.

Adding and Subtracting Money

How can you add and subtract money?

Neta wants to buy a flower pot and a picture frame. What is the total cost of the two items?

? cost in all

$5.47	$6.89

Choose an Operation

$5.47 + $6.89 = ▢

Another Example How can you subtract money?

The items Nancy bought cost a total of $12.36. She pays with $20. How much change should she get?

You can use what you have learned about subtracting across zero in Lesson 4-5 to help you understand subtracting money amounts.

$20

$12.36	?

Step 1

Line up the decimal points. Write $20 as $20.00. Subtract as you would with whole numbers.

```
      9  9
  1  10 10 10
 $2  0. 0  0
-  1 2. 3  6
     7  6  4
```

Step 2

Write the answer in dollars and cents.

```
      9  9
  1  10 10 10
 $2  0. 0  0
-  1 2. 3  6
   $7.  6  4
```

Write the dollar sign and the decimal point.

Nancy should get $7.64 in change.

Explain It

1. Suppose the total cost of the items Nancy bought was $19.36. Write the change she should get from $20 in two ways.
2. Use the prices at the top of the page. Maurice wants to buy a radio and a calculator. How much change should he get from $50?

Step 1

Line up the decimal points in the addends. Add as you would with whole numbers.

$$\begin{array}{r} \scriptsize{1\ 1} \\ \$5.47 \\ +\ \ 6.89 \\ \hline 12\ 36 \end{array}$$

Remember to regroup if needed.

Step 2

Write the answer in dollars and cents.

$$\begin{array}{r} \scriptsize{1\ 1} \\ \$5.47 \\ +\ \ 6.89 \\ \hline \$12.36 \end{array}$$

Write the dollar sign and the decimal point.

The total cost of the flower pot and the picture frame is $12.36.

Guided Practice*

Do you know HOW?

In **1–4**, find the sum or difference.

1. $\begin{array}{r} \$3.85 \\ +\ \ 9.76 \\ \hline \end{array}$

2. $\begin{array}{r} \$10.07 \\ -\ \ 1.68 \\ \hline \end{array}$

3. $17.62 + $4.93

4. $20.00 − $3.64

Do you UNDERSTAND?

5. In the example above, Neta estimated that $13.00 would be enough to pay for the total cost of her items. Would $13.00 be enough? Explain.

6. Use the prices on page 312. Bo wants to buy a clock and a radio. What is the total cost of these items?

Independent Practice

In **7–20**, find each sum or difference.

7. $\begin{array}{r} \$2.87 \\ +\ \ 5.46 \\ \hline \end{array}$

8. $\begin{array}{r} \$6.24 \\ +\ \ 9.97 \\ \hline \end{array}$

9. $\begin{array}{r} \$10.00 \\ -\ \ 7.23 \\ \hline \end{array}$

10. $\begin{array}{r} \$25.00 \\ -\ 14.39 \\ \hline \end{array}$

11. $\begin{array}{r} \$30.00 \\ -\ 27.14 \\ \hline \end{array}$

12. $\begin{array}{r} \$13.06 \\ +\ \ 9.56 \\ \hline \end{array}$

13. $\begin{array}{r} \$0.75 \\ +\ \ 8.49 \\ \hline \end{array}$

14. $\begin{array}{r} \$10.50 \\ -\ \ 3.62 \\ \hline \end{array}$

15. $4.00 − $2.64

16. $20.00 − $6.81

17. $3.75 + $9.82

18. $1.00 − $0.36

19. $40.00 − $28.15

20. $9.09 + $2.83

*For another example, see Set B on page 324.

Independent Practice

In **21–27**, find each sum or difference.

21. $20.00 − 15.37

22. $14.69 + 8.72

23. $0.58 + 6.73

24. $10.00 − 4.91

25. $5.00 − $3.74

26. $15.74 + $7.26

27. $40.20 − $23.10

Problem Solving

Norma and Devon compared the prices of four backpacks. The table at the right shows the prices. Use the table for **28–31**.

Data: Cost of Backpacks

Brand	Cost
A	$24.19
B	$26.09
C	$22.99
D	$20.39

28. Which brand costs more, Brand A or Brand B? Find how much more.

29. Norma will buy Brand B and Brand D. She will pay with $50. How much change should she get?

30. Devon decided to buy Brand A. He paid with $40. How much change should he get?

31. What is the total cost of Brand C and Brand D?

? cost in all

$22.99	$20.39

32. **Algebra** Copy and complete by writing the missing number in each pattern.

25, 50, 75, 100, ▢, 150
75, 70, 65, 60, ▢, 50

33. When the euro became the official money of Europe, $1 U.S. was equal to 0.87 euro. How many euros would you receive for $2 U.S.?

34. Lou used a $5 bill to buy a box of cereal that cost $4.62. How much change did he get?

A $9.62 **B** $1.38 **C** 62¢ **D** 38¢

35. **Think About the Process** Deena bought a pair of socks that cost $3.72. She paid with $10.00. Which number sentence shows how to find how much change she should get back?

A $10.00 − $3.72 = ▢
B $10.00 + $3.72 = ▢
C $10.00 ÷ $3.72 = ▢
D $10.00 × $3.72 = ▢

Enrichment

At Most and At Least

The symbol $\leq$ is read "is less than or equal to."

What whole numbers make this number sentence true?

$\square \leq 6$

The whole numbers 0, 1, 2, 3, 4, 5, and **6** make this number sentence true. The greatest whole number that makes this number sentence true is 6.

The value of $\square$ is ***at most*** 6.

The symbol $\geq$ is read "is greater than or equal to."

What whole numbers make this number sentence true?

$\square \geq 4$

The whole numbers **4**, 5, 6, 7, 8, and so on, make this number sentence true. The least whole number that makes this number sentence true is 4.

The value of $\square$ is ***at least*** 4.

Practice

List the whole numbers that make each number sentence true.

1. $\square \leq 2$

2. $\square \geq 5$

3. $\square \leq 7$

4. $\square \geq 8$

5. $\square \geq 13$

6. $\square \leq 1$

7. $\square \leq 6$

8. $\square \leq 10$

9. $\square \geq 15$

Describe each list of numbers using ***at most*** or ***at least***. Then use $\geq$ or $\leq$ to write a number sentence for each list.

10. 0, 1, 2, 3, 4

11. 9, 10, 11, 12, and so on

12. 0, 1, 2, 3, 4, 5, 6, 7, 8, 9

13. 3, 4, 5, 6, 7, and so on

14. 20, 21, 22, 23, and so on

15. 0, 1, 2, 3, 4, 5, 6

16. Sara started with a package of 12 pens. She gave at least 2 of the pens to friends. How many pens might Sara have left? List all the possible answers. Describe your list using ***at most*** or ***at least***.

17. Miguel is in at least 3 scenes in the school play. The play has 6 scenes in all. Is Miguel in at least half of the scenes? Explain.

Virginia

Lesson 13-4

Prepares for 4.5.c The student will add and subtract decimals.

Problem Solving

Draw a Picture and Write a Number Sentence

Alex earns money by walking dogs. The table shows how much he earned and how much he spent for each of three months. What were Alex's total earnings for May and June?

Data

Month	Earned	Spent
May	\$11.25	\$4.35
June	\$20.25	\$7.80
July	\$13.50	\$5.95

Another Example

In what other kinds of situations can you draw pictures to help choose an operation?

Use Alex's table at the top of the page. In May, how much more was the amount Alex earned than the amount he spent?

Read and Understand

Use a diagram to show what you know.

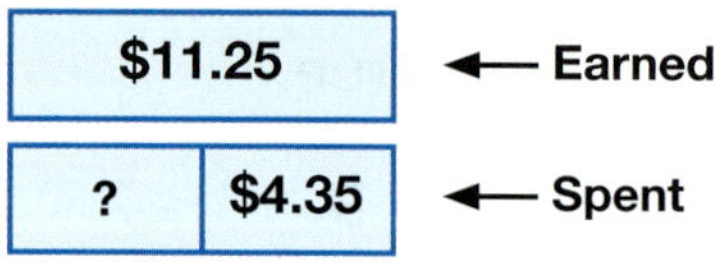

Since you are comparing amounts, you can subtract.

\$11.25 − \$4.35 = ▢

Plan and Solve

Subtract to solve the problem.

$$\begin{array}{r} \overset{0}{\cancel{\$1}}\overset{10}{\cancel{1}}.\overset{12}{\cancel{2}}5 \\ -\ 4.35 \\ \hline \$6.90 \end{array}$$

Alex earned \$6.90 more than he spent.

Explain It

1. Suppose Tammy wrote \$4.35 + ? = \$11.25 for the diagram above. Is this number sentence correct? Explain.

2. Once a month Alex puts \$5 into a savings account. How much does he put into the account in 1 year? Draw a picture and write a number sentence to solve.

Tip *There are 12 months in 1 year.*

Plan and Solve

Use a diagram to show what you know. Then write a number sentence.

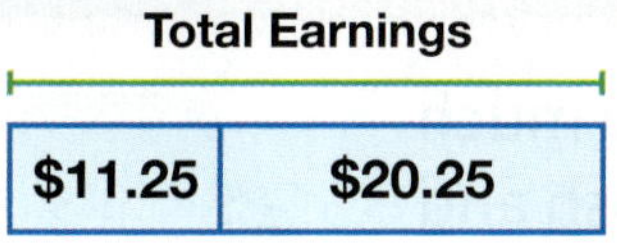

You know the two parts. Add to find the total.

$\$11.25 + \$20.25 = \square$

Solve and Answer

Add to solve the problem.

$$\begin{array}{r} \overset{1}{} \\ \$11.25 \\ +\ 20.25 \\ \hline \$31.50 \end{array}$$

In May and June, Alex earned a total of $31.50.

Guided Practice*

Do you know HOW?

Draw a picture and write a number sentence to solve.

1. Miyoko had a piece of ribbon that was $\frac{7}{8}$ yard long. She cut off $\frac{2}{8}$ yard to make a bow. She used the rest of the ribbon to make a tail for her kite. How much ribbon did she use for the kite?

Do you UNDERSTAND?

2. Anna needs $\frac{3}{8}$ yard of yarn for each bracelet she makes. Explain how to find how much yarn she needs for 2 bracelets.

3. **Write a Problem** Write a problem with fractions that you can solve by drawing a picture and writing a number sentence.

Independent Practice

For **4–5**, draw a picture and write a number sentence to solve.

4. Gus had $10. He spent $3.87 at the hobby shop. How much money does Gus have left?

5. Last week Bev earned $5.75. This week she earned $6.50. How much did she earn in the 2 weeks?

Stuck? Try this....

- What do I know?
- What am I asked to find?
- What diagram can I use to help understand the problem?
- Can I use addition, subtraction, multiplication, or division?
- Is all of my work correct?
- Did I answer the right question?
- Is my answer reasonable?

For another example, see Set C on page 325.

Independent Practice

6. Josh wants to buy some art supplies. How much money does Josh need to buy a paint brush and 4 jars of paint?

Tip *First find the cost of 4 jars of paint.*

Data

Art Supplies	
Jar of paint	$4
Marker	$3
Paint brush	$6

7. Gloria and Louisa both walk to school. Gloria lives 9 blocks from school. Louisa lives 6 blocks from school. How much farther does Gloria have to walk than Louisa?

For **8** and **9**, use the pictograph.

8. Mrs. Riley's class voted on which kind of activity they should do during gym time. The pictograph shows the results. Which activity received the most votes?

9. **Writing to Explain** How do you know that two activities did not receive the same number of votes?

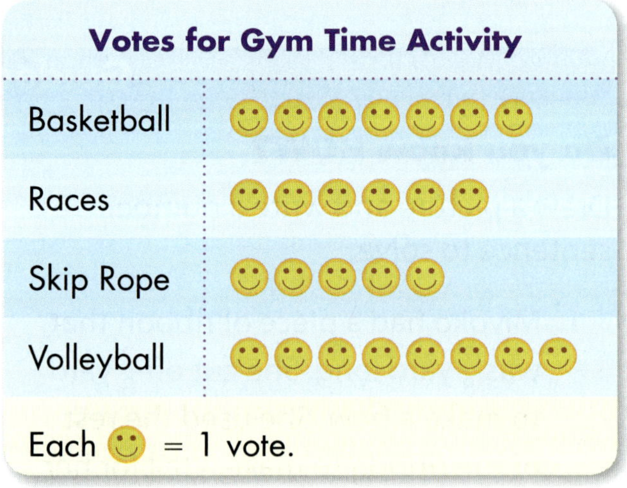

10. Leo colored $\frac{3}{5}$ of a flag blue. Then he colored another $\frac{1}{5}$ of the same flag yellow. What fraction of the flag did he color in all?

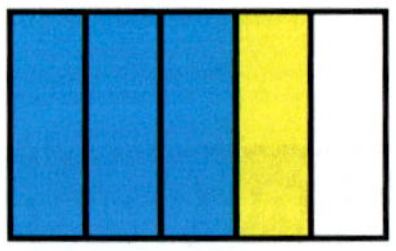

Think About the Process

11. Each week has 7 days. Which of the following is used to find out how many days are in 2 weeks?

A $7 - 2$ **C** $7 \div 2$

B $2 + 7$ **D** 2×7

12. Mr. Wilson's class has 27 students. Mrs. Pak's class has 32 students. Which number sentence shows how many more students are in Mrs. Pak's class than are in Mr. Wilson's class?

A $32 - 27 = \square$ **C** $32 \div 27 = \square$

B $32 + 27 = \square$ **D** $32 \times 27 = \square$

Stop and Practice

Estimate and then find each sum. Check that your answer is reasonable.

1. $\begin{array}{r} 24 \\ +\ 65 \\ \hline \end{array}$
2. $\begin{array}{r} 39 \\ +\ 76 \\ \hline \end{array}$
3. $\begin{array}{r} 638 \\ +\ 823 \\ \hline \end{array}$
4. $\begin{array}{r} 4{,}207 \\ +\ 1{,}985 \\ \hline \end{array}$

Estimate. Then find each difference. Check that your answer is reasonable.

5. $\begin{array}{r} 83 \\ -\ 27 \\ \hline \end{array}$
6. $\begin{array}{r} 285 \\ -\ 89 \\ \hline \end{array}$
7. $\begin{array}{r} 602 \\ -\ 234 \\ \hline \end{array}$
8. $\begin{array}{r} 5{,}413 \\ -\ 2{,}278 \\ \hline \end{array}$

Find each product.

9. 4×7 **10.** 7×9 **11.** 0×8 **12.** 10×6 **13.** 8×5

14. 7×8 **15.** 5×9 **16.** 4×3 **17.** 3×9 **18.** 2×10

Find each quotient.

19. $54 \div 6$ **20.** $40 \div 8$ **21.** $18 \div 3$ **22.** $45 \div 5$ **23.** $72 \div 9$

24. $36 \div 9$ **25.** $63 \div 7$ **26.** $42 \div 6$ **27.** $21 \div 7$ **28.** $18 \div 9$

Error Search Find each sum or difference that is not correct. Write it correctly and explain the error. For **31** and **32**, you may use fraction strips or draw a picture to help.

29. $\begin{array}{r} 183 \\ +\ 127 \\ \hline 310 \end{array}$
30. $\begin{array}{r} 685 \\ -\ 289 \\ \hline 404 \end{array}$
31. $\frac{2}{5} + \frac{1}{5} = \frac{1}{5}$
32. $\frac{7}{8} - \frac{3}{8} = \frac{1}{4}$

Number Sense

Estimating and Reasoning Write true or false for each statement. If it is false, explain why.

33. $3 \times 10 > 300$

34. $27 \div 3 > 10$

35. $90 + 8 < 100$

36. $\frac{1}{4} + \frac{2}{4} > 1$

37. $\$3.65 + 2.95 > \$5.00$

38. $\$6.84 - \$5.00 > \$1.00$

Virginia

Lesson 13-5

Prepares for 4.4.d The student will solve single-step and multistep addition, subtraction, and multiplication problems with whole numbers.

Problem Solving

Missing or Extra Information

Ruth bought one CD, one DVD, and one package of blank tapes. She spent a total of $25 on the CD and DVD. If Ruth started with $45, how much money did she have left?

Guided Practice*

Do you know HOW?

Tell what information is missing.

1. Brad bought 3 tapes for a total of $9. He also bought some CDs that cost $10 each. How much did Brad spend in all?

Do you UNDERSTAND?

2. For Problem 1, make up the missing information and solve.

3. **Write a Problem** Write a problem that has extra information about the cost of school supplies.

Independent Practice

Decide if the problem has extra or missing information. Solve if you have enough information.

4. Pablo collects coins. He has 24 coins from Mexico, 14 coins from Canada, and 6 coins from Italy. How many more coins does he have from Mexico than from Canada?

5. Each minute, the U.S. Treasury Department makes about 30,000 coins and prints about 24,300 bills. What is the total value of the money produced each minute?

Stuck? Try this....

- What do I know?
- What am I asked to find?
- What diagram can I use to help understand the problem?
- Can I use addition, subtraction, multiplication, or division?
- Is all of my work correct?
- Did I answer the right question?
- Is my answer reasonable?

**For another example, see Set D on page 325.*

Plan and Solve

Draw a diagram to show what you know and what you want to find.

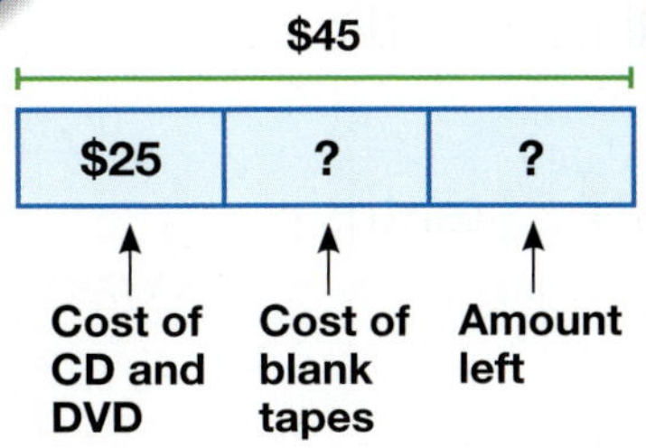

Is any information missing that you need before you can solve the problem?

Yes, I need to know the cost of the blank tapes so I can find the total Ruth spent. Then I can find how much she had left.

Is there extra information not needed to solve the problem?

No, there is no extra information.

For **6–9**, decide if each problem has extra or missing information. If information is missing, make up the information. Then solve.

Use the pictograph for **6** and **7**.

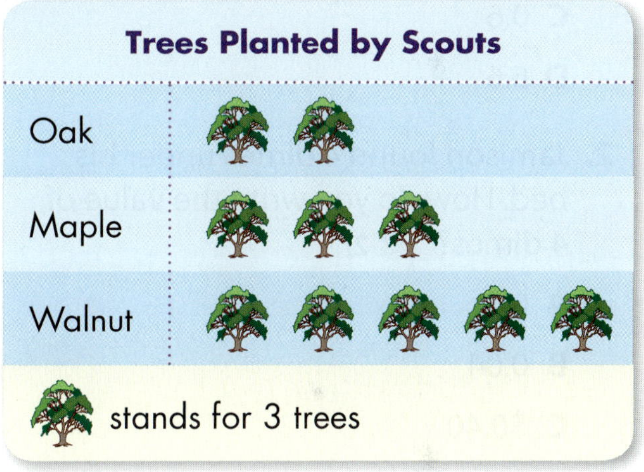

6. The scouts spent 2 hours planting oak trees and 4 hours planting maple trees. How many oak and maple trees did they plant?

7. The scouts also planted twice as many pine trees as walnut trees. How many pine trees did they plant?

8. Stacy spent $24 on 20 yards of material to make curtains. She used all of the material to make 4 curtains, all the same size. How much material did she use for each curtain?

9. Nick is planting 36 flowers in rows in his garden. His garden is 10 feet long and 2 feet wide. How many rows of flowers can Nick plant?

10. Frances has 24 colored pencils and 14 markers. What information is needed to find the number of her pencils that are **NOT** red?

A The total number of pencils and markers

B The number of pencils that are red

C The number of markers that are blue

D The number of markers that are red

1. In the talent show, 6 out of the 10 acts were singing. Larry shaded $\frac{6}{10}$ in the figure. (13-1)

Which decimal equals $\frac{6}{10}$?

A 0.006

B 0.06

C 0.6

D 6.6

2. Jamison found 4 dimes under his bed. How do you write the value of 4 dimes? (13-2)

A 0.4

B 0.04

C $0.40

D $0.04

3. Elena has 6 tennis balls, 12 golf balls, 2 basketballs, and some softballs in the gym closet. What other information is needed to find how many softballs Elena has? (13-5)

A How many balls she has in all

B How many soccer balls she has

C How big the gym closet is

D How often she plays softball

4. What is the missing number? (13-2)

$3.49 = 3 dollars + ☐ dimes + 9 pennies

3.49 = 3 ones + ☐ tenths + 9 hundredths

A 3

B 4

C 6

D 9

5. Celia spent $24.36 on one pair of jeans and $28.65 on a second pair. How much more did the second pair cost than the first? (13-3)

A $53.01

B $5.29

C $4.79

D $4.29

6. How much is $\frac{1}{4}$ of a dollar? (13-2)

A $0.25

B $0.40

C $0.50

D $0.75

7. How much change should Lucia get back from $20 if she spent $9.48? (13-3)

A $9.52

B $10.52

C $11.42

D $11.52

8. Maria spent $11 on a shirt, $25 on pants, $12 on a CD, and $19 on sandals. How much did Maria spend in all on things to wear? (13-5)

A $48

B $55

C $56

D $67

9. Jason wants a shirt that costs $13.89 and a CD that costs $9.95. How much is his total before tax? (13-3)

A $24.84

B $23.85

C $23.84

D $23.74

10. What fraction and decimal represent the part that is blue? (13-1)

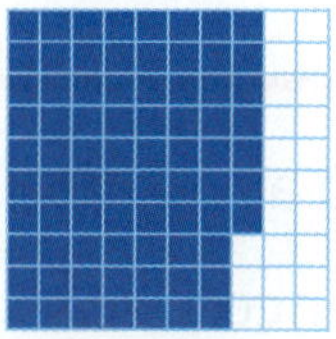

A $\frac{77}{10}$ and 0.77

B $\frac{77}{100}$ and 0.077

C $\frac{77}{100}$ and 7.7

D $\frac{77}{100}$ and 0.77

11. Each day the Video Shop has early morning special prices. From 8:00 A.M. to 10:00 A.M., a CD costs $12.75 and a DVD costs $16.35. At 9:00 A.M., Tia buys a DVD and gives the clerk a $20 bill. What information is not needed to find how much change Tia gets? (13-5)

A The cost of a CD

B The cost of a DVD

C How much Tia gave the clerk

D The time of day

12. Chelle used ham or turkey to make sandwiches. She spent $9.75 on turkey and $3.25 on ham. Which picture models how much Chelle spent on meat for sandwiches? (13-4)

A

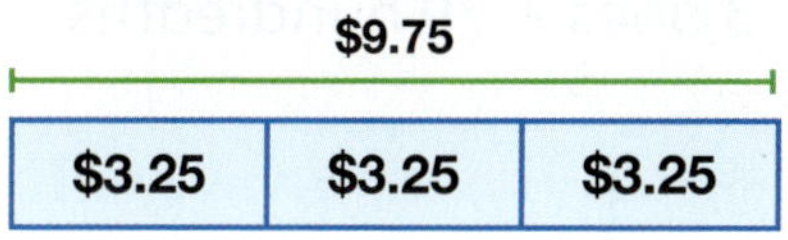

B

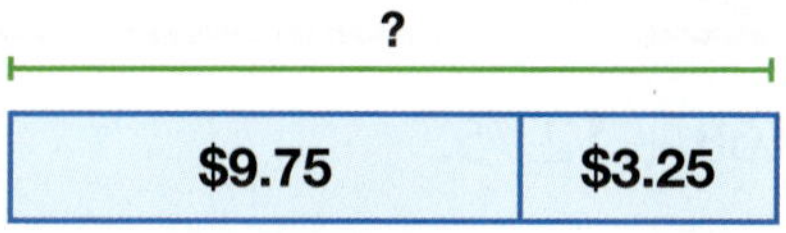

C

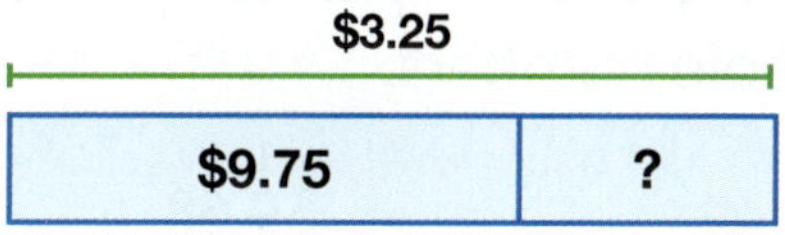

D

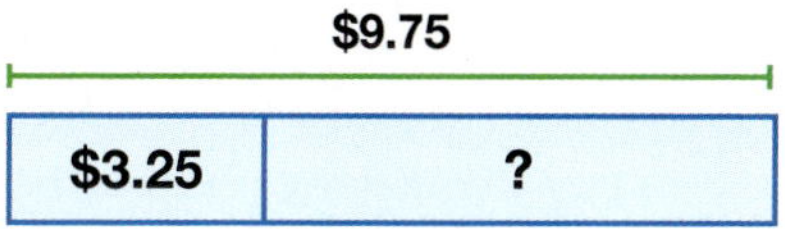

Set A, pages 306–311

Tenths can be written as fractions or as decimals.

$\frac{4}{10}$ or 0.4

Hundredths can be written as fractions or as decimals.

$\frac{23}{100}$ or 0.23

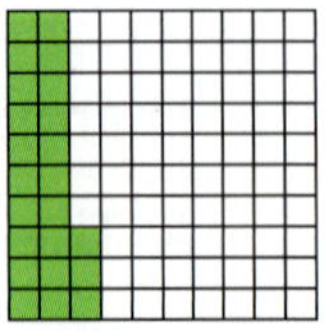

Money amounts are written as decimals.

\$3.79 = 3 dollars + 7 dimes + 9 pennies or
3 ones + 79 pennies

3.79 = 3 ones + 7 tenths + 9 hundredths or
3 ones + 79 hundredths

Remember that tenths are 10 equal parts of a whole. Hundredths are 100 equal parts of a whole.

In **1** and **2**, write a fraction and a decimal for each shaded part.

1.

2.

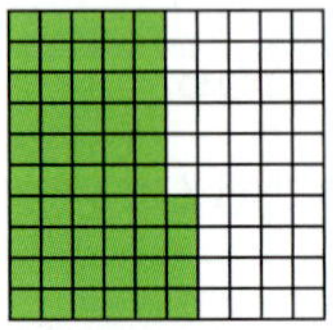

In **3** and **4**, copy and complete.

3. \$5.36 = ☐ dollars + ☐ dimes + ☐ pennies
5.36 = ☐ ones + ☐ tenths + ☐ hundredths

4. \$7.04 = ☐ dollars + ☐ dimes + ☐ pennies
7.04 = ☐ ones + ☐ tenths + ☐ hundredths

Set B, pages 312–314

Find \$9.68 + \$2.75.

Line up the decimal points. Add as you would with whole numbers.

```
   1 1
  $9.68
+  2.75
 $12.43
```

Write the answer in dollars and cents.

Find \$10.00 − \$3.26.

Line up the decimal points. Subtract as you would with whole numbers.

```
      9  9
  0 10 10 10
 $1  0. 0  0
 −   3. 2  6
    $6. 7  4
```

Write the answer in dollars and cents.

Remember to regroup as needed.

Find the sum or difference.

1. \$4.97 + 5.36

2. \$20.00 + 9.28

3. \$18.54 + 4.76

4. \$30.00 − 7.19

5. \$25.00 − 14.38

6. \$12.00 − 9.82

Set C, pages 316–318

Ed has \$6.95. Al has \$8.89. How much more does Al have than Ed?

Use a diagram to show what you know. You are comparing amounts, so subtract.

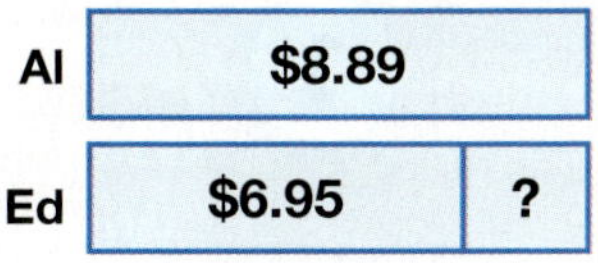

$$\begin{array}{r} \scriptstyle 7\ \ 18 \\ \$\not{8}.\not{8}\,9 \\ -\ 6.9\,5 \\ \hline \$1.9\,4 \end{array}$$

Al has \$1.94 more than Ed.

Remember to draw a picture.

Solve. Draw a picture and write a number sentence.

1. Ira had \$20. He gave \$7.50 to Tom. How much did Ira have left?
2. Kate babysat 3 times last month. She earned \$9.50, \$16.75, and \$12. How much did she earn in all?

Set D, pages 320–321

To solve a problem with a lot of information, follow these steps.

Step 1 Find the main idea and the key facts and details in the problem.

Step 2 Cross out any extra information.

Step 3 Solve the problem if you have enough information.

Does this problem have extra information? Is there missing information that is needed?

Meg collects stamps. She has 36 flower stamps, 24 bird stamps, and more than 20 fish stamps. How many bird and fish stamps does she have?

The number of flower stamps is extra information. The exact number of fish stamps is missing information that is needed to solve the problem.

Remember to make sure you understand what information is needed to solve the problem.

Decide if each problem has extra information or missing information. If there is enough information, solve the problem. If not, tell what is missing.

1. Three friends spent \$24 to buy lunch. They also bought a magazine for \$4. They shared the cost of buying lunch equally. How much did each person spend on lunch?
2. Anna bought 4 yards of cloth to make pillows. She paid \$4 per yard for the cloth. How many pillows can Anna make?

Topic 14 Customary Measurement

1. What is the record length of the "World's Longest Apple Peel?" You will find out in Lesson 14-3.

2. This kind of hat is sometimes called a 10-gallon hat. Does it really hold ten gallons? You will find out in Lesson 14-4.

3

Mark Twain is a famous author. What does his name have to do with a unit of measure? You will find out in Lesson 14-1.

4

Owen, a baby hippo, and Mzee, a giant tortoise, met after a tsunami. When they first met, how much more did Mzee weigh than Owen? You will find out in Lesson 14-5.

Review What You Know!

Vocabulary

Choose the best term from the box.

- estimate
- factor
- fraction
- multiply

1. When you find 3 × 4, you __?__.

2. When you find a number that is about how many, you __?__.

3. If a whole is divided into equal parts, each part is a __?__ of the whole.

Fractions and Length

Find what part of the length of the 1 strip the other strips show. Write the fraction.

4.

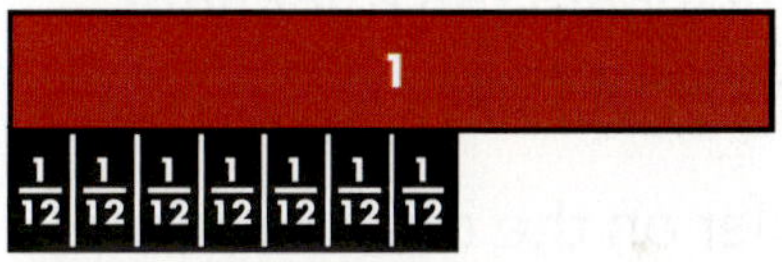

5.

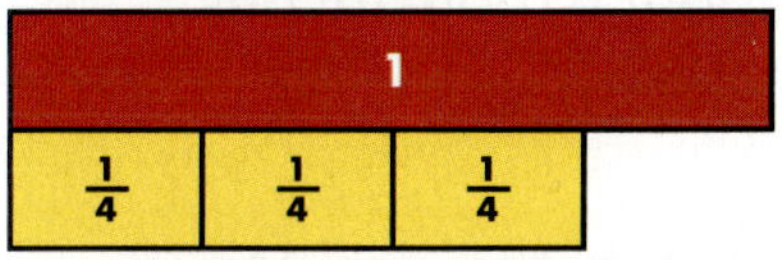

Multiplication

Find each product.

6. 3 × 12 **7.** 6 × 10 **8.** 5 × 3

9. 2 × 11 **10.** 4 × 6 **11.** 6 × 12

12. **Writing to Explain** Kim has had 3 skating lessons each month for 12 months. How many lessons has she had? Explain how an array could help you solve this problem. Then solve the problem.

Virginia

Lesson 14-1

3.9.a The student will estimate and use U.S. Customary and metric units to measure length to the nearest $\frac{1}{2}$ inch, inch, foot, yard, centimeter, and meter.

Understanding Measurement

Hands-On

inch ruler

How can you describe the length of an object in different ways?

Measure the length of your desktop in pencil-lengths and in crayon-lengths.

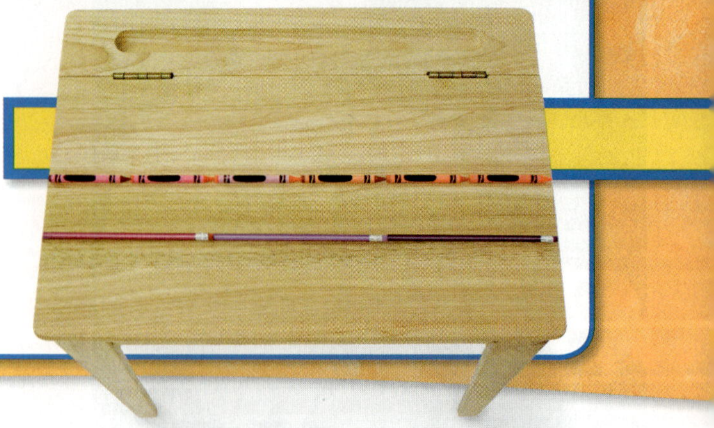

Another Example **How can you use inches to measure?**

Find the length of the desktop in inches.

To use a ruler, line up the object with the 0 mark.

You may need to move the ruler to continue measuring. If so, make sure that you mark where the ruler ends before you move it.

When the ruler on the desk is moved, it will show about 6 more inches.

$12 + 6 = 18$

To the nearest inch, this desktop is 18 inches long.

Explain It

1. Estimate the length of your shoe in inches. Explain how you got your estimate.
2. Find the length of a pen to the nearest inch.
3. Explain why using a ruler is a better way to measure length than using a crayon.

Find the length.
More crayon-lengths than pencil-lengths equal the length of the desktop.

The desktop is 3 pencil-lengths or 6 crayon-lengths long.

Compare the units.
The crayon-length is a smaller unit than the pencil-length.

The smaller the unit used, the more units are needed to equal a given length.

Use a standard unit.
People use standard units to describe measurements.

A standard unit for measuring length is the **inch (in.)**.

1 inch

Guided Practice*

Do you know HOW?

Estimate each length. Then measure to the nearest inch.

1. 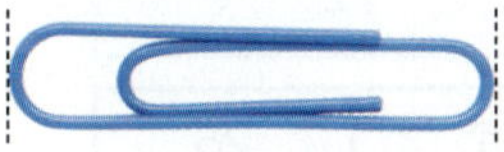

2. 

3. 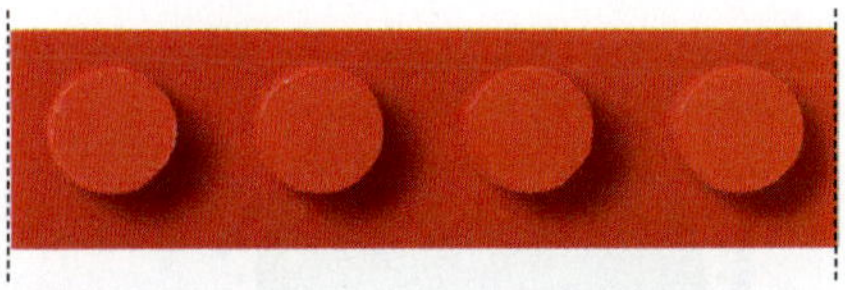

Do you UNDERSTAND?

4. In the example above, are more pencil-lengths or crayon-lengths equal to the length of the desktop?

5. Find the length of your desktop in paper clip-lengths. First estimate the length in paper clips.

6. What is the length of the candle to the nearest inch?

Independent Practice

In **7–10**, estimate each length. Then measure to the nearest inch.

7. 

8. 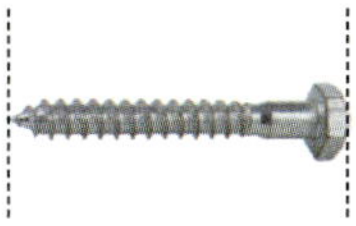

9. 

10. 

DIGITAL
Animated Glossary, eTools
www.pearsonsuccessnet.com

**For another example, see Set A on page 346.*

Independent Practice

In **11–13**, estimate each length. Then measure to the nearest inch.

11. 

12. 

13. 

Problem Solving

14. A marker is 4 times as long as a piece of chalk. The piece of chalk is 2 inches long. How long is the marker?

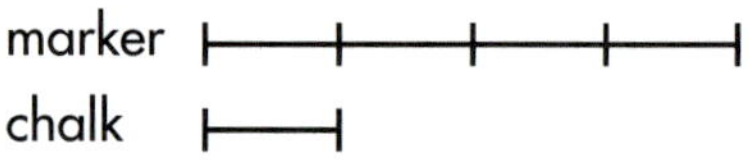

15. Kevin's father is 72 inches tall. He is 26 inches taller than Kevin. How tall is Kevin?

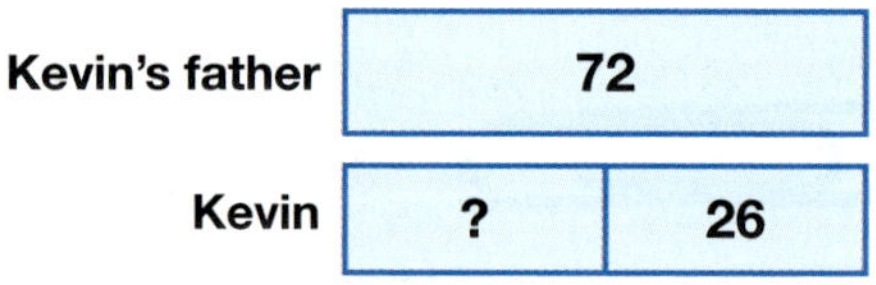

16. **Number Sense** Jeff's hand is 3 large paper clips long. Alan's hand is 8 small paper clips long. Could their hands be the same size? Explain. How would standard units help?

17. **Writing to Explain** You have a piece of string and a ruler. How can you decide how long this curve is?

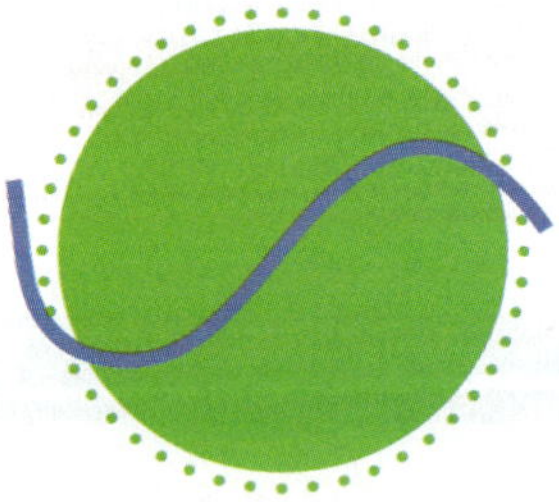

18. **Reasoning** The author Mark Twain's name is taken from riverboat slang. "Mark twain" meant "Mark two" for 2 fathoms. Two fathoms are equal to 12 feet. Which measurement unit is longer, a fathom or a foot?

Algebra In **19–24**, copy and complete each number sentence.

19. 35 + ☐ = 50 + 5 **20.** ☐ − 10 = 38 + 1 **21.** 40 − ☐ = 30 + 1

22. ☐ + 22 = 30 − 2 **23.** 50 − ☐ = 46 + 3 **24.** 32 − ☐ = 20 + 4

25. Without using a ruler, draw a line segment about 4 inches long. Then measure it to the nearest inch.

26. Al fed his friend's dog for 4 days. He used 2 cups of food 2 times each day. How many cups of food did he use?

27. Juan has 15 pennies and 3 dimes. Olivia has the same amount of money, but she has only nickels. How many nickels does Olivia have?

28. Alberto had 104 peacock stickers. He put 68 of them in his old sticker book and gave 18 away. How many peacock stickers does Alberto have left to put in his new sticker book?

29. **Number Sense** Suppose two pizzas are the same size. One pizza is cut into eighths and the other pizza is cut into tenths. Which pizza has larger pieces?

30. **Reasoning** Ken has 8 quarters, 5 dimes, 5 nickels, and 5 pennies. This is all the money he has. Explain why the total value of all of Ken's coins could not be \$2.81. Then find the correct amount he had.

31. Which of the pencil stickers below is 2 inches high? Use a ruler to measure.

SOL Prep

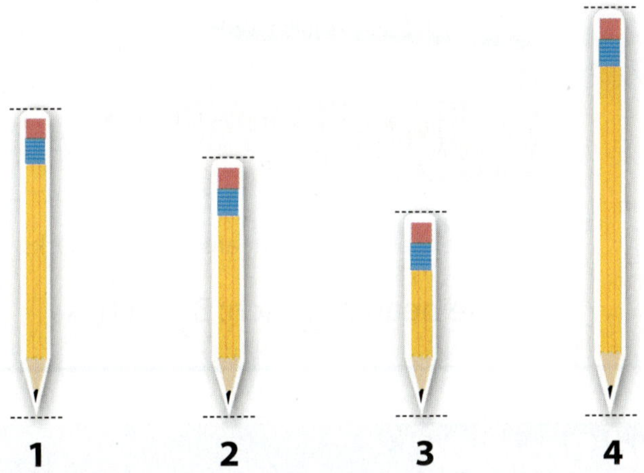

A Sticker 1 **C** Sticker 3

B Sticker 2 **D** Sticker 4

32. Ruth did 63 extra math problems in 7 days. She did the same number of problems each day. Which number sentence would you use to find the number of problems she did each day?

A $63 + 7 = \square$ **C** $63 \times 7 = \square$

B $63 - 7 = \square$ **D** $63 \div 7 = \square$

Virginia

Lesson 14-2

3.9.a The student will estimate and use U.S. Customary and metric units to measure length to the nearest $\frac{1}{2}$ inch, inch, foot, yard, centimeter, and meter.

Fractions of an Inch

Hands-On
inch ruler

How do you measure to a fraction of an inch?

In the picture, what is the length of the red pepper to the nearest $\frac{1}{2}$ inch and to the nearest $\frac{1}{4}$ inch?

Other Examples

The nearest $\frac{1}{2}$ inch and $\frac{1}{4}$ inch can be the same.

In the picture, the length of the green bean is measured to the nearest $\frac{1}{2}$ inch and to the nearest $\frac{1}{4}$ inch.

To the nearest $\frac{1}{2}$ inch:

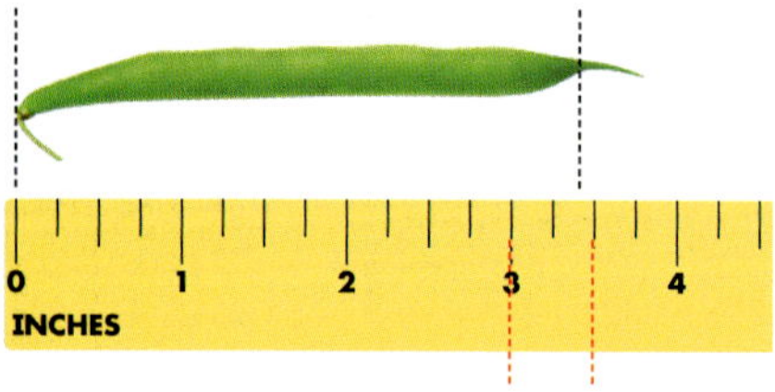

The red marks are the nearest $\frac{1}{2}$-inch marks.

To the nearest $\frac{1}{2}$ inch: $3\frac{1}{2}$ inches

To the nearest $\frac{1}{4}$ inch:

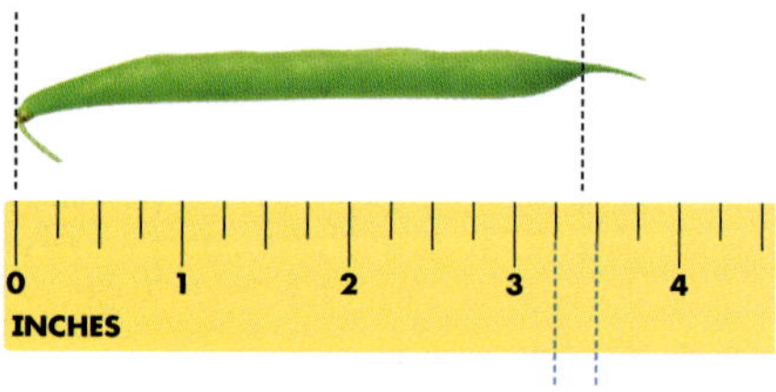

The blue marks are the nearest $\frac{1}{4}$-inch marks.

To the nearest $\frac{1}{4}$ inch: $3\frac{1}{2}$ inches

Guided Practice*

Do you know HOW?

Measure each length to the nearest $\frac{1}{2}$ inch and to the nearest $\frac{1}{4}$ inch.

1. 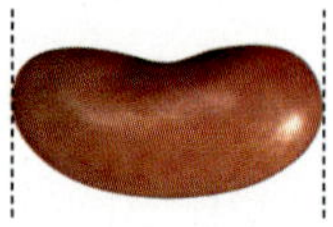

2. 

Do you UNDERSTAND?

3. In measuring the red pepper above, between which two $\frac{1}{2}$-inch marks does the pepper end?

4. Is $2\frac{1}{2}$ inches or $2\frac{3}{4}$ inches nearer to the actual length of the pepper? Explain.

DIGITAL eTools **www.pearsonsuccessnet.com**

*For another example, see Set B on page 346.

Measure to the nearest $\frac{1}{2}$ inch.

The red marks are all $\frac{1}{2}$-inch marks. The nearest $\frac{1}{2}$-inch marks are $2\frac{1}{2}$ inches and 3 inches.

To the nearest $\frac{1}{2}$ inch: $2\frac{1}{2}$ inches

Measure to the nearest $\frac{1}{4}$ inch.

The blue marks are all $\frac{1}{4}$-inch marks. The nearest $\frac{1}{4}$-inch marks are $2\frac{1}{2}$ inches and $2\frac{3}{4}$ inches.

To the nearest $\frac{1}{4}$ inch: $2\frac{3}{4}$ inches

Independent Practice

Measure the length of each object to the nearest $\frac{1}{2}$ inch and to the nearest $\frac{1}{4}$ inch.

5.

6.

7.

8.

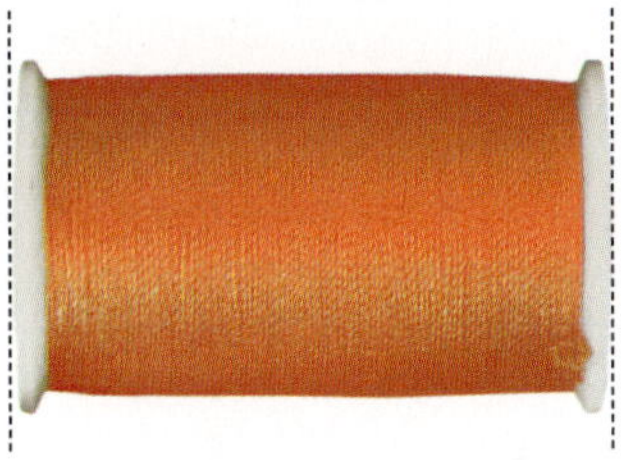

Problem Solving

9. **Reasoning** Can a piece of carrot be 3 inches long to the nearest inch, nearest $\frac{1}{2}$ inch, and nearest $\frac{1}{4}$ inch? Explain.

10. Karina has 3 rows of tomato plants in her garden. There are 9 plants in each row. How many tomato plants are in her garden?

11. What is the length of the asparagus to the nearest $\frac{1}{2}$ inch? Use a ruler to measure.

SOL Prep

A 5 inches **B** $5\frac{1}{2}$ inches **C** 6 inches **D** $6\frac{1}{2}$ inches

Virginia

Lesson 14-3

3.9.a The student will estimate and use U.S. Customary and metric units to measure length to the nearest $\frac{1}{2}$ inch, inch, foot, yard, centimeter, and meter.

Using Inches, Feet, Yards, and Miles

How can you estimate and choose units to measure length?

Joe is writing about fire trucks. What units of length or distance might he use?

Another Example **How can you change from one unit of length to a different unit of length?**

The table at the right shows how some units of length are related.

Data

Customary Units of Length
12 inches = 1 foot (ft)
3 feet = 1 yard (yd)
36 inches = 1 yard
5,280 feet = 1 mile (mi)
1,760 yards = 1 mile

How many feet are in 4 yards?

1 yard = 3 feet

Multiply:
4×3 feet = 12 feet

There are 12 feet in 4 yards.

How many inches are in 3 feet, 2 inches?

1 foot = 12 inches

Multiply, then add:
3×12 inches = 36 inches
36 inches + 2 inches = 38 inches

3 feet, 2 inches = 38 inches

Explain It

1. How could you make a table to help find the number of inches in 3 feet, 2 inches?
2. How many inches are in 2 feet, 7 inches?

Besides the inch, some customary units of length are the foot (ft), yard (yd), and mile (mi).

A loaf of bread is about a foot long.

A baseball bat is about a yard long.

Most people can walk a mile in about 15 minutes.

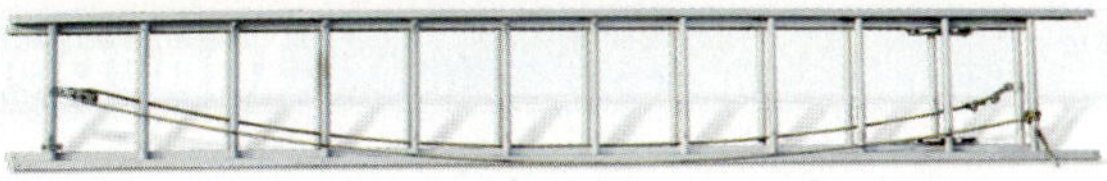

The length of the ladder on the fire truck is best measured in feet.

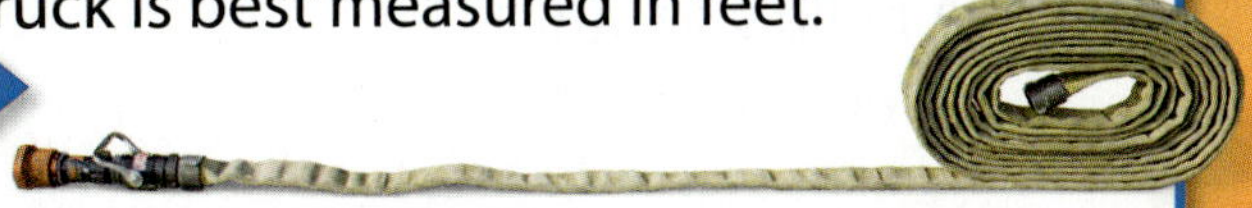

The length of the fire hose is best measured in yards. The width of the fire hose is best measured in inches.

The distance a fire truck travels is best measured in miles.

Guided Practice*

Do you know HOW?

Which is the best unit to use? Choose inches, feet, yards, or miles.

1. The distance between two cities

2. The length of your classroom

Do you UNDERSTAND?

3. In the example above, why would the width of the hose be measured in inches instead of feet?

4. What unit is best used for the height of a bookcase? Why?

Independent Practice

In **5–7**, tell which is the best unit to use. Choose inches, feet, yards, or miles.

5. The length of a toothbrush

6. The distance driven on a road trip

7. The length of a playground

Leveled Practice In **8–11**, change the units.

8. Change 2 feet, 9 inches to inches.
1 foot = 12 inches
2 × 12 inches = 24 inches
24 inches + □ inches = □ inches

9. Change 2 yards, 2 feet to feet.
1 yard = 3 feet
2 × 3 feet = □ feet
□ feet + 2 feet = □ feet

10. How many feet are in 6 yards?

11. 4 feet, 5 inches = □ inches

DIGITAL Animated Glossary www.pearsonsuccessnet.com

*For another example, see Set C on page 346.

Independent Practice

In **12–15**, choose the better estimate.

12. A child's height
4 feet or 9 feet

13. The distance you travel on a train
70 yards or 70 miles

14. The length of a car's license plate
9 inches or 9 yards

15. The distance across your hand
3 inches or 8 inches

Problem Solving

16. Mr. Berry put up the fence shown below.
How many inches long is the fence?

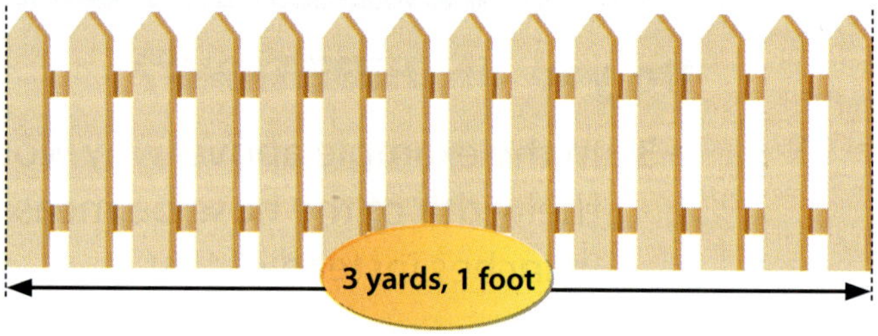

17. Angie needs 8 inches of ribbon for each of the 9 bows she is making. The ribbon is sold by the yard. How many yards of ribbon should Angie buy?

18. **Writing to Explain** West Side Park is 2,000 feet long. East Side Park is 1 mile long. Which park is longer? Explain your answer.

19. Look at the poster below. What fraction of the squares on this poster show food?

SOL Prep

A $\frac{1}{15}$

B $\frac{7}{15}$

C $\frac{8}{15}$

D $\frac{3}{5}$

20. **Writing to Explain** Judy broke one of her shoelaces. She measured the unbroken lace and found it was 2 feet long. She bought a pair of 27-inch shoelaces. How does the length of her new laces compare to the length of her old laces? Explain.

21. **Number Sense** Would you measure the length of a soccer field in yards or inches? Explain.

22. **Geometry** Which shape is a scalene triangle?

SOL Prep

23. In 1976, the world record was set for the "World's Longest Apple Peel," measuring at about 170 feet. Which lettered point best represents the length of the "World's Longest Apple Peel"?

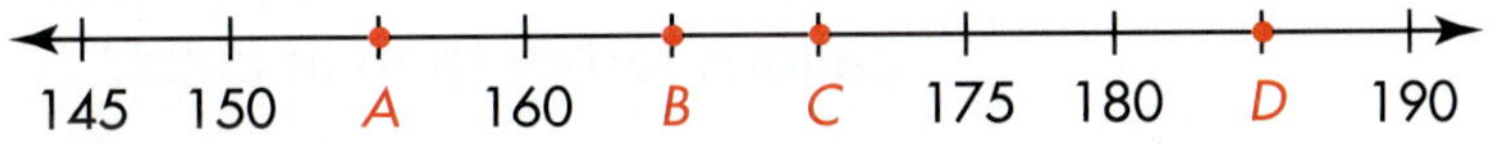

24. The table at the right shows the long-jump distances for Juanita, Tom, and Margo. Write these distances in order from shortest to longest.

Data

Long Jump

Student	Distance
Juanita	2 ft, 4 in.
Tom	23 in.
Margo	2 ft

25. Which measurement best describes the length of a couch?

A 6 miles

B 6 yards

C 6 feet

D 6 inches

26. Which measurement best describes the height of a kitchen table?

SOL Prep

A 1 foot

B 3 feet

C 6 feet

D 12 feet

Algebra In **27–29**, use >, <, or = to compare.

27. 2 yd ◯ 5 ft

28. 3 ft ◯ 36 in.

29. 1 mi ◯ 1,000 in.

Virginia

Lesson 14-4

3.9.b The student will estimate and use U.S. Customary and metric units to measure liquid volume in cups, pints, quarts, gallons, and liters.

Customary Units of Capacity

What customary units describe how much a container holds?

The capacity of a container is the volume of a container measured in liquid units. What is the capacity of this pail?

Guided Practice*

Do you know HOW?

For **1** and **2**, choose the better estimate for each.

1.

1 c or 1 qt

2.

3 pt or 3 gal

Do you UNDERSTAND?

3. **Number Sense** Why does it make sense to measure the pail above in gallons rather than in cups?

4. Find a container that you think holds about 1 gallon and another that holds about 1 cup. Then use measuring containers to see how well you estimated each capacity.

Independent Practice

For **5–12**, choose the better estimate for each.

5.

1 pt or 1 gal

6.

1 c or 1 pt

7.

1 c or 1 pt

8.

1 c or 1 qt

9. kitchen sink
22 c or 22 qt

10. water glass
1 c or 1 qt

11. baby bottle
1 qt or 1 c

12. tea kettle
3 qt or 3 c

DIGITAL Animated Glossary
www.pearsonsuccessnet.com

*For another example, see Set D on page 347.

Step 1

Cups, pints, quarts, and gallons are customary units of capacity.

Choose an appropriate unit and estimate.

The cup, pint, and quart are too small. Use gallons.

The pail looks like it will hold more than 1 gallon.

Data

Units of Capacity
1 pint = 2 cups
1 quart = 2 pints
1 gallon = 4 quarts

Step 2

Measure the capacity of the pail.

Count how many times you can fill a gallon container and empty it into the pail.

The pail holds about 2 gallons.

Choose the better unit to measure the capacity of each.

13. teacup

pt or c

14. swimming pool

pt or gal

15. water bottle

pt or gal

16. pitcher of juice

c or qt

Problem Solving

17. Writing to Explain Can containers with different shapes have the same capacity? Why or why not?

18. Look at the hat at the right. It is sometimes called a ten-gallon hat!

a Can this hat really hold 10 gallons? How do you know?

b Can this hat hold 1 gallon? How do you know?

19. Which measurement best describes the capacity of a bathtub?

SOL Prep

A 50 cups

B 50 quarts

C 50 gallons

D 50 pints

20. Which of the objects below holds about 1 pint?

SOL Prep

A bowl of soup

B punch bowl

C gas tank

D pool

21. Jeanne made 5 pitchers of lemonade. Each pitcher served 9 customers at her lemonade stand. If Jeanne had 1 pitcher of lemonade left, how many customers did Jeanne serve?

Virginia

Lesson 14-5

3.9.c The student will estimate and use U.S. Customary and metric units to measure weight/mass in ounces, pounds, grams, and kilograms.

Units of Weight

What customary units describe how heavy something is?

The weight of an object is a measure of how heavy the object is. What is the weight of this apple?

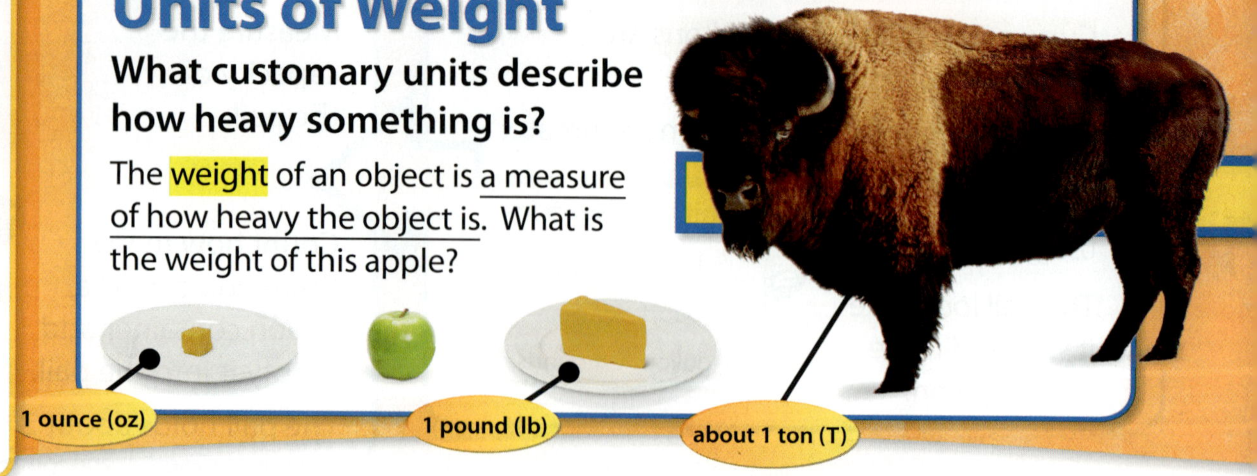

Guided Practice*

Do you know HOW?

For **1** and **2**, choose the better estimate for each.

1.

1 oz or 1 lb

2.

6 oz or 6 lb

Do you UNDERSTAND?

3. **Number Sense** If you buy a bag of 6 apples, what unit would you use for its weight? Explain.

4. Find an object that you think weighs about 1 pound and another that weighs about 1 ounce. Then weigh the objects to see how well you estimated.

Independent Practice

For **5–12**, choose the better estimate for each.

5.

10 oz or 10 lb

6.

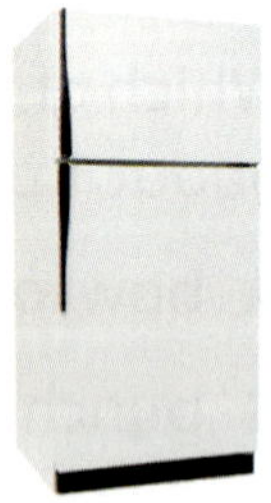

300 lb or 300 T

7.

200 lb or 2 T

8.

2 oz or 2 lb

9. cracker

1 oz or 1 lb

10. television set

30 oz or 30 lb

11. baseball hat

5 oz or 5 lb

12. elephant

30 lb or 3 T

DIGITAL Animated Glossary
www.pearsonsuccessnet.com

**For another example, see Set E on page 347.*

Step 1

Ounces, pounds, and tons are units of weight.

Choose a unit and estimate.

The units pound and ton are too big. Use ounces.

The apple weighs less than 1 pound but more than 1 ounce.

Data

Units of Weight
16 ounces = 1 pound
2,000 pounds = 1 ton

Step 2

Weigh the apple.

Three stacks of three 1-ounce weights balance with the apple.

The apple weighs about 9 ounces.

For **13–16**, choose the better unit to measure the weight of each.

13. student desk
lb or T

14. lemon
oz or lb

15. bicycle
oz or lb

16. truck
oz or T

Problem Solving

17. How much does the orange weigh?

18. When would you use this scale instead of a pan balance?

19. **Number Sense** Which weighs more—a pound of rocks or a pound of feathers? Explain your thinking.

20. **Writing to Explain** Do small objects always weigh less than large objects? Use examples to explain your thinking.

21. When Owen and Mzee first met, Owen weighed 600 pounds. Mzee weighed 661 pounds. How much more did Mzee weigh than Owen when they first met?

22. Which animal weighs about 1 ton?

A squirrel
B giraffe
C wolf
D monkey

Virginia

Lesson 14-6

Extends 3.14 The student will identify, describe, compare, and contrast characteristics of plane and solid geometric figures (circle, square, rectangle, triangle, cube, rectangular prism, square pyramid, sphere, cone, and cylinder) by identifying relevant characteristics, including the number of angles, vertices, and edges, and the number and shape of faces, using concrete models.

Problem Solving

Act It Out and Use Reasoning

Hands-On
cubes

You can use different views of a figure to tell what the figure looks like.

Janet built this figure out of cubes. Then she colored the faces she could see.

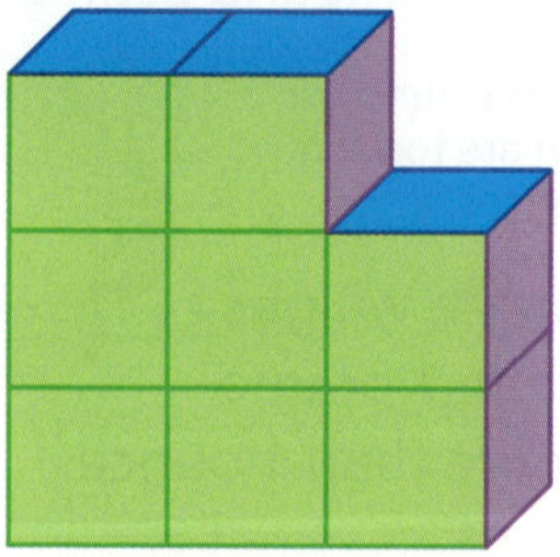

Guided Practice*

Do you know HOW?

1. Use cubes to build the figure shown in these pictures.

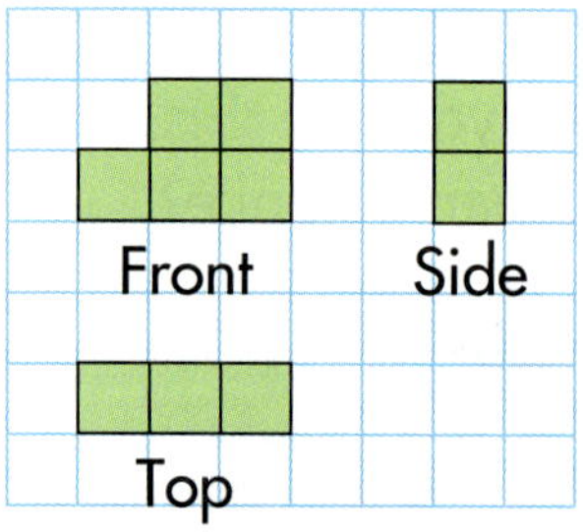

Do you UNDERSTAND?

2. **Writing to Explain** Would a drawing showing the right side of Janet's figure be the same as the drawing showing the left side?

3. Add one more block any place you wish to Janet's figure. Then make drawings to show how each view would change.

Independent Practice

Use grid paper. Draw the front, side, and top views of the figures shown below.

4. 

5. 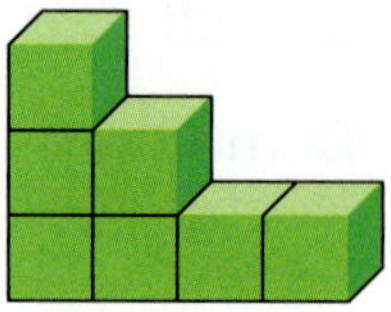

Stuck? Try this....

- What do I know?
- What am I asked to find?
- What diagram can I use to help understand the problem?
- Can I use addition, subtraction, multiplication, or division?
- Is all of my work correct?
- Did I answer the right question?
- Is my answer reasonable?

*For another example, see Set F on page 347.

Here are 3 different views of the figure Janet built.

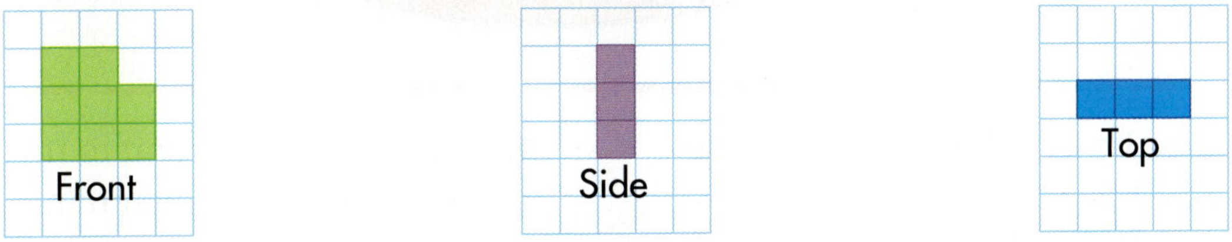

Front View **Left Side View** **Top View**

Use the drawings to help you build the same figure.
You will need 8 cubes.

6. Use cubes to build the figure shown in these pictures.

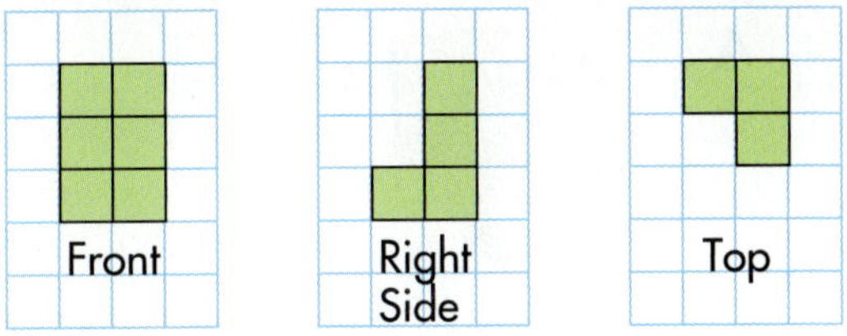

In **7** and **8**, use the figure shown below.

7. Use grid paper. Draw the front, right side, and top view of the figure.

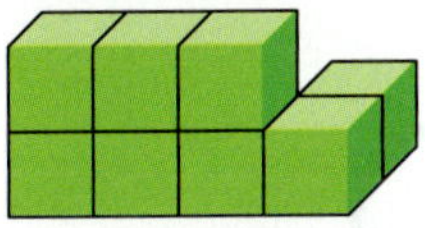

8. How many cubes are used in the figure?

9. Which drawing shows the front view of this figure?

A

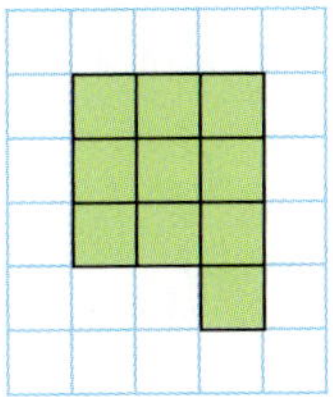

B

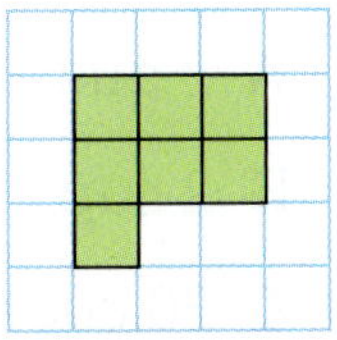

C

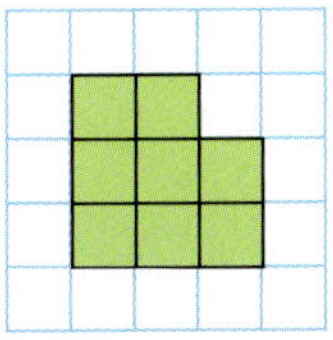

D

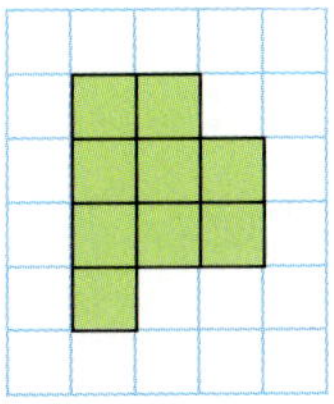

1. What is the length of the leaf to the nearest $\frac{1}{2}$ inch? (14-2)

A $1\frac{1}{2}$ inches

B 2 inches

C $2\frac{1}{2}$ inches

D 3 inches

2. Which is the best estimate of the weight of an adult American bison, also called the American buffalo? (14-5)

A 1 ton

B 1 pound

C 10 pounds

D 10 ounces

3. Emily is 2 feet, 8 inches tall. How many inches tall is Emily? There are 12 inches in a foot. (14-3)

A 28 inches

B 32 inches

C 36 inches

D 98 inches

4. Which is the best unit to measure the capacity of a swimming pool? (14-4)

A Cups

B Gallons

C Pints

D Quarts

5. Which of the following weighs closest to 1 pound? (14-5)

A

B

C

D

6. Which of the following best describes the capacity of a water balloon? (14-4)

A 2 quarts

B 2 cups

C 20 cups

D 20 pints

7. Which is the best unit to measure the length of the Mississippi River? (14-3)

A Miles **C** Feet

B Yards **D** Inches

8. Juana's goldfish is 2 inches long. Which could be Juana's goldfish? (14-1)

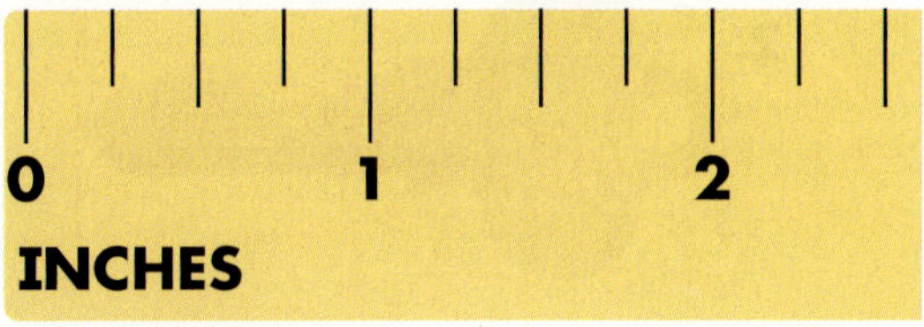

A

B

C

D

9. Which best describes the length of a large school bus? (14-3)

A 12 inches

B 12 feet

C 12 yards

D 12 miles

10. What is the length of the screwdriver to the nearest $\frac{1}{2}$ inch? (14-2)

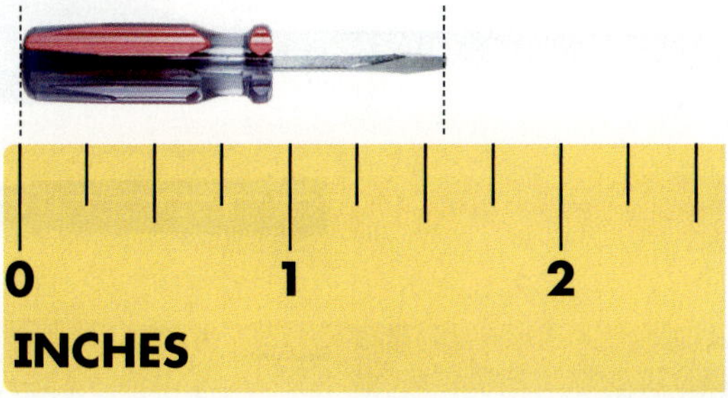

A $1\frac{1}{4}$ inches **C** $1\frac{3}{4}$ inches

B $1\frac{1}{2}$ inches **D** 2 inches

11. Which drawing shows the front view of this figure? (14-6)

A

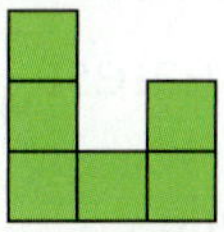

B

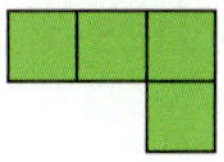

C

D

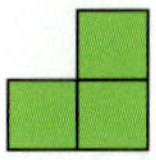

12. Which is the best estimate of the length of the almond? (14-1)

A 4 inches

B 3 inches

C 2 inches

D 1 inch

Set A, pages 328–331

You can use different units to measure length.

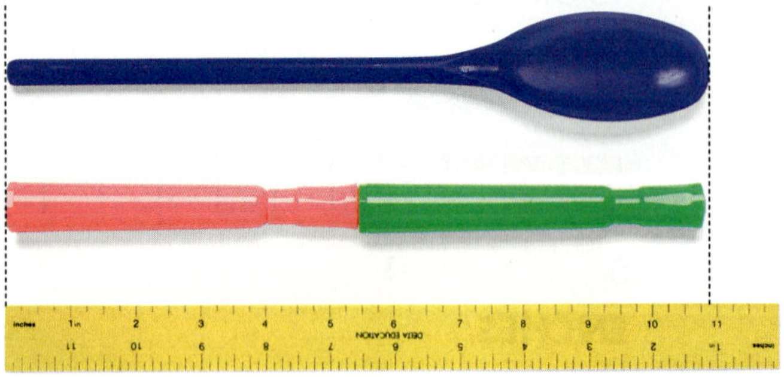

The spoon is about 2 marker-lengths long.
To the nearest inch, it is about 11 inches long.

Remember to line up the object with the 0 mark on the ruler.

Use an inch ruler to measure each length to the nearest inch.

1. 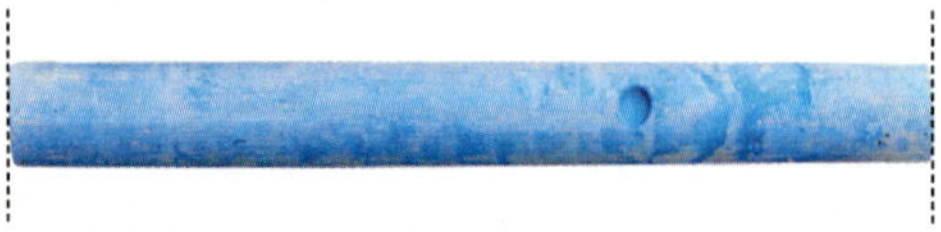

2. 

Set B, pages 332–333

Use the picture to measure the ribbon to the nearest $\frac{1}{2}$ inch and to the nearest $\frac{1}{4}$ inch.

Look for the two nearest $\frac{1}{2}$ inch marks.

To the nearest $\frac{1}{2}$ inch: $3\frac{1}{2}$ inches

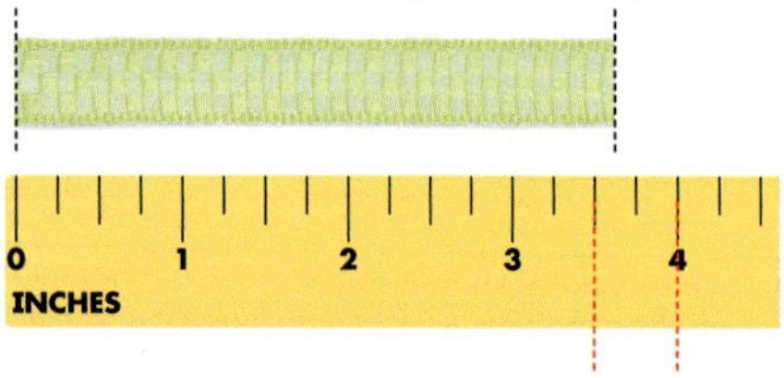

Look for the two nearest $\frac{1}{4}$ inch marks.

To the nearest $\frac{1}{4}$ inch: $3\frac{3}{4}$ inches

Remember that the nearest $\frac{1}{2}$ inch and nearest $\frac{1}{4}$ inch for an object can be the same.

Measure the length of each object to the nearest $\frac{1}{2}$ inch and $\frac{1}{4}$ inch.

1. 

2. 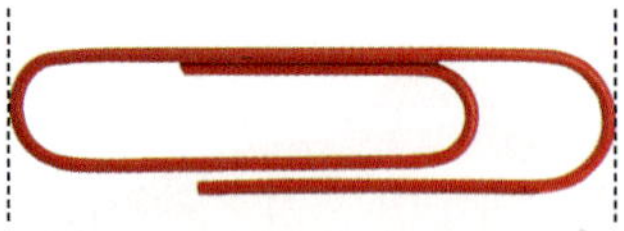

Set C, pages 334–337

Change the units.

2 feet, 6 inches = ☐ inches

Tip *1 foot = 12 inches*

Multiply: 2 × 12 inches = 24 inches
Then add: 24 inches + 6 inches = 30 inches

2 feet, 6 inches = 30 inches

Remember that 1 yard equals 3 feet.

Change the units.

1. 4 feet, 3 inches = ☐ inches

2. 6 feet, 4 inches = ☐ inches

3. 5 yards, 2 feet = ☐ feet

Set D, pages 338–339

What is the capacity of this teapot?

Choose an appropriate unit and estimate.

Gallon and quart are too big. The teapot holds more than 1 pint but fewer than 2 pints.

If you estimate using cups, the teapot looks like it holds about 3 cups.

Remember to use the examples of a cup, pint, quart, and gallon to help you estimate.

1. 

1 c or 1 qt

2. 

30 pt or 30 gal

Set E, pages 340–341

What is the weight of a tennis ball?

Choose a unit and estimate.

A tennis ball does not weigh as much as a ton or even a pound, so estimate using ounces.

The tennis ball weighs about as much as 4 small cubes of cheese, or about 4 ounces.

Remember to use the examples of an ounce, pound, and ton to help you estimate.

Choose the better estimate.

1.  8 oz or 8 lb

2.  20 lb or 20 T

Set F, pages 342–343

Les built this figure with cubes. How can you draw the front, side, and top view of the figure?

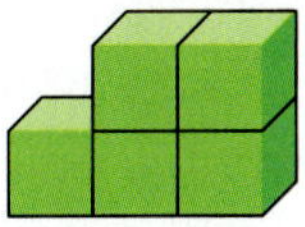

Turn the front of the figure to face you.

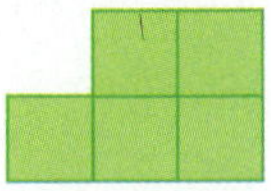

Front View

Then turn the figure to the side.

Side View

Then look at the figure from above.

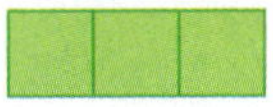

Top View

Remember to check your solution.

Use grid paper. Draw the front, side, and top view of each figure.

1. 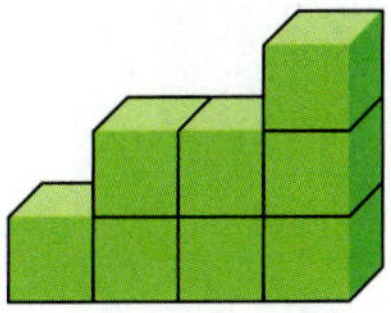

2. 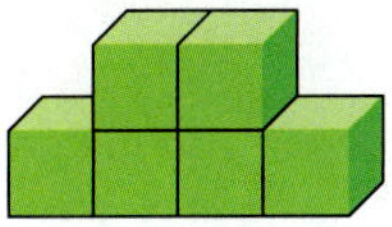

Topic 15

Metric Measurement

1 The sandgrouse soaks up water in its fluffy feathers and carries it many kilometers to its chicks. About how much water can a sandgrouse carry in its feathers? You will find out in Lesson 15-3.

2 What is the length in meters and centimeters of the footbridge on Tower Bridge in London, England? You will find out in Lesson 15-2.

3 Do you know how many grains of sand equal 1 gram? You will find out in Lesson 15-4.

4 What is the length of the world's smallest seahorse? You will find out in Lesson 15-1.

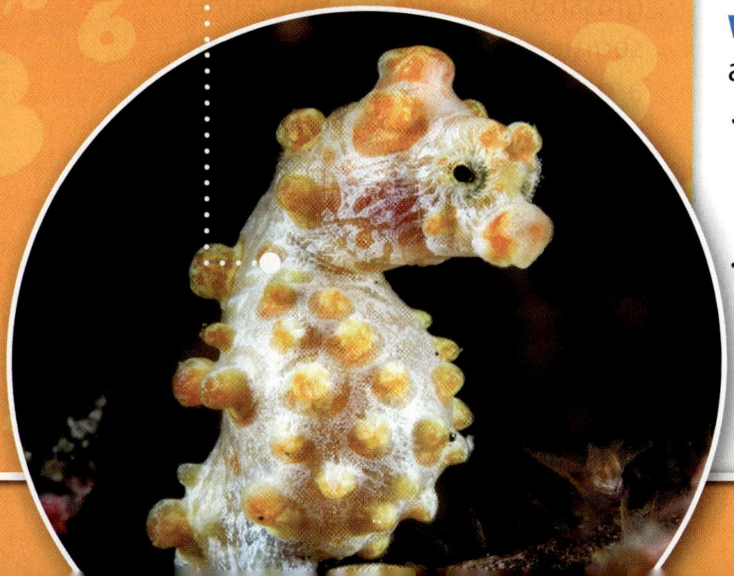

Review What You Know!

Vocabulary

Choose the best term from the box.

- cubes
- feet
- pounds
- quarts

1. You can measure weight in __?__.
2. You can measure a liquid in __?__.
3. You can measure length in __?__.

Compare Measurements

Choose the greater amount.

4. 3 inches or 3 feet
5. 20 quarts or 2 quarts
6. 6 pounds or 60 pounds

Add

Find each sum.

7. 400 + 57
8. 100 + 100 + 36
9. 10 + 10 + 5
10. 1,000 + 1,000 + 1,000

Arrays

Writing to Explain Use the array for **11** and **12**. Write an answer for each question.

11. How can you find the number of dots in the array?

12. Suppose there were 6 dots in each row. How could you find the number of dots in the array?

Virginia

Lesson 15-1

3.9.a The student will estimate and use U.S. Customary and metric units to measure length to the nearest $\frac{1}{2}$-inch, inch, foot, yard, centimeter, and meter.

Using Centimeters and Decimeters

Hands-On: metric ruler

How can you estimate and measure in metric units?

What is the length of the grasshopper, to the nearest centimeter?

Other Examples

Some other metric units of length are the **decimeter (dm)** and the **millimeter (mm)**.

10 centimeters = 1 decimeter
10 cm = 1 dm

This wrench is 1 dm long.

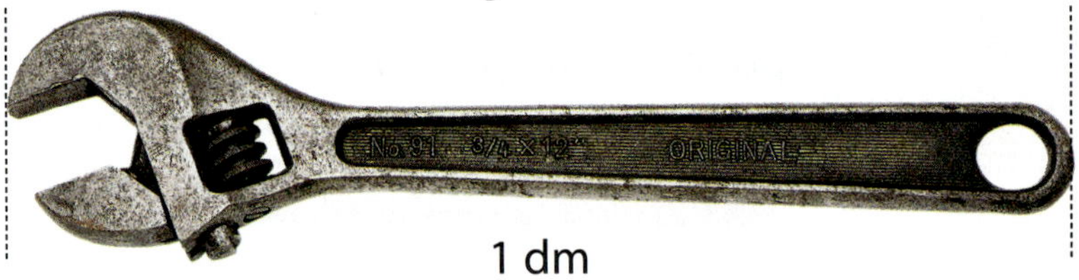

1 dm

10 millimeters = 1 centimeter
10 mm = 1 cm

A dime is about 1 mm thick.

1 mm

Guided Practice*

Do you know HOW?

In **1** and **2**, estimate each length. Then measure to the nearest centimeter.

1.

2.

Do you UNDERSTAND?

3. A cricket is 1 cm shorter than the grasshopper above. Draw a line segment that is the same length as the cricket.

4. What is the length of the clamshell to the nearest centimeter?

DIGITAL Animated Glossary, eTools **www.pearsonsuccessnet.com**

*For another example, see Set A on page 364.

A metric unit for measuring length is the centimeter (cm).

Your finger is about 1 cm wide. Use your finger width to help estimate lengths.

1 cm

Use the centimeter ruler to measure.

The grasshopper is 4 cm long, to the nearest centimeter.

Independent Practice

In **5–7**, estimate each length. Then measure to the nearest centimeter.

5. 

6. 

7. 

Problem Solving

8. What is the length of the flower to the nearest centimeter?

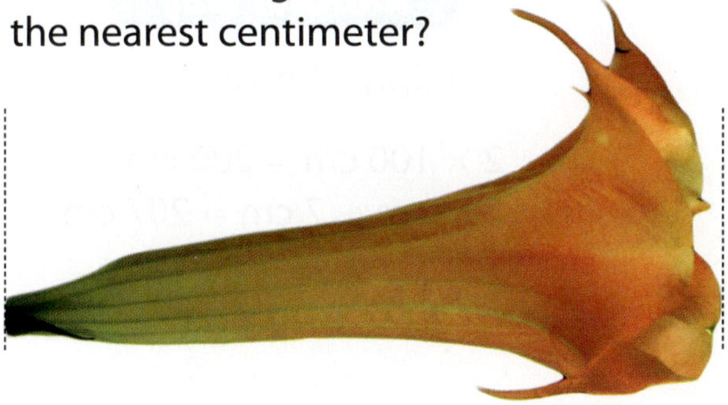

9. What is the length of the world's smallest seahorse to the nearest centimeter?

Algebra In **10–12**, copy and complete each number sentence.

10. 36 = 9 × ▢

11. 7 × ▢ = 56

12. 60 = ▢ × 10

13. Which is the length of the crayon below? Use a centimeter ruler to measure.

SOL Prep

A 1 cm **B** 4 cm **C** 8 cm **D** 1 dm

Virginia

Lesson 15-2

3.9.a The student will estimate and use U.S. Customary and metric units to measure length to the nearest $\frac{1}{2}$-inch, inch, foot, yard, centimeter, and meter.

Using Meters and Kilometers

How can you estimate and choose units to measure length?

Lou needs to tell a friend in another country about the length of a truck and the road it travels on. What units can Lou use?

Another Example How can you change units?

Metric Units of Length
1 meter (m) = 100 centimeters (cm)
1 kilometer (km) = 1,000 meters (m)

Data

2 meters, 7 centimeters = ▢ centimeters

One Way

Make a table that relates meters and centimeters.

Meters	1	2	3	4
Centimeters	100	200	300	400

2 meters, 7 centimeters = 207 centimeters

Another Way

Multiply. Then add.

2×100 cm = 200 cm
200 cm + 7 cm = 207 cm

Explain It

1. How could you make a table to help find the number of centimeters in 6 meters, 5 centimeters?
2. How many centimeters are 4 meters, 17 centimeters?

Metric units used for measuring longer lengths are the meter (m) and the kilometer (km).

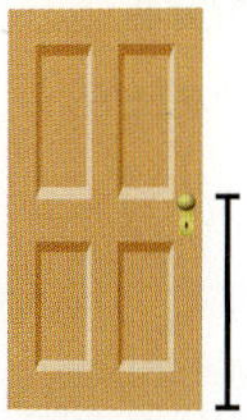

A doorknob is about 1 meter above the floor.

Most people can walk a kilometer in about 10 minutes.

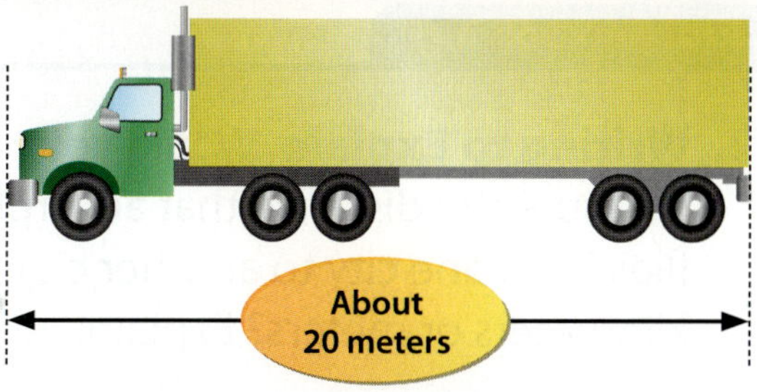

The length of a truck is best measured in meters.

The distance a truck travels on a road is best measured in kilometers.

Guided Practice*

Do you know HOW?

Which is the best unit to use? Choose meter or kilometer.

1. The length of a classroom

2. The length of a table in the lunchroom

3. The distance across your state

Do you UNDERSTAND?

4. In the example above, why is a kilometer the better unit to use to measure the length of the road?

5. **Writing to Explain** Which distance is greater, 850 meters or 1 kilometer? How do you know?

Independent Practice

In **6** and **7** tell if meter or kilometer is the better unit to use.

6. The height of a flagpole

7. The length of a bike trail

In **8** and **9**, change the units. Copy and complete.

8. How many centimeters are in 3 meters, 8 centimeters?

9. 4 meters = ▢ centimeters

In **10** and **11**, choose the better estimate.

10. The height of an adult
2 kilometers or 2 meters

11. The length of your foot
20 centimeters or 20 meters

DIGITAL Animated Glossary **www.pearsonsuccessnet.com**

**For another example, see Set A on page 364.*

Problem Solving

12. Writing to Explain Would you measure the distance that an airplane flies from one city to another city in kilometers or meters? Explain.

13. Number Sense A tree is 4 meters, 10 centimeters tall. Is this more than or less than 500 centimeters? Explain.

14. Change the units. Copy and complete the table to help.

Meters	1	2	3	4
Centimeters	100	200		

a 3 meters, 15 centimeters = ▢ centimeters

b 4 meters, 63 centimeters = ▢ centimeters

In **15** and **16**, use the table at the right.

Sale on Railings (Data)

Length	Price
1 meter	$8
2 meters	$19
150 centimeters	$11

15. Estimation About how much would it cost to buy two 1-meter railings and two 2-meter railings?

16. How much more is the price of one 150-centimeter railing than the price of one 1-meter railing?

17. Which measurement best describes the length of a car?

SOL Prep

A 5 centimeters
B 5 kilometers
C 5 meters
D 5 millimeters

Use the photo at the right for **18** and **19**.

18. The footbridge on Tower Bridge was built so workers could cross the River Thames in London, even when the main part of the bridge was open to let a boat pass. How many centimeters long is the footbridge?

19. Which measurement is a reasonable estimate of the height of each tower?

SOL Prep

A 65 m
B 65 km
C 65 dm
D 65 cm

Going Digital

Changing Metric Units

How many centimeters are in 2 meters, 45 centimeters?

There are 100 centimeters in a meter. To find how many centimeters are in 2 meters, 45 centimeters, multiply 2×100 and then add 45.

Press: 2 [×] 100 [+] 45 [ENTER =]

Display: 245

2 meters, 45 centimeters = 245 centimeters

Changing Customary Units

How many inches are in 4 feet, 8 inches?

There are 12 inches in a foot. To find how many inches are in 4 feet, 8 inches, multiply 4×12 and then add 8.

One Way Multiply first and then add.

Press: 4 [×] 12 [ENTER =]

Display: 48

48 [+] 8 [ENTER =]

Display: 56

Another Way Multiply and add in the same step.

Press: 4 [×] 12 [+] 8 [ENTER =]

Display: 56

4 feet, 8 inches = 56 inches

Practice

1. How many inches are in 3 feet, 9 inches?
2. How many centimeters are in 2 meters, 74 centimeters?
3. How many inches are in 7 yards, 16 inches?
4. How many feet are in 4 yards, 2 feet?
5. How many meters are in 5 kilometers, 25 meters?

Lesson 15-3

3.9.b The student will estimate and use U.S. Customary and metric units to measure liquid volume in cups, pints, quarts, gallons, and liters.

Metric Units of Capacity

What metric units describe how much a container holds?

Two metric units of capacity are milliliters and liters. What is the capacity of this pail?

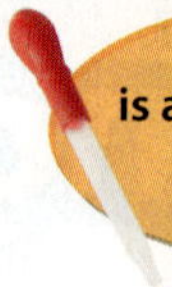

Guided Practice*

Do you know HOW?

Choose the better estimate for each.

1.

250 mL or 2 L

2.

5 mL or 1 L

Do you UNDERSTAND?

3. **Writing to Explain** Suppose the capacity of the pail above is given in milliliters. Is this number greater or less than the number of liters? Explain.

4. Find a container that you predict will hold more than a liter and another that you predict will hold less than a liter. Then use a liter container to check your predictions.

Independent Practice

In **5–12**, choose the better estimate for each.

5.

40 mL or 40 L

6.

15 mL or 1 L

7.

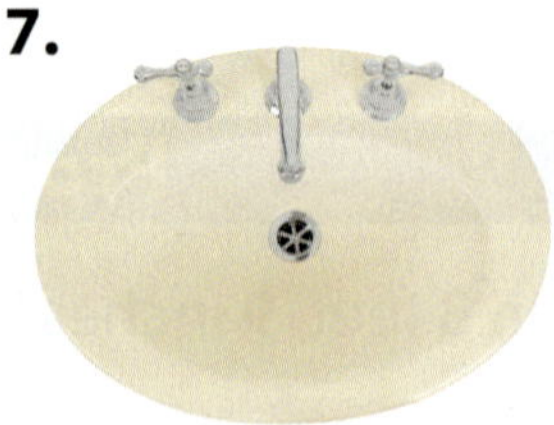

14 mL or 14 L

8.

250 mL or 250 L

9. teacup

15 L or 150 mL

10. bathtub

115 mL or 115 L

11. bottle cap

3 mL or 3 L

12. teapot

1 L or 10 L

DIGITAL Animated Glossary **www.pearsonsuccessnet.com**

*For another example, see Set B on page 364.

Step 1

Choose an appropriate unit and estimate.

Data

Units of Capacity
1,000 milliliters = 1 liter

A milliliter is too small. So use liters.

The pail will hold several liters.

Step 2

Measure the capacity.

Count how many times you can fill a liter container and empty it into the pail.

The pail holds about 8 liters.

In **13–16**, choose the unit you would use to measure the capacity of each.

13. soup can
mL or L

14. water pitcher
mL or L

15. swimming pool
mL or L

16. baby bottle
mL or L

Problem Solving

Estimation For **17–20**, is the capacity of each container more than a liter or less than a liter?

17. large pot

18. glass of juice

19. washing machine

20. mug

21. Reasoning Which cooler has a greater capacity? Explain your thinking.

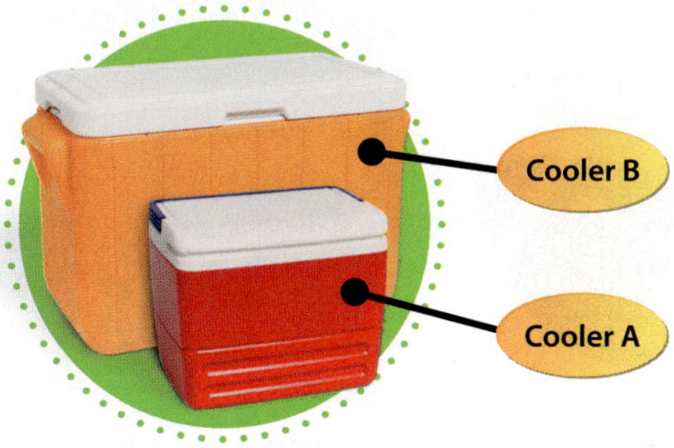

22. Which measurement best describes the capacity of a can of paint?

A 4 mL

B 4 L

C 40 L

D 40 mL

23. Number Sense A sandgrouse can soak up water in its fluffy feathers. It can carry the water many kilometers to its chicks. Does a sandgrouse carry 20 milliliters of water or 2 liters of water?

Lesson 15-4

3.9.c The student will estimate and use U.S. Customary and metric units to measure weight/mass in ounces, pounds, grams, and kilograms.

Units of Mass

What metric units describe mass?

Mass is a measure of the amount of matter in an object. Grams and kilograms are two metric units of mass. What is the mass of this apple?

Guided Practice*

Do you know HOW?

Choose the better estimate for each.

1.

5 g or 5 kg

2.

40 g or 4 kg

Do you UNDERSTAND?

3. **Writing to Explain** There are 10 weights on the pan balance above. Why isn't the mass of the apple 10 grams?

4. Find an object that you think has a mass more than a kilogram and another that has a mass less than a kilogram. Then use a pan balance to see if you are correct.

Independent Practice

For **5–12**, choose the better estimate for each.

5.

100 g or 10 kg

6.

15 g or 15 kg

7.

4 g or 400 g

8.

400 g or 4 kg

9. bicycle

2 kg or 12 kg

10. feather

1 g or 1 kg

11. horse

5 kg or 550 kg

12. penny

3 g or 300 g

DIGITAL Animated Glossary **www.pearsonsuccessnet.com**

For another example, see Set C on page 365.

Step 1

Choose a unit and estimate.

Units of Mass
1,000 grams = 1 kilogram

The unit kilogram is too big. Use grams.

The mass of the apple is less than 1 kilogram but more than 1 gram.

Step 2

Measure the mass of the apple.

Two 100-gram weights, six 10-gram weights, and two 1-gram weights balance with the apple.

The apple has a mass of 262 grams.

Problem Solving

For **13–17**, choose the best tool to measure each.

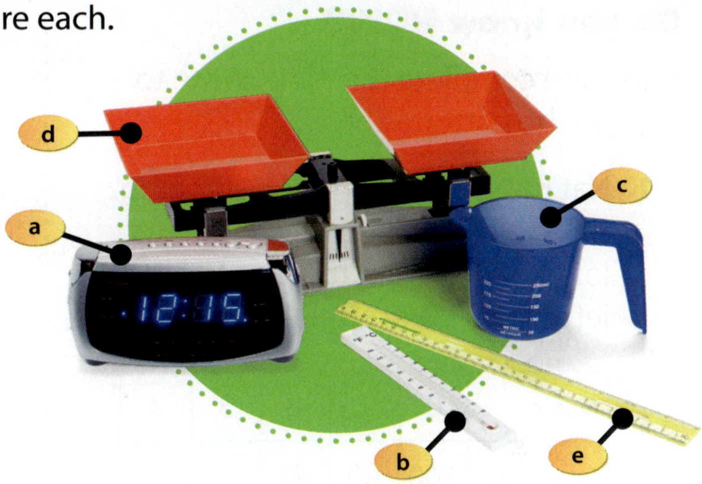

13. the capacity of a glass

14. the temperature of water

15. the length of a box

16. the weight of a pear

17. the length of time you sleep

18. What is the mass of the orange?

19. Correct the mistakes in the shopping list below.

Shopping List
2 L of apples
3 kg of milk
5 cm of flour

20. A bag holds 500 grams of sand. About how many grains of sand are in the bag?

21. Which measurement best describes the mass of a rabbit?

SOL Prep

A 2 grams

B 2 kilograms

C 2 liters

D 2 meters

Virginia

Lesson 15-5

Extends 3.19 The student will recognize and describe a variety of patterns formed using numbers, tables, and pictures, and extend the patterns, using the same or different forms.

Problem Solving

Make a Table and Look for a Pattern

Livia is training for a 25 km walk. She recorded how far she walked each day. If she continues the pattern, how far will Livia walk on Day 4? How far will she walk on Day 5?

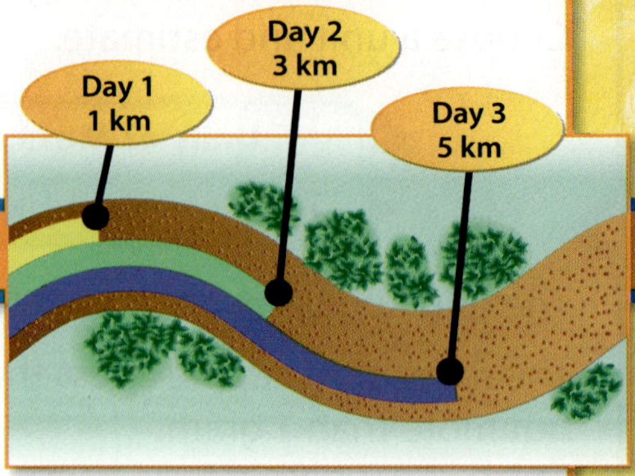

Guided Practice*

Do you know HOW?

Copy and complete the table. Write to explain the pattern. Solve.

1. Nat has a pole that is 1 meter long. He is cutting it into 20-centimeter long pieces. What length of pole is left after 3 cuts? after 4 cuts?

Cuts	0	1	2	3	4
Length (cm)	100	80	60		

Do you UNDERSTAND?

2. In the example above, how did the table help you to explain the pattern?

3. **Write a Problem** Write a problem that you can solve by writing an explanation of a pattern.

Independent Practice

In **4–7**, Copy and complete the table. Write to explain the pattern. Solve.

4. Nola is putting tiles in a row. Each tile is a square and the length of its side is 4 centimeters. What is the length of 4 tiles together? 5 tiles?

Number of Tiles	1	2	3	4	5
Total Length (cm)	4	8	12		

Stuck? Try this....

- What do I know?
- What am I asked to find?
- What diagram can I use to help understand the problem?
- Can I use addition, subtraction, multiplication, or division?
- Is all of my work correct?
- Did I answer the right question?
- Is my answer reasonable?

*For another example, see Set D on page 365.

Plan

You can make a table to show what you know. Then look for a pattern.

Day	1	2	3	4	5
Distance walked (km)	1	3	5		

Explain the pattern you see.

Each day Livia increased the distance she walked by 2 km.

Solve

Use your pattern to complete the table and solve the problem.

Day 3: 5 km
Day 4: 5 km + 2 km = 7 km
Day 5: 7 km + 2 km = 9 km

Day	1	2	3	4	5
Distance walked (km)	1	3	5	7	9

Livia will walk 7 km on Day 4 and 9 km on Day 5.

5. Talia is cutting up a sheet of paper that is 24 centimeters long. She is cutting the sheet into pieces that are each 3 centimeters long. What is the length of the sheet that is left after Talia has made 3 cuts? 4 cuts?

Number of Cuts	0	1	2	3	4
Length Left (cm)	24	21	18		

6. Mr. Lum is putting fence rails together in a row. Each rail is 2 meters long. What is the length of 5 rails together? 6 rails?

Number of Rails	1	2	3	4	5	6
Total Length (m)	2	4	6	8		

7. Evan makes picture frames using wood. For each frame, he needs 60 cm of wood. What is the total length of wood he needs to make 4 frames? 5 frames?

Number of Frames	1	2	3	4	5
Total Length (cm)	60	120	180		

8. Nick earns money doing chores. How much would he earn if he washes windows, washes dishes, and does laundry?

Data

Item	Price
Clean yard	\$8
Do laundry	\$5
Vacuum floors	\$3
Wash dishes	\$2
Wash windows	\$7

9. In the morning, Ray painted 12 windows. By the end of the day he had painted all 26 windows in the house. Which expression shows one way to find how many windows he painted in the afternoon?

A 26 + 12 **B** 26 − 12 **C** 26 × 12 **D** 26 ÷ 12

1. Which unit would be best to measure the mass of a mouse? (15-4)

   A Gram

   B Kilogram

   C Liter

   D Milliliter

2. Pat bought a sub sandwich that was 36 centimeters long. She cut 4-centimeter slices. What was the length of the sandwich left after Pat cut off 5 slices? (15-5)

Slices Cut Off	0	1	2	3	4	5
Centimeters Left	36	32	28	24		

   A 20 centimeters

   B 18 centimeters

   C 16 centimeters

   D 12 centimeters

3. Which animal could be about a decimeter long? (15-1)

   A a turtle

   B a whale

   C an ant

   D a ladybug

4. Which of the following best describes the mass of an orange? (15-4)

   A 20 kilograms

   B 200 kilograms

   C 20 grams

   D 200 grams

5. Which of the following is about 2 meters? (15-2)

   A The length of a bumblebee

   B The distance from your home to your school

   C The height of a one-story house

   D The height of a classroom door

6. What is the length of the apple core to the nearest centimeter? (15-1)

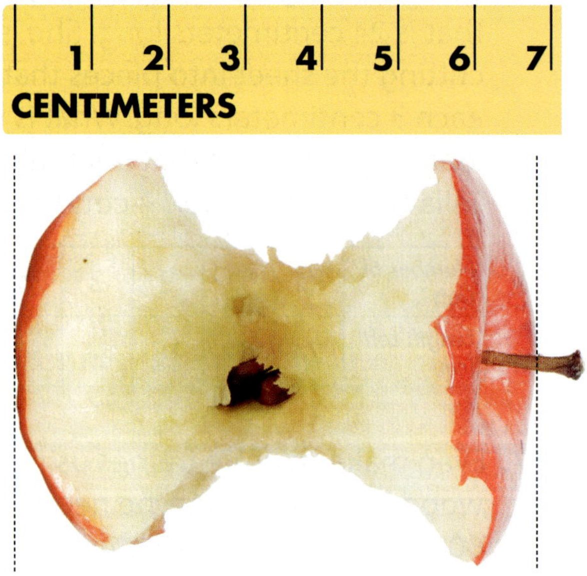

   A 3 centimeters

   B 6 centimeters

   C 7 centimeters

   D 8 centimeters

7. Which is the best estimate of the capacity of a bottle of syrup? (15-3)

   A 709 pints

   B 709 liters

   C 709 cups

   D 709 milliliters

8. Which best describes the length of a crayon? (15-2)

A 7 centimeters

B 7 decimeters

C 7 meters

D 7 kilometers

9. Which of the following would you measure in milliliters? (15-3)

A Capacity of an aquarium

B Capacity of an eyedropper

C Capacity of a coffee pot

D Capacity of a bathtub

10. Which insect could be about 5 centimeters long? (15-1)

A Ladybug

B Flea

C Ant

D Dragonfly

11. Which would be the best to measure in meters? (15-2)

A the distance from California to Hawaii

B the length of a toothbrush

C the length of a soccer field

D the distance a snail can crawl in one minute

12. Trey is practicing for a swim meet. If he continues the pattern, how many laps will he swim on the 6th day? (15-5)

Day	1	2	3	4	5	6
Laps Swam	25	29	33	37	■	■

A 46 laps

B 45 laps

C 44 laps

D 39 laps

13. Which of the following can hold only about 2 liters of water? (15-3)

A Bathtub

B Swimming pool

C Coffeepot

D Medicine dropper

14. Which unit would be best to use for the distance from New York to Chicago? (15-2)

A centimeter

B kilometer

C meter

D millimeter

15. Which is the best estimate of the mass of a golf ball? (15-4)

A 450 kilograms

B 450 grams

C 45 kilograms

D 45 grams

Set A, pages 350–354

Estimate the length of the bead in centimeters. Then measure to the nearest centimeter.

You can use your finger width as 1 centimeter to help estimate.

Estimate: about 3 centimeters long

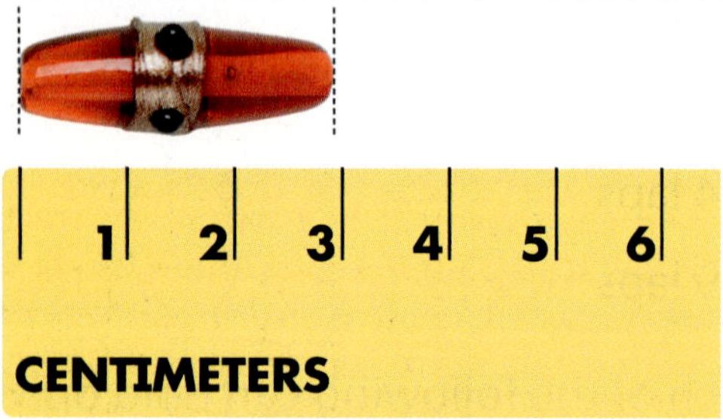

The bead is 3 centimeters long, to the nearest centimeter.

Remember to line up the object with the 0 mark on the ruler.

Estimate the length. Then measure to the nearest centimeter.

1. 

Choose the better estimate.

2. The length of a truck
10 meters or 10 kilometers

3. The height of a house
4 centimeters or 4 meters

Change the units.

4. 5 meters = ___ centimeters

5. How many centimeters are in 4 meters, 3 centimeters?

Set B, pages 356–357

What is the capacity of this pitcher?

Choose an appropriate unit and estimate.

A milliliter is too small, so estimate using liters.

The pitcher looks like it will hold about 2 liters.

Remember that more than one unit can be used to measure the capacity of a container.

Choose the better estimate.

1. 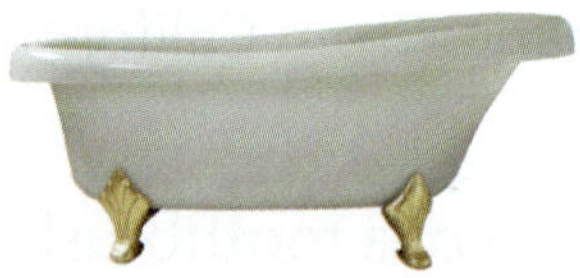

150 mL or 150 L

2. 

5 mL or 5 L

Set C, pages 358–359

What is the mass of this bar of soap?

Choose a unit and estimate.

A kilogram is too much, so estimate using grams.

The bar of soap has about the same mass as 100 grapes, or about 100 grams.

Remember to use the examples of a gram and kilogram to help you estimate.

Choose the better estimate.

1.

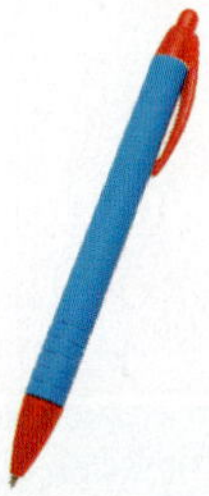

15 g or 15 kg

2.

2 g or 2 kg

Set D, pages 360–361

Vita makes bows using ribbon. She needs 30 cm of ribbon for each bow. What is the total length of ribbon she needs to make 4 bows? 5 bows?

Make a table and look for a pattern.

Explain the pattern you see.
Solve the problem.

Number of Bows	1	2	3	4	5
Total Length of Ribbon	30 cm	60 cm	90 cm	120 cm	150 cm

Vita needs 30 cm of ribbon for each bow she makes. For 2 bows, she needs 30 cm + 30 cm of ribbon. I continued the pattern to find how much ribbon Vita needs for 4 bows and for 5 bows.

Vita needs 120 cm for 4 bows and 150 cm for 5 bows.

Remember to check your answers. Make sure all of your numbers fit the pattern.

Copy and complete the table.
Write to explain the pattern.
Solve the problem.

Ned is training for a 40 km bike race. If he continues his pattern, how far will he ride on Day 4? On Day 5?

Day	1	2	3	4	5
Distance Ned Rode	1 km	4 km	7 km		

Topic 16

Perimeter, Area, and Volume

1 How far would you need to walk to go around the outside of this maze in Williamsburg, Virginia? You will find out in Lesson 16-1.

2 How many different kinds of alligators and crocodiles are there? You will find out in Lesson 16-4.

3 How long is one side of this small chessboard? You will find out in Lesson 16-6.

4

What is the perimeter of the base of this glass house? You will find out in Lesson 16-2.

Review What You Know!

Vocabulary

Choose the best term from the box.

- equilateral
- quadrilateral
- pentagon
- trapezoid

1. A __?__ has 5 sides.

2. A triangle with all three sides the same length is called a(n) __?__ triangle.

3. A rectangle is a special __?__ with 4 right angles.

Multiplication Facts

Find each product.

4. 3×8 **5.** 6×4 **6.** 5×7

7. 2×9 **8.** 7×3 **9.** 4×8

10. 7×5 **11.** 4×4 **12.** 9×8

Geometry

Write the name that best describes each figure.

13. A quadrilateral with only one pair of parallel sides

14. A quadrilateral with four right angles and all sides the same length

15. A triangle with no sides the same length

Arrays

16. **Writing to Explain** Explain how to draw an array to show 3×6. Draw the array.

Virginia

Lesson 16-1

3.9.d The student will estimate and use U.S. Customary and metric units to measure area and perimeter. **(Also 3.10.a)**

Understanding Perimeter

Hands-On

grid paper

How do you find perimeter?

Gus wants to make a playpen for his dog and put a fence around it. He made drawings of two different playpens. What is the perimeter of the playpen in each drawing?

The distance around a figure is its perimeter.

scale: ⊢⊣ = 1 foot

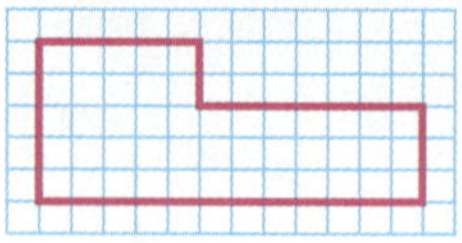

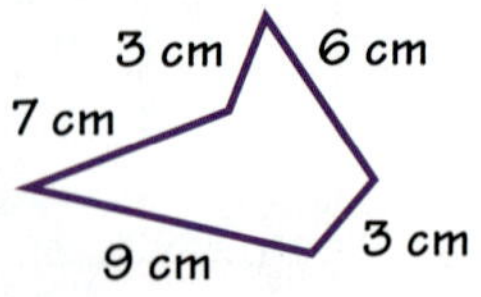

1 cm represents 1 m

Guided Practice*

Do you know HOW?

In **1** and **2**, find the perimeter.

1.

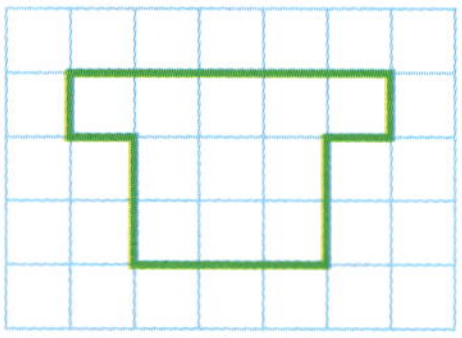

scale: ⊢⊣ = 1 inch

2.

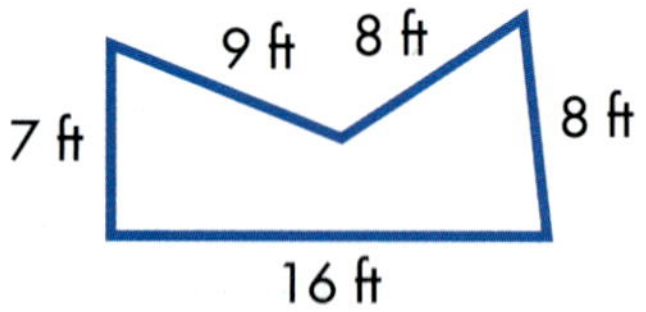

Do you UNDERSTAND?

3. In the example above, how do you know what unit Gus used for the first playpen?

4. What is the perimeter of the garden shown in the diagram below?

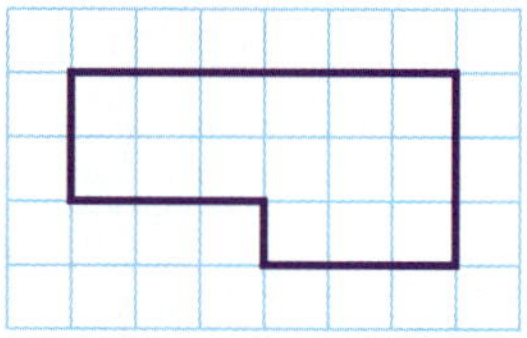

scale: ⊢⊣ = 1 foot

Independent Practice

In **5–7**, find the perimeter of each polygon.

5.

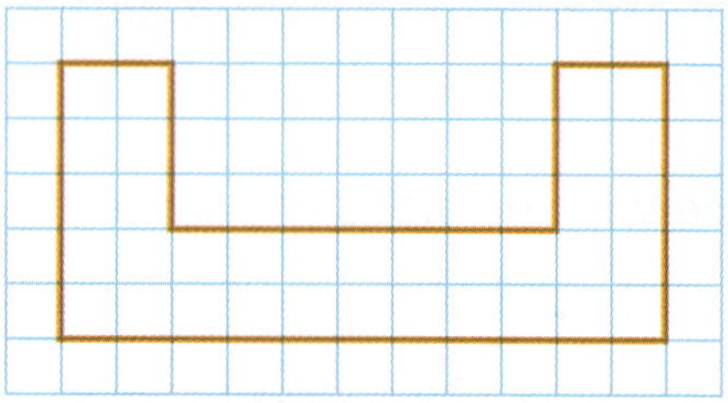

scale: ⊢⊣ = 1 m

6.

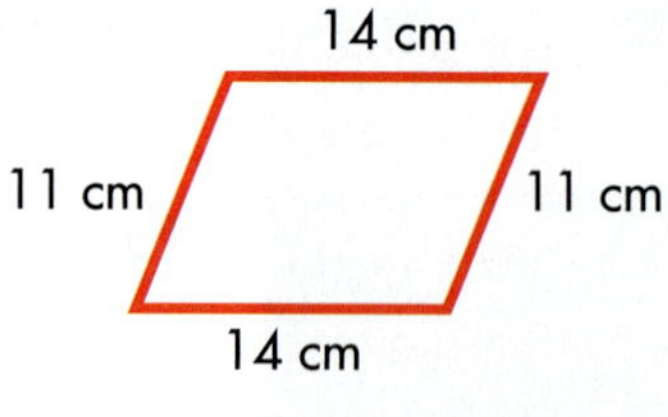

7.

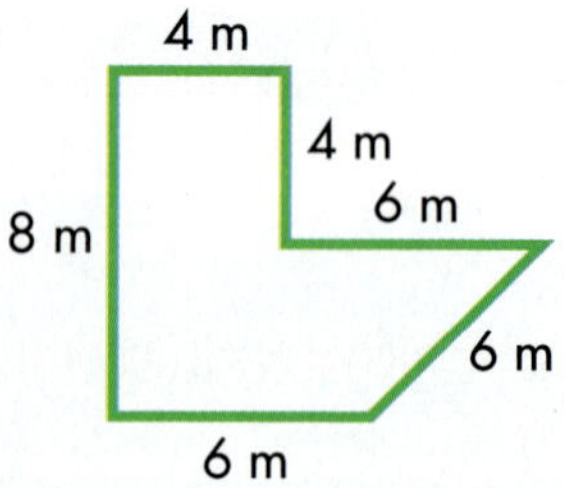

In **8–10**, draw a figure with the given perimeter. Use grid paper.

8. 14 units **9.** 8 units **10.** 20 units

DIGITAL Animated Glossary, eTools **www.pearsonsuccessnet.com**

*For another example, see Set A on page 388.

One Way

You can find the perimeter by counting unit segments.

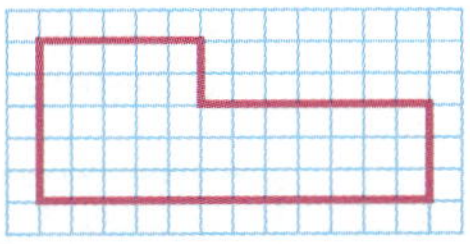

The perimeter of this playpen is 34 feet.

Another Way

Add the lengths of the sides to find the perimeter.

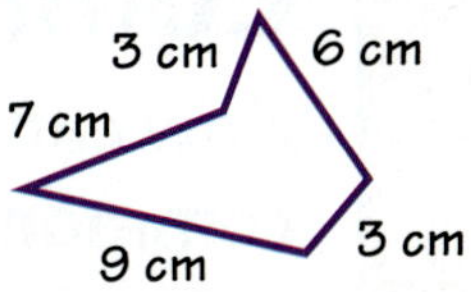

$3 + 9 + 7 + 3 + 6 = 28$

The perimeter of the drawing is 28 cm.
The perimeter of this playpen is 28 meters.

Problem Solving

11. Mr. Karas needs to find the perimeter of the playground to build a fence around it. What is the perimeter of the playground?

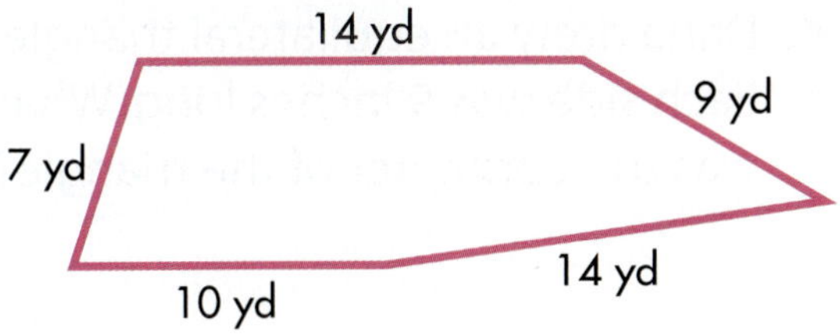

12. Mike needs to find the perimeter of the pool so he knows how many tiles to put around the edge. What is the perimeter of the pool?

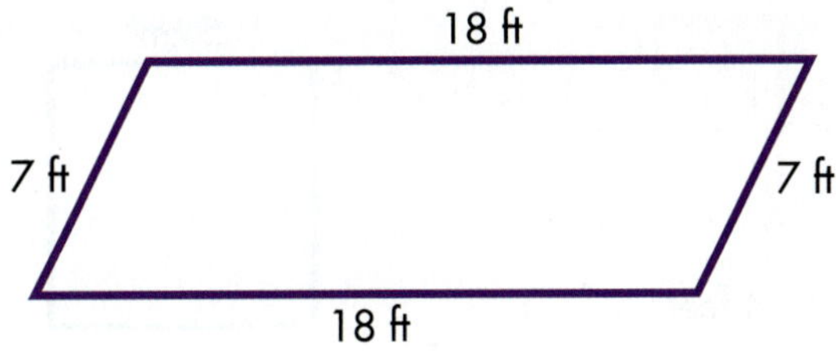

13. The distance around the outside of this maze in Williamsburg, Virginia, is the same as the perimeter of a rectangle. The picture shows the lengths of the sides of the rectangle. What is the perimeter of the maze?

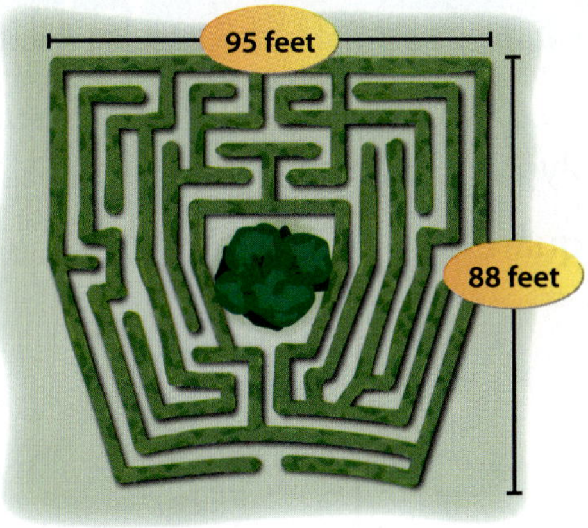

14. Jani has the magnet shown below.

SOL Prep

What is the perimeter of Jani's magnet to the nearest inch? Use a ruler to measure.

A 2 in. **B** 4 in. **C** 5 in. **D** 6 in.

15. **Writing to Explain** Roberto has a magnet that is twice as long and twice as wide as Jani's magnet in Problem 14. Find the perimeter of Roberto's magnet. Explain your work.

Virginia

Lesson 16-2

3.9.d The student will estimate and use U.S. Customary and metric units to measure area and perimeter.

Perimeter of Common Shapes

How can you find the perimeter of common shapes?

Mr. Coe needs to find the perimeter of two swimming pool designs. One pool shape is a rectangle. The other pool shape is a square. What is the perimeter of each pool?

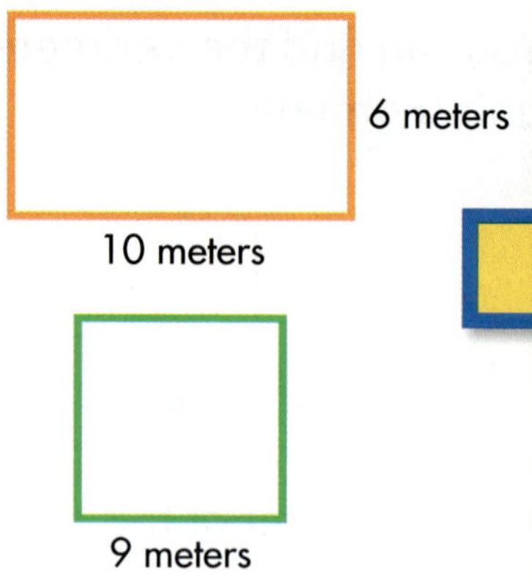

Guided Practice*

Do you know HOW?

For **1** and **2**, find the perimeter.

1. Rectangle

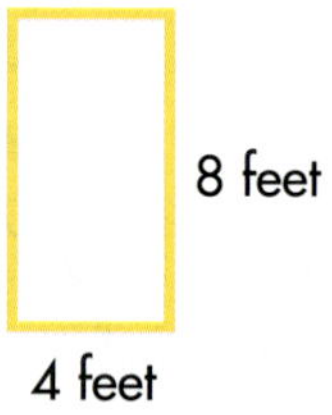

2. Square

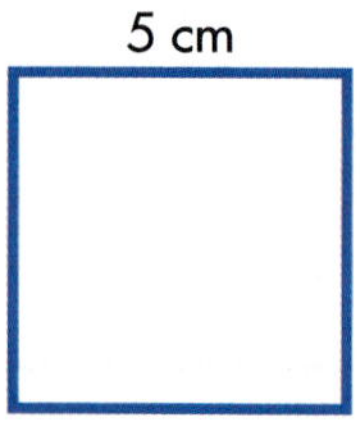

Do you UNDERSTAND?

3. In the examples above, explain how to find the missing lengths.

4. Darla drew an equilateral triangle. Each side was 9 inches long. What was the perimeter of the triangle?

Independent Practice

In **5** and **6**, use an inch ruler to measure the length of the sides of the polygon. Find the perimeter.

5. Square

6. Rectangle

In **7** and **8**, find the perimeter of each polygon.

7. Rectangle

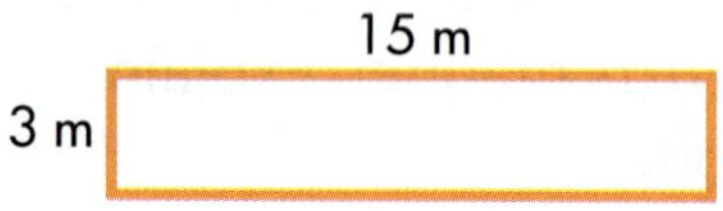

8. Equilateral triangle

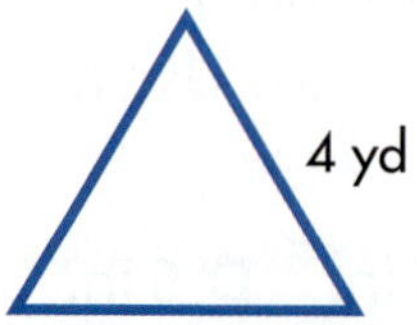

**For another example, see Set A on page 388.*

Find the perimeter of the pool that has a rectangle shape.

Remember: Opposite sides of a rectangle are the same length.

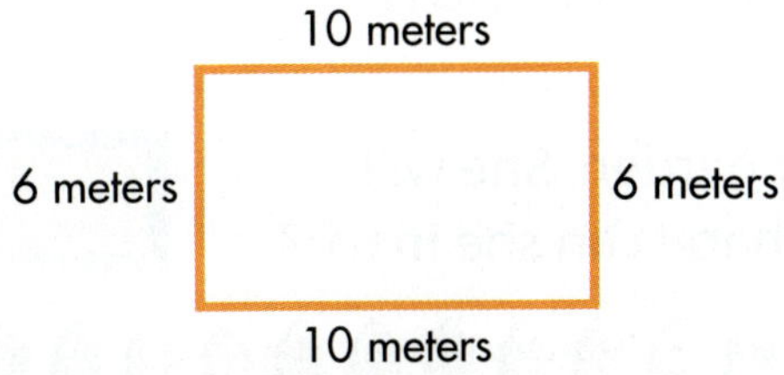

$10 + 6 + 10 + 6 = 32$

The perimeter of this pool is 32 meters.

Find the perimeter of the pool that has a square shape.

Remember: All four sides of a square are the same length.

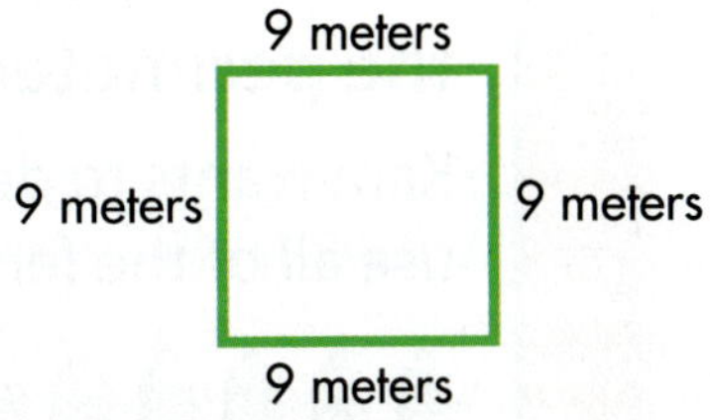

$9 + 9 + 9 + 9 = 36$ or $4 \times 9 = 36$

The perimeter of this pool is 36 meters.

Problem Solving

9. Writing to Explain Cora uses ribbons to make three different sizes of bows. How much more ribbon does it take to make 2 large bows than 2 small bows? Explain how you found your answer.

Data

Size of Bow	Length of Ribbon
Small	27 in.
Medium	36 in.
Large	49 in.

10. The base of Philip Johnson's glass house in New Canaan, Connecticut, is a rectangle. What is the perimeter of the base of the glass house?

11. What is the perimeter of the cloth patch outlined below?

SOL Prep

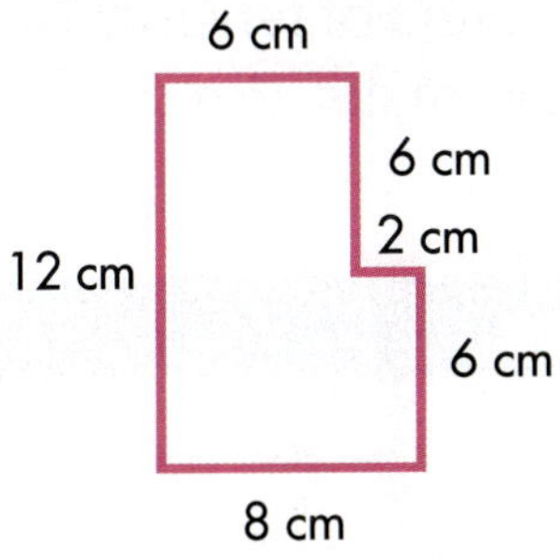

A 96 cm

B 40 cm

C 38 cm

D 32 cm

12. Ami's room is in the shape of a square. What is the perimeter of the room?

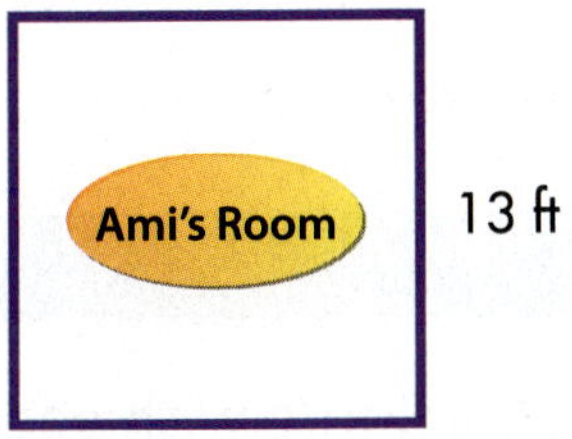

Virginia

Lesson 16-3

Extends 3.9.d The student will estimate and use U.S. Customary and metric units to measure area and perimeter.

Different Shapes with the Same Perimeter

Hands-On
grid paper

What shapes can you make when you know the perimeter?

Kara wants to design a shape for her garden. She will use all of the fencing shown. What shape can she make?

Other Examples

Each of these shapes also has a perimeter of 14 yards.

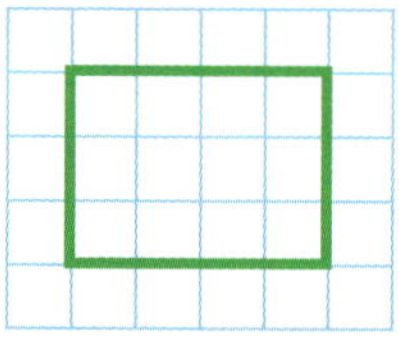

scale: ⊢⊣ = 1 yard

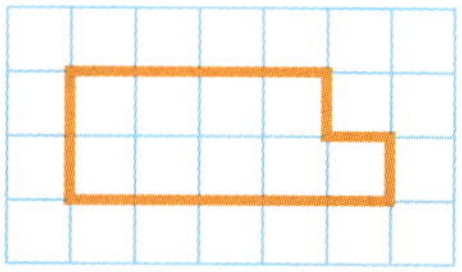

scale: ⊢⊣ = 1 yard

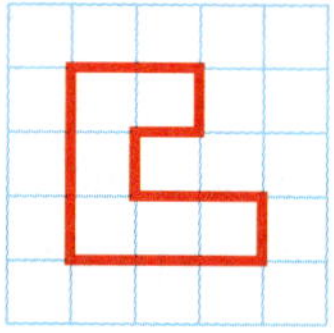

scale: ⊢⊣ = 1 yard

Guided Practice*

Do you know HOW?

Copy and complete each figure to show the given perimeter. Use grid paper.

1. A square
Perimeter = 16 ft

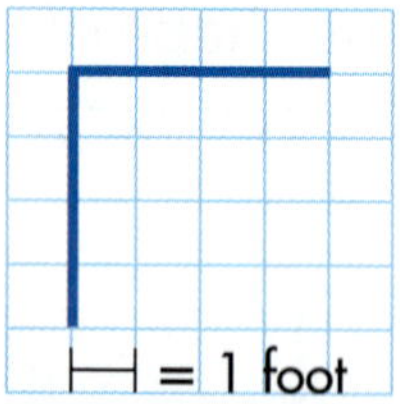

2. A 6-sided figure
Perimeter = 10 m

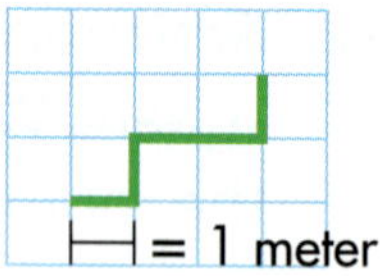

Do you UNDERSTAND?

3. Look at the examples above. Describe the lengths of the sides of a third rectangle that has a perimeter of 14 yards.

4. Mike wants to design a shape for his garden. He wants to use exactly 18 meters of fencing. Draw a shape he can make. Use grid paper.

Independent Practice

In **5–7**, draw a figure with each perimeter. Use grid paper.

5. 12 units **6.** 4 units **7.** 22 units

DIGITAL
Animated Glossary, eTools
www.pearsonsuccessnet.com

*For another example, see Set A on page 388.

Step 1

Draw a picture or use straws to act out the problem.

Each straw is 1 unit. Use 14 straws to make a shape. The perimeter of the shape is 14 units.

Then describe the shape and the length of each side.

The figure is a rectangle. Two sides are each 6 units long, and two sides are each 1 unit long.

Step 2

Check that the shape has the correct perimeter.

Add the side lengths.

$6 + 1 + 6 + 1 = 14$ units

Kara needs exactly 14 yards of fencing to make a rectangle with sides that are 6 yards and 1 yard.

Problem Solving

8. Darius wants to design a birthday card. He has exactly 18 inches of yarn that he wants to glue around the edge of the card. Draw a card design he can make. Use grid paper.

9. Draw 2 different shapes that have a perimeter of 24 units. Use grid paper to help.

Use the pictures at the right for **10** and **11**.

10. Aleesa bought one scarf and three hats. What was the total cost of these items?

11. How much more does a sweater cost than the mittens?

12. **Algebra** Look for a pattern in the table. Copy and complete.

Number of Tables	1	2	3	4	5	6
Number of Chairs	8	16		32		48

13. Which pair of shapes have the same perimeter?

SOL Prep

A

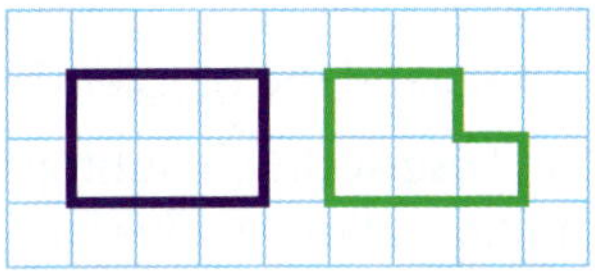

C

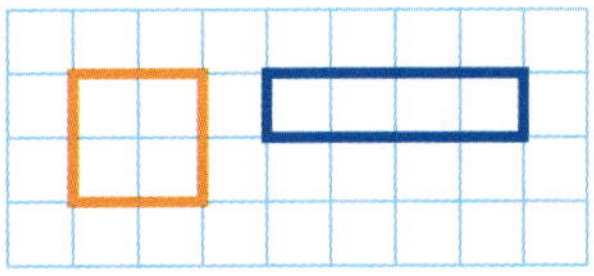

B

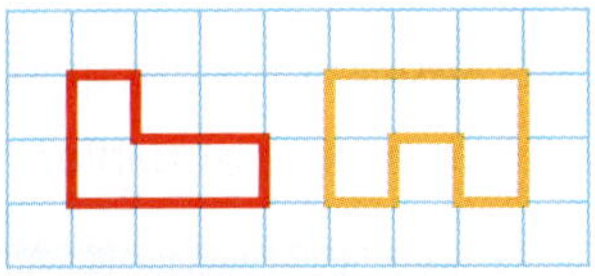

D

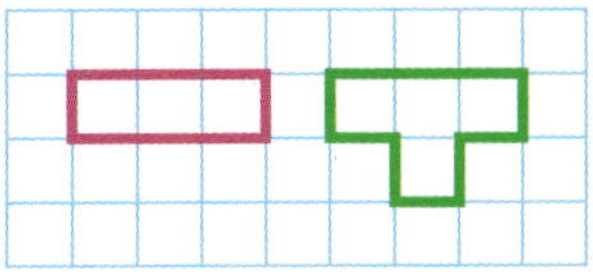

Virginia

Lesson 16-4

Extends 3.4 The student will estimate solutions to and solve single-step and multistep problems involving the sum or difference of two whole numbers, each 9,999 or less, with or without regrouping.

Problem Solving

Try, Check, and Revise

Tad, Holly, and Shana made 36 posters all together. Shana made 3 more posters than Holly.

Tad and Holly made the same number of posters. How many posters did Shana make?

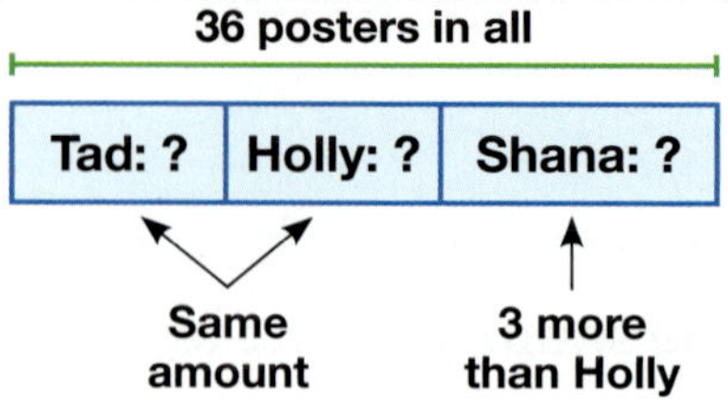

Guided Practice*

Do you know HOW?

1. Peg and Pat are sharing 64 crayons. Pat has 10 more crayons than Peg. How many crayons does each girl have?

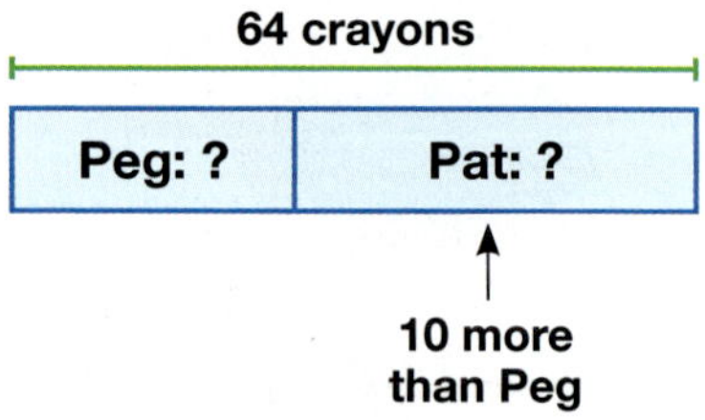

Do you UNDERSTAND?

2. Look at the diagram for Problem 1. Why aren't the two parts of the rectangle the same size?

3. **Write a Problem** Write a problem that can be solved by using reasoning to make good tries.

Independent Practice

4. Rectangles A and B have the same perimeter but different shapes. Rectangle A is 5 inches long and 3 inches wide. Rectangle B is 6 inches longer than it is wide. What are the length and width of Rectangle B?

5. Hanna has 6 coins worth 50¢ in all. Some of the coins are nickels and some are dimes. What coins does Hanna have?

Stuck? Try this....

- What do I know?
- What am I asked to find?
- What diagram can I use to help understand the problem?
- Can I use addition, subtraction, multiplication, or division?
- Is all of my work correct?
- Did I answer the right question?
- Is my answer reasonable?

**For another example, see Set B on page 388.*

Plan

Use reasoning to make good tries. Then check.

Try: $10 + 10 + 13 = 33$

Check: $33 < 36$

Too low, I need 3 more.

Try: $12 + 12 + 15 = 39$

Check: $39 > 36$

Too high, I need 3 less.

Solve

Revise, using what you know.

Try: $11 + 11 + 14 = 36$

Check: $36 = 36$

This is correct.

Shana made 14 posters.

Use the pictures at the right for **6** and **7**.

6. The clerk at the flower store puts all the roses into two vases. One vase has 2 more roses than the other vase. How many roses are in each vase?

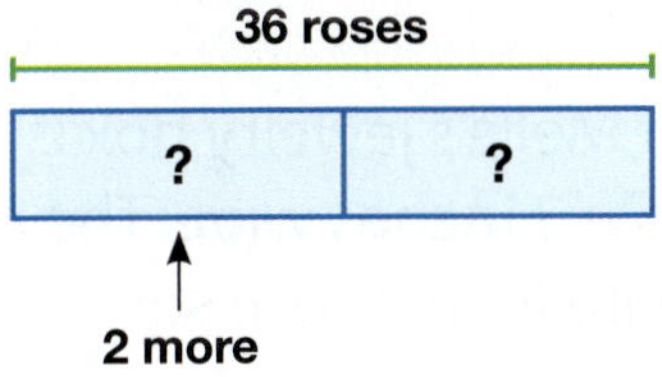

7. Edna, Jay, and Bob bought all of the carnations in the flower store. Edna bought 2 more than Jay. Bob and Jay bought the same number. How many carnations did Edna buy?

8. Mr. Tyler bought one iris for $1.25 and 3 roses for $3 each. How much did Mr. Tyler spend for the roses?

9. Cam bought an iris for $1.25. He paid with 6 coins. What coins did he use?

10. SOL Prep A rectangle has a perimeter of 48 inches. Which of the following pairs of numbers could be the length and width of the rectangle?

A 12 inches and 10 inches

B 8 inches and 6 inches

C 20 inches and 4 inches

D 15 inches and 5 inches

11. Kevin read that there are 22 types of crocodiles and alligators in all. There are 6 more types of crocodiles than alligators. How many types of crocodiles are there? How many types of alligators are there?

Virginia

Lesson 16-5

3.10.b The student will count the number of square units needed to cover a given surface in order to determine area. **(Also 3.9.d)**

Understanding Area

Hands-On: square tiles

How do you find area?

Raj needs to know how many tiles to buy to cover a floor. What is the area of the floor?

Area is the number of square units needed to cover the region inside a figure. A square unit is a square with sides that are each 1 unit long.

☐ = 1 square unit

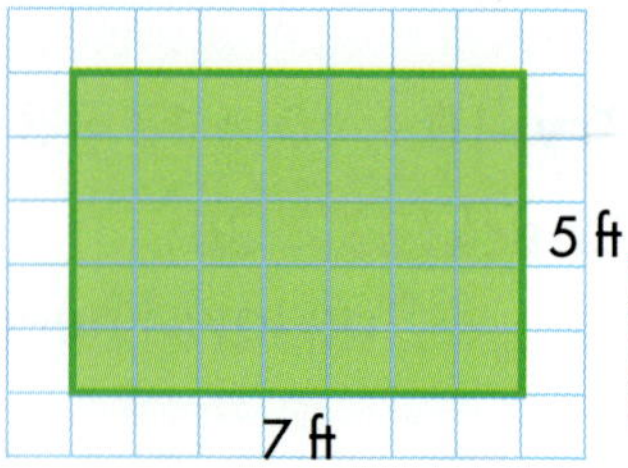

☐ = 1 square foot

Guided Practice*

Do you know HOW?

In **1** and **2**, find the area of each figure. Use square tiles or grid paper to help.

1.

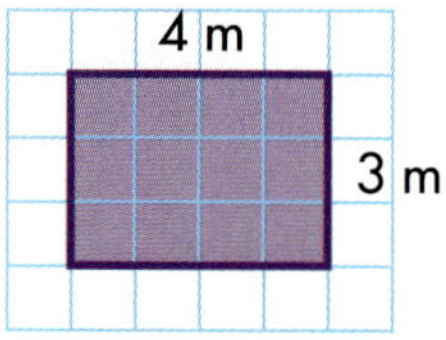

☐ = 1 square meter

2.

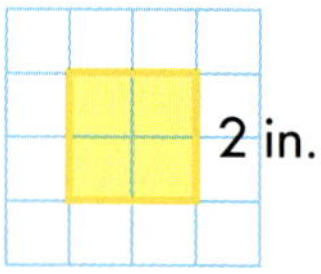

☐ = 1 square inch

Do you UNDERSTAND?

3. Use the example above. Explain how finding the area of a figure is different from finding the perimeter.

4. The lid of Mella's jewelry box is a rectangle 3 inches wide. The area is 15 square inches. Use square tiles to make a model or grid paper to draw a picture of the lid.

Independent Practice

In **5–10**, find the area of each figure.

5.

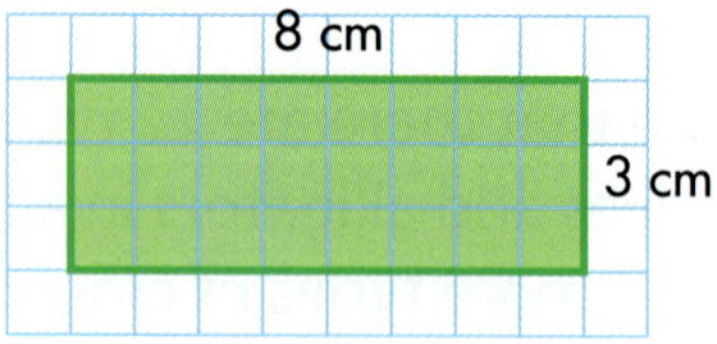

☐ = 1 square centimeter

6.

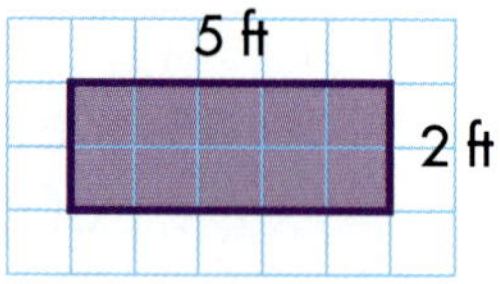

☐ = 1 square foot

7.

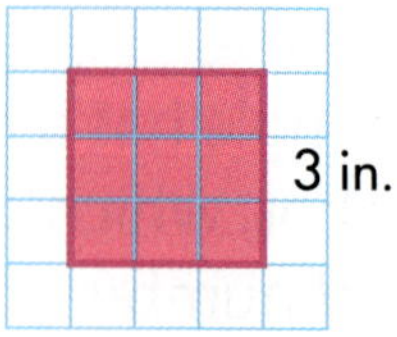

☐ = 1 square inch

8.

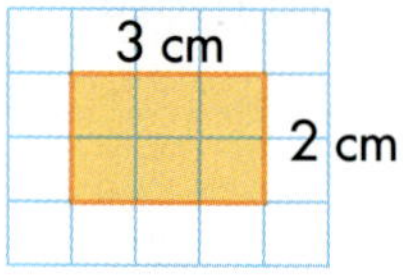

☐ = 1 square cm

9.

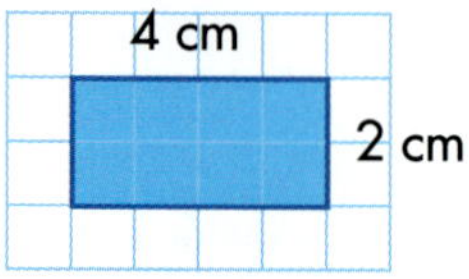

☐ = 1 square cm

10.

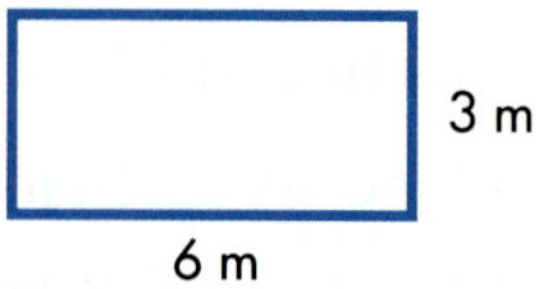

DIGITAL Animated Glossary, eTools **www.pearsonsuccessnet.com**

*For another example, see Set C on page 389.

One Way

Count the square units.

There are 35 square units inside the figure.

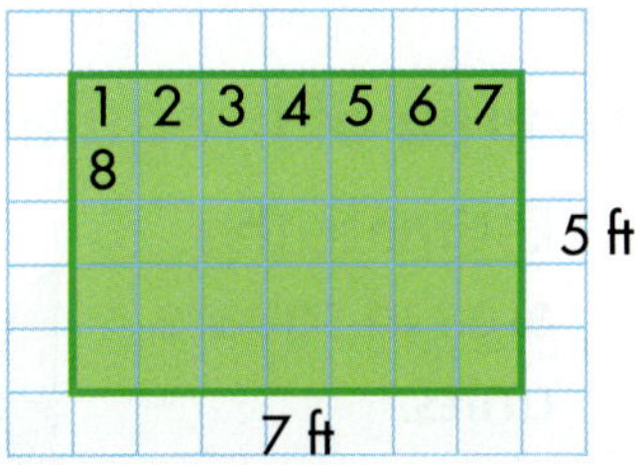

The lengths are given in feet. The area of the floor is 35 square feet.

Another Way

When you find the area of a rectangle or square, you can think of the grid squares as an array.

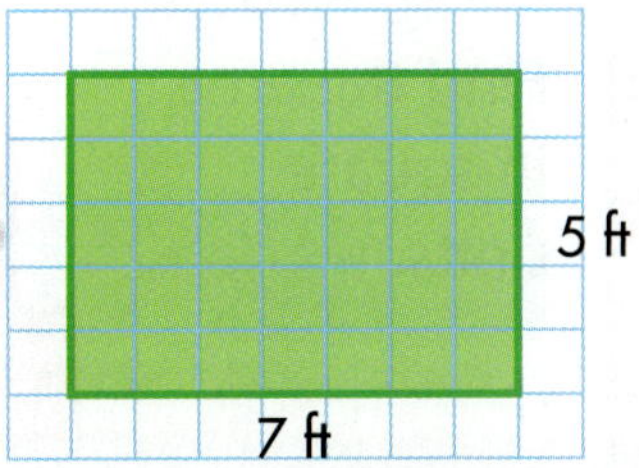

There are 5 rows with 7 squares in each row.

$5 \times 7 = 35$

The area of the floor is 35 square feet.

Problem Solving

A gallery is planning a display of animal photographs. Use the picture at the right for **11–13**.

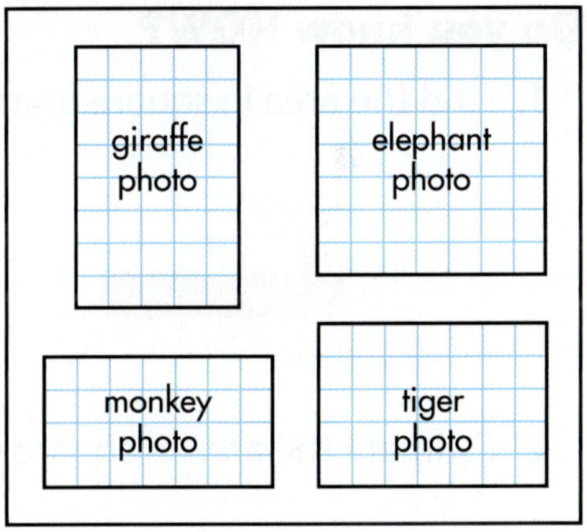

11. Find the area of each photo in square units.

12. Use grid paper. Draw a rectangle that has a smaller area than the giraffe photo and a greater area than the monkey photo.

13. Which has the greater perimeter, the photo of the giraffe or the photo of the tiger? How many units greater is it?

14. Use grid paper. Draw two different figures, each with an area of 24 square units. Find the perimeter of each figure.

15. **Writing to Explain** Tamiya cut a 12-inch piece of string into 3 equal parts. She also cut a 24-inch piece of ribbon into 8 equal parts. Which was longer, a piece of the string or a piece of the ribbon? Explain how you decided.

16. What is the area of the picture Abe made with square tiles?

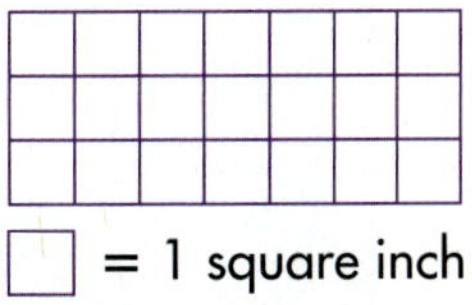

A 20 square inches

B 21 square inches

C 24 square inches

D 30 square inches

Virginia

Lesson 16-6

3.9.d The student will estimate and use U.S. Customary and metric units to measure area and perimeter.

Estimating and Measuring Area

Hands-On
grid paper

How do you find and estimate area of irregular shapes?

Find the area in square units.

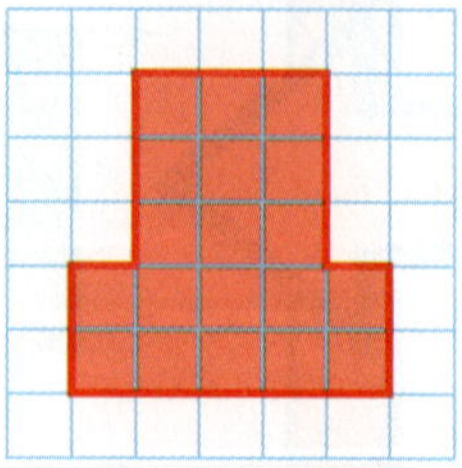

Estimate the area in square units.

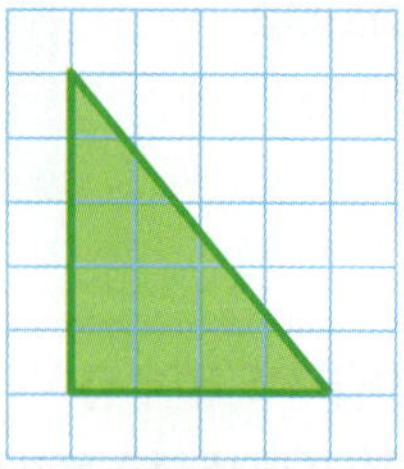

Guided Practice*

Do you know HOW?

1. Find the area in square units.

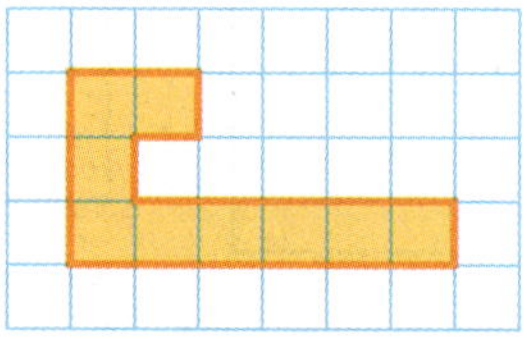

2. Estimate the area in square units.

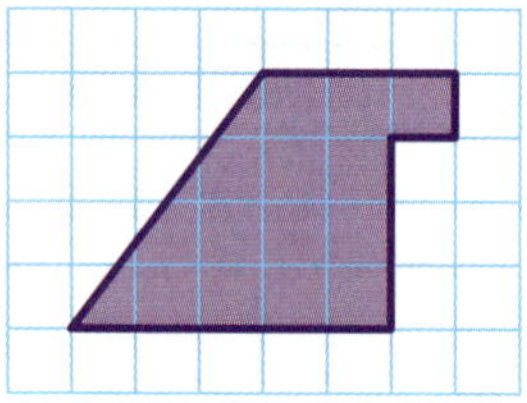

Do you UNDERSTAND?

3. Will partial squares always combine to form whole squares? Why or why not?

4. Kev needs to find the area of the floor so that he knows the number of tiles to buy to cover it. What is the area of the floor?

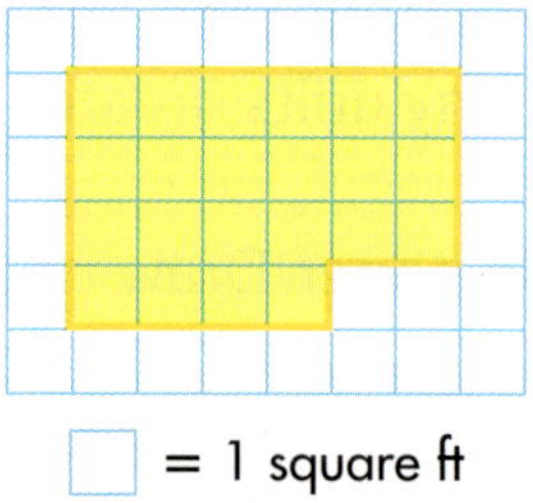

Independent Practice

In **5–7**, find each area in square units.

5.

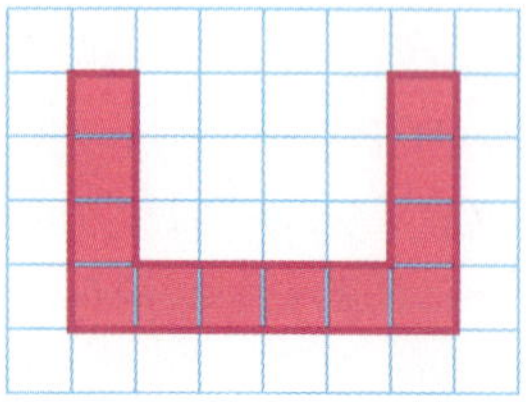

6.

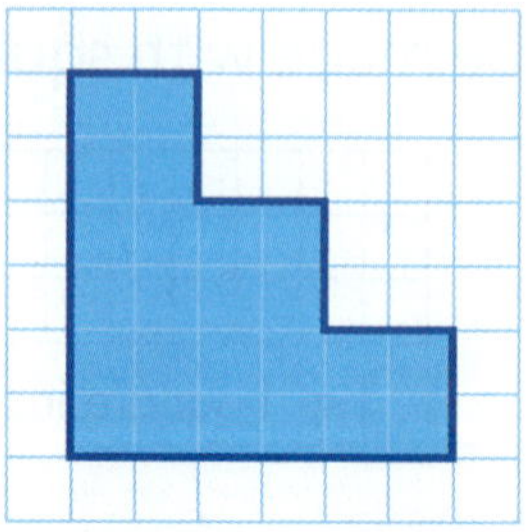

7.

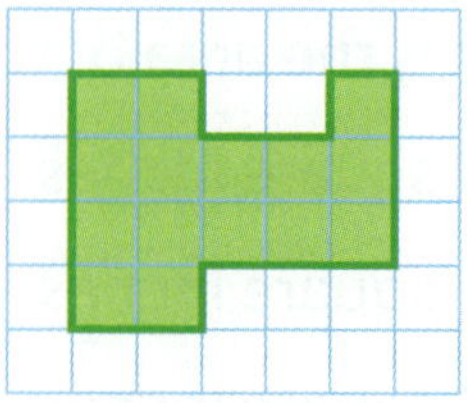

*For another example, see Set C on page 389.

To find the area, count the squares.

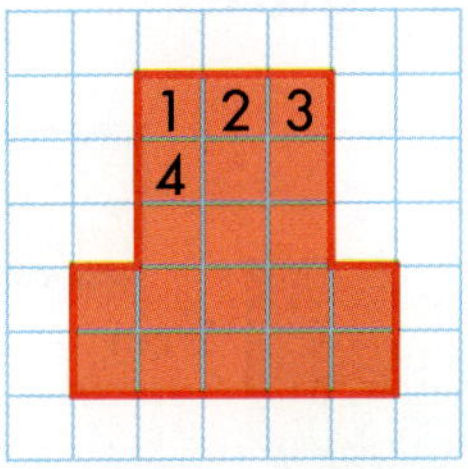

There are 19 square units.

The area is 19 square units.

To estimate the area, count whole squares first.

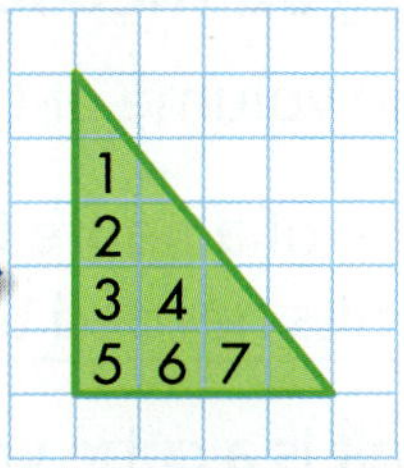

There are 7 whole squares.

Combine partial squares to make whole squares.

The partial squares make up about 3 whole squares.

$7 + 3 = 10$

The area is about 10 square units.

In **8–10**, estimate each area in square units.

8.

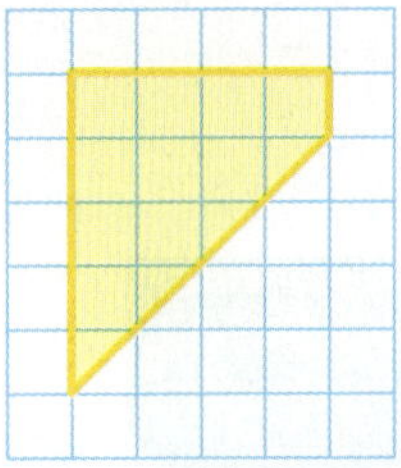

9.

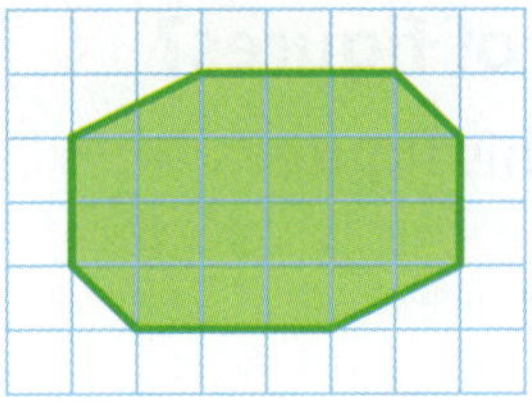

10.

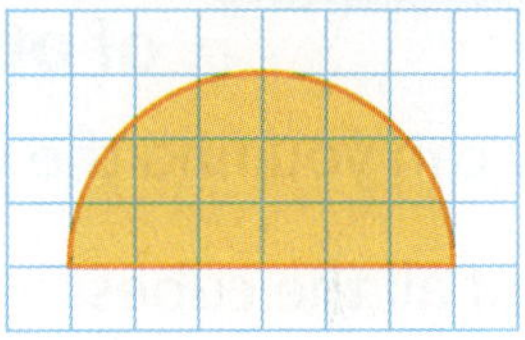

Problem Solving

11. Chen will use tiles to make a picture. He needs to estimate the area of the picture so that he buys enough tiles. Estimate the area of Chen's picture.

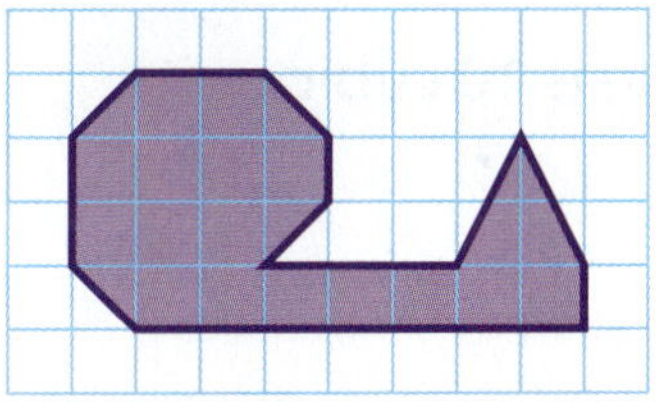

☐ = 1 square cm

SOL Prep

12. Suni put blue tiles on a wall. What is the area of the part of the wall with blue tiles?

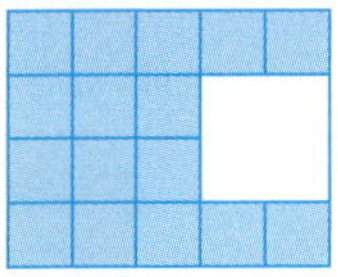

☐ = 1 square foot

A 4 square feet **C** 16 square feet

B 12 square feet **D** 20 square feet

13. **Writing to Explain** Joe says the area of this chessboard is between 1 and 2 square inches. Do you agree? Explain.

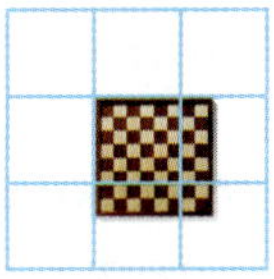

Each side of this chessboard is $1\frac{1}{4}$ inches long.

scale: ☐ = 1 sq. in.

14. **Reasonableness** Bobby estimated that the sum of $138 and $241 is about $480. Is his estimate reasonable? Explain.

Virginia

Lesson 16-7

Prepares for 5.8.a The student will find perimeter, area, and volume in standard units of measure.

Volume

Hands-On
unit cubes

How can you measure the space inside a solid figure?

What is the volume of the box?

The volume of a figure is the number of cubic units needed to fill it.

A cubic unit is a cube with edges that are 1 unit long.

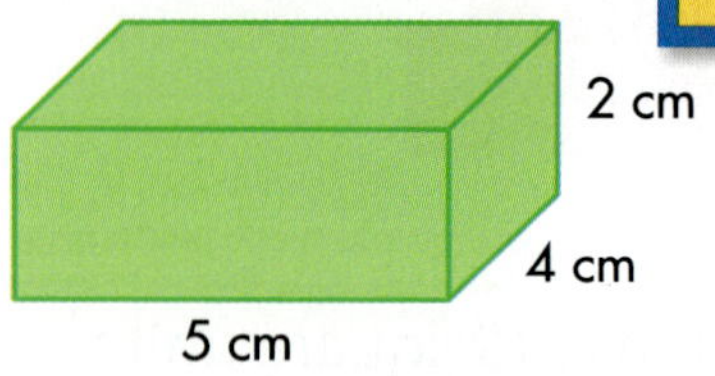

Another Example How can you measure the volume of other kinds of figures?

How can you find the volume of this figure?

Count all the cubes.

The figure has 2 rows of cubes.
There are 8 cubes in the back row.
There are 2 more cubes in the front row.
8 cubes + 2 cubes = 10 cubes

So the volume is 10 cubic units.

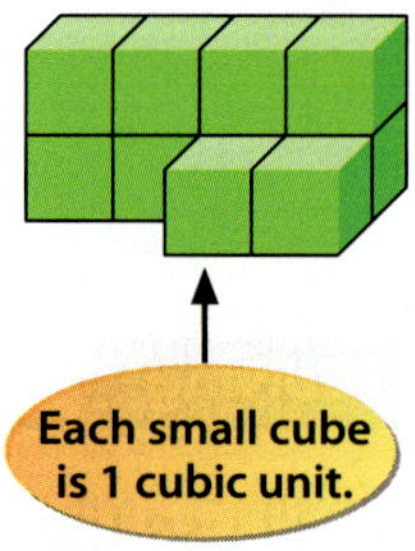

Explain It

1. Describe how to find the volume of the figure below.

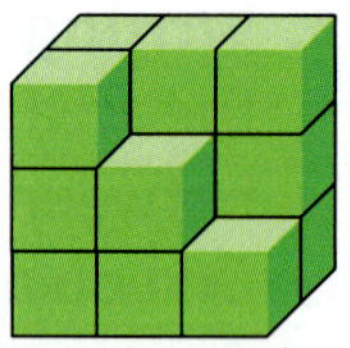

For **2** and **3**, use the figures at the right.

2. How are these two figures the same? How are they different?
3. Find the volume of each of the two figures.

Step 1

Make a model of the box using cubes.

The box is measured in centimeters.

The volume will be in cubic centimeters.

Step 2

Count all the cubes in 1 layer.

There are 20 cubes in each layer.
There are 2 layers.
20 cubes + 20 cubes = 40 cubes

Since there are 40 cubes, the volume is 40 cubic centimeters.

Guided Practice*

Do you know HOW?

Find the volume of each figure in cubic units. You may use unit cubes to help.

1. 

2. 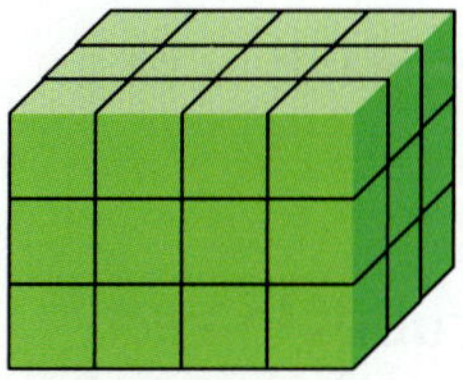

3. 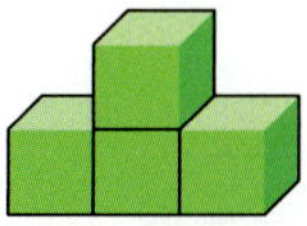

4. 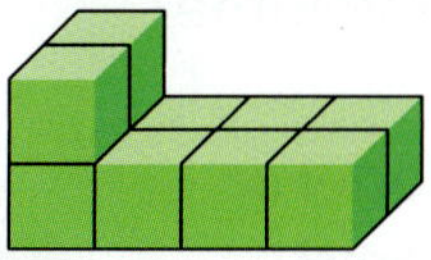

Do you UNDERSTAND?

5. How do you know the volume of the box above is 40 cubic centimeters and not 40 cubic meters?

6. Pedro has a box that is 4 inches long, 4 inches wide, and 2 inches tall. A model of the box is shown below. What is the volume of the box?

Tip *Each cube is one cubic inch.*

Independent Practice

For **7–9**, find the volume of each figure in cubic units.

7. 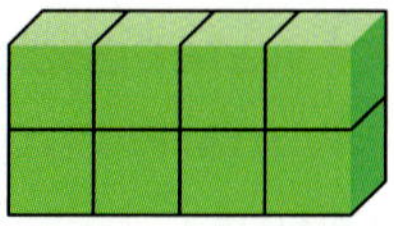

8. 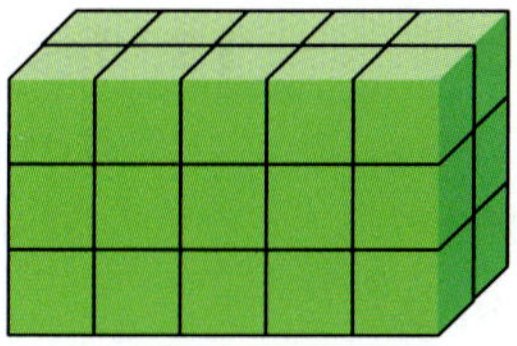

9. 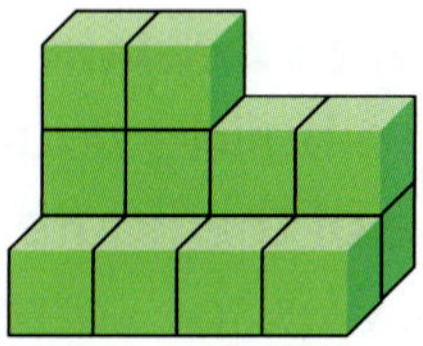

DIGITAL Animated Glossary, eTools **www.pearsonsuccessnet.com**

For another example, see Set D on page 389.

Independent Practice

For **10–12**, find the volume of each figure in cubic units.

10.

11.

12.

Problem Solving

13. **Estimation** Use the cubes shown at the right to estimate the volume of the rectangular prism.

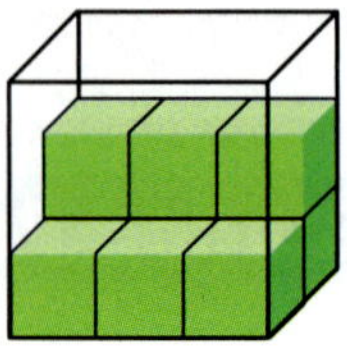

14. Derek made a rectangular prism with 4 layers of cubes. He put 5 cubes in each layer. What is the volume of the rectangular prism?

15. Draw or describe two different solid figures, each with a volume of 16 cubic units.

16. **Reasoning** One rectangular prism has 3 cubes in each of 7 layers. Another rectangular prism has 7 cubes in each of 3 layers. Which prism has the greater volume?

17. Dana has a jewelry box that looks like the model at the right. What is the volume of the jewelry box?

Each  = 1 cubic inch.

A 25 cubic inches

B 34 cubic inches

C 39 cubic inches

D 45 cubic inches

18. **Writing to Explain** Carmen used cubes to build a figure. She said the volume of the figure was 15 square inches. Was she correct? Explain why or why not.

19. Tessa drinks 9 cups of water each day. In one week, how many cups of water does Tessa drink?

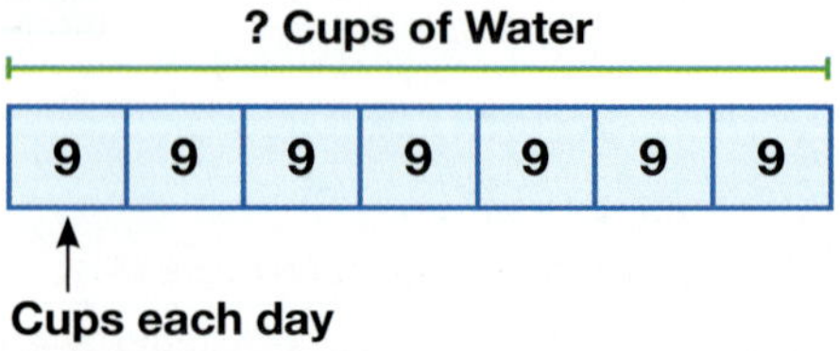

Going Digital

Perimeter and Area

Use e tools

Geometry Drawing

Draw a polygon with an area of 8 square units. Find the perimeter.

Step 1 Go to the Geometry Drawing eTool. Select the Geoboard workspace. Then click on the polygon drawing tool. Click on one point in the workspace. Drag the mouse to a second point 4 units down and click again. Drag the mouse to a point 2 units to the right and click. Drag the mouse 4 units up and click. Finally, drag the mouse 2 units left and click on point A.

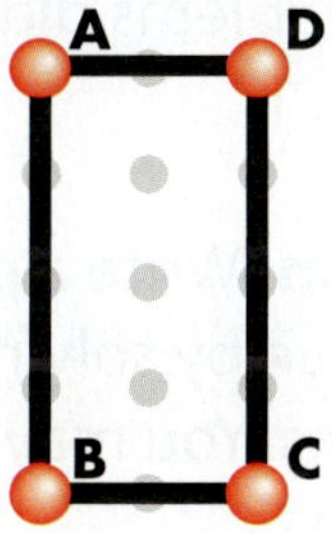

Step 2 Click on the area measurement tool icon and then on the rectangle you just drew. In the lower right corner, under Measurements, the area will appear. Make sure it is 8.00 square units. The area is 8 square units.

Step 3 Click on the perimeter measurement tool icon and then on the rectangle you just drew. In the lower right corner, under Measurements, the perimeter will appear. Make sure it is 12.00 units. The perimeter is 12 units.

Practice

1. Draw two other polygons with an area of 8 square units each. Find the perimeter of each.

2. Use the broom icon to clear the workspace. Draw two polygons with an area of 9 square units each. Find the perimeter of each.

Virginia

Lesson 16-8

Extends 3.10.b The student will count the number of square units needed to cover a given surface in order to determine area.

Problem Solving

Solve a Simpler Problem

Janet wants to paint the door to her room. The shaded part of the figure shows the part of the door that needs paint.

= 1 square foot

What is the area of the part of the door that needs paint?

Guided Practice*

Do you know HOW?

Solve. Use simpler problems.

1. Lil glued square beads on the shaded part of the frame. What is the area of the part she decorated?

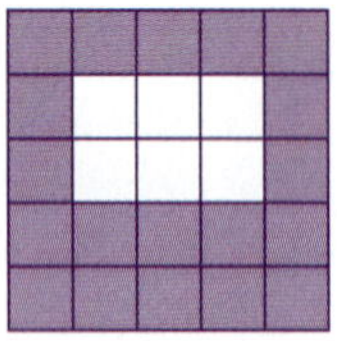

= 1 square inch

Do you UNDERSTAND?

2. What simpler problems did you use to solve Exercise 1?

3. **Write a Problem** Write a problem that you can solve by solving simpler problems. You may draw a picture to help.

Independent Practice

For **4–8**, solve. Use simpler problems.

4. Reg wants to put tiles on a wall. The shaded part of the figure shows the part that needs tiles. What is the area of the shaded part?

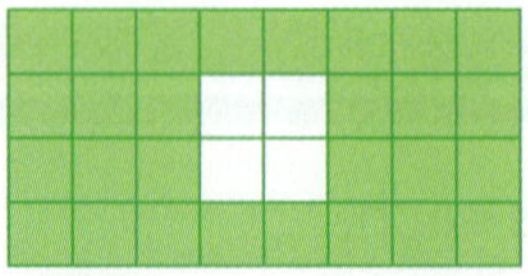

= 1 square foot

Stuck? Try this....

- What do I know?
- What am I asked to find?
- What diagram can I use to help understand the problem?
- Can I use addition, subtraction, multiplication, or division?
- Is all of my work correct?
- Did I answer the right question?
- Is my answer reasonable?

*For another example, see Set E on page 389.

Plan

I can solve simpler problems.

I can find the area of the whole rectangle and then the area of the square.

Then I can subtract to find the area of the shaded part.

Solve

Area of the whole rectangle

7 rows with 5 squares in each row

$7 \times 5 = 35$

Area of the square

3 rows with 3 squares in each row

$3 \times 3 = 9$

Subtract

$35 - 9 = 26$

The area of the part of the door that needs paint is 26 square feet.

5. Jim wants to tile the floor. The shaded part of the figure shows the part of the floor that needs tiles. What is the area of the shaded part?

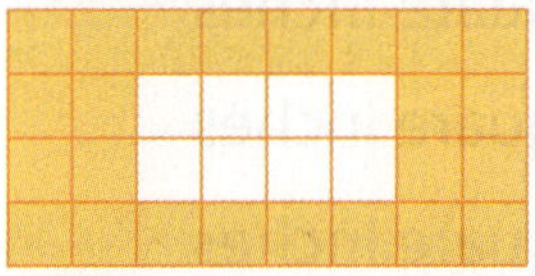

= 1 square meter

6. Dan wants to paint the bottom of a pool. The shaded part of the figure shows the part that needs paint. What is the area of the shaded part?

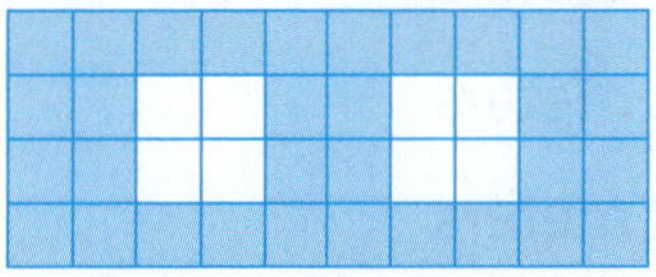

= 1 square yard

7. Macy drew two designs. How much greater is the area of the yellow figure than the area of the green figure?

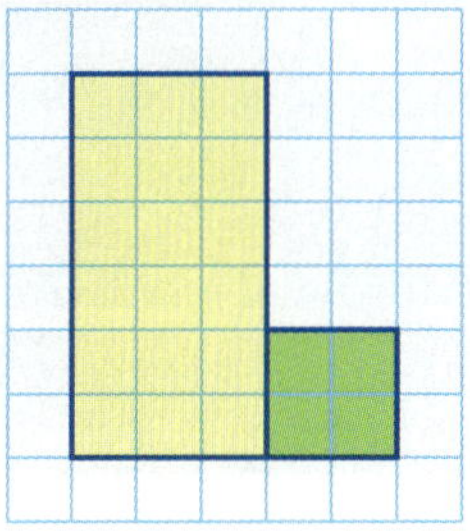

= 1 square in.

8. Mr. Eli grows vegetables in different fields on his farm. What is the total area of the corn and bean fields?

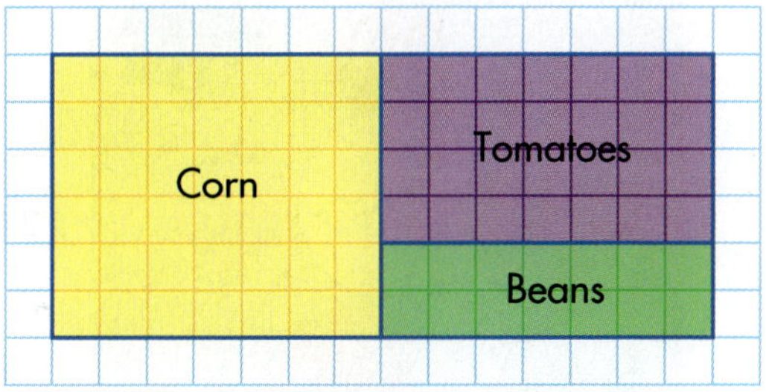

= 1 square meter

9. Neva built these figures using toothpicks. If she continues the pattern, how many toothpicks in all will she use for the 4th figure? the 5th figure?

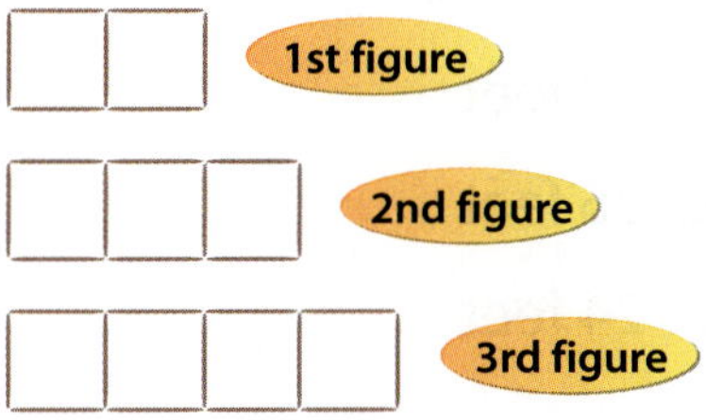

1. A drawing of the rose garden in the park is shown. What is the perimeter of the rose garden? (16-1)

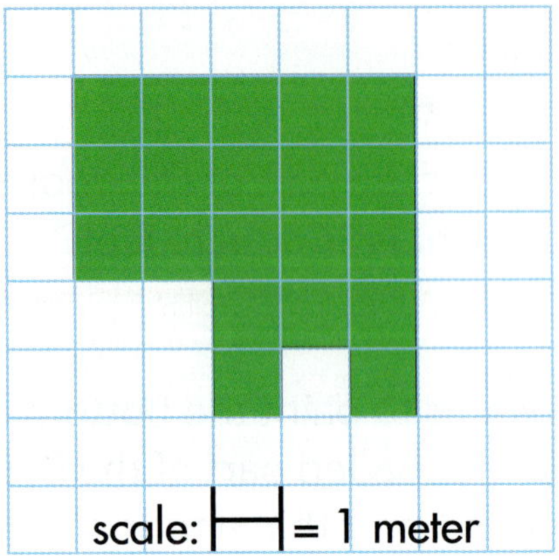

A 26 meters

B 24 meters

C 22 meters

D 20 meters

2. The patio in Marta's backyard is in the shape of a square. What is the perimeter of the patio? (16-2)

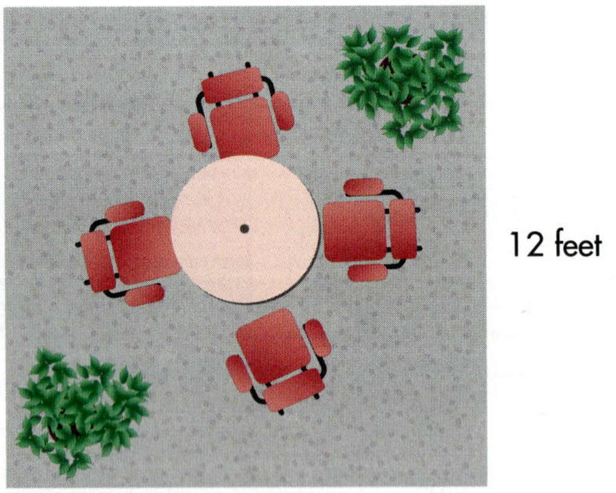

A 144 feet

B 48 feet

C 36 feet

D 24 feet

3. Mrs. Gomez made a quilt for her daughter's doll. What is the area of the doll's quilt? (16-5)

A 50 square inches

B 45 square inches

C 40 square inches

D 30 square inches

4. A swimming pool is drawn below. How many square feet of green tile are around the pool? (16-8)

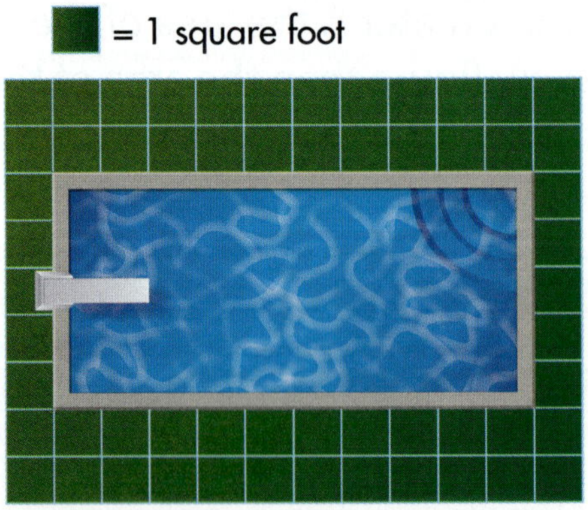

A 108 square feet

B 63 square feet

C 58 square feet

D 50 square feet

5. A model of the box that a toy came in is shown below. What is the volume of the box? (16-7)

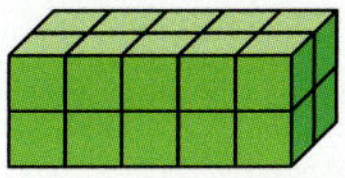

A 15 cubic units

B 16 cubic units

C 20 cubic units

D 24 cubic units

6. Which is the best estimate of the area of the shape shown below? (16-6)

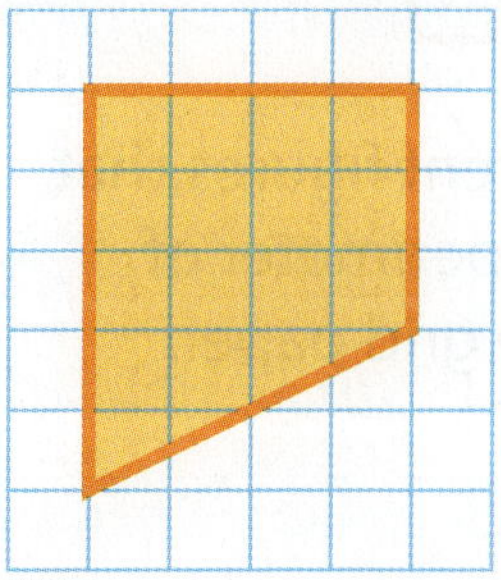

A 23 square inches

B 20 square inches

C 18 square inches

D 16 square inches

7. What is the volume of this figure? (16-7)

A 24 cubic units

B 18 cubic units

C 14 cubic units

D 8 cubic units

8. Each of the 26 students in Carrie's class chose either drums or horns to play during music class. If 4 more students chose drums than horns, how many chose each? (16-4)

A 16 chose drums, 10 chose horns

B 15 chose drums, 11 chose horns

C 14 chose drums, 12 chose horns

D 14 chose drums, 10 chose horns

9. Eugene's garden design is shown below.

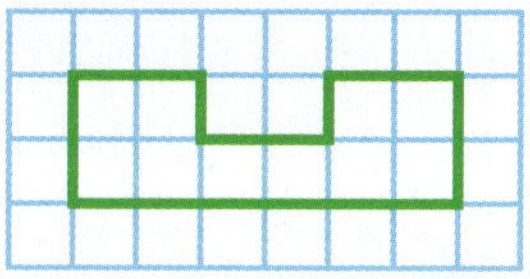

Which other design has the same perimeter as Eugene's garden design? (16-3)

A

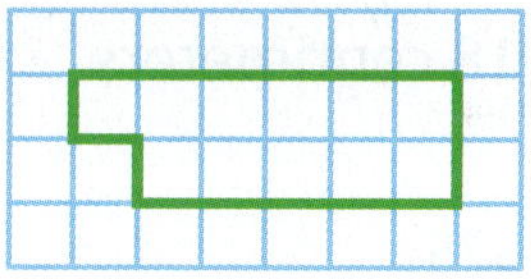

B

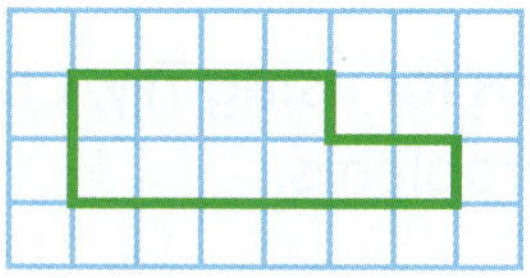

C

D

Set A, pages 368–373

What is the perimeter of each figure?

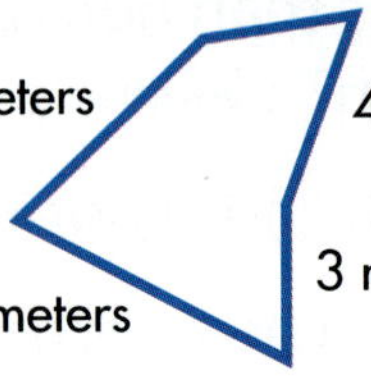

Add the lengths of the sides.

3 + 4 + 3 + 6 + 5 = 21 meters

The perimeter is 21 meters.

Opposite sides of a rectangle are the same length.

6 + 3 + 6 + 3 = 18

The perimeter is 18 centimeters.

Remember that different shapes can have the same perimeter.

Find the perimeter.

1.

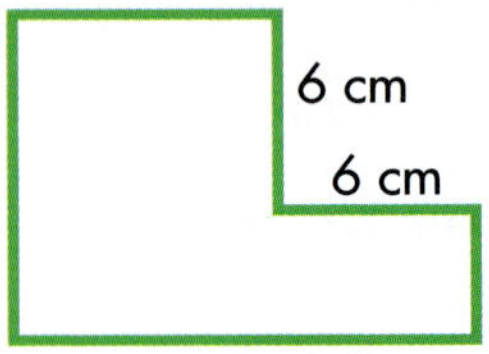

2.

3. Draw 2 different figures that each have a perimeter of 16 units. Use grid paper.

Set B, pages 374–375

Follow these steps for using Try, Check, and Revise to solve problems.

Step 1 Think to make a reasonable first try.

Step 2 Check, using information from the problem.

Step 3 Revise. Use your first try to make a reasonable second try. Check.

Step 4 Continue trying and checking until you find the correct answer.

Remember to check each try.

Use Try, Check, and Revise to solve.

1. Ray and Tony have 32 markers. Ray has 2 more markers than Tony. How many markers does each boy have?

2. The soccer club has 28 members. There are 4 more girls than boys. How many boys are in the soccer club?

Set C, pages 376–379

What is the area of the rectangle?

For a rectangle or square, think of an array.
To estimate area, you can count whole squares and combine partial squares to make whole squares.

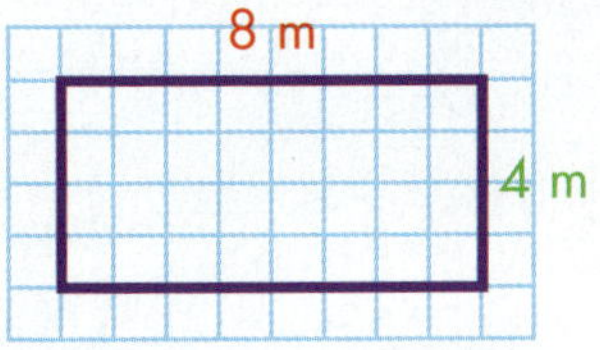

□ = 1 square meter

4 × 8 = 32

The area of the rectangle is 32 square meters.

Remember to give area measurements in square units.

1. Find the area of this figure.

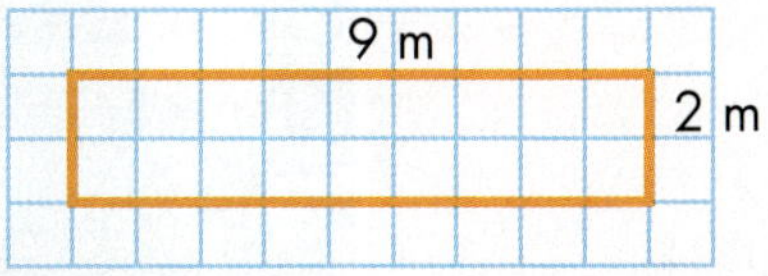

2. Estimate the area of this figure in square units.

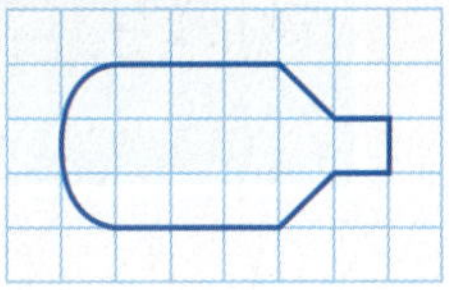

Set D, pages 380–382

What is the volume of the figure in cubic units?

Count the cubes in each floor. Then add.

1st floor, 2nd floor, 3rd floor

4 + 4 + 2 = 10 cubes

The volume is 10 cubic units.

Remember to count all the cubes, even the ones you can't see.

Find the volume of each figure. Write your answers in cubic units.

1. 

2. 

Set E, pages 384–385

Use simpler problems to find the area of the shaded part of the rectangle.

Find the area of the whole rectangle.
5 × 7 = 35

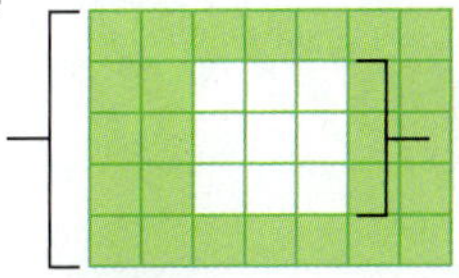

Find the area of the square.
3 × 3 = 9

■ = 1 square inch

Subtract: 35 − 9 = 26

The area of the shaded part of the rectangle is 26 square inches.

Remember to use the answers to the simpler problems.

1. Solve. Use simpler problems.

Walt wants to paint a wall. The shaded part of the wall is the part that needs blue paint. What is the area of the shaded part?

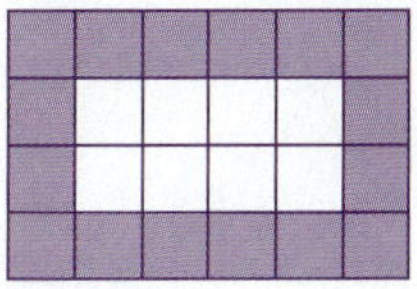

■ = 1 square foot

Topic 17

Time and Temperature

1 The sailfish is the fastest swimmer of all fish. How fast can a sailfish swim? You will find out in Lesson 17-3.

2 How quickly does a Venus flytrap close after catching its next meal? You will find out in Lesson 17-6.

3 How long does the Hubble Telescope take to orbit Earth? You will find out in Lesson 17-2.

4 What is the year-round temperature in Carlsbad Caverns? You will find out in Lesson 17-5.

Review What You Know!

Vocabulary

Choose the best term from the box.

- hour
- minute
- o'clock
- thermometer

1. Luz read the time. She saw that the time was nine _?_.

2. It takes about one _?_ for Anita to tie her shoelaces.

3. Corey will read the _?_ to tell his friend in another state how warm it is.

Time

Write each time.

4. 

5. 

Temperature

Write whether each temperature is hot or cold.

6. 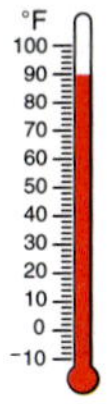

7. 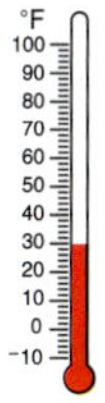

8. **Writing to Explain** Draw a clock face. Draw the hour hand on the 8 and the minute hand on the 12. Write the time. Explain how to read the time on a clock.

Virginia

Lesson 17-1

Prepares for 3.11.a The student will tell time to the nearest minute, using analog and digital clocks.

Time to the Half Hour and Quarter Hour

How do you tell time to the nearest half hour or quarter hour?

The clocks show the time that the bus arrives at school and the time it leaves.

Data

Units of Time		
1 day	=	24 hours
1 hour	=	60 minutes
1 half hour	=	30 minutes
1 quarter hour	=	15 minutes
1 minute	=	60 seconds

Bus Arrives

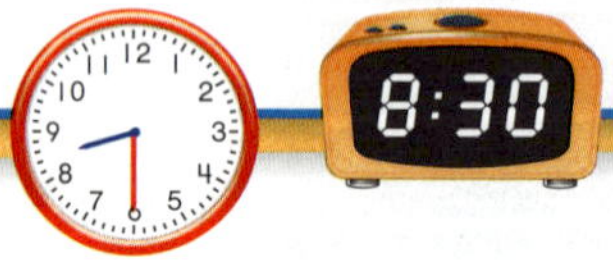

Bus Leaves

Another Example **How do you decide whether the time is A.M. or P.M.?**

The hours of the day between midnight and noon are A.M. hours.
The hours between noon and midnight are P.M. hours.

Would the time the bus arrives at school more likely be 8:30 A.M. or 8:30 P.M.?

8:30 P.M. is in the evening. The bus probably would not arrive at school in the evening. 8:30 A.M. is in the morning.

The bus would more likely arrive at school at 8:30 A.M.

Would the time the bus leaves school more likely be 2:45 A.M. or 2:45 P.M.?

2:45 A.M. is in the middle of the night. The bus probably would not be leaving school at that time. 2:45 P.M. is in the afternoon.

The bus would more likely leave school at 2:45 P.M.

Explain It

1. Why might it be important to use A.M. or P.M. when you give a time?
2. Would you be more likely to leave your home to go to school at 8:15 A.M. or 8:15 P.M.?
3. Would you be more likely to eat lunch at 12:30 A.M. or 12:30 P.M.?

Tell the time the bus arrives.

Write 8:30 in three other ways.

When the minute hand is on the 6, you can say the time is "half past" the hour.

The bus arrives at *eight thirty*, or *half past eight*, or *30 minutes past eight*.

Tell the time the bus leaves.

Write 2:45 in three other ways.

When the minute hand is on the 9, you can say the time is "15 minutes to" or "quarter to" the hour.

The bus leaves at *two forty-five*, or *15 minutes to three*, or *quarter to three*.

Guided Practice*

Do you know HOW?

In **1** and **2**, write the time shown on each clock in two ways.

1.

2.

Do you UNDERSTAND?

3. In the example above, why do you think the fraction word "quarter" is used for the time when the minute hand is on the 9?

4. The clock shows the time that Etta's skating lesson starts. What time does it start? Give the time in 3 ways.

Independent Practice

In **5–7**, write the time shown on each clock in two ways.

5.

6.

7.

DIGITAL Animated Glossary **www.pearsonsuccessnet.com**

**For another example, see Set A on page 408.*

Independent Practice

In **8–10**, write the time shown on each clock in two ways.

8. 

9. 

10. 

Problem Solving

11. The clocks below show the time that the Flying Horse Carousel in Rhode Island opens and closes. What time does the carousel open? What time does it close?

Opens 

Closes 

12. **Writing to Explain** Mr. Boyd gave his students a math test at 10:45. Explain why this time is most likely an A.M. time.

For **13–16**, use the table at the right.

13. **Estimation** Whose bowling score was about 20 points less than Beth's?

14. Whose bowling score was 15 points more than Cal's?

15. What is the order of the friends' names from greatest to least score?

Bowling Scores (Data)

Name	Score
Cal	63
Beth	78
Rusty	59
Pang	82

16. **Algebra** Write a number sentence that compares the total of Cal's and Beth's scores with the total of Rusty's and Pang's scores.

17. Ronaldo delivers a newspaper to the Hong family between 7:00 A.M. and 8:00 A.M. each day. Which clock shows a time between 7:00 A.M. and 8:00 A.M.?

SOL Prep

A 

B 

C 

D 

Enrichment

Roman Numerals

The symbols for numbers, or numerals, used by the ancient Romans are still seen today on some clock faces and buildings. They are used as page numbers at the front of many books, including this one.

Data

Roman numeral	I	V	X	L	C	D	M
Decimal value	1	5	10	50	100	500	1,000

Our number system is called the decimal system. It is based on place value. Roman numerals are based on addition and subtraction.

How to read Roman numerals:

VI = 5 + 1 = 6 When the symbol for the smaller number is written to the right of the greater number, add. No more than three symbols for smaller numbers are used this way.

IV = 5 − 1 = 4 When the symbol for a smaller number is to the left of the greater number, subtract. No more than one symbol for a smaller number is used this way.

Practice

Write each as a decimal number.

1. VII **2.** XX **3.** CV **4.** XIV **5.** LI

6. XXI **7.** XIX **8.** DC **9.** CM **10.** MC

Write each as a Roman numeral.

11. 15 **12.** 30 **13.** 9 **14.** 52 **15.** 60

16. 6 **17.** 110 **18.** 400 **19.** 550 **20.** 40

21. In Roman numerals, the year 1990 is written as MCMXC, and 2007 is written as MMVII. Write the current year using Roman numerals.

22. One movie was made in the year MMIV. Another movie was made in the year MCML. How many years passed between these years?

Virginia

Lesson 17-2

3.11.a The student will tell time to the nearest minute, using analog and digital clocks.

Time to the Minute

How do you tell time to the nearest minute?

The clock shows the time a train is scheduled to arrive at Pinewood Station. What time is the train scheduled to arrive? Give the time in digital form and in two other ways.

Guided Practice*

Do you know HOW?

In **1** and **2**, write the time shown on each clock in two ways.

1.

2.

Do you UNDERSTAND?

3. **Reasoning** In the example above, why is 42 minutes past 12 the same as 18 minutes to 1? Explain.

4. The clock below shows the time that an airplane landed. Write the time in two ways.

Independent Practice

In **5–7**, write the time shown on each clock in two ways.

5.

6.

7.

**For another example, see Set A on page 408.*

Step 1

The hour hand is between 12 and 1. The time is after 12:00 and before 1:00.

Step 2

In 5 minutes, the minute hand moves from one number to the next.

Count by 5s from the 12 to the 8: 40 minutes

Step 3

In 1 minute, the minute hand moves from one mark to the next. After counting by 5s, count two minutes more.

The digital time is 12:42. It is 42 minutes past 12 or 18 minutes to 1.

Problem Solving

8. Toya's family went to see a movie. The clock shows the time that the movie ended. Write the digital time.

9. The Hubble Space Telescope has been moving in its orbit for 1 hour. In 37 more minutes it will complete an orbit. How many minutes does it take the Hubble Space Telescope to complete 1 orbit?

10. **Geometry** Enzo used grid paper to draw a model of a triangle he will paint on a wall. His drawing is shown at the right. Estimate the area of the figure.

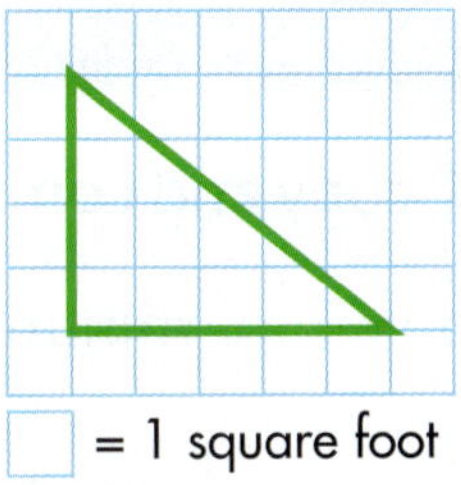

11. **Writing to Explain** Which figure has a greater area, a square with a side length of 4 feet or the triangle Enzo drew? Explain how you found your answer.

12. Ross walks his dog between 3:15 P.M. and 4:00 P.M. Which clock shows a time between 3:15 P.M. and 4:00 P.M.?

SOL Prep

A

B

C

D

Virginia

Lesson 17-3

3.12 The student will identify equivalent periods of time, including relationships among days, months, and years, as well as minutes and hours.

Units of Time

How can you change units of time?

The class is growing a plant from a seed. The project will last for 5 weeks. How many days are in 5 weeks? The picture shows how long the seed has been growing. How many hours is this?

Data

Relating Units of Time
1 week (wk) = 7 days
1 day (d) = 24 hours
1 hour (h) = 60 minutes

Guided Practice*

Do you know HOW?

For **1–3**, copy and complete to change the units.

1. 8 weeks = ☐ days

2. 2 days = ☐ hours

3. How many days are in 2 weeks, 4 days?

Do you UNDERSTAND?

4. In the example above, why do you multiply the number of weeks by 7?

5. At the end of the first week, the class had worked on the science experiment for 6 hours. How many minutes did the class work on the experiment?

Independent Practice

For **6–15**, copy and complete to change the units.

6. 3 hours = ☐ minutes

7. 5 days = ☐ hours

8. 4 hours = ☐ minutes

9. 7 weeks = ☐ days

10. 3 weeks = ☐ days

11. 7 days = ☐ hours

12. How many hours are in 3 days, 5 hours?

13. How many minutes are in 5 hours, 10 minutes?

14. How many days are in 10 weeks?

15. How many hours are in 9 days?

*For another example, see Set B on page 408.

Since there are 7 days in 1 week, the number of days in 5 weeks is 5×7.

5×7 days = ▢ days

$$\begin{array}{r} 7 \\ \times\ 5 \\ \hline 35 \end{array}$$

5 weeks = 35 days

Make a table to find the number of hours in 8 days.

Number of Days	1	2	3	4	5	6	7	8
Number of Hours	24	48	72	96	120	144	168	192

There are 192 hours in 8 days.

Problem Solving

16. In 30 more minutes, the International Space Station will complete an orbit. It has been in this orbit for 1 hour. How many minutes does it take the International Space Station to complete 1 orbit?

17. A group of high school students helped to prepare samples of materials to send to the International Space Station in 2001. The samples were returned to Earth from space after 4 years. In what year were the samples returned?

For **18** and **19**, use the table at the right.

18. Astronauts at the International Space Station took a spacewalk to do tasks outside the station. They finished their tasks in less time than was planned. How many minutes of actual time did the astronauts need?

Data

Spacewalk	
Planned Time	6 hours, 20 minutes
Actual Time	5 hours, 54 minutes

19. **Writing to Explain** How many fewer minutes than planned did the astronauts need? Explain how you found your answer.

20. **Number Sense** A sailfish can swim as fast as 68 miles per hour. In 1 minute can a sailfish swim as far as 1 mile? Explain your answer.

21. What fraction of an hour is 20 minutes? Write your answer in simplest form.

22. How many days are in 6 weeks?

SOL Prep

A 42 **B** 36 **C** 13 **D** 7

3.11.b The student will determine elapsed time in one-hour increments over a 12-hour period.

Elapsed Time

How can you find elapsed time?

Janey took part in a charity walk. The walk started at 7:00 A.M. It ended at 11:20 A.M. How long did the walk last?

Elapsed time is the total amount of time that passes from the starting time to the ending time.

Guided Practice*

Do you know HOW?

For **1–3**, find the elapsed time.

1. Start Time: 11:00 A.M.
End Time: 5:00 P.M.

2. Start Time: 1:00 P.M.
End Time: 4:45 P.M.

3. Start Time: 7:10 A.M.
End Time: 8:00 A.M.

Do you UNDERSTAND?

4. In the example above, why do you count the minutes by 5s as the minute hand moves to each number on the clock?

5. During the charity walk, lunch was served from 12:00 P.M. until 2:10 P.M. How long was lunch served?

6. A movie started at 2:30 P.M. and ran for 1 hour, 45 minutes. What time did the movie end?

Independent Practice

For **7–15**, find the elapsed time.

7. Start Time: 6:30 P.M.
End Time: 9:50 P.M.

8. Start Time: 11:00 A.M.
End Time: 3:55 P.M.

9. Start Time: 5:40 P.M.
End Time: 6:00 P.M.

10. Start Time: 8:10 A.M.
End Time: 10:45 A.M.

11. Start Time: 9:15 A.M.
End Time: 10:45 A.M.

12. Start Time: 10:00 A.M.
End Time: 3:00 P.M.

13. Start Time: 3:20 P.M.
End Time: 6:00 P.M.

14. Start Time: 7:30 A.M.
End Time: 9:45 A.M.

15. Start Time: 12:45 P.M.
End Time: 2:20 P.M.

DIGITAL Animated Glossary **www.pearsonsuccessnet.com**

For another example, see Set C on page 409.

Step 1

Find the starting time.

Step 2

Count the hours.

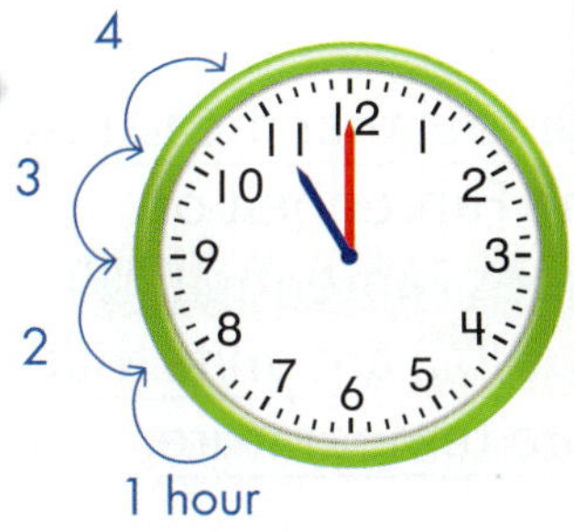

Step 3

Count the minutes.

The walk lasted 4 hours, 20 minutes.

Problem Solving

16. The picnic started at 12:10 P.M. and ended at 5:00 P.M. How long did the picnic last?

17. The baseball game started at 1:15 P.M. It lasted 2 hours, 45 minutes. What time did the game end?

18. The picnic started at 12:10 P.M. Kevin's family had arrived at the picnic 30 minutes earlier. What time did Kevin's family arrive at the picnic?

19. Mr. Parker had $\frac{5}{6}$ of a sandwich. He gave $\frac{2}{6}$ of the sandwich to Mikey. He gave the rest of the sandwich to Ben. What fraction of the sandwich did he give to Ben? Draw a picture.

Mrs. Flores keeps a list of the amount of time it takes for different items to bake. Use the table at the right for **20** and **21**.

20. Which items take less than $\frac{1}{2}$ hour to bake?

21. **Estimation** About how many more minutes does it take to bake the pasta dish than to bake the granola bars?

Item	Baking Time in Minutes
Bread	26
Granola Bars	21
Pasta Dish	48
Vegetables	24

22. The train leaves Carlton at 9:25 A.M. and arrives at Longview at 10:55 A.M. How long is the train ride?

A 1 hour, 20 minutes

B 1 hour, 25 minutes

C 1 hour, 30 minutes

D 1 hour, 35 minutes

Virginia

Lesson 17-5

3.13 The student will read temperature to the nearest degree from a Celsius thermometer and a Fahrenheit thermometer. Real thermometers and physical models of thermometers will be used.

Temperature

How are temperatures measured?

A thermometer is a tool that measures temperature on the Fahrenheit or Celsius scale. Degrees Fahrenheit (°F) and degrees Celsius (°C) are units that are used to measure temperature.

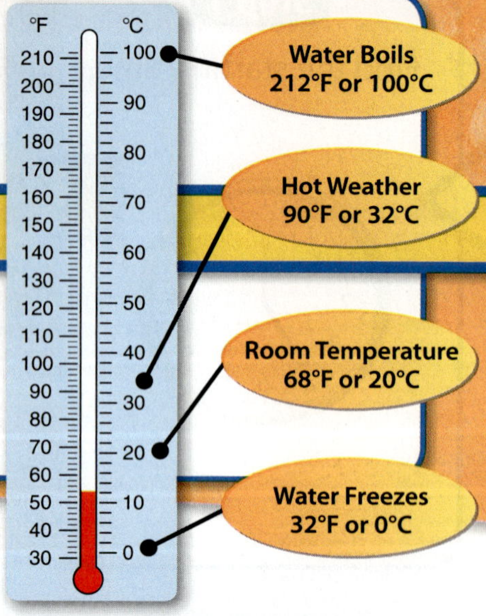

Guided Practice*

Do you know HOW?

In **1** and **2**, write each temperature in °F and in °C.

1.

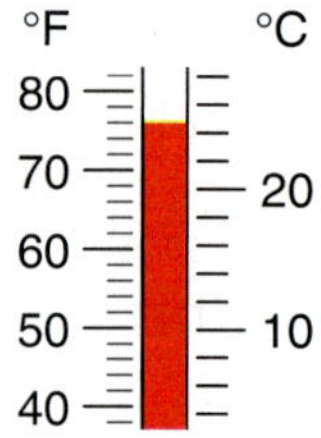

2.

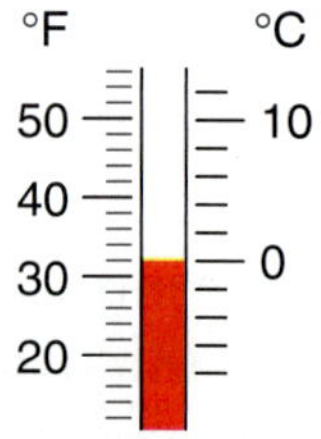

Do you UNDERSTAND?

3. Look at the thermometer above. Would you swim outside if the temperature was 28°C? Explain.

4. **Writing to Explain** Which is the better temperature for bicycling outside, 15°F or 50°F? Explain.

5. Mateo needs to wear a coat to go outside today. The thermometer shows the temperature. What is the temperature in degrees Fahrenheit?

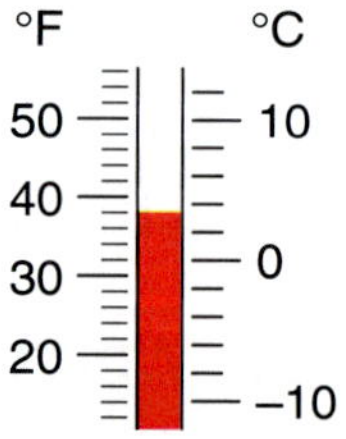

Independent Practice

In **6–8**, write each temperature in °F and °C.

6.

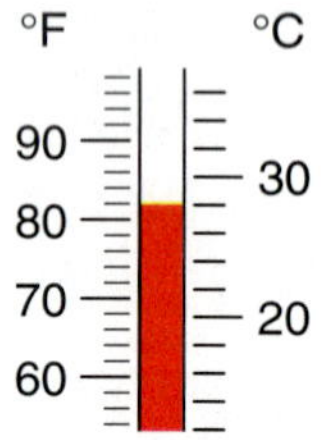

7.

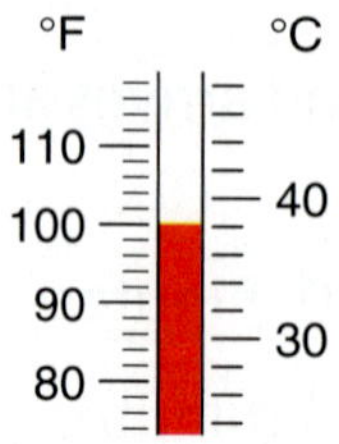

8.

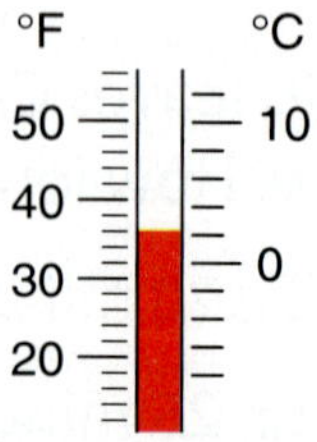

DIGITAL Animated Glossary **www.pearsonsuccessnet.com**

*For another example, see Set D on page 409.

Rita will wear a jacket outside today. What is the temperature outside, shown on the thermometer?

Each line on the scale is 2 degrees. The top of the red column is at 54 on the Fahrenheit scale and at 12 on the Celsius scale.

The temperature is 54°F or 12°C.

Dave will wear a T-shirt outside today. What is the temperature outside, shown on the thermometer?

The top of the red column is at 88 on the Fahrenheit scale and at 31 on the Celsius scale.

The temperature is 88°F or 31°C.

Problem Solving

9. The year-round temperature in Mammoth Cave is shown on the thermometer below. What is that temperature in degrees Fahrenheit?

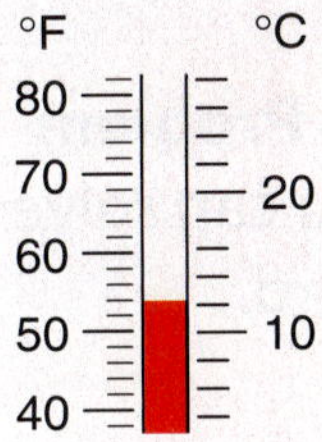

10. **Algebra** The year-round temperature in Carlsbad Caverns in New Mexico is 56°F. Copy and complete the number sentence to compare the temperature in Carlsbad Caverns with the temperature in Mammoth Cave.

56 ○ ▭

For **11** and **12**, use the sign at the right.

Winter Sale

Blanket	$19
Hat	$12
Scarf	$18
Shovel	$23

11. **Reasonableness** Roy says that a scarf and a hat together cost about the same as 2 blankets. Is his estimate reasonable? Explain.

12. **Algebra** What did Jorge buy at the sale if $(3 \times \$19) + \$23$ stands for the total cost?

13. The temperature in Sonora Caverns is always about 70°F. Which thermometer shows this temperature?

SOL Prep

A

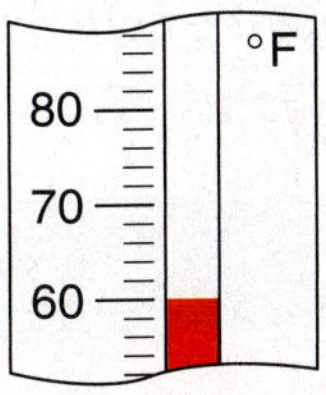

B

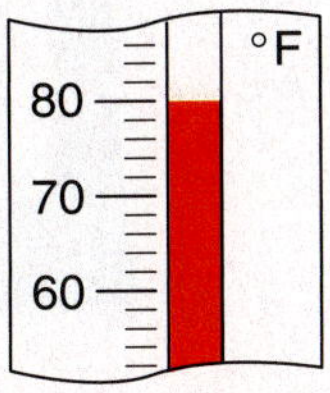

C

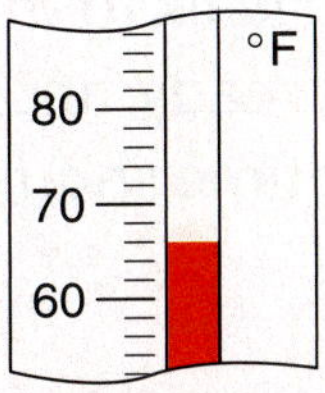

D

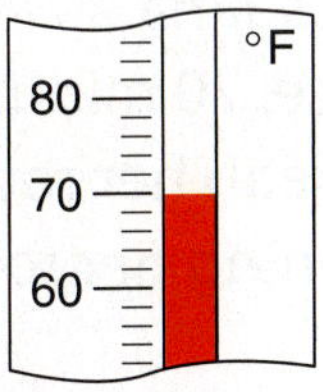

Virginia

Lesson 17-6

Prepares for 4.9 The student will determine elapsed time in hours and minutes within a 12-hour period.

Problem Solving

Work Backward

Eric's family wants to arrive at the movie theater at 2:30 P.M. It takes them 30 minutes to travel to the theater, 15 minutes to get ready, and 30 minutes to eat lunch. What time should the family start eating lunch?

Arrive at Theater

Guided Practice*

Do you know HOW?

Solve the problem by drawing a picture and working backward.

1. The swim meet starts at 10:15 A.M. It takes Abby 15 minutes to walk to the pool. On her way, she needs 15 minutes to shop. It takes her 30 minutes to get ready. What time should Abby start getting ready?

Do you UNDERSTAND?

2. In the example above, why do the arrows in the Solve step move to the left?

3. **Write a Problem** Write a problem that you can solve by working backward.

Independent Practice

In **4** and **5**, solve the problem by drawing a picture and working backward.

4. Emilio read the thermometer one evening. The temperature was 56°F. This temperature was 9°F less than the temperature that afternoon. The afternoon temperature was 7°F greater than the temperature in the morning. What was the temperature in the morning?

5. Jana's dentist appointment is at 4:30 P.M. It takes Jana 20 minutes to walk to the dentist's office, 20 minutes to get ready, and 30 minutes to clean her room. What time should she start cleaning her room?

Stuck? Try this....

- What do I know?
- What am I asked to find?
- What diagram can I use to help understand the problem?
- Can I use addition, subtraction, multiplication, or division?
- Is all of my work correct?
- Did I answer the right question?
- Is my answer reasonable?

*For another example, see Set E on page 409.

Read and Understand

What do I know? Arrive 2:30 P.M., 30 minutes to travel, 15 minutes to get ready, 30 minutes to eat lunch

What am I being asked to find? The time the family should start eating lunch

Plan and Solve

Draw a picture to show each change.

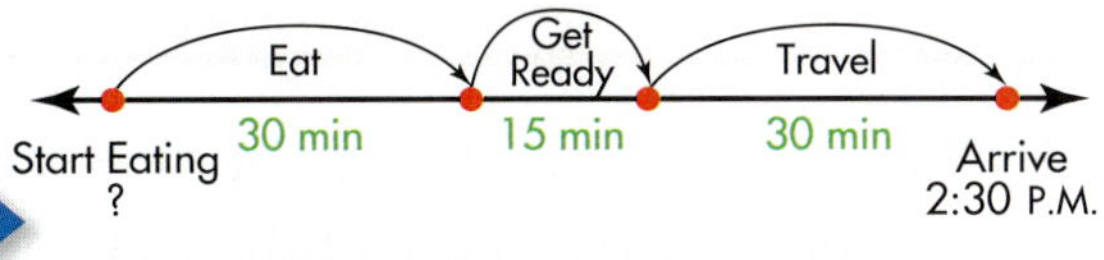

Work backward from the end.

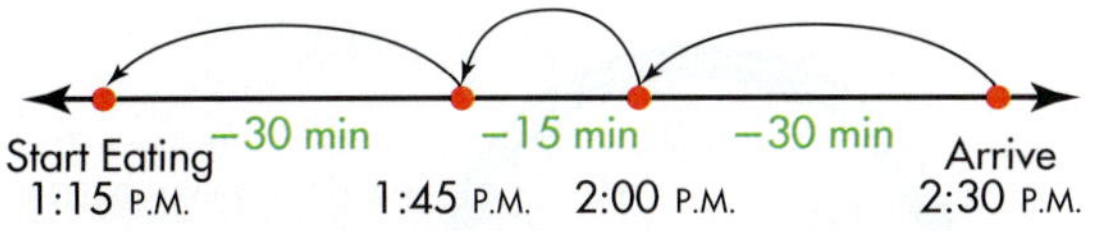

Eric's family should start eating lunch at 1:15 P.M.

6. Kent read the thermometer this evening. The temperature was 65°F. This temperature was 15°F less than the temperature in the afternoon. The afternoon temperature was 14°F greater than the temperature in the morning. What was the temperature in the morning?

7. Corinna read the thermometer at 7:00 P.M. The temperature was 16°C. This temperature was 9°C less than the temperature at 2:00 P.M. The temperature at 2:00 P.M. was 10°C higher than the temperature at 8:00 A.M. What was the temperature at 8:00 A.M.?

8. Wan-li drew these polygons. What is the same in all three polygons?

9. School starts at 8:15 A.M. It takes Shane 15 minutes to walk to school, 20 minutes to eat, 15 minutes to walk his dog, and 15 minutes to get ready. What time should he get up?

10. A scientist recorded the data shown in the table. About how long does it take a Venus flytrap to close after an insect or spider lands on it?

A Less than 1 second

B More than 1 second

C More than 1 minute

D More than 2 minutes

Data

Time Prey Landed	Time Flytrap Closed
2:07	$\frac{1}{2}$ second after 2:07
2:49	$\frac{3}{4}$ second after 2:49
2:53	$\frac{1}{2}$ second after 2:53

1. The clock below shows the time Levi arrived at the doctor's office. What time did he arrive? (17-2)

A 3:42

B 3:37

C 3:35

D 2:37

2. What is one way to write the time shown on the clock? (17-1)

A Quarter to 1

B 15 past 1

C Quarter past 2

D Quarter to 2

3. Anita got to school at 8:05 A.M. She was on the bus 15 minutes, stood at the bus stop for 10 minutes, and took 40 minutes to get ready after she got up. What time did Anita get up? (17-6)

A 9:10 A.M.

B 7:05 A.M.

C 7:00 A.M.

D 6:55 A.M.

4. The temperature outside on Mikal's birthday was 54°F. Which thermometer shows this temperature? (17-5)

A
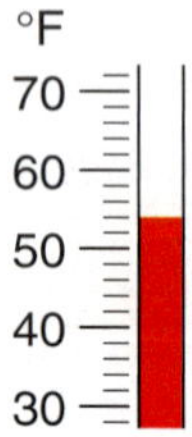

B
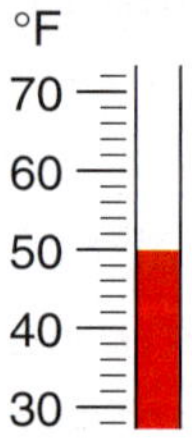

C
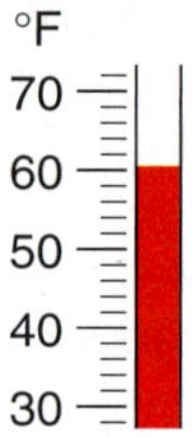

D
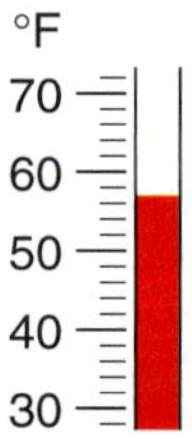

5. Which of the following is a time that Jose would be asleep during the night? (17-1)

A 3:15 P.M.

B 11:45 P.M.

C 10:45 A.M.

D 12:30 P.M.

6. What temperature in °F is shown? (17-5)

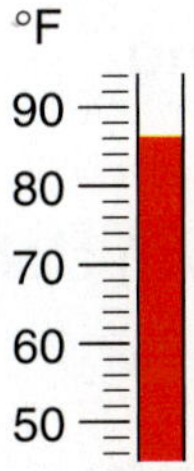

A 88°F

B 86°F

C 84°F

D 83°F

7. Jon arrived home from school at the time shown on the clock.

What time did Jon arrive? (17-2)

A 12:03

B 2:02

C 6:35

D 3:24

8. Olivia left her house at 6:30 to go to the movies. Which is another way to write 6:30? (17-1)

A quarter to 6

B quarter past 6

C half past 6

D quarter to 7

9. The concert in the park started at 11:15 A.M. and ended at 1:50 P.M. How long did the concert last? (17-4)

A 1 hour, 35 minutes

B 2 hours, 25 minutes

C 2 hours, 30 minutes

D 2 hours, 35 minutes

10. How many hours are in 4 days? (17-3)

A 52

B 84

C 96

D 100

11. The 3:00 P.M. temperature was 93°F. This was 8° warmer than the temperature at noon. The noon temperature was 13° warmer than the 9:00 A.M. temperature. What was the 9:00 A.M. temperature in °F? (17-6)

A 72°F

B 73°F

C 88°F

D 114°F

12. Jen was playing in a soccer game. The game started at 11:10 A.M. and ended at 12:40 P.M. How long did the game last? (17-4)

A 30 minutes

B 1 hour, 10 minutes

C 1 hour, 30 minutes

D 2 hours, 30 minutes

Topic 17

VA SOL Reteaching

Set A, pages 392–394, 396–397

To tell the time, find where the hour hand points and where the minute hand points. When the minute hand is on the 9, you can say "15 minutes to" the hour. You can also say "quarter to" the hour.

What is the time to the nearest minute?

The hour hand is between 10 and 11. The time is after 10:00.

Count by 5s from the 12 to the 5.
5, 10, 15, 20, 25 minutes.

After counting by 5s, count the marks by 1.
5, 10, 15, 20, 25, 26, 27 minutes.

The digital time is 10:27.
It is 27 minutes past 10 or 33 minutes to 11.

Remember that the hours between midnight and noon are A.M. hours. The hours between noon and midnight are P.M. hours.

Write the time shown on each clock in two ways.

1. 

2. 

3. 

4. 

5. Lucy saw the sun rise at 6:10. Was this an A.M. time or a P.M. time?

6. At which time is it more likely to be dark outside, 11:00 A.M. or 11:00 P.M.?

Set B, pages 398–399

Change 9 weeks to days.

9 weeks = ▢ days

Change to days.

You know that 1 week equals 7 days.

Multiply: 9 × 7 days = 63 days

9 weeks = 63 days

Remember to use the correct factors for the units you are changing.

1. 6 hours = ▢ minutes

2. 2 weeks = ▢ days

3. 3 days = ▢ hours

4. 1 hour, 41 minutes = ▢ minutes

5. 2 days, 3 hours = ▢ hours

6. 3 hours, 15 minutes = ▢ minutes

Set C, pages 400–401

How long does the hockey game last?
Start Time: 11:00 A.M.
End Time: 2:35 P.M.

- Find the starting time: **11:00 A.M.**
- Count the hours: **12, 1, 2.**
- Count the minutes: **5, 10, 15, 20, 25, 30, 35.**

The game lasted 3 hours, 35 minutes.

Remember to count hours and then minutes.

Find the elapsed time.

1. Start Time: 9:00 A.M.
   End Time: 12:15 P.M.
2. Start Time: 5:00 P.M.
   End Time: 9:50 P.M.

Set D, pages 402–403

The thermometer shows the temperature outside. What is the temperature?

Each line on the scale is 2 degrees.

Count by 2s from the 70 mark up to where the red column ends.
70, 72, 74, 76, 78
Then count on by 1.
79

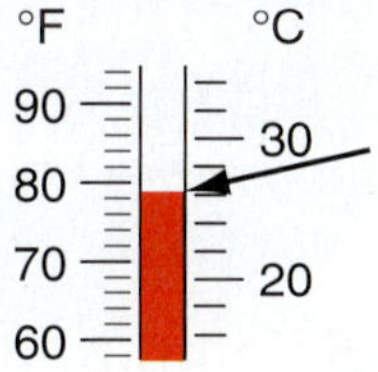

On the Celsius scale, count by 2s from 20.
20, 22, 24, 26

The temperature is 79°F or 26°C.

Remember that each line on the scale on these thermometers is 2 degrees.

Write each temperature in °F and °C.

1.

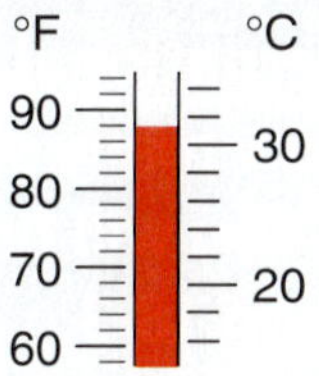

2.

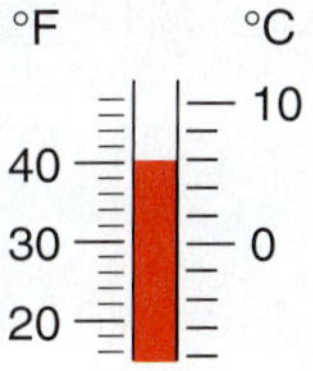

Set E, pages 404–405

Jay's soccer practice begins at 10:00 A.M. He takes 30 minutes to walk to the field. He takes 10 minutes to walk his dog and 10 minutes to get ready. When should Jay start getting ready?

Work backward from the end using the opposite of each change.

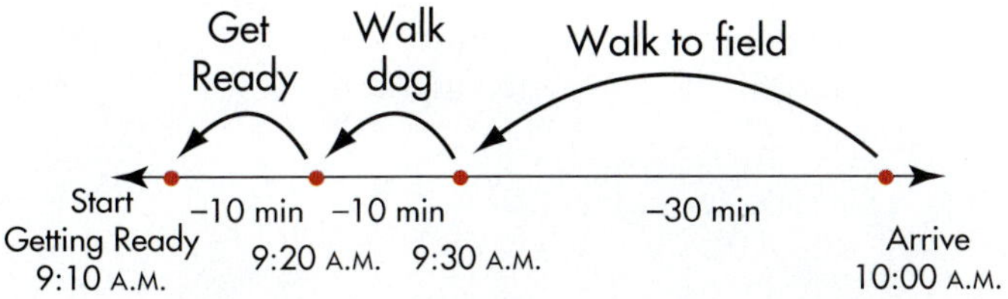

Jay should start getting ready at 9:10 A.M.

Remember to check your solution by working forward.

Solve each problem by drawing a picture and working backward.

1. Hal needs to meet Lou at 1:00 P.M. It takes him 10 minutes to walk to Lou's house, 10 minutes to get ready, and 20 minutes to eat lunch. What time should Hal start eating lunch?

Topic 18 Multiplying Greater Numbers

1 Solar cells on a Solar Array Wing are used to produce electricity for the International Space Station. How many solar cells are there? You will find out in Lesson 18-3.

2 About how much does a manatee weigh compared to a golden eagle? You will find out in Lesson 18-1.

3 How far can a jerboa jump? You will find out in Lesson 18-6.

4 Which has more members, the world's largest accordion band or the world's largest trombone band? You will find out in Lesson 18-5.

Review What You Know!

Vocabulary

Choose the best term from the box.

- addends
- factors
- product
- sum

1. When you add to combine numbers, another name for the total is the ___?___.
2. The Commutative Property of Multiplication says that the ___?___ can be multiplied in any order and the answer will be the same.
3. In the number sentence $9 \times 6 = 54$, the number 54 is called the ___?___.

Multiplication

Multiply.

4. 3×9 5. 8×7 6. 6×6

7. 4×8 8. 7×5 9. 4×2

10. 7×6 11. 8×9 12. 6×8

Arrays

Draw an array of dots for each multiplication.

13. 3×9 14. 4×8

15. **Write a Problem** Write a problem for the number sentence $7 \times 6 = \square$.

Virginia

Lesson 18-1

3.6 The student will represent multiplication and division, using area, set, and number line models, and create and solve problems that involve multiplication of two whole numbers, one factor 99 or less and the second factor 5 or less.

Using Mental Math to Multiply

Hands-On
place-value blocks

How can you multiply by multiples of 10, 100, and 1,000?

You already know how to multiply by 10, as in 5 × 10 = 50.

5 × 100 is 5 groups of 1 hundred or 500.

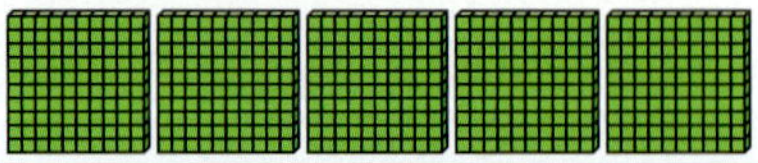

5 × 1,000 is 5 groups of 1 thousand or 5,000.

Guided Practice*

Do you know HOW?

In **1–8**, use place-value blocks or patterns to find each product.

1. 8 × 100 **2.** 7 × 1,000

3. 6 × 1,000 **4.** 9 × 100

5. 6 × 40 **6.** 3 × 700

7. 9 × 50 **8.** 5 × 3,000

Do you UNDERSTAND?

9. In the examples above, what pattern do you see when you multiply a number by 10? by 100? by 1,000?

10. The memory card for Jay's digital camera holds 70 pictures. How many pictures can 4 memory cards hold?

11. Your friend says, "The product 6 × 5 is 30, so 6 × 500 is 300." Is he correct? Explain.

Independent Practice

In **12–27,** use mental math to find the product.

12. 4 × 10 **13.** 9 × 100 **14.** 2 × 1,000 **15.** 3 × 60

16. 8 × 80 **17.** 6 × 50 **18.** 40 × 7 **19.** 900 × 4

20. 500 × 9 **21.** 70 × 5 **22.** 100 × 8 **23.** 2 × 6,000

24. 200 × 8 **25.** 300 × 6 **26.** 4 × 500 **27.** 3 × 400

DIGITAL
eTools
www.pearsonsuccessnet.com

For another example, see Set A on page 432.

Find 3×70.

Use place-value blocks. Remember, $70 = 7$ tens.

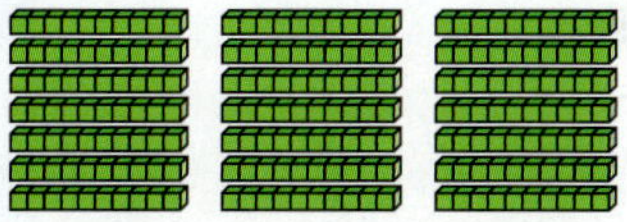

3 groups of 7 tens = 21 tens

$3 \times 70 = 210$

Find 4×300.

Use place-value blocks. Remember, $300 = 3$ hundreds.

4 groups of 3 hundreds = 12 hundreds

$4 \times 300 = 1{,}200$

Find $2 \times 4{,}000$.

Use a pattern.

$2 \times 4 = 8$
$2 \times 40 = 80$
$2 \times 400 = 800$
$2 \times 4{,}000 = 8{,}000$

Notice the pattern of zeros.

Problem Solving

For **28** and **29**, use the table at the right.

28. If you used a washing machine for 3 loads, how many gallons of water would you use? Draw pictures of place-value blocks to show the problem.

29. **Writing to Explain** How much water would you save if you took a 10-minute shower instead of a bath each day for 5 days? Explain how you solved the problem.

Data

Use of Water

Use	Estimated Number of Gallons
Bath	50
Dishwasher (1 load)	10
Shower (10 minutes)	20
Toilet (1 flush)	5
Washing Machine (1 load)	50

30. Each person in the United States uses about 200 gallons of water each day. About 125 gallons are used in the bathroom. How many gallons of water are used in other ways?

31. A golden eagle weighs about 11 pounds. A manatee can weigh 100 times as much as a golden eagle. How much can a manatee weigh?

32. An African elephant drinks about 50 gallons of water each day. How many gallons of water does the elephant drink in 7 days?

33. There are 6 floors in a building. Each floor has 20 windows. Some windows have 2 curtains. How many windows in all does the building have?

A 240 **C** 120

B 122 **D** 28

Virginia

Lesson 18-2

Prepares for 4.4.a The student will estimate sums, differences, products, and quotients of whole numbers.

Estimating Products

How can you estimate products?

Bamboo is one of the fastest growing plants on Earth. It can grow about 36 inches a day. Can it grow more than 200 inches in a week?

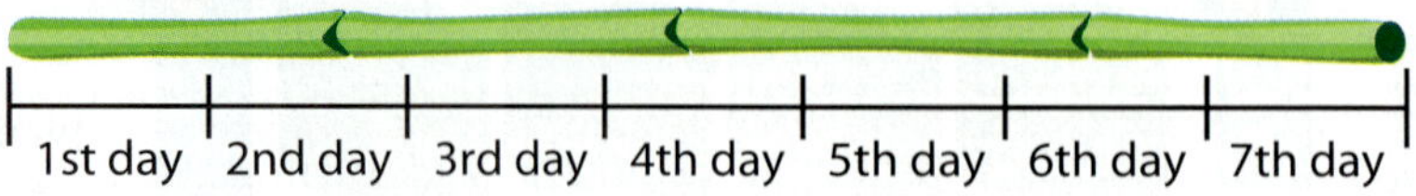

Guided Practice*

Do you know HOW?

In **1–6**, estimate each product.

1. 6×18

2. 3×52

3. 5×79

4. 4×65

5. 7×23

6. 9×37

Do you UNDERSTAND?

7. In the example above, is the exact answer more than or less than the estimate of 280? How do you know?

8. The kudzu plant is a vine that can grow about 12 inches each day. Can it grow more than 100 inches in a week? Explain how to round to estimate.

Independent Practice

In **9–28**, estimate each product.

9. 2×46

10. 8×31

11. 5×84

12. 7×26

13. 4×58

14. 6×19

15. 3×67

16. 9×23

17. 8×44

18. 5×32

19. 9×47

20. 2×64

21. 71×4

22. 98×7

23. 85×6

24. 31×4

25. 56×2

26. 73×5

27. 29×3

28. 47×6

*For another example, see Set B on page 432.

Step 1

An estimate is enough to find out if the plant can grow more than 200 inches in a week.

Estimate 7×36.

Round 36 to the nearest ten.

7×36

↓ 36 rounds to 40.

$7 \times 40 = 280$

7×36 is about 280.

Step 2

Compare the estimate to 200 inches.

$280 > 200$

So, a bamboo plant can grow more than 200 inches in a week.

Problem Solving

For **29–31**, use the graph at the right.

29. **Writing to Explain** Does a giant bamboo plant grow more than 100 inches in 6 days? Explain how to round to estimate the answer.

30. **Reasoneableness** Jim says a eucalyptus tree grows more in 8 days than Callie grass grows in 2 days. Is his statement reasonable? Explain.

31. How much more does giant bamboo grow in one day than Callie grass?

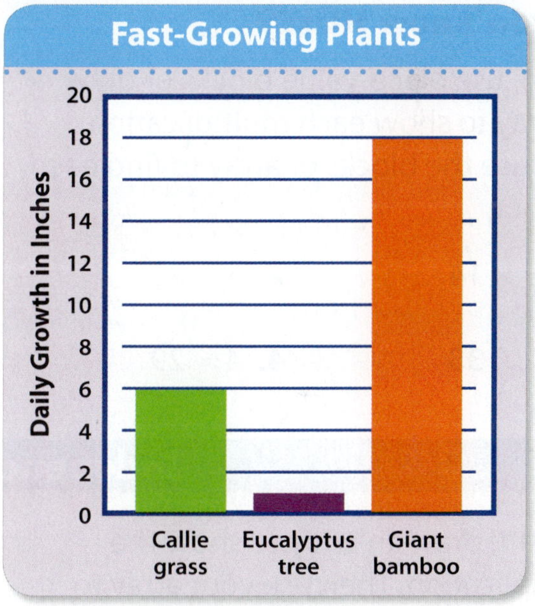

32. **Algebra** Look for patterns in the table. Copy and complete.

2	3	4	5	7	9
40	60		100		

33. There are 22 rows of seats on an airplane. Each has 6 seats. Which is the best estimate of the number of seats on the plane?

A 20 **B** 60 **C** 120 **D** 200

34. **Think About the Process** Jamal is buying 5 books. Each book costs \$19. Which number sentence shows the best estimate of the total cost of the books?

SOL Prep

A $5 \times \$10 = \$50$

B $\$5 + \$20 = \$25$

C $5 \times \$20 = \$100$

D $\$10 + \$20 = \$30$

Virginia

Lesson 18-3

3.6 The student will represent multiplication and division, using area, set, and number line models, and create and solve problems that involve multiplication of two whole numbers, one factor 99 or less and the second factor 5 or less.

Multiplication and Arrays

Hands-On
place-value blocks

How can you use arrays to show how to multiply with greater numbers?

Lava lamps in a store are arranged in 4 equal rows. What is the total number of lava lamps?

Choose an Operation Multiply to find the total for an array.

Guided Practice*

Do you know HOW?

In **1–4**, use place-value blocks or draw an array to show each multiplication. Then use the blocks or array to find each product.

1. 5 × 14 **2.** 3 × 21

3. 2 × 38 **4.** 4 × 29

Do you UNDERSTAND?

5. In the example above, what multiplication fact could you use to find the total number of ones?

6. Light bulbs are arranged in 3 equal rows on a shelf in the store. There are 17 bulbs in each row. What is the total number of bulbs on the shelf?

Independent Practice

In **7–11**, draw an array to show the multiplication. Then use your array to find the product.

Tip *You can draw lines to show tens, and Xs to show ones. This picture shows 23.*

7. 3 × 26 **8.** 5 × 15 **9.** 2 × 18 **10.** 4 × 16 **11.** 7 × 21

In **12–21**, find each product. You may use place-value blocks or draw a picture to help.

12. 2 × 47 **13.** 6 × 28 **14.** 5 × 31 **15.** 3 × 45 **16.** 4 × 32

17. 8 × 15 **18.** 3 × 29 **19.** 5 × 22 **20.** 2 × 38 **21.** 4 × 19

DIGITAL eTools www.pearsonsuccessnet.com

*For another example, see Set C on page 432.

Step 1

Use an array to show 4×13.

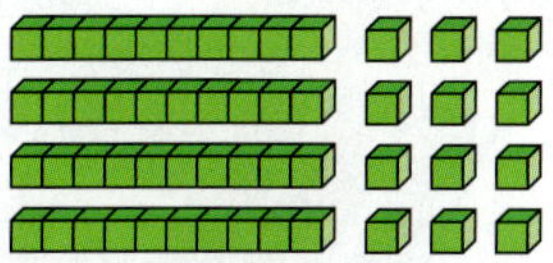

4 rows with 1 ten and 3 ones in each row.

Step 2

Find how many in all.

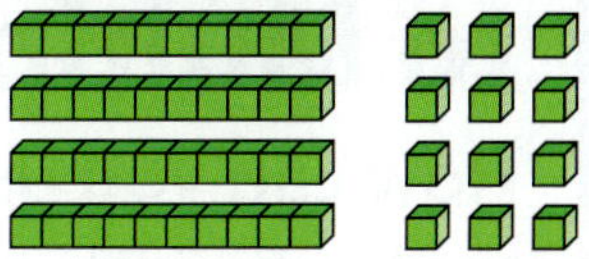

Count by tens and then count on with the ones to find the total.

10, 20, 30, 40

41, 42, 43, 44, 45, 46, 47, 48, 49, 50, 51, 52

There are 52 lava lamps.

Problem Solving

For **22** and **23**, use the table and the tip at the right.

22. Jake walked for 1 minute. How many times did Jake's heart beat?

23. **Strategy Focus** Solve. Use the strategy Try, Check, and Revise.

While doing one of the activities, Jake counted his heartbeats. He found that his heart rate in one minute was greater than 120, but less than 130. Which activity was he doing? Explain how you know.

Data **Jake's Heart Rate**

Activity	Number of Heartbeats in 10 Seconds
Bicycling	21
Resting	13
Running	22
Walking	18

Tip *The number of heartbeats in 1 minute is 6 times as many as in 10 seconds.*

24. **SOL Prep** The soup cans in a store display were arranged in 3 rows. There were 27 cans in each row. Which number sentence describes the array of soup cans?

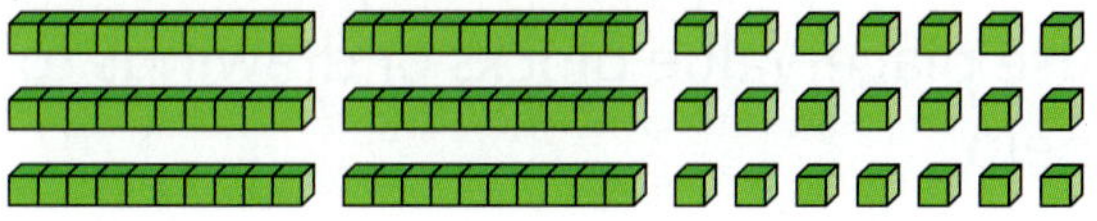

A $3 \times 27 = 81$ **B** $6 \times 21 = 126$ **C** $6 + 21 = 27$ **D** $2 \times 27 = 54$

25. A solar array wing on the International Space Station has 3,280 rows of solar cells. There are 10 solar cells in each row. Write an expression that describes how many solar cells are in the array.

26. What multiplication sentence could you write for the array shown at the right?

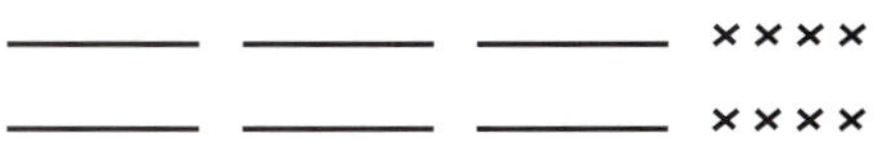

Virginia

Lesson 18-4

3.6 The student will represent multiplication and division, using area, set, and number line models, and create and solve problems that involve multiplication of two whole numbers, one factor 99 or less and the second factor 5 or less.

Breaking Apart to Multiply

Hands-On place-value blocks

How can you use place value to multiply with greater numbers?

A parking lot has the same number of spaces in each row. How many spaces are in the lot?

Choose an Operation Multiply to find the total for an array.

Another Example

The Distributive Property says you can break a factor apart to find partial products. The sum of the partial products is the product of the two factors.

Find 3×16.

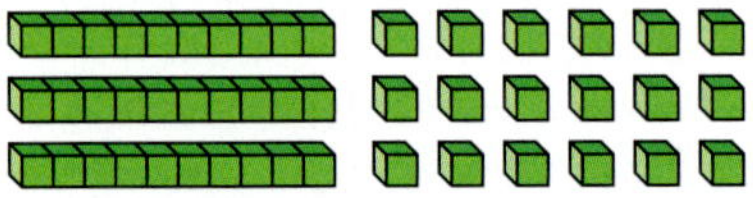

$3 \times 16 = 3 \times (10 + 6)$	Break 16 into tens and ones.
$= (3 \times 10) + (3 \times 6)$	Use the Distributive Property.
$= 30 + 18$	Find the partial products.
$= 48$	Add the partial products.

Guided Practice*

Do you know HOW?

In **1** and **2**, copy and complete. You may use place-value blocks or drawings to help.

1. 4×36

4×3 tens = ☐ tens or 120

4×6 ones = 24 ones or ☐

☐ + ☐ = ☐

2. 5×27

$5 \times (20 + 7) = (5 \times 20) + (5 \times 7)$

☐ + ☐ = ☐

Do you UNDERSTAND?

3. In the parking lot example, what two groups are in the array?

4. The buses at a bus garage are parked in 4 equal rows. There are 29 buses in each row. How many buses are parked at the garage?

5. **Writing to Explain** Why can you break apart numbers to multiply without changing the product?

DIGITAL Animated Glossary, eTools **www.pearsonsuccessnet.com**

*For another example, see Set D on page 433.

Step 1

Use an array to show 4 × 24.

Break 24 into tens and ones.
24 = 2 tens 4 ones

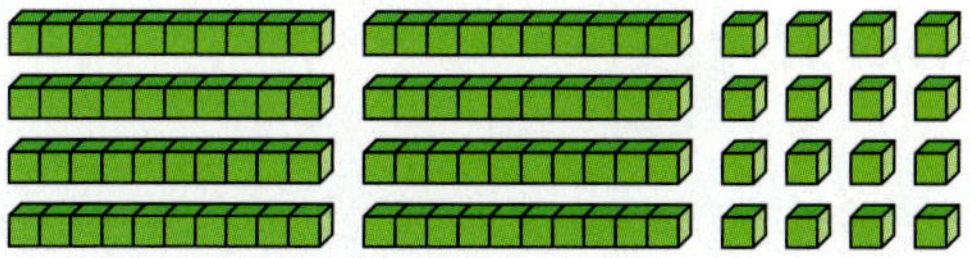

4 × 2 tens
4 × 20 = 80

4 × 4 ones
4 × 4 = 16

Step 2

Add each part to get the product.

4 × 20 = 80   4 × 4 = 16

80 + 16 = 96

80 and 16 are called partial products because they are parts of the product.

4 × 24 = 96

There are 96 spaces in the parking lot.

Independent Practice

In **6–15**, find each product. You may use place-value blocks or drawings to help.

6. 3 × 19 **7.** 4 × 31 **8.** 6 × 23 **9.** 5 × 25 **10.** 2 × 54

11. 3 × 49 **12.** 6 × 27 **13.** 5 × 43 **14.** 7 × 35 **15.** 4 × 62

Problem Solving

For **16–18**, find the total number of miles walked in the number of weeks given.

Data

Kind of Job	Distance Walked in 1 Week
Mail carrier	21 miles
Nurse	18 miles
TV reporter	19 miles

16. Nurse: 6 weeks

17. Mail carrier: 7 weeks

18. TV reporter: 2 weeks

Use the picture at the right for **19** and **20**.

19. **Estimation** Is $80 enough money to buy a chair and a desk? Explain how to round to estimate.

20. Nilda bought a bookcase, a lamp, and a desk. What was the total cost?

A $77 **C** $109

B $104 **D** $123

Virginia

Lesson 18-5

3.6 The student will represent multiplication and division, using area, set, and number line models, and create and solve problems that involve multiplication of two whole numbers, one factor 99 or less and the second factor 5 or less.

Using an Expanded Algorithm

Hands-On
place-value blocks

How do you record partial products when you multiply greater numbers?

How many calories are in 3 peaches?

Find 3×46.

Estimate: $3 \times 50 = 150$

Data

Calories

Fruit	Number of calories in 1 piece
Peach	46
Orange	35
Pear	40

Guided Practice*

Do you know HOW?

In **1** and **2**, copy and complete. Use place-value blocks or draw pictures to help.

1. $\begin{array}{r} 16 \\ \times\ 3 \\ \hline 18 \\ \square\square \\ \hline \square\square \end{array}$

2. $\begin{array}{r} 34 \\ \times\ 5 \\ \hline 20 \\ \square\square\square \\ \hline \square\square\square \end{array}$

In **3** and **4**, find each product. You may use place-value blocks or drawings to help.

3. $\begin{array}{r} 67 \\ \times\ 2 \\ \hline \end{array}$

4. $\begin{array}{r} 54 \\ \times\ 7 \\ \hline \end{array}$

Do you UNDERSTAND?

For **5–7**, use the example above.

5. What factors give the partial product 18? What factors give the partial product 120?

6. What is the next step after you write the partial products?

7. How many calories are in 2 oranges?

Independent Practice

Leveled Practice In **8** and **9**, copy and complete. In **10–12**, find each product. You may use place-value blocks or drawings to help.

Tip *You can draw lines to show tens, and Xs to show ones. This picture shows 27.*

——— ——— ×××××××

8. $\begin{array}{r} 36 \\ \times\ 2 \\ \hline 12 \\ \square\square \\ \hline \square\square \end{array}$

9. $\begin{array}{r} 53 \\ \times\ 4 \\ \hline 12 \\ \square\square\square \\ \hline \square\square\square \end{array}$

10. $\begin{array}{r} 18 \\ \times\ 7 \\ \hline \end{array}$

11. $\begin{array}{r} 42 \\ \times\ 6 \\ \hline \end{array}$

12. $\begin{array}{r} 65 \\ \times\ 3 \\ \hline \end{array}$

DIGITAL eTools **www.pearsonsuccessnet.com**

*For another example, see Set E on page 433.

What You Show

Use place value blocks to make an array for 3 × 46.

46 = 4 tens 6 ones

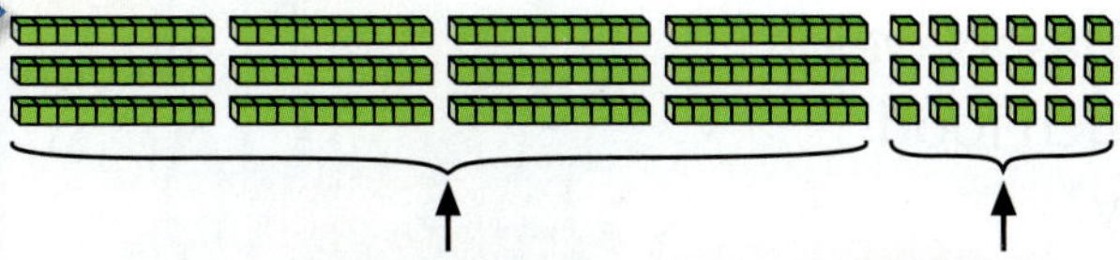

Multiply tens: 3 × 40 = 120

Multiply ones: 3 × 6 = 18

What You Write

$$\begin{array}{r} 46 \\ \times \quad 3 \\ \hline 18 \\ +\ 120 \\ \hline 138 \end{array}$$

Write the partial products. Line up the ones, tens, and hundreds. Add.

There are 138 calories in 3 peaches.

The answer is reasonable because 138 is close to the estimate of 150.

Problem Solving

13. Sam's family is planning a vacation. The table shows the cost of each one-way plane ticket from his town to three different cities.

a How much more is a one-way ticket to Atlanta than a one-way ticket to Chicago?

b How much would Sam's family spend for 3 round-trip tickets to Kansas City?

Tip *A round-trip ticket costs twice as much as a one-way ticket.*

Data

Airfare	
City	**Cost of One-Way Ticket**
Atlanta	\$87
Chicago	\$59
Kansas City	\$49

14. Reasoning How can knowing that 5 × 14 = 70 help you find 5 × 16? Explain your strategy.

15. Algebra The product of this whole number and 25 is greater than 50 but less than 100. What's the number?

16. Estimation Round to the nearest hundred to estimate how many more musicians are in the world's largest accordion band than in the world's largest trombone band.

Data

World's Largest Bands	
Trombone	284 musicians
Accordion	625 musicians

17. Writing to Explain To find 24 × 7, Joel adds the partial products 28 and 14. Is he correct? Explain.

18. Mr. Cruz weighed 8 cartons. Each carton weighed 17 pounds. How many pounds was this in all?

A 25 pounds

B 136 pounds

C 856 pounds

D 8,056 pounds

Virginia

Lesson 18-6

Extends 3.6 The student will represent multiplication and division, using area, set, and number line models, and create and solve problems that involve multiplication of two whole numbers, one factor 99 or less and the second factor 5 or less.

Multiplying 2- and 3-Digit by 1-Digit Numbers

How do you regroup to multiply?

The grass carp fish can eat 3 times its weight in plant food each day. How much food can this grass carp eat each day?

Find 3×26.

Estimate: $3 \times 30 = 90$

Another Example How do you multiply 3-digit numbers?

An aquarium in a large city has about 605 visitors each hour. How many visitors is that in an 8-hour day?

Find 8×605.

Use what you know about multiplying 2-digit numbers for 3-digit numbers.

Step 1

Multiply the ones.
8 × 5 ones = 40 ones
Regroup.

$$\begin{array}{r} {\scriptstyle 4} \\ 605 \\ \times 8 \\ \hline 0 \end{array}$$

Step 2

Multiply the tens.
8 × 0 tens = 0 tens
Add the regrouped tens.

$$\begin{array}{r} {\scriptstyle 4} \\ 605 \\ \times 8 \\ \hline 40 \end{array}$$

Step 3

Multiply the hundreds.
8 × 6 hundreds = 48 hundreds

$$\begin{array}{r} {\scriptstyle 4} \\ 605 \\ \times 8 \\ \hline 4{,}840 \end{array}$$

There are 4,840 visitors in an 8-hour day.

If aquarium tickets cost \$4.75 each, how much would 5 tickets cost?

Find $5 \times \$4.75$.

$$\begin{array}{r} {\scriptstyle 3\ 2} \\ \$4.75 \\ \times 5 \\ \hline \$23.75 \end{array}$$

Multiply as with whole numbers.

Find 5 × 475.

Write the answer in dollars and cents.

$? in all

$4.75	$4.75	$4.75	$4.75	$4.75

Explain It

1. How is multiplying money the same as multiplying whole numbers? How is it different?

Step 1

Multiply the ones. Regroup, if needed.

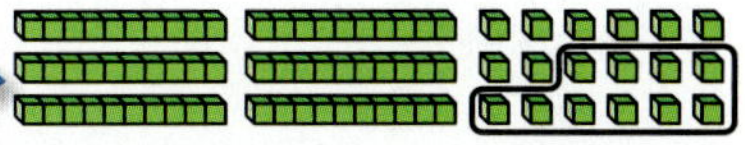

$$\begin{array}{r} {}^{1} \\ 26 \\ \times\ 3 \\ \hline 8 \end{array}$$

3 × 6 = 18 ones
Regroup 18 ones as 1 ten 8 ones.

Step 2

Multiply the tens. Add regrouped tens.

3 × 2 tens = 6 tens
6 tens + 1 ten = 7 tens

$$\begin{array}{r} {}^{1} \\ 26 \\ \times\ 3 \\ \hline 78 \end{array}$$

The fish would eat 78 pounds of food.

Guided Practice*

Do you know HOW?

In **1** and **2**, copy and complete. You may use drawings to help.

1. $\begin{array}{r} 13 \\ \times\ 6 \\ \hline \end{array}$

2. $\begin{array}{r} 124 \\ \times\ 7 \\ \hline \end{array}$

In **3–6**, find each product.

3. $\begin{array}{r} 78 \\ \times\ 4 \\ \hline \end{array}$

4. $\begin{array}{r} \$2.35 \\ \times\ 8 \\ \hline \end{array}$

5. 6 × $1.49

6. 3 × 209

Do you UNDERSTAND?

For **7** and **8**, use the example above.

7. Why is the estimate greater than the exact answer?

8. How much food could this grass carp eat in 4 days?

9. A blue shark can swim 36 feet in 1 second. At this speed, how far would it swim in 3 seconds?

10. Find the total cost of 7 tickets that cost $2.95 each.

Independent Practice

In **11–20**, estimate and then find each product. You may use drawings to help.

11. $\begin{array}{r} 49 \\ \times\ 2 \\ \hline \end{array}$

12. $\begin{array}{r} 37 \\ \times\ 3 \\ \hline \end{array}$

13. $\begin{array}{r} 64 \\ \times\ 5 \\ \hline \end{array}$

14. $\begin{array}{r} 52 \\ \times\ 9 \\ \hline \end{array}$

15. $\begin{array}{r} 46 \\ \times\ 7 \\ \hline \end{array}$

16. 6 × 53

17. 7 × 38

18. 4 × 44

19. 5 × 42

20. 2 × 48

For another example, see Set E on page 433.

Independent Practice

In **21–28**, find each product.

21. 423×9

22. 185×4

23. $\$5.19 \times 6$

24. $\$8.95 \times 2$

25. 291×3

26. 145×5

27. $8 \times \$0.65$

28. $2 \times \$6.85$

Problem Solving

29. The ostrich is the fastest bird on land. An ostrich can run 66 feet in 1 second. The cheetah is the fastest mammal on land. A cheetah can run 94 feet in 1 second. How many fewer feet can an ostrich run in 1 second than a cheetah?

30. The length of the body of this jerboa is shown in the picture. How far can this jerboa jump?

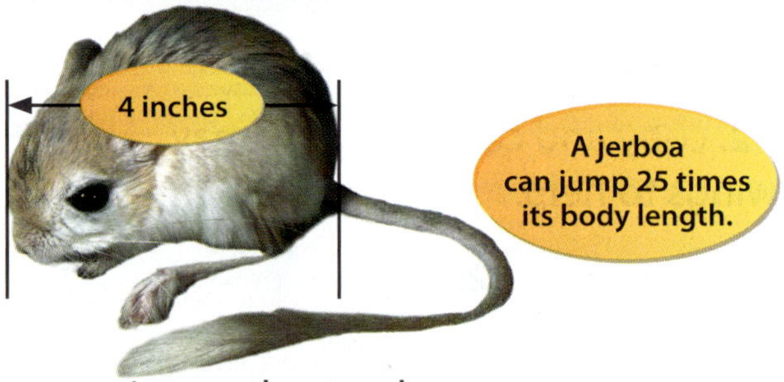

31. **Estimation** Dionne used rounding to estimate the product of 198 and another number. Her estimate of the product was 800. Which number is the best choice for the other factor?

A 3 **B** 4 **C** 8 **D** 10

Algebra For **32–34**, copy and complete. Use <, >, or =.

32. 53×6 ◯ 308 **33.** 19×5 ◯ 145 **34.** 24×4 ◯ 12×8

35. Wanda bought 3 concert tickets that cost $9.75 each. How much did she spend on tickets?

36. Use your answer to Exercise 35. Find how much change Wanda got if she paid with a $20 bill and a $10 bill.

37. At a museum, the visitors formed 8 tour groups to go on tours. Each group had 32 visitors. How many visitors were going on tours?

A 40
B 256
C 246
D 2,416

38. The Great Pyramid of Khufu is square at the bottom. Each side of the square is 751 feet long. What is the perimeter of the pyramid at the bottom?

Algebra Connections

Using Multiplication Properties

Remember to use the properties of multiplication to help you complete number sentences.

Commutative (Order) Property You can multiply factors in any order and the product is the same. $5 \times 9 = 9 \times 5$

Identity (One) Property When you multiply a number and 1, the product is that number. $1 \times 8 = 8$

Zero Property When you multiply a number and 0, the product is 0. $0 \times 7 = 0$

Associative (Grouping) Property You can change the grouping of the factors, and the product is the same. $(3 \times 2) \times 4 = 3 \times (2 \times 4)$

Example: $\square \times 8 = 0$

Think What number multiplied by 8 is equal to 0?

You can use the Zero Property.

$\underline{0} \times 8 = 0$

Example:

$6 \times (9 \times 7) = (6 \times \square) \times 7$

Think What number makes the two sides equal?

Use the Associative Property.

Copy and complete with the number that makes the two sides equal.

1. $10 \times \square = 10$

2. $12 \times 8 = 8 \times \square$

3. $6 \times (2 \times 5) = (6 \times \square) \times 5$

4. $\square \times 8 = 0$

5. $\square \times 7 = 7 \times 11$

6. $(4 \times 3) \times \square = 4 \times (3 \times 8)$

7. $6 \times \square = 9 \times 6$

8. $\square \times 9 = 9$

9. $(\square \times 7) \times 2 = 5 \times (7 \times 2)$

In **10** and **11**, copy and complete the number sentence. Solve the problem.

10. Gemma made 8 rows of stickers on a sheet with 19 stickers in each row. How could she use the Distributive Property to find the total number of stickers?

$8 \times 19 = 8 \times (10 + 9)$
$= (8 \times \square) + (8 \times \square)$

How many stickers did she have in all?

11. Hal and Den each have copies of the same photos. Hal arranges 5 photos on each of 6 pages in 2 albums. Den needs 5 pages in 2 albums for the same photos. How many photos are on each page in Den's albums?

$(6 \times 5) \times 2 = (5 \times \square) \times 2$

How many photos does each boy have?

12. Write a Problem Write a real-world problem to match the number sentence on the right.

$\square \times 12 = 12 \times 3$

Virginia

Lesson 18-7

3.6 The student will represent multiplication and division, using area, set, and number line models, and create and solve problems that involve multiplication of two whole numbers, one factor 99 or less and the second factor 5 or less.

Problem Solving

Draw a Picture and Write a Number Sentence

Oscar bought 5 cases of bottled water. How many bottles of water did Oscar buy?

Another Example

Melody wants to buy a case of juice boxes. There are 3 times as many boxes in a jumbo case as in a regular case. How many juice boxes are in a jumbo case?

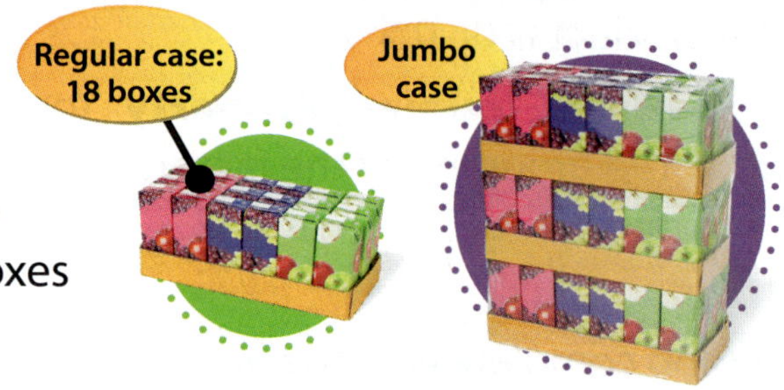

Plan

Use a picture or a diagram to show what you know.

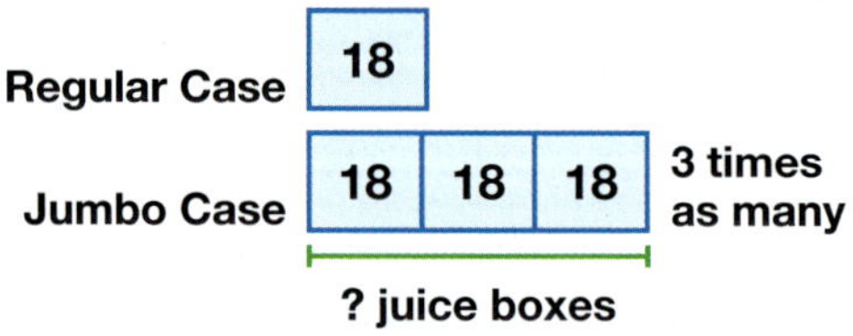

Write a number sentence to find the number that is 3 times as many as 18.

$3 \times 18 = \square$

Solve

Find 3×18.

$$\begin{array}{r} \scriptstyle 2 \\ 18 \\ \times \ \ 3 \\ \hline 54 \end{array}$$

A jumbo case has 54 juice boxes.

Check

Make sure the answer is reasonable.

Estimate to check.

Round 18 to 20.

$3 \times 20 = 60$

The answer is reasonable because 54 is close to the estimate of 60.

Explain It

1. **Number Sense** Why can't you use the same type of diagram for this problem as you used for the problem at the top of the page?
2. Describe another way that you could check that the answer to the problem above is correct.

Plan

Use a picture or a diagram to show what you know.

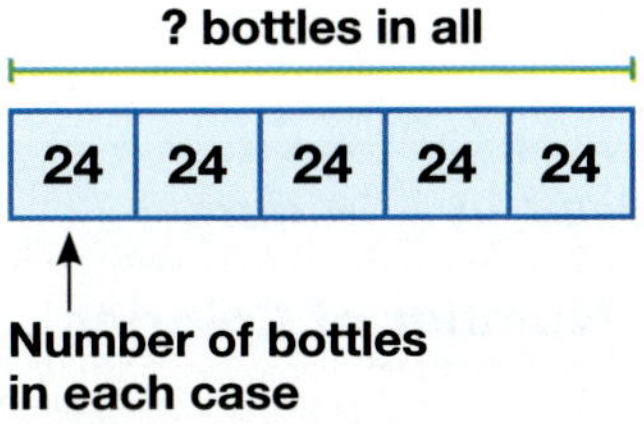

The groups are equal, so multiply to find the total. Write a number sentence.

$5 \times 24 = \square$

Solve

Find 5×24.

$$\begin{array}{r} ^{2} \\ 24 \\ \times\ \ 5 \\ \hline 120 \end{array}$$

Oscar bought 120 bottles of water.

Check

Make sure the answer is reasonable.

Estimate to check.

Round 24 to 20.

$5 \times 20 = 100$

The answer 120 is reasonable because it is close to the estimate.

Guided Practice*

Do you know HOW?

1. A doll collection is displayed in 8 rows with 16 dolls in each row. How many dolls are in the collection?

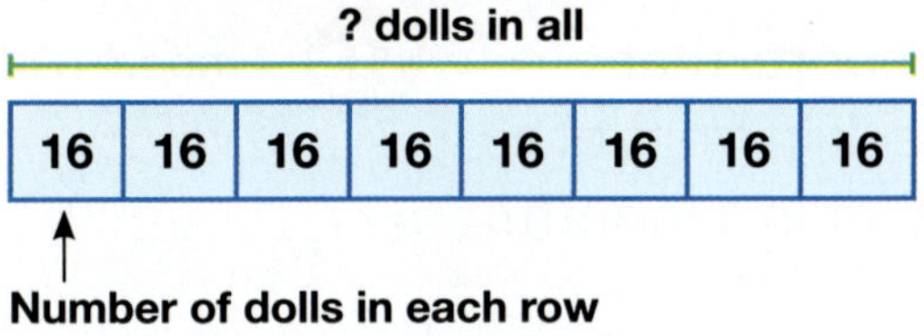

Do you UNDERSTAND?

2. **Writing to Explain** Why do you multiply to solve Problem 1?

3. **Write a Problem** Write a problem that can be solved by drawing a picture. Draw the picture. Solve.

Independent Practice

4. Eduardo has 36 football cards. He has 3 times as many baseball cards. How many baseball cards does he have?

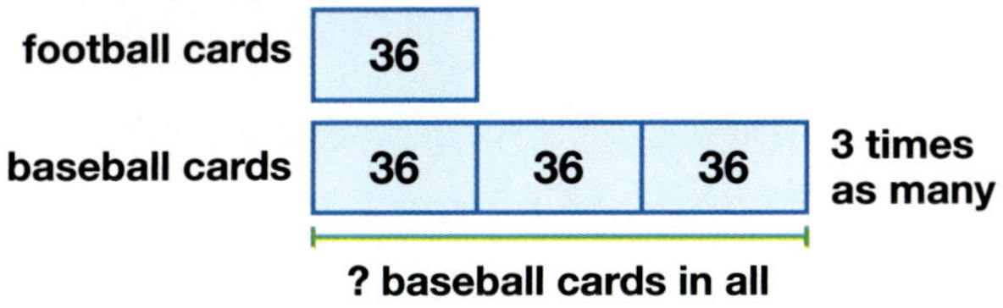

5. **Writing to Explain** Noah has 95 books to put on 4 shelves. If he puts 24 books on each shelf, will all the books fit on the shelves?

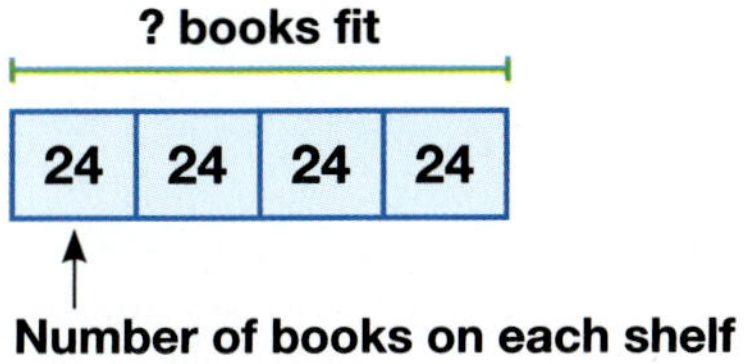

Stuck? Try this....

- What do I know?
- What am I asked to find?
- What diagram can I use to help understand the problem?
- Can I use addition, subtraction, multiplication, or division?
- Is all of my work correct?
- Did I answer the right question?
- Is my answer reasonable?

For another example, see Set F on page 433.

Independent Practice

The table shows about how many calories a 150-pound adult uses doing different activities. Use the table for **6–8**.

6. Martha's mother went jogging for 15 minutes. How many calories did she use?

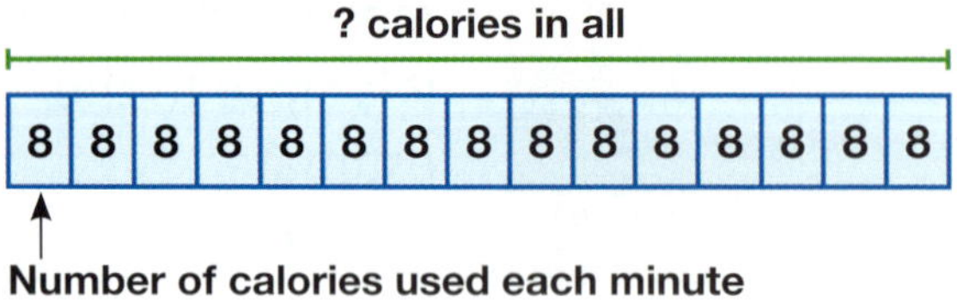

Data

Calories Used in 1 Minute

Activity	Number of Calories
Swimming	10
Jogging	8
Rollerblading	4
Running	9

7. Mr. Lee ran for 25 minutes. Then he swam for 20 minutes. How many calories did he use in all?

8. Miss Nunez plans to swim for 15 minutes every day. How many calories will she use in a week?

9. Frank rode his bike for an hour. Then he went rollerblading for 25 minutes. How many more minutes did he spend riding his bike than rollerblading?

10. **Estimation** The U.S. Department of Health reports that many children spend about 32 hours each week in front of a computer screen. About how many hours is that in a month?

Tip *1 month is about 4 weeks.*

11. Stacy has 3 bags of red beads. Cynthia has 2 more bags than Stacy. There are 24 beads in each bag.

a How many beads does each girl have?

b How many beads do the girls have all together?

Think About the Process

12. Mike earns \$4 an hour doing yard work. He worked 12 hours last week and 23 hours this week. Which number sentence shows how much he earned this week?

A $\$23 + \$12 = \square$

B $12 \times \$4 = \square$

C $23 \times \$4 = \square$

D $(23 \times \$4) \times 7 = \square$

13. Katy read 46 pages of a book on Monday. She read 25 pages on Tuesday. She still has 34 pages to read. Which number sentence shows how many pages are in the book?

A $46 + 25 = \square$

B $46 - 34 = \square$

C $(46 + 25) - 34 = \square$

D $46 + 25 + 34 = \square$

Going Digital

Arrays and Partial Products

Use eTools

Place-Value Blocks

Find 4 × 37. Use an array to tell the partial products.

Step 1 Go to the Place-Value Blocks eTool. Select a horizontal tens block. Click in the workspace 3 times to show the 3 tens in 37. Select a ones block. Click in the workspace 7 times to show the 7 ones in 37. Put all these blocks in one row.

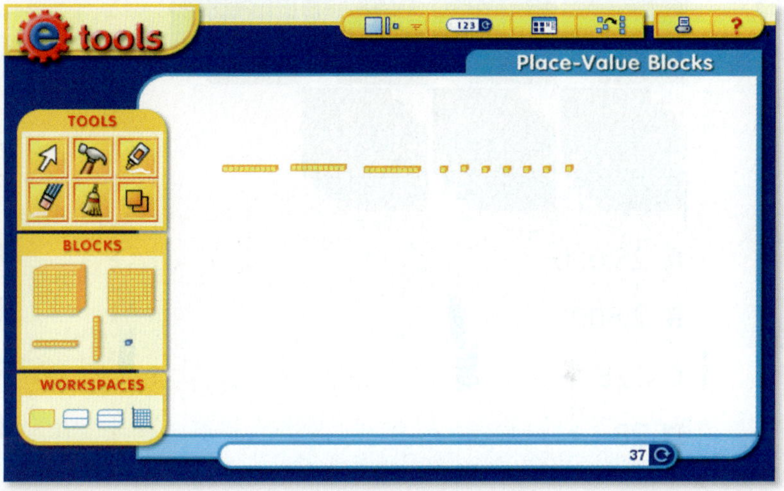

Step 2 Make 3 more rows with 37 in each, so you have 4 rows in all. Click on the odometer style button until you see the partial products 120 + 28 in the odometer. Click on the odometer style button again until the product is shown. The odometer should show 148. Now write a number sentence that shows the partial products and the product.

4 × 37 = 120 + 28 = 148

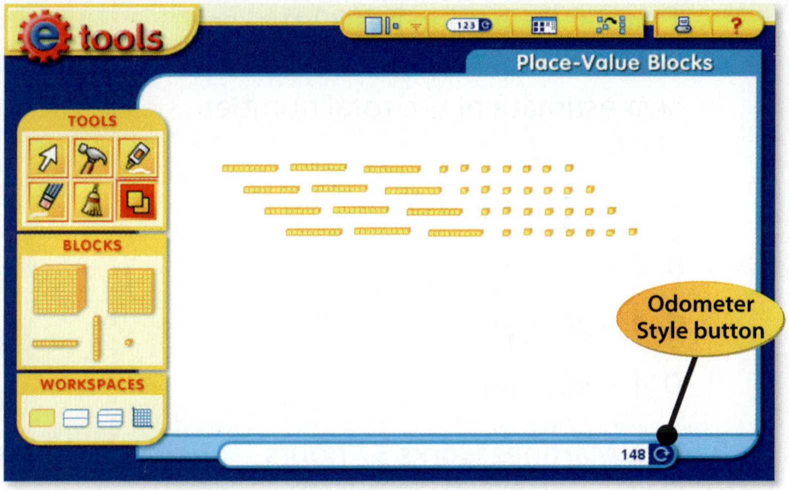

Practice

Use the Place-Value Blocks eTool to find the partial products and the product for each.

1. 3 × 56 **2.** 3 × 29 **3.** 2 × 68

4. 2 × 87 **5.** 3 × 98 **6.** 5 × 17

1. Jillian bought 7 packages of paper. Each package had 400 sheets. How many sheets of paper did Jillian buy? (18-1)

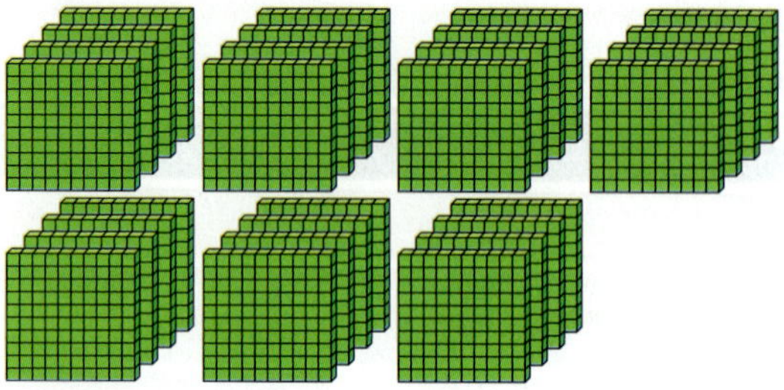

A 28,000

B 2,800

C 128

D 28

2. A package of stickers contains 4 pages. Each page has 32 stickers. Which number sentence shows the best estimate of the total number of stickers? (18-2)

A $4 \times 30 = 120$

B $4 \times 40 = 160$

C $4 + 30 = 34$

D $4 + 40 = 44$

3. Mrs. Martinez works 37 hours each week. How many hours does she work in 6 weeks? Find the product. (18-5)

$$\begin{array}{r} 37 \\ \times \ \ 6 \\ \hline \end{array}$$

A 60

B 122

C 192

D 222

4. Vella's bookcase has 6 shelves. Each shelf displays 3 dolls. Which number sentence shows how many dolls are displayed in the bookcase? (18-7)

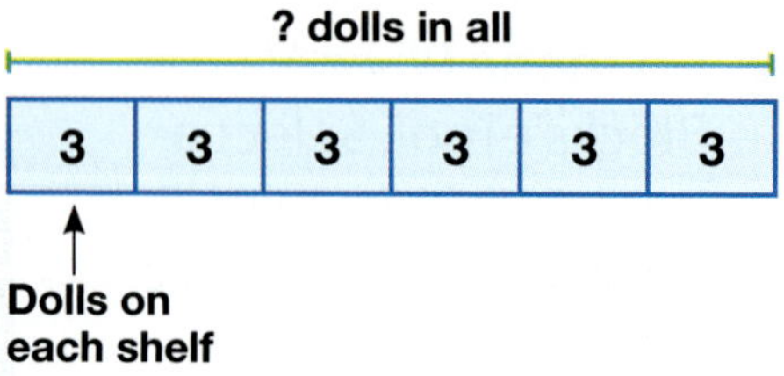

A $6 + 3 = 9$

B $6 - 3 = 3$

C $6 \times 3 = 18$

D $6 \div 3 = 2$

5. Henry bought 3 bags of oranges. Each bag had 16 oranges. How many oranges did he buy? Use the array to solve. (18-3)

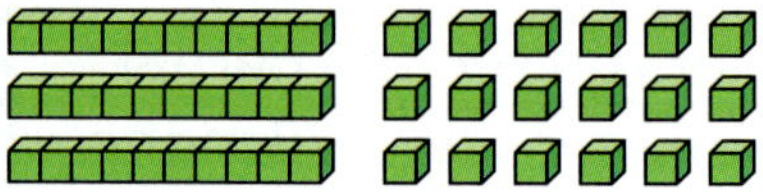

A 19

B 38

C 48

D 54

6. Mr. Gomez bought 26 packages of juice boxes for the school picnic. Each package had 8 juice boxes. How many juice boxes did he buy? (18-6)

A 214

B 208

C 202

D 168

7. Which addition sentence shows how to use partial products to find 5×17? (18-4)

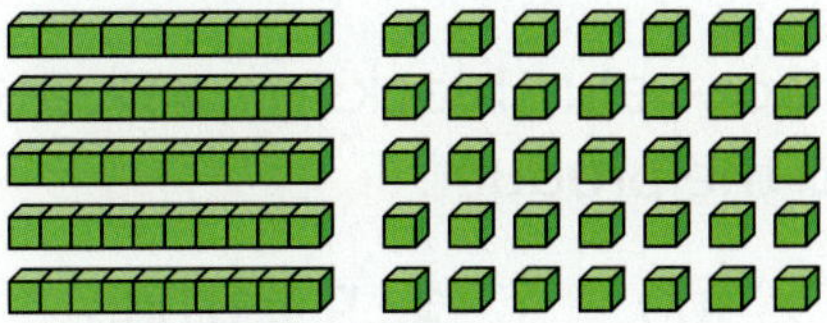

A $50 + 35 = 85$

B $5 + 35 = 38$

C $50 + 45 = 95$

D $50 + 5 = 55$

8. There are 46 students in Grade 3. Each student brought 6 balloons to use on the Grade 3 float in the parade. Which is the best estimate of the number of balloons that will be used on the float? (18-2)

A 50

B 100

C 150

D 300

9. One kind of hippopotamus can eat 130 pounds of food a day. How many pounds of food can this hippopotamus eat in 7 days? (18-6)

A 28

B 91

C 910

D 9,100

10. Which number sentence comes next in the pattern? (18-1)

$8 \times 6 = 48$
$8 \times 60 = 480$
$8 \times 600 = 4{,}800$

A $8 \times 600 = 48{,}000$

B $8 \times 6{,}000 = 48{,}000$

C $80 \times 60 = 4{,}800$

D $80 \times 600 = 48{,}000$

11. Jo drinks 2 to 3 glasses of milk a day. Which is a reasonable number of glasses of milk Jo will drink in 7 days? (18-2)

A Fewer than 14

B Between 14 and 21

C Between 22 and 35

D More than 35

12. Ann needs 20 ceramic tiles to decorate one stepping stone. If she wants to decorate 4 stepping stones for her garden, how many ceramic tiles does she need? (18-1)

A 80

B 24

C 16

D 5

Set A, pages 412–413

Find $7 \times 5{,}000$.

Use basic facts and patterns.

$7 \times 5 = 35$ ← basic fact
$7 \times 50 = 350$
$7 \times 500 = 3{,}500$
$7 \times 5{,}000 = 35{,}000$
} Pattern of zeros

Remember that when the product of a basic fact contains a zero, that zero is not part of the pattern.

Use place-value blocks or patterns to find the product.

1. 7×300
2. $9 \times 6{,}000$
3. $4 \times 5{,}000$
4. 5×200
5. 8×900
6. $3 \times 3{,}000$

Set B, pages 414–415

Estimate 6×57.

Round 57 to the nearest ten.
Then multiply.

6×57
↓ 57 rounds to 60.
$6 \times 60 = 360$

6×57 is about 360.

Remember that you round to the greater ten if the digit in the ones place is 5 or greater. Round to the lesser ten if the ones digit is 4 or less.

Estimate each product.

1. 5×39
2. 8×67
3. 7×42
4. 2×76
5. 4×83
6. 9×25

Set C, pages 416–417

Draw an array to find 3×24.

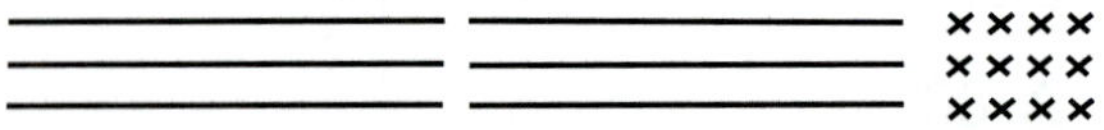

6 tens in all
12 ones in all

Count by tens.
10, 20, 30, 40, 50, 60

Then count by ones to find the total.
61, 62, 63, 64, 65, 66, 67, 68, 69, 70, 71, 72

So, $3 \times 24 = 72$.

Remember to keep your drawings simple.

Find each product. Use place-value blocks or draw a picture to help.

1. 3×27
2. 4×18
3. 5×14
4. 3×32
5. 7×31
6. 4×42
7. 8×22
8. 5×62

Set D, pages 418–419

Find 2×17 by breaking 17 into tens and ones.

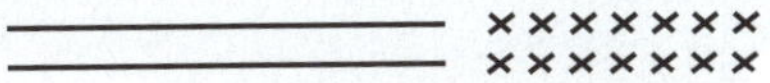

Two rows of 1 ten = 2 tens or 20
Two rows of 7 ones = 14 ones or 14

20 and 14 are partial products.

$20 + 14 = 34$ Add the partial products.

So, $2 \times 17 = 34$.

Remember to include a zero when you record the value of the tens.

Find each product. You may draw a picture to help.

1. 4×73 **2.** 2×59

3. 6×35 **4.** 3×81

5. 7×25 **6.** 5×34

Set E, pages 420–424

Find 27×6.

One Way

$$\begin{array}{r} 27 \\ \times \quad 6 \\ \hline 42 \\ +\ 120 \\ \hline 162 \end{array}$$

42 and 120: partial products

Another Way

$$\begin{array}{r} {}^{4} \\ 27 \\ \times \quad 6 \\ \hline 162 \end{array}$$

Multiply ones.
Regroup.
Multiply tens.

So, $27 \times 6 = 162$.

Remember you can estimate to check that your answer is reasonable.

Find each product.

1. $\begin{array}{r} 29 \\ \times \ 6 \\ \hline \end{array}$ **2.** $\begin{array}{r} 42 \\ \times \ 5 \\ \hline \end{array}$ **3.** $\begin{array}{r} 79 \\ \times \ 4 \\ \hline \end{array}$

4. 9×163 **5.** 8×240

6. $3 \times \$9.67$ **7.** $2 \times \$1.98$

Set F, pages 426–428

Beth has 24 planet stickers. She has 4 times as many flower stickers as planet stickers. How many flower stickers does Beth have?

The groups are equal, so multiply.

$4 \times 24 = 96$
Beth has 96 flower stickers.

Remember that drawing a picture can help you write a number sentence.

Draw a picture to show what you know. Write a number sentence and solve the problem.

1. Ty has his model car collection on shelves in his room. There are 9 shelves with 18 model cars on each shelf. How many model cars are on the shelves?

Topic 19

Dividing with 1-Digit Numbers

1. When Little League began in 1939, there were 30 players. How many teams did they form? You will find out out in Lesson 19-4.

2. The world's largest American flag is 505 feet long. Each star is 17 feet high. About how wide is the flag? You will find out in Lesson 19-6.

3 Skateboarding began in the 1950s. How many skateboards can be made from 38 wheels? You will find out in Lesson 19-5.

4 How much air does a person breathe each day? You will find out in Lesson 19-2.

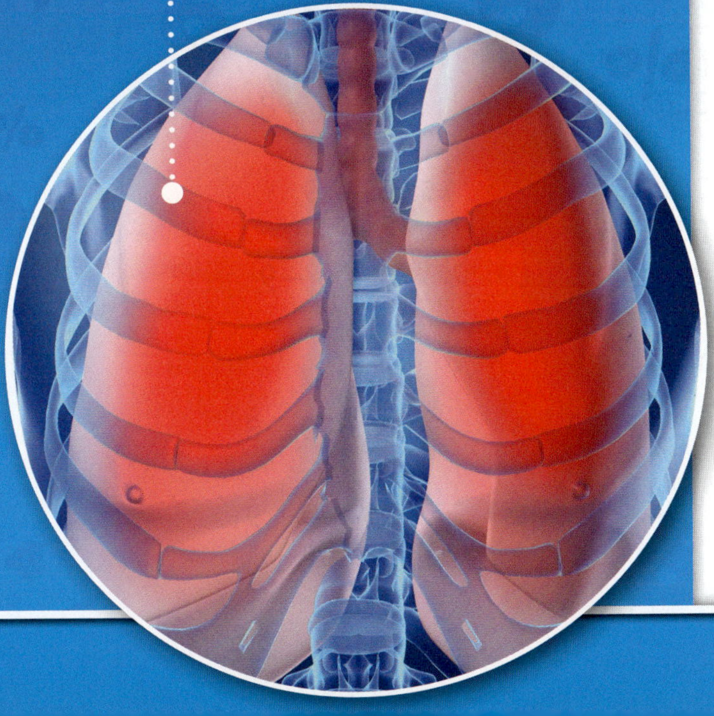

Review What You Know!

Vocabulary

Choose the best term from the box.

- division
- quotient
- fact
- regroup

1. The answer in division is called the ___?___.

2. A ___?___ family shows how multiplication and division are related.

3. When there are not enough ones to subtract, you can ___?___ tens for ones.

Division Facts

Divide.

4. $12 \div 3$ **5.** $18 \div 2$ **6.** $30 \div 6$

7. $54 \div 9$ **8.** $64 \div 8$ **9.** $63 \div 7$

Multiplication

Multiply.

10. 4×19 **11.** 7×14 **12.** 4×23

Subtraction

Subtract.

13. $72 - 60$ **14.** $346 - 200$

15. $1{,}308 - 1{,}200$ **16.** $4{,}275 - 3{,}000$

17. **Writing to Explain** Lea poured 40 ounces of paint into 5 jars. Each jar had the same amount of paint. How much paint was in each jar? Draw a picture and solve. Explain why your drawing helps.

Virginia

Lesson 19-1

Prepares for 4.4.c The student will divide whole numbers, finding quotients with and without remainders.

Mental Math

How can you divide multiples of 10, 100, and 1,000 using patterns?

You know that $12 \div 3 = 4$.

$120 \div 3 = 40$

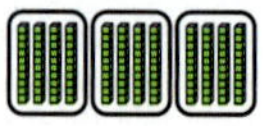

$1{,}200 \div 3 = 400$

$12{,}000 \div 3 = 4{,}000$

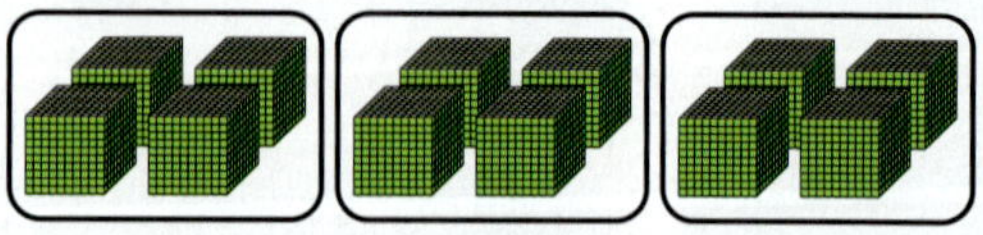

Guided Practice*

Do you know HOW?

In **1–4**, use patterns and mental math to find each quotient.

1. $36 \div 4$
$360 \div 4$
$3{,}600 \div 4$

2. $40 \div 8$
$400 \div 8$
$4{,}000 \div 8$

3. $180 \div 6$

4. $1{,}400 \div 2$

Do you UNDERSTAND?

5. Look at Another Way above. Why are 2 zeros written to the right of 4?

6. What basic fact can you use to find the quotient of $1{,}800 \div 3$?

7. Jay says, "$28 \div 4$ is 7, so $2{,}800 \div 4$ is 700." Do you agree? Explain.

Independent Practice

In **8–15**, use patterns to find each quotient.

8. $15 \div 3$
$150 \div 3$
$1{,}500 \div 3$

9. $54 \div 9$
$540 \div 9$
$5{,}400 \div 9$

10. $32 \div 4$
$320 \div 4$
$3{,}200 \div 4$

11. $72 \div 8$
$720 \div 8$
$7{,}200 \div 8$

12. $21 \div 7$
$210 \div 7$
$2{,}100 \div 7$

13. $12 \div 6$
$120 \div 6$
$1{,}200 \div 6$

14. $20 \div 5$
$200 \div 5$
$2{,}000 \div 5$

15. $63 \div 9$
$630 \div 9$
$6{,}300 \div 9$

In **16–25**, use mental math to find each quotient.

16. $160 \div 2$ **17.** $4{,}900 \div 7$ **18.** $60 \div 3$ **19.** $350 \div 5$ **20.** $5{,}600 \div 8$

21. $3{,}200 \div 8$ **22.** $120 \div 6$ **23.** $80 \div 4$ **24.** $360 \div 6$ **25.** $8{,}100 \div 9$

*For another example, see Set A on page 454.

One Way

Find 2,400 ÷ 6.

Use place value.

2,400 is the same as 24 × 100 or 24 hundreds.

24 ÷ 6 = 4
So, 24 hundreds ÷ 6 = 4 hundreds.

2,400 ÷ 6 = 400

Another Way

Find 2,400 ÷ 6.

Use a rule.

24 ÷ 6 = 4
2,400 ÷ 6 is 4 followed by 2 zeros.

2,400 ÷ 6 = 400

Problem Solving

For **26–30**, use the table at the right.

26. How many times does a horse's heart beat in one minute?

27. How many times does a chicken's heart beat in one minute?

28. In 5 minutes, how many more times does a bat's heart beat than a chicken's heart?

29. In 5 minutes, which animal has 10 times as many heartbeats as a frog?

Data

Animal Heart Rates

Animal	Number of Heartbeats in 5 Minutes
Bat	3,500
Chicken	1,500
Frog	150
Horse	200
Mouse	3,100

30. Write the animals' names in order from fewest to most heartbeats in 5 minutes.

31. Kara leads tours in a museum. During 2 tours she climbed a total of 800 stairs. If the tours were exactly the same, how many stairs did she climb during each tour?

32. The 1,400 people who attended a music concert were equally divided into 7 seating areas. How many people were in each seating area?

A 140 **B** 200 **C** 1,393 **D** 1,407

33. **Number Sense** How many $5 bills make $30? How many make $300?

Virginia

Lesson 19-2

Prepares for 4.4.a The student will estimate sums, differences, products, and quotients of whole numbers.

Estimating Quotients

How do you estimate with division?

The Mills family is planning a car trip that will be 1,764 miles long. The family wants to drive an equal number of miles on each of 6 days. About how many miles should the family drive each day?

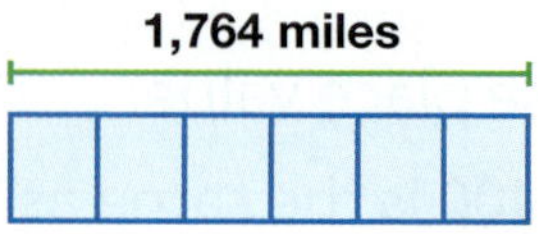

Estimate You need to know *about* how many miles, so an estimate is enough.

Guided Practice*

Do you know HOW?

In **1–8**, estimate each quotient.

1. 83 ÷ 4

2. 248 ÷ 5

3. 572 ÷ 7

4. 4,138 ÷ 6

5. 91 ÷ 9

6. 306 ÷ 5

7. 2,293 ÷ 8

8. 2,710 ÷ 4

Do you UNDERSTAND?

9. In the example above, why is 1,800 ÷ 6 equal to 300 and not 30?

10. What division could you use to estimate 317 ÷ 4?

11. Timmy wants to put 346 toy cars into 5 equal groups. About how many cars should he put in each group?

Independent Practice

In **12–35**, estimate each quotient.

12. 73 ÷ 7

13. 164 ÷ 2

14. 479 ÷ 8

15. 172 ÷ 3

16. 416 ÷ 5

17. 1,983 ÷ 4

18. 361 ÷ 9

19. 505 ÷ 7

20. 7,168 ÷ 9

21. 1,329 ÷ 6

22. 324 ÷ 8

23. 546 ÷ 9

24. 729 ÷ 8

25. 2,036 ÷ 5

26. 697 ÷ 7

27. 812 ÷ 9

28. 364 ÷ 4

29. 206 ÷ 4

30. 427 ÷ 7

31. 489 ÷ 6

32. 278 ÷ 7

33. 8,097 ÷ 9

34. 2,536 ÷ 5

35. 4,917 ÷ 7

*For another example, see Set A on page 454.

Use a division fact.

The family will drive for 6 days. What numbers can be divided evenly by 6?

6, 12, 18, and so on.

1,764 miles is about 1,800 miles.

For division, 1,800 and 6 are numbers that are easy to work with.

Then use mental math.

Find 1,800 ÷ 6.

18 ÷ 6 = 3

1,800 ÷ 6 = 300

The family should drive about 300 miles each day.

Problem Solving

For **36–38**, use the table at the right.

36. The Ramos family wants to take 4 days to drive to River Land. The family wants to drive an equal number of miles each day. About how many miles should the family drive each day?

37. About how many more miles is the trip to Camp Carlson than to Forest Park?

Data

Ramos Family Vacation Ideas
Car Trip Distances

Trip	Number of Miles
Blue Mountain	1,135
Camp Carlson	1,589
Forest Park	473
River Land	766
Sands Point Beach	2,740

38. Reasonableness The Ramos family wants to take 4 days to drive to Blue Mountain. They plan to drive about 300 miles each day. Is this reasonable? Explain.

39. Ashley has 87 insects in her nature collection. She has three times as many leaves as insects in her collection. How many leaves does Ashley have in her collection?

40. SOL Prep Mr. Lowell bought 8 baseball caps. All of the caps were the same price. The total cost was $72. What is the cost of each baseball cap?

A $576 **B** $80 **C** $64 **D** $9

41. Algebra What number makes the number sentence true?

179 × ☐ = 179

42. In 3 days, a person breathes about 9,100 gallons of air. About how many gallons of air does a person breathe in 1 day?

Virginia

Lesson 19-3

3.6 The student will represent multiplication and division, using area, set, and number line models, and create and solve problems that involve multiplication of two whole numbers, one factor 99 or less and the second factor 5 or less.

Connecting Models and Symbols

Hands-On
place-value blocks

How can you model division with greater numbers?

The third graders made 56 sandwiches for a picnic. They put an equal number of sandwiches on each of 4 plates. How many sandwiches are on each plate?

Another Example How can place value help you divide?

Helen has 54 baseball cards. She wants to put an equal number of cards in each of 3 albums. How many cards will go in each album?

Choose an Operation Division is used to find the size of equal groups. Helen needs to find $54 \div 3$.

You have used place value to help subtract. Now you will use place value to help divide.

Estimate Use numbers that are easy to divide: 60 is close to 54 and $60 \div 3 = 20$. There should be about 20 cards in each album.

Draw place-value blocks to show 54.

3)54

Divide the tens into 3 equal groups.

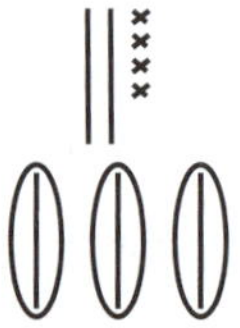

```
  1      1 ten in
3)54     each group
- 3      3 tens used
```

Regroup the extra tens as ones.

```
  1
3)54
- 3
  2      2 tens
         are left
```

Divide the ones into 3 equal groups.

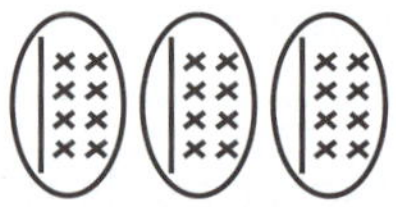

```
  18     8 ones in
3)54     each group
- 3↓
  24
- 24     24 ones used
   0     No ones left
```

There will be 18 cards in each album.

Explain It

1. Why do you trade the tens for ones?

Step 1

Model the problem.

Use place-value blocks.

56: 

Draw rings to show how many equal groups you need.

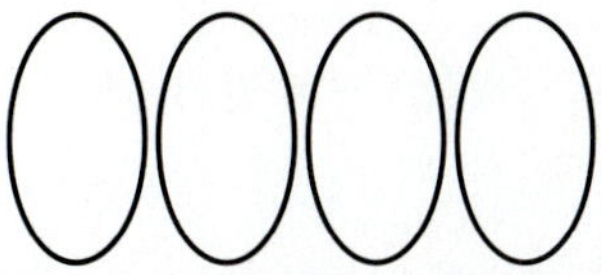

Step 2

Divide the tens.

Put an equal number of tens in each ring. 1 ten and 6 ones are left.

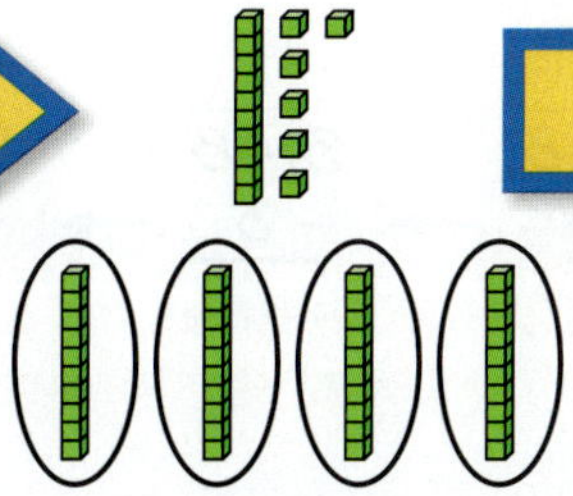

Step 3

Regroup the leftover tens as ones and divide the ones.

1 ten regrouped as 10 ones plus the 6 ones is 16 ones.

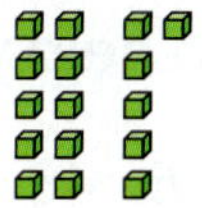

Place an equal number of ones in each ring.

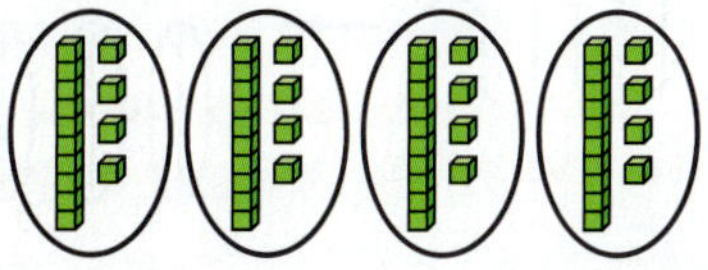

Each plate has 14 sandwiches.

Guided Practice*

Do you know HOW?

Use place-value blocks or the pictures. Copy and complete to find the quotient.

1. 32 ÷ 2

a Draw place-value blocks to show 32.

2)32

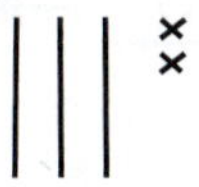

b Divide the tens into 2 equal groups.

2)32
–

c Regroup the extra ten as ones.

2)32
– 2

d Divide the ones.

2)32
– 2

–
0

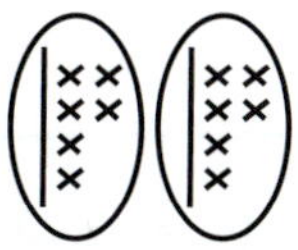

Do you UNDERSTAND?

2. In Exercise 1, how do the pictures help you divide?

3. **Writing to Explain** In the example above, why do you draw four rings?

In **4** and **5**, solve. Use place-value blocks or draw pictures to help.

4. In the example above, suppose the 3rd graders made 68 sandwiches for the picnic. How many would they need to put on each plate?

5. The third graders have 42 straws for a picnic. They want to put an equal number of straws in each of three cups. How many straws should they put in each cup?

DIGITAL eTools www.pearsonsuccessnet.com

*For another example, see Set B on page 454.

Independent Practice

Leveled Practice In **6–9**, use place-value blocks or the pictures to help you find each quotient.

6. 48 ÷ 3

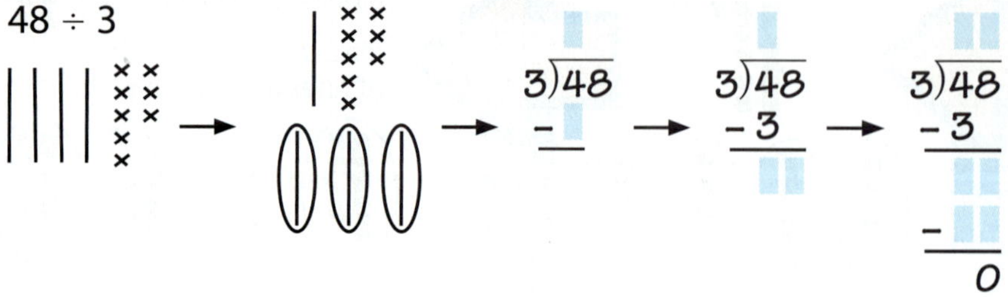

7. 34 ÷ 2

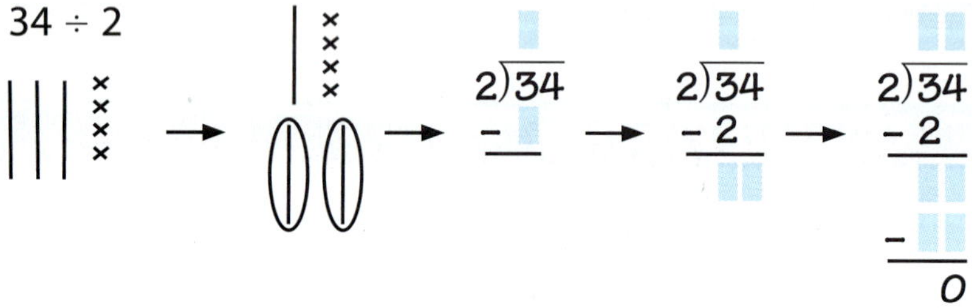

8. 51 ÷ 3

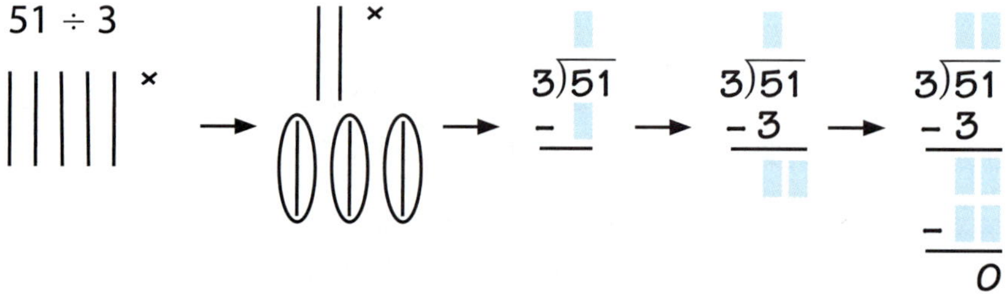

9. 72 ÷ 4

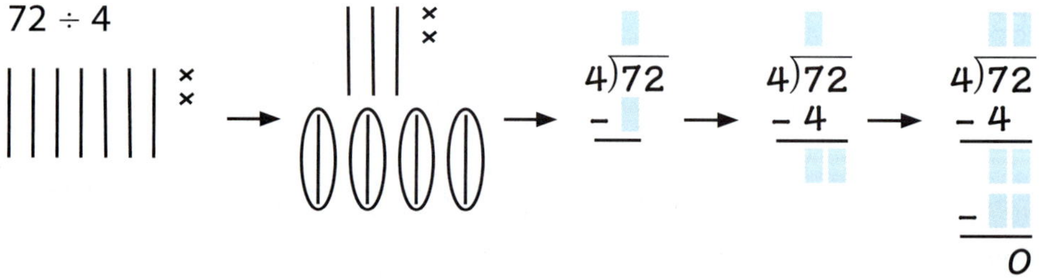

In **10–19**, draw pictures to help find each quotient.

10. 36 ÷ 2 **11.** 68 ÷ 4 **12.** 90 ÷ 9 **13.** 65 ÷ 5 **14.** 84 ÷ 6

15. 42 ÷ 3 **16.** 80 ÷ 5 **17.** 76 ÷ 4 **18.** 42 ÷ 2 **19.** 91 ÷ 7

Problem Solving

20. There are 64 children playing games. They want to make 4 equal teams. How many children should be on each team?

21. **Number Sense** How can you tell if the quotient 46 ÷ 2 is greater than 20 without dividing?

22. Mr. Wen has $42. He wants to give an equal amount to each of his three children. What amount should he give to each child?

23. Indira painted $\frac{1}{4}$ of the length of a board. What is one other way to name $\frac{1}{4}$?

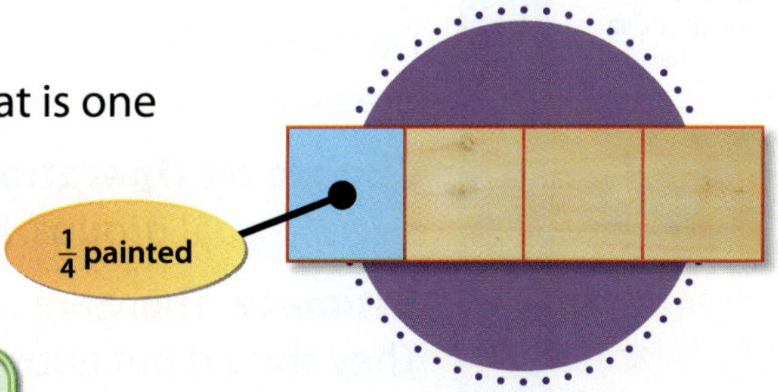

Use the table for **24–26**.

Number of Items in Package

Item	Small	Medium	Large
Paper Plates	36	52	90
Paper Cups	24	48	96

24. Marisol has a medium package of paper plates. She wants to put an equal number of plates on each of four tables. How many plates should she put on each table?

25. Marisol has a large package of paper cups. She wants to put an equal number of cups on each of six tables. How many cups should she put on each table?

26. Suppose Bruce buys a small package and a medium package of paper plates. How many fewer paper plates would he have than if he bought a large package of paper plates?

27. Leslie estimates that it will take 150 hours to paint her house. If Leslie paints for 8 hours each day, about how many days will it take her to paint the house?

A 10 **C** 40

B 20 **D** 60

28. Malik is displaying baseball cards in an album. He can fit 4 cards on a page. How many pages does he need to display 96 baseball cards?

A 20 **C** 24

B 22 **D** 25

29. For a cooking contest, 85 chefs were equally divided into 5 different teams. How many chefs were on each team?

A 17 **C** 80

B 18 **D** 90

30. Mr. Mason bought 3 folding chairs. All of the chairs were the same price. The total cost was $57. How much money did each chair cost?

A $60 **C** $19

B $54 **D** $18

Virginia

Lesson 19-4

Prepares for 4.4.c The student will divide whole numbers, finding quotients with and without remainders.

Dividing 2-Digit Numbers

How do you divide with paper and pencil?

Dara and Toby are dividing each kind of fruit equally into four boxes. How many apples should they put in each box?

Choose an Operation Division is used to find the size of equal groups. Find 76 ÷ 4.

Estimate There are about 80 apples, and 80 ÷ 4 = 20. They should put about 20 apples in each box.

Data

Kind of Fruit	Number
Apples	76
Pears	56
Oranges	92

Guided Practice*

Do you know HOW?

In **1–4**, copy and complete. Find each quotient. Check your answers.

1. 1[ ]
3)48
− 3
1[ ]
− [ ][ ]
0

2. 1[ ]
6)84
− 6
2[ ]
− [ ][ ]
0

3. 1[ ]
2)38
− 2
[ ][ ]
− [ ][ ]
0

4. 1[ ]
5)85
− 5
[ ][ ]
− [ ][ ]
0

Do you UNDERSTAND?

5. In the example above, why is a 1 written above the 7?

6. **Number Sense** Charles says that 68 ÷ 4 = 18. Multiply to find out if he is correct.

7. Use the table above. Dara and Toby are dividing the pears and the oranges equally into four boxes.

a How many pears should they put in each box?

b How many oranges?

Independent Practice

In **8–12**, copy and complete to find each quotient. Check your answers.

8. 3[ ]
2)76
− 6
[ ]6
− [ ][ ]
0

9. [ ][ ]
6)78
− [ ]
[ ]8
− [ ][ ]
[ ]

10. 2[ ]
3)81
− 6
[ ]1
− [ ][ ]
0

11. [ ][ ]
4)92
− [ ]
[ ]2
− [ ][ ]
[ ]

12. 1[ ]
5)95
− 5
[ ]5
− [ ][ ]
0

*For another example, see Set B on page 454.

Step 1

Divide the tens.

7 tens ÷ 4 = ▢

1 ten per group → 1

$$\begin{array}{r} 1 \\ 4\overline{)76} \\ -4 \\ \hline 3 \end{array}$$

4 tens used → − 4

3 tens left → 3

Step 2

Divide the ones.

$$\begin{array}{r} 19 \\ 4\overline{)76} \\ -4 \\ \hline 36 \\ -36 \\ \hline 0 \end{array}$$

9 ones in each group

3 tens 6 ones regrouped as 30 ones + 6 ones

36 ones used

0 ← Nothing left

76 ÷ 4 = 19

They should put 19 apples in each box.

Step 3

Check by multiplying.

$$\begin{array}{r} {}^{3} \\ 19 \\ \times\ 4 \\ \hline 76 \end{array}$$

Also, the answer 19 is close to the estimate of 20.

Problem Solving

For **13–15**, use the table at the right.

Data

Fruits Picked	
Kind of Fruit	**Number**
Lemons	84
Peaches	96
Pears	72
Oranges	79

13. Carla picked the peaches. She put an equal number of peaches into each of eight crates. How many peaches did Carla put in each crate?

14. Justine picked the lemons and put an equal number of lemons into each of three crates. How many lemons did she put in each crate?

15. **Estimation** About how many pears and oranges were picked in all?

16. For the concert, the 64 band members were divided equally into 4 different groups. How many band members were in each group?

17. Little League baseball began in 1939 in Pennsylvania. There were 30 players equally divided among 3 teams. How many players were on each team?

18. **Algebra** Which of the following numbers makes this number sentence true?

8 × 9 > 4 × ▢

A 17

B 18

C 19

D 21

19. Mrs. Adams bought 5 blankets. All of the blankets were the same price. The total cost was $95. How much did each blanket cost?

A $475

B $90

C $19

D $18

Virginia

Lesson 19-5

Prepares for 4.4.c The student will divide whole numbers, finding quotients with and without remainders.

Dividing with Remainders

Hands-On
counters

What happens when some are left?

If 23 members of a marching band march in rows of 4, how many rows are there? How many band members are left?

Division is used to find how many groups. The number left over after dividing is the remainder.

Guided Practice*

Do you know HOW?

In **1–6**, use counters or draw a picture to find each quotient and remainder.

1. 17 ÷ 3 **2.** 22 ÷ 6

3. 25 ÷ 4 **4.** 18 ÷ 5

5. 15 ÷ 2 **6.** 19 ÷ 7

Do you UNDERSTAND?

7. In the example above, what does the quotient 5 R3 mean?

8. There are 20 members in the marching band. Suppose they march in rows of 3. How many full rows of band members would there be? How many band members would be left?

Independent Practice

Leveled Practice In **9–12**, copy and complete. Check your answers.

9. $3\overline{)14}$ = ☐ R ☐; − ☐☐; ☐

10. $2\overline{)17}$ = ☐ R ☐; − ☐☐; ☐

11. $7\overline{)27}$ = ☐ R ☐; − ☐☐; ☐

12. $8\overline{)55}$ = ☐ R ☐; − ☐☐; ☐

In **13–22**, find each quotient and remainder. Check your answers.

13. $4\overline{)21}$ **14.** $6\overline{)46}$ **15.** $5\overline{)48}$ **16.** $9\overline{)41}$ **17.** $9\overline{)64}$

18. $5\overline{)52}$ **19.** $8\overline{)58}$ **20.** $4\overline{)35}$ **21.** $6\overline{)39}$ **22.** $7\overline{)70}$

DIGITAL Animated Glossary, eTools **www.pearsonsuccessnet.com**

*For another example, see Set C on page 455.

What You Show

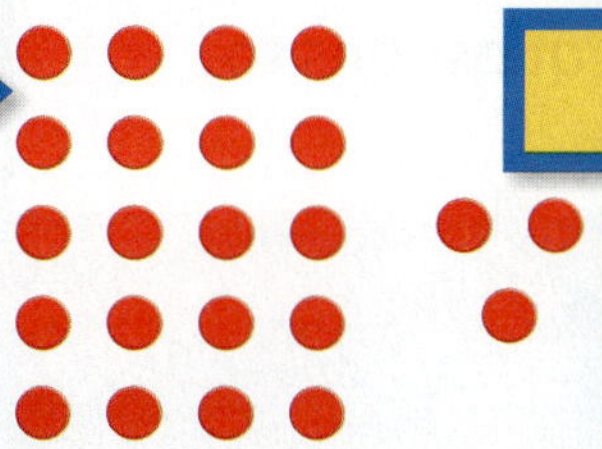

What You Think

If I put 23 counters in rows of 4, I get 5 full rows.

I used 5 × 4, or 20 counters. The 3 counters I have left are not enough for another group of 4, so the remainder is 3.

I can check by multiplying 5 × 4 and then adding 3.

What You Write

$$\begin{array}{r} 5\text{ R}3 \\ 4\overline{)23} \\ -\underline{20} \\ 3 \end{array}$$

Check:
5 × 4 = 20
20 + 3 = 23

There are 5 rows of band members with 3 band members left.

Problem Solving

For **23–25**, use the table at the right that shows all members of the band.

Clayton School Marching Band (Data)

Instrument	Number of Band Members
Drum	23
Flute	14
Clarinet	18
Trumpet	12

23. The flute players march in rows of 3. How many rows of flute players are there? How many flute players are left?

24. The drummers march in rows of 6. How many rows of drummers are there? How many drummers are left?

25. How many band members are there in all?

26. A group of 68 people will be going rafting. Each raft can hold 8 people. The group will fill each raft before using the next one. How many rafts will be needed?

27. **Writing to Explain** Together, Nick and Leslie need to make 9 sandwiches. Nick thinks they will have enough if they each make 4 sandwiches. Do you agree? Explain.

28. **Number Sense** What is the greatest possible remainder you can have if you divide a number by 7? Explain.

29. Melanie has $20. She wants to buy as many cartons of juice as she can. Each carton costs $3. How many cartons of juice can she buy?

SOL Prep

A 6 **B** 7 **C** 17 **D** 23

30. If each skateboard has 4 wheels, how many skateboards can Julian make with 38 wheels? How many wheels are left?

Virginia

Lesson 19-6

Prepares for 4.4.c The student will divide whole numbers, finding quotients with and without remainders.

Problem Solving

Multiple-Step Problems

You have learned that some problems have hidden questions to be answered before you can solve the problem.

A museum collection of 36 dragonflies and 54 butterflies will be used in 2 new displays. There will be the same number of insects in both displays. How many insects will be in each display?

Another Example What is the hidden question?

A store has boxed sets of DVDs for sale. In each box, the DVDs are in 2 rows with 3 DVDs in each row. The total cost of a boxed set is $72. Each DVD costs the same. What is the cost of one DVD?

Plan and Solve

What is the hidden question?

What is the total number of DVDs in each box?

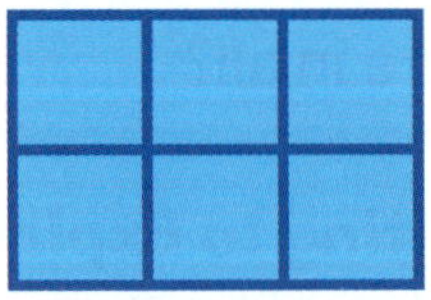

$2 \times 3 = 6$

There are 6 DVDs in each box.

Solve

Use the answer to the hidden question to solve the problem.

What is the cost of each DVD?

$$\begin{array}{r} 12 \\ 6\overline{)72} \\ -\ 6 \\ \hline 12 \\ -\ 12 \\ \hline 0 \end{array}$$

Each DVD costs $12.

Explain It

1. How do you know what the hidden question is in the problem above?
2. Explain how to check the solution to the problem above.

First, you need to find and solve the hidden question.

What is the total number of insects in the museum collection?

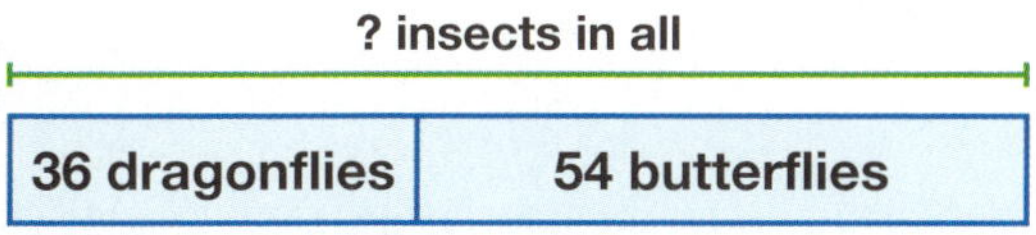

$$\begin{array}{r} {}^{1} \\ 36 \\ +\ 54 \\ \hline 90 \end{array}$$

There are 90 insects in all.

Use the answer to the hidden question to solve the problem.

How many insects will be in each display?

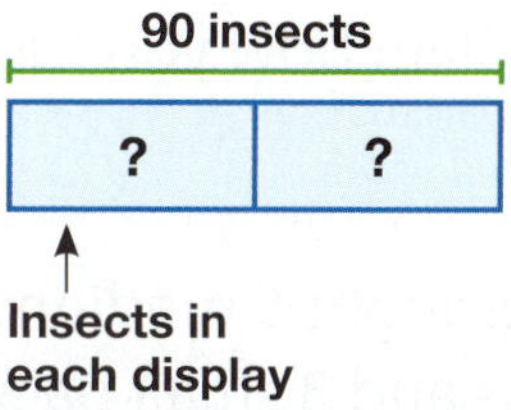

$$\begin{array}{r} 45 \\ 2\overline{)90} \\ -8 \\ \hline 10 \\ -10 \\ \hline 0 \end{array}$$

There will be 45 insects in each of the new displays.

Guided Practice*

Do you know HOW?

Answer the hidden question. Then solve.

1. Twelve friends went camping. All except 4 of them went on a hike. The hikers carried 32 water bottles. Each hiker carried the same number of water bottles. How many water bottles did each hiker carry?

   HINT: Hidden Question—How many went on the hike?

Do you UNDERSTAND?

2. What operations did you use to solve Problem 1?
3. **Write a Problem** Write a problem that can be solved by finding and answering a hidden question.

Independent Practice

Leveled Practice Solve. Answer the hidden question first.

4. Mrs. Lum bought 12 rolls of pink ribbon and some rolls of yellow ribbon. The total cost of the rolls of ribbon is $45. Each roll costs $3. How many rolls of yellow ribbon did Mrs. Lum buy?

   HINT: Hidden Question—What is the total number of rolls of ribbon Mrs. Lum bought?

Stuck? Try this....

- What do I know?
- What am I asked to find?
- What diagram can I use to help understand the problem?
- Can I use addition, subtraction, multiplication, or division?
- Is all of my work correct?
- Did I answer the right question?
- Is my answer reasonable?

*For another example, see Set D on page 455.

Independent Practice

5. **Writing to Explain** There were 24 students in a class. All of the students, except 2, went bowling. What is the total cost the students paid if each person who went bowling paid $5? Explain how you found your answer.

6. Vanya bought 5 medium packages of buttons and 3 small packages of beads. What was the total number of buttons she bought? Use the table at the right.

Data

Number of Items in Package

Item	Small	Medium	Large
Beads	32	64	96
Buttons	18	38	56

7. Mr. Alton wants to buy tickets for a show. The tickets are for seats in 3 rows with 3 seats in each row. The total cost of the tickets is $108. Each ticket costs the same. What is the cost of one ticket?

8. **Estimation** Each stripe of the world's largest American flag is more than 19 feet wide. There are 7 red stripes and 6 white stripes. Each stripe is the same width. About how wide is this flag? Explain your answer.

9. Use the table at the right. Mrs. Casey bought one adult admission ticket and one child admission ticket. Then she bought one adult ticket and one child ticket for a boat ride. What was the total amount Mrs. Casey spent?

Data

County Fair

Kind of Ticket	Adult	Child
Admission	$8	$4
Boat Rides	$2	$1

10. **Think About the Process** Elio had $36 in his wallet. He used $9 to buy a book. Which number sentence shows how to find the amount of money he has left?

A $36 + 9 = \square$

B $36 - 9 = \square$

C $36 \times 9 = \square$

D $39 \div 9 = \square$

11. **Think About the Process** Martin raked 3 lawns yesterday and 4 lawns today. He earned a total of $42. He earned the same amount for each lawn. Which number sentence shows how to find how much he earned for each lawn he raked?

A $42 - 4 = \square$

B $42 + 4 = \square$

C $42 \times 3 = \square$

D $42 \div 7 = \square$

Stop and Practice

Write the fraction in simplest form.

1. $\frac{4}{8}$ **2.** $\frac{4}{10}$ **3.** $\frac{8}{12}$ **4.** $\frac{2}{4}$

Find each sum or difference.

5. $\begin{array}{r} \$3.82 \\ +\ 1.47 \\ \hline \end{array}$ **6.** $\begin{array}{r} \$7.08 \\ +\ 2.93 \\ \hline \end{array}$ **7.** $\begin{array}{r} \$5.86 \\ -\ 1.29 \\ \hline \end{array}$ **8.** $\begin{array}{r} \$4.00 \\ -\ 1.38 \\ \hline \end{array}$

Find each product.

9. $\begin{array}{r} 39 \\ \times\ 8 \\ \hline \end{array}$ **10.** $\begin{array}{r} 56 \\ \times\ 7 \\ \hline \end{array}$ **11.** $\begin{array}{r} 97 \\ \times\ 3 \\ \hline \end{array}$ **12.** $\begin{array}{r} 86 \\ \times\ 5 \\ \hline \end{array}$ **13.** $\begin{array}{r} 300 \\ \times\ 4 \\ \hline \end{array}$

Find each quotient.

14. $3\overline{)78}$ **15.** $6\overline{)96}$ **16.** $2\overline{)56}$ **17.** $4\overline{)76}$

Error Search Find each product that is not correct. Write it correctly and explain the error.

18. $\begin{array}{r} 76 \\ \times\ 4 \\ \hline 300 \end{array}$ **19.** $\begin{array}{r} 39 \\ \times\ 6 \\ \hline 234 \end{array}$ **20.** $\begin{array}{r} 17 \\ \times\ 2 \\ \hline 16 \end{array}$ **21.** $\begin{array}{r} 86 \\ \times\ 3 \\ \hline 258 \end{array}$ **22.** $\begin{array}{r} 15 \\ \times\ 9 \\ \hline 135 \end{array}$

Number Sense

Estimating and Reasoning Write whether each statement is true or false. If the statement is false, explain why.

23. The sum of 128 and 292 is greater than 300.

24. The sum of 910 and 100 is less than 1,000.

25. The difference between 713 and 509 is less than 100.

26. The product of 4 and 29 is greater than 100.

27. The product of 5 and 86 is greater than 500.

28. The quotient of 82 ÷ 2 is greater than 40.

VA SOL Test Prep

1. An auditorium has 2,000 seats in 5 sections. Each section has the same number of seats. How many seats are in each section? (19-1)

A 20

B 40

C 400

D 10,000

2. Mr. Ortiz earned \$6,496 by selling 8 paintings for the same price each. Which number sentence shows the best way to estimate the amount he earned for each painting? (19-2)

A 8 × \$6,400 = \$51,200

B \$5,600 ÷ 8 = \$700

C \$6,400 ÷ 10 = \$640

D \$6,400 ÷ 8 = \$800

3. What is 87 ÷ 7? (19-5)

A 11 R1

B 11 R7

C 12

D 12 R3

4. Don bought \$76 in plants. He spent \$24 on daisies and the rest on rose bushes. If Don bought 4 rose bushes that all had the same price, how much did each rose bush cost? (19-6)

A \$6

B \$13

C \$19

D \$52

5. Which number sentence does the diagram show? (19-3)

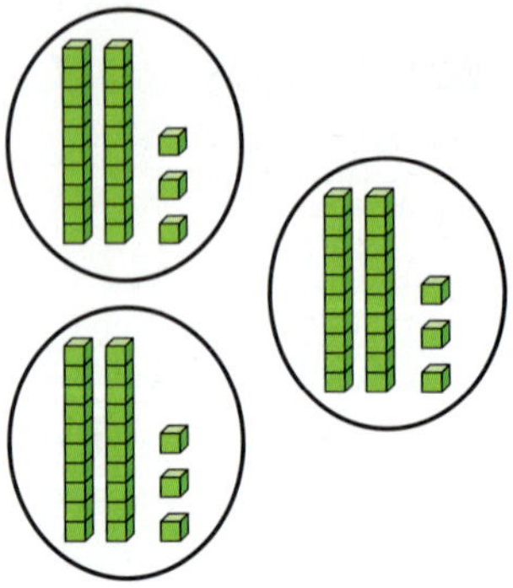

A 69 ÷ 3 = 22

B 69 ÷ 3 = 23

C 69 ÷ 3 = 20

D 60 ÷ 3 = 20

6. For the water balloon toss, 75 students were divided equally into 5 groups. How many students were in each group? (19-4)

A 375

B 25

C 15

D 14 groups with 5 left over

7. Four students stapled 84 school newsletters. How many newsletters did each student staple if they shared the work evenly? (19-4)

A 336

B 92

C 21

D 12

8. The art teacher has 240 cotton balls to use in her art classes. She has 3 classes in the morning and 1 in the afternoon. If she splits the cotton balls evenly among the classes, how many cotton balls would each class have? (19-6)

A 6

B 60

C 80

D 960

9. What is the quotient? (19-4)

```
   □□
3)78
 - □
 ----
   □□
 - □□
 ----
    0
```

A 16

B 23

C 24

D 26

10. Juan practiced the tuba for a total of 235 minutes this week. If he practiced an equal amount of time on 6 different nights, about how many minutes did he practice each night? (19-2)

A 40 minutes

B 55 minutes

C 60 minutes

D 240 minutes

11. What is 38 ÷ 9? (19-5)

A 4 R2

B 4 R3

C 4 R4

D 5 R3

12. To find 96 ÷ 4, Tim first divided the tens into 4 equal groups. What should Tim do next? (19-3)

```
  2
4)96
  8
 ---
```

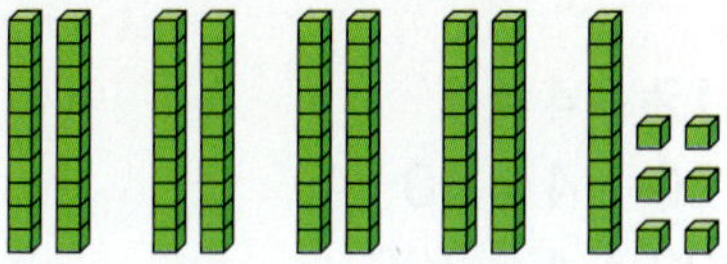

A Divide the ones.

B Subtract 8 tens from 9 tens.

C Regroup the two extra tens as ones.

D Nothing, he is finished.

13. Montgomery uses 7 beads to make a keychain. If she bought a package with 300 beads, about how many key chains will she be able to make? (19-2)

A 60

B 50

C 40

D 4

14. What is 2,400 ÷ 2? (19-1)

A 1,200

B 1,002

C 120

D 12

Set A, pages 436–439

Estimate 1,326 ÷ 4.

Use numbers that are close to the numbers in the problem and easy to divide.

1,200 is close to 1,326. 1,200 can be evenly divided by 4.

Think 12 ÷ 4 = 3

Find 1,200 ÷ 4.

You can use patterns and mental math.

12 ÷ 4 = 3
120 ÷ 4 = 30
1,200 ÷ 4 = 300

Remember that you can use numbers that are close to the actual numbers and easy to divide.

Estimate each quotient.

1. 26 ÷ 3 **2.** 203 ÷ 2

3. 438 ÷ 6 **4.** 3,971 ÷ 5

5. 47 ÷ 8 **6.** 215 ÷ 4

7. 2,946 ÷ 7 **8.** 2,632 ÷ 9

Set B, pages 440–445

Find 57 ÷ 3.

Step 1

Divide the tens.

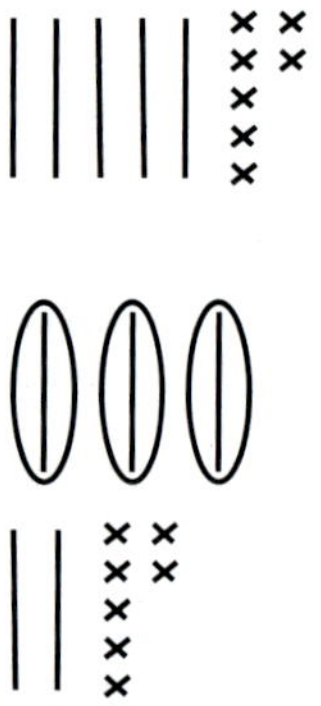

5 tens ÷ 3 = □
1 ten in each group → 1
3)57
3 tens used → − 3
27 left → 27

Step 2

Divide the ones.

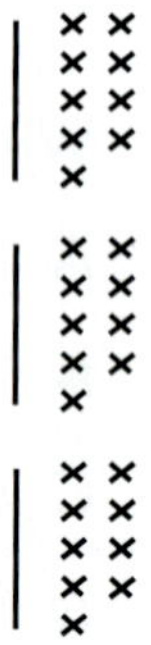

27 ones ÷ 3 = □
19 ← 9 ones in each group
3)57
− 3
27
− 27 ← 27 ones used
0 ← Nothing left

57 ÷ 3 = 19

Remember to first divide the tens by the divisor. Then regroup any extra tens as ones and divide the ones by the divisor.

Copy and complete. You may use place-value blocks or pictures to help find each quotient. Check your answers.

1.
1□
2)38
− 2
1□
− □□
0

2.
1□
4)68
− 4
2□
− □□
0

3.
1□
3)45
− 3
□□
− □□
0

4.
1□
7)91
− 7
□□
− □□
0

Set C, pages 446–447

Mrs. Anderson has 95 ounces of punch for a party. How many glasses can she fill if each glass holds 4 ounces of punch? Is any punch left?

Find 95 ÷ 4.

Step 1

Divide the tens.

$$\begin{array}{r} 2 \\ 4\overline{)95} \\ -\ 8 \\ \hline 15 \end{array}$$

Step 2

Divide the ones. Write the remainder.

$$\begin{array}{r} 23 \text{ R3} \\ 4\overline{)95} \\ -\ 8 \\ \hline 15 \\ -12 \\ \hline 3 \end{array}$$

She can fill 23 glasses. There are 3 ounces of punch left.

Remember to write the remainder in the quotient.

Copy and complete.

1. $$\begin{array}{r} 1\square \text{ R}\square \\ 6\overline{)79} \\ -\ 6 \\ \hline \square\square \\ -\ \square\square \\ \hline \square \end{array}$$

2. $$\begin{array}{r} 2\square \text{ R}\square \\ 2\overline{)49} \\ -\ 4 \\ \hline \square\square \\ -\ \square\square \\ \hline \square \end{array}$$

3. $4\overline{)81}$
4. $3\overline{)42}$
5. $5\overline{)79}$
6. $7\overline{)88}$
7. $8\overline{)98}$
8. $6\overline{)61}$

Set D, pages 448–450

There are 13 girls and 14 boys that will form volleyball teams. Each team needs 6 players. Extra players will be alternates. How many teams can be formed? How many players will be alternates?

Step 1

First find the total number of children.

13 + 14 = 27

Step 2

Use the answer to the hidden question to solve the problem.

Step 3

Solve the problem. Divide 27 by 6 to find the number of teams.

$$\begin{array}{r} 4 \text{ R3} \\ 6\overline{)27} \\ -\ 24 \\ \hline 3 \end{array}$$

There will be 4 teams with 3 players left to be alternates.

Remember to answer the hidden question and use the answer to solve the problem.

Solve.

1. Three friends ordered 2 pizzas. Each pizza was cut into 8 slices. If each person ate the same number of slices, how many slices did each person eat? How many slices were left over?

Topic 20

Data, Graphs, and Probability

1 How fast can a peregrine falcon fly? You will find out in Lesson 20-4.

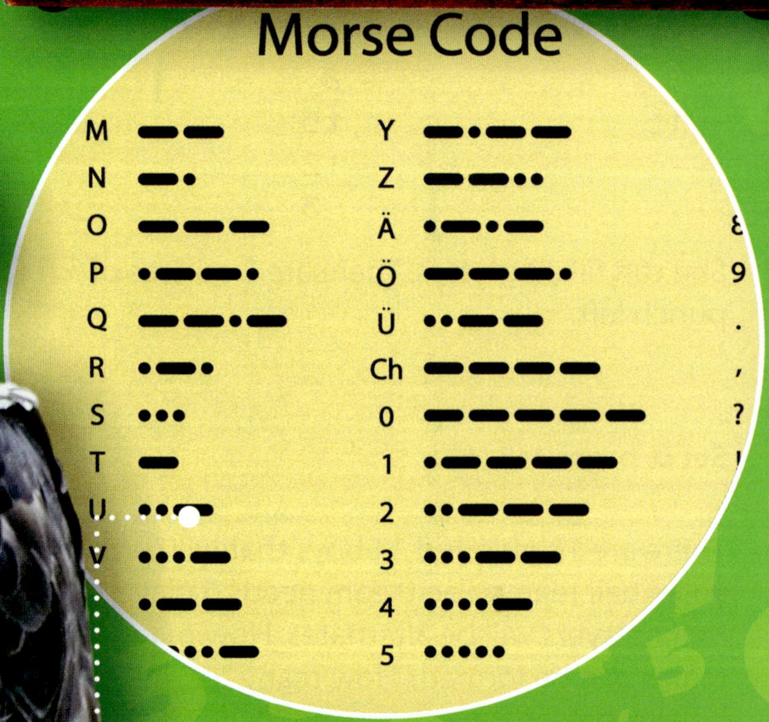

2 In the 1800s, Morse code used a series of dots and dashes to send messages over a telegraph or other machine. How many letters of the alphabet are sent using only dots in Morse code? You will find out in Lesson 20-6.

3

If you put each of the letters in this sign in a bag and took one without looking, which letter are you most likely to get? You will find out in Lesson 20-7.

4

How many gold, silver, and bronze medals did athletes from the United States win in the 2006 Winter Olympic Games? You will find out in Lesson 20-1.

Review What You Know!

Vocabulary

Choose the best term from the box.

- data
- less likely
- more likely
- tally

1. A graph can be used to compare _?_.
2. Elisa is at a library. It is _?_ that she will look at a book than eat lunch.
3. The time is 4 A.M. It is _?_ that you are playing soccer than sleeping.

Order Numbers

Write in order from least to greatest.

4. 56, 47, 93, 39, 10
5. 20, 43, 23, 19, 22
6. 24, 14, 54, 34, 4
7. 65, 33, 56, 87, 34

Skip Counting

Find the next two numbers in each pattern. Write a rule for the pattern.

8. 5, 10, 15, 20, ▢, ▢
9. 2, 4, 6, 8, ▢, ▢
10. 10, 20, 30, 40, ▢, ▢
11. 4, 8, 12, 16, ▢, ▢

Comparing

12. **Writing to Explain** Explain how to use place value to compare 326 and 345.

Virginia

Lesson 20-1

3.17.a The student will collect and organize data, using observations, measurements, surveys, or experiments.

Organizing Data

How can you collect and organize data?

A survey asked students, "What is your favorite after-school sport?"

Information you collect is called data. To take a survey, collect data by asking many people the same question.

Data

Favorite After-School Sport

Swimming	Swimming	Soccer
Softball	Soccer	Swimming
Softball	Softball	Softball
Soccer	Swimming	Softball
Softball	Soccer	Softball
Soccer	Softball	Soccer

Guided Practice*

Do you know HOW?

In **1–2**, use the survey data below.

Data

Favorite Color

Blue	Red	Blue	Blue
Red	Yellow	Red	Green
Blue	Red	Red	Red
Red	Red	Red	Blue

1. Make a tally chart for the data.

2. How many more students chose red than blue as their favorite color?

Do you UNDERSTAND?

In **3–5**, use the tally chart above.

3. What does the chart show?

4. How many students in all answered the survey?

5. Later, six more students answered the survey. Here are their answers.

Softball	Soccer	Softball
Swimming	Softball	Soccer

Make a new tally chart that includes their answers.

Independent Practice

For **6–9**, use the survey data at the right.

6. Make a tally chart for the data.

7. How many people answered the survey?

8. Which kinds of pet were the favorite of the same number of people?

9. Which pet was chosen most often?

Data

Favorite Kind of Pet

Cat	Cat	Dog	Hamster
Fish	Bird	Dog	Dog
Dog	Bird	Hamster	Bird
Dog	Cat	Bird	Fish
Cat	Dog	Dog	Cat
Bird	Cat	Dog	Dog

DIGITAL Animated Glossary **www.pearsonsuccessnet.com**

*For another example, see Set A on page 486.

Step 1

A tally chart is one way to record data. A tally mark is a mark used to record data on a tally chart.

Title the tally chart. Label the columns.

Favorite After-School Sport

Sport	Tally	Number

Step 2

Make a tally mark for each answer given.

Favorite After-School Sport

Sport	Tally	Number
Soccer	𝍸 I	
Softball	𝍸 III	
Swimming	IIII	

Step 3

Count the tally marks. Record the number.

Favorite After-School Sport

Sport	Tally	Number
Soccer	𝍸 I	6
Softball	𝍸 III	8
Swimming	IIII	4

Problem Solving

For **10** and **11**, use the tally chart at the right.

Favorite Sport to Watch (Data)

Sport	Tally	Number
Football	𝍸 𝍸 I	
Baseball	𝍸 𝍸 𝍸 II	
Hockey		8
Basketball		15

10. Copy and complete the chart.

11. Write the sports in order from most to least favorite.

12. **Number Sense** What number is shown by 𝍸 𝍸 𝍸 𝍸 𝍸?

13. Make a tally chart to show how many times the letters *a*, *e*, *i*, *o*, and *u* are used in this exercise.

14. **Writing to Explain** How would you make a tally chart to show what kind of pizza your classmates like most?

15. **Reasoning** Dennis is 2 inches taller than Mica and 1 inch shorter than Rosa. Is Rosa shorter than Mica or taller than Mica? How much shorter or taller?

16. In the 2006 Winter Olympic Games, the United States won 9 gold medals, 9 silver medals, and 7 bronze medals. Which tally chart shows these results?

A U.S. Medals (Data)

Medal	Tally
Gold	𝍸 III
Silver	𝍸 III
Bronze	𝍸 I

B U.S. Medals (Data)

Medal	Tally
Gold	𝍸 IIII
Silver	𝍸 IIII
Bronze	𝍸 II

C U.S. Medals (Data)

Medal	Tally
Gold	𝍸 𝍸 I
Silver	𝍸 𝍸 I
Bronze	𝍸 III

D U.S. Medals (Data)

Medal	Tally
Gold	𝍸 𝍸 II
Silver	𝍸 𝍸 II
Bronze	𝍸 𝍸

Virginia

Lesson 20-2

3.17.c The student will read and interpret the data represented in line plots, bar graphs, and picture graphs and write a sentence analyzing the data.

Reading Pictographs and Bar Graphs

How can you read graphs?

A pictograph uses pictures or symbols to show data.

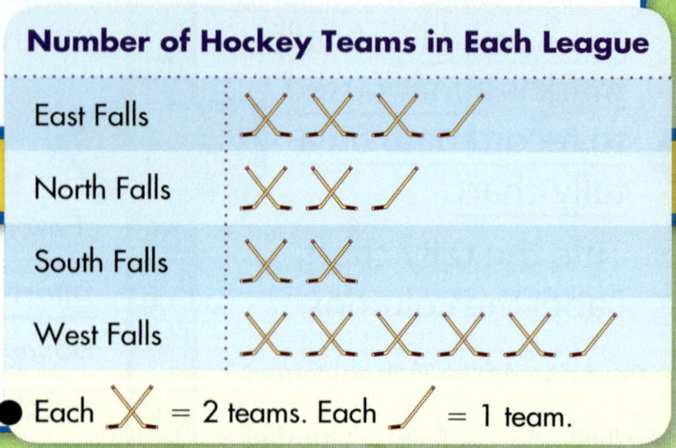

The key explains what each picture represents.

Another Example How can you read a bar graph?

A bar graph uses bars to compare information. This bar graph shows the number of goals scored by different players on a hockey team.

The scale shows the units used.

On this graph, each grid line represents one unit. But only every other grid line is labeled: 0, 2, 4, and so on. For example, the line halfway between 4 and 6 represents 5 goals.

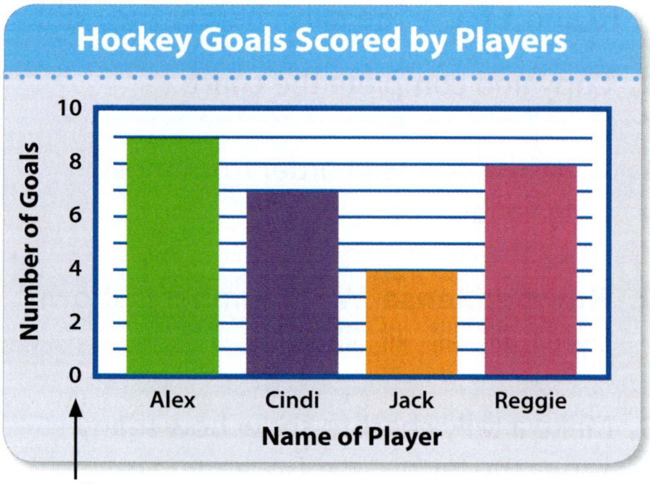

scale

How many goals did Cindi score?

Find Cindi's name. Use the scale to find how high the bar reaches. Cindi scored 7 goals.

Who scored the fewest goals?

Find the shortest bar. The bar for Jack is shortest. He scored the fewest goals.

Explain It

1. Explain how to find how many more goals Alex scored than Cindi.
2. Who scored 8 goals?
3. How many goals in all did Alex and Reggie score?

How many teams are in the East Falls League?

Use the key.

Each  represents 2 teams.

Each  represents 1 team.

There are 3  and 1 .

$2 + 2 + 2 + 1 = 7$

There are 7 teams in the East Falls League.

How many more teams does the East Falls League have than the South Falls League?

Compare the two rows.

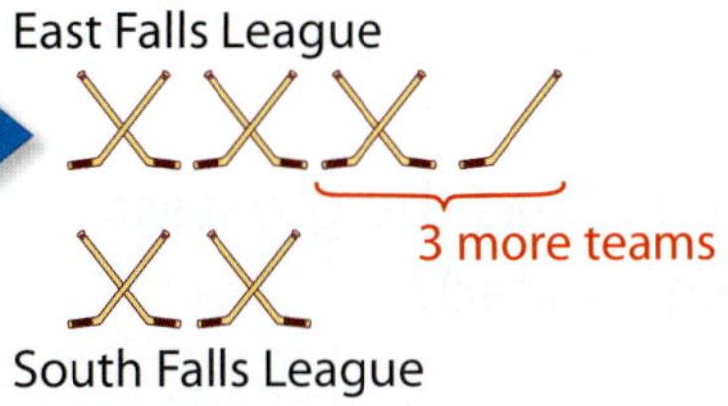

The East Falls League has 3 more teams than the South Falls League.

Guided Practice*

Do you know HOW?

1. Which hockey league in the pictograph above has 5 teams?

2. Which league has the most teams? How many teams are in that league?

Do you UNDERSTAND?

In **3** and **4**, use the pictograph above.

3. Explain how to find which league has the fewest teams.

4. How many teams in all are in the North Falls and West Falls Leagues?

Independent Practice

In **5–7**, use the pictograph at the right.

5. Which area has lights on for the most hours in a week?

6. Which area of the Tri-Town Sports Center has lights on for 50 hours each week?

7. In one week, how many more hours are lights on in the exercise room than in the swimming pool?

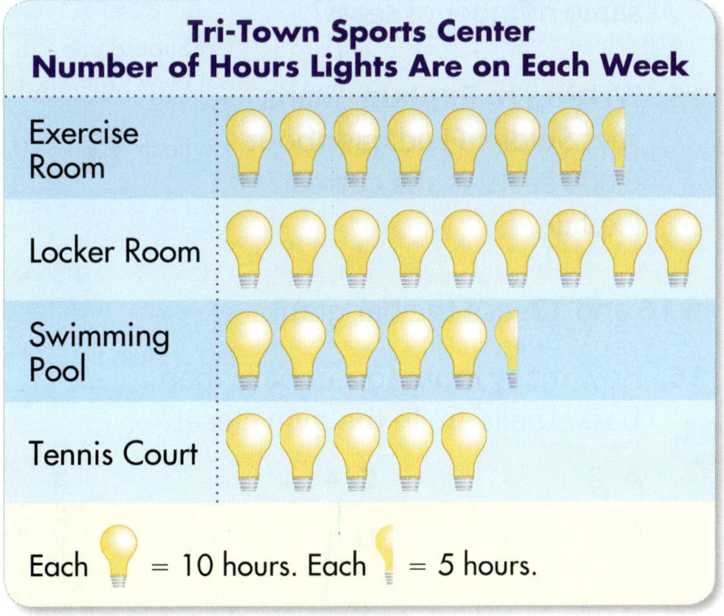

DIGITAL Animated Glossary
www.pearsonsuccessnet.com

*For another example, see Set A on page 486.

Problem Solving

In **8–12**, use the bar graph at the right.

8. How fast can a jack rabbit run?

9. Which animal has the greatest top running speed?

10. Which animal has a top running speed of 50 miles per hour?

11. How much greater is the top running speed of a coyote than that of a grizzly bear?

12. Which animals have the same top running speed?

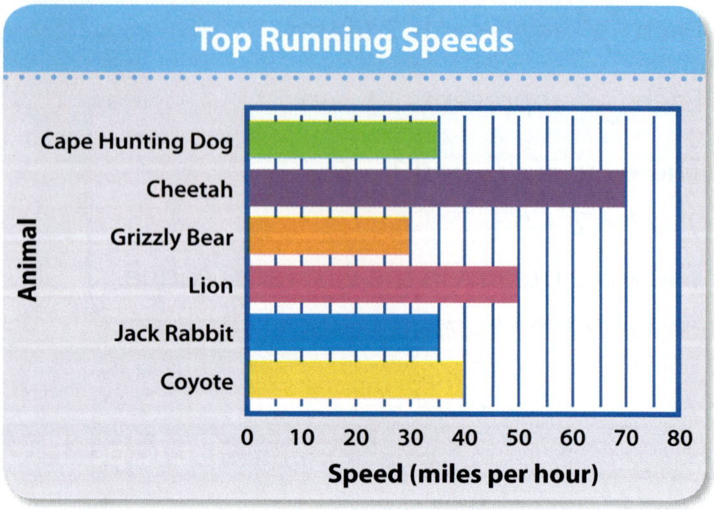

In **13–15**, use the pictograph.

13. To the nearest 10,000, how many seats are in the Rose Bowl?

14. **Estimation** Which two stadiums have about the same number of seats?

15. **Writing to Explain** Maria says Soldier Field has about 6,000 seats. Is she correct? Explain.

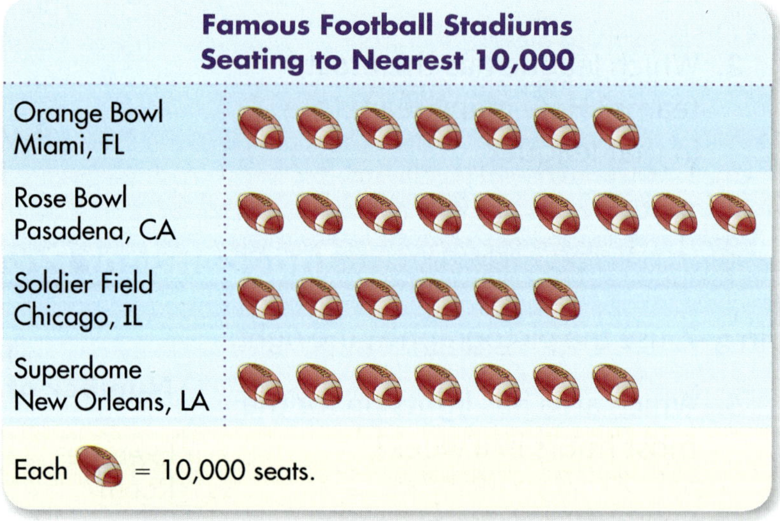

In **16** and **17**, use the bar graph.

16. How many more soccer balls than basketballs are in the gym closet?

SOL Prep

A 8 **C** 4

B 5 **D** 3

17. How many balls in all are in the gym closet?

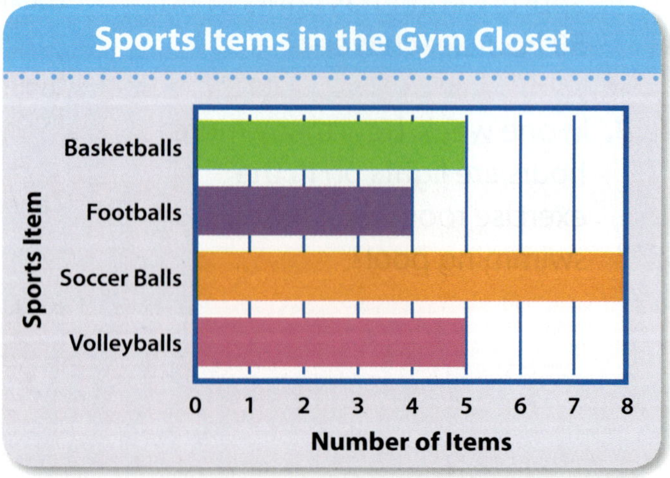

Mixed Problem Solving

Math and Social Studies

The government where you live uses money from the taxes that people pay to provide different kinds of services. The bar graph at the right shows how much money different departments in Park Town receive. Use the graph to answer the questions.

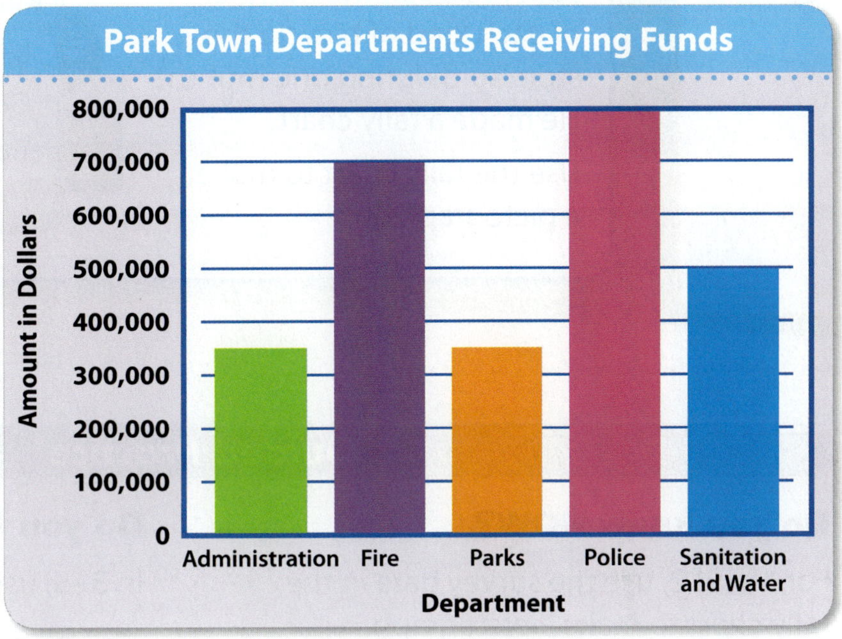

1. Which service in Park Town will receive the most funds?

2. Which two departments will get the same amount?

3. About how much money will the Parks Department and the Sanitation and Water Department receive in all?

4. How much more will the Police Department receive than the Fire Department?

5. Use the table below that shows how the Police Department money is used.

Data

Police Department	
Expenses	**Amount**
Cars	$42,000
Computers	$14,000
Police Equipment	$88,000
Salaries	$643,000
Station Expenses	$13,000

Which expenses are less than $50,000?

6. **Strategy Focus** Solve. Use the strategy Write a Number Sentence.

The state representatives voted on a budget plan. Each representative has 1 vote. There were 86 votes for the plan and 34 votes against the plan. How many representatives voted in all?

Virginia

Lesson 20-3

3.17.b The student will construct a line plot, a picture graph, or a bar graph to represent the data.

Making Pictographs

How do you make a pictograph?

Sam recorded the number of each kind of bicycle the store sold during one month. He made a tally chart.

Use the tally chart to make a pictograph.

Data

Kind of Bicycle	Tally	Number
Boy's	卌 卌	10
Girl's	卌 卌 卌 卌	20
Training	卌 卌 卌	15
Tricycle	卌 卌	10

Guided Practice*

Do you know HOW?

For **1** and **2**, use the survey data in the tally chart to make a pictograph.

Data

Which is your favorite school lunch?

Lunch	Tally	Number
Taco	||	2
Pizza	卌 |||	8
Salad	|||	3
Sandwich	卌 |	6

1. What is the title? What is the symbol for the key? How many votes will each symbol stand for?

2. List the lunch choices. Draw the symbols to complete the graph.

Do you UNDERSTAND?

In **3–5**, use the pictograph above.

3. Explain the symbols that were used for the number of training bicycles that were sold.

4. Suppose 25 mountain bicycles were also sold. Draw symbols to show a row in the graph for mountain bicycles.

5. If the key was △ = 2 bicycles, how many symbols would be used for the boy's bicycles sold? How many symbols would be used for girl's bicycles sold?

Independent Practice

Data

Goals Each Kickball Team Has Scored

Team Name	Tally	Number
Cubs	卌 卌	10
Hawks	卌 卌 卌 卌	20
Lions	卌 卌 卌 卌 卌 卌	30
Roadrunners	卌 卌 卌	15

For **6** and **7**, use the chart.

6. Make a pictograph to show the data.

7. Explain how you decided the number of symbols to draw to show the goals for the Roadrunners.

*For another example, see Set A on page 486.

Write a title for the pictograph.

The title is
Kinds of Bicycles Sold.

Choose a symbol for the key.
Decide what each symbol and half-symbol will represent.

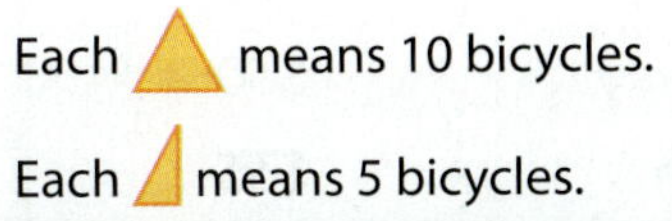

Set up the graph and list the kinds of bicycles.
Decide how many symbols you need for each number sold.
Draw the symbols.

Problem Solving

Ed made a tally chart of the items he picked from the plants in his garden.

8. Make a pictograph to show the data in Ed's chart. Write a title and the key.

9. How many green peppers and red peppers did Ed pick in all?

Vegetables from Garden

Kind	Tally	Number of Items
Green Pepper	||||	4
Red Pepper	||	2
Tomato	~~||||~~	5

10. **Geometry** Ed's garden has a square shape. Each side is 9 feet long. What is the area of Ed's garden?

In **11** and **12**, suppose you are going to make a pictograph to show Simon's Book Shop data.

11. Choose a symbol to stand for 5 books sold. Draw the row for fiction books sold.

12. **Reasoning** Why is 5 a good number to use in the key?

Simon's Book Shop

Kind of Book	Number Sold
Fiction	25
Nonfiction	40
Poetry	20
Dictionary	15

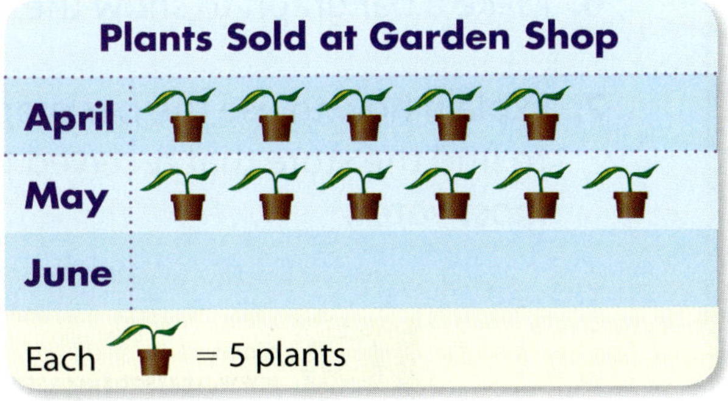

13. SOL Prep Marisol is making a pictograph to show plant sales. There were 35 plants sold in June. How many symbols should Marisol draw for June?

A 5 **B** 7 **C** 11 **D** 35

Virginia

Lesson 20-4

3.17.b The student will construct a line plot, a picture graph, or a bar graph to represent the data.

Making Bar Graphs

Hands-On
grid paper

How do you make a bar graph?

Greg made a table to show the amount of money he saved each month.

Use the data in the table to make a bar graph on grid paper. A bar graph can make it easy to compare data.

Month	Amount Saved
January	$25
February	$50
March	$65
April	$40

Guided Practice*

Do you know HOW?

Use the chart to make a bar graph.

Class	Tally	Number of People Signed Up
Chess	𝍸 I	6
Guitar	𝍸 𝍸	10
Painting	𝍸 II	7
Writing	𝍸 IIII	9

1. Write a title. Choose the scale. What does each grid line represent?

2. Set up the graph with the scale, each class, and labels. Draw each bar.

Do you UNDERSTAND?

In **3–5**, use the bar graph above.

3. In the bar graph above, explain why the bar for January ends between 20 and 30.

4. In which month did Greg save the most money?

5. Suppose Greg saved $35 in May. Between which grid lines would the bar for May end?

Independent Practice

In **6** and **7**, use the tally chart.

Favorite Store for Clothes		
Store	**Tally**	**Number of Votes**
Deal Mart	𝍸 𝍸 𝍸	15
Jane's	𝍸 𝍸 𝍸 𝍸 𝍸 𝍸	30
Parker's	𝍸 𝍸 𝍸 𝍸	20
Trends	𝍸	5

6. Make a bar graph to show the data.

7. Explain how to use the bar graph to find the store that received the most votes.

DIGITAL eTools www.pearsonsuccessnet.com

*For another example, see Set B on page 486.

Write a title.

The title of this bar graph is Amount Greg Saved Each Month.

Choose the scale. Decide how many units each grid line will represent.

Each grid line will represent $10.

Set up the graph with the scale, each month listed in the table, and labels. Draw a bar for each month.

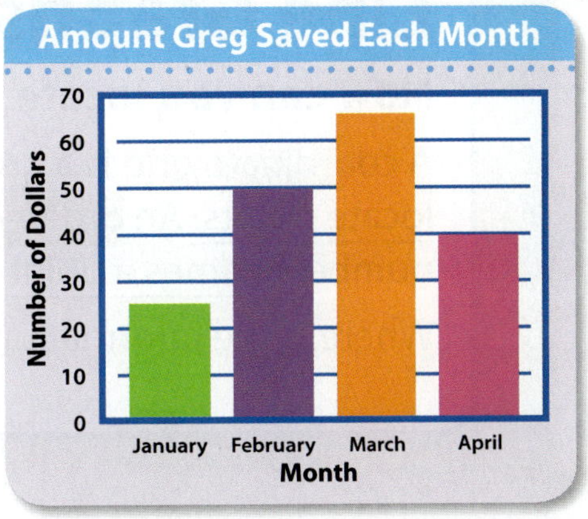

Problem Solving

For **8** and **9**, use the table at the right.

8. Make a bar graph. Write a title. Choose the scale. Draw bars that go across.

Data

Favorite Kind of Movie

Kind of Movie	Adventure	Cartoon	Comedy	Science Fiction
Number of Votes	16	8	10	7

9. **Number Sense** Which two kinds of movies received about the same number of votes?

10. **Strategy Focus** Solve. Use the strategy Draw a Picture.

Each movie ticket costs $8. What is the total cost of tickets for a family of 6 people?

In **11** and **12**, suppose you are going to make a bar graph to show the data in the table.

11. **Writing to Explain** What scale would you choose? Explain.

12. Which would be the longest bar?

Data

Speed of Birds

Kind of Bird	Flying Speed (miles per hour)
Frigate Bird	95
Peregrine Falcon	180
Spin-Tailed Swift	105

13. Luz made this graph to show how many friends wore each color of shoe. Which information does Luz need to complete the graph?

SOL Prep

A How many friends wore black shoes

B The color of shoes with the longest bar

C The color of shoes worn by exactly 8 friends

D The color of shoes worn by exactly 7 friends

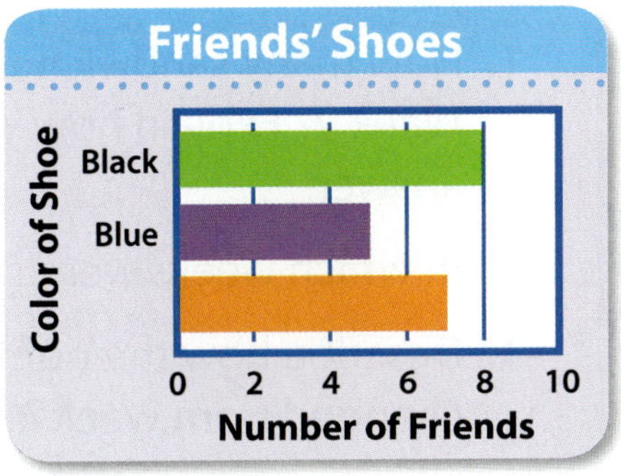

Virginia

Lesson 20-5

Prepares for 6.11.a The student will identify the coordinates of a point in a coordinate plane.

Ordered Pairs and Line Graphs

Hands-On grid paper

How can you locate a point?

A coordinate grid is a grid used to locate points. An ordered pair of numbers names a point on the grid.

Where is the Information desk?

Museum Exhibits

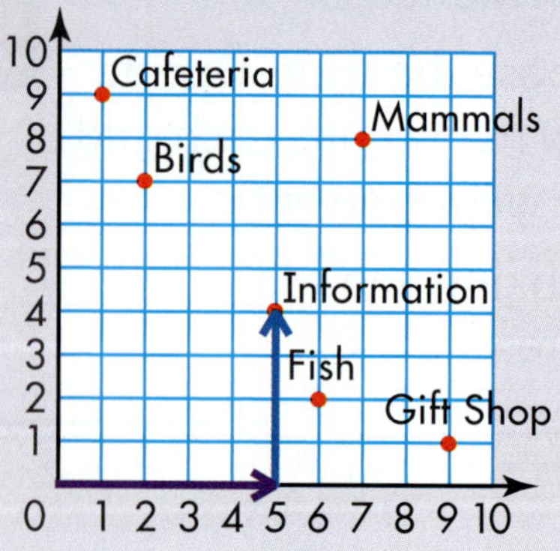

Another Example How can you read and make a line graph?

A line graph shows how data changes over a period of time.

Look at the *Lunchroom Sandwich Sales* graph. To read the data for Week 1, start at 0 and move right until you reach *Week 1*. Move up to the point. Move left to read that 50 sandwiches were sold.

Lunchroom Sandwich Sales

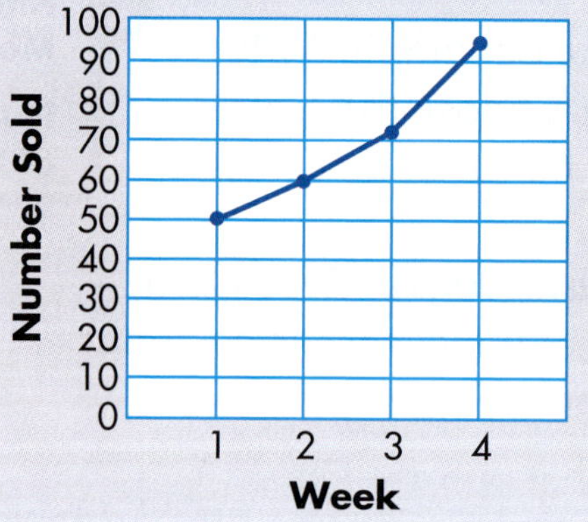

The line graph shows that the number of sandwiches sold increased each week.

To add data for Weeks 5 and 6, plot the following points.

Week 5: 81 sandwiches sold

Week 6: 73 sandwiches sold

Draw line segments to connect the points.

Lunchroom Sandwich Sales

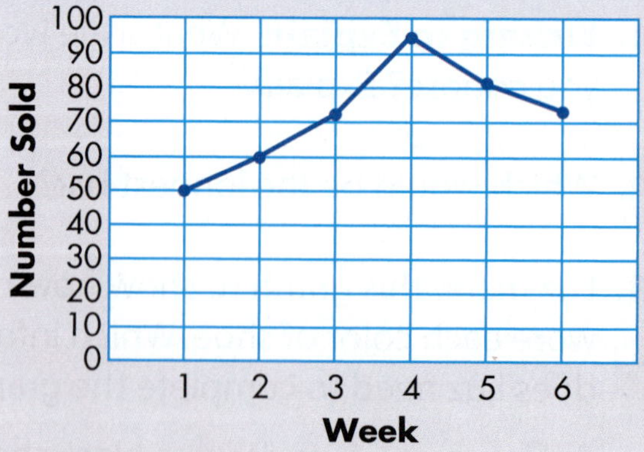

Explain It

1. How many sandwiches were sold in Week 2? Explain how you found your answer.
2. In which weeks were sandwich sales about the same?
3. Describe how the number of sandwiches sold changed from Week 4 to Week 5.

DIGITAL Animated Glossary, eTools **www.pearsonsuccessnet.com**

To name the location of a point:

- Start at 0. Move right until you are under the point labeled *Information*. Count the spaces you moved: **5**.
- Move up to the point. Count the spaces you moved: **4**.

The Information desk is at (5, 4).

To plot a point means to locate and mark the point using the given ordered pair. Plot a point to locate *Reptiles* at (1, 2).

Start at 0. Move 1 space to the right. Move up 2 spaces. Mark a point and label it *Reptiles*.

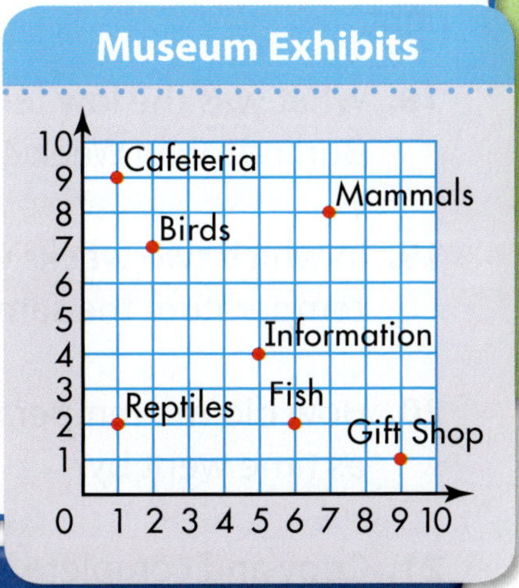

Guided Practice*

Do you know HOW?

For **1–4**, use the *Museum Exhibits* grid above. For **1–3**, write the ordered pair for the location of each exhibit.

1. Fish **2.** Birds **3.** Mammals

4. What is located at (9, 1)?

For **5** and **6**, use the *Luncheon Sandwich Sales* graph in Another Example.

5. About how many sandwiches were sold in Week 4?

6. Between which two weeks did the number of sandwiches sold increase the most?

Do you UNDERSTAND?

For **7–9**, use the *Museum Exhibits* grid.

7. In which direction do you move first to plot a point? In which direction do you move next?

8. Would it be correct to say that the bird exhibit is at (7, 2)? Explain.

9. Explain how to plot a point for the amphibians exhibit at (8, 6).

Independent Practice

For **10–13**, write the ordered pair for each point on the grid.

10. *A* **11.** *C* **12.** *E* **13.** *G*

For **14–17**, write the letter that names each point.

14. (1, 5) **15.** (3, 1) **16.** (2, 4) **17.** (1, 3)

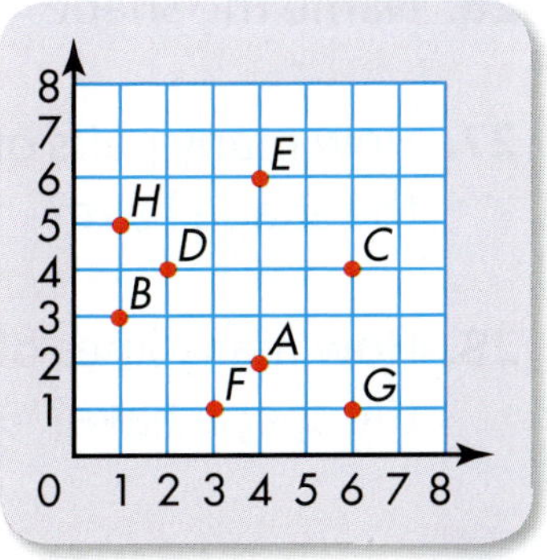

*For another example, see Set C on page 487.

Independent Practice

For **18–21**, use the line graph on the right.

18. What was the low temperature in Burlington in Week 4?

19. In which two weeks was the low temperature the same?

20. How did the temperature change as time went by?

21. Copy and complete the graph to show the Week 6 low temperature of 10°F.

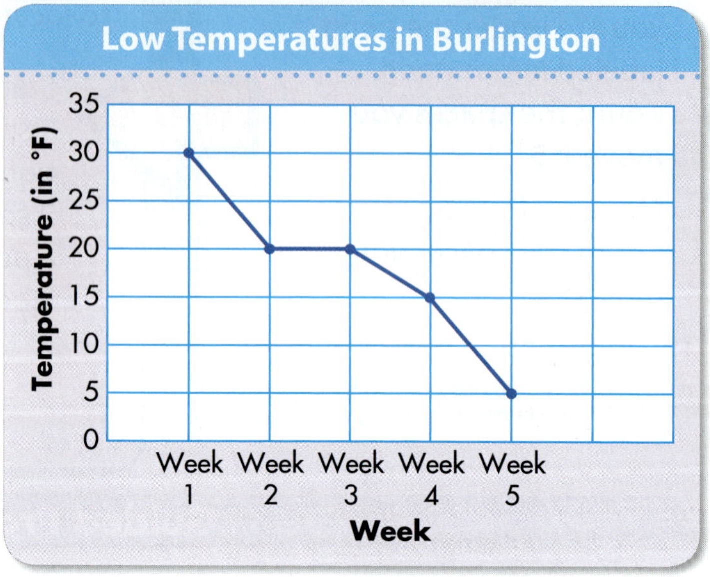

Problem Solving

City maps sometimes use a grid to show where places are located. Use the grid on the right for **22–25**.

22. What is located at point (3, 2)?

23. What is the ordered pair that names the location of the police station?

24. Which building is located three units to the right of the school?

25. **Writing to Explain** Which is closer to the school, the park or the library? Explain how you know.

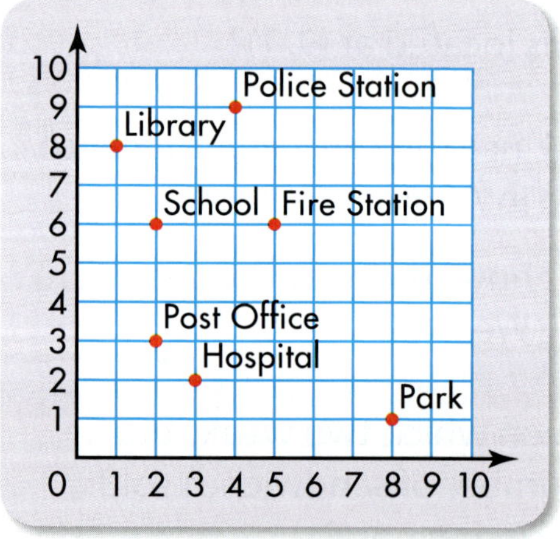

Geometry Jamal drew the shape below. Use the shape for **26–28**.

26. Name the shape.

27. How many pairs of parallel sides does the shape have?

28. How many lines of symmetry does the shape have?

Use the line graph to the right for **29–31**.

29. Copy the line graph that has been started.

a Plot these points on the graph.
8 months: 12 pounds
12 months: 14 pounds

b Draw line segments to connect the points.

30. What was the weight of the puppy at birth?

31. **Writing to Explain** How did the puppy's weight change as time passed?

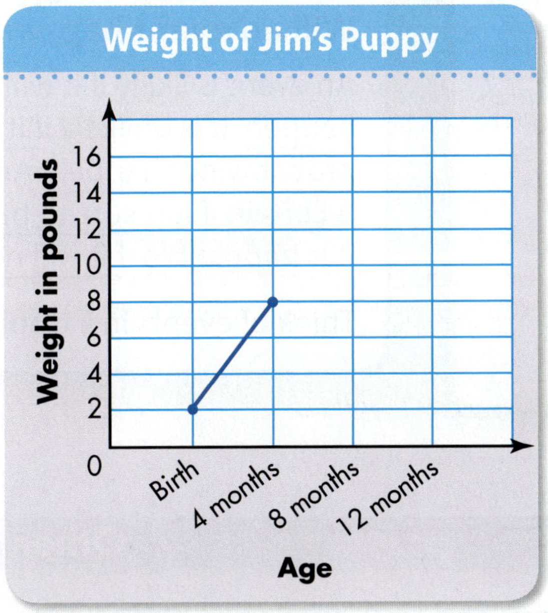

32. Toby has 75 cents. How is 75 cents written as a decimal?

33. SOL Prep The line graph below shows the low temperature each month in Springfield. Which statement best tells how the temperature changed as time passed?

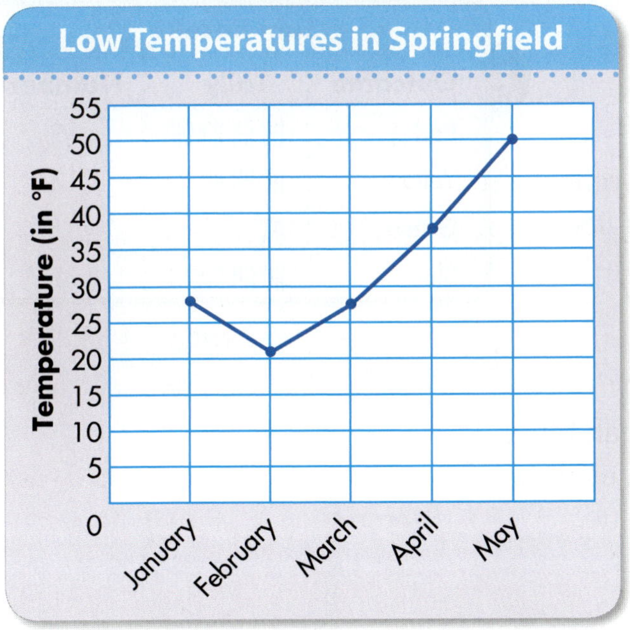

A The low temperature decreased from February to May.

B The low temperature did not change from March to May.

C The low temperature decreased from January to May.

D The low temperature increased from February to May.

Virginia

Lesson 20-6

3.18 The student will investigate and describe the concept of probability as chance and list possible results of a given situation.

How Likely?

Will an event happen?

An event is likely if it will probably happen. It is unlikely if it will probably not happen. An event is certain if it is sure to happen. It is impossible if it will never happen.

Think of events in a tropical rainforest.

Other Examples

How can you compare chances?

Outcomes with the same chance of happening are equally likely.

Sometimes you compare two outcomes.
The outcome with a greater chance of happening is more likely.
The outcome with the lesser chance of happening is less likely.

The tally chart shows the results of 48 spins of the spinner above.

Which outcome is more likely than blue?

A bigger part of the spinner is red than blue. Also, the tally chart shows more red results than blue. So, red is more likely than blue.

Data

Spin Results

Outcome	Tally	Number
Red	𝍸 𝍸 𝍸 ||||	19
Yellow	𝍸 𝍸 |||	13
Green	𝍸	5
Blue	𝍸 𝍸 |	11

Which outcome is less likely than blue?

A smaller part of the spinner is green than blue. Also, the tally chart shows fewer green results than blue. So, green is less likely than blue.

Which outcomes are equally likely?

The yellow and blue parts of the spinner are the same size. Also, the yellow and blue results are nearly equal. So, yellow and blue are equally likely outcomes.

A possible result of a game or experiment is called an **outcome**.

What are the outcomes of spinning this spinner?

When you spin the spinner, the outcome might be blue, red, yellow, green, or a line.

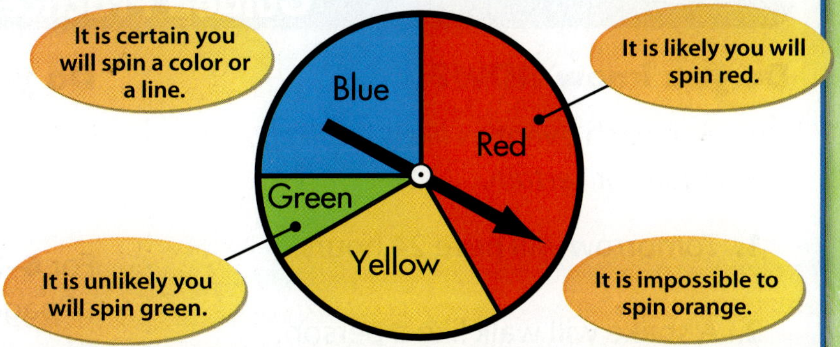

Another Example

Look at the spinner at the right. Which tally chart shows the most likely results of 25 spins?

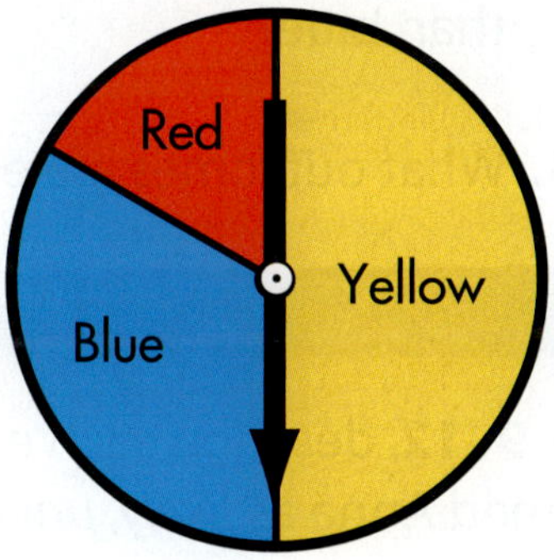

A

Color	Spin Results
Red	卌 IIII
Blue	卌 III
Yellow	卌 III

C

Color	Spin Results
Red	卌 III
Blue	卌
Yellow	卌 卌 II

B

Color	Spin Results
Red	卌
Blue	卌 IIII
Yellow	卌 卌 I

D

Color	Spin Results
Red	卌
Blue	卌 卌 II
Yellow	卌 III

Red is the smallest part of the spinner, so red should have the fewest tally marks. So, **A** and **C** are not good choices.

Look at choices **B** and **D**. The yellow part of the spinner is bigger than the blue part, so yellow should have more tally marks than blue. So, **D** is not a good choice.

Choice **B** shows the most likely results of 25 spins.

Explain It

1. Suppose a tally chart shows spin results. How can you tell if one part of the spinner is much larger than the others?

Guided Practice*

Do you know HOW?

Describe each event as *likely*, *unlikely*, *impossible*, or *certain*.

1. Tomorrow will have 24 hours.

2. A snake will walk like a person.

There are 6 white counters, 12 black counters, 2 red counters, and 6 blue counters in a bag. You take one counter from the bag without looking.

3. What outcome is more likely than blue?

4. What outcomes are equally likely?

Do you UNDERSTAND?

5. What is the difference between a certain event and a likely event?

For **6–8**, use the spinner at the top of page 473.

6. Which outcome is less likely than yellow?

7. Is purple a more likely or less likely outcome than blue?

8. Which outcome is more likely than yellow?

Independent Practice

For **9–12**, describe each event about a third-grader named Anna as *likely*, *unlikely*, *impossible*, or *certain*.

9. Anna will need food to grow.

10. Anna will grow to be 100 feet tall.

11. Anna will travel to the moon.

12. Anna will watch television tonight.

For **13–17**, use the spinner at the right.

13. What outcome is less likely than yellow?

14. What outcomes are equally likely?

15. What outcome is most likely?

16. Name an outcome that is certain.

17. Name an outcome that is impossible.

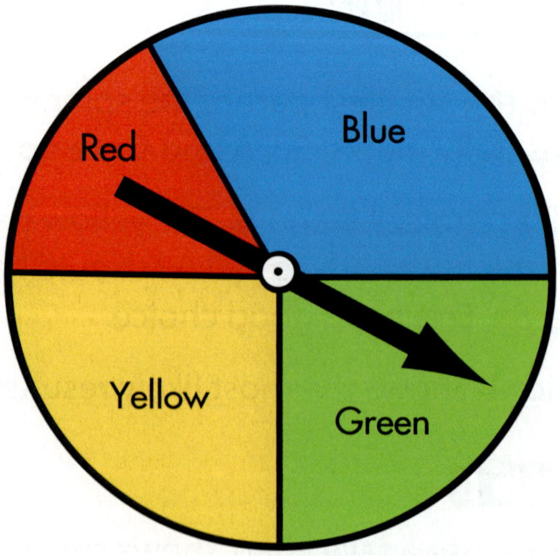

DIGITAL Animated Glossary
www.pearsonsuccessnet.com

**For another example, see Set D on page 487.*

Problem Solving

18. The table shows which letters use only dots and which letters use only dashes in Morse code. All the other letters of the alphabet use both dots and dashes. If you pick one letter from a bag with all 26 letters in the alphabet, are you more likely to pick a letter that uses dots only, dashes only, or both dots and dashes?

Morse Code

Dots Only	Dashes Only
E, H, I, S	M, O, T

19. Writing to Explain How can you tell by looking at a spinner that one outcome is more likely than another outcome?

20. There are 4 medium boxes inside a large box. Inside each medium box, there are 3 small boxes. How many boxes are there in all?

21. Look at the spinner at the right. Which tally chart shows the most likely results of 30 spins?

SOL Prep

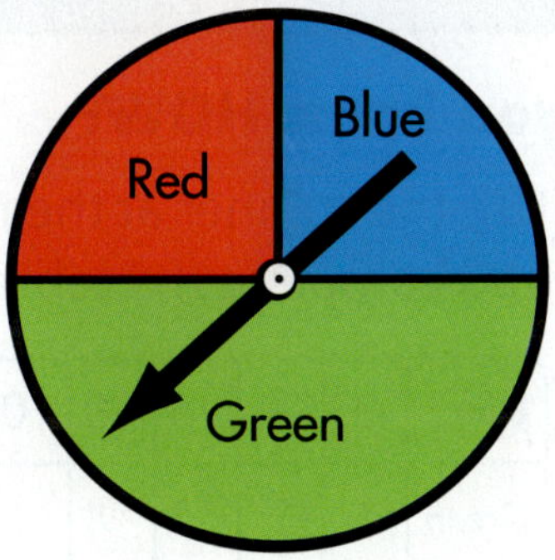

A

Color	Spin Results
Red	𝍸 IIII
Blue	𝍸 II
Green	𝍸 𝍸 IIII

B

Color	Spin Results
Red	𝍸 𝍸
Blue	𝍸 𝍸
Green	𝍸 𝍸

C

Color	Spin Results
Red	𝍸
Blue	𝍸 𝍸
Green	𝍸 𝍸 𝍸

D

Color	Spin Results
Red	𝍸 II
Blue	𝍸 𝍸 𝍸
Green	𝍸 III

In **22** and **23**, use the table that shows the colors of paper clips in a box. Mary will take 1 paper clip out of the box without looking.

Paper Clip Colors

Color	Number in the Box
Green	27
Red	38
Yellow	21
Blue	27

22. Which colors does Mary have an equally likely chance of taking?

A Green and red

B Red and blue

C Green and blue

D Red and yellow

23. Which of the four colors is Mary least likely to choose?

Virginia

Lesson 20-7

3.18 The student will investigate and describe the concept of probability as chance and list possible results of a given situation.

Outcomes and Experiments

Hands-On
spinner

How do outcomes compare to predictions?

In 30 spins, how many times would you expect to spin red? blue?

Spin the spinner. Then compare the results to what you thought would happen.

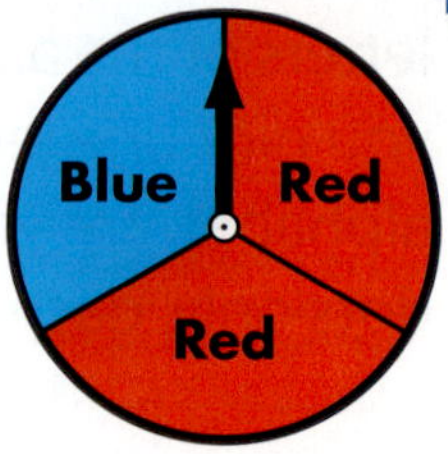

Guided Practice*

Do you know HOW?

1. Use the spinner at the right. Copy and complete the table.

Blue	2	4	6	8	10	20
Green	1	2	3	4	5	10
Red	1	2	3		5	
Total Spins	4	8	12	16		40

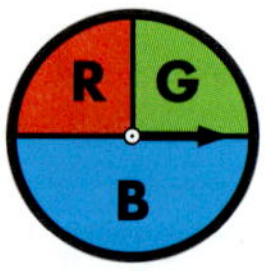

Do you UNDERSTAND?

For **2–4**, use the experiment above.

2. Predict what is likely to happen in 40 spins.

3. Do the experiment. Spin the spinner 40 times. How do the results compare to your prediction?

4. Why should you expect 2 reds and 1 blue in 3 spins?

Independent Practice

In **5–6**, use the table of letter tiles picked from a bag.

A	5	10	15	20	25	30	35	40
B	3	6	9		15	18	21	24
C	2	4	6	8			14	
Total Picks	10	20	30		50		70	

5. Copy and complete the table.

6. Predict what is likely to happen in 90 picks.

DIGITAL
Animated Glossary, eTools
www.pearsonsuccessnet.com

For another example, see Set D on page 487.

Step 1

Predict the results of 30 spins.

To predict is to tell what may happen using information you know.

Red	2	4	6	8	10	20	40	60	80
Blue	1	2	3	4	5	10	20	30	40
Total Spins	3	6	9	12	15	30	60	90	120

The prediction for 30 spins is the spinner will land on red 20 times and on blue 10 times.

Step 2

Spin the spinner 30 times. Do this test 4 times. Compare the results to what you predicted.

Test	*1*	*2*	*3*	*4*	*Total*
Red	22	21	21	20	84
Blue	8	9	9	10	36
Total Spins	30	30	30	30	120

When there are more tests, the results get closer to the prediction.

Problem Solving

In **7–9**, use the spinner to the right and the table below.

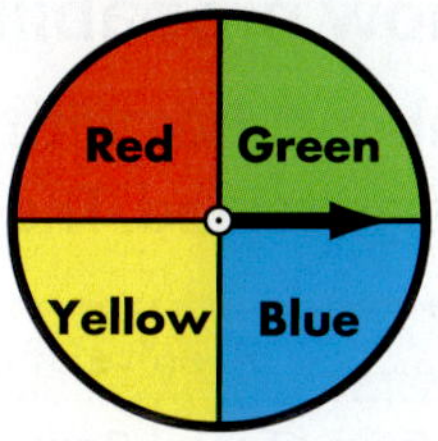

Blue	1	2	3	4		6		8
Green	1	2	3	4	5			
Red	1	2	3	4	5		7	
Yellow	1	2	3			6		
Total Spins	4	8	12	16		24		32

7. Copy and complete the table.

8. Predict the results of 40 spins. Then spin the spinner 40 times. How do the results compare to your prediction?

9. Reasonableness Danny says it is likely that in 40 spins, green will be spun more times than yellow. Do you agree? Explain.

10. Writing to Explain Look at the sign at the right. Suppose you put each of the five letters in a box and take one out without looking. Which outcome is most likely? Explain.

11. In an experiment, the spinner results were 16 blue, 32 green, and 16 red. Which spinner most likely gave these results?

SOL Prep

A

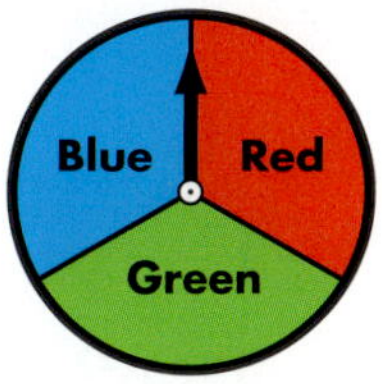

B

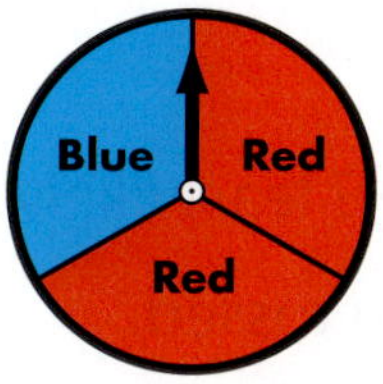

C

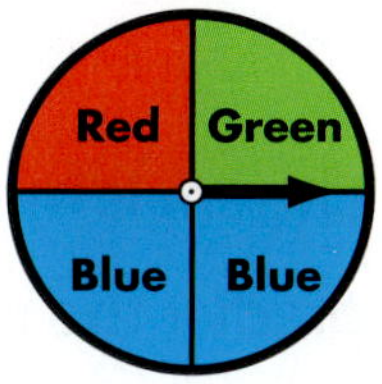

D

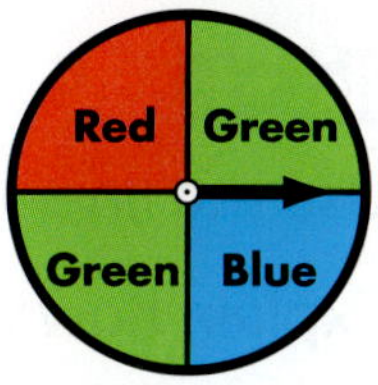

Virginia

Lesson 20-8

3.17.c The student will read and interpret the data represented in line plots, bar graphs, and picture graphs and write a sentence analyzing the data.

Line Plots and Probability

How can you use line plots?

For each day in April, Dara recorded the high temperature on a line plot. What temperature occurred as the high temperature most often in April?

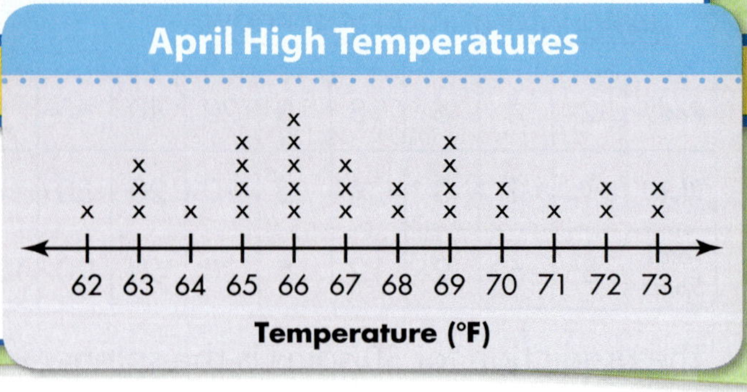

Another Example How can you make a line plot to show probability data?

Ian tossed two number cubes with sides labeled 1 to 6 and added the numbers he tossed. The table shows his results.

Data

Results of 30 Tosses

Toss	Sum	Toss	Sum	Toss	Sum	Toss	Sum	Toss	Sum	Toss	Sum
1	8	6	5	11	10	16	7	21	10	26	8
2	8	7	5	12	7	17	6	22	8	27	9
3	7	8	7	13	9	18	8	23	4	28	7
4	12	9	11	14	6	19	5	24	7	29	7
5	6	10	3	15	9	20	5	25	6	30	7

Steps to make a line plot:

- Draw a line.
- Below the line, list in order all the possible outcomes of the sum of the two number cubes.
- Write a title for the line plot.
- Use the data table. Mark an X for each time that sum was the outcome.

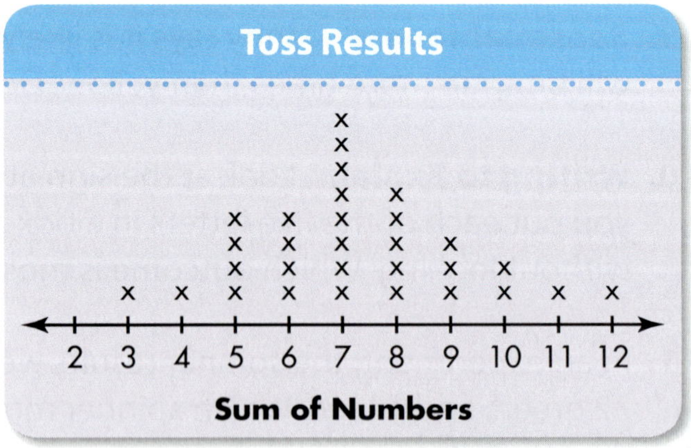

Explain It

1. Use the line plot. Which sum is most likely? least likely?
2. Explain how you can predict the next sum tossed.

A line plot is a way to organize data on a number line.

To read a line plot, look at the numbers below the line. Then count the Xs above each number.

On Dara's line plot, each temperature is labeled below the line. Each X represents one day.

Since there are 2 Xs above the 68, the high temperature was 68° on two days.

Which temperature has the most Xs?

There are 5 Xs above the 66, so the high temperature was 66° on five days.

The temperature that occurred as the high temperature most often in April was 66°.

Guided Practice*

Do you know HOW?

Sixteen 3rd-grade students entered the long jump event. The results are shown in the table below. Use the data for **1–3.**

Data

Student	Distance (Inches)	Student	Distance (Inches)
1	27	9	30
2	31	10	26
3	28	11	28
4	26	12	30
5	30	13	31
6	33	14	26
7	29	15	33
8	31	16	30

1. Make a line plot to show the data.

2. How many Xs should be drawn for the number of students who jumped 33 inches?

3. Suppose another 3rd-grade student enters the long jump event. Predict the distance that student will jump. Explain.

Do you UNDERSTAND?

4. In the example above, what was the highest temperature recorded in April?

5. Use the line plot below. Which high temperature occurred most often in August?

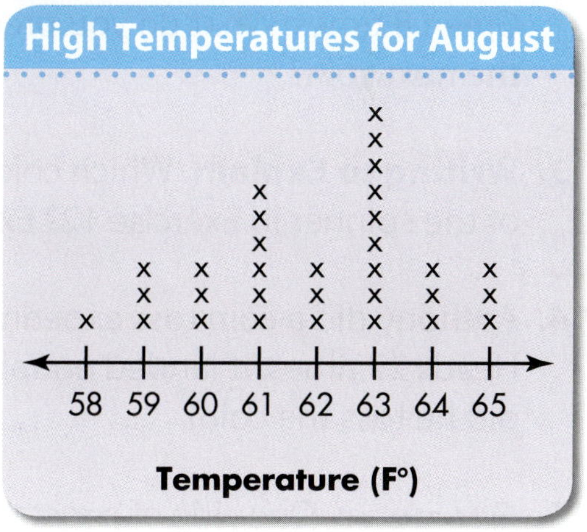

6. In Exercise 5, which high temperature occurred least often?

DIGITAL Animated Glossary **www.pearsonsuccessnet.com**

For another example, see Set E on page 487.

Independent Practice

Amelia recorded the number of people riding in each of 30 cars that passed by. Use the data to the right for **7–11**.

7. Make a line plot to show the data.

8. How many Xs should be drawn for 3 people in a car?

9. Which number of people occurred in two cars?

10. Which number of people in each car occurred most often?

11. What do you predict will be the number of people in the next car?

Data

Number of People in Each Car

Car	Number of People	Car	Number of People	Car	Number of People
1	2	11	3	21	1
2	3	12	1	22	2
3	2	13	2	23	2
4	1	14	4	24	4
5	4	15	1	25	1
6	1	16	3	26	3
7	1	17	1	27	1
8	5	18	2	28	1
9	4	19	6	29	5
10	1	20	1	30	2

Problem Solving

12. A spinner has two unequal parts. Janice spun the spinner 10 times. The spinner landed on Red 2 times. It landed on Green 8 times. What do you predict will be the outcome of the next spin?

13. **Writing to Explain** Which color is most likely the larger part of the spinner in Exercise 12? Explain your answer.

14. Anthony did a coin toss experiment. The coin landed on Heads 27 times. It landed on Tails 35 times. How many times did he toss the coin?

15. **Geometry** One side of a rectangle is 5 inches long. Another side of the rectangle is 7 inches long. What are the lengths of the other 2 sides of the rectangle?

16. **Algebra** One print of a photograph costs 36¢. Two prints cost 72¢. Three prints cost $1.08. If the cost of each print remains the same, how much would 4 prints cost?

Use the line plot at the right for **17-21.** It shows how long it took each of 28 people to run a mile.

17. Which amount of time was used by the greatest number of people?

18. How many more people took 10 minutes than 5 minutes?

19. How many people took less than 8 minutes to run a mile? more than 8 minutes?

20. Suppose another runner joined this group. Predict that runner's time for 1 mile.

21. **Number Sense** Cory said that the fastest runner in this group took 13 minutes to run a mile. Is this reasonable? Explain.

22. **Algebra** Copy and complete each number sentence by writing $<$, $>$, or $=$.

a $3 \times 18 \bigcirc 6 \times 9$ **b** $76 \div 4 \bigcirc 64 \div 4$

23. In an experiment, with a spinner that had 4 numbered sections, results were 3, 1, 4, 1, 4, 2, 1, 3, 4, 4, 3, 2. Which line plot matches the data?

A

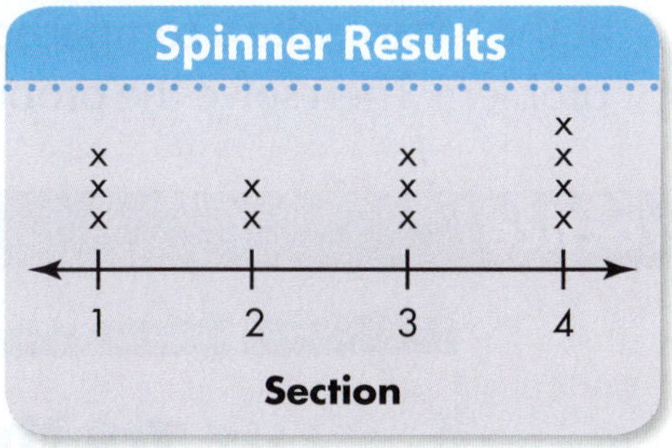

C

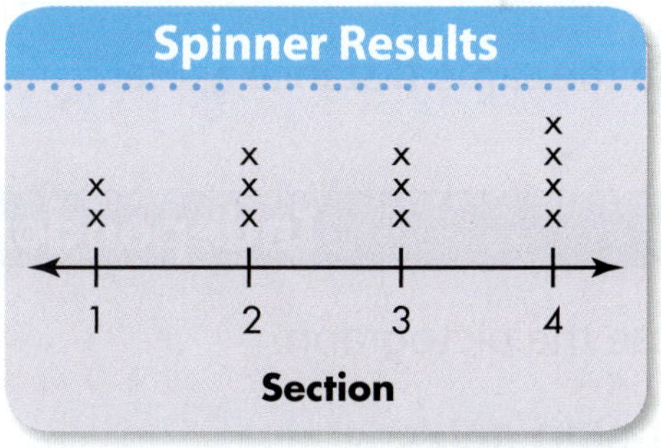

B

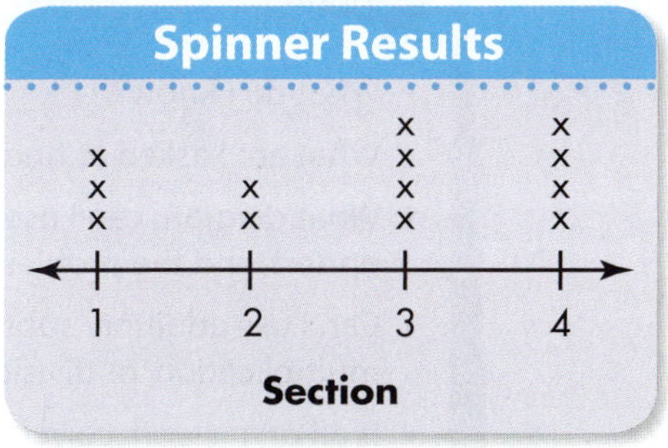

D

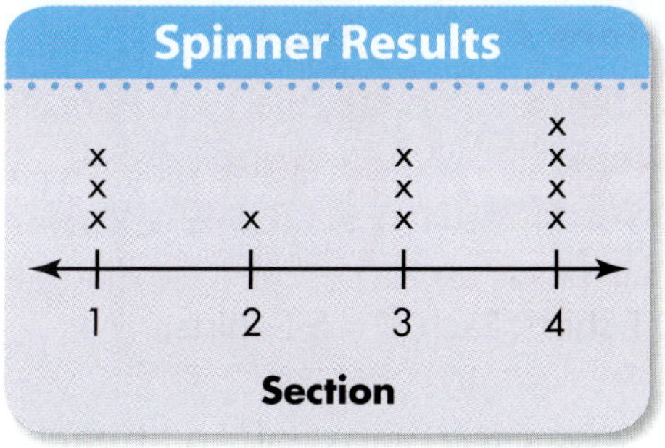

24. Which digit is used most often in whole numbers less than 20?

SOL Prep

A 9 **B** 1 **C** 5 **D** 2

Virginia

Lesson 20-9

Extends 3.17.c The student will read and interpret the data represented in line plots, bar graphs, and picture graphs and write a sentence analyzing the data.

Problem Solving

Use Tables and Graphs to Draw Conclusions

The tally chart shows data about the favorite hobbies of two Grade 3 classes. Compare the hobbies of the two classes.

Data

Favorite Hobbies

	Class A		**Class B**	
Hobby	**Tally**	**Number**	**Tally**	**Number**
Model Building	|||	3	𝍸	5
Drawing	𝍸 𝍸 ||	12	𝍸 ||	7
Rock Collecting	||||	4	||||	4
Reading	𝍸 |	6	𝍸 ||||	9

Guided Practice*

Do you know HOW?

Data

Bicycle Club Miles

Member	Victor	Rosita	Gary	Hal
Number of Miles	20	35	30	20

1. Which club member rode exactly 10 miles more than Hal?

2. Who rode the same distance as Hal?

Do you UNDERSTAND?

3. How do the bars on a bar graph help you to compare data?

4. What is the favorite hobby of Class A above? of Class B?

5. **Write a Problem** Use the tally charts or graphs above or the table at the left to write a comparison problem. Then solve the problem.

Independent Practice

For **6** and **7**, use the pictograph.

6. What color was sold most often at each store? equally at both stores?

7. Where was blue sold more often?

Stuck? Try this....

- What do I know?
- What am I asked to find?
- What diagram can I use to help understand the problem?
- Can I use addition, subtraction, multiplication, or division?
- Is all of my work correct?
- Did I answer the right question?
- Is my answer reasonable?

*For another example, see Set B on page 486.

Plan

Make a bar graph for each class.

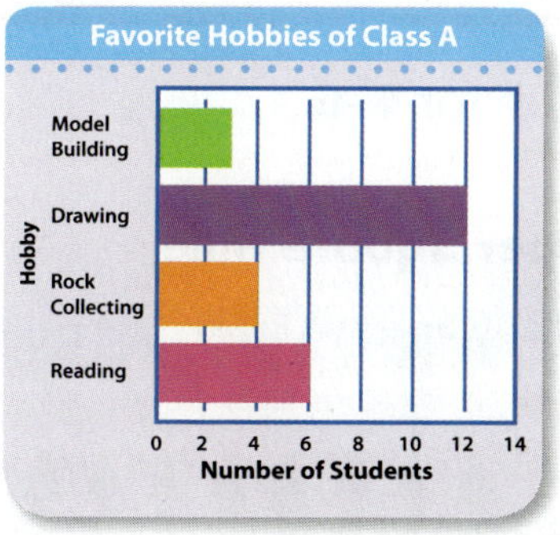

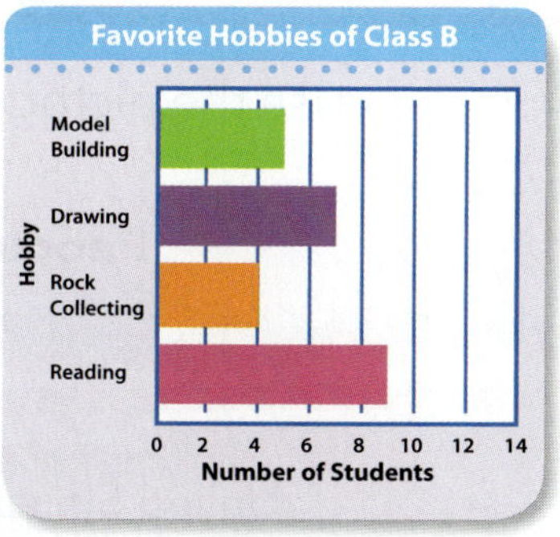

Solve

Now read the graphs and make comparisons.

- More students in Class B like model building than in Class A.
- The same number of students in each class like rock collecting.

For **8–10**, use the bar graph at the right.

8. How many people in all voted for their favorite type of exercise?

9. How many more people voted for gymnastics than for jogging?

10. **Write a Problem** Write and solve a word problem different from Exercises 8 and 9.

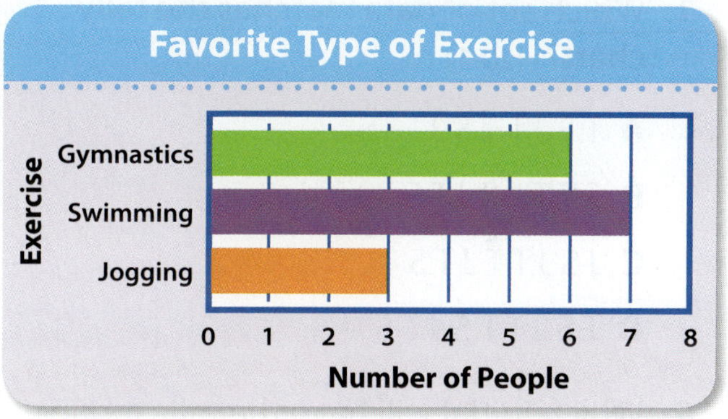

For **11–13**, use the tally chart.

11. Make a graph to show the data. Choose a pictograph or a bar graph.

12. Who read exactly ten more books than Sandra?

13. Write the members in order from most to fewest books read.

Data

Books Read by Reading Club Members

Member	Number of Books Read
Daryl	卌 卌 卌 |||
Alice	卌 卌 卌 |
Sandra	卌 |||
Helmer	卌 卌 ||||

14. **Strategy Focus** Solve. Use the strategy Make a Table.

At the farmer's market, Matt gives 2 free apples for every 6 apples the customer buys. If Lucinda buys 24 apples, how many free apples will she get?

15. **Write to Explain** What kinds of comparisons can you make when you look at a bar graph or a pictograph?

Trudy took a survey and made the tally chart shown. Use the chart for **1** and **2**.

First Initials (Data)

Initial	Tally
J	||
S	|||
T	||||

1. Which set of data matches the tally chart? (20-1)

A T S J T T S J

B S T T J S J T S

C J S J T T J T S

D T S J T T S J T S

2. Which initial will have the tallest bar on a bar graph of Trudy's data? (20-4)

A J

B S

C T

D S and T will be the same.

3. What was the temperature at 9 A.M.? (20-5)

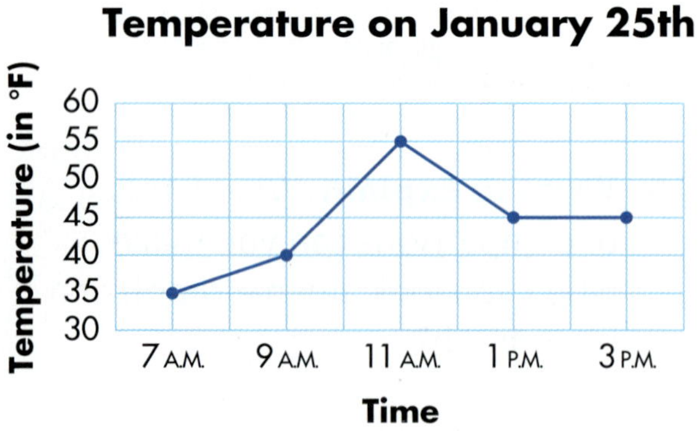

A 35°F

B 40°F

C 45°F

D 50°F

Use the pictograph for **4–6**.

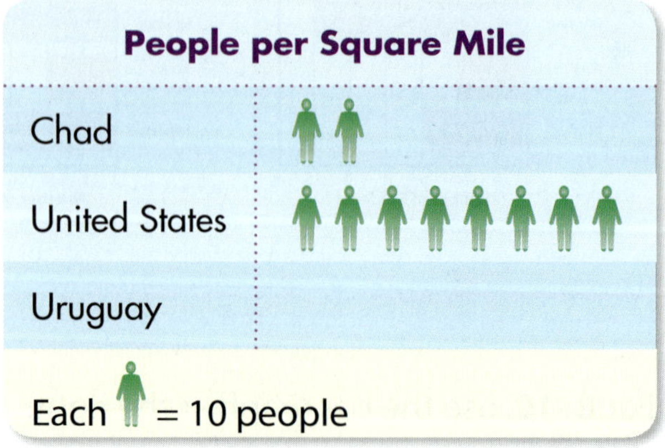

4. How many people per square mile does Chad have? (20-2)

A 80

B 20

C 10

D 2

5. How many more people per square mile does the United States have than Chad? (20-2)

A 6

B 20

C 60

D 100

6. If Pedro knows Uruguay has 50 people for each square mile, how many symbols should he draw for Uruguay? (20-3)

A 5

B 10

C 25

D 50

7. Use the bag of tiles and the table to answer the question below.

Heart	3	6	9		15	
Moon	2	4	6	8		12
Star	1	2	3			6
Total Picks	6	12	18	24	30	36

Which is the best prediction for how many moons will be picked in 30 total picks? (20-7)

A 12 moons

B 10 moons

C 8 moons

D 5 moons

8. Jose spun a spinner 12 times. The line plot below shows his results.

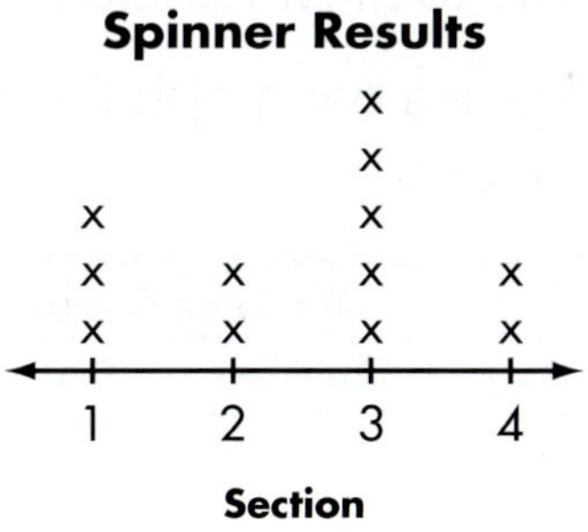

Which is the best prediction of the section Jose will spin next? (20-8)

A 1

B 2

C 3

D 4

9. Which statement is true about the data in the graphs? (20-9)

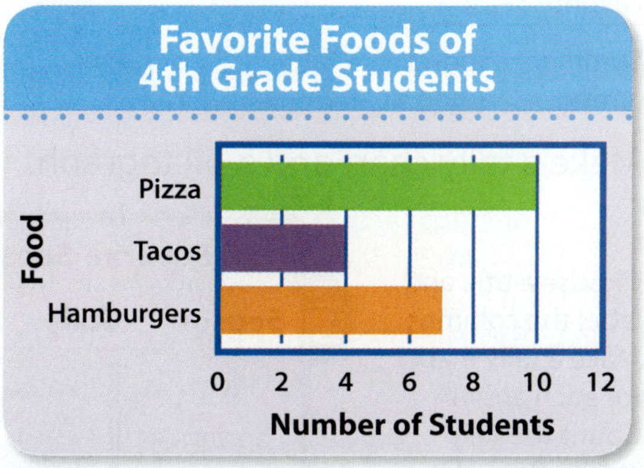

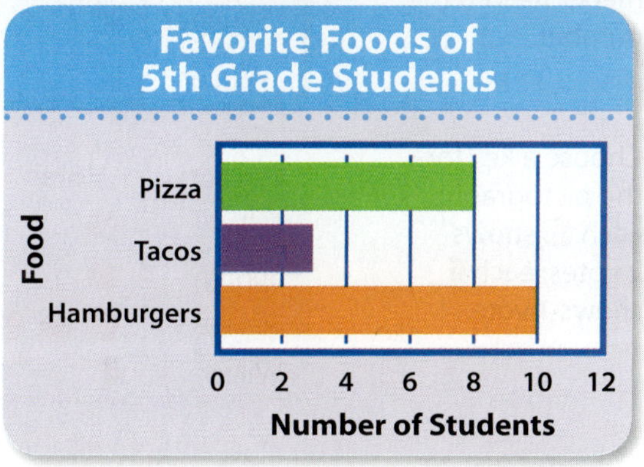

A Pizza is the favorite in both grades.

B The same number of students in each grade like tacos.

C More students in Grade 4 than in Grade 5 like hamburgers.

D More students in Grade 4 than in Grade 5 like pizza.

10. At the fair, the fish pond has 15 red fish, 9 blue fish, 10 yellow fish, and 5 orange fish. If Tammy hooks a fish without looking, what color fish is she most likely to get? (20-6)

A Blue

B Orange

C Red

D Yellow

Set A, pages 458–462, 464–465

What is the favorite season of these students?

Favorite Season

Summer	Spring	Fall	Summer	Summer
Spring	Summer	Winter	Fall	Summer

Make a tally chart and a pictograph.

Choose a title and label the columns. Make a tally mark for each answer. Count the tally marks. Record the number.

Favorite Season

Season	Tally	Number
Fall	||	2
Spring	||	2
Summer	𝍸	5
Winter	|	1

Choose a key for the pictograph. Each ● shows 2 votes; each ◖ shows 1 vote.

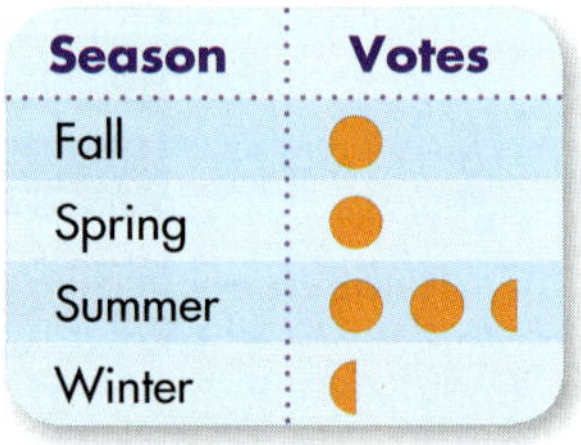

Remember to make sure your tally marks and the symbols in the pictograph match the data.

For **1–3**, use the Team Name data.

Votes for Team Name

Aces	Fire	Aces	Fire	Aces
Aces	Fire	Fire	Aces	Stars
Fire	Stars	Fire	Fire	Fire
Aces	Aces	Aces	Fire	Stars
Fire	Fire	Fire	Aces	Fire
Stars	Fire	Stars	Fire	Aces

1. Make a tally chart for the data.
2. How many more players voted for Fire than Stars for their team name?
3. Choose a key and make a pictograph to show the data.

Set B, pages 466–467, 482–483

How can you make a bar graph to draw conclusions about how much Don saved?

Month	Amount	Month	Amount
January	$20	March	$30
February	$35	April	$15

Choose 10 for the scale. Amounts with a 5 in the ones place will be halfway between 2 grid lines.

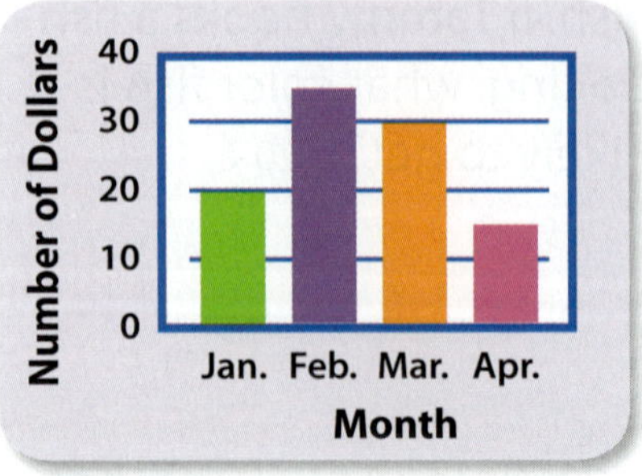

The longest bar in February shows the most.

The shortest bar in April shows the least.

Remember that you can compare the bars to draw conclusions.

1. Make a bar graph for the data below.

Pennies Saved

Day	Number	Day	Number
Mon.	25	Wed.	15
Tues.	20	Thurs.	10

2. Suppose the bar for Friday is as long as the bar for Tuesday. What conclusion can you draw?

Set C, pages 468–471

Add $15 earned in July to the line graph.

Amount Earned Doing Chores

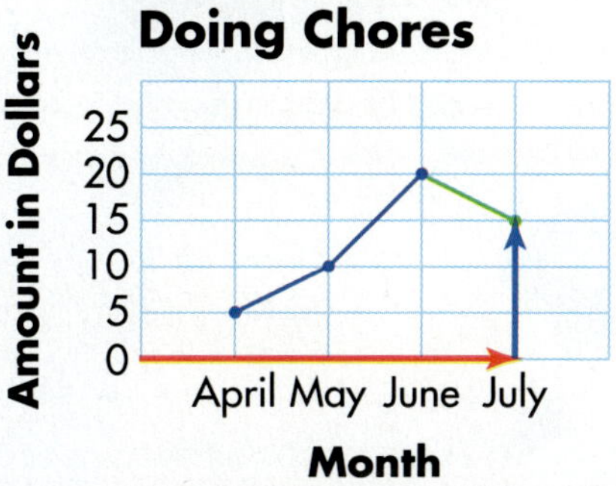

- Start at 0. Move along the bottom to July.
- Move up to the line for 15. Mark a point.
- Connect the points with a line segment.

Remember that to plot a point, go across, then up.

1. Explain how to plot (3, 2).
2. Copy and complete the graph to show the data for Friday.
   Friday: 20 books collected

Books Collected

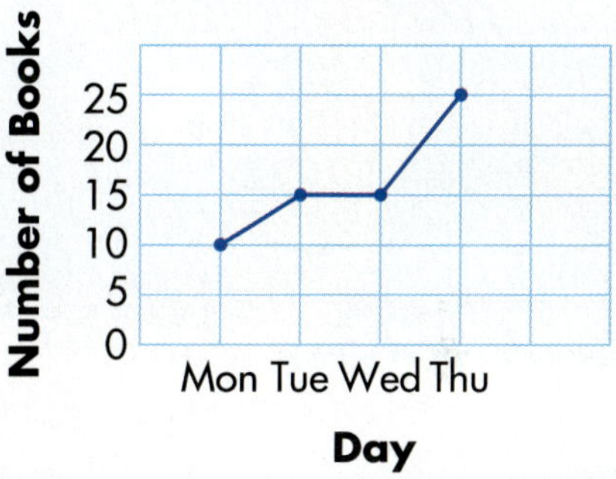

Set D, pages 472–477

When you spin this spinner, what outcome is likely? unlikely? impossible? certain?

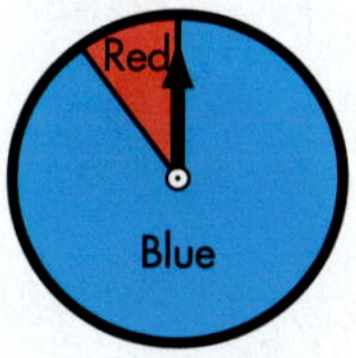

It is likely you will spin Blue.
It is unlikely you will spin Red.
It is impossible to spin Green.
It is certain you will spin a color or a line.

Remember that you are deciding what will probably happen.

1. What outcome is likely on this spinner?

2. In 3 spins, Lisa spun 2 Gs and 1 Y. Predict what is likely in 30 spins.

Set E, pages 478–481

Which high temperature occurred most often in June?

High Temperatures in June

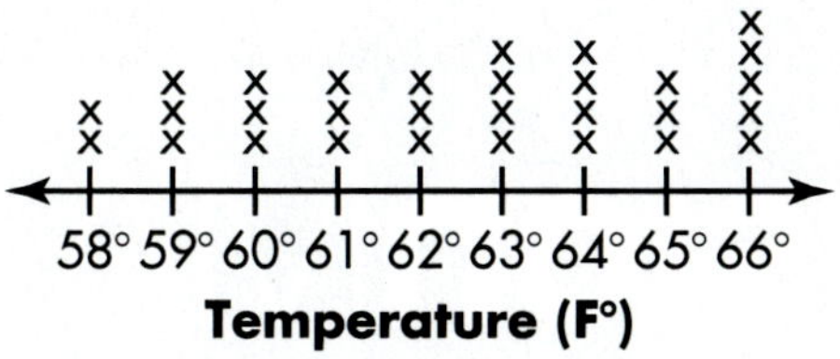

A high temperature of 66° occurred most often.

Remember that each outcome gets an X on a line plot.

Spin Results

Spin	Section	Spin	Section	Spin	Section
1	3	4	2	7	1
2	2	5	1	8	2
3	2	6	2	9	2

1. Make a line plot of the data. Then predict the section of Spin 10.

Scott Foresman·Addison Wesley

enVisionMATH™

Virginia

Virginia Handbook

Lessons

VA SOL Practice

Virginia

Lesson VA-9

3.3.c The student will compare fractions having like and unlike denominators, using words and symbols (>, <, or =).

Comparing Fractions

How can you compare fractions?

Flo and Rita had identical sheets of paper. Flo shaded $\frac{1}{3}$ of her sheet. Rita shaded $\frac{3}{5}$ of her sheet. Who shaded more of her sheet of paper: Flo or Rita?

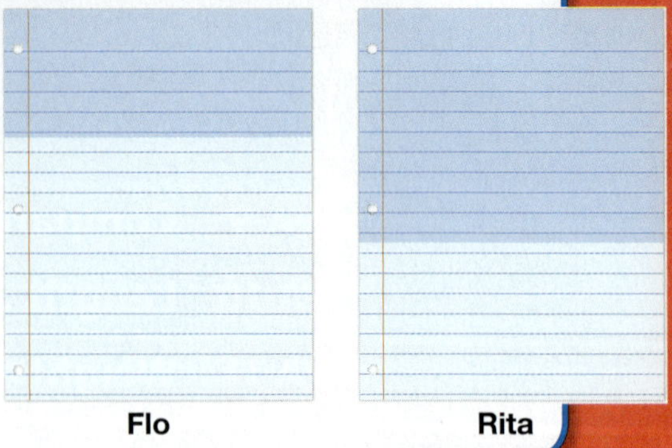

One Way

Compare the fractions using fraction strips.

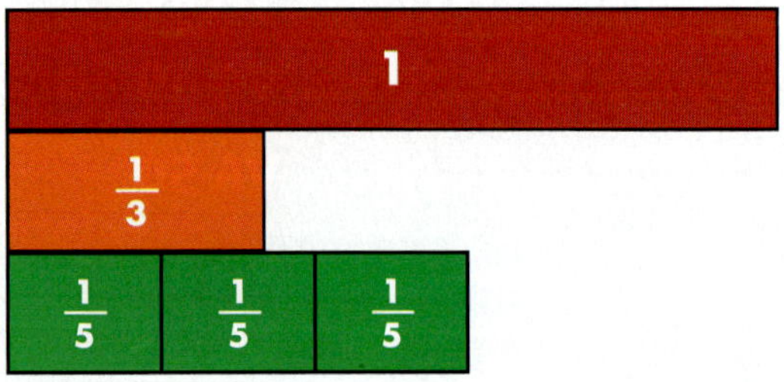

Another Way

Compare the fractions on a number line.

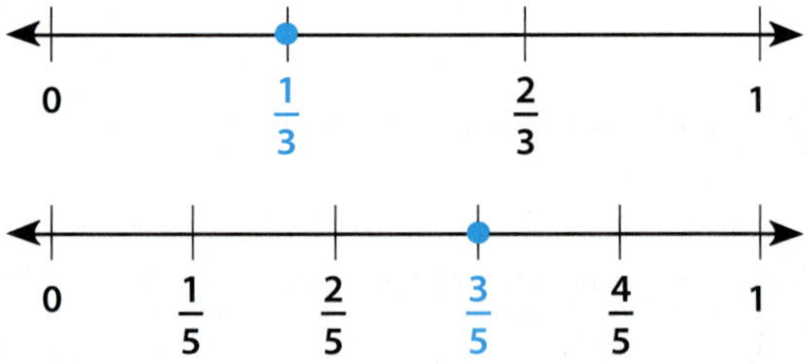

Both ways show that $\frac{1}{3}$ is less than $\frac{3}{5}$, or $\frac{1}{3} < \frac{3}{5}$. Flo shaded less than Rita.

Guided Practice

Do you know HOW?

In **1** and **2**, compare. Write >, <, or =. Use fraction strips to help.

1. $\frac{3}{4} \bigcirc \frac{2}{4}$

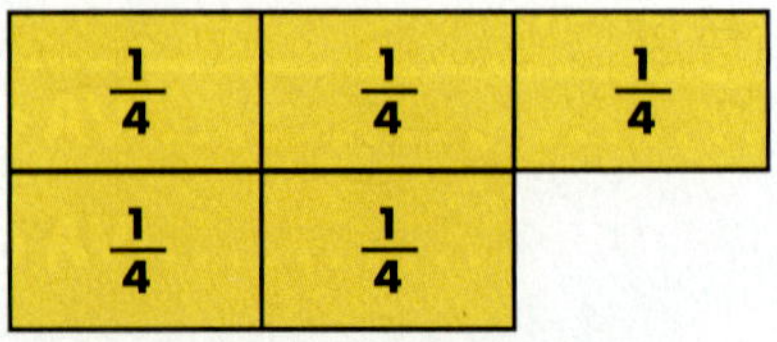

2. $\frac{4}{6} \bigcirc \frac{2}{3}$

Do you UNDERSTAND?

3. In the example above about Flo and Rita, how can the picture of the sheets of paper help you solve the problem?

4. The girls kept shading until Flo shaded a total of $\frac{3}{4}$ of her paper and Rita shaded a total of $\frac{2}{3}$ of hers. Write a number sentence to compare $\frac{3}{4}$ and $\frac{2}{3}$. Who shaded more? Draw a model to help.

Independent Practice

Compare. Write >, <, or =.
Use fraction strips or a number line to help.

5. 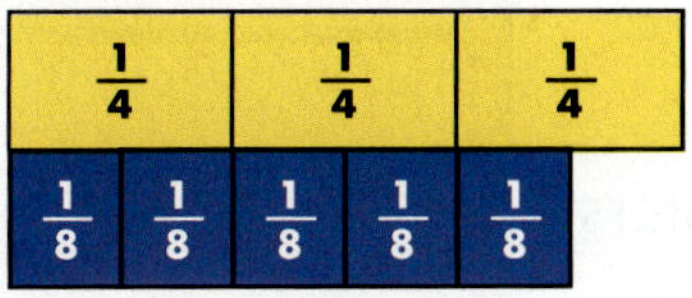

$\frac{3}{4} \bigcirc \frac{5}{8}$

6. 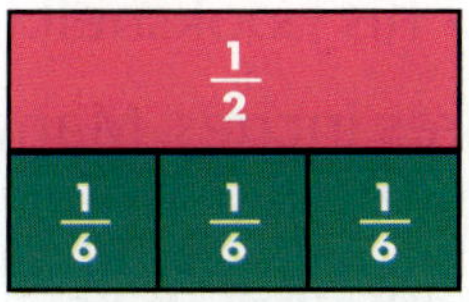

$\frac{3}{6} \bigcirc \frac{1}{2}$

7. 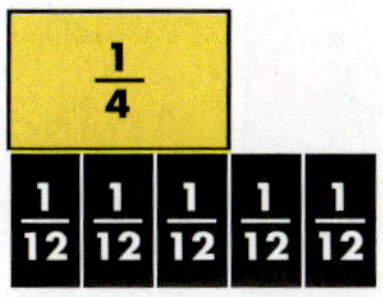

$\frac{1}{4} \bigcirc \frac{5}{12}$

8. 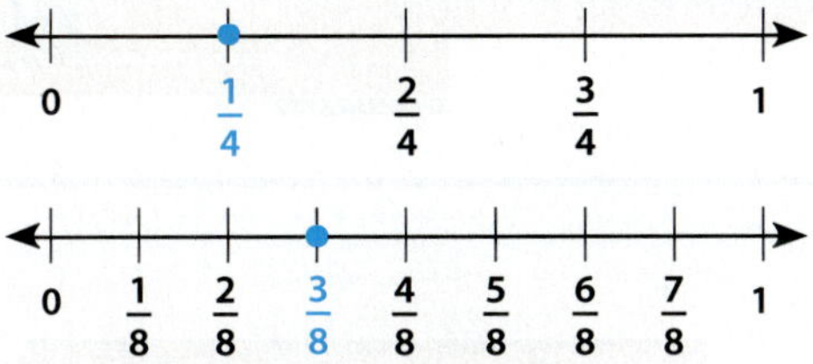

$\frac{1}{4} \bigcirc \frac{3}{8}$

9. 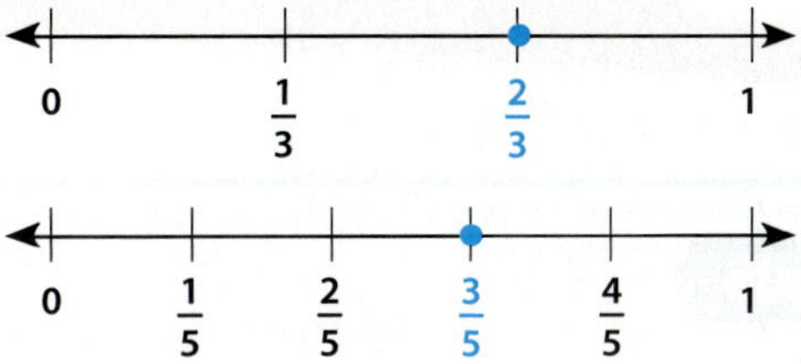

$\frac{2}{3} \bigcirc \frac{3}{5}$

Problem Solving

For **10**, use the set of green stars and the set of red stars at the right.

10. Eric has 10 green stars, and Susan has 10 red stars. Eric drew white stripes on $\frac{7}{10}$ of his stars. Susan drew white stripes on $\frac{4}{5}$ of her stars. Write a sentence that uses the words *equal to*, *greater than*, or *less than* to compare $\frac{7}{10}$ and $\frac{4}{5}$.

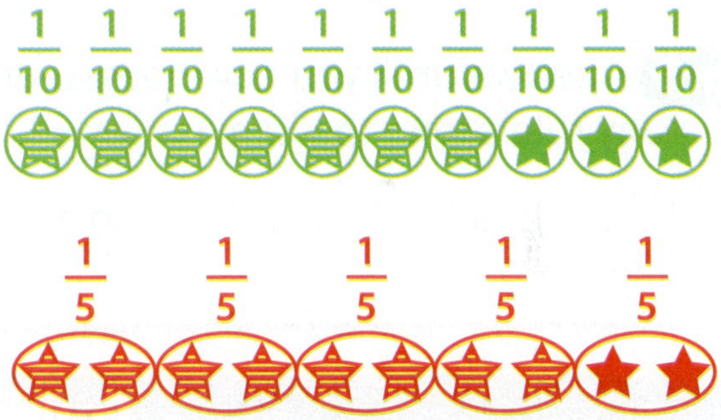

11. Melissa had $26.54. She spent $13.90 of it at the store. How much money did she have left?

12. **Geometry** What kind of triangle has no sides that are the same length? Write *equilateral*, *isosceles*, or *scalene*.

13. Gia eats $\frac{3}{4}$ of a granola bar. Lance eats $\frac{7}{8}$ of the same kind of granola bar. Who eats more? Draw number lines to solve.

14. Draw what comes next in the pattern.

15. Which figure shows more than $\frac{5}{8}$ shaded?

A 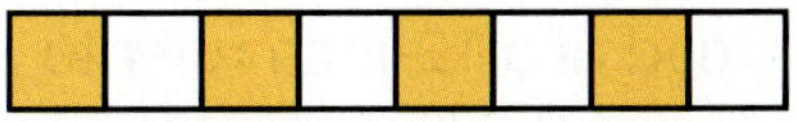

B 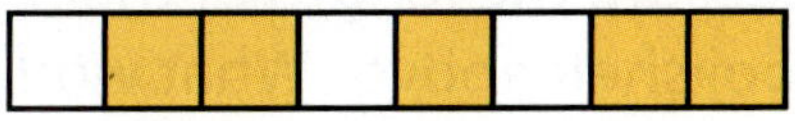

C 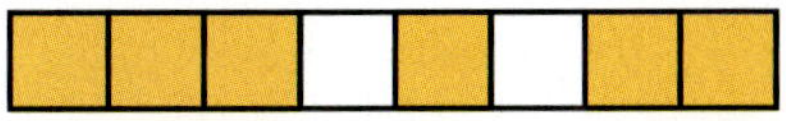

D 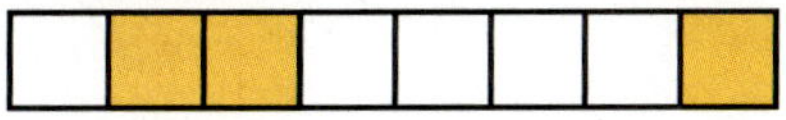

Virginia

Lesson VA-10

3.9.a The student will estimate and use U.S. Customary and metric units to measure length to the nearest $\frac{1}{2}$-inch, inch, foot, yard, centimeter, and meter.

Length

How can you measure length?

Bob uses a 12-inch ruler to measure the length of his bookshelf. What is the length of his bookshelf in feet?

An inch ruler measures inches. Many inch rulers are 12 inches, or 1 foot long. These rulers can measure inches and feet. A yardstick is 3 feet long. It can measure inches, feet, or yards.

Example

Step 1 Line up the zero mark of the 12-inch ruler with the left edge of the object you want to measure.

Step 2 Mark the right edge of the ruler. Slide the ruler to the right. Line up the zero mark of the ruler with your mark.

Step 3 Repeat until you have measured how many rulers long the item is.

The bookshelf is 3 rulers long, so it is 3 feet long.

Guided Practice

Do you know HOW?

1. Use a ruler to measure the width of your desk. What is the width of your desk in feet?

2. Use a yardstick to measure the height of your classroom door. What is the height of your classroom door in yards?

Do you UNDERSTAND?

3. Why should you first line up the zero mark of a ruler or yardstick with the edge of the object you are measuring?

4. **Estimation** How could you use a ruler to estimate the length of a rug to the nearest foot?

5. How could Bob use a yardstick instead of a 12-inch ruler to measure the length of the bookshelf above? What would the measurement be in yards?

Independent Practice

For **6** and **7**, measure each object in feet.

6. What is the width of a window in your classroom?

7. What is the height of a student's chair in your classroom?

For **8** and **9**, measure each object in yards.

8. What is the length of the shortest wall in your classroom?

9. What is the length of the longest wall in your classroom?

Problem Solving

For **10** and **11**, use the picture at the right.

10. Tamika used a ruler to measure a poster in her bedroom. What is the width of the poster in feet?

11. What is the height of Tamika's poster in feet?

12. A school theater has 12 rows of seats with 8 seats in each row. If people are sitting in 79 of the seats, how many seats are empty?

13. How many edges does a cube have?

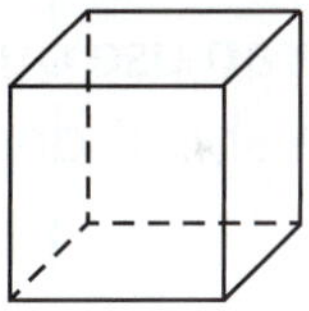

14. Write six hundred thousand, seventy-three in standard form.

15. Find a classroom object that is about 2 feet long.

16. What number comes next in the pattern below?

87, 91, 95, 99, ▢

17. Paul has read $\frac{3}{12}$ of a new book. What is $\frac{3}{12}$ written in simplest form?

18. **Reasoning** Rachel and Eric measure the length of the same mural. Rachel writes how many feet long it is. Eric writes how many yards long it is. Which student writes a greater number? Explain.

19. **Estimation** Which shows the best estimate of the height of a classroom wall?

A 1 foot

B 1 yard

C 3 feet

D 3 yards

Virginia

Lesson VA-11

3.9 The student will estimate and use U.S. Customary and metric units to measure
b) liquid volume in cups, pints, quarts, gallons, and liters;
c) weight/mass in ounces, pounds, grams, and kilograms.

Weight and Capacity

How can you measure how much an object weighs or how much a container can hold?

Cara fills the container on the right to the line shown. How much liquid is in the container?

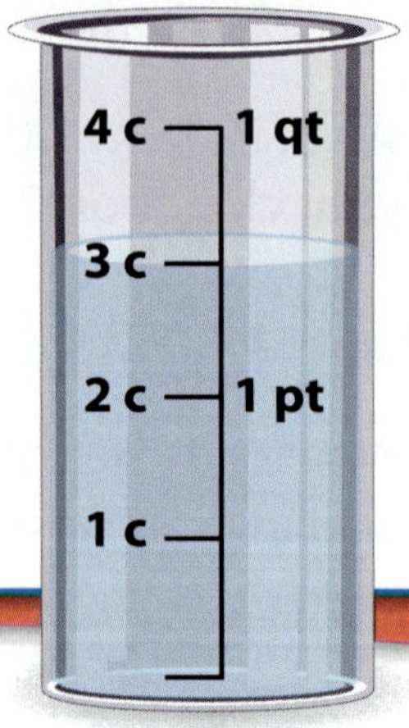

Cara's Container

Example Decide how much liquid is in the container.

The container is marked in three customary units: cups (c), pints (pt) and quarts (qt). Cara filled the container up to the line marked 3 c, or 3 cups. So, there are 3 cups of liquid in the container.

A liter (l) is another unit commonly used to measure capacity. It is a part of the metric system.

You can also measure how heavy an object is. To measure weight, you can use ounces (oz) and pounds (lb). A slice of cheese might weigh about one ounce. A loaf of bread weighs about one pound.

The scale measures in pounds. So, the rock weighs about 5 lb.

Guided Practice

Do you know HOW?

Tell how much liquid is in each container.

1.

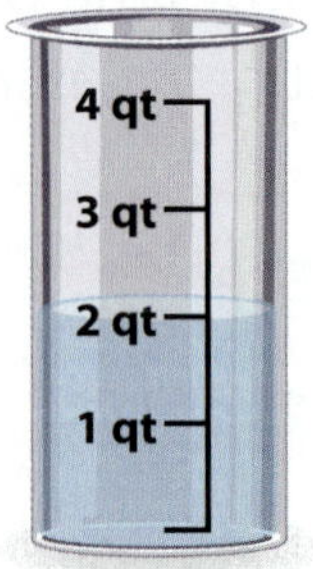

2.

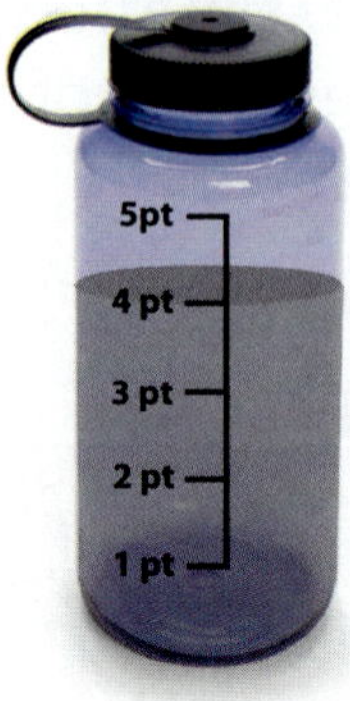

Do you UNDERSTAND?

3. Why must you write a number and the unit to tell how much something weighs or how much it holds?

4. Cara weighs a pine cone. How much does the pine cone weigh?

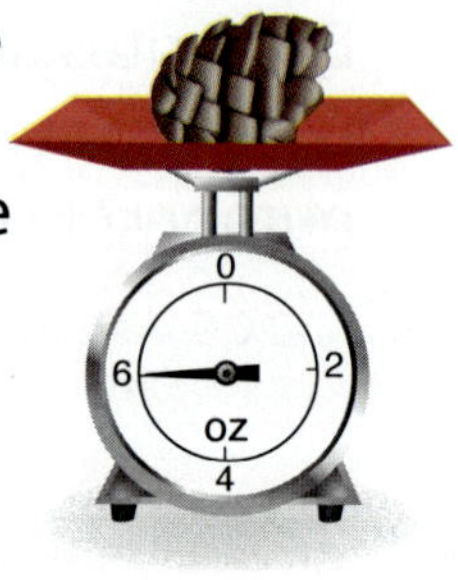

Independent Practice

Tell how much liquid is in each container.

5.

6.

7.

8.

9.

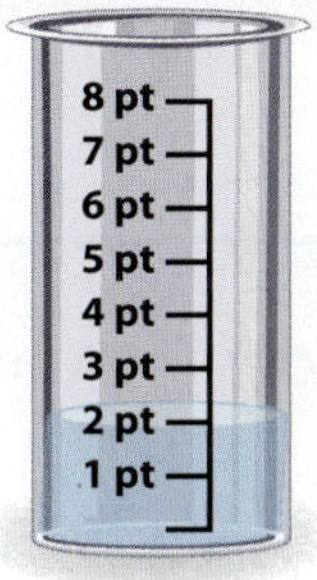

10.

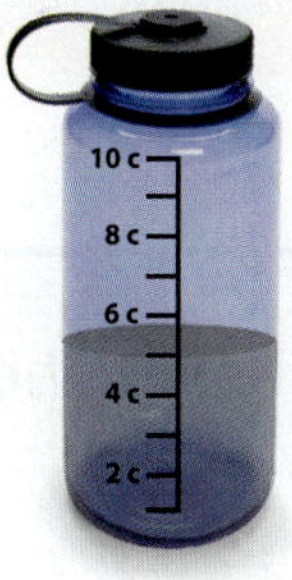

Tell how much each object weighs.

11.

12.

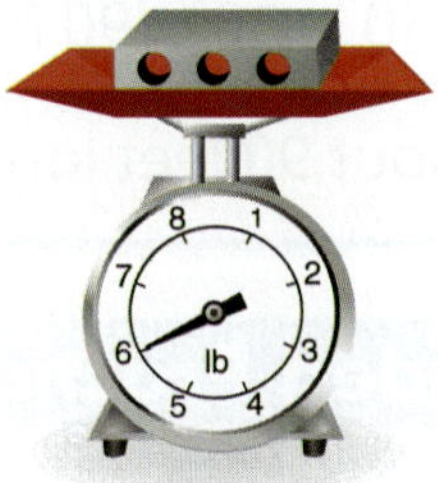

13.

Problem Solving

14. Mr. Evans is 72 inches tall. Ms. Blair is 6 inches shorter than Mr. Evans. How tall is Ms. Blair?

15. A pail has lines showing 2 gal, 4 gal, and 6 gal. The water in the pail is halfway between the 2-gal and 4-gal marks. How much water is in the pail?

16. Three dogs weigh 24 pounds, 18 pounds, and 27 pounds. How many pounds in all do the three dogs weigh?

17. Which weight is shown on the scale?

A 25 pounds　　**C** 20 ounces

B 20 pounds　　**D** 20 pints

Virginia

Lesson VA-12

3.9.d The student will estimate and use U.S. Customary and metric units to measure area and perimeter.

Estimating Perimeter

How can you estimate perimeter?

Ava has a triangle-shaped garden. Each side of the garden is 29 feet long. Estimate the perimeter of Ava's garden.

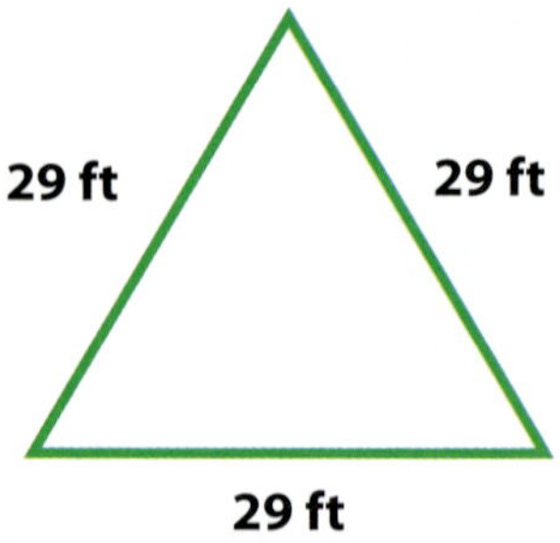

Example Round the lengths of the sides to numbers that are easy to add.

First, round 29 to 30.

Then, add the estimated lengths of the sides.

$$30 + 30 + 30 = 90 \text{ ft}$$

The perimeter of Ava's garden is about 90 feet long.

Guided Practice

Do you know HOW?

For **1** and **2**, estimate the perimeter of each figure.

1. Square

2. Rectangle

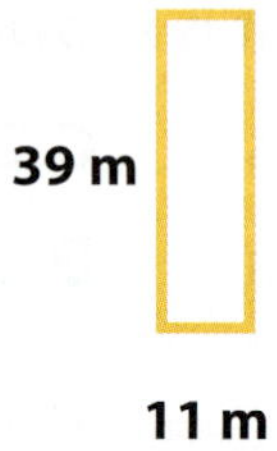

Do you UNDERSTAND?

3. When rounding to the nearest ten, how do you know if you should add 1 to the rounding digit?

4. How did you estimate the perimeter of the square in Exercise 1?

5. **Strategy Focus** Tell how to estimate the perimeter of a rectangular city that is 21 miles long and 28 miles wide.

6. Ava's neighbor has a triangular garden with sides of 11 feet, 19 feet, and 12 feet. Estimate the perimeter of her neighbor's garden.

Independent Practice

For **7–10**, estimate the perimeter of each figure.

7. Rectangle

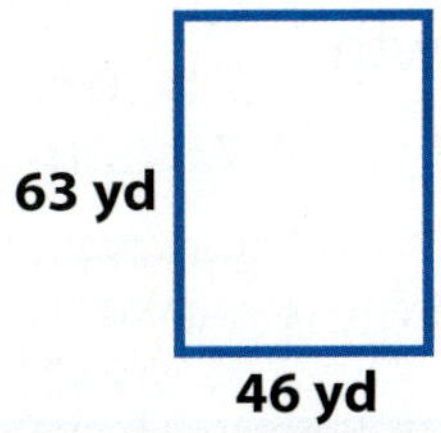

8. Isosceles Triangle

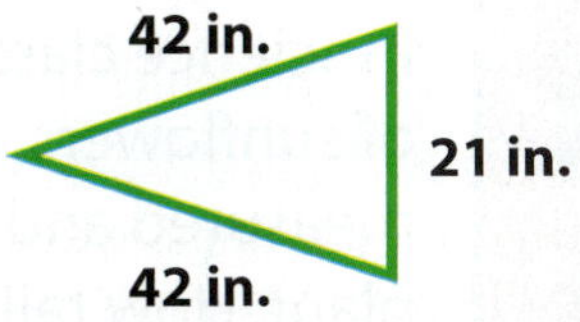

9. Square

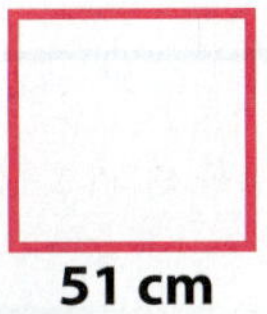

10. Rectangle

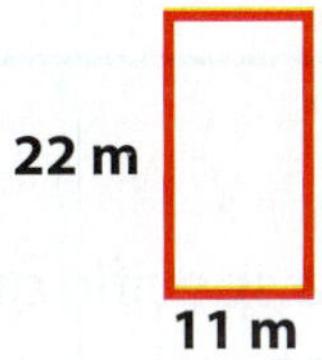

Problem Solving

For **11** and **12**, use the rectangle at the right.

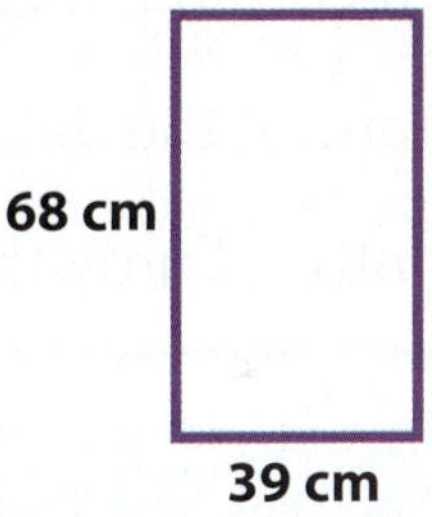

11. Estimate the perimeter of the rectangle.

12. **Reasoning** If the length of each side of the rectangle were doubled, what would happen to the estimate of the rectangle's perimeter?

13. **Geometry** How many vertices does the rectangular prism have?

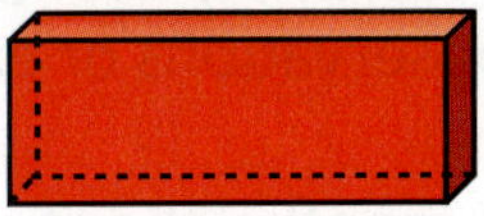

14. Mr. Jensen bought movie tickets for 6 children. Each child's ticket cost $5. He also bought movie tickets for 4 adults. Each adult's ticket cost $8. How much money did Mr. Jensen spend in all?

15. Thomas built a rectangular fence around his barnyard. Estimate the perimeter of the fence.

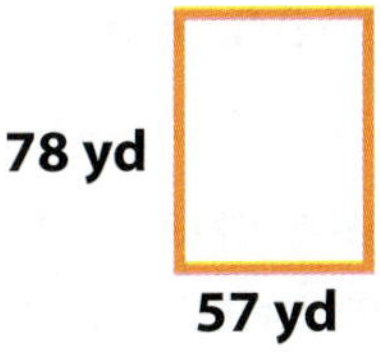

16. Tillie measures the length of one side of a square. It is 19 inches long. Which shows the best estimate of the perimeter of the square?

A 20 in.
B 40 in.
C 80 in.
D 400 in.

Virginia

Lesson VA-13

3.17.a The student will collect and organize data, using observations, measurements, surveys, or experiments.

Ways to Collect Data

How can you collect data from an experiment?

Observations are things you see or notice.
Experiments are scientific tests.

In science class, students observed the growth of sunflowers. After 3 months, the students measured and recorded the height of each plant. How tall were most of the sunflowers?

Sunflower Heights

7 ft	6 ft	7 ft	7 ft	7 ft	6 ft
7 ft	6 ft	6 ft	5 ft	7 ft	7 ft
7 ft	7 ft	7 ft	7 ft	6 ft	6 ft

Example

Step 1 Ask a specific question that the experiment will answer: *How tall are sunflowers 3 months after the seeds were planted?*

Step 2 Perform the experiment. Make a tally chart to record the measurements.

Step 3 Interpret the data.

Data

Sunflower Heights After 3 Months	
5 feet	|
6 feet	𝍸 |
7 feet	𝍸 𝍸 |

After 3 months of growth, most of the sunflowers were 7 feet tall.

Guided Practice

Do you know HOW?

For **1** and **2**, use the tally chart below.

Data

Seeds' Growth After 1 Week	
Did not sprout	𝍸 |
Less than 1 inch	𝍸 𝍸 ||||
At least 1 inch	||

1. How many seeds were planted in this experiment?

2. How many seeds grew to be less than 1 inch tall after 1 week?

Do you UNDERSTAND?

3. **Writing to Explain** How can a tally chart help you organize data from observations or experiments?

4. After 6 months, the students recorded the sunflower heights again.

Sunflower Heights

8 ft	7 ft	9 ft	8 ft	9 ft	7 ft
9 ft	7 ft	8 ft	7 ft	8 ft	7 ft
8 ft	8 ft	9 ft	8 ft	7 ft	7 ft

Make a tally chart to record the new measurements.

Independent Practice

For **5–7**, use the tally chart at the right.

5. The students saw 2 more sparrows than finches. Draw tallies to show how many sparrows the class saw.

6. Including the sparrows, how many birds in all did the class see?

7. The class saw fewer than 6 of which types of birds?

Data

Birds that Mr. Lunt's Class Observed at Nature Center	
Blue Jays	||||
Cardinals	卌
Finches	卌 ||||
Hawks	||
Sparrows	

Problem Solving

For **8** and **9**, use the tally chart below.

Data

February Temperatures

Noon Temperature	Number of Days
31°F and below	卌 卌
Between 31°F and 50°F	卌 卌 卌
50°F and above	|||

8. **Write to Explain** Tell how a class could collect the data used for the tally chart.

9. **Reasoning** Can this tally chart help you find the temperature on February 12? Explain.

For **10** and **11**, use the tally chart at the right.

10. How many rock samples were weighed in this experiment?

11. Erin put all of the rocks that weighed 3 ounces and over into 3 bags, with an equal number of the rocks in each bag. How many rocks did Erin put in each bag?

Data

Weight of Rock Samples	
Under 1 oz	卌 卌 |
Between 1 oz and 2 oz	卌 |
Between 2 oz and 3 oz	卌 卌 ||||
3 oz and over	卌 ||||

12. **Estimation** A bucket holds about a gallon of water. Will it take more than 9 buckets of water to fill a 15-gallon aquarium? Explain.

13. A carpenter cuts a $\frac{3}{8}$-foot piece off a board that is $2\frac{1}{4}$ feet long. How long is the board now?

A $1\frac{2}{4}$ feet

B $1\frac{3}{4}$ feet

C $1\frac{7}{8}$ feet

D $1\frac{15}{8}$ feet

Virginia

Lesson VA-14

3.17.b The student will construct a line plot, a picture graph, or a bar graph to represent the data.

Constructing Line Plots

How do you make a line plot?

Students in a third-grade class at Henley Elementary measured the heights of all of the plants in their school garden.

Use the data they collected to make a line plot.

Data

Heights of Plants in School Garden

Height in Feet	Number of Plants
1	𝍸 II
2	𝍸
3	𝍸 III
4	
5	III

Example Title the line plot "Heights of Plants in School Garden."

Label the number line with all possible values for plant heights. Include 4, even though no plants were 4 feet tall.

Write "Feet" below the number line.

Use the tally chart to draw the correct number of Xs above each height.

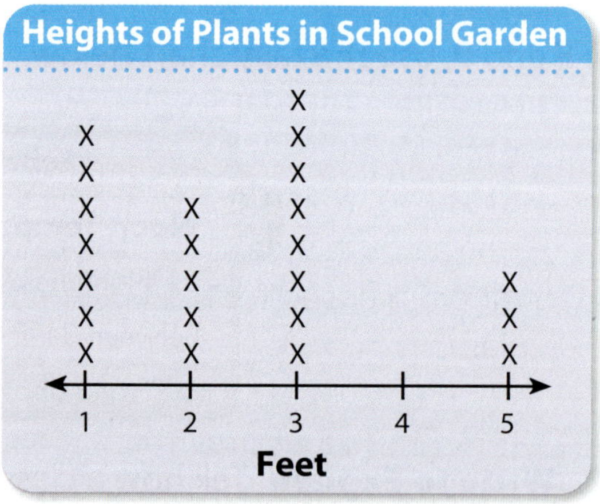

Guided Practice

Do you know HOW?

For **1** and **2**, use the data in the tally chart.

Data

Volunteer Gardeners

Age	Number of Volunteers
8	𝍸 IIII
9	𝍸 𝍸 II
10	𝍸 I

1. Draw the number line. What label and numbers do you use?

2. Write a title. Complete the line plot by drawing one X for each tally.

Do you UNDERSTAND?

3. **Writing to Explain** How does a line plot help you find the most common and least common values in a set of data?

4. In the line plot above, what was the most common height of plants in the school garden?

5. One third grader wanted to make a bar graph of the data in the tally chart at the top of the page. How will the bar graph be the same as the line plot? How will it be different?

Independent Practice

For **6** and **7**, use the tally chart at the right.

6. Make a line plot that shows the data. Write a title. Draw a number line and use Xs to plot the data. Label the units.

7. How many apples in all were weighed?

Data

Apple Weights

Weight in Ounces	Number of Apples
8	III
9	𝍸 II
10	𝍸 III
11	IIII

Problem Solving

For **8** and **9**, use the list at the right.

8. This list shows students' quiz scores. Make a line plot that shows the data.

Quiz Scores

15	15	15	16	16	16	16
20	17	19	19	19	19	19
20	20	20	20	20	20	20

9. **Reasoning** No student scored an 18 on the quiz. Will 18 appear on the number line used for the line plot? Explain.

10. Derrick draws a design on a note card by tracing a quarter five times. Are the five circles in Derrick's drawing congruent? How do you know?

11. Johanna starts soccer practice at 4:00 P.M. Soccer practice ends 1 hour, 15 minutes later. At what time does Johanna's soccer practice end?

12. Manuel's family ordered a large pizza. They ate $\frac{3}{5}$ of the pizza for lunch and $\frac{1}{5}$ of it later in the day. What fraction of the pizza did they eat in all?

13. **Draw a Picture** Lisa draws a model of a rectangular garden. The perimeter of the model is 24 units. Draw a rectangle that has the same perimeter as Lisa's model. Use grid paper to help.

14. Moe measured the lengths of the baseball bats in the gym closet. He recorded the data in the tally chart at the right. Then he made a line plot of the data. How many Xs did Moe draw in all?

A 4 **C** 26

B 12 **D** 32

Data

Length of Baseball Bats in Gym Closet

Length in Inches	Number of Bats
28	IIII
30	𝍸
32	III

3.3.b The student will model fractions (including mixed numbers) and write the fractions' names.

Showing Fractions (See Lesson 12-3 for help.)

In a fraction, the numerator shows the part of the whole or the part of the set. The denominator shows the total number of equal parts.

Examples:

Show the mixed number $2\frac{3}{4}$.

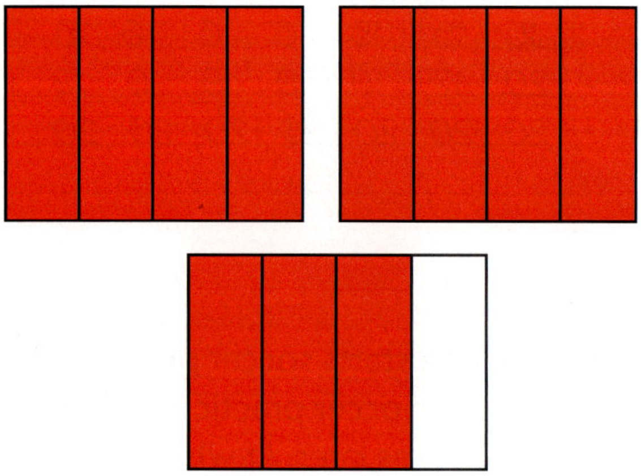

$2\frac{3}{4}$ squares are red.

Show the fraction $\frac{3}{5}$.

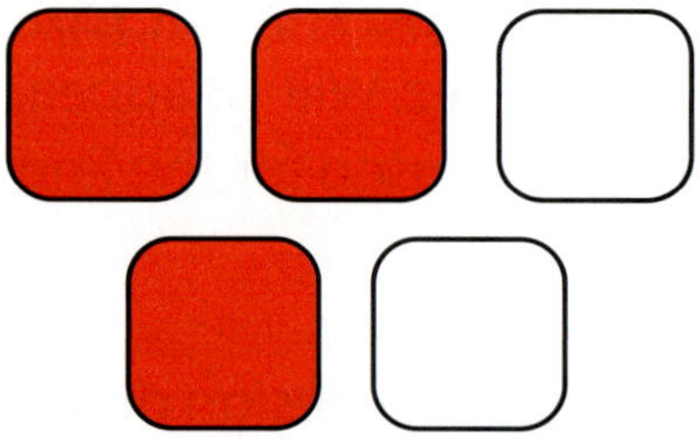

$\frac{3}{5}$ of the set is red.

Practice

For **1–4**, draw a set of counters to show the fraction given.

1. $\frac{2}{7}$ **2.** $\frac{4}{6}$ **3.** $\frac{3}{4}$ **4.** $\frac{1}{2}$

For **5–7**, copy and shade the figures as many times as is needed to show the mixed number.

5. $3\frac{2}{3}$ **6.** $1\frac{7}{8}$ **7.** $2\frac{1}{4}$

VA SOL Practice

3.3.c The student will compare fractions having like and unlike denominators, using words and symbols, (>, <, or =).

Comparing Fractions (See Lesson 12-6 for help.)

You can use fraction strips or number lines to compare fractions.

Examples:

Use fraction strips to compare $\frac{3}{4}$ and $\frac{3}{5}$.

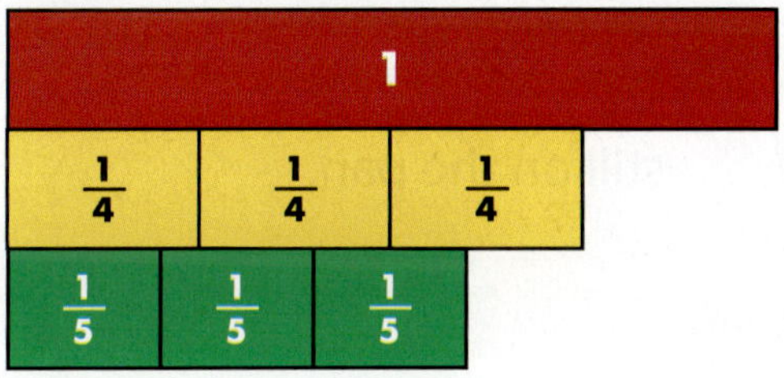

$\frac{3}{4}$ is greater than $\frac{3}{5}$.

$\frac{3}{4} > \frac{3}{5}$

Use number lines to compare $\frac{2}{4}$ and $\frac{1}{2}$.

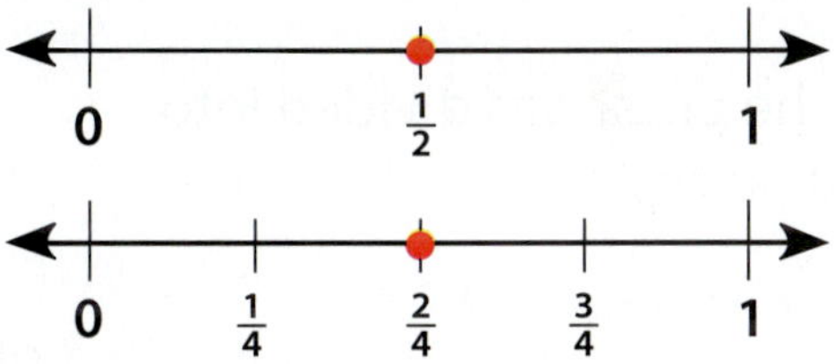

$\frac{2}{4}$ is equal to $\frac{1}{2}$.

$\frac{2}{4} = \frac{1}{2}$

Practice

Compare. Write >, <, or = in each ◯.

1.

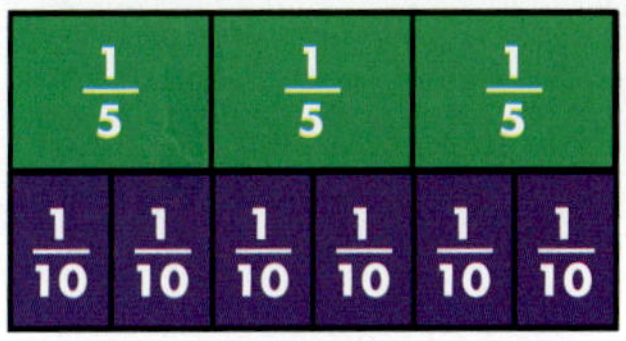

$\frac{3}{5}$ ◯ $\frac{6}{10}$

2.

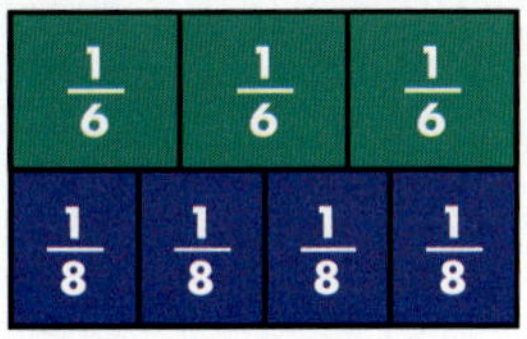

$\frac{3}{6}$ ◯ $\frac{4}{8}$

3.

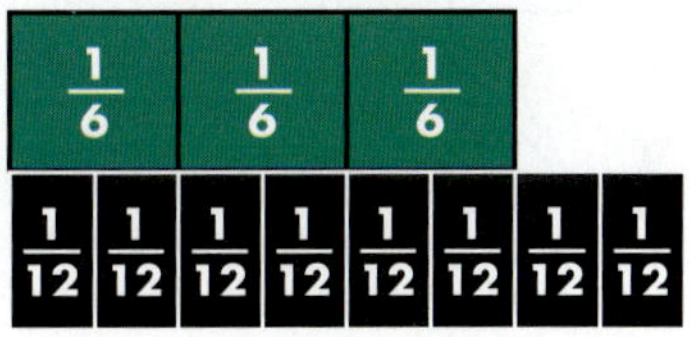

$\frac{3}{6}$ ◯ $\frac{8}{12}$

4.

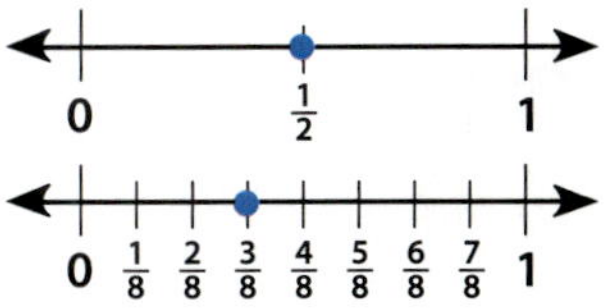

$\frac{1}{2}$ ◯ $\frac{3}{8}$

5.

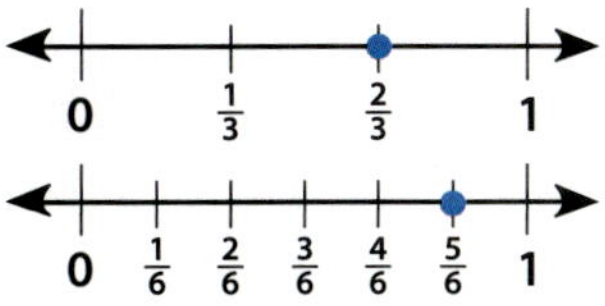

$\frac{2}{3}$ ◯ $\frac{5}{6}$

6.

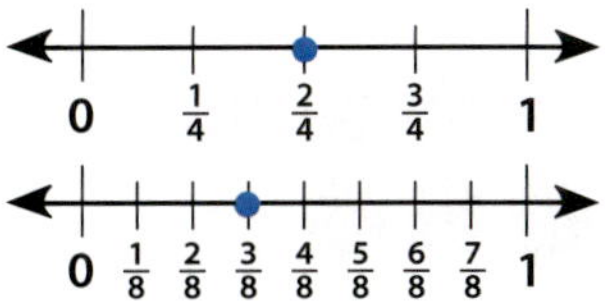

$\frac{2}{4}$ ◯ $\frac{3}{8}$

3.3.a The student will name and write fractions (including mixed numbers) represented by a model.

Naming Fractions

(See Lesson 12-7 for help.)

To write a fraction, think about the number of equal parts and how many equal parts are described.

Example:

What fraction of the pizza is left?

The pizza was divided into 8 pieces.

There are 5 pieces of pizza still on the pan.

$\frac{5}{8}$ of the pizza is left.

Practice

For **1–4**, name the fraction of the figure that is shaded.

1. 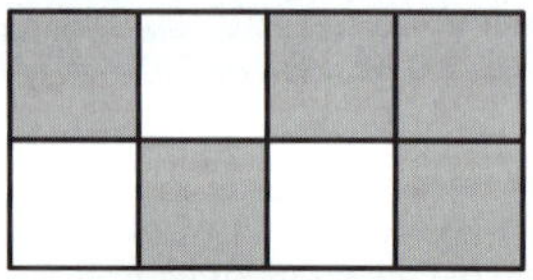

2. 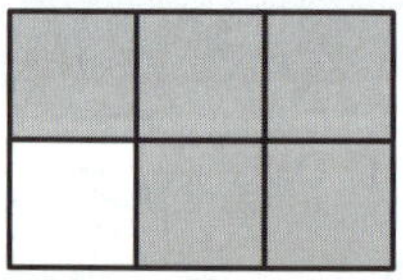

3. 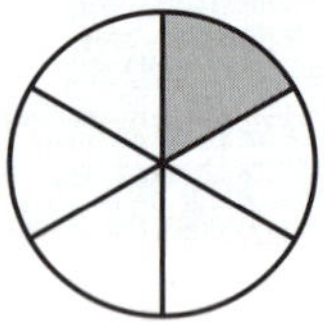

4. 

For **5–8**, name the fraction of the counters that are red.

5. 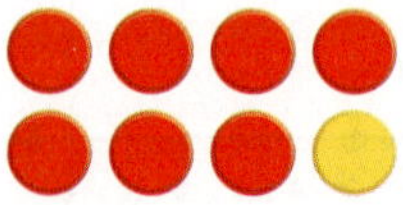

6. 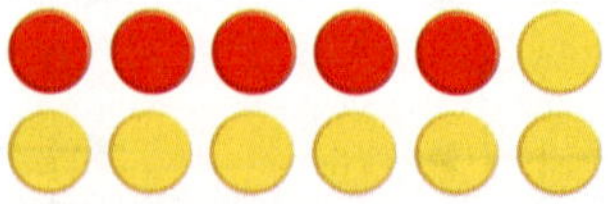

7. 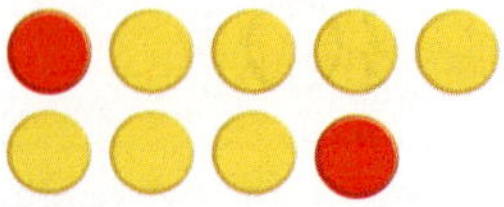

8. 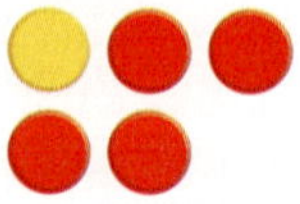

VA SOL Practice

3.7 The student will add and subtract proper fractions having like denominators of 12 or less.

Adding and Subtracting Fractions

(See Lesson 12-9 for help.)

To add or subtract fractions with like denominators, just add or subtract the numerators and keep the denominator the same.

Examples:

Add: $\frac{5}{12} + \frac{4}{12}$

Add the numerators.

$5 + 4 = 9$

$\frac{5}{12} + \frac{4}{12} = \frac{9}{12}$

Simplify.

$\frac{9}{12} = \frac{3}{4}$

Subtract: $\frac{6}{6} - \frac{4}{6}$

Subtract the numerators.

$6 - 4 = 2$

$\frac{6}{6} - \frac{4}{6} = \frac{2}{6}$

Simplify.

$\frac{2}{6} = \frac{1}{3}$

Practice

For **1–15**, add or subtract. Write the answer in simplest form.

1. $\frac{1}{8} + \frac{5}{8}$

2. $\frac{8}{12} - \frac{5}{12}$

3. $\frac{3}{10} - \frac{1}{10}$

4. $\frac{4}{9} + \frac{3}{9}$

5. $\frac{5}{6} - \frac{3}{6}$

6. $\frac{2}{5} + \frac{3}{5}$

7. $\frac{10}{11} - \frac{8}{11}$

8. $\frac{4}{8} + \frac{3}{8}$

9. $\frac{11}{12} - \frac{2}{12}$

10. $\frac{7}{8} - \frac{2}{8}$

11. $\frac{5}{10} + \frac{3}{10}$

12. $\frac{1}{6} + \frac{2}{6}$

13. $\frac{8}{9} - \frac{5}{9}$

14. $\frac{7}{8} - \frac{4}{8}$

15. $\frac{1}{3} + \frac{2}{3}$

16. Carlo makes a recipe. He uses $\frac{3}{8}$ cup of cake flour and $\frac{3}{8}$ cup of all-purpose flour. How much flour does Carlo use in his recipe in all? Write the answer in simplest form.

17. Petra has a piece of ribbon that is $\frac{11}{12}$ inch long. She cuts $\frac{5}{12}$ inch off the end of the ribbon. How much ribbon does Petra have left? Write the answer in simplest form.

VA SOL Practice

3.9.a The student will estimate and use U.S. Customary and metric units to measure length to the nearest $\frac{1}{2}$-inch, inch, foot, yard, centimeter, and meter.

Length (See Lesson 15-2 for help.)

Centimeters and meters are metric units used for measuring length.

Example:

Find the length of the stamp, to the nearest centimeter.

Use a centimeter ruler.
Line up the zero mark of the ruler with the left end of the stamp.

The stamp is 3 centimeters long.

Practice

For **1** and **2**, estimate each length in centimeters. Then use a centimeter ruler to measure.

1. 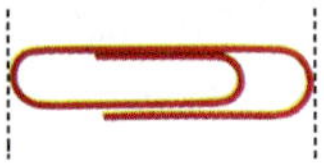

2. 

For **3** and **4**, measure each length to the nearest meter.

3. What is the height of your classroom door?

4. What is the length of one wall in your classroom?

For **5–10**, tell which units are more appropriate to measure each length: *centimeters* or *meters*.

5. The length of a mouse

6. The length of a fork

7. The width of a building

8. The height of a flagpole

9. The height of a rabbit

10. The distance a soccer player kicks the ball

For **11–14**, tell whether each estimate is *reasonable* or *not reasonable*.

11. A bedroom door is about 20 meters high.

12. A car is about 5 meters long.

13. A flashlight is about 21 centimeters long.

14. A telephone pole is about 120 centimeters high.

3.9.b The student will estimate and use U.S. Customary and metric units to measure liquid volume in cups, pints, quarts, gallons, and liters.

Capacity (See Lesson 15-3 for help.)

Capacity is the amount of liquid a container can hold.

Example:

How many units of water are in the water bottle?

This container is marked in pints.

The water reaches the 5-pint mark.

So, there are 5 pints of water in the water bottle.

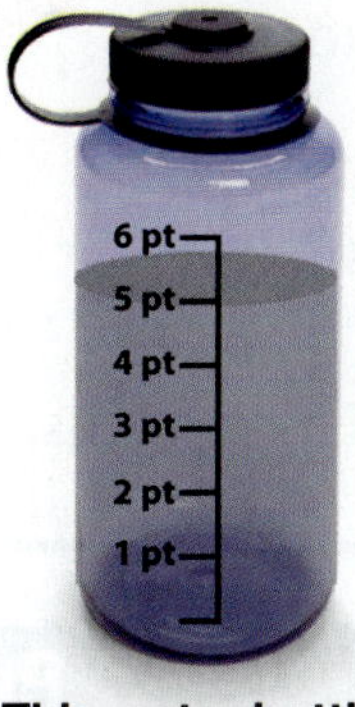

This water bottle holds up to 6 pints.

Capacity Abbreviations

c = cup

pt = pint

qt = quart

gal = gallon

l = liter

Practice

Tell how many units of liquid are in each container.

1.

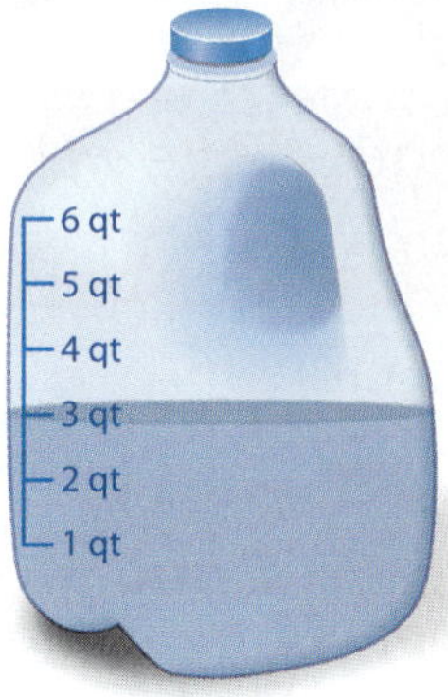

2.

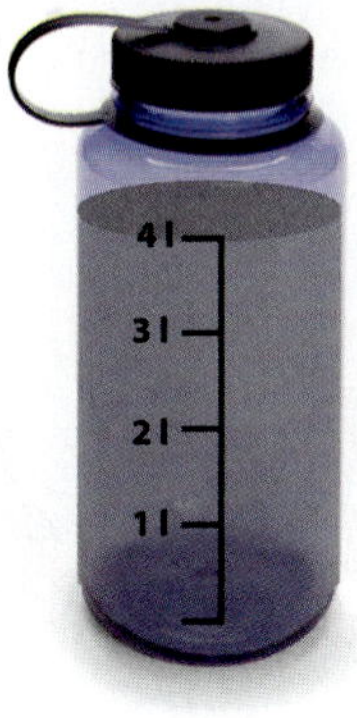

3.

4.

5.

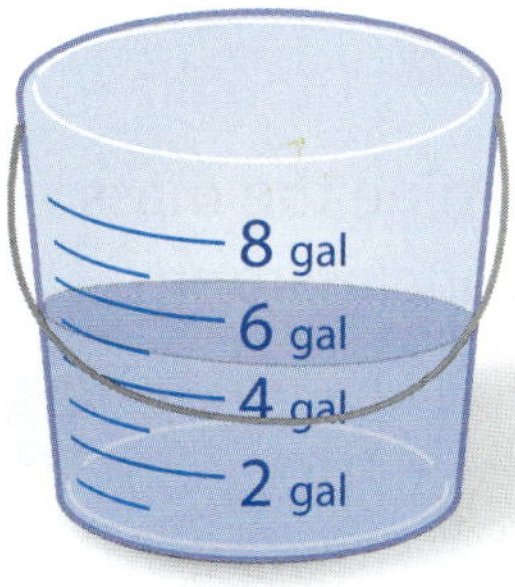

6.

VA SOL Practice

3.9.c The student will estimate and use U.S. Customary and metric units to measure weight/mass in ounces, pounds, grams, and kilograms.

Mass (See Lesson 15-4 for help.)

You can use a balance scale to find the mass of an object.

Example:

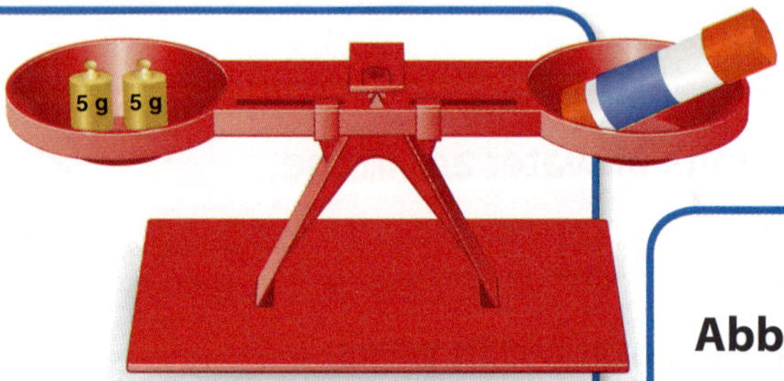

What is the mass of the glue stick?

Add the metric weights to find the total mass of the glue stick.
5 g + 5 g = 10 g
The mass of the glue stick is 10 grams.

Mass Abbreviations

g = gram
kg = kilogram

Practice

For **1–4**, find the mass of each object.

1.

2.

3.

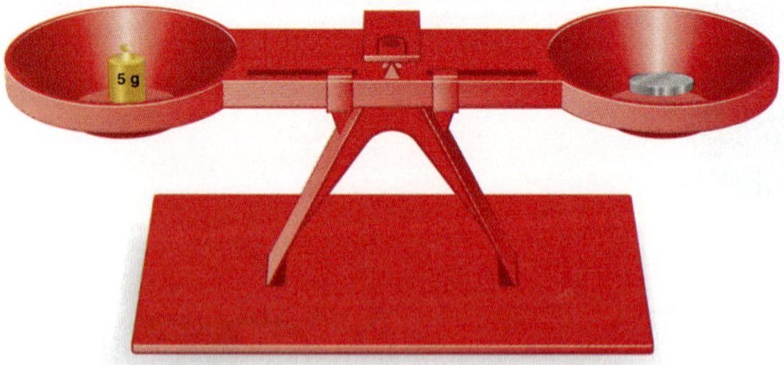

4.

For **5** and **6**, use a balance to determine the mass of the object. Find the object in your classroom.

5.

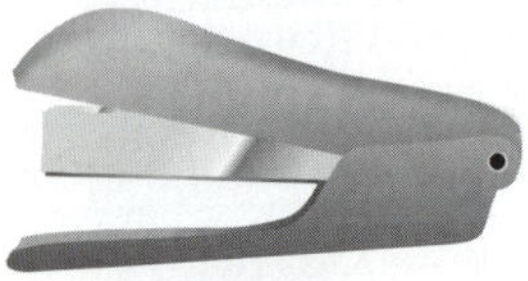

Stapler

6.

Crayon

3.9.d The student will estimate and use U.S. Customary and metric units to measure area and perimeter.

Estimating Area and Perimeter (See Lesson 16-6 for help.)

You can estimate the perimeter and area of a figure by rounding the lengths of the sides.

Examples:

Estimate the perimeter of the square at the right.
First, round the lengths of the sides.
Round 17 to 20.
Then add all four sides.
$20 + 20 + 20 + 20 = 80$
The perimeter of the square is about 80 centimeters.

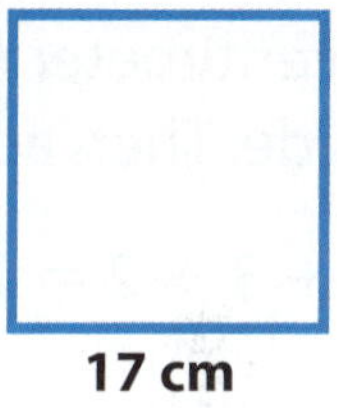

Estimate the area of the rectangle at the right.
First, round the length of the greater side.
Round 13 to 10.
Multiply the length times the width.
$3 \times 10 = 30$
The area of the rectangle is about 30 square centimeters.

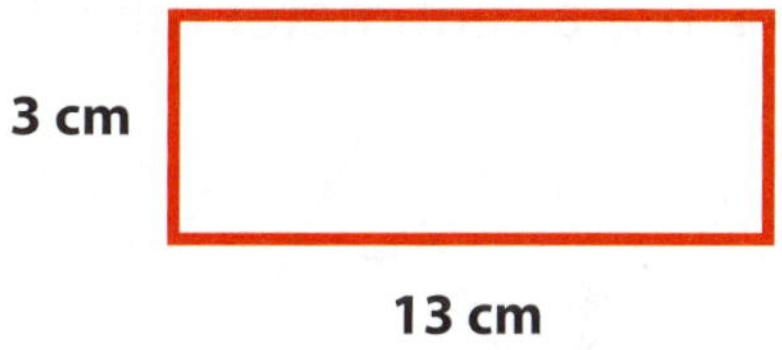

Practice

For **1** and **2**, estimate the perimeter of each figure.

1.

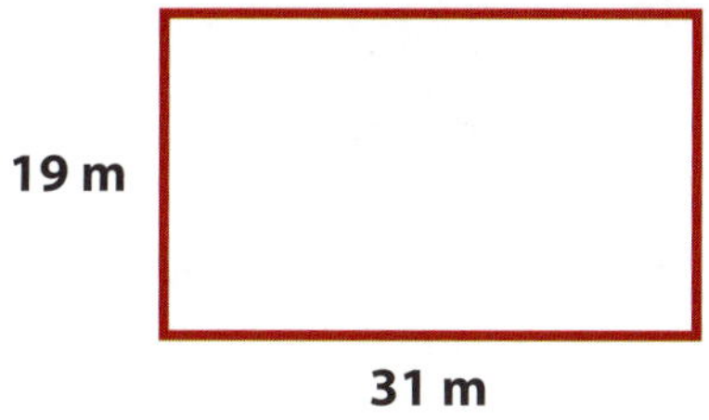

2.

For **3** and **4**, estimate the area of each figure.

3.

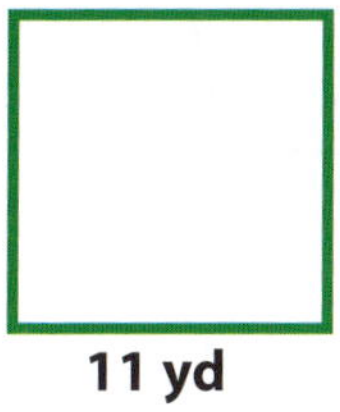

4.

3.10.a The student will measure the distance around a polygon in order to determine perimeter.

Finding Perimeter (See Lesson 16-1 for help.)

Find the perimeter of a figure by adding the lengths of its sides.

Example:

What is the perimeter of the figure?

Use a centimeter ruler to measure each side. Then add.

$3 + 2 + 3 + 2 = 10$

The perimeter is 10 centimeters.

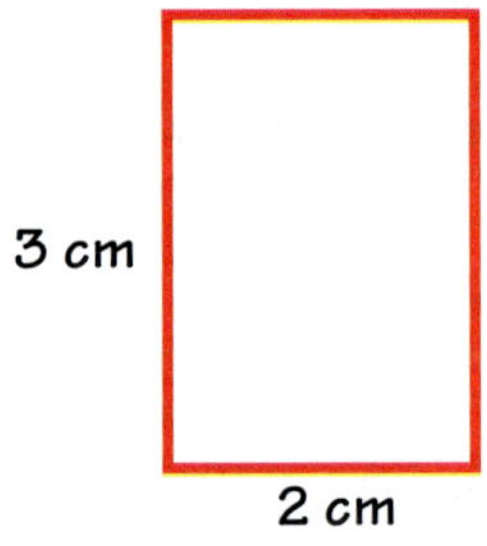

Practice

For **1–4**, use a centimeter ruler. Find the perimeter.

1.

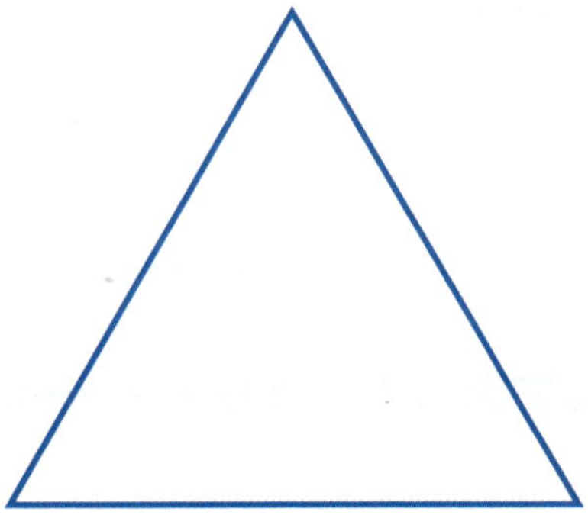

2.

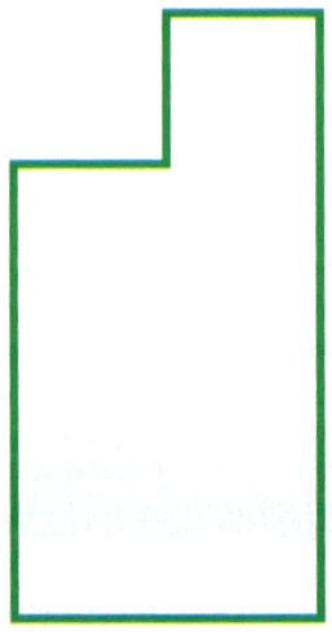

3.

4.

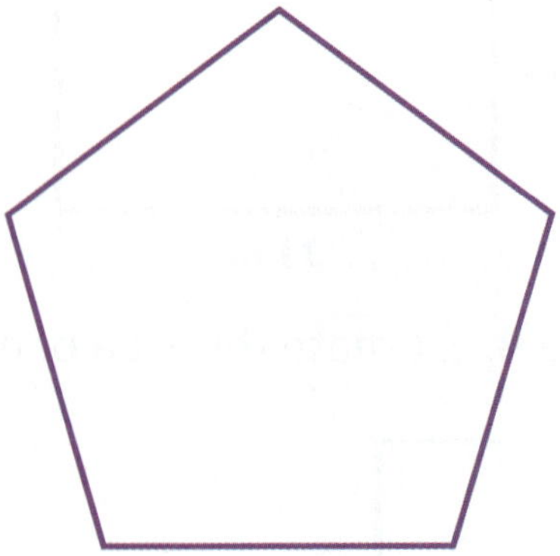

3.10.b The student will count the number of square units needed to cover a given surface in order to determine area.

Finding Area (See Lesson 16-5 for help.)

To find area, you can count the number of square units that fill the inside of a figure.

Example:

What is the area of the rectangle?

There are 12 squares inside the rectangle.
Each square is 1 square inch.

The area of the rectangle is 12 square inches.

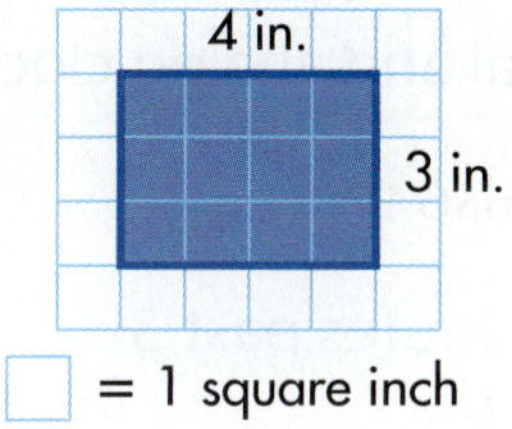

Practice

For **1–6**, find the area of each figure.

1.

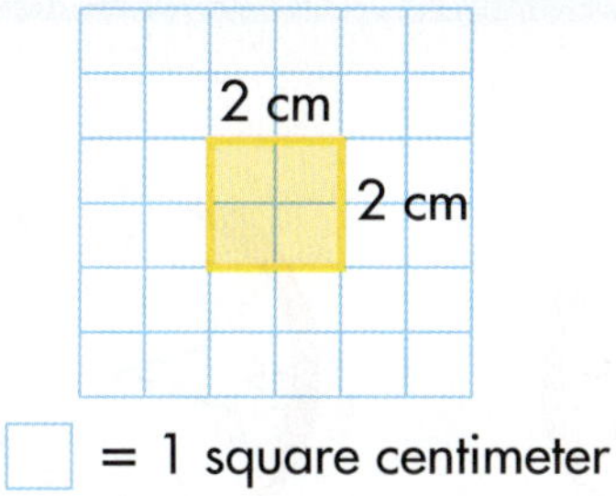

2.

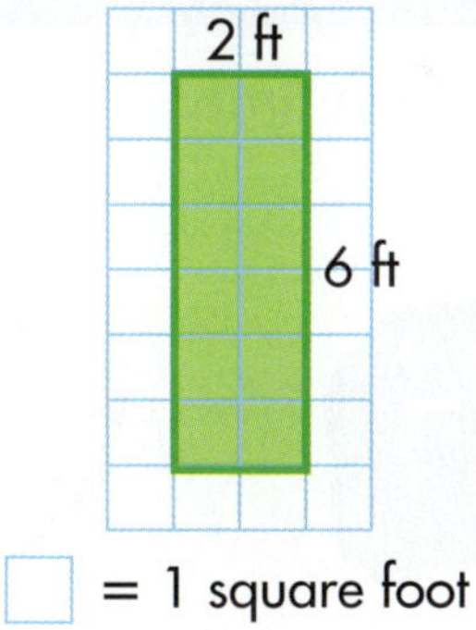

3.

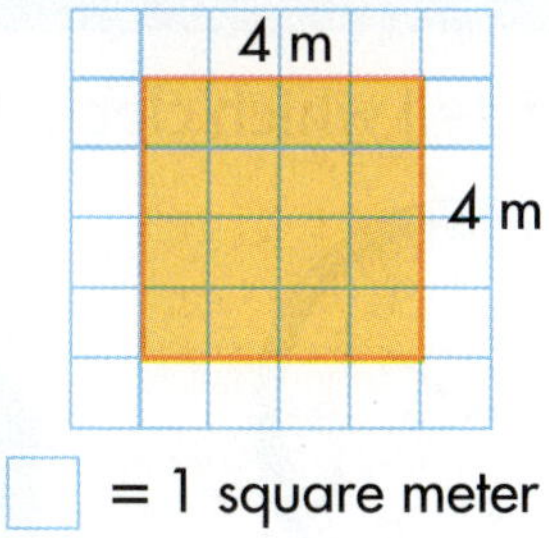

4.

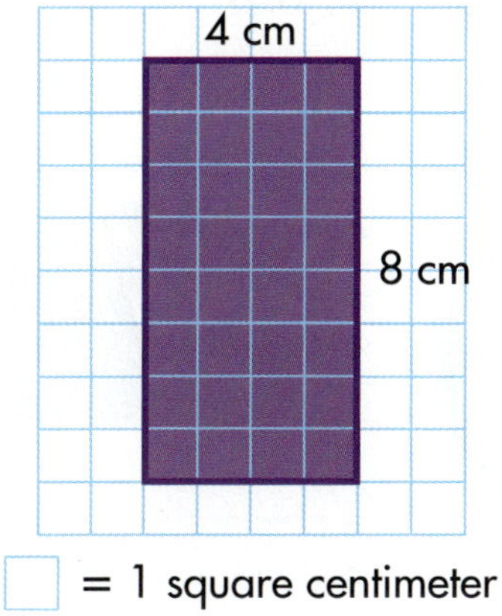

5.

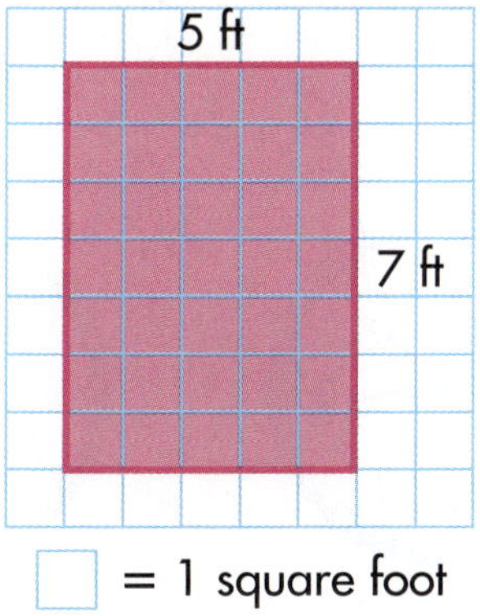

6.

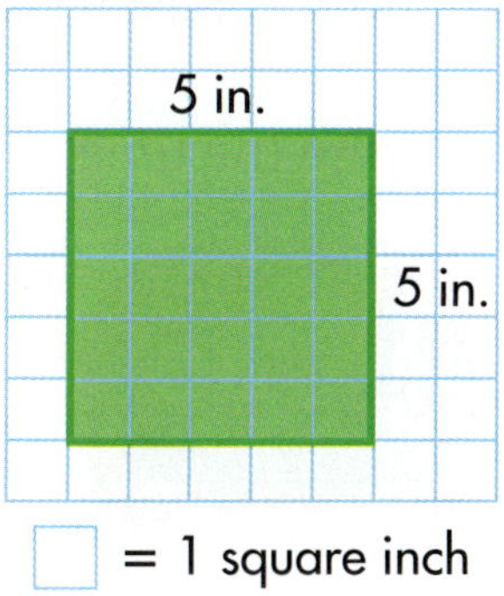

VA SOL Practice

3.11.a The student will tell time to the nearest minute, using analog and digital clocks.

Telling Time (See Lesson 17-2 for help.)

Example:

What time do the clocks at the right show?

The digital and analog clocks both show 3:45.

You can also say:

- 45 minutes past 3
- 15 minutes to 4
- quarter to 4

Practice

For **1–4**, tell which clock shows the given time.

A

B

C

D

1. 42 minutes past 9 **2.** 14 minutes to 2 **3.** 7 minutes past 11 **4.** 6:28

For **5–8**, write the time shown on each clock in two ways.

5.

6.

7.

8.

VA SOL Practice

3.12 The student will identify equivalent periods of time, including relationships among days, months, and years, as well as minutes and hours.

Time (See Lesson 17-3 for help.)

When you convert from smaller units of time to larger units of time, divide. When you convert from larger units of time to smaller units of time, multiply.

Example:

There are 28 days in February 2011.
How many weeks are there in February?

There are 7 days in one week.

$28 \div 7 = 4$

There are 4 weeks in February.

February 2011

		1	2	3	4	5
6	7	8	9	10	11	12
13	14	15	16	17	18	19
20	21	22	23	24	25	26
27	28					

Practice

For **1–3**, use the calendar above.

1. If the date today is February 6, what will be the date 2 weeks from today?

2. It is February 2011. Jane will go to Space Camp in February 2012. How many months are there before Jane leaves for camp?

3. The temperature was below freezing for exactly 3 weeks in February. How many days was the temperature below freezing?

For **4–9**, copy and complete to change the units.

4. 3 hours = ☐ minutes

5. 8 weeks = ☐ days

6. 2 weeks, 5 days = ☐ days

7. 10 hours = ☐ minutes

8. 35 days = ☐ weeks

9. 2 days = ☐ hours

3.11.b The student will determine elapsed time in one-hour increments over a 12-hour period.

Elapsed Time (See Lesson 17-4 for help.)

Elapsed time is the amount of time that passes between the beginning and the end of an event.

Example:

Soccer practice started at 4:15 P.M. and ended at 6:15 P.M. How long did soccer practice last?

The top clock shows the start time of 4:15 P.M.

In one hour it will be 5:15 P.M.

In one more hour it will be 6:15 P.M.

Soccer practice lasted for 2 hours.

Start

Finish

Practice

For **1–8**, find the elapsed time.

1. Start: 6:00 a.m.
   Finish: 9:00 a.m.
2. Start: 4:35 p.m.
   Finish: 8:35 p.m.
3. Start: 2:07 p.m.
   Finish: 9:07 p.m.
4. Start: 6:43 a.m.
   Finish: 11:43 a.m.
5. Start: 2:58 p.m.
   Finish: 8:58 p.m.
6. Start: 8:16 a.m.
   Finish: 11:16 a.m.
7. Start: 2:49 a.m.
   Finish: 8:49 a.m.
8. Start: 1:15 a.m.
   Finish: 11:15 a.m.

For **9–12**, write the time each clock will show in 5 hours.

9.

10.

11.

12.

VA SOL Practice

3.13 The student will read temperature to the nearest degree from a Celsius thermometer and a Fahrenheit thermometer. Real thermometers and physical models of thermometers will be used.

Temperature (See Lesson 17-5 for help.)

Degrees Fahrenheit (°F) and degrees Celsius (°C) are units that measure temperature.

Example:

Read the thermometer. What is the temperature in °F? What is the temperature in °C?

Match the top of the red column with the scale marks on each side of the thermometer.

The temperature is 85°F and 30°C.

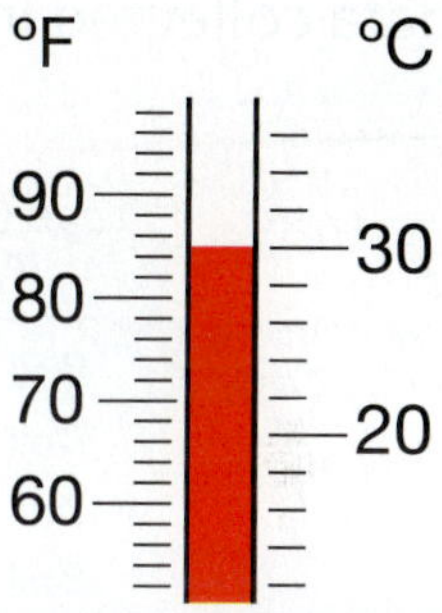

Practice

For **1–3**, write each temperature in °F or °C.

1.

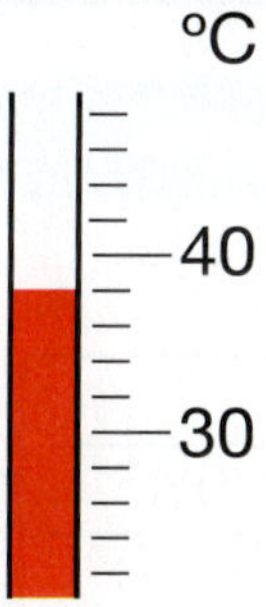

2.

3.

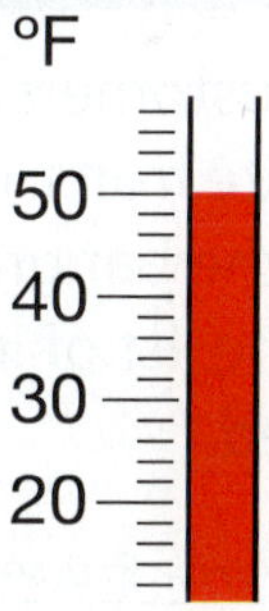

For **4–6**, write each temperature in both °F and °C.

4.

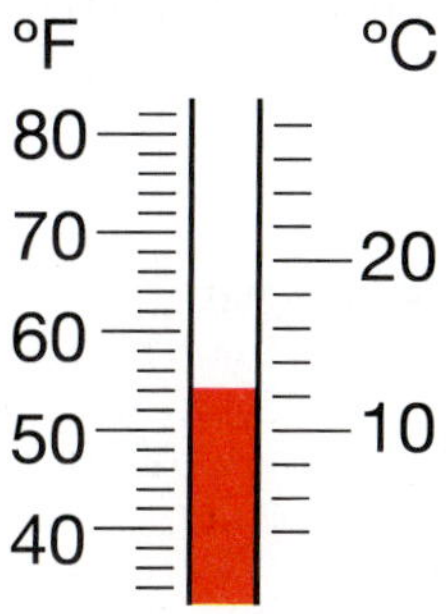

5.

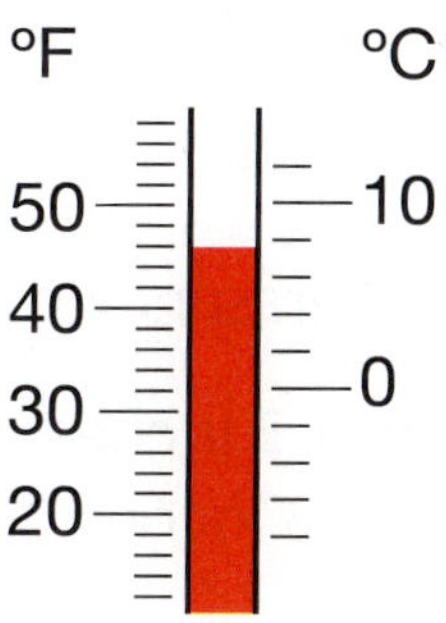

6.

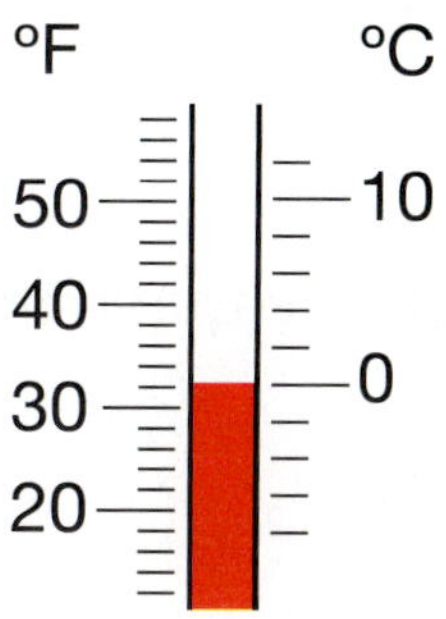

3.17.a The student will collect and organize data, using observations, measurements, surveys, or experiments.

Organizing Data (See Lesson 20-1 for help.)

A bar graph is one way to organize information.

Example:

The data collected in the list has been organized using a bar graph.

Toys Collected at Toy Drive	
Ball	Truck
Doll	Truck
Ball	Ball
Ball	Truck
Board Game	

Practice

1. Mr. Hall's customers named their favorite fruits. Copy and complete the bar graph to organize the list of information he collected.

Favorite Fruits		
Pears	Oranges	Bananas
Apples	Pears	Oranges
Pears	Bananas	Bananas
Bananas	Pears	Bananas
Apples	Bananas	Oranges

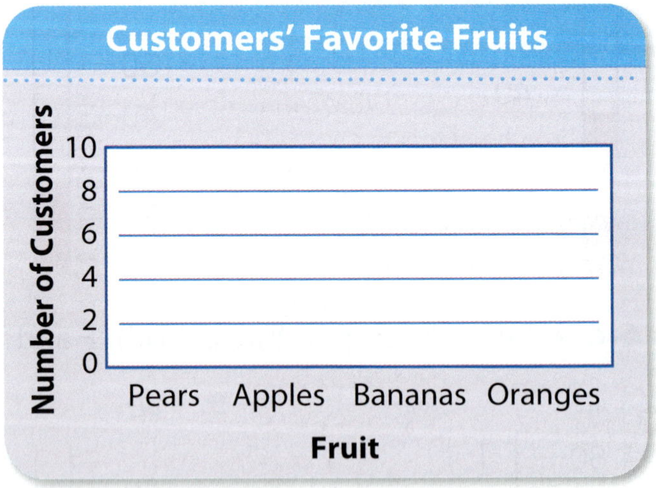

2. Charlie measured the lengths of 10 erasers. He listed the lengths below.

2 inches, 3 inches, 3 inches, 2 inches, 4 inches,
1 inch, 2 inches, 3 inches, 2 inches , 2 inches

Create a tally chart to organize the lengths of the erasers.

3.17.b The student will construct a line plot, a picture graph, or a bar graph to represent the data.

Constructing Graphs (See Lesson 20-4 for help.)

You can make a graph to display data clearly.

Example:

The bar graph shows the data in the tally chart below.

Number of Games Teams Won (Data)

Team	Games Won
The Spiders	卌 |||
The Hawks	卌
The Bears	卌	

Practice

For **1** and **2**, use the table at the right.

1. Set up a bar graph to show the data. Include a title and labels. Choose a scale. Draw a bar for each color.

2. What scale did you use for the graph?

Shirts Sold Last Week at Shirt Shack (Data)

Color	Number Sold
Blue	10
Green	5
Red	10

For **3** and **4**, use the table at the right.

3. Set up a bar graph to show the data. Include a title and labels. Choose a scale. Draw a bar for each sport.

4. Which of the sports was voted for the most?

Class 302's Favorite Sports (Data)

Sport	Votes
Baseball	卌 |||
Basketball	卌 卌
Soccer	卌 卌 ||

VA SOL Practice

3.18 The student will investigate and describe the concept of probability as chance and list possible results of a given situation.

Probability (See Lesson 20-7 for help.)

An outcome is an event that might happen. Probability is the likelihood, or chance, that an event will happen.

Example:

If you choose one of the tiles without looking, you can predict some outcomes.

- It is *certain* that you will select a letter.
- It is *impossible* that you will select a number.
- It is *likely* that you will select the letter P.
- It is *unlikely* that you will select the letter Y.
- Selecting a U and selecting a Y are *equally likely*.
- Selecting a U is *as likely as* selecting a Y.
- Selecting P, U, or Y are all of the possible outcomes.

Practice

For **1–4**, use the cards at the right. Decide whether each outcome is *certain*, *impossible*, *likely*, or *unlikely*.

1. Selecting a shape **2.** Selecting a circle

3. Selecting a star **4.** Selecting a square

For **5–7**, use the marbles at the right.

5. What are all of the possible outcomes?

6. Which outcome would be *as likely as* selecting a blue marble?

7. Name an outcome that would be *equally likely* as selecting a green marble.

VA SOL Practice

3.17.c The student will read and interpret the data represented in line plots, bar graphs, and picture graphs and write a sentence analyzing the data.

Interpreting Graphs (See Lesson 20-8 for help.)

You can read and interpret data in a graph.

Examples:

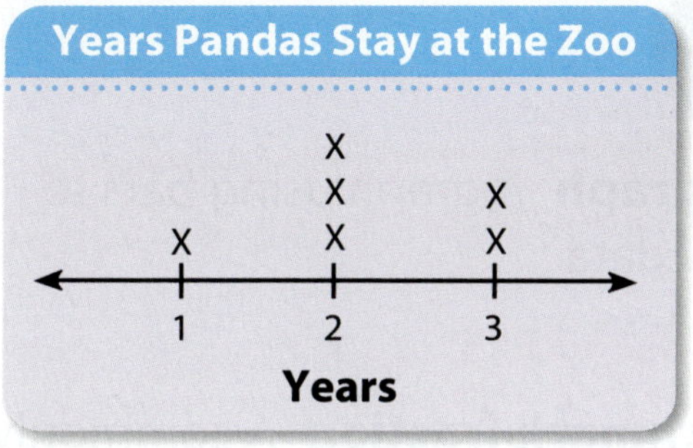

More pandas stay at the zoo for two years than stay for 1 year.

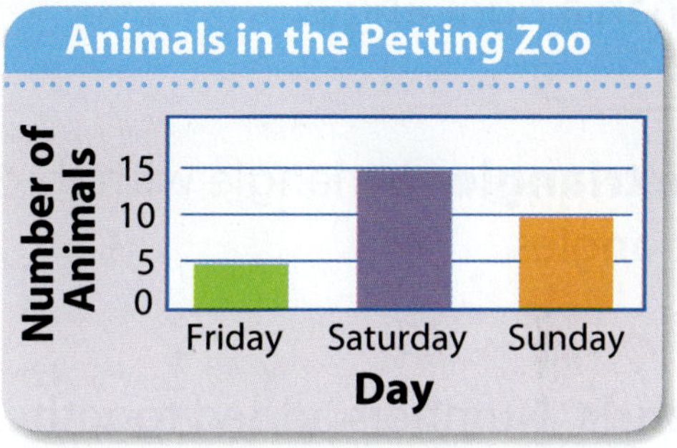

There are 10 animals in the petting zoo on Sunday.

Practice

For **1** and **2**, use the line plot at the right.

1. What is the most common height for gorillas at this zoo?

2. Explain why there are no Xs above the number 2.

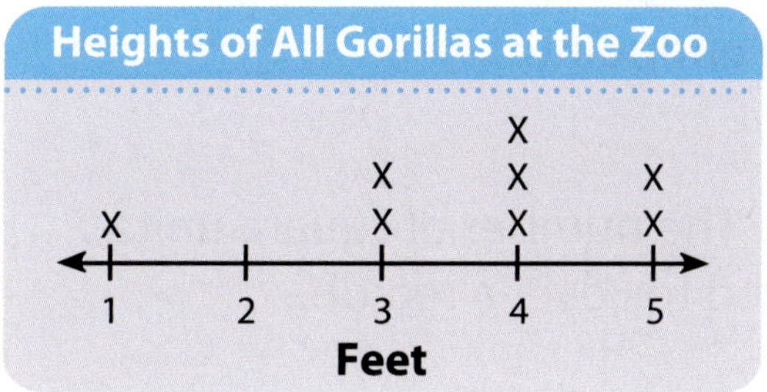

For **3–5**, use the bar graph below.

3. How many penguins are at the zoo?

4. How many more King penguins than Chinstrap penguins are there?

5. Write a sentence about the penguin data shown in the graph.

Glossary

A

A.M. Time between midnight and noon.

acute angle An angle that measures less than a right angle.

acute triangle A triangle with three acute angles.

addends Numbers added together to give a sum.
Example: 2 + 7 = 9 (2: Addend; 7: Addend)

angle A figure formed by two rays that have the same endpoint.

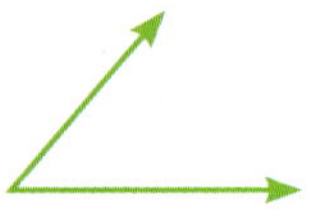

area The number of square units needed to cover a region.

array A way of displaying objects in rows and columns.

Associative (Grouping) Property of Addition The grouping of addends can be changed and the sum will be the same.

Associative (Grouping) Property of Multiplication The grouping of factors can be changed and the product will be the same.

B

bar graph A graph using bars to show data.

benchmark fraction A commonly used fraction such as $\frac{1}{4}$, $\frac{1}{3}$, $\frac{1}{2}$, $\frac{2}{3}$, and $\frac{3}{4}$.

C

capacity The volume of a container measured in liquid units.

centimeter (cm) A metric unit of length.

certain event An event that is sure to happen.

Commutative (Order) Property of Addition Numbers can be added in any order and the sum will be the same.

Commutative (Order) Property of Multiplication Numbers can be multiplied in any order and the product will be the same.

compare To decide if one number is greater than or less than another number.

compatible numbers Numbers that are easy to add, subtract, multiply or divide mentally.

cone A solid figure with a circle as its base and a curved surface that meets at a point.

congruent figures Figures that have the same shape and size.

coordinate grid A grid used to show ordered pairs.

corner The point where 3 or more edges meet in a solid figure.

cube A solid figure with six faces that are congruent squares.

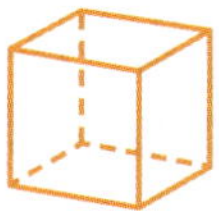

cubic unit A cube with edges 1 unit long, used to measure volume.

cup A customary unit of capacity.

cylinder A solid figure with two congruent circles as bases.

D

data Pieces of information.

decimal A number with one or more digits to the right of the decimal point.

decimal point A dot used to separate dollars from cents in money and ones from tenths in a number.

decimeter (dm) A metric unit of length. 1 decimeter equals 10 centimeters.

degree Celsius (°C) A metric unit of temperature.

degree Fahrenheit (°F) A customary unit of temperature.

denominator The number below the fraction bar in a fraction, the total number of equal parts in all.

difference The answer when subtracting two numbers.

digits The symbols 0, 1, 2, 3, 4, 5, 6, 7, 8, and 9 used to write numbers.

Distributive Property One factor in a multiplication problem can be broken apart to find partial products. The sum of the partial products is the product of the two factors.
Example: $(4 \times 28) = (4 \times 20) + (4 \times 8)$

dividend The number to be divided.
Example: $63 \div 9 = 7$
↑ Dividend (63)

divisible Can be divided by another number without leaving a remainder.
Example: 10 is divisible by 2.

division An operation that tells how many equal groups there are or how many are in each group.

divisor The number by which another number is divided.
Example: $63 \div 9 = 7$
↑ Divisor (9)

dollar sign ($) A symbol used to indicate money.

E

edge A line segment where two faces of a solid figure meet.

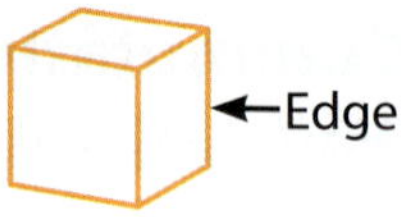

eighth One of 8 equal parts of a whole.

elapsed time Total amount of time that passes from the beginning time to the ending time.

equally likely outcomes Outcomes that have the same chance of happening.

equation A number sentence that uses = (is equal to).

equilateral triangle A triangle with all sides the same length.

equivalent fractions Fractions that name the same part of a whole, same part of a set, or same location on a number line.

estimate To give an approximate number or answer.

even number A whole number that has 0, 2, 4, 6, or 8 in the ones place; A number that is a multiple of 2.

expanded form A number written as the sum of the values of its digits.
Example: $2{,}476 = 2{,}000 + 400 + 70 + 6$

F

face A flat surface of a solid that does not roll.

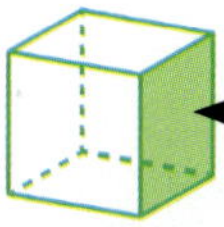

fact family A group of related facts using the same numbers.

factors Numbers that are multiplied together to give a product.
Example: $7 \times 3 = 21$
(7: Factor; 3: Factor)

fifth One of 5 equal parts of a whole.

flip (reflection) The change in the position that picks up and moves a figure to give a mirror image.
Example:

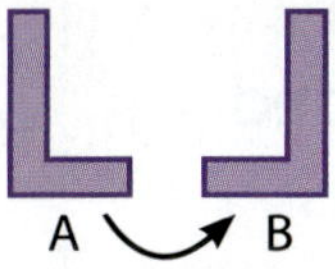

Figure A is flipped to make figure B.

foot (ft) A customary unit of length. 1 foot equals 12 inches.

fourth One of 4 equal parts of a whole.

fraction A symbol, such as $\frac{2}{8}$, $\frac{5}{1}$, or $\frac{5}{5}$, used to name a part of a whole, a part of a set, or a location on a number line.

G

gallon (gal) A customary unit of capacity. 1 gallon equals 4 quarts.

gram (g) A metric unit of mass, the amount of matter in an object.

H

half (plural, halves) One of 2 equal parts of a whole.

half hour A unit of time equal to 30 minutes.

hexagon A polygon with 6 sides.

hour A unit of time equal to 60 minutes.

hundredth One of 100 equal parts of a whole, written as 0.01 or $\frac{1}{100}$.

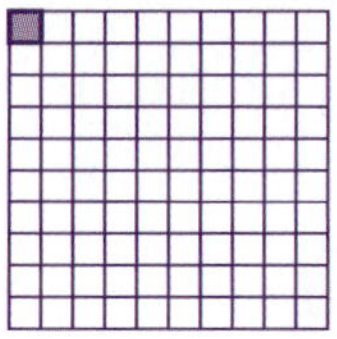

I

Identity (One) Property of Multiplication The product of any number and 1 is that number.

Identity (Zero) Property of Addition The sum of any number and zero is that same number.

impossible event An event that will never happen.

inch (in.) A customary unit of length.

inequality A number sentence that uses $<$ (is less than) or $>$ (is greater than).

intersecting lines Lines that cross at one point.

isosceles triangle A triangle with at least two sides the same length.

K

key Explanation of what each symbol represents in a pictograph.

kilogram (kg) A metric unit of mass, the amount of matter in an object. 1 kilogram equals 1,000 grams.

kilometer (km) A metric unit of length. 1 kilometer equals 1,000 meters.

L

likely event An event that will probably happen.

line A straight path of points that is endless in both directions.

line graph A graph that shows how data changes over a period of time.

line of symmetry A line on which a figure can be folded so that both parts match exactly.

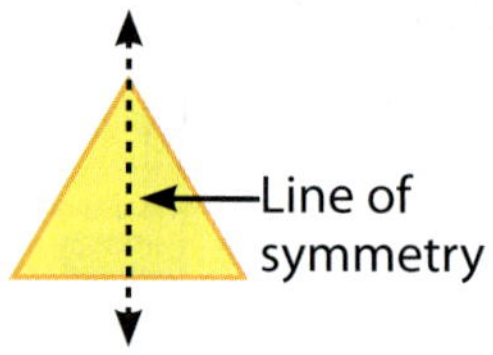

line plot A way to organize data on a line.

line segment A part of a line that has two endpoints.

liter (L) A metric unit of capacity. 1 liter equals 1,000 milliliters.

M

mass A measure of the amount of matter in an object.

meter (m) A metric unit of length. 1 meter equals 100 centimeters.

mile (mi) A customary unit of length. 1 mile equals 5,280 feet.

milliliter (mL) A metric unit of capacity. 1,000 milliliters equals 1 liter.

millimeter (mm) A metric unit of length. 1,000 millimeters equals 1 meter.

minute A unit of time equal to 60 seconds.

mixed number A number with a whole number part and a fraction part.
Example: $2\frac{3}{4}$

multiple The product of the number and any other whole number.
Example: 0, 4, 8, 12, and 16 are multiples of 4.

multiplication An operation that gives the total number when you put together equal groups.

N

number line A line that shows numbers in order using a scale.
Example: 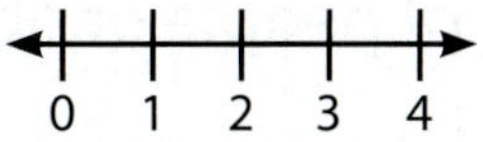

numerator The number above the fraction bar in a fraction.

numerical expression An expression that contains numbers and at least one operation. A numerical expression is also called a number expression.

O

obtuse angle An angle that measures more than a right angle.

obtuse triangle A triangle with one obtuse angle.

octagon A polygon with 8 sides.

odd number A whole number that has 1, 3, 5, 7, or 9 in the ones place; A number not divisible by 2.

order To arrange numbers from least to greatest or from greatest to least.

ordered pair Two numbers used to name a point on a coordinate grid.

ordinal numbers Numbers used to tell the order of people or objects.

ounce (oz) A customary unit of weight.

outcome A possible result of a game or experiment.

P

P.M. Time between noon and midnight.

parallel lines Lines that never intersect.

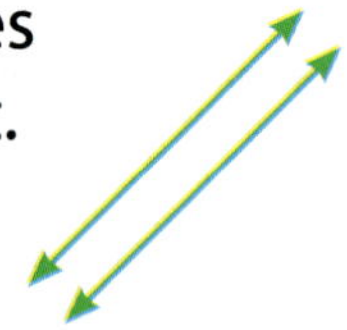

parallelogram A quadrilateral in which opposite sides are parallel.

pentagon A polygon with 5 sides.

perimeter The distance around a figure.

period A group of three digits in a number, separated by a comma.

perpendicular lines Two lines that intersect to form right angles.

pictograph A graph using pictures or symbols to show data.

pint (pt) A customary unit of capacity. 1 pint equals 2 cups.

place value The value given to the place a digit has in a number. *Example:* In 3,946, the place value of the digit 9 is *hundreds.*

plot Locate and mark a point on a coordinate grid using a given ordered pair.

point An exact position often marked by a dot.

polygon A closed figure made up of straight line segments.

possible event An event that might or might not happen.

pound (lb) A customary unit of weight. 1 pound equals 16 ounces.

probability The chance an event will happen.

product The answer to a multiplication problem.

pyramid A solid figure whose base is a polygon and whose faces are triangles with a common point.

Q

quadrilateral A polygon with 4 sides.

quart (qt) A customary unit of capacity. 1 quart equals 2 pints.

quarter hour A unit of time equal to 15 minutes

quotient The answer to a division problem.

R

ray A part of a line that has one endpoint and continues endlessly in one direction.

rectangle A quadrilateral with four right angles.

rectangular prism A solid figure with faces that are rectangles.

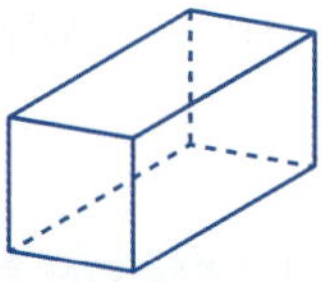

regroup To name a whole number in a different way.
Example: 28 = 1 ten 18 ones.

remainder The number that is left over after dividing.
Example: 31 ÷ 7 = 4R3
↑
Remainder

rhombus A quadrilateral with opposite sides parallel and all sides the same length.

right angle An angle that forms a square corner.

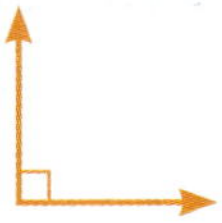

right triangle A triangle with one right angle.

round To replace a number with a number that tells about how much or how many to the nearest ten, hundred, thousand, and so on.
Example: 42 rounded to the nearest 10 is 40.

S

scale The numbers that show the units used on a graph.

scalene triangle A triangle with no sides the same length.

second A unit of time. 60 seconds equal 1 minute.

side A line segment forming part of a polygon.

simplest form A fraction with a numerator and denominator that cannot be divided by the same divisor, except 1.

sixth One of 6 equal parts of a whole.

slide (translation) The change in the position of a figure that moves it up, down, or sideways.
Example: 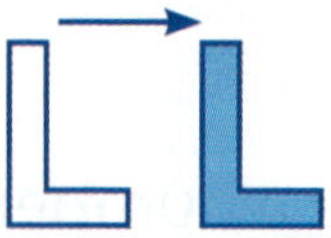

solid figure A figure that has length, width, and height.

sphere A solid figure in the shape of a ball.

square A quadrilateral with four right angles and all sides the same length.

square unit A square with sides 1 unit long, used to measure area.

standard form A way to write a number showing only its digits.
Example: 3,845

sum The answer to an addition problem.

survey Collect information by asking a number of people the same question and recording their answers.

symmetry A figure has symmetry if it can be folded along a line so that both parts match exactly.

T

tally chart A chart on which data is recorded.

tally mark A mark used to record data on a tally chart.
Example:  = 5

tenth One of 10 equal parts of a whole, written as 0.1 or $\frac{1}{10}$.

thermometer A tool used to measure temperature.

third One of 3 equal parts of a whole.

ton (T) A customary unit of weight. 1 ton = 2,000 pounds.

trapezoid A quadrilateral with only one pair of parallel sides.

triangle A polygon with 3 sides.

turn (rotation) The change in the position of a figure that moves it around a point.
Example:

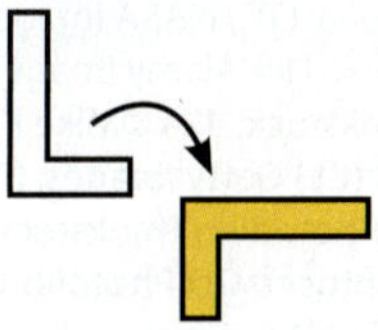

twelfth One of 12 equal parts of a whole.

twice Two times a number.

U

unit fraction A fraction with a numerator of 1.
Example: $\frac{1}{2}$

unlikely event An event that probably won't happen.

V

vertex (plural, vertices) The point where two rays meet to form an angle. The points where the sides of a polygon meet. The points where 3 or more edges meet in a solid figure that does not roll. The pointed part of a cone.

volume The number of cubic units needed to fill a solid figure.

W

week A unit of time equal to 7 days.

weight A measure of how heavy an object is.

word form A number written in words.
Example: 9,325 = nine thousand, three hundred twenty-five

Y

yard (yd) A customary unit of length. 1 yard equals 3 feet or 36 inches.

Z

Zero Property of Multiplication The product of any number and zero is zero.

Illustrations:

8, 12, 16, 38, 54, 146, 350 Dick Gage; 10, 11, 76, 88, 117, 122, 123, 140, 143, 144, 166, 168, 237, 265, 267, 271, 281, 282, 283, 298, 301, 302, 345, 369, 386, 414, 422, 446, 448 Leslie Kell; 55, 92, 124, 146, 174, 331, 336, 351, 352, 353, 360, 386 Neil Stewart; 195, 279, 280 Joe LeMonnier; 251 Rob Schuster.

Photographs:

Every effort has been made to secure permission and provide appropriate credit for photographic material. The publisher deeply regrets any omission and pledges to correct errors called to its attention in subsequent editions.

Unless otherwise acknowledged, all photographs are the property of Pearson Education, Inc.

Photo locators denoted as follows: Top (T), Center (C), Bottom (B), Left (L), Right (R), Background (Bkgd)

Cover:

Luciana Navarro Powell

Front Matter:

X ©Corbis/SuperStock, Getty Images/ Jupiterimages/Thinkstock, (TL) surpasspro /Fotolia; xi (TL) Getty Images/Jupiterimages/ Thinkstock; xii (TL) Gallery of the Republic, (BR, BC) Glass Crab Sculpture by Jackie Leatherbury, assisted by John Douglass/ ©Jackie Douglass; xiii (BL) Getty Images, (TR) megasquib/Fotolia; xiv (TCR) Mark Markau/ Fotolia, (BR) thinkstock/Getty Images; xv (T) Sven Weber/Fotolia; xxiv Getty Images/ Jupiterimages/Thinkstock;

2 (TR) 2010/Photos to Go/Photolibrary, (CL) Comstock/Thinkstock; 3 (L) sculpies/Fotolia; 6 (TR) Eric Isselée/Fotolia; 14 (CR) ©Brad Perks Lightscapes/Alamy, (CR) Comstock/ Thinkstock, (BC) Getty Images, (BC) Jupiter Images; 17 (R) ©WizData, inc./Alamy, (CC) 2010/Photos to Go/Photolibrary, (CL) Comstock/Thinkstock, (CC) steve estvanik/ Fotolia; 21 (TR) Labrador/Fotolia; 30 (B) Getty Images, (CL) John Foxx/Thinkstock, (TR) Ken Usami/Getty Images; 31 (L) Goodshoot/Thinkstock; 35 (BL) 2010/Photos to Go/Photolibrary; 38 (C) Getty Images, (CL) IT Stock Free/Jupiter Images; 42 (BR) Goodshoot/Thinkstock, (CR) Thinkstock; 44 (TR) ©Royalty-Free/Corbis; 49 (BR, BL) ©photolibrary/Index Open, (BL) Getty Images, (C) Index Open, (CL) Stockdisc; 56 (TR, CR) ©imagebroker/Alamy, (TC) hotshotsworldwide/Fotolia; 57 (BR) ©John Luke/Index Open; 64 (BL) DM7/Fotolia, (L) Michael Rosskothen/Fotolia, (TR) NASA Image Exchange; 65 Getty Images, (TL) Getty Images/Thinkstock, (BL) Jefery/ Fotolia; 70 (BL) Getty Images, (BL) Getty Images/Thinkstock; 73 (CR) Jefery/Fotolia; 84 David R. Frazier Photolibrary, Inc./Alamy Images, (TR) Getty Images, (CR) Hemera Technologies/Thinkstock; 85 (TL) 2010/ Photos to Go/Photolibrary, (BL) 2011/Photos to Go/Photolibrary; 94 (B) David R. Frazier Photolibrary, Inc./Alamy Images; 106 (TR) ©Jill Stephenson/Alamy, (B) 2010/Photos to Go/Photolibrary; 107 (BL) 2010/Photos to Go/Photolibrary, (TL) Dusty Cline/Fotolia; 115 (BR) Photos to Go/Photolibrary; 138 (TL) ©Geoff du Feu/Alamy, (B) Dmitriy Elyuseev/ Fotolia; 139 (BC) Getty Images/Thinkstock, (BL) Hemera Technologies/Thinkstock, (TL) NASA/JPL-Caltech/M. Kelley (Univ. of Minnesota)/NASA; 162 (TR) Getty Images, (B) NASA; 163 (C) Thinkstock/Getty Images; 182 (Inset) Library of Congress, (TC) Living Legend/Fotolia, (B) Saty Bha/Fotolia; 183 (BL) Getty Images, (TL) Rubberball/Getty Images; 184 (TL) Getty Images; 185 (TR) Getty Images; 198 (C) hotshotsworldwide/Fotolia, (CR) PB/Fotolia; 204 (TR) ©Directphoto/ Alamy, (B) Ablestock/Thinkstock, (CL) Photos to Go/Photolibrary; 205 (L) Getty Images; 209 (CR) ©Directphoto/Alamy; 210 (TR) Jupiter Images; 214 (CR) Eric Isselée/Fotolia; 232 (B) 2010/Photos to Go/Photolibrary, (TL) poco_bw/Fotolia; 233 (CL) Henryk Sadura/Fotolia; 234 (BR) ©photolibrary/Index Open, (BL) Jupiter Images; 235 (BC) ©photolibrary/Index Open, (BL) ©Vstock/Index Open; 236 (BR, BC) Getty Images, (CR) Jupiter Images, (C) Stockdisc; 243 2010/Photos to Go/Photolibrary; 247 (BL) Henryk Sadura/Fotolia; 258 (B) Getty Images, (CL) Photos to Go/Photolibrary, (B) Photos/Thinkstock; 259 (T) Getty Images, (BL) Index Open; 267 (BL) Index Open; 274 (TCR) 2010/Photos to Go/Photolibrary, (BL) Getty Images, (TR) Michael Pettigrew/Fotolia; 275 (BL) Dream Maker Software, (T) Photos to Go/Photolibrary; 281 (BL) Keith Levit Photography/Photos to Go/Photolibrary; 283 (BC) Photos to Go/Photolibrary; 293 (TR) ©Creatas, (TC) ©Stefan Sollfors Insects/Alamy, (TRC,) Hemera Technologies/Thinkstock, (CR) Jupiterimages/Thinkstock; 297 (BC) 2010/Photos to Go/Photolibrary, (BR) Cathy Keifer/Fotolia; 305 (TL) ©Simon Belcher/ Alamy; 308 (TR) ©Vstock/Index Open; 310 (BL) Getty Images; 327 (BL) 2010/Photos to Go/Photolibrary, (BCL) Eric Isselée/Fotolia, (TL) Library of Congress; 329 Jupiter Images; 332 ©photolibrary/Index Open, (CL) Corbis, (BL) Getty Images; 333 (B) ©Mistral Images/ Index Open, (CR, CL) Index Open, (TR) Jupiter Images; 335 (TL) Getty Images; 338 (CR) ©Image Source Limited, (BL) Comstock Inc., (BR) Jupiter Images; 339 (CR) ©Simple Stock Shots; 340 (BR) ©D. Hurst/Alamy, (T) ©Mark Duffy/Alamy, (TR) ©Royalty-Free/Corbis, (CL, BR, BL) Getty Images, (BL) Jupiter Images; 341 (BC) 2010/Photos to Go/Photolibrary, (BCL) Eric Isselée/Fotolia; 344 (TCR) ©Vstock/Index Open, (BR) Corbis, (BC) Getty Images; 345 (BR) Corbis, (TR) Getty Images; 346 (BR) Getty Images, (CR) Index Open, (TR) Stockdisc; 347 (BR) ©Lew Robertson/Corbis, (CR) Index Open, (CL) Jupiter Images, (TR) Stockdisc; 348 (TC) EcoView/Fotolia, (B) Getty Images; 349 (BL) Frogkick/Fotolia, (TL) Getty Images; 350 (TR) ©Creatas, (CL) ©photolibrary/Index Open, (BR) Foodcollection/Getty Images, (CL) Getty Images, (BL) Hemera Technologies; 351 (TR) ©Creatas, (C) Frogkick/Fotolia, (C, BL) Getty Images, (R) Jupiter Images, (CL) Pat Lalli/Fotolia; 354 (BR) Pat Lalli/Fotolia; 356 (CL) ©photolibrary/Index Open, (BR) ©Simple Stock Shots; 357 (BR) Amur/Fotolia, (BC) Simple Stock Shots; 358 (BC) Getty Images, (BL) Jupiter Images, (CR) Stockdisc; 364 (CR) MIXA/Getty Images; 365 (C) ©photolibrary/ Index Open, (TL) Getty Images; 366 (CL) Christopher Dodge/Fotolia, (BL) Photo courtesy of Pleasant Time Industries; 367 (BL) Anup Shah/Thinkstock, (TL) Jupiterimages/ Thinkstock; 371 Jupiterimages/Thinkstock; 390 (Inset) Geza Farkas/Fotolia, (B) Thinkstock/Jupiter Images, (T) unamarina/ Fotolia; 391 (BL) Getty Image/Photos/ Thinkstock, (TL) NASA Image Exchange; 398 (TR) Getty Images; 403 (TR, T) Getty Images, (B) Jupiter Images; 410 (BR) Getty Images/ Comstock/Thinkstock, (BL) Julia Mashkova/ Fotolia, (TC) NASA Image Exchange; 411 (TR) ©Mike Hill/Alamy Images, (BR) Stockbyte/ Thinkstock; 424 ©Mike Hill/Alamy Images; 434 (CL) Getty Images, (CL) judwick/Fotolia, (B) Photodisc/Thinkstock; 435 (BL) 2010 /Photos to Go/Photolibrary, (TL) 2011/Photos to Go/Photolibrary; 456 (TR) ©Hot Ideas/ Index Open, (C) cristi180884/Fotolia, (BL) Sir_Eagle/Fotolia; 457 (B) Galina Barskaya/ Fotolia, (TL) Ingram Publishing/Jupiter Images; 472 (TR) Getty Images/Thinkstock; 477 (BR) Ingram Publishing/Jupiter Images.

Index

A

B

C

D

E

F

K

L

M

N

Q

R

S

T